Through These Eyes

By Denny Noland

PART II - FALLEN HERO

1991-2011

"I tried to please you, make you proud, but I never heard a cheering crowd. I forgot to polish my halo, but it seems that only my horns show. I think that by now you all know that I was never cut out to be your hero..."   -Denny Noland
"Draven" From my song "Childhoods End" 1999-2000   Copyright 2014

INTRODUCTION

It was like any other night. I drive to my favourite bar to have a few drinks and more importantly, to pick up a gram of cocaine. As soon as I walk in, I notice that they have done a little renovating and redecorating. I order a drink from the new bartender, and I scan the room to find my dealer, who is the head chef, but he is nowhere to be found. As a matter of fact, I don't recognize *anyone* which is very bizarre. I keep walking through the bar, looking at all the patrons but I can't find a familiar face.

Then just as the music stops, the spotlight is redirected toward the entrance, the door opens, and there she is, looking as stunning as ever. She looks so beautiful in fact that everyone in the room has stopped whatever they were doing to watch her enter the room, but she doesn't seem to care. Her eyes are fixed on me and no one else seems to exist. It has been a very long time since she has looked at me like this and my heart is melting. She was the first of only three women I have truly been deeply in love with in my life. I call them my "Holy Trinity". At this moment, though, there was only the one, and she was coming to take what was hers.

I can't believe that she is standing there right in front of me. I have fantasized about this scene so many times but it never happened until tonight. She grabs my hand, while gazing deep into my eyes, and says "I need to have a talk with you, come with me..." She leads me outside to her car and she sits up on the hood, facing me, like she has so many times in the past, and starts pulling me closer. She wraps her legs around me tightly, grabs my face, and leans in like she is about to kiss me passionately. But just as our lips are about to meet, she says, "Look down, I have something for you..." I look down at her breasts, which at some point have worked their way out of her top and almost seem to be glowing in the moonlight. They are covered with perfectly chopped lines of cocaine. She says, "I tried to love you...but I couldn't" and hands me a straw. I snort a huge line and then I hear, "Freeze! Put your hands up in the air!"

I am terrified and frozen like a deer in the headlights. My second reaction was to run for my life and try to reach my truck. I know that if I get arrested, it will ruin my life, so I try to escape. I sprint through the parking lot and finally get to my vehicle. I can hear the cops closing in but I'm already a step ahead. As I'm driving away, I look in the rear view mirror, and there's about ten cops standing there in my dust. As I race down the street, overtaking everything in my path, I start wondering if this was another set up, another betrayal. It happened before, it could happen again. I kept driving until I reached my grandparent's house which was just down the road from my parents' house. The front door was open, which I thought was strange, but I entered anyway and locked the door. There were lights on, but it seemed like no one was home. I hear sirens in the distance and a helicopter overhead. There are lights shining in the windows. I crouch down in the corner, close my eyes, and say a little prayer. I know my life is over.

Out of nowhere, I hear a familiar Creed song playing in the background, which turns out to be the alarm clock, and I open my eyes. Its morning and I'm lying in the bed next to my beautiful wife Sepi. I have just had *another* nightmare. I've been clean from drugs and alcohol for nearly ten years but I still dream about them almost every night. The dreams are different now, than they used to be, but they still torment me. In the first couple of years after I beat my addiction, I would wake up every night in a cold sweat, usually reaching for a crack pipe. My first instinct was to go get some dope but I was always able to fight it. Most of the time, the dreams aren't too farfetched from reality, even the dream I just experienced is like a remake of an event in my life. The girl I spoke of in the dream really exists and choosing drugs over her really happened in almost the same fashion. I have no feelings for her anymore but she seems to be the face of my demons and I have no explanation why. The dreams are really about drugs, mostly cocaine, not about her. I did love her once but that part of me is dead forever, except in my subconscious, where time seems to always rewind back to 1999 to 2001 when she was a significant part of my life.

9:11 hit the snooze button. The rooster is crowing, and the birds are singing. I already feel like shit, just want to stay under my *blanket*, **I don't even feel like moving…1:43**
There will be a knock at the door, or the phone's going to start ringing. Give me more nicotine, more caffeine, so I can go to work for a boss who is a jerk, I'm so fucking over this routine…4:20 I'm going to be the life and death of another party. I'll probably stay up too late and forget to masterbate, when I should have just gone to bed. Now that I'm wide awake, without a pill to take, I guess I will sleep when I'm dead…
-Denny Noland "Draven" From my song "Insomnia" 1999-2000 Additional lyrics 2013   Copyright 2014

    I believe that some people are truly blessed when they come into this world, and some are dealt a bad hand from the start. I am one of the latter. You see it happen in the movies all the time, a person gets pushed to the edge and decides one day that it is time for a change, so they go somewhere to make a fresh start, to reinvent themselves, to make the wrong things right. There always seems to be a happy ending…but that's not reality.

There have been many people who have committed suicide over the years who went through far less than I have in my life. I even knew a few who have done so. I will admit, however, that the thought has crossed my mind many times in the past but either I didn't have the guts to go through with it, or I was holding on to some false hope that things have to get better, so I kept pushing forward. I wasn't too concerned about what would happen to my soul, since I've been in hell my whole life anyway. Some say that when bad things happen, you are being punished for your sins. I used to say "Sometimes, I feel like a modern day Jesus Christ. Not only have I been punished for any sins I might have committed, but ones that I haven't even thought of yet. Maybe I'm paying for everyone else's as well."

There were triumphs, but when I would try to cherish them, they would often be overshadowed by tragedies. There was always someone or something there to ruin the moment...to rain on my parade. After a while, I just wanted to throw in the towel. Even today, when I'm excited about something, it only lasts a few minutes, then I start getting depressed because "nothing lasts forever" and I know I will lose it one day. That's what happens when you have lost *everything* on more than one occasion. I never leave the house in a good mood either because there will be some asshole whose sole purpose that day was to piss me off, so why let my guard down and send them an invitation? It's better to be prepared than to be caught unaware.

The irony of it all was that, when I was a kid, I wanted to be a super hero who saved the world. I loved life and humanity back then...before I came out of my bubble and entered a society that rejected me. I really tried to reach out to people at first, pretending to be pleasant and likeable, as well as being full of confidence, but it rarely worked. Most people could see right through me and would slap my hand away. However, there would be a few people who saw something special about me, a light that shined brightly underneath all of the darkness on the surface. They believed in me and saw the potential to be much more than I thought I was capable of. Some of them, in time, realized that they were wrong about me and chose to write me out of their lives. Others, although few and far between, still remain loyal despite how many mistakes I have made.

2

There was a preacher man who told me years ago, "God gave me a vision about you last night. He has big plans for you. You have a higher purpose…but I don't really know what it is yet." Several years later, at the local Wal-Mart, an elderly lady asked me for help so I obliged. She touched my hand afterwards and told me, "You will be a great leader one day. We will all depend on you to guide us in the dark days ahead. You are an important and beautiful person, whether you realize it or not. Maybe, it has not been revealed to you or anyone else yet, but one day everyone will know who you are. Thank you for your help, and I look forward to seeing you again one day." I think that they were probably both senile. It's hard to be a leader, when no one is willing to follow you.

I've had opportunities to be in the spotlight if I was willing to put the time and work into it, but I'm notorious for not finishing anything that I started. First, there was the world of professional wrestling. It used to be my dream to be a wrestler when I was a teenager. But years later, when I started working in the local strip club circuit, I found myself working with and for a lot of them. Hell, I even lived with a couple of them for a few years. I had family in the business as well, and a ring to train in for free at a local wrestling school, so my way in was served to me on a silver platter. Many people would have given anything to have all those resources. There were several reasons why I didn't cease the moment. First, I was already working as a bouncer in a strip club where I was fighting for *real* on a nightly basis. I didn't see the point in voluntarily having someone kick my ass for very little money. I didn't feel like starting at the bottom as a "jobber", I wanted to be a star right now. I wanted to skip the whole "paying my dues" part. I felt like I was too old to work my way up the ladder and have a successful career where I could make a good living. Then fate made the decision for me with a couple of painful injuries, one would leave unable to walk properly for a few weeks. That dream was dead...

    There was something else that I fantasized about when I young...being a rock star! Music is in my blood. My father is a lead singer and plays the guitar, my sister plays the piano, and my mother also sings. My parents have even recorded a couple of gospel albums that sold fairly well locally. It seemed only natural that I would pick up the bass guitar but my singing voice could make flowers wilt. I took lessons from a teacher who tried to teach me all about reading music, but all I cared about was learning how to play my favourite songs so I could show off in front on my friends. I was in a garage band called "Valkyrie" for a while until I got into trouble at school and was grounded. As part of my brainwashing, I was volunteered to play at the local church with my parents. Every mistake I made on stage, whether obvious or hidden, was exposed by my dad when he would turn around and look at me when he heard them...right in the middle of playing the song! After redeeming myself, I returned to the garage band that was now on the brink of breaking up. My absence had caused the band to go their separate ways. Although I had no band, I still kept writing songs over the years, waiting for right musicians to come along to play my music. I was always stoned and drunk in those days, so when I would put another band together, we would spend all of our time getting high and reading my lyrics. We were always going to work on the music tomorrow, but there was always another party to go to, so we never had time to practice. I even went to breakfast with a record producer one morning, who was interested in signing me because of how I looked, and how I had structured seven albums in vivid detail. He wanted me to be the singer as well. I said, "The only way anyone will offer to pay me for my singing, is if they were paying me to stop." He said I had the perfect cheekbones to be the front man, I would make the ladies wet, and I could always take lessons. I don't know if he was actually trying to sign me or coming on to me. I never called him. Then one day I woke up, and I was 32 years old, wondering what the hell I have been doing, and where all the time went. I still kept the faith that I was still going to make it all happen someday. I was now off the drugs, so I dug up those old songs to see what I could use. I could now see why people didn't really understand what the songs were about, now neither did I. I decided to rewrite the whole lot, starting with the first album, which was going to be all about love and sex, called "Loverseas". After the songs were finished, I sent them off to Washington, DC to have them copyrighted. I also wanted to copyright the name "Draven" which had been my nickname for years due to my love of "The Crow" movies, and the band name "Melancholia" which had been with me since the breakup of the first garage band. Two weeks after my certificate arrived, I received several offers from various record companies wanting to use my songs for some of their lesser known bands which that already had under contract. They all just wanted at least $300 first. I was about to send the money to one company in particular, just to get my music out there, when I decided to get a few second opinions first. Everyone suspected a scam, especially when one record company specifically sent me a contract for my song "Black Leather" and everyone read the details and the so called "fine print". We did a little research on this company to see if they were legit or not, which they were, but the problem was that they used the songs, but did very little promoting, if any, so they didn't have to pay out very many royalties. If the album didn't sell, they still made $300 off every sucker who fell into their trap. I was advised to "never send money to anyone who claims that you won something but needs your money to process it or get the ball rolling...if you actually won something, they pay you...you don't pay them!" All of my excitement turned to anger. I sent them all letters declining all of their offers, but if they were willing to waive their fees, I might reconsider. They returned my songs, usually with a letter saying "the offer is no longer on the table but as always, we wish you the best of luck with your future endeavours". My final attempt at putting "Melancholia" together ended shortly after that when my guitar player was fired and taken to jail for shoplifting from the place where we were both employed.

3

Without a shadow of a doubt, the best years of my life were the club years that spanned a full decade from 1994-2004. Ironically, I call this era my "Decade of Self-Destruction" due to it being my downward spiral from being a casual, social drinker and drug user to my peak as a fully blown drug addict and alcoholic. It was also when I went from being a shy, somewhat naïve, and innocent young man who had only been with a handful of women to a confident, arrogant "man-whore", who went through women like some people go through their underwear. I started out as a customer who came in every weekend to basically give my pay-check away to one or several ladies who had convinced me that they actually *liked* me, and wasn't just using me for my money. I fell for their bullshit many times. I did hook up with several of the ladies while I was a customer, but never the ones that I really wanted to be with, so I just settled for whoever was willing then I would cast them aside like yesterday's garbage afterwards. One day it dawned on me that I was being used and abused and I wanted a little payback, not only emotionally, but financially as well. The only way to pull this off was to leave my lucrative factory job of 5 years and start working at the club. After being accused of something that I didn't actually do and being threatened by my manager that "if it happens again, you are gone…" I was bitter and disgruntled, and ready to walk out. Later on that week, I made what became a life changing decision, but the way I did it was possibly the worst way imaginable and could have been catastrophic. I took a day off work and never came back, which would burn a bridge that did come back and "bite me on the ass" years later. I also made a critical error that left me without an income for several weeks. I assumed that I would be welcomed into the strip club fold with open arms, since I thought I had developed a healthy, yet slightly unstable, friendship with the owner over the past year. I had even helped the bouncers throw out a few customers to earn their trust and respect. When I met with him, he told me that although he did promise me that he had a spot for me at the club before I left the factory, there had been a change in management since then. The new manager was named "Tommy". He owned his own construction business and was a local professional wrestler. Tommy had already handpicked his own staff, which included other wrestlers and local competitive bodybuilders, to fill all the vacancies, including my position. I was about to sell my house, pack my bags, and leave town, had it not been for my parents and a girl I was dating from a rival club who talked me out of it. Just before my nest egg was completely drained, I got that phone call that I was waiting for. One of the bouncers was going to leave so he could spend more time with his family, so they wanted me to start the following night. I thought I was prepared for what I was getting into since I knew the bar staff and most of the girls. I was also not afraid to brawl, if necessary, after I have been *drinking*. I had this...or so I thought.

It had only been a few weeks since I have been in the club, and in that short period of time, everything had changed. The first thing I noticed as I was driving into the parking lot was the sign. The club had changed not only its name but apparently it was now a nude club instead of a topless one. In fact, it was the *only* nude club in this city. When I walked into the building and met up with the owner, he told me to train with the doorman who I had struck up a friendship with over the past several months. The first thing he warned me of was the crowds. Since we were the only nude club, people were coming from everywhere to check us out and some of them were just looking for trouble, so "keep your eyes and ears open, and never let your guard down". Little did I know how big of an understatement that actually was, as the club would go on to resemble the "Double Deuce" in the movie "Road House" over the next couple of years until we weeded out all of the riff raff. As I watched the girls coming in to work, I realized that most of the girls who worked here that I knew, and spent so much money on, had apparently moved on because " they wasn't comfortable doing nudity". We did, however, have the most beautiful ladies from all of the other clubs who wasn't afraid to take it to the next level to make much more money. I also felt that this was a great career move for them, as well as myself, due to all the celebrities, feature dancers, models, wrestlers, rappers, and bands who would visit our club quite frequently who would often leave us their calling card. This place was like heaven and hell rolled up in one flickering package.

    I used to be afraid of confrontation, which was another reason why I wanted to become a bouncer. In this scenario, I couldn't walk away, and I had to win at any cost. It was my way of not only growing a set, but becoming a man in general. I was also determined to look fabulous doing it...spending all my spare time in the gym and the tanning bed even before I broke into the business. My hard work paid off when I was confronted in the lobby on my second night by a doped up customer who sucker punched me when I asked him to have a seat. I not only took his shot, which ripped out one of my earrings, but I recovered and grabbed him by the throat, choke slammed him, and squeezed until he was not only turning blue, but I could see his life leaving his eyes. Tommy (as he would go on to have to do many other times in the future) pulled me off before I would earn myself a life sentence. It got easier after that, as I would go on to leave a long trail of victims behind me over the next few years.

I had heard many rumours about all of the sex that happened behind closed doors between staff and dancers and even dancers with other dancers but I was shocked when I began witnessing it firsthand. My first night, I kept seeing management and the owner, slip off with one or more of the girls through the side door of the lobby into the unused section of the club then return quite a while later. It didn't take a rocket scientist to figure out what was going on. However, on my second night, I was not only watching, but participating as well. Although, I wasn't sleeping with near as many ladies as some of the other guys were, I did quite well for myself. By the time I walked away from the club, I had participated in nearly every sexual act imaginable, from threesomes to gangbangs to having sex with a man's wife, while he watched. I did all of this while being under the influence of probably every drug you have ever heard of and even some that, at the time, hadn't be named yet. I very rarely used protection either, which led to many sleepless nights but luckily, I never caught anything or knocked anyone up.

At first, I enjoyed living like a rock star. I had unlimited access to any drug of my choice. I had girls walk up to me and ask if they could blow me for no reason whatsoever. Some even offered to spread their legs for me if I would do *them* a favour. Hell, one of the girls even offered me $300 to spend the night with her, which I considered at first because I wanted the money, but later would politely decline because I knew I would feel like a whore afterwards. Then one day, the strangest thing happened...I didn't want it anymore. I wanted to settle down with one girl who actually *loved* me. I started to see the grim reality that was my life after

I did 3 grams of crystal meth by myself, over the course of only a day, and ended up in the emergency room with my kidneys shutting down. When I got out of the hospital, I came home to an empty house. I would have given anything for someone to be there to look after me, but no one even called me to see how I was feeling. I was in and out of the hospital several times that year, and every single time I had to take care of myself. For everyone around me, life just went on, as if nothing ever happened. I used to love the fact that I just had sex with the ladies, remembering birthdays and anniversaries, raising kids, even having dinner with them was someone else's problem. I was just there to get them off, and I was ok with that…until now.

4

You will read about my relationships in vivid detail throughout the course of this book, but if I had to sum it all up with one sentence it would be, "Blondes, brunettes, and redheads…I've tried them all." If you lined up every woman I have ever shared an intimate moment with, you would notice one thing straight away. There was never any group that I favoured… no pattern, no trend. All of them were unique in their own way, with very few similarities. It had got to the point that my theory of "everyone has someone who was put on this earth just for them" was being really tested. I thought my soul mate must have died at birth. There were two scenarios that always seemed to play out. I was either very attracted to my significant others, but didn't have anything in common with them, which usually resulted in not being able to have a decent conversation over dinner or I really enjoyed their company but found them repulsive, so intimacy was out of the question. If only I could find that one woman who was attractive and didn't annoy me, I would do *anything* that I had to do to spend the rest of my life with her.

By December 2009, my health had already started to deteriorate. First it was acid reflux disease in 2003, and then in the summer of 2006, I was diagnosed with Type 2 Diabetes. It seemed like the longer I stayed off drugs, the sicker and weaker my body became. I also had been through two failed marriages and an impressive list of exes who had lived with me at various times which had left my credit rating far less than desirable. I had just come out of a four year relationship with a girl who was almost young enough to be my daughter and was feeling like no one "noticed" me anymore, no matter how many hours I spent in the gym. I was a piece of chewing gum that has lost all of its flavour, in this town at least. I had become so desperate for companionship that I broke my own golden rule. I started dating a woman who had already fucked me over in the past. History would repeat itself, just as I predicted, as I spent the next few months chasing a ghost. Around Christmas, she brought out her tarot cards and did a reading of my future. She told me that "in the month of March, an important lady was going to come into my life". She couldn't tell me if she was a family member, an old friend, or my next wife but I must admit I was a little intrigued and very excited even if I didn't really believe in all that bullshit. I very foolishly assumed that she was talking about herself, finally surrendering and giving herself to me. On New Year's Day in 2010, I found out the hard way that wasn't the case, when she rang me from jail, and told me that she was getting back together with her husband…the same asshole I tried to get her away from ten years ago. "He must still care about me since he posted my bail" was her defence. That was the second time she chose him over me, even if she always claimed to hate him and blamed him for ruining her life. Fool me once, shame on you. Fool me twice, shame on me. I felt like the biggest fucking idiot on the planet. I dropped down on my hands and knees and prayed for whoever God chose for me to come along. I was sick and tired of these fucking mind games. I was ready for my ship to finally come in.

In February, 2010, my niece moved in with me to help me out financially. She brought her computer with her which was a bonus, considering I didn't have access to one after my last girlfriend moved out and took hers with her. For years, I used to complain and make fun of her for having a Facebook account. I vowed that I would never have one of my own, and I meant that. As soon as my niece logged in, she went to check *her* Facebook account. I was thinking "Am I the only person in the world that wasn't on Facebook?" Out of boredom and curiosity, I asked her to help me create my Facebook page. I even wrote a short version of my life story on my information page so people could decide for themselves whether to welcome me into their world or avoid me at all costs. It was originally intended to be just for finding old friends and doing some catching up since I haven't seen or heard from them in years. It took only a couple of days to realize that I haven't really missed anything at all... in fact the majority of them bored me to tears and was soon deleted. I tried to give the others, who I didn't like, a chance to prove me wrong with the hope that maybe they have grown up and matured over the years, and that I might have misjudged them. Some of them didn't even want to interact with me at all by refusing to accept my friend request, and others who did add me, usually didn't stick around for long even after I did everything I could to keep from offending them. One day I decided to build my friend list to the maximum 5000 friend limit by raiding my friends' lists and sending requests to anyone who looked interesting, especially if they were of the opposite sex. Within a couple of weeks, I had almost 4000 friends and climbing, and about 80% of them were attractive ladies aged 16 to 50. One warm morning in March, I came home from work to find a personal message from a young lady who was about the same age as my last girlfriend when we *started* dating, which meant there was now an age difference of about 16 years at this point instead of 12. She said that she could relate to my story because she used to have a drug problem as well. She also said that "she couldn't believe that I listed "Little House on the Prairie" and "Sweet Home Alabama" as two of my favourite tv shows and movies just as she did so it must be fate that we found each other. I am single, and I assume that you are too, so I would like to get to know you better." When I showed it to my niece, she said, "I know her! I used to go to school with her." I started feeling like a dirty old man for a minute till I looked at her photos and saw how attractive she was. I emailed her and asked her out, despite the fact that the age difference was greater than before, which was inevitably the downfall of my last relationship. I apparently didn't learn my lesson.

   We only dated for a week before she broke it off for unknown reasons. She said it was because "I pretended to be a Facebook celebrity" but I know that it was more than that. I took all the responsibility and made a very public apology to her on Facebook to try to win her over that pretty much made me look like a total loser in front of everyone. She was impressed that I would do that for her and wanted to try again. That lasted another two days before she found something else wrong with me and this time I snapped and called her a "fucking bitch". She would go on to say that I was someone who "probably beat women" which obviously hit me below the belt after what I went through as a child. The last thing that she said to me was to "enjoy all the popularity that you have on Facebook…that's the only place you will ever have it".

The first thing that I thought of after she said that was the tarot card reading. I was hoping that she wasn't the one that was supposed to come into my life in March. In the next week, I would talk to several women on a regular basis. Two of them were from England and another was from Germany. I seemed to be extremely popular overseas for some reason. The English girls were just about harmless flirting, but the German girl took it a step further by telling me what she would be willing to do to me in bed. She even called me once which was quite hilarious since she couldn't understand what I was trying to say with my thick Southern accent. I wasn't willing to move overseas and the only thing we had in common was our love for professional wrestling, which was never brought up in a conversation anyways, so we drifted apart. Talking dirty to me all the time will only get you so far after all.

However, there were two ladies who were in a category on their own. One was a beautiful single mother who lived in Baltimore named "Christie" and the other was an exotic looking goddess from parts unknown named "Sepi". I talked to both of them quite regularly, and I must admit I was very attracted to both equally. I also did my fair share of flirting with them and they gave it right back. I knew that one of these girls was going to be that "important lady that was going to come into my life" that I have been waiting for nearly a month.

Sepi made an attempt to take herself out of the running because she had already been talking to another guy in Texas for several months and they had agreed to take things to the next level before I came along and made her have doubts. I respected her decision and agreed to back off…at first. My focus shifted to Christie and we began talking seriously about meeting up somewhere and see what happens…what might develop. She couldn't deny the "spark" between us but voiced her concerns about what happens if we really hit it off while living so far away from each other. Would I be willing to give up my house and move to Baltimore if things got serious? I remember telling her that "I wanted to live in Gettysburg after I visited there, and if I moved to Baltimore, I would only be a couple of hours away, so of course I would." We both had a good laugh but I'm not sure that was the answer she needed to hear.

Then the strangest thing happened…Christie had put some space between us and I found myself talking to Sepi again. She hadn't heard from her partner in a couple of weeks either, so we started confiding in each other and getting closer. The more we talked, the more we realized that our lives paralleled each other. We were definitely kindred spirits…like a mirror reflection but of the opposite sex. We were both writers and artists, we both loved heavy metal music, horror movies, and wrestling, and if that wasn't enough of a connection, we were both diabetics with a number of health problems to boot. I fell ill not long after we started talking and I was in need of an operation. As I prepared for this operation, Sepi was recovering from one of her own. We were there for each other, day and night, even if it was only on a computer. When I got out of the hospital, we finally took a step forward when we exchanged phone numbers. We would talk for hours, forgetting about it being long distance or just not caring. After the bills started rolling in, we decided that perhaps a web cam would be a wiser choice, so I purchased one. Now we could spend as much time together as we wanted, which usually meant until we fell asleep, or sometimes even beyond that. The worst part was when we would hang up and log off, we didn't know "when" or "if" we would be able to talk again.

No matter how close we seemed to be or felt like we were, in reality, we couldn't be much farther away. We were on the opposite sides of the planet to be exact. I was still living in my hometown of Maryville, Tennessee and she was in Canberra, Australia. The situation got even more complicated when I asked her to be my girlfriend and she accepted. Now all we had to do was figure out how this was going to work. Sepi was all about coming to the States but it would take a year before she got through all the red tape just to be able to board the plane. I also knew that with all of her health problems and no health care, we would never have a future in America. I spent the next few weeks looking for other options, but in my heart I knew that there was only one all along. All of the events in my life had been leading up to this moment and I knew what I had to do.

In June 2010, I made a decision that would change both of our lives forever. I was going to walk away from everyone and everything that ever meant anything to me, and never look back. I was moving to Australia in two months to be with Sepi, and likely never to return. You would think that would be a difficult decision for an ordinary person to make and you are probably right, but it was an easy one for me. If you haven't noticed, I'm not exactly an ordinary person.

For the past six years, I had been working the same job at a local grocery store with no chance of advancement within the company. I was also buying a house with no legal contract to prove it, and was frustrated with my surroundings and all the people who dwelled within them, so I wasn't afraid of the direction or detour that my life was taking me. I welcomed it.

I made the announcement to Sepi first and she was ecstatic except for her concerns about whether this was what I really wanted or was I just doing it for her. I convinced her that it was kind of a combination of both. My parents were not impressed at all and made me feel like I "disappointed" them again and was making a terrible mistake. They made it crystal clear that if it doesn't work out "don't call us...we won't be there." The reaction I received from everyone else was a combination of every emotion imaginable. Some people were very supportive of me, while others thought I was insane. But what bothered me the most was the ones who didn't seem to care either way. They just completely stopped talking to me, not even considering the fact they may never see or hear from me again. They were even a few who thought that it was all bullshit, just some stunt to draw attention or create drama. If there is one thing that I pride myself with, it's that I tell the truth and never fabricate a story to impress anyone, yet some people still think that I've been in the States all along, just staying out of sight, as ludicrous as that sounds.

For the next couple of months, I said my goodbyes, packed up everything that I wanted to keep in storage, and sold everything else to pay for my passport, visa, and plane ticket. I even worked at the store up to the night before I left to make as much money as possible to take with me. Those who seemed unaffected from the initial shock of hearing that I was leaving the country in August were stunned when they heard the news that I had also asked Sepi to be my wife. Although I had said numerous times that I was *never* getting married again, when I thought about everything I was willing to sacrifice in order to be with her, I felt like now was the time to reconsider, so I proposed over the webcam and she accepted. Now I needed an engagement ring, and she deserved the best that I could afford. I would buy a few rings, upgrading each time, until I found one I thought would be suitable for my love. When I rang her to tell her, she was very upset. Her landlord had sold her house and the new owners, although they promised that they wouldn't when they met with her, had decided that *they* were moving in and she had three weeks to find a new place. That meant that we would be moving a week after I got there. She thought that I would change my mind when she told me but I said, "I'm coming whether we live there, or in your car. You can't get rid of me that easily." When she heard that, she seemed instantly relieved, like a large weight was lifted off her shoulders.

    The days seem to pass quickly and finally August 18 arrived. I had everything sorted except for finding a home for my two cats "Gabriel" and "Azreal". I had to go a couple of days without any contact with Sepi because my phone and internet had already been disconnected so it was a very stressful time indeed. I went over to my parents' house that morning to park my van which was filled with my keepsakes and said my final farewell to my mother who was very upset. She spent most of the morning yelling at me then vanished before dad and I left to fill my prescriptions at the store. Dad dropped me off at my house afterwards, hugged me, said a few parting words, and left. There I sat, in an empty house which by now had no electricity, with my two suitcases and my two cats, waiting on my cab. They could sense that something was going on and were freaking out. Then a miracle happened. An old friend called me and offered not only to drive me to the airport but to take the cats as well. I was almost in tears. I wanted the cats to go to a good home and no one wanted them until now. I did not want to have to take them to a shelter. Now everything was finally coming together.

Before he arrived, I held the cats one last time, apologizing to both for abandoning them, and telling them everything was going to be ok. They had always been there for me for several years, loving me unconditionally, and they deserved better than this which broke my heart. Then I heard him pulling in the driveway. We caught the cats, put them in their carriers, then I took one more look throughout the house, and off we went. The cats were crying in the back of his truck so loudly, we could hear them in the front. When we got to the airport, I petted the cats one last time, shook my friends hand and told him how much I appreciated what he has done. I stood there waving as he drove away, still hearing the cats until he was out of sight.

After I got through customs, I was informed that my flight to Dallas had been delayed which was very disturbing news considering how tight my schedule already was. I called my mother who had finally calmed down enough to talk and we finally parted on peaceful terms. I also started second guessing myself but I've had too many "what ifs" in my life already. I knew that if I backed out now, I would regret it the rest of my life. We were brought together for a reason, and made it through a lot of tough times to get here. I knew it must have been God's plan and I never questioned it again.

I had never flown before so I was a bit nervous the weeks leading up to that day but surprisingly I was calm and relaxed on the plane. First, I arrived in Dallas, then Los Angeles, and finally Sydney before catching a bus down to Canberra. Sepi picked me up at the bus station, we grabbed a bite to eat, and then we arrived at my new but temporary home. That night, after dinner, I dropped down on bended knee, and properly proposed. As I placed the ring on her finger, it felt different than the two previous times I did it, this time it actually felt *right*.

We were married on October 29, 2010 and we are still happily married four years later. We have been through many hardships over the years but we overcame them all. My life outside of marriage, however, has been a fucking nightmare filled with hatred, hostility, racism, and madness. When I thought I had seen it all, I realized that I had seen nothing. I've had to deal with issues beyond anything I could have ever imagined... but that's a story to be told later in another book.

5

This book is the second of three books that I am writing about my life. It is called "Through These Eyes Part II- Fallen Hero" and it spans from 1991-2011. In case you are wondering why this book was written first, I will explain. This particular era of my life defines me. It created me...moulding me into this person I have become. You will read about everything from all of my past relationships, to my rise in the club years that led to my fall into the world of drugs and alcohol that left me unrecognizable. You will also read about my experiences in the paranormal that has made me a believer. I know that this has been a very long introduction but I can assure you that I have only "touched" on these subjects. You don't have the whole story. The real stories lie within and will go much deeper to fill in any remaining gaps and lapses. (NOTE: Although the stories and events in this book are all true, some of the names have been changed, to protect certain people's identities and privacy)

    Some people think of me as a hero, for sacrificing everything, and coming so far to be with the woman I love. They said I gave them faith in true love again, and hope that there is someone out there who would do the same for them. Others think I'm either insane, or just a fool, for even taking the risk in the first place, saying the no one is worth it in the long run. Either way, I just followed my heart, and this is where it led me. By the time you finish reading this book, you will have a better understanding of who I am, where I came from to get here, and where I plan to go in the future. You will see some of Sepi's amazing drawings and read some of my most heartfelt poetry. I'm not saying that my opinions and views are right or wrong, that's just how the world looks "Through These Eyes" and now your journey begins...

–DJN

CHAPTER I- *"THE CROSSROADS"*

1991

Although "the Brotherhood" left for Myrtle Beach as a tight unit, by the time we made our way back to Tennessee, we were barely speaking to each other. When we reached the state line, we had already forced Byron out of the car so he would have to catch a ride the rest of the way back with the girls. We couldn't stand the sight of him any longer. That would be the last time I would speak to him until just before I left for Australia almost two decades later.

It breaks my heart how it all ended. After all those years of friendship and all that we have been through together, once we left school, only two of us stayed in touch. Everyone else went their separate ways. All it took was a week of friction to erase twelve years or longer of being like "brothers". After everyone's true colours were seen, we realized that we didn't really know each other at all.

As soon as we arrived home, I immediately went back to work to take my mind off things. I told my aunt that I wanted to be a full time cashier at the S-Mart instead of being just a part-time filler. I started working day shift to learn the ropes but would be eventually moving to nights to work with a quite attractive, yet married, older woman. If there was anything that I learned from past experiences at this age, it was that older women seemed to be more attracted to me than girls my own age. There were a number of ladies who were coming into the store regularly who would look at me like they were undressing me with their eyes. One in particular, was a beautiful brunette, who usually came in wearing a two piece bathing suit with a flannel shirt tied around her waist. From the first time I saw her walk up to the counter, I had many sinful thoughts about what I would do to her if I ever had the opportunity, especially after how she would look at me and lick her lips. There was a slight problem though...she was not only married but married to a biker nearly twice my size! I knew he would probably kill me if he saw me staring at his wife, or saw how she looked at me, so I never lets things progress. I thought it would be a wise choice to keep her in my fantasies. That decision probably saved my life.

So when I heard that I was going to work nights with an older woman, I knew it was going to be a recipe for disaster. I was catnip for women her age, so I had a feeling that this was not going to end well, and unfortunately I was right. Any hopes I might have had of her being an ugly hag went right out the window when I met her. She was an attractive blonde haired, blue eyed woman with a nice rack. It all started innocently enough, with the exchange of pleasantries with not only her but her husband, son, and daughter as well. They would keep us company throughout the night for the first week or so until she got settled in or maybe it was until her husband trusted me enough to leave her alone with me, or perhaps a combination of both. I would later find out that her mother and older sister would also be working there on other shifts and that started making me a little uncomfortable.

Nothing happened for a few days, then she started coming on to me when we were the only two people in the store. At first, it was just playful flirting, and then some touching, but it all led to her asking me for a kiss. I declined the first time she asked because I really liked her husband and I saw how affectionate they were toward each other when customers weren't around. Besides, I earned his trust. He knew that she was safe with me otherwise he would still be hanging around. But was she safe *from* me? That was the question…and soon everyone would find out the answer.

Being an 18 year old with hormones raging and all too easy erections, I couldn't resist for very long, so one night when she started trying to kiss me, I didn't turn away from her advances. It was a simple dry kiss but it led to another and another until finally a customer turned up to spoil the moment before we could go any further. I knew that what we were doing was wrong, but for some reason I no longer cared. When her husband came to pick her up, they made out like any other time, as if nothing happened. He had no clue, suspecting nothing, and she obviously didn't have a guilty conscious. The strangest part was that neither did I.

Now I couldn't stop thinking about her, which made me want more. So when we had a lady training with us overnight, I finally had the opening to get another fix. We were now free to leave the front counter and work in the back together without interruption. I seized the moment when I planted a deep, passionate kiss on her soft lips. Afterwards she told me that I was "a very good kisser" and "that we could keep doing this as long as we kept it a secret." Apparently, the kiss was so good that she had to tell someone about it. Within a couple of days, I was not only being questioned by my aunt about what was going on between us, but was accused of having an affair by her mother and sister. I was now so angry and embarrassed that I wanted nothing to do with her anymore. The more I rejected her, the more she seemed to want me. Then one day she told me that her teenage daughter had a crush on me so I should ask her out.

When I said that I wasn't interested, what she said next sounded like something straight out of a porn movie or some teenage boy's fantasy. She said, "You don't have to like her, just pretend that you do so you can have *me*. You will have an excuse to be around the house then. Everything would be so much easier. If you do start liking her, then you could have the best of both worlds. Like having your cake and eating it too." I was shocked. I couldn't believe what I was hearing. If this scenario played out several years later, I would have probably jumped at the chance but not now. I was so freaked out that I stopped talking to her at all, and soon after she would quit working there, as did the rest of her family. I would only see her two other times in my entire life. Once was a couple of months later at the store when she stopped in to get beer. When I looked out the window before I attempted to greet her husband, I noticed that she was with another man. She must have seen the expression on my face, because she quickly insisted that "you never saw me here" line and they peeled out of the parking lot together with two cases of beer in tow. The other time would be about a year later, when I was at the park in Louisville trying to clear my mind. As I walked past the picnic area, I heard a familiar voice calling out to me. I knew who it was straight away and was very hesitant to go anywhere near her, until I saw that she had company, a *female* companion. Curiosity got the best of me, and I approached their table. We talked for about an hour and although a few hints about a possible threesome were tossed around, nothing actually developed. I was both relieved and disappointed. I would never cross paths with her again. I would go on to work with three other ladies on the nightshift at the store without incident. One was even around my age, and just like any other girl my age, she didn't show any interest in me whatsoever. I must admit that I did share a kiss with one of the other older women, but that's as far as it went. There was simply nothing there. She, like all the others, didn't stick around very long. When I saw her again a few months later, she was visibly missing a few teeth, which made me glad that I dodged that bullet. I wasn't ready for a woman yet anyways. I needed to get my shit together before I brought someone else into my life. This was my time to find out not only who I was, but who I wanted to become.

2

I believe that when you are at this age, fresh out of school and ready to face the world, you are at a "crossroads" in your life. The decisions that you make of whether to go to college, serve your country, or start working will affect the rest of your life. This is a very critical time…and if you make the wrong choices, there will be serious repercussions. I chose to go straight to work and fool around with a married woman. I could live with that because one day I was going to be the biggest rock star on the planet, so what I did in the meantime didn't really matter.

If I was going to play the role, then I needed to start looking the part as well. I already had the long hair, but I needed something more. There was no way that I was ever going to get my ears pierced in this lifetime because I thought that would be too feminine. The answer became obvious…I needed to get a tattoo. I had wanted to get one since I was in high school but without parental consent, most respectable artists won't touch you. My dad had always spoken openly about his dislike for tattoos, and the people who had them. He always tried to discourage me by saying if I ever got one, I would regret it when I got older. Obviously, they were never going to sign off on that, so there was no point in wasting my time to ask. But that was then…this is now. I didn't need anyone's permission to do anything anymore, so it was time to pick out what I wanted to get. I really liked the symbol on the single "I Don't Want Your Love" by Duran Duran which was a simple heart with an "X" through it. That just seemed appropriate for how my luck with women had been so far. That would be my first tattoo but it certainly wouldn't be my last. No one warned me of how addictive they were, as I would go back to get three more as soon as that one healed. My second and third would be the Japanese symbols for "evil" and "darkness" and my fourth would be an ankh, which represented eternal life. I was content…at least for a little while.

3

Just as I was starting to make progress in my personal life, I found myself in a difficult spot at the workplace literally fighting to keep my head above water. First, I learned that due to the high turnover rate of employees on the night shift, I was now going to be working alone. Then, I was informed by my aunt that I was going to day shift for a week so she could train me on how to do everything since I would no longer have anyone around to help me out. The second reason why I had to go was so one of the owners of the business could meet me. My uncle Jay had already warned me about both owners but told me that I would probably only ever see one of them. The other very rarely looked in on this store. Apparently, they owned a chain of these stores scattered across several counties and they split up who went to which location. I had managed to avoid them so far, but if I was going to be solely responsible for their money six nights a week, that was about to change. Jay let me know beforehand that the one I was going to meet was named "Leon", and that he was very "old school… set on his ways". I wasn't sure what he meant but I would soon find out. I just smiled and said "I got this."

When that day finally came, I arrived at work early as usual. I had only been late once and that was due to my truck overheating on the way. Although I was only a half hour late, my aunt gave me a lecture about being late and told me that "if you had left the house even earlier than you already do, you might have still been on time. It better not happen again." I thought that speech was hilarious considering she was late *every* single day herself. What angered me the most about that was the fact that she lived next door to me so the distance was almost exactly the same. Maybe, *she* should have followed her own advice.

As I approached the building, I saw an older gentleman standing near the minnow tank. I knew it had to be Leon, going by how my uncle Jay had described him to me. He saw me and started walking toward me with hand outstretched for a shake. He introduced himself and we talked for quite a while before going inside. I found him to be a very humble, likable fellow despite what Jay had told me. I was very confident that I made a great first impression because I can normally pick up a certain vibe when someone doesn't like me, and this time it was noticeably absent. I immediately thought that Jay was just "messing with me" and I didn't think about it anymore. I was convinced that I was working for a great man who might just be getting a bad rap. I wouldn't have to wait very long for the truth to be revealed.

When I came in the next day, my aunt was waiting for me. She said that she wanted to have a chat with me in private before I began my shift and I probably wouldn't like what she was going to tell me. Apparently, Leon told her to fire me, but she talked him out of it. If I was going to continue to work there, I would have to complete about two dozen tasks *each* day before I went home and still do my job and if I didn't comply, I would have to seek employment elsewhere. I asked if my work performance had anything to do with this punishment and she said, "Denny, you are doing a great job. You are never more than a couple of dollars short or over on your register if you are off at all. Everyone else is all over the place. I don't know why he wants me to get rid of you. I asked him but he wouldn't give me a reason." He never admitted it to anyone, but we all knew the reason. He didn't like my appearance, which was quite ironic considering that he sold the business years later to a long haired biker, who didn't have to deceive people, he was just genuinely nice. I must admit that I did think a lot about quitting, especially after I saw that cleaning the outside toilets was on that list. They looked like they hadn't been cleaned in years, and the stench alone was enough to make me want to vomit. I also thought about the fact that it was a minimum wage job so anything else that I found would definitely pay more. But there was one problem though…I wasn't ready to leave yet so I wasn't going anywhere.

    For about a month, I did everything on that list, even cleaning the outside bathrooms till they were as spotless as the ones on the inside. No one ever offered to help because they were too busy worrying about the latest gossip, smoking cigarettes, and sitting on their asses. For the first week, my aunt would check behind me to make sure I had done everything. By the second week, she started slacking and only checked certain things.

However, after a month, she stopped checking *anything* so I started doing less and less and eventually stopped all together. Strangely, no one noticed or seemed to care. I had won this battle, but there was no way to win the war. I was still a victim of discrimination and humiliation. He had made an example out of me for everyone else's amusement. I made a goal for myself right then and there. I was leaving for sure but if I made it a year, I would receive my paid vacation. I felt like the old bastard owed me that much. Things were starting to get back to normal, but little did I know that there was a "storm" just over the horizon that was going to tear my life apart. It had actually been there all along. Watching…and waiting…

-DJN

CHAPTER II- *"STORMCHILD PART I"*

1991-1992

Since high school, I had been labelled a "junkie" by practically everyone in my hometown. But, honestly, nothing could be further from the truth. Other than a few sips of beer here and there when I could get it, I actually lived a very clean lifestyle despite what everyone thought. There were only two incidents where I experimented a little, and I got caught both times. That was all it took to destroy my reputation and make me an outcast in that community even to this day. It's funny how I was supposed to be getting high all the time, yet no one ever saw me intoxicated. Despite having no evidence, they still found me guilty as charged. After I graduated from school and started working, I usually spent my spare time sitting in my parents' camping bus watching horror films, not getting stoned. I was still a good kid, not very outgoing at all. I loved quiet evenings at home and avoided as much contact with other people as I possibly could, and that included the ladies. I had been in only one relationship, which lasted a whole month, and despite a few close calls, had yet to lose my virginity. That was *all* about to change...

After another case of "she didn't say no, but she didn't say yes either" with a regular customer, I decided right then and there that I wasn't asking anyone else out. Someone was going to have to practically come out and tell me that they liked me or I wasn't wasting my time anymore. I would rather be alone than get rejected again. There are two sayings that could be used to describe what was about to happen next. One is "sometimes even when you aren't looking for trouble, it will find you" and the other is "be careful what you ask for, you might just get it." I was about to find out the true meaning of both.

For weeks I stood my ground. No matter how tempted I was to approach an attractive girl, I refused to make the first move. The way I saw it was if someone liked me enough and realized that I wasn't going to take notice, they would eventually say or do something to break the ice to grab my attention. One day, someone did just that...and looking back I wish that she hadn't.

There she stood...across from me at the counter like she had been numerous times before. I always thought that she was hot, but there was just something about her that made me feel uncomfortable. Maybe it was the fact that she always looked wasted or perhaps it was how she came on to me whether she was alone or with a younger lad who I had assumed was her boyfriend. Whatever it was, something just didn't feel right. The signs were there, but being as superficial as I was then, I foolishly chose to ignore them.

She started with her usual small talk but it was different this time...she wasn't leaving. It took her a little while but she eventually told me the real reason why she was still hanging around. She wanted to let me know that she thought *I* was hot and she wanted to get to know me better by inviting me over to her house for a drink. Since I was underage, I think it was the lure of alcohol that won me over in the end, not her, yet having both was definitely a bonus. I was not only going to take her up on her offer, but I was ready and willing to do so as soon as possible, which turned out to be the following day.

She lived in a trailer park about five minutes from the store. I was so nervous before I got there...playing out every possible scenario in my head and how I would deal with each one if I found myself in that situation. I had already decided that sex was out of question, no matter how worked up we got. By the time I arrived, the butterflies were gone. I was calm and confident as I knocked on her door. She was dressed down quite a bit, and had on far less makeup than what she usually wore when I saw her, but that seemed to make her look even hotter, which was starting to intimidate me a little. She greeted me with a hug and a peck on the cheek, before inviting me in.

She insisted that I take a seat on her couch while she turned on some music and poured us a couple of drinks. I was pleasantly surprised when she turned on heavy metal music instead of something romantic. Between the good tunes and the alcohol, I was starting to really feel relaxed until she asked me that question I would be asked many times in my life, and would ask others myself numerous times..."Do you get high?" I wanted to say no since I didn't but I didn't want to seem like a prude either so I lied and said, "of course, who doesn't?"

As she was rolling the joint, I started having second thoughts. Then I thought about my reputation, that scarlet letter I was already wearing within the community, and how now at least, I would be living up to it. I tried it, and I must say that I wasn't exactly impressed. I never liked *anything* about marijuana. The smell, taste, even the way it made me feel didn't agree with me. But what I disliked the most was being around people who smoked it regularly. They are too sure of themselves, thinking that the drug is making them smarter. You can't tell them anything either, because they know everything already. If you don't want to take my word for it, just ask one of them, they will tell you themselves. But the sad reality is if you spend enough time around them, you will see that it's *actually* doing quite the opposite, but you will never convince them of that. May I present Exhibit A? She was a perfect example…

The higher we got, the more she opened up to me. She believed that she had life all figured out. Her name was Salena and she was a 24 year old single mother who got her home through her divorce. She didn't work so she lived off of welfare, food stamps, and child support. Oh, and that guy who comes into the store with her sometimes, his name was Derek and he was indeed her boyfriend… providing yet another source of income. He had just recently started working out of town and was only home on the weekends, leaving her free to spend time with me during the week. Now I wasn't sure if we were actually dating, or if I was just auditioning to be his future replacement.

The longer the conversation went, the stranger it got. She told me that thunderstorms arouse her, which would inspire me years later to write the first version of "Stormchild" which no longer exists after I decided that she didn't *deserve* a song written about her. She also tried to convince me that she only had six lovers in her life, which I find very interesting since she had three lovers that I know of, in the single year that I knew her. But it was when she said, "I'm much more intelligent than everyone thinks I am. I just trick people into believing than I'm not" that left me scratching my head. I rest my case.

I thought that she was never going to stop talking but eventually she had to come up for air. When she did, she looked me in the eyes with a look that used to make me melt. It was obviously rehearsed, and was so convincing that her performance could have won her an Oscar. Then we started kissing passionately, as our hands began to explore each other's bodies. This went on for at least an hour before I glanced down at my watch and realized that I needed to get home immediately. I still had a curfew even if I was almost 19 years old. My dad used to say, "As long as you live under our roof, you will follow our rules no matter how old you are" plus I was still stoned and drunk and didn't need to get home late and draw any suspicion. What I did next was what any guy would love to do at least once in their lifetime. I got a girl so worked up that she was dripping wet, then told her that I had to leave and did just that. I know that she had to pleasure herself that night, and that made her want me more.

2

The next day, I went back to her house and this time she had company. One was a lady named Mallory and the other was a guy named AC who I had only met once before years ago through my father yet I could barely remember him. He still claimed that he knew me and had been "putting a good word in for me" all along to try to persuade Salena to leave Derek and get with me instead. He had known Salena his whole life and they were pretty close, so having him in my corner early on gave me the edge I needed ,but I think that his hatred for Derek played a bigger part in my push than anything else, whether he would admit it or not.

This time there were four of us, partying hard and having what we thought was an intelligent conversation, but Salena was determined that history wasn't going to repeat itself. She grabbed my hand and led me down the hall to her bedroom fairly early on so there would be no excuses this time, which left AC and Mallory to entertain themselves for a while. She pushed me down onto her bed, pulled my pants off, and started performing oral sex on me. There were not many things she knew how to do in life, but she had mastered this skill. She was so great at it, in fact, that if she charged money for this service, she would have become a very wealthy woman. I've never been with anyone who came close to her expertise in that department. She said that her former husband had taught her how men liked it and now I was going to benefit from it. Of course, with her remarkable talent, and my lack of experience, you can probably guess what happened next. Let's just say that a couple of minutes later, I was smiling and she was wearing a frown, due to her disappointment and frustration.

After a quick spit and a gargle, not only had the mood in the room totally changed, but I was already starting to regret the first orgasm that I ever had. Now I was angry and verbally criticizing myself as we left the room. I completely forgot about AC and Mallory being outside, so as soon as they heard the commotion, they knew exactly what happened. AC didn't say a word but Mallory gave me a few words of encouragement by saying, "At least you got it up. I've been with a few guys who couldn't even do that." Now the focus was off of me, as they started sharing stories about that topic, which let me off the hook to hide in the background.

3

The third night was indeed the charm…that night a boy became a man. It was exactly the same sequence of events with only one difference: minimal fellatio. She got me extremely hard, then warned me that she had been told that she was "really big down there" on more than one occasion. She blamed it on the fact that she has given birth to a child. When I reached for a condom, she said, "Don't worry about it. I can't get pregnant anyway unless I roll over on my back and put my legs behind my head. That's how I got pregnant with my son." Being the naïve kid that I was, I didn't use protection this time or *any* other time we were ever intimate.

Now it was the moment of truth. She crawled on top of me and placed me inside of her. I could only feel her for an instance before her body's natural lubrication made it nearly impossible to feel anything. I couldn't even tell if I was still inside of her or not. Despite this numbness, I still managed to get off within just a few minutes. I had such a feeling of release and accomplishment that I didn't really care if she got anything out of it or not. Back then, it was all about me…

Afterwards, when I informed her that she was my first, I didn't get the reaction that I expected from her. At first, she didn't believe me, even if I didn't know what the hell I was doing, then after I convinced her that I wasn't lying, she said, "That's not good…if we become a couple, you know that our relationship would be doomed cause no one stays with their first." I assured her that this time would be different, despite all of the problems we were already having without any kind of commitment. There were so many red flags that I had missed along the way that everyone around me saw, yet I was too blind to see the writing on the wall for myself. Anyone who tried to warn me or attempted to bring them to my attention was forced to either apologize or be removed from my life…no questions asked. This was the road I was willing to take even if it was full of potholes.

4

When the weekend came, I welcomed the break. It had been an emotional week and I was both mentally and physically exhausted. I was basically going back to work to get some rest. I was confident that I wouldn't see her since Derek was back in town. You would think that they would be inseparable, attached at the hip or somewhere else, since they haven't been around each other all week. I really had no idea where her heart was or what she was capable of but I was about to get a sample. She would not only come into the store both days but she also brought Derek with her each time. There was no reason for her to do this considering how many other stores were within a mile or two of her house in any direction. She was fucking with me and it worked. I was not only furious but jealousy was starting to rear its ugly head as well. Now I was thinking about Derek having sex with her and it was bothering me. I had never been in this situation before so I didn't know how to deal with it. For the first time in my life, I couldn't wait until Monday...

On Monday, I think I set a new speed record getting to her house. The first thing I asked her was if they had sex over the weekend. She said that he wanted to but she resisted...whether or not she was telling me the truth, I will never know. I told her that she needed to make a decision soon about who she wanted to be with because I couldn't keep going on this way. She said that she needed a little more time to think about it then kissed me... and we ended up having sex again. We must have inspired AC and Mallory because they hooked up too. Her house had become a place to socialize a bit, and afterwards everyone spent the rest of the night naked. We never went anywhere or did anything outside of her door for the whole week, and before we knew it, the weekend was upon us again.

This time around, everything was different. I didn't see her either day which was unusual and that concerned me a little. When I asked her that same first question on Monday, she gave me a different answer...the one that I feared all along. She admitted that she had given in by having sex with Derek and her reason was because he was getting suspicious that something was going on behind his back so she had to. He even took her out to dinner afterwards, serenading her with Bryan Adams "Everything I Do (I Do It For You)" while it was playing on the jukebox. I was so hurt that I got back into my truck and went for a drive to clear my head. I drove for hours, then went home and took the phone off the hook. I tried to avoid her all week by not answering her calls and even taking a different route home so I wouldn't be going near her house. When Friday arrived, I had something special planned that she would never forget. It would haunt her for the rest of her life...

She said, "When I saw your aura, I saw a vampire, in a fog like nimbus, out of an age of anti-individualism and into the Age of Aquarius. You know the meanings in stones, by watching an insect's behaviour. You can read the power in leaves, by listening to the rooks, and the manner of their chatter." Every year, I can gaze into my crystal ball and predict the weather, to write your calendars and almanacs. Every day, I can read your mind, or palm, to predict your future, write your horoscope from the zodiac. When I meditate, I am on another plane. Oh, how it stimulates, but it's a high that I can't sustain. I've been to all levels of infinity and up ten stages of enlightenment. Want my advice? Just ring me up at 1-800---each minute

is three dollars and fifty cents.   –Denny Noland "Draven" From my song "The Clairvoyant" 1999-2000   Copyright 2014

<u>5</u>

For years, I had been interested in the topic and a collector of books on the subject, yet I have only had the desire to dabble into the occult once. There was a book that I was reading at the time which was about "psychic self defense" that really grabbed my attention. It taught you how to go into a type of trance or self- hypnosis right before or as you start falling asleep, which allows your spirit to leave your body and "travel" to other places while your physical body is left behind. I don't remember the whole procedure to get into this state of mind, but I know that it involved the imagining of following a rope with many knots and a black hole that either grew larger or smaller until it fills the frame or simply vanishes. When one of these things happens, your journey begins...

I must admit that I was always sceptical about these abilities, believing that probably 99% of it was bullshit until I became part of that 1% who experienced it for real. I followed the directions then I was able to see Salena and Derek lying in their bed while I was somewhere else. It felt more like watching a security camera than having a dream. There was no dialogue or storyline. Then I heard a knocking on my door and my mother's voice saying "Wake up! You have a phone call." I opened my eyes and my bedroom was illuminated by sunshine. It seemed like only a few minutes had passed, but it was actually several hours. Somehow, it was morning already and I felt like I hadn't slept a wink. Although I wasn't speaking to Salena, for some reason I decided to take this particular call. Her voice was shaken and she sounded like she hadn't slept well either. She told me that she was awakened by a sound in the middle of the night and when she opened her eyes and took a look around, she saw my face on her wall, staring back at her. It was so bright that it lit up that corner of the room. She was so frightened that she woke up Derek and he witnessed it too. It was only there for a few minutes then it disappeared. They were both so freaked out that they have both been awake all night. I couldn't believe what I was hearing...it actually worked! I thought it would be better if she didn't know what I have done. I just told her that it was all in her imagination. I didn't want to scare her any more than I already have.

    I never intended to use this skill ever again, but just playing around with it in the first place seemed to open doors that I couldn't close which changed it from a "gift" to a "curse". I would do it at random times over the years without having to use the steps beforehand whether I wanted to or not. I had no control over it anymore. On one occasion nearly a decade after this incident, it really got to me. I was having a horrible nightmare one night and suddenly realized that none of it was real and tried to wake myself up. When I opened my eyes, I wasn't in my bedroom...I was in my old bedroom at my parents' house! The strangest part was that although I was lying there looking toward the door like I did for many years, there wasn't actually a bed there anymore. I was levitating! The room looked very different as well, like it had been rearranged or redecorated. I explored for a few minutes before I realized that I wasn't supposed to be there and once again told myself to wake up. This time when I woke up, I was in my own bed. When I visited my parents later that week, they told me that they have changed my old bedroom into a study and insisted that I look at what they have done with it. I was shocked when it looked exactly like it did in my "dream".

6

About midweek, I was informed that Salena had made her decision…she chose me! I was ecstatic until she told me the bad news which was that Derek would be stopping by from time to time to pick up the rest of his belongings. AC told me not to worry about it since he was going to be staying at Salena's house for a while until he found a place of his own. If Derek tried anything at all, he would not only let me know, but would be more than happy to take care of the problem himself. During our first day as an "official" couple, he did drop in to pick up a few boxes. AC and I watched him like a hawk…waiting for him to cross that line but he never did. He would get all of his stuff out without incident. I was almost starting to feel a little sorry for him… almost.

When Salena and I finally took a minute to just sit down and discuss our new relationship, I brought up one major concern that was bothering me: our age difference. There was a six year gap between us and I wanted to make sure that wasn't going to be a problem. Her response was both soothing and slightly disturbing. She said, "I can assure you that it won't be. Derek is actually a couple of years younger than you are." I said, "That's makes him 16 years old and a minor!" She replied, "Yeah, but his parents were cool with it so it's ok." I was stunned and didn't know what to say so I let it go, never to be brought up again.

We also decided that it was time to reveal ourselves to the rest of the world starting with our parents. I met her parents first. I stayed sober all day, out of respect, so they would have one less reason to disapprove. It seemed to go fairly well for the most part, but when she met my parents, it was a whole different story. She insisted that she had a few drinks to "loosen her up" before we got there and although I didn't want her to, she was determined to do it anyway and she did. She was one of those girls who didn't wear her alcohol well. If she had one drink, she smelled like she drank an entire case. It was on her breath so intense that I not only made her brush her teeth and gargle but chew gum as well. Nothing seemed to cover up the scent. As soon as we walked into their house, I could tell by their reaction that they knew that she had been drinking. Her lack of respect for my parents overshadowed all the charm that she displayed and it became a total disaster. Needless to say, we weren't off to the great start I had hoped for with my parents but I was old enough to make my own decisions and they realized that. They just voiced their concerns and wisely backed off to let me learn from my mistakes.

    Now that we didn't have to sneak around anymore, and could be seen in public together, we took advantage of it. It was very rare if it was just the two of us since AC was still staying at her place. He was still dating Mallory so she would often tag along as well. It was always an adventure when the four of us went somewhere together and one more trip down that dreaded Lake Road immediately comes to mind. There was a steep dirt hill on the side of that road that had tire tracks obviously made by ATVs, or something of that nature, that went right up the middle, into the woods. You would have to be insane to attempt to climb it in a regular car as many have tried and failed. However, AC was sure that Salena's car would make it, so we all loaded into her car and handed him the keys. After a slight struggle, we made it to the top which led to a continuation of the one lane road, or trail, deeper into the bush. For years, we had heard rumours of a satanic cult that performed certain rituals somewhere on the property but we all thought that they were just stories made up to frighten teenagers away and keep them from trespassing. We soon learned that was not the case. As we drove along, we reached a clearing that had a bizarre rock formation in it. We got out of the car to take a closer look and what we saw left us shaken for days afterwards. The formation was actually an altar, but it was what was on that altar that freaked us out the most. It was covered with animal hair and fresh blood! We just stood there frozen for a few minutes until I suggested that we should leave in case they were still there. We were also losing daylight quickly, and if we turned up missing, no one would ever find us. They wouldn't even know where to start looking since we didn't tell anyone where we were going. Everyone agreed and we got the hell out of there and never went back.

7

A couple of weeks later, AC started going through a series of changes when his old friend "Bobby" got out of jail and re-entered his life. Bobby came from a wealthy family but had his own personal issues. He was always in trouble with the law, partly because he knew that his parents would usually get him out of it. The first time that he came over to Salena's house, he was cool to Salena and me but we were both appalled by how he treated AC. He had a sneaky way of making fun of him or using sarcasm to insult him constantly without making it obvious. Sometimes AC would pick up on it and usually laughed it off and other times he either didn't, or pretended that he didn't, yet he never did anything about it. Here was a guy that I used to admire, who took no shit from anyone, now appearing to have lost his balls somewhere along the way. When Mallory tried to intervene, AC dumped her almost immediately. No one ever discovered the real reason why Bobby had AC wrapped around his finger, but whatever he had on him stood the test of time, and AC was never the same again.

    It would only be a matter of time before Bobby did something to really get on my bad side. It was inevitable. One night he decided to bring an old "white trash" schoolmate of mine over to Salena's house. This guy spent the whole night either bragging about just getting out of prison or flirting with Salena. I don't know if he was just fucking with me or really trying to fuck her, but either way I was furious! AC no longer had my back as he just sat there like a zombie, but Bobby *did* which was very out of character for him. When things went too far, he told the idiot to "shut the fuck up" and got him out of the house. As he was leaving, he told Salena that "he would be back later to take care of her" and winked. She knew that I was about to snap so she quickly kissed me to try to calm me down, but it had little effect on me. I wanted to knock the few remaining teeth out of his mouth, but cooler heads prevailed and he left without incident and with all of his teeth. AC was just watching the whole time and did nothing. I was waiting for him to make popcorn. He probably would have if we had any food in the house. I don't know which made me angrier...the things that he said or the fact that I still had a curfew and couldn't be there when he promised to return. It was the same ole routine. I called her the next morning to see if he came back or not, and she replied, "I don't know. I went to bed right after you left. If he did, he didn't bother to wake me up." As I would find out in time, loyalty was not one of her best qualities, so who knows if she was telling the truth or not.

8

With Mallory out of the picture, AC quickly moved on to Salena's cousin "Kathy" who had started hanging out with Salena again. AC had run the gauntlet with all of Salena's female friends and family members over the years, but never touched her. If you asked him why it never developed, he would tell you that "they talked about it, but decided not to because it might wreck their friendship." If you asked her, she would tell you that "there was no chance in hell because she didn't find him attractive at all." For whatever reason, I always trusted him around her but now he was drifting away…spending less time with us and more time with Bobby and Kathy. Eventually, he just moved out and we would rarely cross paths with him in the weeks to come.

The last time I saw him was at a drug dealer's house that was a friend of Bobby's. We all had a little too much to drink, so I was in no condition to drive. That's when Bobby brought out a little baggie of white powder and said, "Try some of this shit. It will sober you up." When we asked him what was in the bag, he told us it was called "crank." Salena might love to drink and smoke a lot of weed but she was terrified of speed…especially cocaine. Since this wasn't cocaine, she let her guard down for a minute and grabbed a straw. She did a line then passed me the straw and I didn't hesitate. I was sick of being drunk and I needed to be "picked up" before I got behind the wheel. A couple of lines later and I became straight as an arrow. I was always a speed freak so I naturally loved the way it made me feel but Salena let me know immediately that this was only going to be "a one time thing" so don't get any ideas. True to her word, we never did it again. If only I knew how important of a role this drug was going to play in my future.

9

When AC and all of the people associated with him were out of our lives, that's when we *really* got to know each other. It was great at first, with her coming by the store daily to give me a kiss... which usually turned into a make out session either in the stock room where all those dangerous liaisons took place with the married woman months before, or pinned against the wall on the side of the building in front of God and everyone. When I would go to leave her place at night, it was very much the same result. We would share a goodnight kiss on her balcony, lose track of time, and I would usually get home late which was creating more friction between me and my parents. There was so much passion between us in those days but unfortunately, it wouldn't last.

The closer we got, the more I was starting to dislike her. It started when she talked me into taking her into town so she could smoke a joint with some random guy who turned out to be one of her former lovers. She didn't bother to tell me that until we were on our way back home. Then she informed me that she was very spiritual but not in a Christian way. It was more like a pagan or Wiccan kind of way, which would be cool except that she came across as a complete idiot. I must admit that I enjoyed our trips to the local lake on overcast days which created a beautiful gothic setting, or hiking through the woods until we found old hidden graveyards to explore, but when she brought out the Ouija board, that's when things became ridiculous. When we used it, I was always the one moving it. She was always too wasted to notice, so she would continue to talk to the "spirit". I played along until my hands and wrists started getting sore then coincidentally, the "spirit" would leave. She never saw the connection. This would only be a prelude to one of the biggest acts of stupidity she would perform during our so called "relationship".

It happened one evening while I was at work. She decided to go out to a local bar, alone, to meet an old friend who lived just down the road from her parents named "Aaron" for a couple of drinks before my shift ended. I had a bad feeling about this when she told me but there was no point in trying to talk her out of it because that would make her more determined to go just as an act of defiance. I just thanked her for being honest and told her to "have a great time but drive responsibly." She promised that she would. When I got to her place, I was pissed when she wasn't home yet, but my anger turned to concern when she still hadn't arrived several hours later. Finally, I gave up and went home because I was tired of waiting. When I got home, my parents knew that something was wrong, especially since I was home *early.* They made a noble attempt to console me by claiming that there was probably a logical explanation for why she never showed, but I knew better. I knew her...

She called the next morning...from jail. She told me that the cops found her passed out in her car on the side of the road with no recollection of how she got there. She had apparently hit *something* because there was a significant amount of damage to her car. She was also covered in mud which made no sense to her whatsoever. She claimed that Aaron was coming on to her all night and that she thought that he must have slipped something in her drink when she wasn't looking. That would explain why she couldn't remember anything that happened after she left the bar. She was also convinced that Aaron was actually the one who was driving the car because her keys were missing, and that he must have bailed after the accident so he wouldn't be held responsible. But the plot thickens. During the investigation, it was determined that the accident happened somewhere else besides where the found her car. It was like someone had driven as far from the scene as possible until the car broke down and could go no further. Either way, she was charged with DUI, which meant that she had lost no only her car, but her license as well. She would also have to serve 48 hours in jail. There was no evidence to link Aaron to the crime whatsoever, especially with her theory being possible yet so farfetched that it seemed highly unlikely. The whole incident brought up more questions than answers. It would impact both of our lives in the long run, and definitely not for the better either. Things were about to go from bad to worse.

10

Now that she was forced to depend on me as her transportation, she had no other choice but to introduce me to not only her circle of friends but to her dealer as well. His name was "Maurice" and he lived in an old, abandoned, two room shack with no electricity down on the lake. He used kerosene lanterns to provide light, and the fireplace for heat. It was what it was…a roof over his head and not much else. That didn't really deter people from coming there, as there was always a revolving door of visitors there on a daily basis. Some of them I would get to know and become great friends with over time. Maurice and I really seemed to hit it off immediately but that didn't set well with Salena. She was always trying her best to ensure that I remained an outsider. It was as if she felt threatened that Maurice might actually start liking me more than her. I think that she was worried that we might start talking or doing something behind her back. I'm sure that all the weed she was smoking, was making her a little paranoid as well. She also used to remind me of how close Maurice and Derek used to be and probably still are which made me be more thoughtful and cautious of what I said before I said it. I was trying to fit in after all, so it wasn't my intention to offend someone if at all possible.

    The rest of the "circle" consisted of "Ralph", "Gary", and Gary's girlfriend, who everyone called "Red" due to her long, red hair. They were all fun people to party with but it was Maurice's stepbrother "Joey" that was always the centre of attention. Joey had just got out of prison for good behaviour after serving a lengthy sentence on a murder charge. He had apparently killed a man who was stalking and beating his former wife and mother of his children. After he told me his story, I understood his reasoning and wasn't sure if I wouldn't have done the same thing if I had been in that position myself. He was like the court jester, who entertained everyone with his crazy antics. Maybe he was just happy to be a free man again and that was how he expressed himself...who knows? His behaviour would inspire me to show my comedian side as well, which made us very competitive. We were always trying to top each other, and that led to some hilarious, unforgettable moments. Like when I was telling a funny story and jumped up to demonstrate something, forgetting about a low hanging lantern above my head. I nearly knocked myself unconscious on that damn thing. Needless to say, I didn't finish the story...everyone was too busy laughing after they found out I was ok. Then there was the time that I challenged Joey to a drinking contest. We were building pyramids with our empty cans and I made a tremendous effort but just couldn't hang with the big dog. My head was spinning and I wanted to pass out, but Joey looked after me. I was terrified that I was going to vomit in front of everyone, but I never did. I had only been sick like that once, which was back when AC and Mallory was still in the picture. That morning, I woke up feeling ill and thought that I just had a hangover. The four of us got into Salena's car and headed down to the lake. For some reason, I agreed to sit in the backseat, which normally makes my stomach turn on a good day. That's why I *always* ride shotgun. Salena noticed that I was taking a turn for the worse and asked AC to pull over. They both insisted that I drink a few beers and smoke a little weed and the "hair of the dog" would make me feel better. The problem with this was that I wasn't hung over, I had a stomach virus...so everything that I was consuming was making me sicker instead of helping me. Let's just say that the party was over before it even started that day. However, on this day, it was self-inflicted which made it worse. I learned my lesson though...don't let my mouth write checks that my body couldn't cash anymore.

    Another incident that sticks out in my mind was the night that a few people were tripping on acid at Maurice's shack. There were the usual suspects, but there was also a new face there as well. He was just a guy who happened to be riding his bicycle around the lake and was invited in. No one knew his name, so they called him "the Outdoorsman". When

Salena and I arrived, he was acting normal, but as time passed, he started constantly fucking around with the fireplace. He would keep sticking the poker into the fire, then pull it out and ask me, "Do you see them?" I didn't know what the hell he was talking about but I played along anyway. At first, we didn't know what was going on, but we eventually figured it out. At some point, he snuck out, got back on his bike, and headed down the road. No one really noticed that he was gone. We thought he might have stepped out for a piss or was just staring at the hill behind Maurice's shack again that he vowed to climb one day. It wasn't until Gary and Red left to make a beer run, that we found out where he had went. As they were driving down the road, they noticed something large lying in the middle of the road. They slammed on the brakes just before impact then got out of the car to see what it was. They were stunned to find out that it was the Outdoorsman. He was still alive but unconscious. He had passed out and flipped his bike. They found it in the ditch several feet away from his body. They loaded both he and his bike onto Gary's truck and brought him back to Maurice's place. He spent the night there and left the next morning. It was a miracle that he hadn't been killed before they found him. We never heard from him again.

    One of many "close calls" with law enforcement occurred just a few days later. We were all at Maurice's shack partying hard as usual, with Joey and I doing our usual loud talking over everyone else when I noticed Maurice's look of concern as he reacted to hearing something outside. He went out to investigate and was gone for a few minutes. He always knew when someone was outside whether anyone else noticed or not. I reckon that's a skill that all drug dealers have…it's a necessity. When he came back in, the room fell silent except for me who was still acting like a moron. When I looked up, I saw two men standing with him wearing camouflage and holding firearms staring directly at me. I thought it was time to sit down and shut my mouth like everyone else. They identified themselves as FBI agents and flashed their badges at us. We all knew that we were fucked. There were so many drugs in the house and some of them were sitting right out in the open for them to see. We weren't only going to jail...we were going under the jail. But they weren't interested in all of that. They were searching for two escaped convicts who had been spotted in the area. They showed each of us mug shots of the two felons, and asked us if we had seen them which we hadn't. They thanked us and told us that if we saw these guys anywhere, to let them know. As they were leaving, one of them turned around and said, "Don't worry. This isn't a narcotics raid so party on." After they left, everyone let out a sigh of relief, but their buzzes were gone. It made me stop and think about how many times I have driven home intoxicated on roads that were notorious for road blocks and checkpoints without getting caught. I counted my blessings, yet still continued to take the risk nearly every night.

    I would unknowingly take it all a step further the next day, when our friend "Opie" stopped at the store fresh out of jail on drug charges. I talked to him as I normally would about partying without a second thought. He seemed to be acting a bit strange but I wasn't sure what would be considered "normal" behaviour after just getting out of the pen. When I told Salena about talking to him, she said, "I hope you didn't say anything that would incriminate anyone. They made him wear a wire because he refused to rat. I forgot to tell you." I had not only mentioned our drug use in front of him but also Maurice's name as her dealer since he was Opie's dealer as well. I spent weeks worrying about what I said and if it was going to be used against either me or someone else or even both. Luckily, it never was and I learned another valuable lesson. I definitely needed to be much more careful or I was going to fuck up my life beyond repair.

11

A few days later, Salena dropped a bombshell on me. She was going to sell her trailer, and move back in with her parents. I was overjoyed, because this would put a greater distance between her and the lake. This was a huge step in the right direction to get her life back on track and to re-establish her relationship with her estranged son. After her trailer was sold, I volunteered to help her move so she could start her new life as soon as possible. As we were moving, I met her little sister, who was absent the day I met her parents. She looked like a younger, better version of Salena with every quality that I wished that Salena had. She was actually closer to my age than Salena was, and her boyfriend was the same age as me. At that moment, I realized that I was definitely with the wrong sister. If only I would have found her first, life could have been so much different...but it wasn't meant to be.

It would only take a few days before Salena got bored and wanted to see her friends. I would oblige and take her which was all we needed to fall into the same routine except now I had to drive much further every night than before. But her friends on the lake would be the least of my worries. There was a bigger problem lurking just down the street that was about to resurface.

I had completely forgotten about Aaron living near her parents until she mentioned it one day when I came to pick her up. Since she was going to be home alone quite frequently with both of her parents working and her sister still in high school, she was concerned that he would take advantage of it. It wouldn't take long for him to make an appearance. According to her, he showed up and rang the doorbell. When she opened the door, he forced his way in and then on her. She claimed to have fought him off and threatened to call the cops, only then did he leave the premises. I was so angry that I made her show me where he lived... I was going to take care of him once and for all. Unfortunately, he had fences and a huge gate that stopped me in my tracks. Since I couldn't get to him, there was only one other thing I could do to keep her safe and it would be the beginning of the end...

12

If the living wasn't enough to worry about, she started seeing spirits in the woods across the road as well. I must admit that those woods were creepy, in a Sleepy Hollow kind of way, but I never saw anything unusual. She told me that they were part of ancient Indian burial ground but I never followed up on it to verify. She kept asking if I knew where her Ouija board was and I would lie and say that it must have been lost in the move, when in reality it was safely hidden behind the seat in my truck. That was where it would stay until I disposed of it. All of this added to the Aaron visit was enough to make me speed up the whole process of doing something drastic to save her from not only him...but from herself. It was time to put my plan in motion. It was time to fix this.

The first part of my plan was to find her an affordable apartment somewhere near both her parents and her child's father. Since she was unemployed, the second part was that I was going to live there as well. Her parents thought that it was a great idea, but my parents obviously didn't approve. They did make an effort to talk some sense into me before it was official but they quickly realized that it was pointless. If that was what I wanted to do, there was really nothing that they could do or say to stop me. The third part was for her son to split his time with both parents equally. If we found a place in this particular area, it would work. The father had already stated that he would be willing to drop the kid off personally if we lived nearby. In the weeks to come, I would make all of this happen. I was determined to get Salena's life back in order even if it killed me.

    Life was good for a little while. I was bonding with the kid by taking him with me when I went places, playing with him when I could, and even buying him nice things. Salena seemed happy and content for once and even got herself a job as a clerk at the local supermarket. For about a month, she really tried to change but the temptation was too great to convert back to her old ways. It all started when she decided to have "a drink or two" before her shift started one day, just as she had the night she met my parents. A few minutes after she got there that day, someone smelled it on her breath and reported it to one of the managers. He would approach her later on and fire her on the spot. Her ex-husband was so pissed off after he heard the news that he asked her if she would sign off on him having full custody of the boy. At this point, I started agreeing with him. We both thought it would be best for him to stay away from his mother. She couldn't take care of herself, much less her kid. She was always fucked up and he didn't need to be around that. It was much harder to get Salena to see that but I managed to pull it off somehow and she signed those papers. She would then turn it around until she became the victim by saying that she" did it for me because she knew that he was a burden to me" which was a total lie. At the end of the day, everyone knew that I didn't really factor in on her decision at all...she did this for *herself.*

13

The first thing that she wanted to do afterwards was to go to the lake and get high. Maurice wasn't available for some reason so we looked up another old friend of hers. This guy was a complete loser who met us in a van outside of his parent's house. He obviously had a thing for Salena and was trying constantly to impress her by acting and talking tough, which only made him look and sound pathetic since he was a skinny, nerdy guy who wore thick glasses. He kept saying things like "I trust you Salena cause you are like my sister, but I don't know him." Then he would look at me and say, "If you tell anyone about this, I'm going to be paying you a visit." I wanted to either punch him in the face or just bust out laughing but I did neither, because she kept feeding his ego by telling him that I was cool and didn't want any trouble. When we got back to my truck, I let her have it. "Look at this fucking clown, how am I supposed to take him seriously? What if I did tell someone about him? What would he actually do about it? Let me answer that for you sweetheart...not a damn thing that's what!" I warned her that if she wasted my time with a moron like him again, I wasn't going to be held responsible for what happens next. She never did that again, but she wouldn't need to...

14

    Our apartment after the kid left had went from a safe haven to a warzone literally overnight. We only had one really bad fight before this and it was back at the trailer, in the early days of our relationship, when we were both drunk. That night she slapped me in the face and I grabbed a butcher knife out of the drawer. I wasn't going to use it, I just wanted to scare her but the crazy bitch grabbed my hand and put the knife up to her own throat and kept screaming "Do it motherfucker! Do it!" I dropped the knife on the floor and embraced her to calm her down and then off to the bedroom we went so we could work all of this aggression out in a different, more enjoyable and pleasurable way. Although, it never got physical like that again, with the exception of when she would accidently hit me in her sleep that is, I would go on to learn that the things that would come out of her mouth hurt me much more than her fists ever could. Once she figured out how to push my buttons verbally, her mouth became a powerful weapon. Instead of saying things that were constructive and positive like she once did now she was always saying destructive and negative things about me every time something didn't go her way. Suddenly, everything was my fault. I started feeling incompetent and no longer good enough for her, which was exactly what she was striving for. It all started behind closed doors, but she wasn't satisfied with that. She wanted the whole world to watch her humiliate me. She wanted everyone to know that I was beneath her.

    We couldn't even take a simple trip to the lake to sunbathe without her finding a way to fuck with my head. She thought that it would be a great idea to only lie on one side the entire day despite me trying to reason with her and after she got partially burned to a crisp, tried to justify it by saying that we were coming back the next day so she "do the other side". I was embarrassed to be the seen with her... she looked like a half- baked cyborg for god's sake. When I couldn't lie there any longer, I jumped in the lake to have a swim. I saw that girl that I used to go to school with, the one who sat behind me in class, who had a crush on me way back then, swimming under the bridge with her family. I approached them and when I got close, found myself headed straight for her. Now we were only inches from touching each other. We gazed deep into each other's eyes but said nothing. I had never really paid attention to how beautiful she actually was until just now...in this moment. Then she gave me that same seductive smile that she used to that I always took for granted. It was like we were frozen in time and everyone else had disappeared. I wanted to kiss her and I knew that she was going to let me but then I heard a familiar voice that brought me back to my grim reality. Salena was ready to go get high with a couple of neighbours who we had only recently met. I left without even saying goodbye. This was the world I knew and there wasn't a damn thing I could do about it.

15

There was a young couple downstairs, who she had befriended that were in college and just happened to like to get stoned as well. When she was around them, she became a completely different person. It was almost like she thought that she was a fucking rocket scientist all of a sudden. When I was present, she would make fun of my grammar, my education, my upbringing, and even my job (you know...the one that kept a roof over her head, food on the table, paid all of her bills, even paid for and supported her habits) in front of them for their amusement. That night, they had invited us over for dinner and a movie. The dinner was ok, but they chose some silly science fiction movie about a large eye to watch that was not only boring but the story made no sense whatsoever. Salena usually hated watching these types of flicks but the more weed we smoked, the harder she pretended to like it. She was putting on such a front that my stomach was starting to turn. It was hard enough for everyone to keep a straight face as it was considering how ridiculous she looked, yet she never missed a beat. I'm sure that they had a great laugh after we left. When we got home, I made the mistake of mentioning how I didn't understand the plot of the movie, and she quickly jumped to their defence by saying that "only people with very high intelligence like them or herself would get it." Then I challenged her to tell me what it was all about since she was so smart but she didn't want to talk about it anymore and walked away. The worst part was that now we didn't have to drive down the lake to get weed, there just happened to be a dealer living in the house beside of the complex. This was valuable information provided to us courtesy of our new friends downstairs. All of those weeks of trying to steer her away from drugs was down the drain. Hell, now I could just walk across the parking lot and buy some for her without her having to leave the house. I didn't need her to be there anymore...

    Salena would always annoy me with her interpretations of song lyrics, even when the meanings or messages were already crystal clear, yet she would take a step further after that night and start doing it with movies as well. She seemed to be obsessed with those erotic films like "Wild Orchid" or "9 And a Half Weeks". She would study the female lead's behaviour throughout each frame by not only taking notes, but explaining to me how the men were only puppets and the women were always pulling their strings using sex to keep them under control. I was too naïve to understand where she was going with this or why was she telling me all of this in the first place. She was basically showing me on film what she was doing to me and even Derek before that. No wonder she always went for the younger guys, we were much easier to manipulate. This was her way of making a confession without just coming out and saying it but I just didn't take the hint.

16

This was about the time that she made me her personal guinea pig. She introduced me to one of her best friends in high school who was now happily married with children yet still carried around a dark secret. When this woman was still a teenager, her father did unspeakable things to her body that she learned to enjoy… which included incest. She made me swear not to say anything because even her husband didn't know. Then there was her cousin "Michelle", who had just arrived from out of town to visit. She was drop dead gorgeous with a great personality to boot. I was attracted to her instantly. A couple of days after she left town, Salena suggested that we have a ménage a trois to spice up our sex life a little. When I asked her who would that include, since I found none of her girlfriends very attractive at all, she replied "I can get Michelle." The first question that popped in my head and out of my mouth was "So…you would do your own cousin?" She said, "Not do her…we would just touch each other, maybe kiss for a few minutes…play around a little to arouse you." I was thinking that I must have died and went to heaven and I was confident that I wouldn't have any problems getting it up for those two beauties but I wasn't about to say anything. Unfortunately, due to the chain of events that was about to be set in motion, we didn't even ask her and it never happened. I often wondered how this would have played out if we had and I can only speculate on whether she would have participated or not but now we will never know.

   We would get a call from another one of Salena's closest friends shortly after that, inviting us to the Metallica concert in Knoxville. Her name was "Ann" and I had heard a lot about her but never met her due to her boyfriend "Dan" being such close friends with Derek. Salena asked me if I was going to be comfortable being around them or if it was going to be too awkward. I wasn't sure at first, until she told me that they had two spare tickets to Metallica then I saw it from another angle and thought "why not?" This was during the "black" album tour so they were going to be playing a three hour set with no opening act. I wouldn't miss that for the world! We accepted their offer and were so excited up until the day before the show and then the phone rang...it was Ann, starting the conversation with a question. "Have you got your tickets yet?" she asked. Salena replied, "What do you mean? I thought you had two spare tickets." Ann said, "I never said that." Salena had just assumed that they had the tickets and never actually asked them. They assumed that we already had tickets and was just calling to see if we wanted to go with them. Now I was going no matter what. I knew that there would be scalpers outside the venue and we would be able to score some tickets there. On the day of the show, Dan and Ann came over early so we could get stoned and have a few drinks. Dan had only a couple and said that he was cutting himself off there. He then told us why.

He had hit the bottle hard once before a show and got so drunk that he passed out in the backseat. His friends had tried to wake him up but couldn't so they went inside and left him there to sleep it off. He missed the entire show. We all stopped drinking after that and off to the show we went.

    I paid twice the money that Ann paid for our tickets and our seats were shit. With a little luck, we might be able to look down and see Dan and Ann from up there in the clouds but at least we were going to see the show. When we got seated, we actually *could* see them and we had a good laugh. Then the weed and alcohol really kicked in and we barely said anything until Metallica appeared on the big screen above the stage. We both thought that it was genius how they interacted with the audience from backstage before they played. They had a couple of hot local girls back there with them and although I obviously had no way of knowing it at the time, one of them was going to play a significant part in my future about 8 years later. She would become the real "Storm Child" and the inspiration for the lyrics in the final version of the song. It's a small world indeed...

    The show was, without a doubt, one of the best concerts I have ever seen. It was also the only time I ever saw Dan and Ann, or had a great time with Salena without taking our clothes off first. Then when we got home, instead of talking about how great of a time we had, Salena chose to discuss how Ann was feeling deprived because Dan wasn't as "well endowed" as she would like him to be. Unfortunately, that statement would be used for ammunition and echoed by Salena against me in the not so distant future when the gloves came off and we stopped pulling our punches at the very end of our relationship.

17

    For almost a year, I hadn't heard from any of my "brothers" but one of them was about to resurface not a minute too soon. Kaine and I had run into each other at the shops one day, as we always seem to do when one of us is going through a crisis. He was eager to introduce me to his new girlfriend so we arranged to meet at the Dairy Queen in Lenoir City then he was going to follow us home to stay overnight. When we got back to our place, the girls disappeared after a few minutes so they could talk in private. As the night progressed, we all got very drunk and ended up calling it a night a bit early. Kaine and his girlfriend stayed out in the living room while Salena and I staggered off to the bedroom. As soon as we got settled in, we could hear them fooling around outside, so in typical Salena fashion, she started telling me all of the dirt on Kaine that his girlfriend had told her. I started noticing a pattern here. She was always focusing on the negative, like she thrived on it. She never had anything good to say about any man. She was always the first one to point out any flaws that they might have, and it was really starting to get on my nerves, so our discussion became an argument. Then out of nowhere, she wanted to have sex. As soon as I got stripped down and naked, she started lashing out at me like never before. "Your penis doesn't satisfy me…I'm used to being with very large men. My ex-husband was hung like a horse and Derek was even longer but not as thick. When you go down on me, I get off every time but I'm yet to have an orgasm when you are inside of me." She concluded by saying that my dad must be small too because guys usually inherit that from their fathers and that I was "probably too small to satisfy *any* woman." I was completely caught off guard and that made me totally speechless. I was praying that they weren't hearing any of this outside the room and thinking that this type of abuse was a common occurrence between us on a regular basis. To this day, I don't know what got into her. She hadn't been the same since she talked to Ann, and just when I thought that she had said everything in the book, she kept pushing the knife deeper. She continued to criticize me until she passed out which was just as well since I couldn't get it up now if I wanted to.

Sex became a torture device after that night. Since we had been having unprotected sex for nearly a year, I asked her what happens if we have an "accident" and she got pregnant. Her response was "If I found out that I was pregnant with *your* child, I would throw myself down some stairs to take care of it." This statement would really hurt most people, but at this point, nothing she said really shocked me anymore. It was like I had built up this immunity to her, and was numb to everything. I suggested that we start using some form of birth control and take every possible precaution to prevent this from happening. I saw how she was as a mother and would rather cut off my own balls than allow her to have my child. She wouldn't take the pill or use anything so I tried using a condom later that night. My dad used to say, "Wearing a condom is like taking a shower with your socks on…it just doesn't feel natural." I suppose that the acorn doesn't fall far from the tree because I soon found out that I struggled to use them as well. Not only was I dealing with her being offended that I wanted to be safe, but I had problems keeping an erection once it was on. I've only used a condom a handful of times my whole life and the only reason that I wore them then was because the girls in question gave me the ultimatum to either wear them or I wasn't getting laid. The sad part is that these particular girls were the ones that I really cared about, the ones that I wished I hadn't wrapped up for, because to me, it felt like I wasn't actually *with* them.

After she witnessed the shrinkage that the condoms created, she insisted that I just go back to "pulling out." She always wanted to be on top so she could be "in control" and this night would be no different…or so I thought. As soon as she mounted me, she started going fast and hard like she was double parked. She was restraining me by forcing my hands behind my head like I was being arrested. Obviously, I wasn't going to have much endurance with this much intensity and she knew that. When I started getting sensitive just before, I told her that I was going to come but she ignored me and didn't stop. I told her again but she kept going with a strange grin on her face which made her look almost demonic. I couldn't hold it in any longer and before I could free myself, I came inside of her. After a few seconds, she let go of me and jumped off, acting like she was petrified about what just happened. "Why didn't you tell me that you were about to?" she screamed. I was puzzled and didn't really know what the hell she was talking about. I knew that she heard me *both* times. Hell, I was even trying to break loose as I was saying it. She was up to something but after her actions that night I never had sex with her again so I was going to have to wait a while to find out what it was. Luckily, the wait wasn't going to be as long as I expected…

18

I started taking stupid risks at work, without thinking about the consequences, because I felt that I couldn't sink any lower. When a couple of regular customers asked if I wanted to step outside and get stoned, I went. Unfortunately, the cops just happened to be driving by and thought that three men standing on the side of the building looked suspicious so they stopped in to investigate. I saw them coming and started walking back toward the front. When the two guys saw me walking, they just threw the joint on the ground. I didn't get very far before I was told to stop. When I turned around, I saw two cops standing there with flashlights pointed on me, one of which I usually provide with free coffee and have developed a friendship with. When he saw me, the expression on his face was one of frustration and disappointment. He wanted to arrest the two customers but didn't want to take me in so he was in quite a dilemma. He had no other choice but let us all go to keep me out of trouble even if he not only found the still lit joint on the ground but was holding it in his hand. I felt terrible about putting him and his partner in that situation, and never did any kind of narcotics on the premises again.

    Although I never officially *stole* beer from the store, I did drink old beer that they were planning to throw out anyway when I stocked the coolers. I was about to take that up a notch in order to take beer home. I would sell myself beer, pay for it, and figure out a clever way to get it into my truck without anyone noticing. This was going to be difficult with customers always around and cops usually parked close by which would, at any other time, be a welcomed sight. I developed a genius plan to get it passed everyone without looking suspicious. Every night when I stocked the coolers, I usually took heaps of empty boxes to the bin but if I parked my truck in front of the bin, I could put them in it instead. Even if someone saw me, it looked like I might have been moving house and needed boxes for storage. The catch was that in one of the boxes at the bottom of the pile was not only beer but any other supplies that I was able to write down for "store use" to save money. Even if I got pulled over on the way home, how many cops would bother looking through three stacks of empty cardboard to find the evidence at the bottom? My plan for the beer worked to perfection but somehow someone figured out what I was doing with the supplies but they couldn't prove it so they didn't have a leg to stand on. I only did all of this out of spite and hatred for the owner after how he treated me and I never felt any remorse for doing it. I always find a way to get my revenge...

However, the one risk that I didn't take, but should have, was ceasing the opportunities to cheat on Salena when they presented themselves. I already regretted not acting at the lake that day with an old flame but now another test was about to come my way. A girl from Leon's home store who I admired from a distance came into my store one night and was totally wasted. As soon as she walked in, she came around the counter and started coming on to me. She asked me if I would go back to that infamous stockroom so she could "show me something." When we got back there, she threw her arms around my neck and asked me if I would dance with her. I placed my hands around her waist and slow danced with her but as she leaned in to kiss me, I turned away. For some reason, I was still loyal to Salena even after all she had put me through and just couldn't do it no matter how much I wanted to. I also didn't want to take advantage of a girl who maybe wasn't coherent enough to realize what she was doing and probably wouldn't remember anything the next day. Then there was Leon. What if she told someone about it and it got back to him? I was already on thin ice as it was. Instead of giving in to her advances, I sat her down and made her drink some coffee until she sobered up. I looked after her until I felt she was ok to drive home then sent her on her way. I felt like a complete idiot for doing the right thing but maybe she would appreciate what I did one day. Most guys would have used and/or abused her in that state but tonight, at least, one didn't...

<u>19</u>

 By the time Kathy started coming around again, fresh from her split with AC, our relationship was on life support. She was now with a new guy and wanted Salena to party with her new circle of friends without me. Every night when I got home from work, the house would be empty and I would have no idea where Salena was. All I knew was which street that Kathy's boyfriend lived on and would usually start looking there. Sometimes I would find Salena passed out on the couch, other times they didn't even know where she was. When I did find her, I would usually have to carry her because she was unable to walk. When I couldn't find her, someone would just drop her off randomly at our doorstep and drive away. I pleaded with her to be more responsible and she promised that she would but as the sun started to set, she would repeat the cycle. I didn't know what else to do.

 She was out of control and I started blaming myself. I was the one who pushed her away from her friends at the lake who looked after her and cared about her. I trusted *them* at least. I thought that if I took her to see them, maybe they would become top priority and her new friends would slowly fade away. It couldn't have backfired worse than it did. She insisted that the two groups meet each other and although Maurice had no interest, Joey and Red, who were now dating, were game.

This led up to them accompanying us to a party near the airport. When the alcohol started running low, everyone seemed to have errands to run leaving Joey and me alone at the house. There was an aquarium in the living room that caught Joey's eye. He grabbed the fish food and poured the whole container into the tank. Then he noticed the bloodworms and dumped all of them in there as well while he laughed and screamed "Have some God damned bloodworms, you fuckers!" This was the side of his personality that concerned me. I had seen a glimpse of it when his mother would stop by the store every morning with Maurice and him to pick up snacks and drinks on their way to work. Maurice would just pay for his items and leave but Joey, on the other hand, would pay for the stuff he sat on the counter but would see something that he wanted on the way out the door and just stick it in his pocket. He would always say, "Put it on my tab." The problem was that he didn't have one so I would have to pay for it myself since other customers were watching. He had absolutely no respect for other people's property and I despised him for that. Here we were… in a stranger's house who had been nothing but a pleasant host, trusting us enough to leave us alone in his house with all of his personal belongings, while he is buying more beer for us to drink with his own money, and we show our appreciation by killing all of his fish. I stepped out for air and never returned. When Salena and Kathy came back, she told me that there was someone else that she wanted me to meet. His name was "Craig" and he lived in the trailer next door to the one Joey had just trashed. As soon as we walked in, I could tell that he had a problem with me right off the bat but I didn't know why. Salena and I sat on his couch and he sat on the sofa directly across from us. He kept saying things to try to make me feel uncomfortable or to try to intimidate me. Salena had failed to mention that he, like Joey, had just got out of prison for a murder charge and that he had a thing for her as well. He pulled a pistol and sat it on the coffee table between us. He told me about his stint in prison and how that he could "blow my brains all over the wall without a second thought and take my girl." What he didn't expect was that I wasn't scared, and didn't really react at all to his statement. I just sat there and stared a hole through him while Salena begged for my life. Then I just snapped and said, "Go for it, asshole! Don't pull that fucking thing out if you don't intend on using it. I'm waiting..."His whole demeanour changed and he put the gun away. Then I said, "That's what I thought. Salena, let's go. And Craig, go fuck yourself! That's the only way you are going to get laid. I'm going to fuck her like I do every night" and we left. When we got outside, we could hear Joey laughing about what he had done in front of an angry mob. I took Salena home and vowed to never go around these people again.

    The following Sunday, we were awakened by someone knocking on our front door. It was Joey and Red which was very bizarre considering that they had never been to our place before. I didn't even think that they knew where we lived. It was kind of funny that Joey and Red had started dating considering how Joey used to say that she was a "road dog" because she was so easy. They brought over a couple of cases of beer, a shitload of weed, and quite a wad of cash. I was wondering where Joey had got all of this money from since he wasn't coming into the store every morning with Maurice anymore, and was supposed to be unemployed. He offered to pay for *everything* if we went to party with them at the lake. This was a first...and an offer that we just couldn't refuse. He stressed that he needed to stop by at a particular store, on the way, to pick up a pack of cigarettes. We thought nothing of it at the time but we would find out why he chose that store about a week later.

    There had been a series of robberies all up and down the highway for the last couple of weeks. The culprit had hit every store except for ours, making my aunt very concerned about my safety. I always worked alone on the overnight shift and if you did the math, there was a high probability that our store would be next…but it never happened. Salena rang me at work one night to let me know that she saw on the news that Joey and Red had been arrested and charged with all of the robberies. Apparently, Joey would do the actual holdup and Red would drive the getaway car. Now it all made sense. Not only did we know where he got all of that money, but also why he was so keen to stop at the one particular store after we had just passed several others to get there. He had only robbed that store the night before and this was his way of mocking them or giving them the proverbial "slap in the face" by returning to the crime scene. Hell, he even bought those cigarettes with their money! It was only then that we realized why our store was spared. He may have taken things right in front of me but chose not to do it at gunpoint in case something went wrong and he had to put my life in danger. I was deeply saddened that I lost a friend but what upset me the most was thinking about his young daughter who he was just starting to know. Now there's a chance that he will never see her again. This was one instance that I was glad to know some of the hoodlums of society…it might have saved my life. I must admit that I would have loved to have handed Leon's money to anyone under those circumstances. The bastard would have deserved it.

20

    I was weary of making any new friends after the whole Joey fiasco, but there were two guys who I met at the store that still managed to win me over somehow. Their names were "Floyd" and "Sam" and they used to keep me company throughout the night which gave me a slight sense of security. I told Salena about them and every time that I had arranged for them to meet, something would come up and someone had to cancel. I cherished their friendship because I really had no one to talk to about my issues at home. They were more than happy to lend me their ears, and I valued their opinions, which made them a godsend during those uncertain times. But things aren't always what they seem...

    It was only a few days later that my life was literally going to come unglued. Salena had now stopped coming home at all and since Kathy was dating a new guy, I didn't even know where to start looking anymore. I had just put in for my vacation that I had busted my ass for a year to get, and I had plans to use it to try to rekindle the spark between Salena and I that was close to being extinguished. But those plans went right out the window when she had been gone for several days without even giving me a simple phone call. I searched for her the first couple of days but her trail had gone cold... none of our mutual friends had seen or heard from her. Just as I was about to call the police and file a missing person's report, she came wandering in the front door. The first words out of her mouth were that we needed to talk, so we sat down, and she told me everything. She had not only met someone but she had been having sex with him for the past few days. Then she had to let me know how much she enjoyed having sex with *him.* I was heartbroken and tears were starting to roll down my cheeks so I did what any stupid kid would do...I begged her not to leave me and took full responsibility for pushing her towards infidelity. At first, it wasn't working but the more I poured my heart out to her, the more I could see her walls starting to come down. Then I kissed her, and although I could feel her pushing away at first, she eventually started to kiss me back. That was all it took to weaken her defences. She agreed to end her affair and give our relationship another chance.

We were starting over with a clean slate. We had weathered the storm and came out on the other side. It was a new day. When I left for work, she kissed me and said "I love you. Have a great night. I will see you when you get home." I asked her if she really meant it this time and she assured me that it came from her heart. "I will see you in the morning" she repeated. I stared up at her one last time before I reversed, to see her standing on the balcony... watching and waving. This was the first time in months that I had a positive outlook about our future. Too bad I had forgotten that her trademark phrase was that she "tricks people" and I was about to pay the ultimate price for it.

21

When I got home, my darkest fears had come true... she was nowhere to be found. This time it was the end of the line for me. I called Kathy the next morning at her grandparents' house where she was staying and she gave me directions to their place so I could pick her up. I think that although she may have planted the seeds for Salena to cheat on me, she realized that the way she went about it was wrong and it was time to end this once and for all. When I got there, her senile grandfather tried to pick a fight with me because he didn't want her leaving the house. We just ignored him, got into my truck, and drove away while he stood there waving his fists and calling me every name in the book.

I wasn't surprised at all that she knew exactly where Salena was. It was probably a twenty minute drive away so I had a few minutes to think about what I was going to say and do when I finally saw her. At first, I was going to fight for her but then I started remembering all of the significant moments over the past year when she made me feel like a piece of shit, and as they passed before my eyes, I realized that she wasn't worth it and I had a last minute change of heart. I was just going to say goodbye… nothing more. To be honest, she didn't even deserve that.

When we walked in, I was relieved to see two familiar faces shooting a game of pool with a third guy that I didn't know. It was my new "friends" Floyd and Sam but they didn't appear to be as thrilled to see me as I was to see them. I nodded my head to greet them but they just seemed to glare at me for some reason. Then I saw Salena, walking toward their table with a round of drinks in her hand. I approached their table as well and got there about the same time that she did. When she looked up and saw me standing there, the look on her face was priceless. As soon as he saw her reaction, the third guy figured out who I was, and stood at Salena's side while Floyd and Sam snuck up behind me. Suddenly, I was surrounded and I knew that this could get ugly pretty quick if I didn't handle it right. It was obvious who her new guy was by how he was clinging to her, but I didn't know how Floyd and Sam fit into the puzzle yet.

I asked Salena if we could talk somewhere in private which made her new boyfriend become very uncomfortable and defensive. Of course, I knew from my own personal experiences with her that if she wanted to go, she was going whether he supported her decision or not. She knew that this was it, the perfect opportunity to break clean, so she agreed. It started with me asking her if this was what she truly wanted and if he made her happy which she answered with a very resounding "Yes!" At this point that was all that I really needed to hear. I replied with a simple "Ok" and that was all that I had on this day. Then I just had to ask how Floyd and Sam were involved in all of this. That's when she informed me that Floyd was actually her new boyfriend's brother. They were coming in the store every night to basically spy on me and make sure that I didn't leave work early while his brother was fucking my girlfriend. I think that their betrayal hurt me more than what she did. Then her new boyfriend decided that we had been out there long enough so he came out to make a complete ass out of himself. I didn't get a chance to say anything before she put him in his place. She told him that I was being cool about everything so he should basically "shut the fuck up." She knew my temper and my lack of tolerance pretty well and although I'm calm at the moment, that could all change at the drop of a hat. Luckily for him, he got the message. I shook his hand and told him to take very good care of her, then hugged Salena, and left. Hopefully, Kathy didn't want a ride home because I completely forgot about her and left her there.

    I don't think that it actually hit me until I got home and I just lost it. I trashed the house and then ran up her phone bill so much that it would have to be disconnected. After I packed my things, I took one last look around the apartment which now looked like a tornado had hit it then closed this chapter in my life. I'm not sure if I even locked her

front door. It's funny how life works out sometimes. I lost her in the same manner that I got her in the first place. What goes around comes around I suppose...
-DJN

Chapter III – *"THE CROSSROADS PART II"*

1992-1993

Finally, she was gone... and what I didn't think about, but should have been, was where I was going to live. Now I was officially on vacation as well and had no intentions of going back to that cesspool once it was over either. I just needed somewhere to rest my head while I licked my wounds and my parents' house was not an option. My parents were old school which meant that you went to work as soon as you turned 16 and could drive. You should also be out of the house at 18, and no matter what the circumstances were, don't come back...you were on your own. I had a little money put back so I pretty much lived at the mall until it closed, then slept in my truck overnight. I had never felt so alone in my entire life.

Then I saw someone at the mall one evening who understood what I was going through probably more than anyone else on the planet...Derek. I approached him and extended my hand as a gesture to make amends, then told him what happened. He wasn't surprised and quickly changed the topic. We talked about everything and realized that we had a lot more in common than just her. I knew now that I was wrong about him all along and apologized. We ended up hanging around together the rest of the evening then he asked me if I had a place to stay for the night which I didn't. He invited me over to his parents' house where he had been living since I took his girl away. When we got there we talked and listened to music, then went out to his backyard so he could build a large bonfire and have a few drinks. I was really starting to like Derek and I could tell that the feeling was mutual. His parents were also very cool as they socialized with us a bit then went and did their own thing which was very refreshing considering what I was used to. We sat out there for hours and when we were over it, went back inside to crash. Before we passed out, Derek told me about a small party that he was going to the following day and told me that I was more than welcome to join him and his friend if I could give them a ride. My schedule was free so why not? I was honoured and more than happy to oblige.

    I met them at the mall and found Derek's friend to be as charming and likeable as he was. We hit it off immediately as I usually did with any other fellow head banger wearing a mullet in those days. I drove them to a house where three girls were waiting...two very attractive and an ugly one. Strangely, the ugly one was the only one who had a boyfriend, and it was *her* house. The lines were clearly drawn where the boys stood and I was supposed to be the odd man out. When our host brought out a bottle of whiskey, I chugged about half of it in one drink to impress not only the girls but Derek as well which inspired him to say, "Dude, you were around Salena way too long. I don't think we're going to have enough liquor to go around."

    The more I drank, the more obnoxious I became. Within minutes, I was not only sitting beside both of the attractive girls, but I had my arms around each of them. One was very receptive and moved closer to me but the other not so much. If this disrespected the boys, they didn't show it as they decided to go get more alcohol and leave me alone with the girls. By the time they got back, I was wasted and the bottle was almost empty. As I went to take one last drink to polish off the bottle, the unthinkable happened. I started vomiting and everything turned black. Apparently, I kept vomiting even while I was unconscious which is very dangerous. The fact that I hadn't eaten anything all day had come back to bite me on the ass. All that I remember about the next few hours was the concern on everyone's face when I initially got sick, and in and out memories of Derek and his friend dragging me back and forth to the toilet a couple of times. Everything else was a complete blur.

When I woke up the next morning, I was disorientated and lying face down in a puddle on the floor in a different room. Their decision to place me in that position probably saved my life. When I tried to raise my head, I realized that my face was firmly stuck to the floor so trying to break free was going to look like that scene in the first "Hellraiser" movie when Frank's remains were being resurrected by the blood. My armpits were extremely sore and as I would notice in the shower later that morning, heavily bruised as well. At first, I didn't know where I was until I saw everyone staring at me from down the hall and then it all came back to me. I peeled myself off the floor, dusted myself off, and approached them not knowing what I was going to say when I got there. The only words that managed to come out were "Are you guys ready to go home?" I didn't offer to clean up the mess I made or even apologize. I just walked out the door. It was a quiet ride home that day because we all knew that we probably wouldn't ever do this again…and we didn't.

2

Since my attempt to make new friends was an epic fail, I turned to an old one: Kaine. I asked him if I could move in with him until I got my shit together, and he seemed to like the idea. He had a place in Lenoir City which meant that I was about to be reunited with two more of my "brothers" from school who lived in the area "Tony" and "Mason". I hadn't seen them in over a year so it felt great to have them back in my life again. We spent most of our time drinking and jamming in the basement which Kaine and I had devoted to our guitars and amps and nothing else. I must say that just being around my "brothers" helped to put the nightmare that was my life for the past year behind me.

However, Kaine had a new, younger girlfriend who wasn't exactly the easiest person to get along with. She didn't seem like the fact that I was living there or anyone being around the house that might draw a little attention away from her. When Kaine got home every morning, she was always with him. She would usually come in first and make her rounds to find something to complain about to create friction between Kaine and I or the boys when they spent the night. It wasn't like the house was clean before and we wrecked it, it always looked like a tornado had just hit it. Only once was her accusations justified and that was when Mason nearly knocked the fridge over in front of Kaine in a drunken stupor. Knowing Kaine as well as I did, I knew that my days there were numbered.

Kaine and his girlfriend decided to take it upon themselves to "put me back on the market" or help me "play the field" so to speak by trying to set me up on a couple of double dates with their single friends. The first girl was quite attractive but had just recently split from her boyfriend and was clearly using me to rebound. When I was alone with her on the couch, in the moonlight, I made my move and kissed her, hoping that would take her mind off of him. I did this several times and I could tell that she liked it by the way she was kissing me back, but every time I stopped, she started talking about him again. I eventually got frustrated and just walked away. The second girl was just as attractive but was a single mother which was already one strike against her to me. I had just got out of that situation and wasn't ready or willing to give it a chance again anytime soon, especially after her son started calling me "daddy" as soon as he saw me. We had a great time shooting pool and at dinner but by the time we got back to her place, I had no interest in her whatsoever. I don't know what it was, but we just didn't click. I didn't even want to sit near her so I kept my distance. Kaine and I did manage to drink all of her alcohol and even gave the kid a few sips so we could laugh as we watched him stumble around. There was a sigh of relief when she decided to turn in for the night and not ask me to join her. This was one occasion that I was more than happy to sleep on the couch. It would be one of the smartest decisions I ever made.

    The next morning, I was startled by someone violently pounding on the front door. I wasn't going to answer it considering that it wasn't my house and whoever was out there definitely wasn't there to see me but when I realized that they weren't leaving until they spoke to someone, I had no other choice but to open the door. There stood a young woman who looked like she was ready to kill someone. The first words that came out of her mouth were "Ok, where is that little slut hiding?" I said, "Excuse me?" She responded with "Do you know that your girlfriend has been having an affair with my husband?" I replied "She's not my girlfriend… I actually just met her last night. I don't know where she is either. I did hear her leave early this morning but I have no idea where she went." Then she said "I hope you didn't fuck her because she gave my husband crabs and he spread it to me. That's how I found out that he was cheating on me." I told her that I didn't and that I was very sorry about everything but I don't really know what else to say. She thanked me and told me "When you see that fucking bitch, tell her that I know about her and I will get her one day when she least expects it." I said I would pass along her message and closed the door.

Kaine and his girlfriend woke up about an hour later and joined me downstairs. I had been awake since that woman left and I couldn't wait to tell them what happened and get the hell out of there. After I informed them, they agreed that it was probably time to leave. A couple of days later, Kaine told me that both he and his girlfriend had crabs now as well. Apparently, they caught it from the sheets on the bed in her guest room where they had sex that night. I felt like my guardian angel had put in some overtime this week…that could have easily been me.

Those two experiences made me weary of dating again and someone was about to suffer for it. Kaine had warned me that his cousin had taken a liking to me and she was coming to our next party. She was a wholesome girl, different from anyone else I had been involved with in the past, so I was looking forward to meeting her. When that night came, the boys wanted to go cruising around Lenoir City in Tony's jeep before we started drinking and I wasn't going to miss that for anything in the world. That left her in an awkward situation. She could either sit at the house alone or tag along with us and she chose the latter. She sat beside me in the backseat the entire time, quiet as a mouse, while we drooled over all the hot chicks on the strip and didn't seem to mind. When we got back to the house, I decided to plant a kiss on her to see if I could feel anything there. I have kissed countless women in my day but this girl kissed me harder than *anyone* ever has…it actually hurt! Her braces left my mouth bleeding and sore for days afterwards. As she was leaving, she handed me her number and said, "Call me sometime." Even with Kaine constantly urging me to do so, I never dialled that number. I wasn't ready for a relationship yet so I just let it all fizzle out and die, not taking into consideration or caring that I probably hurt her feelings in the process.

    Between me and Kaine consistently hitting the comic book shops or the flea market every weekend and my idea of adding HBO to our monthly cable package at my expense, my reckless and careless spending had drained my savings. I was so desperate for money that I searched through my baseball cards to see if I had anything of value to sell. I found a Cal Ripken rookie card and since he made history when he broke the Ironman record, it should bring a hefty price according to my guides. Kaine even gave me a protective cover for it to make it more presentable. When I took it to the shop, the owner was more than happy to buy it from me…for only a fraction of what it was worth. Although it was in mint condition, he claimed that it had many flaws even if I couldn't see them, and that made its value drop significantly. Unfortunately, I needed cash and voluntarily let him rip me off. I had to get a job very soon because this was getting ridiculous.

3

    When I spoke to my parents later that week, I asked them to keep an eye on the newspaper and let me know if there were any new job listings. A few days later, my mom called and told me about a lawn and landscaping job just down the road from our house, and even offered to take me down there to talk to the owner in person. I met the owner just outside a recycling plant that his father-in-law owned and operated and where he worked as a truck driver. The interview was only two questions, "Are you at least 18 years of age?" which I was and a second one that I wasn't expecting. He looked me straight in the eyes and asked me "Are you gay?" I busted out laughing thinking that he was joking but he was dead serious. I said, "No, I'm not." Then he replied "Good! You're hired. You start tomorrow morning. This is where we meet every morning because this is where I store all of the equipment. Be here at 8am and don't be late or we're leaving without you." I thanked him and we left.

    I was thrilled and couldn't wait to tell Kaine the good news but when I got there, he was already asleep. His girlfriend was just sitting on the couch watching television and asked if I would care to join her. This seemed odd considering that it was obvious to everyone that we didn't like each other. After a few minutes, she asked if I would watch some pornography with her out of the blue. Something was fishy, but I agreed for some reason. She put a tape in the VCR and we watched for a short while before the whole scenario started making me feel very uncomfortable, but it was about to get far worse. What she asked me next was completely inappropriate. "Do you want to fuck?" I was speechless. Then she added "Kaine will never know unless you tell him." I couldn't believe what I was hearing. I declined and locked myself in my room until morning.

    When Kaine got home the next morning, I told him what happened. He seemed to appreciate that I told him and didn't seem surprised. He wished me luck at my new job and said that he was going to take care of this once and for all. I was very confident that he was going to do the right thing and give her the boot and that there was going to be a much easier road ahead for both of us. When I got home, it was exactly the opposite. He told me that they were getting married and I needed to be out by the end of the week. Here I was, trying to be honest and show my "brother" that he could trust me, and he betrayed *me* for my efforts. Now I was about to be homeless again, but I wasn't about to live in my truck again. It was time to just take my ball and go home...

4

    I felt like such a failure for turning to my parents for help but at least I had a job that was a definite step up from that damn store. The pay wasn't great for the amount of work I was expected to do and the hours were long. I was literally working from sunrise to sunset but at least I was working outdoors which was a plus. My partner was making twice my salary, and since he had the title of "manager" did very little work as well. I thought that since there were only three of us in this company and two of them had titles were ridiculous but since I was the low man on the totem pole, there wasn't much I could do about it. Whether we were mowing lawns or doing landscaping, I did all of the physical labour while they did all of the lighter work.

    After about a month, it was all starting to take a toll on my body. I had been stung by yellow jackets countless times due to accidently hitting their nests while mowing, including nearly a hundred stings in just one incident on my right leg which made it painful to walk for nearly a week. The sun had scorched my skin to a degree that every time we came inside the office at the end of the day I would nearly pass out as soon as I felt cooler air whether I was standing or sitting at the time. Yet, I never complained or missed a day of work unless it was raining and no one worked then anyway. The only real problem I had was seeing the grass when there was not a significant length being cut from it due to my poor eyesight. The guys had noticed this issue and asked why I was taking so long to finish. They said that it was like I was going in circles over the same area, which meant that I was wasting time, money, and gas. They had no idea that I was almost legally blind, and I felt that it was more beneficial to me if it stayed that way.

For the most part, I got along with both of the other guys. I loved their sense of humour. The manager loved to play golf so he would always channel his inner "Caddyshack" and quote Bill Murray's lines from the movie. He had obviously practiced a lot, because he had the voice down perfectly. The owner, although he rarely went out on a job with us, would always sing along with whatever song was playing on the radio while we were travelling. He would sing so high pitched that it actually hurt my ears. He also used a lot of sarcasm while dealing with customers as well. On one occasion, an older woman asked us the best way to clear the jungle beside her house. The owner replied, "Have you ever considered using napalm?" His expression never changed and I was holding back laughter as hard as I could. Her response was "I think I've heard of that. It sounds very interesting. How much do you think that will cost?" It was all we could do to keep a straight face while he kept running with it. When we got in the car, we could hold it back no longer.

My nights were usually spent hanging around the mall with my friend "Jack" playing "Street Fighter" or "Mortal Kombat" in the arcade or hitting the air hockey table with a vengeance at the pizza place. We would hit the puck so hard that when it flew off the table and hit the wall, it would either dent it or knock a hole in it. They had to put rails on both sides of the table because of us but it still didn't help. When we nearly hit a woman carrying an infant with a flying puck, the manager had finally had enough and asked us to leave. I was unbeatable at that game for many years, dominating anyone who dared to challenge me. Jack was the only person I ever played who could beat me in those days, and that wasn't very often. We would then go cruising which was usually quite boring due to Jack's shyness. Most of the night, I would be pretty much talking to myself and when he did say something, it would usually just one sentence and then he was quiet again. He never had much to say, but he was a great friend and a fierce competitor.

5

Back at work, it was still all fun and games until we were asked to mulch a massive flower bed for the man who supposably "owned the Nickelodeon Channel and used to own MTV." Just mowing his lawn each week was a full day chore, and when he requested that we trim his expensive, fragile trees, it took at least two. Since his driveway wrapped around the hill that the bed was on, the plan changed from the manager working with me to him just picking up a load of mulch in his air conditioned truck, dumping it at the top of the hill and then leave to pick up another while I spread it down the hill and around the trees with a rake by hand. It was a hundred degrees plus outside and since mulch actually absorbs heat, I felt like I was standing on the surface of the planet Venus. I had no access to water and no one even bothered to offer me a drink. About every 30 minutes, I tried to find some of the limited shade to get out of the boiling sun but I was so dehydrated that I felt sick and weak regardless. The manager only helped me late in the evening as the sun was starting to set and it was cooling down. This went on for 3 treacherous days until the job was finished, and the more I thought about the whole situation, the madder I became. I had to say something to someone or it would never stop.

    I felt like I had a healthy enough relationship with the owner to be able to be open and honest about any concerns or issues that I was having, so when I had the opportunity, I told him how I didn't appreciate doing all of the work when the manager and I was supposed to be working *together* as a team. His response was "I thought that was what was going on. I will have a talk with him about pulling his own weight more. I am very sorry about all of this." The next two days we didn't work because of the heavy rain, so I was surprised when I received a phone call from him late in the evening on that second day. He opened the conversation by telling me that he rang me to inform me of some changes that he was forced to make. At first, I was very optimistic, thinking that *finally* something was going to go my way for once but this was not about just any ordinary person, this was *me* that we're talking about here. The next words that came out of his mouth were more like what I had grown accustomed to. He said "I don't want to but I'm going to have to let you go. Business is getting slow and I just can't afford to keep you on." The first thought that popped into my head was how this felt like a case of deja-vu. Another person stabs me in the back with a lame bullshit excuse. It was the middle of summer for crying out loud and business was actually picking up. Once again, honesty wasn't the best policy, and this time it costed me my job.

6

I wasn't looking forward to telling my parents that I was unemployed again. There was already enough tension in the house without throwing another log on the fire. My parents resented me for being there, and I regretted coming back after that guilt trip that they put on me after I fell on my ass in the real world. I was also furious at my father for a more personal reason. On the day that I moved back home, I noticed that something was missing but I just couldn't put my finger on what it was at first. It wasn't until I had unloaded the truck and was sitting down having a bite to eat that it hit me. *"Where were the dogs?"* No matter how long between visits, those dogs were *always* there to greet me when I came home...always happy to see me. They loved me unconditionally even if I did leave them behind for a piece of ass. But this time, there was no sign of *any* of them, including mom's dog "Pooh", who never strayed far from the front yard. I asked mother where they were, already preparing myself mentally for the worst possible answer before she had time to respond. "Your dad put them down. They had been chasing around a bitch in heat for days and when they came home, they were already agitated and acting quite aggressive. When Pooh came up to them and starting playing around with them as he always did, they turned on him and ripped him to shreds right in front of us. Your dad was so furious that he shot them both and buried all three of them together in an unmarked grave in the hills." Looking back on it now, I can understand *why* he did it but back then, there was nothing he could say that would make up for what he did.

It was the way that he lured them up to those hills that bothered me the most. The dogs used to go everywhere with me. They enjoyed that more than anything in the world and dad knew that. When I moved away, dad took my place and started taking them with *him.* All he had to do was lower the bucket on the tractor and say "Load up" and the dogs would jump in but little did they know that this ride was one that they were never coming back from. He drove the unsuspecting dogs up to the spot where they would take their last breath and where Pooh's remains were lying uncovered in a hole and put a bullet in both of their heads. To this day, I still feel that this was inappropriate. The one thing in life, the one perk that brought them such joy and happiness was used against them and led them to their deaths. Although, in time I learned how to deal with the fact that I was never going to see them again and never even got to say goodbye, I still haven't forgiven my father for how he went about it.

7

As soon as I told my mother that I lost my job, she suggested and made arrangements for me to have an interview with a local temporary agency. After I had spoken to the lady and had found out more information about what they do, and how their process actually works, I didn't want any part of it. They already had a job lined up for me before I even walked through the door at a nearby industrial park. They also had the paperwork ready to go so they could take out a portion of my hourly wages that I would work for to fill their own pockets since they "found" this position for *me.* The only reason I agreed to these terms was that there was a possibility that I could be a permanent employee if I did well through my 90 day probation period and impressed the company enough with my work ethic. I still thought that this was a scam...a way to save the company money and deceive the employee with false hopes of advancement and benefits but I promised my mother that I would go through with it, so leaving empty handed wasn't an option. As I was leaving I was told to "only wear plain, white t-shirts because I wasn't representing *myself*, I was representing *them*." I was starting to dislike this arrangement more and more with each passing second.

In a bizarre twist, I actually liked my job and got along with all the people I worked with. Although I had heard horror stories about most of the other departments, the shipping area where I worked was gravy. The only thing that I didn't like was the breaks. We had two 10 minute breaks (one in the morning, the other in the afternoon) and an hour long lunch break. Since it took nearly 5 minutes to even get to the *closest* break room, by the time you got seated, it was almost time to go back. The fact that no one ever included me in their conversations didn't help either. Lunch was actually worse, because my whole crew scattered, leaving me to fend for myself in a room full of strangers. The guys would all go to the picnic area by the lake just down the road and not once did they invite me to join them. The two women on our crew would go eat with their friends in other departments, leaving me all alone.

One of my old classmates recognized me one day and started sitting with me for a week or so until I found out that she was having an affair with one of the married men on my crew. I thought that it was probably a bad idea to be the new kid on the block stepping on someone else's toes by eating lunch everyday with his mistress, so I started avoiding her like the plague. She did, however, give me some great advice beforehand. She told me that my position has been a revolving door over the past year and that was probably the reason that my crew felt like it was a waste of time to get to know me. She also told me that my supervisor gets a larger bonus if my position is never filled, so don't get too comfortable. She also made me aware that I probably knew quite a few people that worked there, but due to the sheer size of the building, I would probably never see them. But if I did, ask them to help you transfer to another department before my probation was over.

 I was determined to prove them all wrong. When the supervisor came around to ask if anyone could stay back and work overtime, everyone refused, except for me. I did everything in my power to show them how much this job meant to me through my hard work and dedication. I never questioned anything that I was told or asked to do, I just did it. I was confident that they would decide to keep me. I just hoped that the guys already had a spot at the picnic table reserved for me.

 When that day finally came, I was called in to the supervisor's office to discuss my role and future with the company. I was both nervous and excited but I tried not to show it by just acting natural. He just got straight to the point. "Things just aren't working out so your services are no longer required." I was almost in tears when I asked him what I did wrong, especially when he couldn't even provide an answer. I asked him if I could have another chance and he said "You already had your chance, and besides your replacement starts tomorrow. It's a done deal. I couldn't do anything about it now even if I wanted to." At this point, not only was I getting emotional and it seemed that even he was also. I had to get out of there before I did shed a tear, and by the time I got to my truck, I couldn't hold them back any longer. I knew that my performance had nothing to do with his decision, greed did. I drove away feeling like a piece of shit and vowed to *never* work for another temporary agency again and that was one promise that I made myself that I managed to keep. Ironically, that recruiter called me the following week with another job offer and I pretty much told her to "go fuck herself" and that "I would rather starve or live on the streets than work for you vultures again." After saying all of that I felt much better…as you could probably imagine.

8

It was time to start doing something that always made me feel better both mentally and physically…going to the gym. I jumped back into it with a passion, spending at least 3 hours a day with the heavy weights and about 30 minutes of cardio. There was also a new girl working at the front desk in the evenings who caught my eye, so for several weeks I spent as much time talking to her as I did training. She was a busy girl to say the least…not only working at the gym but had a job at Dollywood as well. She was also going to college to complete her studies and get her degree so maintaining this schedule for a long period of time was impossible. Before I could build up the courage to ask her out, she was already gone, which was probably a good thing. Now I could really focus on my body instead of hers. I also started tanning every other day to give my skin a little colour to make me look even better. I was starting to get my confidence and swagger back.

I began to surround myself with people who motivated me and who I could draw energy from. Two of them, I would develop a close friendship with. One was a 60 year old, retired military officer who was in better physical condition than most 20 year olds. His son was one of my old classmates who had decided to follow in his father's footsteps and enlist as well. Sometimes, when he was on leave, he would come to the gym with his father and they would train together. The other was the deacon at a local church that seemed to care more about chasing tail than working out, which would be ok, if he wasn't already married with a couple of small children. He started getting really close to a beautiful brunette and would often disappear without saying anything and return in a much better mood a half hour later. It wasn't really a surprise when I got word that he was stripped of his membership after being caught in a very compromising position with that girl on the premises by the owner of the gym. This wasn't a big loss considering that he only lifted weights when there was a lady present and after he got a good pump, would usually approach her and strike up a conversation. He was more of a distraction than an inspiration, so I felt that it was time for him to leave anyway.

    Summer was coming to an end so my dad suggested that we go on what would be our last family vacation. First, we thought about going back to my second home: Clearwater Beach, Florida. Then dad suggested a change of scenery. He wanted to see New Orleans, and then follow the coast up to Panama City so we could see a part of Florida that we hadn't seen before. I was all for it, especially since the Panama City area was the old stomping grounds of my "brother" Tony, so I packed up my video camera and other necessities and off we went. We drove across Tennessee one more time and headed south straight through Mississippi, then across to Louisiana while I was filming everything that I thought was interesting. When we got to the welcome center just across the Louisiana state line,

I was blown away. On the wall were numerous pictures of haunted tourist attractions like old plantation houses and even older cemeteries, and underneath each one told us not only where they were, but provided directions on how to get there. I wanted to see them all but I knew the parents weren't interested in seeing *any* of them, so I was "shit out of luck" as they say. At least, New Orleans was filled with haunted locations so there was a slight chance I might be able to talk them into taking a tour once we got there.

    Everyone was having a great time until dad chose to come off the main highway and take the "scenic route." Like what happens in countless horror films, we got lost…but we didn't come across a family of cannibals or a serial killer wearing a mask, we ran into something far worse in my dad's eyes at least: the state police. After we stopped at a gas station to fill up and ask for directions, the cops in the parking lot noticed that we had Tennessee plates so they decided to tail us for a few miles. Dad *always* carried a firearm with him when he travelled, which is illegal, so he started to panic. My mother tried to get him to relax but that seemed to make him angrier, and eventually it led to an argument. They never pulled us over but the incident changed the whole mood of the trip.

    There are only two things in this world that I *know* my dad is afraid of…the cops and severe weather. We had just dealt with the cops and now we were hearing reports on the radio that there was a tropical storm headed toward the gulf coast and New Orleans. The sky was getting darker the closer we got to the Big Easy and I could tell that my dad was thinking about turning around, but my mother and I kept encouraging him not to. By the time we got there, we were in the heart of the storm and stuck in a traffic jam. We pleaded with dad to just get a room for the night but he was determined to get away from this storm as quickly as possible, so he basically turned around and headed back in the direction we came. The further we got from New Orleans, the clearer the skies were. By the time we got to the coast, the sun was shining yet the beaches were empty with the exception of one buxom blonde in a bikini walking on the shore that I caught on camera. It was such a cool scene that it looked like a painting. We must have passed a dozen hotels on the coast but dad wanted to go further inland to be on the safe side. We ended up on the outskirts on Biloxi before dad decided to stop and get a room.

    The place he picked was a fucking dump filled with cockroaches, a stagnant pool, and a television that was probably older than me. Mom and I teased him about picking this shithole after we passed so many luxurious hotels to get to this one and even dad had to laugh. "At least, we have a pool" he joked. After fumigating our luggage, I decided to take a walk to get some fresh air. I strolled around the complex until I reached the second level and noticed a room with the door open. As I passed it, I noticed two girls either my age or slightly older sitting on the bed having a conversation. I made it a point to walk past it again to get a closer look. When I did, one of the girls yelled out "Hey dude, come here!" My heart was racing as I anticipated what *could* happen when I got there. They asked me to come inside and close the door which made me start getting an instant erection whether I wanted one or not. "You're cute. Do you smoke weed?" she asked. "Of course" I replied. "Do you want to get high with us?" she asked. Although, I was fully aware of the kind of trouble I would be in if my parents found out, there was no way I was going to say no to these two goddesses. We talked about a little bit of everything while they rolled up the joint, and even as we passed it around, but not in a hundred years would I have expected what happened next. As soon as we put it out, they asked me to leave so that they could be alone. Any potential that this was going to be the best vacation *ever* went right out the window. This incident just added to the way the rest of the trip had gone so far…a Clark Griswold- like disaster! I don't know why I thought that my luck was about to change.

    Now I had a bigger problem facing me. I was stoned and had to figure out a way to get past my parents and make it through the next couple of hours without them noticing that I was high. As I walked past the pool I heard "Denny! Come here so we can have a talk." For some reason, dad was sitting on a lawn chair at the pool having a cigarette and his sense of timing couldn't have been worse. He had picked up smoking again recently so we often went for a smoke *together* which still didn't feel natural after years of butting heads over them. He offered me one and I accepted it to help cover up the scent of marijuana on my clothes. He had a nose like a bloodhound when it comes to those things, and I was desperate to cover my tracks. Even if my scent was covered, I was still paranoid that he would notice my red, bloodshot eyes considering that this was someone who had never been high in his life so he knew what to look for. I don't know whether it was the dim lighting or the cigarettes, but there had to be some divine intervention at work because he never suspected or detected anything. We ended up having a pleasant conversation about the road ahead to Panama City. He even apologized for how everything was going on this trip so far. It was definitely one of those rare, bonding moments that didn't come around very often over the years.

After a good night's sleep, we headed down the coast the next morning. We all enjoyed the scenery of beautiful beaches and thick swamps along the way but when we reached Panama City, we were shocked by what we saw. Apparently, the storm that we avoided in New Orleans had swept across Panama City on its way and although all of the structures were still intact, the beach looked like something out of an apocalyptic movie. There were seaweed and fish carcasses everywhere, and the stench was unbearable. No one was in or near the water, and there were only a handful of people walking along the beach who seemed to be just going back and forth to the pier. Dad had finally seen enough and was ready to start heading home. We got back into the van and headed north into Alabama and didn't stop until we reached Fort Payne where we would spend the night before coming back to Tennessee. This had definitely been a trip for the ages, and luckily, I had caught most of it on film.

9

As soon as we got back home, I got a part time job working at the local K-Mart. I was part of the "replenishment" team as they called it, which basically meant that I was nothing more than a glorified "filler" or "stocker." I also became a number instead of a name and had to wear that stupid red vest. My team was under the guidance of a woman who was so obsessed with tanning that she looked about a decade or two older than she actually was. She insisted on being called the "replenishment supervisor" instead of a manager and was one of those people who constantly insulted you or made fun of you with a smile on her face to make it seem that she was kidding when you knew that she wasn't. She seemed to have taken a "liking" to me personally, and invited me over to her house to tan in her bed almost every single day without fail. She would try to entice me in by saying "Why are you wasting your money paying for visits at your gym when you can use my bed anytime you want for free?" I never went because I had a feeling that her tanning bed wasn't the only bed that she wanted to share with me, and in time that would be verified.

Although I wasn't interested in screwing around with another married woman, I was lonely and finally ready for female companionship once again. The first girl who interested me was already in a relationship with someone I knew, which made her off limits. The second turned out to be a single mother which disqualified her. The third was practically engaged, but I didn't know the guy and that meant that she was not safe from me. I knew from the beginning that she was attracted to me but didn't want to act on it and that seemed to make me want her more. I was sure that if I got her alone, she wouldn't be able to resist me and I was right. On that day, I saw on her in the back with no one around and started working my magic. I started kissing her softly on the neck which caused her to breathe heavy and let out a soft moan, then worked my way to her lips. There was no hesitation on her part as we started making out. It seemed like she had forgotten all about her fiancé for a few minutes before she stopped me and said that "she couldn't do this anymore." That would be her only chance, as I completely lost interest and never pursued her again. I saw no other prospects in my immediate future but that was about to change. Inside of this building was one young lady who was going to make me do something that I swore that I was *never* going to do in my lifetime...and we were on a collision course.

10

    In the meantime, all I did was turn people against me. It all started when Tony invited me to wander around Gatlinburg with him on one of my nights off. We had a great time there but when we got back to Maryville, I insisted that we pop a few over the counter speed pills. I had experimented with these on several occasions back when I still worked at that convenience store for a quick fix after some overnight parties. Since we sold these at the store, I always had access to them anytime I wanted them. However, there was one downside...when I came off of them they usually made me sick to my stomach. Someone suggested to me once that I should try chopping them up and snorting them through a straw but all that ever accomplished was fucking up my nose, making it difficult to breathe. After taking about four apiece, I was feeling great until we headed home...then it hit me. I asked Tony if we could stop to get a jug of milk because I had also heard, probably from the same source, that milk would "settle my stomach" if the pills started to make me feel unwell. After downing the whole bottle I only got sicker, and this time I started spewing before Tony had a chance to pull off the road. My head was out the window, going about 55mph, and chunks were flying...all over the side of Tony's car! He was furious and stopped at the nearest car wash so I could wash it off. When I got out of the jeep, I was surprised that the entire side was covered with a white substance that looked like snow. The combination of pills and milk didn't look like your typical vomit, it was actually quite pretty, but unfortunately it did smell like it. I washed it off and we crashed at Tony's place. This was the last time that we would ever go anywhere together in his car.

    I managed to piss off most of my crew at work as well. I was responsible for the pet department and had a great idea on how to get rid of all of the old stock that had been collecting dust in the back. I would build a huge display that featured all of these items because I knew that we would never sell this crap if it wasn't on the sales floor. Everyone was very supportive until the unthinkable happened. As I was placing the final items on the top shelf, the whole thing collapsed! There were pet shampoo and medications spilled all over the floor and everyone was staring at me. Several customers gave me hand to pick up the debris off the floor, but my fellow staff members didn't offer to help at all. They were too busy either laughing or telling me in passing that "I should grab a mop because someone might slip and fall." On a positive note, at least I found a way to get rid of all of that old stock.

    I made even more enemies once I saw the girl who lived in that house that I trashed at Derek's party was working at K-Mart as well. Just seeing her again inspired me to start telling that story to anyone who was willing to listen. One day, I told it in front of the wrong people and nearly lost my job. I was sitting in the smoker's break room talking louder than I thought and just assumed that the old ladies, who were talking among themselves, weren't listening to me. To make things worse, the guy who I was telling the story to was actually that girl's boyfriend and no one warned me ahead of time. I'm sure that he enjoyed hearing me say that I didn't clean up my mess because "she was an ugly bitch anyway." He just sat there with the same expression on his face the entire time, and even laughed afterwards so I didn't have a clue of who he actually was. He never said a word to anyone but someone else did. One of the old ladies, who annoyed the hell out of all of us daily by talking about her son "Dustin" (who I would work with years later and have a filthier mouth than I ever had) being such an angel, *was* listening and decided to complain to management. The store manager approached me on the sales floor about an hour later and asked me to follow him to the back so "he could talk to me about something." He was known to do this quite frequently when he had a specific task for me to do so I didn't suspect anything. However, this time he took his glasses off and got into my face when he turned around. Then he started yelling at me and threatened to fire me "if I ever used that language in his store again." It wasn't what he said that infuriated me because I had that coming, but approaching me in such a confrontational manner was a coin toss which could have ended with both of us being unemployed if I had reacted violently. He looked like he was prepared to fight and having the explosive temper that I have, we were both damn lucky that I managed to keep my cool. I don't know what he thought that he could do if I turned on him, because I was built like a tank and he was short, fat, and severely out of shape. There is no doubt in my mind that I would have kicked his ass and probably ended up in jail. Fortunately for him, I chose to be professional instead and promised him that it would never happen again. He later suggested that I should apologize to all of the women who were present that day, and although I said I would, I never did. "Don't press your luck old man" I thought to myself. **-DJN**

CHAPTER IV- *"TIL DEATH DO US PART PART I"*

1993-1994

Ever since she was a little girl, she decided to wait, till she found her soul mate, her Mr. Right, stay the teasing virgin, who didn't give in, until her wedding night.

She wears that white dress, the one she's getting married in. Do you think I'm going to confess, because wanting her is a sin?

On bended knee, I proposed, asking her to marry me, the veils and diamonds, the vows of chastity...then I gave up my career, to start a family. When she asked, "Where do you see us in five years?" I said, "Who knows? Probably another bride and groom, in the courtroom, I've committed adultery, been having an affair with my secretary, now we're dividing everything equally, alimony...palimony...fighting over custody.

40 carats to inreconcilable differences, it all comes crashing down...no happily ever after. "Where's my red house and white picket fences?" I burned them to the ground. OJ may get away with murder, but I'll get the death sentence.

Like something out of Shakespeare, the pain I just could not bear. Her blood was on my hands, and it never disappears. No matter how much I wash, it's still there. I'm nothing more than Picasso, when his paints are dry...Romeo, watching as his Juliet dies.

"The trash is starting to stink, there's a pile of dishes in the sink... you're never here for breakfast, never home for Christmas." As a result of my labours, I'll be dead by thirty. She can thank me later, for my life insurance policy.

Another disagreement leads to a fight, apparently I'm never right. When she says "Get out of my sight" I know I'll be sleeping on the couch tonight.
Sometimes people change, want to get some strange, sometimes the estranged, must be rearranged, used to make a few booty calls, now I don't come around at all. My world trembles, ready to collapse, all my hopes and dreams are down the drain. All the feelings we once had, we will never regain. Today she learned a valuable lesson, in this life, you can't trust anyone.
-Denny Noland "Draven" From my song "Til Death Do Us Part" written on September 11, 2006 Copyright 2007

Now it was time to get a new car. Dad took the old truck back and I bought an 81' Thunderbird. It ran like a motherfucker but still had its share of problems. The motor leaked oil which caused a lot of smoke when it got hot. The digital speedometer wasn't right so I never knew how fast I was going so I usually just tried to stay in the flow of traffic. Then there was the car alarm...I never had one nor did I know anyone else who did either at the time so I was very excited about that. I was so excited that I invited Tony to take a spin with me into town to show it off. We made it there without incident but when we headed home the alarm started going off while we were going down the road. I tried to shut it off but it wouldn't stop. People were staring at us as we drove past, probably thinking that we stole the car, so I decided to pull into an abandoned gas station and pop the hood to see if there was a way to disconnect it. Neither of us knew a damn thing about cars so we did the only thing that came natural...we yanked the fucking thing out, threw it on the ground, smashed it into a thousand pieces and drove away. To this day, I've never owned another car with an alarm.

A couple of weeks later, I overslept one morning making me run late for work. It was pissing rain and foggy as hell and I was driving way too fast on the back roads trying to get to work as soon as I could. As I got to the top of the hill and started my descent, the car lifted off the road causing me to lose control. For a couple of seconds, the world seemed to move in slow motion. The only thing that was going through my mind was how substantial of a drop that it was going to be once I veered off the road. If I survived crashing into the trees, the creek would probably finish me off, so I closed my eyes and waited…but it never happened. I did feel the impact of hitting trees but there was no fall. Due to how fast I was going and how I had the wheels turned, I had made it to the bottom of the hill before I came off the road. When everything stopped, the car was resting against a tree about 10 feet from the creek. I had taken out several small trees along the way which had slowed the car down significantly which probably saved my life. After I pulled myself out of the wreckage, I still had the presence of mind to start walking home to get help. When I got home, my parents wanted to take me to the hospital but I was more concerned about the car and how I was getting to work. Dad took me back to the crash site on the tractor so we could try to pull the car out. When we got there, the cops had arrived and were shining their flashlights into my car expecting to find an unconscious or dead body inside. They were shocked that I had not only survived the crash but walked a half of a mile afterwards. They asked if we needed a tow but dad said that wasn't necessary because he was going to take care of it which he did. When we got the car back up to the road and took a good look at it, strangely, there was barely a scratch on it so I ended up driving it into work. At first, they wanted to send me home as a precautionary measure but I wasn't leaving. That incident alone changed a lot of people's perception of me. I had finally gained their respect.

2

Fresh off the adrenalin rush from cheating death one more time, I was feeling confident enough to walk up to the cute girl in the electronics department named "Angela" and strike up a conversation with her. The first thing that she noticed was the mud all over my clothes so she couldn't help herself from cracking a joke about it. After I told her that I had just been in an accident so I didn't exactly have enough time to change my clothes, the joke was no longer funny anymore. After a few minutes of small talk, I felt that it was time to reveal the real reason why I approached her in the first place: to ask her out on a date. Although she didn't know me that well and we had never really talked until that day, she accepted without hesitation. We went out later in the week and had a great time, ending the night with a kiss. From that night on, we were inseparable. I finally had a new lady in my life.

I would soon find out that one of her closest friends was the single mother that I had passed on earlier. She was now dating a fellow employee as well and they had to be the most dramatic couple in the store with the exception of the warehouse manager that was having an affair with one of the office girls who always came back from "lunch" with her hair looking like a birds nest and her lipstick smeared. We would see the same scene play out in the parking lot each day with him stomping out to his car and her chasing after him, usually crying, while begging him not to walk away. He was a nice enough kid, but I always thought that she could do better. As pretty as she was, she shouldn't be chasing *anyone*, they should be chasing *her.* Even when we went over to her place for dinner, we could tell that they had been fighting before we arrived. You could just feel the tension in the room. I just didn't get it at all, but at the end of the day, it was none of our business so we would just watch the fireworks from afar and shake our heads.

3

Something else that was acting strange in 1993 was the weather. In late February, it was unseasonably warm so everyone thought that spring had arrived early, which would become a grave mistake. One day, my parents asked if I wanted to meet them and my aunt at a friend's new bar and grill to shoot a few games of pool. I thought that it sounded fun so I attended. When I walked in the door, I saw an old schoolmate, who I used to have a crush on, sitting at the bar with some dude that I didn't know. He was all over her and eventually they started making out so hot and heavy that even my parents noticed them and were offended. I thought that they were actually going to have sex right then and there, and was tempted to do my best Rusty Griswold impersonation by saying "I think he's going to pork her dad!" but was too disgusted to do so and decided to leave instead. Then I got in my car and drove down to the Lenoir City Park so I could feed the ducks and clear my head. After an hour or so, the skies darkened over the lake as a vicious storm started blowing in. The sun was still shining in the direction of Maryville and

I needed to work out so I decided to head that way before the storm hit. As I was driving up Highway 321 near the city of Friendsville, there was a tornado warning issued on the radio for not only Lenoir City but Maryville and Friendsville as well, which basically meant that I was stuck in the middle of the super cell. As I was passing Friendsville, I didn't see a funnel cloud but there was debris blowing around in the sky which made me want to get off the road as soon as possible… so I floored it! When I got to the gym in Maryville, which was cleverly built on the side of a hill, I thought that I had outran the storm but in reality, it had been closely following me the entire time. By the time I got down to the free weights room, which was for the first time in memory, completely empty, it was right on top of us. The wind ripped into the side of the building so hard that the glass in the windows were bending inwards which freaked me out. I started backing slowly toward the inner wall when I heard the announcement over the speakers from the front desk that everyone should head upstairs where it had a stronger foundation and was more secure, so I sprinted up there as fast as I could and waited out the storm with the others.

It wasn't until the next day that I realized that I could have just cheated death for a second time in a month after watching the local news. Only minutes after I had left Lenoir City, an F3 tornado tore a path of destruction right through the heart of the city and lifted just before reaching the house that Kaine and I used to live in. There was a second smaller tornado that spawned from the same storm, hitting Friendsville as I passed by it, which explains why I saw all of the debris in the air. The funnel was just on the other side of the trees, hidden from my view at the time, so I had no way of knowing the danger that I was in. I was damn lucky to have been on the move when I was, and not a few minutes later, or I may not be here today to tell the story.

In March, the weather got even worse. The meteorologists were calling for a blizzard and since we hadn't had a decent snowfall in years, no one believed that it was going to happen...including yours truly. The weather was still very spring- like in the days prior so it seemed like a ridiculous prediction, which meant that no one took it very seriously...except for Angie. She was so concerned, in fact, that she was afraid to go to work that night so I volunteered to drive her myself and pick her up afterwards. It began snowing a couple of hours before her shift ended but I still wasn't concerned about it very much. I thought that it would stop before there was any significant accumulation like it always does, and we would probably be laughing about it tomorrow. However, when I went to pick her up, there was probably 2-3 inches on the ground and it wasn't showing any signs of stopping. If anything, it seemed like just the opposite. I got her home safely but nearly slid off the road turning into her driveway. It wasn't until I got out of the car to open her door that I realized that another couple of inches had fallen during the commute home. My tires were partially submerged in the snow already, so now it was obvious that I had, like so many others, underestimated Old Man Winter. I knew that I would never make it home in a 4x4, much less my car, so I called my parents and told them the situation. My dad responded with sarcasm in his voice. "So, you are stranded at your girlfriend's house. How convenient is that?" I tried to convince him that I didn't plan this to happen but he still didn't buy it. "Well, have fun I guess. I'll see you in a few days hopefully." My parents were covered but it was her parents that I was concerned with. Her parents were unique to say the least. Her dad was a wild man, a former pool hustler, who had found religion and barely spoke even under the best of circumstances. Her mother was an outspoken, fearless, tell it like it is, weed smoker. They were stranded up in the mountains near Gatlinburg and even though they had a four wheel drive vehicle, they weren't going anywhere for a few days either, so that bought me a little time to write my will before they got back. When Angie called them to let them know that she was safe, they didn't seem bothered that I was there too, which was a relief to both of us. Maybe it was because we weren't alone in the house. There were also two elderly people that lived in the house who Angie's mother got paid to take care of, that were confined to beds. One was a retired general, who suffered from Alzheimer's Disease, and the other was his sister who had her own health problems. There was also a nurse present to look after them. They needed around the clock attention so it wasn't exactly going to be a walk in the park…especially if we lost electricity.

4

The big question mark was going to be the sleeping arrangements for the night. Angie and I hadn't had sex yet so sharing a bed with her might be a bit awkward. I was prepared to sleep on the couch until she invited me into her room. Once we got into bed together, we cuddled for a while, then one thing led to another and we started making out. Before anything else could happen, we were rudely interrupted by the nurse knocking on Angie's bedroom door. She just wanted to ask Angie where something was, but I think that she was just being nosy as usual. She was curious about what we were doing more than anything else so that was the only excuse that she could think of to have a look. Before we could attempt to pick up where we left off, there was a power outage, so now everyone was scurrying around looking for candles or lanterns. Now there would be no further disturbances from the nurse as she had her work cut out for her for the rest of the night.

Angie's bedroom had become a city of candles, which created a more romantic setting for what was about to become a very special night. Within minutes, we were making love and I can honestly say that it was the first time that I really enjoyed sex. It was almost magical, and so different from any other experiences that I have had. It was no longer about just getting my rocks off... there was emotion and feelings there for once. We went at it most of the night and were wearing smiles on our faces the next morning...until we looked outside.

5

There was an additional several inches of snow that had fallen overnight and it was *still* snowing, plus the temperature had plummeted to below freezing, yet these factors were the least of our problems...we were running out of food. Back then, no one rushed out to their local supermarket, like they do now, to buy milk and bread at the first mention of the word "snow", because it didn't stay on the ground long enough to be concerned with. We were in serious trouble and although there was a small market just down the road, more than likely, it wasn't going to be open. We had no other choice but to try regardless, so Angie and I bundled up and headed out on foot. The snow, which had reached more than 12 inches deep by this time, made it difficult to see where the road began and ended, so we were constantly pulling each other out of snowdrifts which made the journey very difficult and extremely dangerous. When we finally reached the store, it was open, which was a miracle to say the least. We bought enough supplies to last for several days and carried them back to the house, which left us both exhausted, but the reward was well worth the risk.

We lived off of peanut butter sandwiches and had sex anytime that we wanted for the next two days before I received a double dose of bad news. It started when we found out that Angie's parents were on their way home. The snow may not have melted enough for me to get out but apparently it had for them and their 4 wheel drive. This meant no more sex, or even kissing for that matter, and I would be sleeping on the couch at night. After they got home, it felt weird to still be stranded there. I was ready to leave even if we did now have better meals and heating. Cabin fever had finally set in, making me feel as if I had worn out my welcome in this household. Yet just when I thought it couldn't get any worse, one phone call from my parents took this misery to a whole new level.

6

My Papaw "Octo", who had been suffering from emphysema for the past couple of years, had come down with a case of double pneumonia as a result of this extreme weather. He was now fighting for his life at the hospital, needing a machine in order to breathe. They couldn't get an ambulance down to the "Old Homeplace" so they had to fly a helicopter in to take him there. The doctors had already told mother that "he was going to spend the rest of his days on life support" and at some point Mamaw would have to make the decision on whether or not to "pull the plug." I knew that Mamaw wouldn't hesitate to make that call when the time came, so it was a race to get to see him one last time and say goodbye before he left this world forever.

    Octo had done something very clever several months prior to ensure that the land stayed in the family long after he was gone. He knew that if he divided up the land equally with all of the children, they would sell their shares to the highest bidder the first chance they got because that's just how they were. There was only one person that he could trust and that was my mother, so he sold her the land with one condition: that Mamaw could live in the house for as long as she wanted or until she died…whichever came first. No one knew about this except for my parents, Mamaw, Octo, and me, and we all also knew that it was going to be a war zone once the family found out that he had changed his will at the last minute. They had already started pouring into town when they heard that he was on his deathbed. The stage was set for things to get really ugly…fast!

7

    The weather finally improved enough for me to get my car out later that week. It was strange because the roads were dry and it was warm enough to wear a t-shirt yet in the shady areas on the road and off, there was still at least 6 inches of snow still on the ground. I wanted to get to the hospital as soon as possible but I desperately needed a shower and a change of clothes first. I had been reeking of sweat and sex for a full week. It was a miracle if Angie's parents didn't smell the stench on either one or both of us but I wasn't taking any chances around *my* folks. When I got to the hospital, I went up to Octo's room and my mother was still by his side. I was horrified as I watched him struggle to breathe. He was too sick to even open his eyes when mother told him that I there...he just nodded his head to acknowledge that he heard what she said. For a brief moment, I wanted to throw my cigarettes away, but as soon as I got out of the building, the first thing that I did was light one up. Mamaw decided a few days later to take him off life support and put an end to his suffering. Now it was time to let the rest of the family in on his dying wish and no one knew what to expect or how anyone was going to react to it.

    Octo wanted all of the male grandchildren to be pallbearers after he died so we all rode together to his funeral. This was the first time that we had spoken to each other since Octo's and Mamaw's 50th anniversary several years earlier so it felt like we were more like strangers than family. We talked mostly about what our plans for the future were and how wrong it was to think about how a certain female cousin had really blossomed into a beautiful young woman. We had all noticed her and wished that we weren't related to her so we had a good laugh about the whole thing. By now, everyone had found out that my parents were the sole owners of the house and land so there was a lot of tension in the air between my parents and all of my aunts and uncles. Some of them had refused to even speak to my parents at all. I thought that it was pathetic how all of this had overshadowed the real reason that we were all here: to mourn the passing of one of the greatest men that any of us had ever known. But that was just how my family operates. They only get together when someone dies and it becomes more of a party than a wake, with people going around saying things like "Is this Denny? The last time I saw him, he was only about this tall" and bragging about their wealth and success over a few cases of beer or liquor. It always made me sick to around all of this bullshit but I always felt obligated to attend. Hell, it was the least I could do.

The funeral was a touching ceremony, with a preacher who was an old friend and neighbour of the family, doing the sermon. One of his daughters was my second kiss and nearly took my virginity back in high school, so unfortunately, every time that I saw him, it reminded me of her, even in this atmosphere. You would have thought that there wouldn't have been a dry eye in the house, but it was actually just the opposite. The only person I saw crying was my mother who was probably closer to Octo than anyone…everyone else just sat there without showing any emotion whatsoever. It was like they were fucking zombies! Mamaw seemed totally unaffected and couldn't wait for it to all be over so she could get some chicken from KFC. All that had happened in the past week had just made me want to put even more distance between me and my family and I vowed to do just that.

8

The first person that I ran to after it was all said and done was Angie. I hadn't seen her since Octo died and I missed her dearly. She did offer to go to the funeral with me, but I didn't want to drag her into that mess so I decided that I would deal with it myself and not get her involved. We got a motel room in Lenoir City and spent the entire evening having sex. This would become an expensive, weekly routine for the next couple of months. The funny thing about it all was how careful we were not to get caught all those times, yet when her family had a reunion later on and the entire immediate family was present, including her parents, we had sex in the pool right in front of everyone while they played a game of touch football around us without anyone noticing, and didn't care if they figured out what we were doing or not. There were moments when someone was only a couple of feet from us but we kept going at it anyways. It was a huge risk but I think that the danger factor made it more exciting and enjoyable for both of us.

9

    Now it was time to meet all of these people that I had heard so much about including one that I could have done without: her ex- boyfriend. We ran into him at Wal-Mart one day and all he did was stare at Angie and avoiding eye contact with me. He didn't say anything to either of us but sat in his car, watching and waiting for us to come out of the store. When we got into our car, he did a couple of donuts around the car, then proceeded to spin his tires as he tore out of the parking lot leaving only skid marks, the scent of burnt rubber and a cloud of smoke behind. Angie seemed a little shaken but I never even looked at the idiot or acknowledged his act of cowardice, which surprised her. She asked, "Does that not bother you?" I responded back with "He's not worth my time. He didn't have the balls to confront me when he had the chance. Instead, he waited until he was safely in his car before he did something. To even give him the time of day is just sinking down to his level." She was impressed and even told her parents about my act of "maturity." We never saw that gutless bastard again or at least I didn't.
    Then there was the cousins, one of them Angie grew up with and was considered to be one of her closest friends, the other a younger girl named "Greta" who looked up to Angie like a big sister. The latter often stayed with Angie to get away from the

chaos of an overcrowded house and irresponsible parents. The other was a lovely girl who smoked a lot of weed and had a fiancé who was just like her. We hung out with them a couple of times where I ended up sharing a joint or two with them and we were even invited to their wedding. They were such stoners that they had to get high before they said their vows which made the ceremony one of the most comical and entertaining weddings that I had ever been to. We lost touch with them not long afterwards. I found her on Facebook in 2010 and sent her a friend request which she refused. Apparently, she has fried too many brain cells and can't remember who I am.

Although Angie eased me in to meeting her best friend from high school by having me meet her sister first, I couldn't wait to finally see "the girl who used to try to steal all of her boyfriends and who she used to practice her kissing with." Angie was hesitant about having the two of us in the same room because she was certain that she would try to seduce me. Finally, we crossed paths by accident at her sister's house one night and she had either grown up and changed her ways or didn't find me attractive because she didn't try anything at all. I didn't know whether to feel relieved or feel insulted. We would never see her again either.

Meanwhile, back at the workplace, Angie was informed by one of her male friends that my "replenishment supervisor" and two other middle aged married department heads were talking about me in the lounge in front of him recently. They were saying things like how they would "wear me out sexually" and how much they appreciated my body and even took a shot at Angie by saying that "I could definitely do better." When he tried to get them to stop by reminding them that they were married and shouldn't be talking about me in this manner, they responded with "We can still look and fantasize can't we? We're not hurting anybody." Angie was disgusted but I was quite flattered. In fact, I had more than a few sinful thoughts about them over the past few months as well so this just gave me more ammunition. One of those women was the stepmother of one of my old classmates and most of my "brothers" had admired her from a distance for years so just thinking about her thinking about me made my imagination run wild. Hell, I am only human.

10

After this isolated incident, Angie felt that just being my girlfriend wasn't good enough anymore, so she brought up the topic of marriage. At first, I didn't think much of it and hoped that it was just a passing phase but every single day she became a little more persistent. I knew I wasn't ready or mature enough to be someone's husband and, to be honest, I wasn't even sure that she was the one that I would have picked to spend the rest of my life with in the first place. In reality, we hardly knew each other. We had only been dating for a few months, and to me, that just wasn't enough time. I was also concerned that she wouldn't know how to survive considering that she had never been on her own before. Despite all of these concerns, I would go on to buy her an engagement ring and propose to her at the Greenbelt Park in Maryville. It wasn't going to be a long engagement…only about a month, with the date set for July 3, 1993.

That gave me only a few weeks to sort a few things out. First, I needed a new job. K-Mart had cut back everyone's hours to about 12 a week and I had already tried to pick up a few extra shifts to no avail. There wasn't anything anyone could do to help me out, so I had no other choice but to turn in my notice. Luckily, one of Angie's cousins, "Ken", got me a job working at a plant down in Vonore with several other members of her family just a few days later. I would start there in a couple of weeks, literally going from one job into the next with no break in between. Now, I needed to find a house that we could afford. One of the cashiers at K-Mart told us about a two bedroom house in the city that one of her relatives owned that was up for rent. When we looked at the house, we fell in love with it instantly, but it wasn't exactly in our price range. That's when Angie's mother offered to help out with the monthly payments so we could get it. Before the ink had even dried on the contract, the old lady who owned it was already demanding money which we didn't have yet. We wouldn't be moving in until after the wedding and after I had settled into my new job, but she didn't care. It needed to be deposited into her granddaughter's "trust" fund immediately…no exceptions. I managed to come up with the money for the deposit and the pieces began to fall into place.

 I wasn't happy about leaving K-Mart so those last few days were quite depressing. I wanted someone to offer me a new role and ask me to stay but it wasn't happening and I knew that so I decided to make the most of it and have a little fun before I left. There was an arrogant jerk, who worked in the shoe department that had been a thorn in my side the entire time that I had been working there. He always made smartass remarks whenever I said anything and had a tendency to flirt with Angie when I wasn't around. When he started his bullshit one day, I basically told him what I thought of him. "Why are you such an asshole?" I asked. Before he could respond, I interrupted "At the end of the day, you are just a shoe salesman…like Al Bundy. Is that the profession that you used to dream of when you were a kid? Are your parents proud of you or are you a disappointment?" For the first time, he was speechless and soon after, left the room. Everyone laughed and was so happy to be there when someone finally put him in his place. I was starting to like no longer having restrictions or giving a fuck. What were they going to do? Fire me? I was going to tell that woman who ratted me out for my language what I thought of her as well but changed my mind after she told Angie after hearing of our engagement that "she approved even if I did need my mouth washed out with soap." I had one more person that I wanted to say something to: that luscious redhead working in the clothing department that I had been perving over for quite a while without her knowledge. I approached her and said "I don't mean anything by it. You are married and I am about to be married, but I must tell you that you are one of the most beautiful women that I have ever seen." I was expecting a simple "Thank you" or a least a smile but got neither. In fact, she only looked at me for a split second then continued hanging clothes like I wasn't even there. I was totally embarrassed and didn't know what else to do except walk away with my tail between my legs. I guess she didn't know how to take a compliment. She would be the first of many…

11

I didn't know Angie's cousin "Ken" very well, but he told the plant manager "Chance" that I was a great worker which was quite a compliment coming from the hardest working, most respected guy in the whole damn building. I walked in with all of these expectations and accolades and was determined to live up to all of them. What we did at this plant was to take clear plastic and add colour to it through a number of procedures for companies like Mayfield Dairies and Hoover. We would make thousands of pounds of these plastic pellets per day and had two 10-12 hour shifts, one during the day and the other overnight, which meant that the machines ran around the clock, four days a week. We usually had Friday, Saturday, and Sunday off unless we got behind on orders which rarely happened. It was a sweet gig and I could see myself staying there for the long haul. I often wondered if Ken would have brought me into the fold had he known that Angie and I made love in his pool at that family reunion.

    It was, without a doubt, the dirtiest job that I ever had. The pigments would get into your hair, be absorbed through your skin and pores, and even find its way into your lungs whether you were wearing a respirator or not. On more than one occasion, when I would break a sweat over the weekend, my skin would change colours to match whatever I was running earlier in the week. We were required to take a shower before we left the premises but it really didn't matter. You could only wash what you could see, and the rest would sometimes take days to work its way back to the surface. I started in perhaps the filthiest section of the plant: the "dry colour" room. In this area, we blended the pigments together to get a certain colour to send out to the production lines and repaired "off-colours" by taking a dab of this and a smidge of that and placing it in Zip-lock baggies to be mixed with the original material to correct the problem. My first order was to make about 100 of these in black as quickly as possible, because the colour wasn't right and the line was shut down and supposably waiting until I was finished. As if this wasn't enough pressure, it was Ken's line and his operator just happened to be another one of her cousins named "Brad" so I wasn't just letting down the guy who got me the job but another family member as well. They got impatient, grabbed a handful of the baggies, and started up the machine. Within minutes, they had caught up with me, so someone had to come and help which made me feel like a worthless piece of shit. By the end of the week, Chance had decided to move me to the production lines to see what I was really made of. I was about to surprise everyone...

12

    The following weekend was spent preparing for the wedding. Angie's parents had decided that we were having the ceremony at their house and the preacher was going to be an old friend of their family who I had never met. I had no input on the planning of the big day whatsoever. That was made apparent by the fact that no one ever bothered to ask my opinion about a damn thing. The night before the wedding, Angie's dad and I took Angie's nephew to see the fireworks in Pigeon Forge and pre-book the suite for our honeymoon. I found a beautiful room on the top floor of the hotel right on the strip. It was going to cost a lot of money but it was our special day so I beared no expense. I put down a deposit for a 3 day stay then we headed off to watch the show. I didn't really enjoy the fireworks because I was starting to get really stressed out about all of the things that could go wrong on the following day. It didn't help that Angie's dad barely spoke to me under normal circumstances, so he definitely didn't know what to say to me the night before I married his daughter. It was one of the most uncomfortable trips that I had ever taken in my life. We got back to Angie's parents' place around midnight, and everyone was still waiting up for us. Angie and her parents went to bed shortly afterwards, leaving me alone to crash on the couch. A million things raced through my mind causing me to start getting cold feet about the whole thing but realized that there was no turning back now. Needless to say, I didn't sleep a wink that night...

    The next morning, we had a nice breakfast and watched as all of the guests started pouring in. Most of Angie's immediate family was in attendance, including Ken and his wife, Greta, and even Angie's estranged brother made an appearance. Although, I had seen Angie's nephew countless times, I had yet to meet her brother until this day. He seemed to be a really nice guy, and even offered to help us with the moving process into our new home, including using his big truck, which was "an offer that I just couldn't refuse." When it came to my side of the family, I was only expecting my parents to show up, but Papaw and Nanny Noland also attended which was a pleasant surprise. Seeing my relatives sitting out there did relax me a bit but I was still freaking out, especially while I was getting dressed. I had never worn a tie in my life so I had to ask Angie's father to help me out which made the whole situation worse. When I was finally ready and stepped out in front of everyone, my stomach was in knots making me feel like I needed to throw up. I just stood there like a statue looking out at the audience, shaking like a leaf, waiting for the music to cue and my bride to join me. Then I heard the piano start playing that tune that symbolizes one of the most important and emotional events in your entire life, and the collective sound of everyone rising up out of their seats...it was time to make this official.

If the series of events that happened next wasn't an omen of things to come, I don't know what was. As Angie and her mother walked towards the door to enter the room, Angie got her veil stuck in the door…yanking it off of her head. Apparently her mother, who was walking behind her, closed the door before she was clear leaving an unsuspecting Angie one step away from humiliation. She handled it like a pro and laughed along with everyone else. I'm sure that she was already regretting her decision to have the whole ceremony videotaped as a keepsake. Now it was my turn. Before I could say my vows, lightning struck again. The preacher, who had to write down my name to remember it since he had no idea who I was, called me "Denise" instead of "Dennis" which made the whole room erupt with laughter. I was so angry at this point. This whole event was a fucking nightmare that belonged on either a comedic movie script or America's Funniest Home Videos. I just wanted to get it all over with and get to the honeymoon which was evident when I couldn't even repeat what the preacher said without screwing that up as well. I can laugh now when I watch it on film, but on that day, I didn't find it very funny at all.

After all of the post wedding festivities which included countless photo opportunities, hugs and handshakes from everyone in the room, opening of the gifts, and the cutting of the cake, I was ready to get the hell out of there. It wasn't until we got into the car to leave that it really hit me that we were actually married now and just the concept of that terrified me. All I wanted to do was get to the room, have a lot of sex and drink that bottle of bourbon that Angie's mother had bought me as a wedding gift. I was more than a little concerned that I wasn't feeling as happy and enthusiastic as I should be under these circumstances, but I was sure that would change in time. I just thought that everyone probably felt this way at first, so it was perfectly natural. In a few short hours, I would figure out what my heart was trying to tell me all along...

13

We arrived at the hotel in Pigeon Forge late in the evening. Angie was impressed at how nice our room was but didn't waste any time looking around...she was ready to consummate this marriage. We spent a couple of hours having sex and probably would have kept going if we weren't so damn hungry. We ordered room service and had a fantastic dinner before going at it again. Now I was exhausted and wanted to pour myself a drink of bourbon to celebrate this special occasion. I didn't think that Angie would care or that I would need to ask for her permission since she never had a problem with me sharing a joint or a bottle with her mother or other family members before. She didn't say anything until I got drunk and wasn't in the mood to have sex anymore, then she snapped and lashed out on me like I had never seen or heard her do before. The argument got so intense that I left the room and held on to the guardrail outside as I screamed back at her in a drunken rage. Eventually, I just started crying because I already knew that this marriage was a fucking mistake and that I was a total idiot for not listening to my gut feelings and coming to my senses before taking this plunge. I was on the top floor of this massive hotel and wanted to jump to my death to end all of this only a few hours after making everything right in the eyes of God. I had really done it this time and there wasn't going to be an easy fix for it either.

14

When we got back from our honeymoon, I stayed at Angie's parent's house until we got into our own place. I was working 12 hour shifts during the day again, which meant that I would have to move all of our stuff in the dark leaving me with about three hours to sleep each night until we were finished. This lasted for a few days and by the time we got moved in, I was so exhausted that all I wanted to do was collapse. My fatigue had also affected my work performance since I was always too delirious to even think straight, which could have been a total disaster considering that this was all occurring during my 90 day probation period. Once we got settled in, I was determined to make my mark at the plant, and silence any critics that I might have had. I was also devoted to making my marriage work no matter what it took or how much shit I had to put up with along the way. When I said "forever" I meant it, even if I was fully aware that I fucked up.

It didn't take long before the fighting started again. Angie was quite content to only work 12 hours a week and would usually start screaming at me as soon as she walked in the door after completing her gruelling 4 hour shift. It didn't matter that I was working long hours in conditions that she could only imagine in her nightmares, apparently I was supposed to cook and clean the house as well. I would usually just get up and leave, usually on foot, and return when I calmed down to avoid being pushed too far. I don't know what happened to her after I placed that ring on her finger or what she thought a marriage was about, but she had become a totally different person than the woman I used to love once she became my wife. I was growing to despise her more each and every passing day.

15

    Our little white house with a picket fence wasn't all it was cracked up to be either. The old woman who collected the rent turned out to be a total bitch as we found out the first time she showed up at our doorstep. She tried to blame us for pre-existing scratches and cracks and went off on me about keeping the hedges trimmed which meant that I had to spend money that I didn't have on equipment and accessories to maintain the property and keep her happy. She also informed us that she wouldn't accept *any* excuse for being even a day late on the rent, which would come into play the following month, when Angie's mother got into financial trouble after both of her live in clients passed away within days of each other, which left me trying to figure out how I was going to come up with the entire amount by myself. I was making good money now but the monthly payments on that place were ridiculous even for that location. If only it was due a couple of days later when I would get paid again, giving me the full amount, but that's how it always went and there was only one thing that I could do about it: I was going to have to face that wicked witch and ask for an extension on just our second month of living there. This wasn't going to be fun...

    When we got to her house and knocked on the door, it was the granddaughter who actually owned the house that we lived in that answered the door, with the old lady peering around the corner to see who it was. As soon as she recognized us, she got a stern look on her face and knew why we were probably there. I didn't waste any time getting to the point, "I'm a little short on rent but I get paid on Thursday. Can I just pay you then? I'm sorry." The granddaughter didn't seem to think that it was a big deal but the old woman went off on a long rant and gave us both a lecture about the terms of the lease and how her granddaughter was relying on that money to be in her "trust fund" every month. I was starting to wonder who the money was actually for and suspected that the old lady was doing something dodgy with it, but it was really none of my business. She eventually agreed to wait till Thursday, like she really had a choice, but did warn us that "this better not happen again" as we were leaving. I gave her my word that it wouldn't.

16

Now I was starting to hate the plant less than being at home. Although the guy who I was replacing tried to intimidate me by telling me how many people have quit after looking at all the buttons and lights on the panels of the machines, I welcomed the challenge. I made many mistakes at first but went on to become one of the best Banbury operators in the company's history. I would even eventually break the record of how many pounds of pellets produced in a single shift by nearly 5000 pounds! I also admired and respected all of the men and women that I worked with even if most of them were stoners and alcoholics and usually high or drunk while they were working. We were like a family and *always* had each other's backs. Even when you were called up to the office to get a royal "ass chewing" using words that would make a sailor blush, you didn't take it personal, you just made damn sure that whatever you did never happened again. You just had to roll with the punches and take it like a man then have a beer with the boss after work like nothing ever happened. That was just how we rolled...

The only difficult thing about the job for me was working with several members of Angie's family and other people who knew her and not being able to talk to anyone about the problems we were having at home without the risk of it getting back to her. If that wasn't bad enough, most of them knew Salena too. In fact, one of my supervisors had been intimate with her a couple of times since we broke up which was met with mixed emotions from me. I got satisfaction from hearing that it obviously didn't work out with the guy that she dumped me for, but just knowing that she had been around me all of this time when I thought that she was farther away, made me a bit nervous. He then dropped another bombshell on me by letting me know that although it was over with her, he was now in a relationship with her cousin Michelle, and they were living together. For some reason, I was jealous that he had slept with both of them…probably since I was offered to have that threesome that never happened. But I must admit that when I found out that Angie's cousin Brad was also in a relationship with Salena's friend Ann, that news probably hit closer to home than anything else. Here was a direct link from my ex to my wife and I was starting to think that although Angie claimed that they had never met, maybe she was lying to protect me.

17

Back at home, we tried everything to make our marriage work but it wasn't happening. We got a dog named "Chelsea", named after Jane Fonda's character in the film "On Golden Pond", which is one of my favourite drama movies of all time, to give Angie a companion while I was away at night. It wasn't long before the dog had become more of a liability than a pet. It was chained up in the backyard day and night usually spending its time barking and digging holes which caused a lot of problems with not only the landlord but the neighbours as well. When that wasn't working, I encouraged Greta to stay at our place more often which meant that she was practically living with us at that point. We went everywhere together like a family but after a while she started getting on Angie's nerves too. One memory that really sticks out in my mind was when Angie would yell at her like a mother would, if she kissed the nephew on the lips too much, saying that it was "inappropriate" even if she got the idea from watching Angie do it.

    She had become heavily influenced by everything that she saw us do and wanted to try it all...including drinking hard liquor. One night, I decided to give her a few sips and she got plastered. Eventually, she started getting sick so she went to sit on the steps outside to get some fresh air. I joined her, feeling terrible about what I have done. It was freezing cold so I put my arm around her and after apologizing, tried to persuade her to go inside where it was warm. She eventually went inside, and I remained outside for a few minutes to have a smoke. When I entered the house, Angie was waiting for me with fists clenched and rage in her eyes. I thought that she was angry about Greta being sick but that wasn't it at all. Before I could apologize to her, she interrupted with "Greta told me that you hugged her! How dare you come on to my little cousin! She's only 13 years old! I'll fucking kill you if you ever touch her again!" I couldn't have ever imagined how an act of compassion could be so blown out of proportion or taken the wrong way in such a manner, but it did. I tried to defend myself but she didn't want to hear my side of the story and probably wouldn't have believed it anyway so I just walked away with my head down, feeling like I had just molested someone that I knew I didn't.

18

    There would be another incident a couple of weeks later involving alcohol that caused a bigger riff between Angie and I. Kaine had contacted me for the first time since our falling out and wanted to get together on the weekend while Tony was still on leave from the military. They came over with a bottle and we started playing quarters. I could tell that although Tony claimed that he could out-drink everyone in his platoon including his drill sergeant, he wasn't handling his liquor very well on this night. He was being obnoxious and arrogant and proceeded to say inappropriate things to Angie leading to her turning in early, and leaving us alone to deal with the situation however we saw fit. Kaine and I both felt that he was out of line but chose to wait until he passed out to get our revenge instead of beating the hell out of him. We wouldn't have to wait long as he was out on the couch only a few short minutes after Angie went to bed. Kaine and I can be quite evil on our own but when we are together, even the devil himself would be impressed with the ideas that we came up with. Unfortunately for Tony, he passed out with his mouth open which made things much easier. First, we grabbed a camera and posed like we were getting head from him, then snapped a few pictures. Then I decided to take it a step further to avenge Angie. I had a bandage of my leg that had dried blood and pus on it from an infection that I was recovering from that found its way into Tony's mouth. We obviously had to take a few photos of that as well. I still have all of these pictures to this day as a warning to show anyone beforehand of what happens when you cross that line. I usually add "If I would do this to a "brother", imagine what I would do to you."

Angie's reaction the next morning wasn't exactly what I was expecting. She verbally criticized Kaine and me for our retaliation and made Tony the sympathetic figure or "victim". Everything I tried to do to please her, seemed to blow up in my face, yet she wasn't putting in any effort at all. There were two incidents that really got under my skin and made me question if she had any feelings for me at all. One was the night that I offered to fill up her car with gas so she could stay home and rest, fully unaware that she had a faulty battery since she "forgot" to tell me.

The closest station was only a few minutes away but in a rough part of town. It's not somewhere that you would want to spent a significant amount of time at, especially at night. It was going smooth until I tried to start the engine after paying and it wouldn't turn over. No one had cell phones back in those days but luckily there was a phone booth nearby so I immediately rang Angie but there was no answer. I tried to call several more times but still couldn't reach her. I had no other choice but to approach strangers and ask if they had any jumper cables but who would be willing to help *anyone* out at this time of the night in this neighbourhood? I was freaking out since I was blocking the pumps and running out of options quick. Then I heard a voice that didn't exactly bring me any relief whatsoever, asking if I was having car trouble. It was my estranged sister, who I hadn't seen in years, and for good reason. She didn't waste any time taking shots at me by saying things like "I heard you got married. Where is your wife?" and "So she won't answer her phone? Well that's not good. Just remember that your sister was here when she wasn't." It was the same old song and dance with her that I have heard or seen a hundred times in my life. She didn't come to help me, I just happened to be there in the middle of a crisis and she showed up out of the blue, in the right place at the right time, yet in *her* mind she was the hero of the day. She was able to get me a boost from one of the customers, and I knew that she would never let me live that down but it was worth it just to get the hell out of there. When I got home, I found Angie asleep on the couch near the phone. She looked up at the clock and asked me where I have been for the past hour. I couldn't believe that she fell asleep literally five minutes after I walk out the door and was in such a deep sleep that she couldn't hear the phone ringing only a couple of feet away. Of course, it led to yet another argument and us sleeping in separate rooms, refusing to talk to each other. She would do exactly the same thing, only a few days later, when I was on my way to work one snowy morning and slid off the road into a ditch. I had to walk to the closest house and ask to use their phone. When I knocked on the door, I heard a familiar voice on the other side: it was my old bandmate "Crimson", who I hadn't seen or heard from since high school. He didn't recognize my voice, and was hesitant about opening the door, which was understandable. I had to spent a couple of minutes trying to convince him of who I was before he believed me and let me inside. I called Angie first to let her know and once again she didn't answer because that might mean that she would have to get out of bed, which was quite embarrassing, especially in front of an old friend. Then I called my boss to tell him that I was going to be late and finally my reliable father who, for the second time in a year, had to pull my car out so I could drive on into work.

19

Although it was great to see Crimson again, he wasn't the same person that I used to know. He had found God and turned from rock n roll to gospel. He was so different that I felt like he was a total stranger. He didn't talk to me much at all while I was waiting for dad and neither did his wife. It was almost as if he felt that I wasn't worthy to talk to him or be in his house and didn't do *anything* to make me feel welcome. It didn't help that he had enough crucifixes around the house to keep an entire nest of vampires away and just being there made me want to drop down to my knees and repent. I didn't interact with him again until many years later when I found him on Facebook. He had a joint account with his wife. He never used the account but his wife was always on there, talking about Jesus and how many souls were saved at church the night before. She made an unnecessary comment on one of my posts about how my love for Sepi made me not want to live another day without her. She said something about how this so called love "didn't really exist" and "that she had never heard of such a thing" and ended with "The only love that you can't live without is Jesus..." I didn't appreciate her sticking her nose in my business and was about to tell her off when she deleted me before I could respond. I have never heard from either of them since, which I consider a real "blessing."

    I was so angry at Angie when I got home but we ended up having great makeup sex, as we always did, to smooth things over. Sex seemed to be the answer to everything back in those days. It was so important, in fact, that we decided to rent a video camera and film ourselves in the act for our own amusement. This was 1993, so it wasn't the quality of a Kim Kardashian or Paris Hilton sex tape with different angles and a money shot, it was much more amateur. Angie was primarily featured, with many incriminating shots of her throughout, but myself on the other hand, unintentionally avoided any frontal shots through the duration of the film. You can see great footage of my back and ass and that's about it. I thought that there was only one copy of this film made, and I destroyed it after we split, but apparently there was a second copy made by Angie which is still in her possession, that I'm not exactly thrilled about. This would be the first of two sex tapes that I was featured in, and the only one that I willingly participated in.

Of all of the ceaseless bickering and verbal abuse that we had bestowed upon each other over the past few months, there were two things that we could always say which was that we never lied to each other and our fights had never become physical. I guess that once you are pushed to your limits and can't take anymore, at some point, you will snap. It started when I clearly stated to Angie that I wasn't ready for kids, yet she decided to lie about taking her birth control pills with the hope that maybe an "accident" would happen. When I found those pills in her dresser drawer without the seal even being broken, I thought about all of the times that we had unprotected sex over the past few months and how it was a miracle that she never got pregnant somewhere along the way. Now I was hesitant to even touch her after that trust was gone. When you take away the only thing that we had going for us, the volcano is going to erupt. The fighting increased and became unbearable in the weeks to come, and with me no longer willing to leave the house, the stage was set for something terrible to happen.

After getting home from a particular bad day at work, all I wanted to do was lie on the couch and watch television for a little while to take my mind off things. When Angie came through the door about an hour later, it was the same ritual. She started yelling at me about something that I didn't do, as usual, but this time, decided to yank the remote out of my hand and turn the television off. I wasn't in the mood to put up with that shit on this day. I rose from the couch to grab the remote off the stand when Angie saw me coming and intercepted me. As I was returning, with remote in hand, she was trying to wrestle it away from me, so I picked up her little frame and tossed her against the wall. Then she came at me again and I took her to the ground this time. I drew back to hit her and as I was coming down in the direction of her face, realized what I was doing, and pulled the slap back to where it made a minimal impact. She barely felt a thing but the *idea* of me hitting her would become salt on the wound and give her ammunition to try to rally everyone over to her side and make me out to be the bad guy. Within hours, she had blown the whole incident out of proportion to her family and then called my parents in an attempt to turn them against me too. My parents *knew* that I would never strike a woman and suspected that her story must have been fabricated to some degree and wrote her off at that moment, changing their opinion of her forever. Over time, the story changed several times, probably never told correctly, and eventually evolved into me "beating" her, and although she had no bruises or even scratches to back up these claims, everyone, with the exception of my parents, seemed to believe her and turned on me anyway.

20

This would push me into the arms of a much older woman. I had been drawn to her since we first met at work and often imagined what it would be like to kiss her. One day, when we were alone in the break room, I just went for it. To my surprise, she not only went along with it, but stuck her tongue down my throat in the process. We would meet at pretty much the same time every day and passionately make out but not once did I try to seduce her. I was still married at the end of the day and wasn't interested in having an affair. In fact, the person who benefited from this the most was probably Angie... because I was already horny when I got home and she benefitted from that. I would never sleep with this woman, even after my marriage had dissolved. If anything, once I was single, she seemed to lose interest in me completely. She would become the first of many to join that exclusive club of women in my life who were more than willing to make out with me or give and receive oral, but refused to let me inside of them. The irony was that she had slept with several of guys at work, including seven of them in one night as they ran a train on her, but still didn't let me touch her. Before I left the plant several years later, she start having sex with one of the most feminine guys on the roster that we had all assumed was gay which left me scratching my head and wondering what was wrong with me. Go figure...

By Christmas, the marriage had become nothing more than just a piece of paper...it meant nothing. Due to my schedule, I couldn't go to the landlord's house that month to pay the rent, so I gave the money to Angie and asked her to do it instead. Although I didn't trust her, especially with money, my hands were tied so I had no other options. When I got home, I noticed extra presents under the tree but didn't think much of it. Maybe Angie had saved up some money and didn't tell me. I asked her if she paid the rent and she said that she did, and like an idiot, I believed her. Christmas came and went, and a new year was upon us before we knew it and that's when I got the call from the hag asking why she hadn't received the rent. I defended Angie thinking that there must be some mistake and told the old woman that there was probably a logical explanation and that I would call her back after I talked to Angie. When she got home, she came clean and told me that she had bought Christmas presents for her entire immediate family with the rent money that I gave her. At this point, I had enough. I called my parents and asked if they knew of any places to rent in their neck of the woods that was much cheaper than living in the city. They told me about a trailer park right off Highway 411 that had a few vacancies. I was interested straight away but Angie wasn't keen, thinking that she was too good to live in a mobile home. Unfortunately for her, she had no say in the matter since I was the breadwinner. I met with the owner, who happened to be an old friend of the family, and signed the contract. Even before the ink dried, I let the old woman know what was going on and agreed on a financial settlement for the duration of the move. Although she didn't deserve it, I felt like it was the right thing to do as I always try not to burn my bridges if possible. Now I was going to be much closer to my family, her family, and the plant and paying *half* as much money per month to do so. Angie would have to drive further but since she rarely went to work, I didn't even factor that into my decision.

21

The trailer wasn't in the best condition but it would do. I was a little concerned about the neighbours considering that just behind us was a Hell's Angel, and his family, who had already let me know that they didn't like cops coming into the park, so if I had an issue, don't get them involved under any circumstances. Angie's mom came over after we got settled in and got me stoned which helped me relax until she started tripping out over Angie's father deciding to stop in to see our new home unexpectedly when the place smelled like weed. When I saw him coming down the driveway, I bolted to the back and stayed out of sight until they left. I didn't know that Angie had already told him about the big fight and that he had went from considering me to be part of the family to hating my guts literally overnight. I had forgotten that he had asked me the night before the wedding to never hit his daughter and I had assured him that would never happen. Now, in his eyes, I was a piece of shit...no longer worthy to be married to his little girl.

This would become pretty evident when I decided to drive Angie's car to work one day unaware that her tires were worn so thin that they were split in several places, exposing the tube inside. One of the guys from work noticed them as he passed by the car on his way to the picnic tables to eat his lunch, and was shocked that I even made the trip in without having a blowout. Dad came to my rescue once again and put two new tires on before I headed home, thinking that Angie or her dad would pay him back or at least offer to eventually... which never happened despite Angie's dad's so called "religious" beliefs. As a matter of fact, her dad never even returned my dad's calls when he asked for payment. At this point, not only were Angie and I not getting along but neither were our families. It was obvious that we weren't going to make it...just too many obstacles to overcome that was standing in our way and we didn't have enough fight left in us to rise above them.

Then Angie came home one day and told me something that would be the final nail in the coffin. She admitted that she still had feelings for her ex and had been considering giving him another chance. This gave me that excuse to file for divorce that I had been searching for a very long time. I told her to get her belongings and get the fuck out of my house immediately and she did so without argument. I didn't bother asking if she had been cheating on me or not...it would have been irrelevant anyway. For the first couple of weeks, I allowed her to come by from time to time to pick up some of her things but grew tired of it quickly and gave her an ultimatum...either get it all out or I was going to dispose of it all myself. She didn't listen so I left it all in the front yard, hoping that someone would take them but with a Hell's Angel living so close, no one took *anything.* I eventually burned any remnants of my life with her in the middle of the front yard except for a pair of her panties, which I would hang right beside a pair of Salena's that I kept after we broke up, on the rail outside the kitchen. This would become my personal trophy case that I would add to over the years until one of my later girlfriends convinced me to dispose of them or she was going to leave me, much like how Angie got me to get rid of what would now be an expensive Playboy magazine collection when we got married. Doing this for *anyone* should be an unwritten rule, like getting your partner's name tattooed on your body, that you should *never* agree to willingly... in my opinion.

22

For the first time in my life, I was truly a bachelor and I loved it! I loved not having to get someone's permission before I did something, eating what I wanted, and not feeling obligated to socialize with anyone if I didn't want to. Over the years, I have lived alone nearly as long as having people around me. This stage in my life was definitely hard to adapt to considering that my house was now filled with furniture that I didn't even have a hand in picking out yet I agreed to take over the debt from my former wife so I had *something* in the house to sit on, sleep in, cook with, etc. I also had Chelsea because I felt like Angie wasn't responsible enough to take care of herself…much less an animal. The poor dog lived in a cage during the night while I worked and was tied up in the yard during the day while I slept which was no life for a puppy and I was about to fix that. I let Papaw Noland have her so she could do what she was bred to do: hunt. He knew a man up north who could train her and give her a life that I never could so I let her go. It really wasn't a difficult decision at all and getting rid of her gave me a clean slate to start over…again.

    One of the first lessons that I would learn was when you got horny and there wasn't exactly a line of women outside of your door, don't call the ex and arrange a "booty call" to get a nut. Sometimes, it can complicate things or even stir up those old feelings that you were trying to get out of your system so don't risk it. I made that mistake with Angie. We agreed to meet up and do it one more time for "old time's sake" and it would have been better if I had just stayed home and masterbated. We made out for a few minutes and as we went for it, Angie stopped me. She said that now she knew that she was over me because the emotion and feelings were no longer there. I couldn't really get upset about what she said because I was feeling the same way. So I gathered my things, gave her one last kiss and left. We never made that mistake again. If I needed to get my rocks off bad enough and no one was around, I would just grab one of my Christy Canyon, Traci Lords or Ginger Lynn videos with a jar of vasoline and problem solved.

23

We didn't have any further contact until we saw each other in court. It was an easy divorce since we had already divided everything beforehand so the judge praised us both for attending when only one of us was required to be there. I was hopeful that she would just go away and I would never see her again but that was just wishful thinking. In the months to come, she would marry a guy who works with Kaine and, just like Salena, fall pregnant within weeks of our split. She had filled her new husband's head with lies about how I abused her during our marriage which caused him to tell Kaine daily that he was going to "kick my ass if we ever crossed paths." This was hilarious considering that if he wanted a piece of me that bad, he knew where I lived and worked. I wasn't hard to find. Hell, I even stopped in to talk to Kaine several times when he was in the same building and he never confronted me. This would go on for several months until Kaine transferred to a different store. I am still waiting…

Several years later, when I was working the club circuit, I went into my old stomping grounds of K-Mart and ran into Angie by accident with child in tow. I literally turned the corner and there she was. After saying hello, she informed me that she had heard that I was working in a strip club and she bet that I was having a lot of fun working *there.* I couldn't deny it but I did cut the conversation short and pretended like I was in a hurry to get away from her. I managed to avoid her like the plague for the next few years until I received a phone call from my parents letting me know that they had heard that she had been in a terrible car accident and was in critical condition. A part of me wanted to visit her but I just couldn't do it. However, when she recovered, she called my parents and apologized for all of the hell that she had put me through then asked for my number. My parents wouldn't give it to her so she sent a message instead. She said that when she was close to death, she started to think about her life and decided that if she pulled through she was going to tell everyone the truth about us. At this point, I still had no idea of how many enemies that I had because of her and wouldn't know for several more years. I didn't really want to hear an apology from her, or anything else for the matter, I just wanted her to come clean and clear my name which she eventually did. In 2010, when I joined Facebook, I found her and wanted to do the right thing by sending her a friend request so we could clear the air once and for all. She accepted and we talked via messages for a few hours. She did apologize to me and even took some of the responsibility for why we couldn't make it work, which was very enlightening. She also told me that her dad was on his deathbed and wanted to see me before he passed so that he could apologize for being wrong about me and hating me for all of these years. I just couldn't bring myself to visit him so I told Angie to let him know that I forgave him to give him some closure. Angie and I would then move on to talk about the great sex that we use to have and even the videotape that we made which gave me a strange vibe considering that she was now single as well. I was hoping that this wasn't triggering any nostalgia that would give her any crazy ideas but I didn't really stick around long enough to find out where this was all going. I would also see her one last time about a week before I came to Australia at Hastings in Maryville. I was selling some of my dvds at the front counter when she walked up to return some that she had rented. She had to have seen me but didn't acknowledge by making eye contact which was refreshing to me at least. We never said a word to each other and that was fine with me. There was such a feeling of relief when she walked out that door into oblivion and I knew that there was absolutely no chance that we would ever be in the same building, at the same time, again.

24

(UPDATE: In January 2015, after posting on Facebook an update on the status of how this book was coming along, I received a private message from Angie. She wished me luck with the book and hoped that I didn't say too many bad things about her. I reminded her that I wasn't using her real name so she shouldn't be too concerned and if she came out and told everyone that this chapter was written about her, she just incriminated herself. Don't blame me. She then came out of nowhere and asked me why I never had kids and before I could even answer, let me know that she needed to tell me a secret that she had been keeping for over 20 years. "Do you remember when I working at K-Mart and I doubled over in pain and started bleeding really bad? You were already working in Vonore at that time. You got a call letting you know that they were taking me to the hospital." I told her that I didn't remember this incident at all, which was the honest truth, but I got chills because I had a feeling that I knew where this was going. She continued, "You had to come to Blount Memorial and pick me up. It was in November, 1993. I will never forget. I told you they said that I had cysts that were rupturing on my ovaries. I lied to you and I am very sorry for that. I was actually pregnant and had a miscarriage from pulling those pallets of oil and stuff at K-Mart. I didn't know I was pregnant until I had the miscarriage. They said I was about two months along. It was yours...and only me, and my mom and dad, knew about it. I never told you because I was afraid that you would think that I got pregnant on purpose, which I didn't, especially since I wanted kids and you didn't." I was both shocked and angry when I heard this but there was still a part of me that didn't believe any of it. If she was indeed telling the truth now, that meant that she had been lying to me for the last two decades. How can I distinguish between the truth and the lies? If it had been anyone else, I would have had an easier time accepting it but she has spent her entire adult life deceiving me. She also made a few claims later on that I knew were total bullshit and made me doubt her even more. Those things are not even worth mentioning. I went back and forth on whether to even bother writing any of this into the book but just in case she *is* actually telling the truth this time, it changes everything. The sad part is that there is absolutely no way to prove it one way or the other now as all of the evidence died along with my possible son or daughter long ago.)

-DJN

CHAPTER V - "SUCH DEVOTED SISTERS"

1994-1997

Within just a few weeks after the dust had settled, I had money in the bank and a second vehicle. Life was just easier to balance without that so called "special" someone in it. I never went anywhere or did anything so I always had money burning a hole in my pocket and that's where Kaine came in. He would ring me at the crack of dawn, when I had only been asleep for an hour or two and ask me if I wanted to hit various retail stores around Knoxville in search of various toys and comic books to add to our impressive collections. I always went whether I felt like it or not, because I had a bad habit of agreeing to almost anything if I wasn't fully awake as many telemarketers would later find out and take advantage of. I would usually feel like shit at work that evening but when I got home the next morning and looked around the house, I realized that the sacrifice of sleep was well worth it.

That summer Kaine and I would also attend our first MLB game in Atlanta. That's when I realized that it was better to just watch the game on television. I was bored shitless...especially between innings when nothing was going on. I thought that if I had a few beers, it might make the experience a little more exciting so I started drinking and ended up getting hammered. To this day, I don't remember if the Braves won or not. Hell, I can't even remember who they were playing but I had a blast anyway. It's funny how alcohol can sometimes turn the night around even if you can't remember anything afterwards.

2

    I hit the gym pretty hard that summer as well. Unhappy with the lack of "serious" bodybuilders at my old gym, I would get a second membership at another gym across town that was strictly for hardcore weightlifters. They didn't have an aerobics room, sauna, swimming pool, or racquetball courts, only two levels of free weights and machines. As soon as you walked in, you heard the grunts and groans of men and women pushing their bodies past their limits, and occasionally even the sounds of steel bouncing off the floor or walls due to failure. It was intense...and just what I needed. I would attend both gyms equally for the next few years depending on which equipment I wanted to utilize or what mood I was in.

    There was a girl at the front desk of my new gym that caught my eye instantly. She was practically a mirror image of the girl that got away at the other gym a year prior. They may have looked different but that was about it. When it came to their ages or backgrounds, there were exactly the same. They even attended the same college and both were only working at their gyms on a temporary basis. I was determined not to make the same mistake twice so I immediately started getting to know her and wearing her down. She was a tough cookie though, already scorned by an ex and not really looking for anything serious. I spent endless hours just listening to her problems and giving her advice and could feel myself being pulled into that dreaded "friend zone" so I changed my approach and started ignoring her. She would then catch me as I was entering or exiting the building and pull me into the office for a chat. That's when she told me that she had made out with one of the guys who worked there and now he didn't want anything to do with her anymore. She obviously liked him and was genuinely hurt by this rejection but I wasn't the shoulder to lean on this time. I just told her the truth…that he just used her and apparently didn't feel the same way about her that she did him. That would be the end of the chase. Now when I saw her car parked out front, I didn't stop, I just kept driving until it was no longer there. I would see her at the local Wal-Mart a couple of years later…with a baby! I don't know whether it was hers or not and wasn't about to ask. Luckily, she never saw me and I even headed in the opposite direction to avoid her so we wouldn't have any interaction. It's ironic that this whole fiasco ended the same way as it did with the girl from the other gym as well…she would leave before I ever built up the courage to actually ask her out. Another big question mark in my life…

3

The next woman to enter my life pretty much just walked right up to my front door and presented herself to me. As I was getting into my car to go to work one afternoon, I noticed an attractive woman walking directly toward me from one of the other trailers across the driveway. I was expecting her to be having car trouble or possibly be looking for someone else but that wouldn't be the case at all. She introduced herself and immediately started coming on to me, letting me know that she had been admiring me for a while but was afraid to approach me…until today. I hadn't been laid in a couple of months and this woman was ripe for the picking so I told her "I don't have to work tomorrow. You can come over then if you like for a drink or something." I must admit that I wasn't expecting her to show, thinking that this was just someone's idea of a joke so I was totally shocked when she kept her word and came over the following day. However, she didn't come alone...she had her two kids with her as well. She told them to play outside while she visited with me for a while. I poured her a drink of bourbon and we started talking about life in general. She told me that she had just recently filed for divorce from a man who used to slap her around then basically just walked out on her and the kids without saying anything. I was amazed that all of this domestic violence was going on literally right under my nose without me knowing but we were both eager to change the topic before it affected the mood. She was then drawn to my movie collection and picked a couple that she wanted to borrow. I was hesitant about loaning them to her but then I started thinking "What's the worst that could happen? She lives only a few feet away for God's sake..." so I reluctantly agreed. After a couple of short interruptions from the kids, I felt that the time was right to get to the real reason why I invited her into my home. I planted a kiss on her and she responded in kind which was a relief. We started ripping each other's clothes off and were so into it that we never even made it to the bedroom...we did it right on the couch. I could tell that she wasn't very experienced by how she reacted when I was going down on her and how she wasn't comfortable in any position other than missionary. It was like everything was a first for her. We went at it for nearly an hour then she got dressed and left with a smile on her face. We had planned to meet up again soon and exchange bodily fluids once more but with all the crazy shit that I had already seen in my brief sex life, even I couldn't have seen what happened next coming. When I got home from work the following morning, not only was she gone but so was her trailer! There was just an empty lot there where it once stood. The sad part was that the first thing that I thought of was that I was never going to get those movies back. It didn't bother me at all that *I* was used sexually, just that I would have to replace those damn VHS tapes. I was already showing signs of the man I was about to become...

4

I used to say "Tattoos are contagious...you can't have just one" which means that there is always something else that you want after you get your first. I was ready for more ink and this time I wanted to be more creative...no more symbols and emblems. I saw a vampire chick on the wall at the tattoo shop and had to have it. I wanted to put it near the ankh on my right arm to connect the two into one single piece especially since they are linked together in legend and folklore. Only a few weeks later, I got my fifth tattoo which was going to be put on my left arm. I had picked a photo of one of my childhood heroes, "Skeletor", took it in and got it done. I used to say that "Skeletor was a great role model for kids, because no matter how many times he tastes defeat at the hands of He-Man, he never gives up." Unfortunately, the artists that had collectively done all of my other work was absent that day so I had a heavy handed substitute who constantly had to stop to answer the phone which made this tat more painful than it should have been. He put the colours in so deep that it scarred my arm and even bled so much that I had to wear extra bandages on it that night at work to keep it from getting infected. By the end of my shift, the bandages were stained with blood. It was worth it in the end as the colours have yet to fade.

5

A couple of weeks later, after my arm healed, I had already found a new place to tan. The beds at the gym weren't strong enough so I thought that going to a proper salon seemed like the best option at the time. The girls who worked there were quite attractive too which reassured me that I had made the right choice. I wanted to ask out the cute blonde who worked the evening shift until I found out that she was already taken so I set my sights on the older chick who opened in the morning. I started with casual conversations for the first few days then moved on to buying her a dozen roses *every* morning. I was sweeping her off feet but still didn't have the confidence to ask her out so I never did. I was hoping that she would take the hint and ask me out instead but that wasn't happening either so I just kind of vanished into thin air...never showing my face in that salon again. The way I saw it, if she did like me, she should have said so before it was too late. It was 1994 after all. Women didn't have to be old fashioned anymore. That might sound a little arrogant on my part, but that was how I felt so it would be a while before *I* pursued a woman again. It just wasn't worth my time.

6

Walking through that door is like walking into another world. We have quite a collection, a large selection, an open bar and VIP section. We have anything that you are looking for. We have thirty beautiful girls and one ugly one. We promise that you will leave with an erection.

Most exotic of feminine splendour, most erotic of her gender, they treat her like royalty as she

walks down that runway to the pole. In someone's fantasy, she plays the starring role.

Down on all fours, she crawls across the floor, undressing him with her eyes. Nothing personal, just business as usual, he thought he was something special, but she does that to all the guys.

Tight spandex, fake breasts, white lace, black leather, what's your pleasure? Lap dances, and last chances, he was her best customer, until he mistook friendly gestures for sexual advances.

When she sits at your table, remember she's a trained professional. I'm not going to tell you twice, "You can give her a tip, to watch her strip, but you must follow one simple rule: keep your hands off the merchandise."

Never ask to hear her story, should be kept unread, should be left unsaid, "He used to cheat on me, beat on me, now I prefer women instead."

Nothing in this world is free, it's all about dollars and cents…dead presidents…having fun at his expense. She loved only money, was sweet as honey, until it was all spent. She picked him clean of anything green then off she went…

Last call for alcohol! After he pays his tab, better call him a cab…

At the end of the day, she wonders if it's all worth what she goes through, it feels so degrading…always worried about what she's going to do when her looks start fading…

-Denny Noland "Draven" From my song "Black Leather" Written on August 27, 2006 Copyright 2007

When Kaine transferred to a different job, he befriended a guy who we called "Bones" that introduced him to the world of strip clubs. He was addicted straightaway and insisted that I go with them some weekend and have a look for myself. I refused several times but curiosity started getting the best of me and I finally gave in. He sweetened the pot by letting me know that model/exotic dancer Alyssa Alps was going to be featuring at a particular club, which I will just call "The West Club" in west Knoxville, the following Saturday so it would be a perfect time for me to make my debut into the adult entertainment business. Little did I know that attending this show was going to literally change how I viewed the world forever…

When we walked into the building that night, I was overwhelmed by what I saw. Never had I seen so many beautiful women under one roof in my life. In this environment, I felt like a god as women approached me nonstop without me having to do anything or use any pathetic lines. I barely noticed that they were leaving just as quickly as they came once they realized that I wasn't going to give them any money. Fortunately for those who stuck around long enough for me to get drunk, I am much more generous after a good buzz in the right conditions. I spent a shitload of money on a couple of the girls as I impatiently waited for main attraction to hit the stage. By the time Alyssa did her set, I was hitting the closest ATM to dip into my savings. I threw money on her like it grew on trees and was ecstatic when I found out that she was autographing her posters and posing for pictures after her final performance. I bought several of her signed photos and had my picture taken with her. She was a gorgeous woman with the biggest breasts that I had ever seen outside of a magazine. She was also a real sweetheart who didn't seem to mind that I kept trying to kiss her on the lips. She just politely turned her head enough each time so I got her cheek instead. By the end of the night, I was just thrilled that I got to pose with my hands holding those massive breasts for the world to see. As we were driving home, we discussed the events of that night. I had a great time but had no plans of ever venturing into that domain again so I let the boys know that. They didn't believe me and continued to make jokes about me "being so drunk that I couldn't find our table on the way back from the bathroom" which did happen I might add.

By the time the next weekend rolled around, Kaine was inviting me to a different strip club a little closer to home. It was called "Bambi's" and it catered more to the working man than the suits that the girls flocked to in west Knoxville. I told him once again that I wasn't interested which echoed what I said the previous week in the car on the way back from the other one. However, he kept pressing, even promising that if I didn't like this club, he would never ask me again. I reluctantly agreed and away we went.

When we entered this place, I felt right at home which wasn't good. The music was better, the girls were more approachable, and the overall atmosphere made me feel much more comfortable. The first girl on stage was a beautiful girl who we will call "Sara". She was in her mid-twenties, was quite tall and had flowing brown locks down to her ass. I was smitten right away and invited her over to our table after I tipped her. She came over afterwards and took a seat beside me. We talked about everything and I was really feeling a connection with her so I asked her if she would like to go out sometime. She was definitely a player, not really saying yes but not saying no either. I was starting to sense that she wasn't near as interested in me as I was her but I didn't want to admit it. Women like "confident" men or so I've been told. Needless to say that she didn't show up at the Waffle House that night and had a great excuse for why she couldn't make it, as they always do. It was a heartbreaking lesson and the nature of the business you might say. Unfortunately, I couldn't see the forest for the trees and would make the same fucking mistake over and over again with many different girls before it finally sunk in.

    I took a different approach on trying to pick up girls from the club after realizing that my original strategy wasn't working. I thought that if I got close enough to the owner and manager, the girls would think that I was someone important which would generate some kind of interest in wanting to get to know me better. I approached them while they were having a drink at the bar and introduced myself. They were both quite friendly but I could tell that they just wanted me to go away by the way they responded with as few words as possible. An example was when I told the owner, who was named "Gene" by the way, that he had "the best club in Knoxville" and all he could say was "we try harder" which would become his catch phrase every time anyone complimented his club. The girls weren't buying into this whole fiasco and continued to treat me like I was just another customer which angered me somewhat. The more I drank the madder I got and eventually acted on it by getting into the Gene's face on several occasions when I didn't like how he handled certain situations. I had the bouncers following me around like my own personal security guards just itching to throw me out. I even tried to pick a fight with Gene one night and dared him to ban me from the club which didn't work either. He actually told me that he would never do that because I spent too much money and he didn't want to lose my business. He also said that he knew that I had a great time at his club but just couldn't handle my liquor. I couldn't deny this and eventually went back to being that model customer again. There was someone else who was watching all of this with great interest and taking notes: Gene's best friend, "James", who was at the club practically every night too and even worked there occasionally when they were short staffed. I would find out a short time later how this guy had my back the entire time without my knowledge.

Although I was on my best behaviour when Gene was around, I was still a little obnoxious in the trenches. One example was when a young lady joined Kaine, Bones, and I at our table and let it slip that she was getting married the following day. It became a quest for me to see how loyal this chick was going to be to her future husband, so I pulled out all my ammunition in an attempt to seduce her. As usual, I had a little too much to drink and the room was starting to spin so I went to the bathroom and threw up. When I got back to our table, she insisted on giving me a private dance and led me to the closest couch. I was trying not to get too close so she wouldn't smell the vomit on my breath and it was working until the song finished. She then grabbed my face and planted a deep, wet kiss on my lips, tongue and all. If she tasted anything, she never acknowledged it which was a relief. I started feeling guilty and avoided making any suggestions about hooking up with her for the rest of the night. I know I could have had her but wasn't in any condition to act on it so we just talked about other topics to let it all settle down. She did kiss me once more at last call then disappeared into the back for the final minutes before closing. She never returned to dancing after getting married which was probably a good thing after all that had happened that night.

Eventually, my luck would change and I would go out on a series of dates with a number of the girls. However, each would turn out to be a fucking nightmare. The first would be with the waitress who was much older than me. We went to a club called "Late Nights" which opened after all of the other clubs closed which explains why it was called what it was. Anything could happen in a place like this since everyone was already drunk before they walked in the door...including yours truly. It didn't help that this woman didn't drink or do drugs so we already had a problem right out of the gate. I focused on partying the entire time while she would often go up to the dance floor on her own since I didn't dance. We ended up leaving and parking somewhere so we could make out. After a lot of kissing, we had a conversation and the topic of drugs came up. I was totally honest about everything and she wasn't impressed...telling me that she didn't want to be around or in a relationship with anyone who got high due to a bad experience in a past relationship and I respected that so it ended before it ever got started. I wasn't a heavy drug user yet, but I knew that under the right circumstances I probably would be. I was already drifting into the wrong crowd and knew what the future held for me. I did this poor woman a favour by cutting her loose before it all went down.

About a week later, I asked out a cute, yet skinny, blond girl who had just started working at the club. I was supposed to pick her up in Farragut but got lost trying to find the exit and ended up driving about an hour and a half out of the way making it too late to go anywhere by the time I got back. I promised to make it up to her the following day by taking her to Cades Cove in the Great Smoky Mountains National Park. The trip up there was fine but we got stuck in traffic on the way out of the Loop and spent the next couple of hours moving at a snail's pace as the temperature started dipping below freezing. She even got out of the car once, walking up ahead to stretch her legs and when I finally caught up with her she said, "It would be quicker to walk out of here. Too bad it's so damn cold!" Although she wasn't discouraged about how terrible the past couple of days had went, I was...and never asked her out on another date.

 These two incidents were nothing compared to what would happen next. I had spent the entire evening getting to know a pretty little brunette named "Dakota" and at the end of the night, she asked me if I would like to go home with her. This was not only against the rules, but against the law as well yet she somehow managed to get the green light from the club to make it happen. She drove me to the other side of town, and stopped at the local Waffle House to get some breakfast before heading to her place. After we had finished eating, a random guy walks in, heads straight over to our booth and starts yelling at her. I jumped up to her defence and felt like a fool after I found out that this guy was her *husband* when I was told that she wasn't married. He grabbed her hand and dragged her to the door leaving me stuck in a strange place with no car. I said to him "How am I supposed to get back to my car? I rode out here with *her*." "That's not my problem" he replied as they were leaving. The staff at the Waffle House saw the whole thing and rang me a cab. I could see that they felt sorry for me especially after they told me that she had called him on one of her trips to freshen up and told him where she was and who she was with so this was obviously a set up. A few minutes later, my cab showed up and even the cab driver felt bad for me after he asked why I was stranded so far away from my car and gave me a discount. To this day, I don't understand why all of this happened but my story with her was far from finished. I would get my revenge in time.

7

I decided that a change in scenery was in order so we visited the other strip club just down the road from Bambi's that I will just call "The South Club." We had heard that the clientele there was a definite step down from what we were used to but we wanted to try it anyway. One of the first girls that I saw there was Sara, who had either quit or been fired from Bambi's a week or two prior. This would start the whole cycle up again and take it all to the max. She had surrounded herself with two gorgeous twin sisters named "Autumn" and "Sasha" who, by the way they were acting, were more than just friends to her. I think that it was the groping and making out in front of everyone that gave it away, but being young men in their early 20's, Kaine and I was eating it up. Kaine grew close to Autumn and would eventually start seeing her outside the club while I tried to reconnect with Sara. I had a fondness for Sasha as well, so when Sara wasn't around, I worked on her as a backup or "Plan B" if case Sara started playing her tricks again. It wouldn't take her long to do just that.

After Kaine got played by Autumn, he took a little break from the club scene leaving me to fly solo for a while. One of my first nights there alone ended in a catastrophe. There was a customer who Sara was looking at with a certain look…a look I had wished that she gave me but never did. Whether she was on stage or off, this dude had her full attention. I was quickly becoming just a figure standing in the background and I wasn't happy about it. I spent the entire night with Sasha pretending that this wasn't bothering me, but I went home very upset. The next night, he was in there once again so I did what any jealous, nosy guy would do: I bought him a drink and joined him at his table. He seemed like a cool enough dude so I just asked him if he had anything going on with Sara. He responded with "Not really. I just met her last night and she threw herself at me. She ended up coming back to my place and we went at it like two barnyard animals." I was sorry I asked but played along like I didn't care. That was the final straw. I gave up on Sara which didn't really matter since she didn't stick around this club for long either.

I would embarrass myself further by falling for the same bullshit with another buxom goddess who turned out to be a lesbian. She would stick her tongue down my throat and even hold my hand throughout the night with the promise of going out to breakfast with me afterwards. She would completely change when her butch other half came in and not even glance in my direction for the rest of the night. She did this to so many vulnerable guys as I would observe over the next year. She ended up hating my guts once I figured her out which didn't surprise me. But the worst rejection came in the form of a cute little blonde girl who hand-picked me to be her punching bag about a week later. She told me that she was single, but when I asked her out, she got offended and rang her boyfriend to tell him what happened. Here I was... standing at the bar talking to some bimbo's boyfriend on the phone about why I would hit on his girl after she had just shown me her tits for a dollar. I didn't even raise my voice because I felt like a damn fool. I probably even came across as apologetic, because after a few minutes he wasn't even angry anymore and started asking me personal questions about myself. I was started to believe that I was the biggest loser on the whole fucking planet.

But if you take enough shots, you are eventually going to score a basket. I hit it off with an older stripper at the club a few days later who was very attracted to me and wanting to do me as soon as she got off work. A smart man would have stopped drinking so there wouldn't be any "problems" downstairs during their performance... but not this guy. I kept partying until last call and was pretty wasted by the time I got behind the wheel. It was a miracle that we made it to the motel without getting killed but somehow we managed. After about an hour of foreplay, I finally entered her with only a semi-hard dick which wasn't going to be easy to maintain. As soon as it started going soft, I panicked which made any chance of getting it back up nearly impossible. It wasn't helping that she was voicing her frustrations to me while I was trying to concentrate. I eventually just gave up and took her back to my place, which was a fucking mess I might add, and tried again. Once again, I only lasted a couple of minutes before the shrinkage occurred and this time she had enough and was ready to go home and forget that this night ever happened. I only saw her one other night at the club and begged for a chance to redeem myself but she wasn't having it. She said "I thought that there was something there... between us... but now I *know* I was mistaken." She would disappear just like everyone else not long after...

    I would hook up with another stripper the following week. She was just as interested in me as the one before but the feeling wasn't mutual. She was hot but there was just something about her that I didn't like so when I took her to my crib, I went on all of the back roads so she wouldn't know where the hell she was in case she was one of *those* girls you just can't get rid of. Of course, I was drunk and even stoned this time but I rooted her like a champion regardless, which pissed me off even more about my performance the week before. The next morning, I couldn't wait to drop her back off at her car because her talking was really starting to annoy me. I made it clear that this was just a one night stand, and she seemed ok with that until about a month later. As I was resting on my couch late one night, I kept hearing a car going up and down the park driveway like they were looking for something. I started getting a sick feeling in the pit of my stomach because I knew it was *her*. Call it psychic ability, a premonition, intuition, who knows? But somehow I *knew*. Then I heard the car getting closer and moving much slower until the engine shut off…right in my parking space! I didn't wait until I heard knocking to open the door. I was right…it was her. I was planning on telling her to leave until she said "I'm moving back to Detroit in the morning. I just wanted to be with you one more time before I go. And I brought weed…" I was just going to get stoned and not have sex with her but somehow I ended up rooting her hard again. I blame the weed. And just like that, she was gone…

8

Kaine and I returned to Bambi's soon after which meant that now we were alternating between the two clubs depending on the mood we were in. With Sara gone, I set my sights on a pair of sisters named "Monica" and "Natasha" and their friend "Sydney". Monica was the older sister who had a better body but gave no indications that she would be interested in me whatsoever…only my money. She usually worked the crowd until she felt there wasn't any money to be made then she would join her little sister and Sydney at our table. She rarely said anything, just listened to what Kaine and I were discussing and either nodded her head or chuckled. I would get her to dance for me sometimes just to stay on her good side in case I needed help winning her little sister over. To say that Natasha was flat chested would be an understatement. I used to call her breasts "mosquito bites" because that's what they looked like but I would never say that in front of her. Usually, that would be a major turnoff for me, but the way she would look at you and work her body was so sexy that it made you want her despite her flaws. Her choice of music just fit her persona, making her irresistible to males and females alike. She also wore a perfume that matched her body chemistry so well that it made you think that she must be some kind of divine being. I actually went out a bought a bottle for myself so I could sniff it myself and think of her.

    I had it bad I must admit, and she used that to her advantage. When Kaine and I took our vacations, instead of going somewhere out of town, we ended up going to Bambi's *every* single night and practically giving our money away...me especially. I went through my entire savings that week by tipping big and buying as many private dances as possible. All it accomplished was receiving an invitation to meet the girls at Late Nights after work which didn't necessarily mean that they were going to hang out with us and they rarely did. We would usually get there first and sit by a window waiting for them to arrive and usually spotted them because they were already dancing while they were still in line outside the building. Once they got inside, we would chat for a few minutes then the sisters would usually vanish, with Sydney sometimes staying back for some reason. One of those nights we found out why when she stuck her tongue down my throat as we were all saying goodbye before heading home. I had never paid her much attention because she had short hair and I *hate* short hair on women so if she had been eyeing me in the entire time, I wouldn't have noticed. I was more shocked because she did it in front of everyone including Natasha, who she was fully aware that I had a thing for. I enjoyed the kiss but wanted to be with someone else, so I never spoke of it or acted on it which was probably very insulting to Sydney but I didn't really know how to handle it differently.

Back at The South Club, Kaine started dating a lovely blonde chick and I was talking to a black girl who was volunteering to be my first interracial sex partner. It was one of those things that I wanted to check off the list and I was flattered that one approached me and made the offer. One problem though: she had short hair. I wrestled with that the entire night and just couldn't go through with it for that reason and that reason alone, so I reluctantly told her that I couldn't do it but wisely chose not to tell her why. She seemed very disappointed and in parting said, "Promise me something will ya? When you decide to be with your first black woman, please don't pick some Shaka-Zulu looking bitch ok?" I promised her not really knowing what she meant. At times, I still kick myself over that one but I just don't find short hair attractive on *any* woman. That's just how I am.

Once again, we would find ourselves at Late Nights with a different cast of characters. We didn't bring enough beer so we started stealing out of people's buckets when they weren't looking and nearly got into a brawl with a group of rednecks who almost caught us. Kaine and his girl disappeared to the car to have sex, leaving me to fend for myself for a majority of the night. Then I bumped into someone that I wasn't expecting: Sara. She was acting a bit weird about seeing me but grabbed a seat at my table anyway. I was so drunk that I asked her if she wanted to dance and that's just something that I don't normally do but luckily it was a slow song which made it easier. The whole time we were dancing, she wouldn't look into my eyes, choosing to look around at everyone else instead, which, even in my state of mind, hurt my feelings. After the song finished, I returned to my table alone as she headed off in a different direction without saying a word. Kaine and his girl had seen the entire thing and she warned me that "If you don't stop crowding her, she is going to tell you off." I don't know what the hell I supposable done but apparently I did something because everyone saw it except for me. I was so over people criticizing me, especially in public, so I approached the dance floor once again…alone. I started dancing in the corner, if you want to call it that, oblivious to everyone and everything around me. Even when a country song was played and everyone started line dancing, I still did my own thing. I had no rhythm or skill and probably looked like someone having an epileptic fit but I didn't give a fuck. What I didn't notice, however, was that this horrific display was taking place in front of the DJ booth and he was snapping photos to put up on his wall of fame or shame depending on how you looked at it. He was loving it, and kept encouraging me to continue but I was thirsty and felt like I was about to pass out if I didn't cool off, so I returned to the table to a standing ovation. We left soon after, and I didn't see Sara again after our dance together, not that I was really looking.

    Kaine would eventually break up with and replace his girl with another blonde, this time from Bambi's. Now we were bouncing back and forth quite frequently between clubs which meant that we were drinking quicker and more excessively, and that would often backfire on one or both of us. One example was when the beer at The South Club was a little warmer than Kaine's stomach could handle and we were about to get into the car to head down to Bambi's after having a few and he started hurling in the parking lot. I thought that he was down for the count but he started feeling better and was ready to go on down the road. Once we got into Bambi's, he immediately ordered a beer and chugged it saying that he just needed a cold beer to settle his stomach down which seemed to work like a charm. Another incident was when I started feeling sick on the way home one night and Kaine suggested that if we stopped and got something to eat, it might keep me from suffering from a hangover the next morning. As we were going through the drive-thru, I couldn't hold it any longer and spewed out the car window all over the bushes of the Pizza Hut next door. The worst part was that there was a family eating pizza in that booth and they saw me throwing up on the other side of the glass which probably made them sick as well but we didn't stick around to find out. We used to do some crazy shit like drive at dangerous speeds in thick fog to get home after leaving the clubs while still quite intoxicated. When I was driving, it was even more risky since my eyesight was so bad already that I couldn't see well even under normal driving conditions. I even went to the clubs one night that the weather man had advised everyone to stay off the roads unless it was an emergency because there the fog was so thick that it left zero visibility. *Nothing* could stop me from going when my head was set on it and miraculously I always got there and made it back home safely.

9

I was always a fan of Joe Montana. So when we heard that he was going to retire at the end of the season, we checked the Chiefs' schedule and saw that they were playing the Atlanta Falcons in Atlanta so we had to be there. We got several tickets which would allow each person to bring along a friend or guest. Kaine was bringing his new girlfriend, Bones was bringing his little brother, and I asked Natasha to come with me. She agreed to come, saying that "It sounded fun" but of course she was a no call no show on the day of the game so I was already in a bad mood from the outset. Bones had rented a big van so we could all ride together in style and I chose to sit in the very back of it, stretched out on the couch, nursing a beer. Kaine had given his underage girlfriend a couple of drinks and she was already feeling quite tipsy inspiring her to start flashing her tits back at him. Unfortunately, Bones was watching the show in the rear view mirror and not watching the road so when he looked up, he noticed that traffic had stopped just ahead of him and we were going way too fast to keep from hitting the car in front of us. He took evasive action and swerved around the cars, missing each one of them without driving off into the ditch. He probably not only saved us from going to jail but saved our lives as well yet if he had been paying attention to the road, we could have avoided this scenario altogether so we let him have it, then thanked him for using his Jedi-like reflexes and mad driving skills to avoid a potential fatal accident. Needless to say, everyone was sober and on their best behaviour for the remainder of the trip.

    When we got there, we were shocked that there weren't many Falcons fans there...everyone was cheering for Joe and he didn't let them down. The Chiefs beat them to a pulp to a rousing ovation and I was drunk as a skunk by the end of the game. My kidneys felt like they were going to burst but I couldn't be bothered waiting in line to take a piss, so I chose to wait till we got to nearest fast food joint not taking into consideration how much traffic would be pouring out of the stadium. We were practically in a gridlock and although the restaurant was in sight, it was going to take a very long time to get there. Someone handed me a bottle so I could try to relieve myself in the car so I pulled out my penis in an attempt to let it flow, but nothing was coming out. The cars that were sitting beside us could see everything but I was in too much pain to care. Finally, I pulled my pants up and decided to writhe in pain until we got to the local McDonalds. When we got into the parking lot, I lunged out of the car before it even stopped moving and shoved people out of my way until I reached the urinal. Once again, nothing came out. After about five minutes of standing there holding my dick, listening to the sinks running and toilets being flushed, it finally started and didn't stop for several minutes. I promised myself *that* day that I will always attempt to use the bathroom before I went anywhere, especially if I had been drinking, just in case.

10

Another mutual interest that we shared was wrestling…and this was an exciting time for both of us as the Monday Night War was in full effect. When we heard that WCW was doing a house show at the Civic Coliseum in Knoxville, we purchased our tickets immediately. Kaine and I hadn't been to a live wrestling show together in a few years so this was a rare treat indeed. The two things that I remember most was the Public Enemy/Steiner Brothers match and the Scott Hall vs Lex Luger main event match. During the tag match, the Steiners were supposed to be the babyfaces but the Knoxville crowd was cheering Public Enemy instead which pissed Scott Steiner off. Throughout the match, he dropped several loud f-bombs toward the audience which was hilarious. But that would be topped by Lex Luger later on when he attempted to run around the ring before his match and slipped on a wet spot on the floor… falling right into the steel stairs leading up to the ring! Even Scott Hall and Sean Waltman, who were already standing in the ring, were laughing their asses off. It was a decent show, even if most of their biggest stars weren't in attendance.

    Of course, we would have to stop by Bambi's afterwards and have a few drinks. We assumed that some of the wrestlers would be dropping by considering that the club sat between the arena and the airport and one of them actually did: Vincent. He didn't mingle much with the crowd. He just stood quietly near the bouncer at the front door with his arms crossed like he did when he worked as "Virgil" in the WWE years before. Kaine and I approached him with our "too sweet" hand gestures up in the air and touched fingers with him before starting a brief conversation. He seemed like a man of few words so we didn't stick around long enough to annoy him. We knew that he probably had a flight to catch anyway so we let him enjoy the show before he had to leave. Overall, it was a great night that I will never forget.

11

    A few weeks later, Kaine married his girlfriend and although he made a few appearances at the club every now and then, it wasn't with me. He had started resenting James since he was the one who discovered his new bride and got her into the business and I tried my hardest to keep the peace. It wasn't easy considering that I had started drinking Everclear, which was the strongest liquor that was legal, instead of beer, which altered my moods and caused me to go through every emotion in a single night. I was harassing customers, being obnoxious to the girls, and challenging the bouncers to toss me out. On one occasion, after the club had closed, I started talking shit to the morbidly obese DJ, and instead of just laughing about it as he usually did, decided to shove me as hard as he could down the concrete stairs which could have seriously injured me. I was in no condition to defend myself, which pissed the bouncer off who saw the whole thing, and nearly caused a fight between staff members. I had vowed to come back and kick that fat bastard's ass but he quit shortly after and never showed his face there again.

    My drinking had gotten so over the top that I was having a few beers before work and staying back on Thursday nights with the guys at the plant to get hammered before heading home in the morning. I had also increased the amount of Everclear I was putting down to two bottles a night on the weekends which is enough to stop a heart from beating. Without anyone around to moderate or monitor what I was doing, I was drinking myself to an early grave. I didn't realize how bad it actually was until one Sunday when I was driving to Lenoir City and because my blood alcohol level was still so high from the night before, began hyperventilating on the highway making it impossible to even grip the steering wheel. I had to pull over to the side of the road to get my breathing under control before I passed out. But I still didn't stop or even slow down, as I had become a full blown alcoholic.

    Every now and then, I would go out of my way to help someone without any reward or recognition like when a new girl started at Bambi's and was so uncomfortable with stripping that she had to have a few drinks just to get uninhibited enough to take her clothes off. She sat at my table and told me throughout the night how she felt out of place in this environment and couldn't believe how low she had stooped to even be doing this in the first place. I simply told her "If you have to get drunk in order to go through with all of this, then this is not the job for you. Not everyone can cope with this lifestyle, and do this type of work, so if you find it too difficult, maybe you should get out of this business and never look back." She listened to my advice and walked out, eventually getting her life back on track without having to resort to dancing naked in front of strangers to make ends meet. I felt like I had just saved someone from going down a path that they would regret for the rest of their life and it might bring me some good karma, when my life was already turning to shit.

12

Sometimes when something terrible happens, you don't realize that there was a blessing hidden within… until days, weeks, or even years later. This would be the case in December of that year when I attended the annual Bambi's Christmas party. I had purchased two bottles of Everclear earlier in the night and managed to polish off one of them before I got behind the wheel to drive home. I was driving very careful and cautiously, especially since it was the holiday season and cops were everywhere. I made it from Knoxville to Maryville without a problem, but as I was driving through a green light at an intersection in town, I got hit head on from a car running a red light right on the driver's side of my truck so hard that it totalled it and actually spun my vehicle around to where it was facing Knoxville again. I was so disoriented that I didn't know what happened until an eyewitness stopped to check on everyone and filled me in. He rang the cops and an ambulance then stuck around so he could tell them who was at fault which I greatly appreciated but it was what he did next that probably saved my ass. As the sirens began to wail in the distance, he asked me if I wanted a cigarette. I politely declined. Then he said, "You *need* a cigarette. I could smell the alcohol on you before I ever got near you. If the cops smell it on you, *you* will be the one at fault not *him* because that's how the law works." I chose to smoke that cigarette as the cops pulled in and filled out their report. I got extremely nervous when the cop recognized the kids in the other car who hit me and knew their parents on a first name basis. Apparently, they confessed to playing a game where they attempted to cross the intersection through oncoming traffic without getting hit, kind of like Russian roulette with a car instead of a gun. They claimed to have done this many times before without incident and felt confident that they had mastered this skill. They had not been drinking which surprised both me and my eyewitness but the cops still had to search my vehicle too. I had forgotten about that second bottle of Everclear that was in my seat at the time of the accident and if the cops found it, I was probably fucked! In a shocking turn of events, the cops not only didn't see the shattered bottle but didn't smell the stench in my truck either which was nothing short of a Christmas miracle especially when I had a look myself afterwards and saw the glass all over my floorboard right there in the open and smelled alcohol as soon as I opened the passenger side door. I just didn't understand how they missed it, especially when they were tearing my truck apart with flashlights searching for *anything* to incriminate me instead. My eyewitness came up to me once again and said, "You're almost home. Just hang in there, keep calm, and you got this" then he turned and walked away before I had a chance to thank him for everything. That night, this mystery man was my guardian angel and I never even caught his name.

After not finding any visible evidence or doing any kind of sobriety tests on me, the cops offered to drive me to the police station to call my parents. As they finished up, they left me in the car with the heater going full blast. Now I knew that the heat and my profuse sweating were going to make me reek of liquor but somehow they didn't smell it on me then either. Before we could drive away, the paramedics strongly insisted that I go to the hospital to get checked out because I was showing signs of a possible concussion but I refused since I knew I had no head injury…I was just shit faced drunk. I didn't need anyone examining me and figuring that out so I rejected any and all medical attention. On the way to the station, the cop kept trying to start a conversation and every time I spoke, I turned my head so he couldn't smell my breath. When we got to the station, I was still expecting to be locked up, thinking that this was some new technique to get offenders to the station without cuffing them or meeting any resistance but it was all legit. I rang my parents to let them know what happened and they picked me up and took me back to their place against my wishes since the cop told them to as a precaution. Dad stayed up with me for a while and even *he* didn't suspect that I was drunk but *did* notice that something wasn't right. I slept it off and didn't spend very long away from the club as I was back there the following week in my new truck, a 1991 black Ford Ranger!

It was sad to see that little truck go to the junkyard so I took a few pictures before it got demolished. Dad had put so much work into it in the short time that I had it including putting a cover over the dashboard with my name on it which I did take it back out after the accident. I had even driven it as far as Crossville to visit a freshly divorced Kaine who had relocated there before this all went down. It had very little power and struggled across the Cumberland Plateau on that journey but it made it. My first visit to Crossville to see Kaine helped me more than he will ever know. We had fun without visiting a strip club, even if we did surface at the local bar once or twice and even ran into an ex waitress from Bambi's who was now working there, but it wasn't the same. I missed my friend and I had already started my descent into darkness without him being around. This trip would lead to many others but the Denny that would show up the next time would be a completely different person altogether.

13

I had become a laughingstock over the past few weeks before the accident. Another customer and yours truly had developed a friendship built on our mutual lust over a new girl at the club who broke every rule in the book when she danced for us. I think we would have shared her if she offered because we were *that* obsessed with her. She literally took our money and ran as she just vanished without saying anything to either of us. The other guy was so disappointed that he stopped coming in as well. Then I nearly scored with a female customer who was missing her front teeth. I didn't notice this flaw until they turned the lights on at the end of the night and I was petrified after I saw her smile. The look on my face probably said it all. Gene sat at the bar the entire time laughing his ass off. But when I nearly scored with a *guy* without knowing, that was the end of the line.

After watching an older gentleman and a younger guy who looked like Jim Morrison having a great time from a distance, I decided to join them at their table. It was very close to the stage with a bird's eye view of the girls coming down the runway, possibly the best seat in the house, so why not? They were both very cool and friendly, but I noticed a few of the girls just staring and laughing at us but I wasn't sure if I was just imagining things or not so I just ignored it. The older gentleman offered to buy me a beer which won me over immediately and continued to buy both me and the young guy drinks until last call. I thought that this was a kind gesture and thought nothing more about it. When the lights came on, the old gentleman asked "Would to like to join us back at my place for a drink?" Here was a man who had spent a lot of money on keeping my buzz going without asking for anything in return so I didn't see any reason to decline so I accepted his offer. When I went to take a piss before leaving, one of the girls pulled me aside. "You know that those two guys are gay right? They come in here every now and then. The young guy is bisexual and likes to look at beautiful women sometimes to get himself aroused for the old man. When you came up and sat down at their table, he started getting you drunk so he could possibly add you into the mix. I just thought I would warn you, in case you didn't know." I really did it this time. I hid in the bathroom until those two were tired of waiting and left without me and when I came out, everyone was gone except for the staff. Gene said, "We were wondering how far you were willing to go. It was funniest thing we have seen in here in a long time. Why do you think I stuck around till closing and not go home early like I usually do?" Even Natasha threw in her two cents by saying, "I can't believe you didn't know..." before leaving. That night was one that I wished that I could have erased from history and no one was going to let me live it down.

14

Although I had been humiliated in front of the entire staff, I still had the balls to show my face in there the following night. I wasn't really in the mood to drink so I just sat quietly at the bar and watched the show from a distance. After about an hour, all hell broke loose in the DJ booth and the music died…literally! Apparently, one of the ladies accused the DJ of having cocaine hidden in his cd case resulting in the manager making accusations and demanding to search his personal belongings. Needless to say, the DJ wasn't happy about it and ended up walking out… in the middle of a song! When I saw how little this fellow was, I was impressed that he didn't back down and stood his ground against the much larger manager without any regard for his own personal safety. He could have been beaten to a pulp but he took his chances and it paid off. He left looking like the hero instead of the villain and won not only my respect but everyone else's that witnessed it that night.

When the following weekend rolled around, I decided to stop in at The South Club just down the road and there he was in the DJ booth. I went straight up to him and introduced myself and we became fast friends. His name was "Paul" and in a cool twist of sweet irony, he just happened to be dating Kaine's ex squeeze Autumn. They would later invite me to attend a party with them after the club closed. He also informed me that Sasha was probably going too and could be my date for the night with a little luck. I told them that I would love to and away we went. Sasha ended up backing out at the last minute so I became the proverbial third wheel which made me feel even more awkward amongst strangers. I had no idea of the repercussions that going to this party was going to have on the rest of my life.

When we got to the guy's house, one thing that stood out to me was his love for pornography. There were two strippers going at it on the couch just inside the door and several sexual paintings on his wall. He also had two other lesbian strippers living with him and I knew both of them personally. I had no idea at this point that he was a drug dealer, even if he did look the part with the Miami Vice bald head and thin ponytail. He told me that his name was "Buck" and treated me as if he had known me his entire life. In a matter of a few minutes, I saw Paul give him a wad of money and he left the room shortly after. When he came back, he had a baggie with a white powdery substance in it and began cutting out lines on a small mirror. I'm not an idiot... I knew exactly what it was and didn't hesitate when they passed the straw to me. From the moment the cocaine's effects hit my body, I was addicted. I fucking loved how it made me feel even if I was talking nonstop and breathing loud and quickly due to my nose running constantly. This might have been the first time that I did cocaine but I knew already that it was certainly not going to be the last.

As the night progressed, my personality and behaviour began to change. Every time they would dump the coke on the mirror, they would have one pile that they would divide into smaller lines for us to do and when it was my turn, I would snort that line "by accident" so I would get twice as much as everyone else. No one said anything because they knew better. If I went on a rampage, no one would be able to stop me. I had also started rambling on about how I would never "sell Buck down the river" meaning that I wouldn't tell anyone about Buck or "rat him out." I must have sounded like a broken record but everyone was too afraid to call me on it. I went home that morning feeling like a million dollars and couldn't wait to do it all again.

    I wouldn't have to wait long as we were back at Buck's place the next night. This time everyone wasn't so eager to share their dope as they were the night before so I offered to pay for everything myself. I literally bought Buck's entire stash and had to put my trust into one of the girls to keep the party going. I gave her money to pick up some from another source and after a couple of hours, we all realized that she wasn't coming back. This would piss me off to the point that I never went back over there. I would, however, get my money back from an unlikely source: the culprit's girlfriend who never liked me. She apologized and told me that what her partner did was wrong and vowed that it would never happen again. Eventually, the thief herself would cross paths with me in the clubs and attempt to apologize but I told her off instead. I did, however, thank her for teaching me a lesson in trust and never sent *anyone* out to pick up more drugs with *my* money ever again.

15

    Paul would always find a party to go to and people to hang out with. On one occasion in particular, we were in an apartment near the UT campus with a group of college kids. The biggest guy started talking about Peyton Manning, who was our star quarterback at the time, and how angry he was at the fact that Manning never had to go to class yet still had passing grades. He and his group of disgruntled misfits started planning an attack on Manning's leg in an attempt to end his football career so "he would be just like everyone else." I was enraged and appalled by what I was hearing and decided to take a stand. I told him that "If I hear that *anything* has happened to Manning off the football field, I will go straight to the cops and tell them what you just told me so you better pray that he doesn't get hurt." The guys knew that I had them by the balls and quickly changed their tune. Whether I had just saved a legend and future NFL Hall of Famer's career is debatable. Maybe it was just the drugs talking but I wasn't taking any chances.

16

Paul would only stick around Knoxville for about a month after this incident before packing his things and moving back to Myrtle Beach, South Carolina where he was originally from. Our last night of partying was just the two of us, since he had broken up with Autumn and already dating someone else. We only had a small amount of coke and I divided it all up into about 30 very small lines to make it seem like there was much more. Paul thought that it was a brilliant idea and I responded back with "It's all in your head...mind over matter. You don't need a lot of dope to have a great time. You just need to create an illusion and play along with it and by the end of the night your body and mind will never know the difference." That was total bullshit...as I would find out the more I used but at least it sounded good at the time. I did see him the day that he left, as I helped him and his new girlfriend pack their things then stood there waving as they drove away into the sunset. I envied his free spirit and ability to just make a snap decision and follow through with it, not afraid of taking a risk. I remember thinking to myself that I wished I had the balls to do that, obviously unaware that I was not only capable but would go on to take it to a whole new level that he could probably never imagine.

17

    Back at the plant, I discovered that my supervisor "Cody" was a crack addict himself so we would sneak outside every chance we had to get high. Crack made me work relentlessly, unlike when I smoked weed with the boys occasionally and was always either paranoid that someone would notice or that I would make a mistake, which I usually did, and ended up getting made fun of afterwards for being stoned. This drug was different. It placed me in my element and made me a fucking machine. I started coming over to Cody's house in Madisonville after work several times a week as well so I was doing drugs pretty much every single day…no matter where I was. The only time that I slowed down was when I went on the weekend shift, where I was working only Fridays, Saturdays, and Sundays and off the rest of the week. I loved having four days off in a row but hated going in at 10 pm at night. I would still go to the clubs early to get my fix and end up having to leave just as the party started going. It was an hour long drive to work from the clubs, which meant that I actually passed my house on the way there and was always saying "This is stupid. I'm not doing this anymore" yet I would still do it again the next night anyway. Luckily, this shift wasn't available for very long and I was back with my crew only a few short weeks later.

18

    However, when I got back, there was a new drug floating around: crystal meth. It seemed like everyone was sampling it, including Cody himself. I didn't like it as much as cocaine, but it was cheaper and lasted a helluva lot longer so I started doing it for a while. I stopped eating and would usually be up for a couple of days before I came down enough to sleep. It was during this time that I met a guy named "Jonah" at the clubs. He looked much like Buck, with the bald head and ponytail, and always came with an entourage. He was an arrogant asshole who threw money around like he had an endless supply. Our first encounter was at The South Club and we didn't exactly hit it off immediately. As a matter of fact, I nearly punched him in the face and he responded by handing me a $100 bill. I took it at first, then thought about for a minute and threw it back at his face, leading to an apology from him. He was known for three things...never coming in alone, never coming in without a bottle of rum, and *always* having cocaine on him. You never knew what was going to happen when he was around...especially at Bambi's, which seemed to bring out the absolute worse and best in him. Sometimes he would bring someone with him who would try to pick a fight with Gene or the staff and have to be removed, and other times when I was too drunk to deal with his shit, he would tell Gene that "we were going outside and will be back in a few minutes" which basically meant that he was going to give me a few lines to sober me up. Gene knew exactly what was going on and seemed ok with it. But when I got on the meth, and Jonah would offer me some blow, I refused, telling him that "Meth was so much better, and that he should try some of my stash." He became concerned straight away and warned me of the dangers "of using household chemicals and poisons found under your sink to get a buzz" and that I should "get off that shit immediately." I didn't listen and continued using it to replace my "true drug of choice" cocaine.

I resented that people were so against me taking something that made me feel indestructible and I needed to get away.

19

It was time to take a break from Bambi's to let things cool off, so the following weekend I took a road trip back to Crossville. Kaine had invited me there several times when certain female adult stars were featuring at Deja-Vu in Nashville and for some reason I had never gone. First there was Christy Canyon, who I was a big fan of for years that I had to miss out on due to fatigue and sickness. Then he rang me and told me that a new girl named "Jenna Jameson", who he claimed was the hottest up and comer in the business, was coming into town. I had never heard of her and was quite annoyed with his offer to see someone who was, in my own words, "going to be a shooting star, forgotten in a year or two like so many others before her." I would regret later not only saying that but not meeting these two beautiful adult icons when I had the opportunity, so when he informed me that Lisa Lipps was going to be there, I wasn't missing it for the world.

I was very impressed with the roster of girls at Deja-Vu. I don't believe that we saw the same girl on stage twice that night. I also figured out where Gene got the phrase "30 beautiful girls and one ugly one" that he had on the Bambi's sign near the highway. He had stolen it from Deja-Vu! They even used it on their t-shirts, so I had to buy one just so I could rub it in Gene's face that I knew that he didn't come up with it himself. There was one girl who both Kaine and I favoured who danced by "Dusty" that wore the whole cowboy hat, country-western attire and had long flowing brown hair. It was no secret that we both had a thing for brunettes and still do as far as I know. We bought a few dances from her while we waited for Lisa to bless us with her presence. When she came out, I was somewhat intimidated because I had actually seen a couple of her films and knew who she was beforehand unlike Alyssa Alps. After her set, we got in line to get pictures taken with her and buy some autographed memorabilia. I was behind Kaine and watched nervously while he posed with her awaiting my turn. As I approached her, she warned me that "If you touch me inappropriately, I will have your ass thrown out of here in a second" then proceeded to sit her naked body on my lap, place my hands on her massive boobs while spreading her vagina with her other hand. I started wondering what the hell she meant by "touching her inappropriately" after how she posed for the photo, and started feeling offended, especially after I asked Kaine if he received the same threat before his turn and he said no. I felt that this comment was unnecessary and inappropriate. It affected how I felt about her and made me no longer a fan. I still have the picture in one of my albums, although the thought of burning it did cross my mind more than once. She was the only adult star or model to *ever* threaten me and I have met and worked with many over the years. I don't know whether she didn't like how I looked or what, but I didn't appreciate her actions whatsoever. It pretty much ruined my entire night, like a dark cloud hovering overhead. I was ready to go home...

20

Back in those days, my fondest memories were when Kaine and I hung out with a trio of guys who were into the same things as us. Their names were "Bill", "Will", and "Travis." Kaine used to work with

Bill when he took a part-time job at KB Toys for extra money and they hit it off. Then Bill brought Will and Travis into the fold and last, but certainly not least, Kaine introduced me to them. Before Kaine moved to Crossville, we would get together on Sundays to watch the wrestling pay-per-views on the box. Every once in a while, we would attend local house shows when WCW and WWE came into town and eventually moved on to other events like Dragon-Con in Atlanta since we were all collectors of toys and comic books as well. My first time to Dragon-Con was like a walk into an alternate universe…I didn't know what to think. I had never been around so many people in costume or this many celebrities in my life. My main reason for going was to get James O'Barr's autograph, since I was such a fan of "The Crow", but I never found him and couldn't be bothered looking for him among the masses. I remember discussing this with Kaine, unaware that I leaning against Lou Ferrigno's table, yet I wasn't interested in getting *his* autograph, even if he was staring directly at me with marker in hand. We even planned to go to see GWAR, who was playing there later that night, but changed our minds at the last minute and hit the road instead. I left without any autographs but *did* spend a lot of money on a car load of comic books, toys, posters, and books that day.

    When Kaine moved to Crossville, it was just too convenient to catch significant events in Nashville since we were already half way there. Bill, Will, and Travis would usually carpool while I would drive separately, meeting up at Kaine's house a day or two before the show. We would use this strategy to go to Starrcade 96' which pitted "Hollywood" Hulk Hogan against "Rowdy" Roddy Piper in the main event. As we were standing in line to enter, we saw Sean "Sixx" Waltman walking on the second level looking down at us, pretending to be videotaping us with the camera that he used to carry as a part of his gimmick. When we got inside, we purchased our New World Order t-shirts as did three quarters of the audience and immediately slipped them on. The boys had made a "Mike Tenay is God" sign that we not only had a difficult time hauling in the car but it took all five of us to hold this damn thing up when "The Professor" walked out. When he saw it, he appeared to be very flattered and waved at us, which was cool even if Kaine and I wasn't really fans and had nothing to do with it except for helping to hold it. The show itself was incredible, with highlights that included being in the right place at the right time when "Sting" came out, with his Crow makeup on, to attack Rick Steiner during his match. Kaine poked me on the shoulder as he passed right by us and at first, I didn't think that it was the real Sting, considering how many lookalikes that were in the audience. When the crowd reacted, I knew he was legit and patted him on the back before he got out of reach. If you watch the footage, you can see us several times throughout the course of the show, especially as Sting was coming through the crowd. Other highlights would have to been seeing Scott Hall & Kevin Nash against The Faces of Fear and, of course, Piper vs Hogan. The pyro when they came out rained down on the audience and I foolishly stared up at it and got something in my eye causing me a lot of pain during the opening moments of the match. It stopped hurting in time to see Piper put Hogan to sleep to win the match, but not the belt since it wasn't on the line... apparently. The audience was confused when Hogan left with the belt especially since we were all led to believe that we were watching a title match. Anyway, we all had a great time and headed off to the motel to chill for the night.

The following day, we headed to the mall to do some shopping before heading home. I still had my New World Order t-shirt on, which created a small gathering of kids who started following us around the shops. Apparently, they thought I was Kevin Nash and one of them even came up to me to ask me just that. I did have the same hair length and colour, tattoos, a goatee, and was built like a wrestler at the time but that's where the similarities ended. I was nowhere near as massive as he was, but trying to tell that to a disbelieving, disappointed little kid was impossible. I ended up signing several autographs that day for the kids but I didn't charge anything since I had a conscious and only wanted to be left alone. I don't know how celebrities do it but I had a newfound respect for them afterwards.

21

I started off as a social drug user but evolved into an around the clock addict who was just as content sitting at home writing songs with music blaring all night long as living it up at the local club amongst so called friends. I was obviously disturbing the neighbours but didn't really give a damn as no one would dare to knock on my door and ask me to turn the volume down. Not even the Hell's Angel wanted to risk the consequences. I could have easily killed someone if I felt threatened in any way and everyone knew that. Eventually, when the landlord came to collect the monthly rent, he politely asked me if I would take into consideration that some people were trying to sleep late at night and I was making it extremely difficult. For the moment, I saw their side of the story and agreed to be a little more mindful of other people schedules but by nightfall, that all went out the window. I was back to my old tricks and this time no one said a word about it.

But it wasn't just the neighbours who were suffering from my newfound erratic behaviour. After a night of partying with Jonah, I got home and started coming down really hard and decided to ring Cody to get a quick fix. It was already 3am in the morning so I was probably the last person whose voice he wanted to hear at that hour. He very calmly told me to sleep it off and he would see me on Monday. I was embarrassed that it had even come to that and apologized for disturbing him. I ended up passing out on the bathroom floor underneath the sink and woke up the next morning with no recollection of how I got there. It wasn't until Monday when I saw Cody that my memory started coming back and I didn't like what I saw. It was just the first step in a long journey that many never return from...alive.

Because of incidents like this, when something strange and unexplained happened to me, people generally thought that it was only in my imagination or I was just too high. One of these experiences occurred while I was sober and yet no one believed me. It happened late one night while I was sleeping on the couch near the window. I was awakened by a bright light shining down on me from the sky. I immediately sat up and looked directly at it wondering what it could be. I was both concerned and curious at the same time so I decided to walk out on my front porch to get a closer look. I was left with more questions than answers once I stepped outside. It was just a large, pulsating light hovering in one spot directly overhead that made no sound. I watched it for long enough to wonder if anyone else was seeing it and even thought about waking up the neighbours before it just quickly sped away faster than anything I had ever seen in my entire life. I have no explanation for what I witnessed that night and when I told people about it, no one took me seriously since I was known to be on drugs 99% of the time. This just happened to have occurred in the other one percent but since I didn't have any visible evidence to show to back my story, everyone thought I was making it up to gain attention. Nothing could be further from the truth. I know what I saw but even to this day, I still don't have a fucking clue about what it was. I've never seen anything like it since then and to be honest, I don't want to either.

22

There was only one strip club that I hadn't been to in West Knoxville so I wanted to check it out for a change. This particular club won't be mentioned by name for an entirely different reason than the others: I fucking despise it and don't want it to gain any publicity from me writing about it. Over the years, they have banned me and even had the cops escort me out in the middle of a private dance just because of my affiliation with Gene and his club. I have been accused of "recruiting" girls to work at our club when I've never done so. However, at this point and time, I am still a customer so I was allowed entry. I was blown away by the beautiful women that worked there but the building itself just had a bad vibe that wasn't welcoming.

But when a certain girl named "Jessie" took the stage, I think I actually blushed. She was just stunning and I was so attracted to her that I developed a crush on her straight away. No other girl in the building could hold a candle to her in my eyes and that's saying a lot considering that several of my future exes and even one of my future wives were performing that night as well. I was so smitten with Jessie that I couldn't even look her in the eyes when I tipped her or say a complete sentence when she came around to my table to thank me afterwards. I actually had to leave to keep from making a fool of myself because I was sure that she would reject me and the irony was, as I would find out years later, she developed a crush on me that night as well. I would never see her again in that building but our paths would cross once more only a few weeks later and destroy any feelings that we might have had for each other. Today, she and her husband are two of my closest friends in the world and I love them to death and for the record, Jessie and I did make out several times later on but never slept together or been involved with each other romantically even if I have fantasized about what it could have been like many times over the years.

23

After leaving there, I stopped in at Bambi's and noticed that the club itself was going through a lot of changes and renovations. Not only had the name of the establishment been changed from "Bambi's" to "The Last Chance", but Gene had hired a brand new manager and bar staff to boot. I had heard rumours that Gene's lawyer, who was one of the sleaziest yet respected names behind the scenes in the adult entertainment business, had found a loophole in the system that would allow The Last Chance to become the first nude strip club in Knoxville. This would put Gene's club in a position to begin the largest talent "purge" this city had ever known and destroy his competition. Who's going to go to a club to look at just breasts when they can see the entire package somewhere else? There was a helluva lot of money to be made here and I wanted to be a part of it somehow if I could only find a way...

Gene had already followed in the footsteps of The West Club, by bringing in big name "feature" dancers to draw larger crowds. He even had a live band once that played between sets. Business had picked up so much that he had opened up the other side of the building and expanded the club which allowed people to walk back and forth as he had two girls on stage simultaneously, or in the case of having a feature there, used the second stage for photo opportunities while the show went on upon the main stage. The first girl that I met there was a beautiful redhead named "Mallesia Renee" who worked for Hot Body International. She was a sweet girl who I would have the pleasure of working with down the road. We posed together on a Harley-Davidson motorcycle that Gene had brilliantly placed on the second stage and I must admit that it is one of my favourite pictures that I've ever had taken.

The following week they had a girl named "Michelle Fox" who was billed as Courtney Love's lesbian partner in a scene from "The People vs Larry Flynt". She was also a sweetheart and posed for an autographed photo with me as well. Within a few weeks, I had gained quite a vast collection of autographed memorabilia to add to my portfolio but it still wasn't enough. I was about to set in motion a chain of events that was going to allow me to reach up and grab that brass ring for myself instead of just being a spectator to someone else taking it. It was my time at last…

24

It all started with a simple phone call from Kaine. He was thinking about moving back home and invited me to Monday Night Raw in Nashville as one last hurrah before leaving Crossville. Since it was on a Monday, it meant that I had to work and since I didn't have enough time to request it off, my hands were tied... so I had to decline. When I went to the plant that day, I looked around and wanted to hurl. My supervisor was out to get me and did everything in his power to either make me quit or get me fired. He tried to stop me from getting raises by giving me bad reviews even bragging to one of my mates that "When Denny sees what I put down about him, he's probably going to leave." However, Chance had the final say and I got a raise anyway, giving me the last laugh. The problem was that Chance believed that I made too much money to still be a machine operator and against my wishes, decided to promote me. For the past few months, I had been working with Cody on the small machine that ran special orders of expensive material. It wasn't as physical as the other machines but cleaning up between orders was critical to prevent contamination. The biggest problem I faced there was getting the kerosene out of my hair at the end of the shift. Now I was going back to where I started but this time I was responsible for someone else. The worst part was that they stuck all the new people on this machine and since I had no fucking idea what I was doing, there was a million things wrong with this picture. To make matters even worse, the guy who I trusted to look after the machine while I was eating lunch ran a box of bad product that was soaking wet and didn't tell me to save his own skin. By the time I got out there, he had filled the top of the box with good material so I had no suspicion that there was anything wrong with it and signed off on it. A few days later the customer sent it back and I nearly got fired. It was displayed in front of the entire plant and I came out looking like an idiot... lucky to still have his job. This disaster put me on eggshells for the rest of my stay there. When I tried to sleep, I had nightmares about running that damn machine which made me feel as though I was working 24/7 and it was really starting to take its toll on me both physically and mentally. That place was killing me in more ways than one and I wanted out but the pay was still the driving force to make me punch that timecard every day. I couldn't decide what I wanted to do but it was time to either suck it up and keep going or move forward into finding a new career.

    I still hadn't made my mind up by Friday so I did my normal routine of scoring a couple of grams of meth from my buddy for the weekend. He almost didn't let me have it due to his dealer getting busted and was probably about to go to prison for a very long time. He knew that meth was about to vanish in that county so it took a lot of persuading to get him to let any of it go. This would be the final time I would do meth for the next couple of years until it resurfaced into my life once again from a new source. However, when I look back at it, it could have heavily influenced the life-altering decision I was about to make, but then again, maybe it didn't. Who knows?

    I stayed home that night but made an appearance at The Last Chance on Saturday when I heard that Gene had brought in yet another feature dancer: a gorgeous redhead who I would also have the pleasure of working with in the future, "Raquel Darringer." She, like Mallesia Renee, was as beautiful on the inside as she was on the outside. I didn't look or smell very healthy when I walked in the door and Jonah immediately knew what I was on. He said, "You really need to get off that stuff before it kills you." I was sweating profusely all over my body but my hands were literally pouring. When I walked up to Raquel to have my picture taken with her, I tried to pose without touching her but she grabbed my sweaty hands and placed them on her massive cleavage. After the flash, she looked me in the eyes and said "You know, I've been all over the States and this is the first time I have *ever* had to force a guy to touch me" and then chuckled. I didn't really want to tell her that I've been dangerously high on meth for two days so I just laughed and walked back to my table. I must have drunk a case of beer trying to come down a little bit but I couldn't feel the alcohol at all. It was like I was drinking water...no effect whatsoever. I was starting to think that I might have overdosed but tried to stay calm because I knew that panicking would make it ten times worse. It was at that moment that I had an epiphany, which provided me with the information necessary to propel myself to the next level and never look back at it to second guess myself again. I made the call.

    I headed to Crossville first thing in the morning with no sleep and no food in my stomach but I felt great. The fatigue didn't really affect me until I got to Kaine's house and finally ate something. I didn't sleep a wink that night either as the meth was still racing through my veins. It wasn't until we got to Nashville that it started wearing off but then the adrenaline of a live audience picked me up and I was wide awake again. I don't remember much about the show because my mind was elsewhere. The past five years started replaying in my head and the fear of the unknown was beginning to creep in, leaving me in an emotional wreck. Kaine could tell that something was bothering me but I didn't want to talk about it. The guilt of what I had done was eating away at me and there wasn't really anything he could possibly say that was going to make me feel better so I just kept him in the dark about the whole thing. I finally slept that night and rose early the next morning to start my trek home. I was eager to get the ball rolling as soon as possible to put my restless mind at ease.

    While I was driving, the memories started whirling in one after another. There was the time that the older woman who wanted me bad from the plant told me that she was going to be tanning on the beach in Vonore after work and like a fool, I showed up and she wasn't there. Yet when one of my fellow workers, who was still married at the time, invited her to lunch in the middle of a shift, she didn't think twice about it. He came back and told me that they skipped lunch and had sex all over his van while parked in the picnic area near the lake. I thought about when Chance, Ken, Brad and me loaded up in Chance's truck to take a company field trip to Mayfield's Dairy in Athens. It was like we were crammed into a clown car but once we got there, it was a fascinating experience seeing how one of our biggest clients takes our material and makes jugs and cartons out of it. I must admit that was the cleanest fucking building I had ever been in. As a bonus we all got free ice cream after the tour. This was also the first job I had where everyone had a nickname. Mine was "Arms" or "Arnold" depending on who you were talking to, since I probably had the biggest biceps in the building at the time. Then there were all the mishaps and incidents that would happen on the road to work like when Brad insisted that we carpool to work together to save gas. Other than smoking a joint with me, he never paid me a dime. I wasn't saving money on gas because I was still driving the same distance with someone who had a tendency to annoy me at times in my car so his "great idea" only lasted a couple of weeks before I pulled the plug on it. I would get him back by catching up with him at night and tailgating him, making him think that I was a cop. My Thunderbird did look like a police car in the dark and with him already stoned and paranoid, he was easy prey. He would always flip me a bird and yell obscenities at me when I would decide to overtake him. There was also times when karma caught up with me like when I was driving past the weigh stations on the way home one night and a German Shepard, which obviously belonged to the guy whose truck was parked there, ran out in front of my car and got hit at 55+ mph, making me lose control of my car and spin until I finally came to a stop in the median. After I came to my senses, I turned around to survey the damage and there were pieces of dog all over the road for about 100 feet. There was even flesh and bone stuck in my engine and blood all over my hood but not a single scratch on the Thunderbird itself. The dog's owner was asleep in his cab and never heard a thing so I made my getaway, leaving him to clean up the bloody mess when he woke up the next morning. After my first wreck in the snow, I lost my confidence for a while and tried to catch a ride with a buddy from work who had a 4x4 jeep. It was the same routine, he would assure me as he was driving that the roads weren't too bad until we reached the bridge and hit the ice, then he would say "Ok, now this is bad." Meanwhile, I would see other workmates burning a joint before heading down the road without a care in the world and make it home safely every time. I spent five years in that place, and leaving with a clear conscious was going to be much harder than I thought it was going to be.

    I went to the club to talk to Gene that evening. I waited until he got a few drinks in him to approach him then made my move. I informed him that I had left the plant and was a "free agent" if he needed any help. I was very confident that he would welcome me in with open arms considering that I had actually "worked" there for the past two years, unofficially, throwing people out. But I could tell by the expression on his face before he even spoke that he wasn't going to. "I'm sorry Denny, but I don't really need anyone right now. I have a full staff and nowhere to put you at the moment. However, I will keep you in mind if anything comes up." I was crushed... and now unemployed, without anything lined up to make enough money to pay the bills. I gave him my number anyway and walked out of the club before I burst out into tears in front of God and everyone. To put it into terms that everyone can understand, I was fucked!

    I spent the next few weeks contemplating about what my plans were for the future. I was still stopping in at the club almost every night trying to bond with the new manager "Tommy" who was actually responsible for filling all of those jobs with his own handpicked staff members who were either professional wrestlers or jacked up weightlifters twice my size. I resented him for keeping me on the outside looking in. Hell, I even helped *them* toss people out to get on their good side and actually bonded with the biggest bouncer "Adam" who later campaigned to bring me into the fold himself. The other bouncer who we will call "Bear" wasn't sold and tried to discourage me by saying things like "If you don't have any money, why do you come in here all the time?" As all of my savings were quickly dwindling away, I started asking myself that same question and stopped visiting so frequently. There's only so many times you can have doors slammed in your face and keep rolling with the punches. I vowed to myself that I was not going to enter that building again unless I was working there and that was one promise I did keep.

25

I did, however, still continue to drop by the South Club and eventually started semi-dating a girl there named "Blair". We would go to dinner together and even go to Lenoir City once to have a swim at the lake. We never slept together nor did either of us make an attempt. The only time that we shared a kiss was when we were picking up supplies at the local market before heading to the lake that day. She actually came out and asked me for a kiss and pointed at her cheek but when I leaned over to plant one on it, she moved her head quickly and kissed me on the lips. "Gotcha!" she said. I never tried to kiss her after that because I wasn't looking for a girlfriend or even a "friend with benefits." I had decided that I was going to sell my trailer and two vehicles and fulfil a dream I've had since I was a child: moving to Clearwater Beach, Florida which I considered my second home. When I told my parents about my plan, they weren't very supportive. "What if you go down there and fall on your ass and end up coming back here with *nothing?* What if you can't find work straight away? That money is not going to last forever you know." I thanked them for their concern but my mind was made up. I was going come hell or high water. When I mentioned that I was seeing Blair, they weren't very happy with that either. "I know her. She used to ride my bus. She's a little troublemaker." dad said. I knew that Blair went to the same school as me but was quite a few years younger than me which made me think that maybe my dad didn't know her but dad knows everyone in that town and doesn't like most of them. It changed from a civilized discussion to a full blown argument in the blink of an eye and I left my parent's house pissed off once again.

Blair, on the other hand, took a totally different approach to the whole thing. She was just intent on having a great time with me before I left. She did, however, give me a few words of advice that made me rethink everything. "I know that you are going through a rough time, but things always seem to have a way of working out. Things always get better. You just have to persevere. But if you are determined to leave this town anyway, I totally respect and support your decision." Those words of wisdom spoken from the mouth of that young lady changed my mind and made me want to keep fighting. I never thanked her for what she did but she will always have a special place in my heart. Within just a few days, as I was down to my last few dollars, my phone rang. I recognized the voice on the other end, it was Gene. "Are you ready to come to work?" he asked. I said, "Absolutely! I will be there tomorrow." I could hear a sigh from the old man, "Fuck that! I want you to start today. Be here at 5:00 and don't be late." I told him that I would be there and thanked him for the opportunity. I took a deep breath because I knew everything was going to be ok. I wanted to call Blair and tell her the good news but chose instead to cut her loose and set her free. I don't know if it was the right thing to do, but it could have been, considering how my life was about to change. This was my shot to become the man I always wanted to be, with the potential to become a legend. I owed it to myself to at least try and that's exactly what I did…

-DJN

CHAPTER VI - *"THE KISSING PLACE"*

1997-1998

I came in with a huge chip on my shoulder. I was an angry, bitter kid with not only something to prove to myself and everyone else around me but I felt like the world owed me something. But as soon as I walked through that door, I realized that no matter how ready I thought I was, I was way out of my league. The club I knew had become something entirely different. No longer a topless club, it had evolved into a nude club with an entirely different roster of girls than the ones that I knew and was accustomed to. Sydney was gone and out of the business and Natasha had relocated to the club that I hated to avoid doing nudity. On the flipside, we had gained a majority of the top names from all of the rival clubs, including Jessie, and had a line-up capable of holding its own against larger, more renowned clubs around the country. On any given night, we would have 20-30 girls working which was a vast improvement from what Gene had before. Business was about to pick up in a major way but it wasn't the Garden of Eden that I expected it to be.

The guy training me wasn't very happy about seeing me walk through that door, especially as his replacement. We had words a couple of times in the past and apparently still had beef between us so he just showed me the basics in the rudest and most unenthusiastic manner possible and then went to a different station to avoid me for the rest of the night. It didn't really bother me since I was fully aware that this was his last day and I would probably never see him again anyway. I just kept thinking about all of those times when I was giving Gene a hard time and he was right there, just waiting to pounce on me the first chance he got but

Gene wouldn't allow it. I think that made him hate me even more. But, looking back at it, I wish he would have given him the green light just once so I would have had an excuse to lay him out.

One thing that I noticed was how different it was working there than it was just being a customer. Not being able to drink was a killer because alcohol enhances the whole experience and makes you more aggressive and confrontational. Being a bouncer, your focus shifts to the crowd instead of the show which takes the fun out of being there in the first place. I was only there for a couple of hours then I was sent home after I was shown the ropes. Gene promised to call me the following day and tell me my schedule for the rest of the week. That call never came as I would later discover that Tommy had someone else in mind for the role and I was kicked to the curb. It was over...or so I thought.

I would receive another phone call from Gene a couple of weeks later with an apology attached. He explained to me that Bear had wanted more days and when the guy I was replacing left, he took his shifts as well. He used his friendship with Tommy to his advantage and assumed my position, pushing me out of the immediate picture. However, karma bit him in the ass as his wife wasn't pleased with the increase of hours, leading to a big fight and his resignation. Now I was already trained and replacing Bear instead, so for once I was in the driver's seat. I wanted to turn down his offer but couldn't for some reason. Now I had officially arrived...for real.

2

My first full night at Last Chance was interesting indeed. I hadn't been there but a few minutes when a lovely young lady named "Harley" came over to welcome me. She would eventually just pull up a chair and sit beside me which gained Gene's attention. He walked over and told her to leave me alone and to get back to work. Then a gothic chick came and sat in the chair that she left behind and tried to strike up a conversation with me as well. She was a pretty girl but her teeth were as repulsive as her vanilla scented perfume. Combine that with her short, black hair and sickly pale skin and any attractiveness that she might have had wasn't even noticeable anymore. Gene walked over this time with purpose and yelled, "If you want to fuck the new guy, do it after work. Right now, he has a job to do and so do you so get busy." He walked away just shaking his head. I was already nervous and all of this drama wasn't helping. I didn't want to mess the gig up after going through so much crap to get it. I was praying that no one else came over to socialize and get me into deeper trouble on my first day.

    Throughout the night, I was seeing both girls and bar staff going back and forth to the other side of the building which was sealed off during the weekdays. I kind of had an idea of what was going on but I wasn't sure until Tommy came up to the window and said, "It's your turn. I'll watch the door for you. Go on. She's waiting." I wasn't about to refuse, even if I wasn't comfortable hooking up with a girl on cue, unexpectedly. Let's get one thing straight, Gene didn't provide health insurance or a retirement 401k plan, but the job did come with certain "benefits" that other jobs didn't have. It was the most honest environment I've ever worked in. People acted on their fantasies and escaped the real world that they had to face every day. It could be paradise or purgatory…in the same night. It was up to you and your point of view to make it whatever you wanted. I was about to make that first step into a world I didn't believe existed.

When I entered the room, there sat a girl who I had known for quite a while and even bought private dances from over the years, waiting for me. There was no greeting or conversation. She just started unzipping my pants and pulled them down to my knees. I just sat back on the couch and stroked her hair, while she gave me head for as long as I wanted. What I lack in size, I make up in endurance. When I'm in the zone, it's almost impossible to give me an orgasm so after about a half of an hour, I asked her to stop cause it wasn't happening. I pulled up my pants and went back over to the other side. When I got to Tommy, he smiled and said, "Welcome to the family. We're all related by proxy now. That girl blew all of us today. We're all about sharing here at the Last Chance." Then he walked away, only to be passed by Gene, who had something to say to me as well. "That was one of the perks of being in this business, but don't let it get to your head" he said. "Because if she was willing to do this for all of us, she has probably blown half of Knoxville in her lifetime" he continued. It all made sense to me and at that moment, I saw the world in a different light. I learned how to keep myself from getting emotionally attached to every woman I was about to sleep with.

The next day, I came in early and James was already there. He had worked his way up to being the assistant manager from being just a customer, like myself, and was close friends with Gene. He approached me and formally welcomed me into the fold. "I really went to bat for you" he said. "Gene was hesitant about bringing you in because he felt that you were a bit of a loose cannon and I just kept telling to give you a chance. The selling point was when I said, "One day that guy is going to snap. Wouldn't you rather have him on your side than against you?" I saw something in you and I felt like you would be a great asset to the club. Don't make me look bad ok?" I thanked him and promised him that I wouldn't let him down. Unfortunately, that was one promise that I wouldn't keep.

3

It didn't take long to figure out who truly owned the place in my eyes. Gene paid me a base wage of $60 a night, but the girls were making up the rest with their tips. That meant that I not only protected them but I did the little things like start their cars when it was cold outside and carried their bags if need be to make them feel like they were royalty. In other words, I kissed their asses because they were where the real money was to make a decent living in this business. That's why when Gene would run off the girls when they tried to socialize with me, especially Harley, who was one of my best tippers, I didn't appreciate it. Harley and I had become close friends and that made Gene think that we were a couple so he began teasing me about it every chance he got. Although we had kissed several times, that's as far as we ever went. She even called me "Hercules" due to my resemblance to Kevin Sorbo's portrayal of him on the popular show. But Gene didn't approve of our friendship at all which became a problem. He would always come up to me and say, "You work for me not them. I pay your wages so what I say goes." I always thought to myself, "Yeah, but they pay me *more* and that's what matters the most to me." But I just kept my mouth shut and reluctantly agreed.

There were two girls who refused to tip me and both were from the old club. One was "Dana" who was the club snitch and the other, my old friend Monica. Dana always used the excuse that Gene told her that the only person she was obligated to tip was the DJ. I eventually won her over and she would let go of two measly dollars every night, no matter how good of a night she had. This would go on for many years. She would always look at me like I had just won the lottery which made it quite humorous. Monica, however, wouldn't even do that, which was an insult, considering how much money I gave her and her sister over the years. One night I said something to her about it and she went off. She used the Dana excuse first then went on to say that I never have to do anything for her anyway, so she didn't feel the need to give me anything. When neither of those excuses worked, she reached into her bag, grabbed a couple of dollars, and threw them at me before driving away. I never brought it up again as she quit a few days later, never to return. I would see her at West Town Mall quite a few times over the coming years, working in a yogurt bar or something, but never bothered to say anything to her. It wasn't worth it. One of the main reasons I got into this business was to make back some of the money I had given away over the years and she denied me that. She was nothing to me anymore.

<u>4</u>

    Thought I had died, and gone to heaven, felt like god's gift to women, with more lip service than Richard Dawson...had my bachelor's degree, and she was my trophy, on the rebound, in between beaus, under the mistletoe, with her eyes closed, and her tongue down my throat.

When she wants her daily dose of protein, she works her way south. With all that sickness and no vaccine, she kisses her mother with that mouth...

Had to play hard to get, always thought I was cute, but I had to initiate it, repeating like a film, playing in an endless loop, we never finished what we started.

Under a waterfall, in a hot tub, up against the wall, in the mall, or a bathroom stall, of a night club... Mile high, up in the sky, on a plane, in a dark pine forest in the rain, in Paris, or on sun kissed beaches, or cross country on a train...

The pen is mightier than the sword, yet I need the sword, for when the pen fails...I'd like to say, "Welcome aboard" to all those so eager to ride on my coat tails...

Sometimes I would rather watch, than participate, so I lay my head back, and squeeze her tight, so afraid, when she pulled down the shades, of things that go bump in the night.

Sometimes it feels so good being bad, never underestimate me, (nice guys finish last), we may start strong, but fizzle out in the matter of weeks, go from being the best I ever had, to ancient history...

On the kitchen counter, in the shower, at the chalet, in front of the fireplace, at a rave on ecstasy, in a limousine, with a sliding screen, in the backseat of my car, under the stars, or the bright lights of the city...

Sometimes you're the windshield, sometimes you're the bug. Sometimes the dummy fails the crash test. When kissing cousins, are a dime a dozen, I'll leave the stain of incest...

-Denny Noland "Draven" From my song "The Kissing Place"

Written on October 31, 2006   Copyright 2007

One thing that I've struggled with over the years is my eyesight. I had bluffed my way through school, various jobs, and especially driving at night or in the rain by squinting enough to get by but in this line of work, vision was critical. If I missed something, it would not only affect my money but someone could actually get hurt in the process. I was pretty self-conscious about what I would look like wearing glasses, so I avoided the eye doctor like the plague. But one incident at the club was about to change all of that. While one of the girls was dancing for a guy near the stage, he was trying to reach his hand between her legs. Not only did I not see what he was doing but I didn't even notice that the girl was motioning for me to come over there by waving her hands up in the air even though I was looking directly at her. Adam saw it from the other side of the room and rescued her, leaving me looking like I was too scared or just didn't care about the girl's safety. When the dance was over, she came over and let me have it as expected. She was one of my best tippers and I let her down. This wasn't going to happen again.

The following day I rang my parents and asked them if they wanted to go to the eye doctor with me. They took me and I ended up getting glasses. It was a whole new world to me being able to see clearly. I wore them to work that night and everyone complimented me on how they looked as any decent person would do but I wasn't convinced. I went back and got fitted for contact lenses the next day. Although I struggled getting them out the first time and ended up scratching my eye, one trip back to the doctor to help remove them was all I needed. The doctor said, "You are going to have to learn to do this on your own. What are you going to do? Come here every time you want to take them out? We will show you one last time how to do it properly and then you are on your own." I practiced until I perfected it and can now take them out without even looking.

My eyes turned out to be the least of my worries. I woke up from dead sleep with a feeling that something wasn't right. Within minutes, I was doubled over in the floor in severe pain. I felt like I needed to piss but nothing would come out. I never had kidney stones before but I had heard enough horror stories about them to self-diagnose myself. I called my parents because I needed to go to the doctor and I was in no condition to drive. My mother chose to take me all the way to the clinic in Loudon instead of the one in Maryville which was probably half the mileage. When we got there, the nurse asked me to go into the bathroom and try to piss in a cup. I didn't think I was going to have success but as soon as made an attempt, I felt something hard shoot out of my penis and into the cup, then out came a solid stream. I had passed the stone before I ever saw the doctor. I immediately felt better and was released but they still charged me for a full visit even though I wasn't even examined. I told mother that I wasn't ever going back to that clinic again and I didn't. This time I got lucky but it would be the only time I was that fortunate.

I felt that this was probably the best time to tell my parents the truth. They had suspected that I was no longer at the plant by how I had been acting lately and I had made the decision already to come clean about everything so they wouldn't have to hear it from someone else. I told them about the drug use, the details of my volatile relationships, and where I had been working for the past few weeks. It felt good to spread everything out on the table and just live my life without any secrets. My parents though, were sorry they asked by the time I was finished but at least I wasn't pretending to be someone I wasn't. Within the next several weeks, *everyone* knew my story and although I wasn't proud of it, I wasn't exactly ashamed of it either. It was very liberating to get it all out and I have no regrets about anything.

5

On New Year's Day, I make a resolution to start a revolution...We had faith in our leader, as he raised his right hand and made promises. But when he became president, and formed his government, all he did was raise taxes.

The lamb is crippled, watching the demise of his empire. Man will always be lured in, by his creature comforts and carnal desires.

This is the playground of the demented...the great theatre, where the net is cast, and the dice are thrown. This is the playground of the demented...if you are not the traitor, or the dictator, you will be his stepping stone. Legend has it... I was brought by a stork that ate my placenta and chewed off my umbilical cord. Into every generation, a slayer is born. Within every generation is the passing of the sword.

I'm here to kill a king, and his kingdom will be overthrown. When the skies darken... black as a sackcloth of hair, the face of the beast will be known.

Like Nostradamus, I will make a prediction: once you have faith in a leader, he will be assassinated. Then his enemies will leave the soil scorched, and the water contaminated.

> The lamb is crippled… now let's see it walk on water… no longer the spiritual to my material…no longer the sacred to my secular.
> Like all the available sources are biased, and he can't find community status or prestige. Like being unchallenged by the lethargic populace, then suddenly feeling besieged.
> I'm here to kill a king, for I am the heir to the throne. The rain will fall red from the heavens, and the streets will be white with unburied bones.
> Farewell to a legend…it's you know who, he-who-cannot-be-named, the pride of a nation…Farewell to a king…modified for his ongoing campaign, for world domination…
> -Denny Noland "Draven" from my song "…To Kill a King" 1999-2000   Copyright 2015

As with any job, this looked better on paper than it actually was. The longer you worked there, the more you noticed the patterns in each girl's performance. They always danced the same steps to the same songs in the same order every single night. Even the DJs had "catch phrases" that they repeated night after night as well. Then there was the fighting. Let's be honest, I took a lot of shit over the years because I didn't stick up for myself. I avoided confrontations if I could unless I had been drinking. Accepting this role, I had to grow up fast and conquer my fears, which was one of the biggest reasons that I wanted it so bad. With a jacked up powerhouse, suffering from roid rage like Adam working with me, I wouldn't have to wait very long to get my hands bloody.

My approach was to try to get the customers out without touching them while Adam chose to just grab the guy or guys and walk them often leading to a brawl once we got outside. To make it worse, it seemed like we were always seriously outnumbered. So many times he would get in over his head and depend on me to have his back, which I always did, but on one occasion in particular, I arrived too late. After we tossed a guy out who was nearly the same size as Adam, he stood at the bottom of the concrete steps talking shit and spitting on the ground while staring directly at Adam. This caused Adam to snap and grab the guy in an attempt to slam him on the steps. Unfortunately, Adam lost his balance and the guy landed on *him* injuring his arm. I had to choke the guy out to break his grip on Adam. When it was over, Adam, in his own way, tried to make me feel guilty about the injury and even though he brought it on himself. This led to some internal trust issues between the two of us, and made us both question each other's guts and loyalty. In the meantime, Adam's friends started hanging out at the club which actually made me feel safer and intimidated the hell out of the customers. They were all massive and usually stood near Adam the entire time which at times even intimidated the employees as well. That was enough to make Gene want to hire them to work at the club but they all refused because they all had bigger fish to fry as I would later find out.

    Despite the fact that although there were all of these internal problems between Adam and me, I stood by his side whether I agreed with his methods or not but when the roles were reversed, he didn't return the favour. That weekend he would get his so called "revenge." There was a customer who was acting very bizarre most of the night but really started freaking out when he saw the cops come in for a "free show." He hid in the hall between the two sections of the club and was shaking hysterically. Tommy saw this and told me to walk over there and tell him to sit down at a table like everyone else... so I did. When I tapped him on the shoulder to get his attention, he spun around and threw a roundhouse at me, hitting me in the ear. A few months prior, against my father, workmates and even my own approval to some extent, I got my left ear pierced. The irony of that was that I had vowed that I would never wear an earring because I felt that it was too feminine and often criticized other grown men who chose to wear them themselves. But I was evolving and practically overnight, I changed my opinion on it entirely. What I didn't realize was that piercings in this line of work was a huge bullseye...and this guy's punch was living proof. It completely ripped my earring out causing blood to start pouring out all over my clothes. When I came to my senses and saw my own blood, I grabbed him by the throat, which was my trademark, and slammed him to the floor. I was literally choking the life out of him when I felt someone trying to pull me off of him. It was Tommy...probably saving me from a murder charge, as he would many other times in the future. When I let the guy up, he instantly apologized and told me that he thought I was one of the "pigs." He was obviously strung out on coke and was extremely paranoid, thinking that those cops were there to get him. I still made him leave because he attacked me but I was angrier at Adam than I was him. Where was he during all of this? Sitting in his chair watching the fireworks pretending like he didn't know what was going on. His only response was "I thought something was going down but when I saw Tommy go over there too, I knew everything was under control." I wanted to say that Tommy doesn't get paid to do that...he does, but I just kept my mouth shut to avoid yet another argument.

We would form a close friendship over time after we realized that we were more alike than we originally thought. We were both hitting the gym very hard, liked the same music and had a mutual fondness for cocaine. I would have never guessed the latter by his physical appearance but it was true. We also got on the same page at the club as well, often trying to outdo each other with violence and brutality on the poor, unsuspecting customers. Much of this happened outside so there would be no witnesses. We broke the law every night and didn't care. One incident that I do regret was when a young guy purchased a private dance and had actually ran out of money and couldn't pay for it. We grabbed this kid and dragged him out into the lobby where we beat him senseless but Adam took it a step further. He pulled out the boy's wallet, emptied it all out on the ground, and looked for anything that might be valuable to accommodate for his lack of payment. When he couldn't find anything, he continued to kick him until I convinced him to stop. If I hadn't been there, I can only imagine what could have happened. He only got worse when he and Tommy took a liking to the same girl. He had the upper hand but Tommy was persistent and really didn't care whether Adam liked her or not. Eventually, he started dating the girl, which caused him to be overprotective of her and her sister, who worked there as well, and more aggressive to customers to try to impress them. It was just throwing gasoline on a fire and I was the only bucket of water to put it out with.

I wasn't having the same kind of luck with the ladies. Jessie was already spoken for so there was nothing going on there. There was, however, the re-emergence of a certain girl who broke the rules as she danced for me back in the day that gave me hope. She remembered me and was still very flirtatious. We even made out once while she was waiting for her boyfriend to pick her up. The last thing I said to her as she sucked on my neck was jokingly "If you don't stop, I'm going to rape you." She replied "You can't rape the willing baby!" That was the last time I ever saw her. She was probably only there for a week or so before vanishing again. I don't even think that my customer friend, who adored her as well, even had a chance to see her before she was gone.

    Then there was "Missy", a beautiful blonde haired girl with brown eyes. She was one of the top money makers in the club, a real hustler. Her nightly performance of Savage Garden's "To the Moon and Back" made guys melt and fill up her garter which is what I remember most about her. I liked her but so did Tommy, who had rebounded to her when Adam took his last quest away from him. I never pursued her because I didn't believe that I had a fighting chance. Every now and then, she would throw a possible hint in my direction that she might be interested but I needed to know for sure before jumping to conclusions as I had so many times before. It wasn't until I walked her and a couple of the other girls to her car one night that she just came out and asked me for a kiss. I planted one on her sweet lips and she was smiling from ear to ear afterwards. I could tell that she definitely liked it and was planning my next move when she quit dancing a couple of days later after her boyfriend demanded that she "get out of the business or else." When I found out that she was gone too, I was crushed...especially after Harley told me that she had a crush on me all along a little too late. Several years would go by until I saw her again, working at the Department of Transportation. I was in there with Tommy, who was picking up new plates and as soon as he saw her, he did all the talking. I barely even got to say hello. She would come out to the club a few years later, when she was going through a difficult time in her life, to get drunk and hit that stage one last time to her trademark Savage Garden tune. I did something that night that I never had the chance to do before: I tipped her. It was a moment still frozen in time when she turned around and saw me standing there. It was like we were the only two people in the room as she crawled up to me, buried my head under her hair, and gave me a long lingering kiss out of sight from everyone except for the DJ, who was teasing me about it over the microphone. It would be a kiss goodbye, as we never saw each other again.

6

At this point and time, I still had a life outside the club. Kaine had just moved back into town, and I even went to a few conventions with Bill, which was once unheard of, when Kaine wasn't able to go himself. On one of these ventures, I ran across an unopened, mint condition "Castle Grayskull" still in the box. I was a little short on money and didn't have the total amount for the asking price so I was feeling a little sick about letting it go. Bill, knowing how bad I wanted it, made up the difference and I was able to bring it home. It was the centrepiece of my collection for years…my pride and joy. Kaine was even impressed when I showed it to him. It was a damn shame how I ended up letting go of it a few years later.

This was also around the time that we all gathered together to attend one final wrestling show: Wrestlepalooza 98' at the Cobb County Civic Center in Marietta, Georgia. For years, we had all wanted to attend an ECW show but they never came to our neck of the woods... until now. So we loaded up for this unforgettable road trip and away we went. We got down there early enough to watch "The Dudleys" pull up to the arena together, and see "Sabu" turn in after them, already dressed in his full wrestling attire. Once inside, I bought the "Sandman", "Beulah", and "Francine" t-shirts as well as their personally autographed photos. It was already the coolest show I'd ever attended due to the interactions between the stars and the fans. The action didn't disappoint either. After their match, "Balls Mahoney" and "Axl Rotten" signed autographs at the concession stands, but I didn't find out about it till they had already returned to the back. During "Taz's" run- in later in the show, he was handcuffed by "Georgia's Finest" and arrested by storyline, and as he was being escorted out, walked right by us, which allowed a quick pat on his back as he went past. Everyone in the crowd got Styrofoam heads to shake during "Al Snow's" entrance in the main event as well, which was awesome sight when you look back at it on dvd. By the end of the show, we definitely felt like it was worth the drive and the money spent. "Paul Heyman" even came out with the entire roster that was still in the building (some had to go to the hospital) and entered the ring in the closing minutes of the show to thank everyone for coming. It was a special moment. Then we looked around and noticed how bent the guard rails were from all of collisions between steel and bone. It was unbelievable. As we were leaving, Kaine suggested grabbing a bite at "Abdullah the Butcher's House of Ribs" on the way home, but then in typical Kaine fashion, just drove right past it like he never mentioned it. Overall, it was an epic night and a great memory. **-DJN**

CHAPTER VII- *"CRUEL SUMMER"*

1998

    Over the years, I had run into quite a few people at the club that I used to either go to school with, or worked with at the plant, when I was still a customer. There was a guy I used to work with who would ask me every Monday if I saw his little brother at the South Club over the weekend then try to convince me that the girls' panties would literally be dripping wet at the mere sight of him. He would sometimes come with his brother and sit there staring and smiling at me the entire night. Sometimes I wondered if he was actually there to see the girls or me. I didn't really understand why he kept hyping up his sibling so much when I saw him leaving empty handed every single time.
    Then there was the night I saw one of the girls that used to be in my class at school come into the South Club with a couple of guys. She was looking great and I had to let her know about it so I walked up to her and started flirting relentlessly. It was very well received as she started flirting back and agreed to go home with me if she could find a way to ditch the guys she came with. I eventually ran out of patience and snuck out while she was in the ladies room and went home. It just wasn't worth my time.
    But the most intriguing incident was when I ran into my cousin at the South Club. He came in with a couple who I had seen in the club on a regular basis that I didn't even know he knew. I partied with them until last call and then began wandering about to sober up. When I turned toward the stage, instead of seeing a girl dancing, I saw my cousin slow dancing very close to that guy's wife while he watched from the table. What made it even more

shocking was that the staff didn't seem to mind, unlike the time Paul let me be the DJ one night while I was drunk. On that particular occasion, because I didn't know what the hell to say and when I did speak I was slurring badly, I just kept repeating the same phrases on the microphone over and over again which annoyed not only the manager, but the girls and customers alike. This led to my departure from the booth and the end of my brief DJ career. At least Paul found it amusing…

Occasionally, Kaine and I would come across other old friends from school and end up joining them at their table and at some point try to drink them under it. Most of the time they would be alone and supposably happily married… just needing to blow off some steam. They always appeared nervous that someone they knew was also in the building, but we would assure them that as far as we were concerned, we never saw them and we kept our word. But that was a whole different situation when we fast-forward to 1998. Now I not only had control of who came into the club and how long they stayed, but how they left the building as well. A few bruises and a little blood would be pretty hard to explain to your better half when you got home. Now I was the one who controlled their fate and that scared the hell out of people, leading to interesting scenarios.

The first schoolmate I let in basically just sat in the corner and would come up to me every now and then to kiss my ass. The second was a little more personal. He was a guy named "Rat" that I didn't get along with in school and the girl he brought with him named "Holly" had hurt my feelings many years ago by telling me that I was "ugly" for no reason at all. They both grew up in my old neighbourhood and I must say that I was delighted to see them come through that door...together. As soon as they recognized me, they invited me to join them at their table...bad mistake. They were talking to me like I was one of their best friends which almost made me sick. However, what they didn't know was that I used to work with Holly's former husband who was much older than her and quite wealthy, at the plant. Money was apparently the driving force in the relationship...the glue that held it together. When the money ran out, so did she. Once I mentioned that, the mood completely changed and I went back to work, leaving them to ponder with probably the darkest chapter of their lives. They wouldn't stick around much longer which disappointed me because I was just getting started. They never came back to the club for some reason.

The next one that I saw used to come in *with* his wife to see a specific girl every weekend. I don't really know what kind of arrangement that they had, but I must admit that it was a bit intriguing. However, when another one of my former workmates from the plant came in, named "Rocky", obviously without his quite attractive wife, I was both thrilled to see him again and wondering what the hell he was doing there especially with it being so far from home. A few weeks prior, when I turned on the TV late one night and the Jerry Springer show was on, I saw a girl who looked like our mutual friend and fellow employee Cody's girlfriend on stage telling her story about her boyfriend having an affair with an 80 year old woman. I wasn't sure if it was her until I saw the "video evidence" of Cody walking into the bingo hall in Madisonville, approaching this little old lady, and making out with her on camera. Then of course, they brought Cody out to join her on stage to an astounding roar of boos and bleeped out obscenities. The audience made their usual stupid remarks like asking Cody how he could possibly cheat on such a beautiful woman (which was probably the most shocking moment of the entire show considering how hideous she actually was) and if he was going to do so, why with such a fossil. One guy even took it a step further and offered to take Cody's girlfriend off his hands. Cody's response to be called sick and disgusting was "Don't knock it til the try it, brother." Finally, they brought the old woman out which whipped the audience into a fucking frenzy, especially after she gave Cody about a 10-15 second French kiss right in front of his girlfriend. It was a disturbing, yet believable segment especially for anyone who knew Cody in person. I had wondered if any of it was true for weeks and I knew Rocky would know the answer. "It was all bullshit" he said. "Cody just wanted to get a free trip to Chicago and make some money while doing so. Springer's people came up with this crazy storyline and he and his girlfriend just went along with it. Hell, several of the guys have been on the show multiple times for various things. I'm surprised you didn't recognize any of them." I couldn't believe what levels certain people would stoop to for their "fifteen minutes of fame."

    Would you be my shrink, my shoulder to cry on? I'm defected but plain, neglected and in vain, yet my worst foe lies within, not on the surface. Can't rekindle old flames, or repair my ruined reputation. I'm the has been, that never was, fading into oblivion…
    Break up with an ex, then have make up sex, its either a bed of roses or a bed of nails…All women wear haloes till their horns start to show, sometimes it's heaven, and other times it's pure hell.

Thought I had her figured out, knew what she was all about, used to get positive feedback, in the sack, then that Lizzie grabbed an axe, and gave me forty whacks, throwing stones at my glass house…

I'm the man of glass, into a thousand jagged fragments I shatter, she's the only one who can pick up the pieces, she's the only one who can put me together…

Laughing in sorrow, crying in lust, I'm haunted by her wavering voice. Hear the horns of Jericho, and remember "sound without focus, is the definition of noise."

Today is a good day to die…been thrown from the saddle, been up the creek without a paddle, now I'm ready to sever all ties. Had all I can take, and I'm about to break, I've outgrown that fucking lullaby.

I've been ostracized, burned all of my bridges, for her amusement. I've ebonized, when I was prejudice, just to make a statement. I've thrown all my pennies in the wishing well, but fools like me never win. I'm so weak and frail, with no one to mend what is broken.

Each feeling a magnet, each frame of mind, a woman's intuition is a man's migraine…Each lay a regret, each love is blind, one man's fortune, is another man's pain. The thing about magic, there's always consequences…if I don't make it back alive she'll find her name in the credits…

-Denny Noland "Draven" From my song "The Man of Glass" Written on November 7, 2006 Copyright 2007

2

It was July 4th 1998 and I had to work. It was going to be an extremely slow night and we were all wondering why we were even open. As the girls came up for the 7:00 roll call, a young lady who danced by the name "Justice" came out of the back wearing something either made out of leather or some other material that looked like it. It was no secret that leather drives me fucking insane to the point that seeing a girl wearing it could even change my perception of them entirely. I had worked with this girl for quite a while and although I thought she was very beautiful, I never really noticed her until at that moment. As she was returning to the back to finish getting ready, she walked past my desk and must have noticed me checking her out, because she gave me a cheeky smile which only made things worse. I had managed to steer clear of potential future girlfriend material till now whether I meant to or not but the little voice in my head was telling me that I was in trouble...serious trouble.

As the night progressed, I left the door and took a seat at the bar. I didn't even realize that Justice was sitting right next to me with her head down half asleep until I had been there for several minutes. I started up a conversation by mentioning how dead we were and how it wasn't fair that we were forced to work on such an important holiday. She agreed and told me about how she had other plans but Gene told her that if she didn't come in, he would fire her. We talked about many things throughout the night and eventually I built up the courage to ask her out to breakfast after work. She kindly accepted and the wheels were put in motion.

Since we both lived in Maryville, there were only two places that you could grab a bite to eat at that time of the night that was on our way home: Waffle House or Krystal's. I let her choose and we met each other in the parking lot at Krystal's. I told her to get anything that she wanted cause it was all on me even if I wasn't sure if this was considered an official "date" or not. I was the one who invited her so it only seemed fair.

The longer we sat there and got to know each other, the more we realized that we were a combustible element that just wasn't going to work. There was a significant age difference between us which showed when discussing our outlooks on life even if she was no stranger to being in serious relationships with much older men or "father figures." She told me that when she was only around 16-17 years old, she dated a guy in his forties who just happened to work for a local legend that my mother used when *she* was just a teenager herself. She also came across as a high maintenance diva that grew up privileged, with young parents that treated her more like a "best friend" than a daughter, which didn't really appeal to me much either. I was starting to wonder what the hell I was doing there and was confident that I had made a terrible mistake. It all came to a head when she only took a couple of bites of her food and said she was full, which prompted me to ask "Are you going to waste all that food when there are children starving in Africa?" The look on her face said everything. I could tell that she was beyond offended which inspired me to call it a night.

I walked her to her car not expecting to get a kiss and wasn't planning to attempt one either. Just a simple goodbye seemed appropriate this time around, but she had other plans. She leaned out for what I thought was going to be a light peck on the lips, and I'm sure that was her intentions, but it became much more than that. As soon as our lips met, we both felt something that neither of us was expecting. It was almost magical...electric even. Although there was no tongue involved, we shared a much longer and more passionate kiss than we planned to. It was so intense that it left us both intoxicated and made us rethink every conclusion that we had come to earlier in the night. We must have both went home with our minds racing and smiles on our faces.

The next few weeks were fucking insane. We did everything that normal couples do. We went to the gym together, went out to dinner and the clubs together, hell, I even met her parents but we still weren't actually "together." There were times when I thought that we had made a breakthrough, like when Adam chewed her out for "dancing too close" to a customer which made her so upset that she started crying hysterically. At the end of the night, it was pouring rain, so I grabbed an umbrella and led to her to my truck so we could talk. That turned into about an hour long make out session that made her forget about all of her problems. Yet the next day it was like nothing ever happened. This would go on for several weeks until cocaine came into the picture. That was when she really started fucking with me.

3

I had developed a friendship with one of the DJs at the club named "Dewayne." We had become quite the party animals. He lived with a black girl, who danced by the name "Daisy", in a kind of hippie suburb not far from the club that wasn't very accepting to outsiders. I had been friends with Daisy since my days as a customer. She was the only black girl I knew who only dated white guys and only listened to hard rock or heavy metal music. She would have also been a worthy candidate for my first black girl but I never looked at her that way for one reason or another. She was also very close friends with Justice, so you can probably see where this is all going.

We met up late one night at their house to snort a few lines of coke as we had done several times before but for some reason the girls started getting a bit more "playful" than usual. Justice decided to give Daisy a lap dance that ended up with them making out either for our amusement, or to make me jealous or both. Dewayne was enjoying the show and cheering them on but I wasn't so impressed so I demanded them to stop. I wasn't about to watch someone else, male or female, kissing the girl I had spent so much time trying to win over myself. They both thought it was funny and appeared to be surprised that I wasn't turned on by their antics. We left shortly after and I went home once again in need of a cold shower. The next day Dewayne told me that the two girls had "been together" at least once before to his knowledge and that I was out of line and shouldn't have overreacted. He also warned me that my actions made it pretty clear that Justice was both in my head, and my heart, and now that she knows that as well, she's probably going to use that against me somewhere down the road. I should have listened.

    Now that she was fully aware of my feelings for her, I decided to take a chance and become a bit more aggressive to see if she felt the same way. One day at her house, I made a few advances that led to me performing oral sex on her. She was holding my hands as I went down on her, squeezing them tight every time I would hit a sensitive spot. I could tell that she was getting into it. Then all of a sudden, she started freaking out and told me to stop before I had a chance to finish her off. She claimed that she had taken a hit of acid before I got there and it was starting to kick in. To this day, I'm not sure if she was telling the truth or not but it did make me think twice before doing anything like that again.

4

One thing that really annoyed me about this business was how the strippers placed the DJs above the bouncers in their pecking order. They loved their DJs, tipping them a huge percentage of their earnings while giving the bouncers their "loose change." They all believed that whoever was talking on the mic and spinning their discs while they were on stage were more valuable than those who protected them, which to me, was complete and total rubbish. Any bouncer can work the lights and the CD player… all they need to learn is what to say to promote the ladies. But does the DJ have the balls to step into a crowd of intoxicated thugs looking for a fight with fists clenched and odds never in their favour? Not many would be the correct answer but that, to them, was irrelevant. Sometimes we appeared to the girls as nothing more than "white trash" or "rednecks" that should consider ourselves lucky that we breathed the same air as them until they needed us for something. This meant that the DJs sat just under the owner and manager on the totem pole, which made them quite a "catch." Some guys weren't really interested in this as they were more motivated by money yet others chose to take advantage of it.

Dewayne's backup decided to leave the club for personal reasons which meant that there would be a revolving door of DJs until Gene found the perfect fit as his replacement. One of those was a guy named "Caleb" and he would become a thorn in my side almost immediately. He was nothing special to look at but was a player who knew the game well enough to go through women like I went through underwear. He didn't have a car so he would always talk one of the girls into giving him a lift home. Once they got back to his place, he would get them stoned and turn on the charm until he got their pants off and would move on to a different victim the next day. I didn't have a problem with him at first, but Gene who had a strict rule of "keep your hands off the merchandise or it could cost you your job" hated him straight away. Adam didn't care for him much either after he found out that his own girlfriend used to be in a relationship with him not long before she came to our club. I knew that his days were numbered, so I tried to get along with him as best I could until he got fired. I even found myself protecting him from Adam, who wanted to kick his ass for obvious reasons. It wasn't until he had worked his way up to and went after the wrong girl that he got on my bad side.

The first time I saw him get into Justice's car, my heart sunk down into the pit of my stomach. I knew what was going to happen but there wasn't anything I could do about it but watch. I was certain that she knew what he was up to, especially after Daisy had already been tossed aside after he was through with her, and informed Justice beforehand. Their little charade only lasted a few days but it felt like an eternity. When I asked her what was going on she would say, "He smokes weed with me and it makes me feel funny then things just happen." When I asked him if they were dating he would just say "Not really. We're just...talking." Eventually Gene would fire him and add him to the growing list of casualties but his brief stint with us made a lasting impression on me.

I would adopt his very distinguished look by getting my other ear pierced, and adding yet another earring to my left ear, as well as a cartilage piercing at the top of my left ear. The cartilage piercing would be short lived as it kept getting infected and became more a burden than anything else. I would follow that up with getting my tongue pierced which was very taboo at the time. I had only seen a handful of people with it done as this was before it really went main stream. It made me very popular with the girls at the club. They had heard how it was supposed to enhance oral sex and was curious if that was just a myth or not. They also wanted to French kiss me to see how it felt in their mouths. Let's just say I was more than willing to oblige them on either subject. I adapted quite well to having this new object in my mouth. I even stopped by McDonald's after I had just got it done for a hamburger and fries against my better judgement and my tattoo artist's advice. The only times that it really annoyed me was when I would accidently bite down on it and it would come loose or when I got very high and my tongue would take on a life of its own, clanging against my teeth nonstop until it wasn't just annoying me but anyone around me as well.

5

With Caleb out of the picture, I thought that Justice was within reach but I was wrong once again. Now I was seeing less of her because she had started working for Jonah on the side. Gene told me that he had opened up a "Peep Show" business on the other side of town and had recruited a few of the girls to perform behind the glass for extra money. Justice just happened to be one of those who accepted the job. I knew that they were pretty close because she used to tell me about the "cocaine parties" he would throw at his parents' house for the wealthy socialites of Knoxville that she always attended. I tried to go with her once or twice but was told that I couldn't get in unless Jonah invited me personally, which he never did. I never felt like he was any kind of threat to take Justice away from me with his old wrinkled skin, lack of charm, and overall hideous appearance but I underestimated the power of money and what people would be willing to do to obtain it.

That was when I started hearing rumours circulating around the club that Jonah and Justice were more than just friends or business partners. At first, I didn't believe any of it because gossip spread like the plague around that place constantly and most of it was total bullshit. When Justice did make an appearance at the club, she gave no indication that anything was going on at all. She even stopped by to see me one night before attending one of Jonah's parties and was quite friendly with me in the parking lot. She said, "Kiss me with that pierced tongue" before she got into her car, since she hadn't shared a kiss with me since I had it done. She kissed me so passionately that it erased any doubts I might have had about her loyalty. There was absolutely no way she could kiss me like that and have feelings for someone else as well. It just wasn't possible. She was mine at last...and only mine I thought.

Then I got a rude awakening the night I came out to the club on my night off to see Justice and brought a bottle of Everclear. She normally didn't drink since she was still underage but for some reason, decided that she wanted to take a few sips from my bottle on this particular occasion. I was hesitant at first, due not only to her age but if Gene found out, I could possibly lose my job. To make a long story short, I reluctantly poured her a couple of drinks and she couldn't handle it. She was hurling all over the back and was unable to work for the rest of the night. This angered not only Gene and Tommy but Jessie as well. She came to my table and started yelling at me for getting her drunk and told me that I should be ashamed of myself for what I have done. Part of me wanted to just leave and spare myself any further embarrassment, but this was Justice, so

I decided to stay till closing to take care of her. I waited in the parking lot for her to come out so I could take her home but when I saw that Jessie was still by her side, I knew that wasn't happening. As soon as Jessie saw me standing there, she ripped into me a second time. "Why are *you* waiting out here? I'm going to call Jonah" she said. I replied, "Why would you call *him?* What does *he* have to do with any of this?" She snapped back with, "That's *his* woman so he has everything to do with it." I just stood there stunned...especially when Justice didn't say a word. I watched as Jessie rang Jonah several times and got no answer then decided that *she* would drive Justice to his house personally against her wishes. I still wasn't buying this whole charade even with all of the evidence right there in front of me. "Well, she didn't want Jessie to take her there for some reason and maybe she didn't deny that she was *his* girl cause she was wasted after all" I thought to myself. I wasn't sure if it was just wishful thinking or I already knew the truth but was in denial. I was sure that I wasn't going wait long for the truth to come out: that she was really *my* girl and everyone else was gravely mistaken. A lot of people were going to owe me a fucking apology when this was over.

6

One of the advantages of this business was that it gave you an outlet to release any anger that might be building up on other people without a lawsuit. I was enraged over this so called "love triangle" that I was caught up in and someone was going to bleed over it. Gene knew what was going down and let me know that "If Justice does anything wrong, I will take care of it myself so you don't have to get involved. I know that you guys have been seeing each other and I can tell that you care very much for her. But remember if she crosses that line, I won't hesitate to let her go, no matter if you have feelings for her or not." I nodded my head in appreciation. I was one of the few bouncers who Gene looked at like a son at times. He knew that I had broken every rule that he made and he would usually just turn a blind eye toward it yet he would sack anyone else who tried their luck. But even Gene couldn't stop me from unleashing my wrath on some poor bastard who caught me at the wrong time.

    Two victims who bled was a couple of customers who came in when I was the only bouncer on duty. I warned them once and they didn't listen so I grabbed one of them by the throat and dragged him kicking and screaming toward the door. Once I got him outside, I just tossed him down the concrete steps to the pavement. Pete Rose would have appreciated the head first slide through the gravel which opened up several cuts on his chest and arms. When his buddy saw the brutality in which I displayed on him, he voiced his displeasure which was a huge mistake. Before he even finished his sentence, I grabbed *him* by the throat and pushed him against the handrail. Gene was pleading with me to let him go and get back inside but it fell on deaf ears. I proceeded to choke slam him over the rail to a very resounding thud. If he hadn't landed right, I could have easily broken his neck. Gene was petrified and ordered me back inside before I killed someone. This time I listened and went back to my seat on the door. I had made a statement to everyone who witnessed it and no one got out of line the rest of the night. My only regret was that Jonah and Justice wasn't there to see it.

    Later that week, Jonah came in with his bottle and joined Gene at the other end of the bar as he usually did. I just sat on the door staring a hole through him the entire time. He was in a very good mood and actually left early which I found a little suspicious. Tommy would come over a few minutes and let me know that Jonah said that he was heading over to Justice's place to help her "study." He even gave Gene a wink and a smile after he said it to indicate that there probably wasn't going to be any books involved. I asked Tommy if I could leave to get to the bottom of this once and for all and surprisingly he gave me the green light. I drove like a bat out of hell to her place and saw Jonah's van parked outside in her visitor's parking space. As I got out and approached the front door, I noticed that all the lights were turned off but both cars were there. "How are they studying in the dark?" I sarcastically asked myself. I pounded on the door and there was no answer. I tried again and still nothing. After a third try, I gave up and headed back to my truck, partially relieved that no one actually came to the door because I hadn't put any thought into what I would have said if they did. I went back to work even madder than I was when I left. I still wasn't ready to accept that I had lost her to someone, who if they weren't wealthy, probably wouldn't have had a snowballs chance in hell with her.

 Within a couple of weeks, I found out what I needed to know straight from the horse's mouth. As we were closing up for the night and all the girls had safely left the building, I walked back inside to see Jonah sitting at the bar with Tommy, Adam, James, and Dewayne. He was obviously shit faced drunk and had tears rolling down his cheeks. I joined them, not because I was really concerned but because I was delighted to see Jonah suffering and was curious about what was causing him such pain. He would cut to the chase. "As you guys have heard, I've been dating one of the girls that works here: Justice." I felt a sharp pain in my chest and you could have probably lit a match off my face after hearing those words that I never wanted to hear. I looked at Adam first and he never looked back which was probably a good thing. Then I looked at all the other guys who also knew how I felt about her, and no one would look directly at me, which was, without a doubt, the kindest thing that they could have done. Jonah continued, "Well, she dumped me and I don't really know why. I was in love with her and she broke my heart." His rambling would go on for what seemed like forever as he told us all the details of the relationship: how it started, how much money he had spent on her, where they shared their first kiss etc. By the end of his sob story, I knew everything…even shit that I really didn't want to know. But for some reason, I didn't feel sorry for him. Instead, one thought came across my mind. "It couldn't have happened to a nicer guy, motherfucker!" For a brief instance, I wasn't mad at Justice…I wanted to thank her for putting this arrogant jackass in his place. Someone needed to. As far as I was concerned, "Justice was served," but the whole experience had taken its toll on me. I was going to suffer more from this than anyone else in the months to come…

-**DJN**

CHAPTER VIII- "SIDE EFFECTS"

1998

   Those little white lines, I hurt for like a junkie. I'm getting old before my time, looking like a fucking zombie. Lost in the shuffle, needing to be discarded, they are like a swarm of bees, seeping their stingers into me, yet I'm ready to get this party started.
   At the bottom of the bottle, going against the grain, drown in a sea of liquor and wash up on a beach of cocaine.
   Take a bump, take a peek, nothing is clear without a streak. Take a drag, take a toke, and watch it all go up in smoke.
   The trees are flame and the water is still, everything is so brown and lifeless. The sky is overcast and the air tastes damp and decayed... no better setting for my purpose. (The sun only shines for some, for the rest its stormy weather)
   My friends eventually became foes, leaving me no one to confide. In boredom, I turn on the TV or radio but nothing kept me occupied. If we cross paths on the streets, don't even bother to stop and say hello, just let me hide.
   I used to see only with my fingertips, had an open mind to your views. Now I don't care about the bullshit and gossip, no prying mind for the latest news.
   When I'm this comfortable, I can't raise my weary head. When I'm this comfortable, you can raise the nearly dead...
   I have tried rehab, detox, even cold turkey but always fell off the wagon. Always found myself back at that pharmacy, filling me prescription. There's always a needle for another shot, or a sheet for another hit. I usually have sores on my

face, reeking of vomit and sweat, as my body runs hot, causing a certain stench to come from my armpits...

My eyes and ears are of stone, and my thoughts are a million miles away. My body is breaking down, my ass is dragging the ground, since I haven't eaten or slept in days.

They say I have a problem, because I can never say no. All I know is that I'm going to die young and be wasted when I go...
-Denny Noland "Draven" From my song "Candy Man"
Written in 1998-1999   Copyright 2015

I started seeing Jonah in the club more frequently as time passed on, especially after Justice took some time off to work on other projects. He was still heartbroken and not really himself. He invited me and a friend over to his hotel room one night to do a little free coke, and of course anyone who really knew me can tell you that was an offer that I just couldn't refuse. When we got there, he was just sitting there on the bed like a statue staring at the TV in deep thought. He had a fat bag of cocaine on one nightstand and a bottle of liquor on the other. It didn't take long before he mentioned Justice's name and began sobbing uncontrollably once again. For some reason, unbeknownst to me at the time, I decided that this would be the perfect time to let him in on a little secret that he needed to know. I told him all about Justice and me spending time together, even kissing, while he was seeing her too. I didn't lie or even stretch the truth. I even told him that we had never slept together, which I thought that he would be relieved to know, but it didn't really help. Just hearing that I was part of the "love triangle" made him even more upset. I felt like a piece of shit after telling him and started thinking that maybe I should have just kept my mouth shut. For the first time, I felt pity for him and tried a different strategy to cheer him up by quickly changing the subject.

    The higher we got, the more we bonded. He claimed that he used to think that I was just a burned out redneck but now he saw a different side of me. He said that he was impressed by how intelligent I was under the surface. He admitted that he was wrong about me and for that he apologized. He even thanked me for doing something that all of his so called "circle" of friends couldn't do: make him smile again. In a bizarre twist, we became very good friends that night, instead of bitter rivals unknowingly fighting for the affections of the same woman.

2

    Of all the drugs that I had sampled at this point, there was one drug that I had no desire to try: heroin. I hadn't really been around anyone who did it, or even tried it to my knowledge, but Dewayne was about to change all of that. I had no idea that he was into that shit until the night he asked me to drive him out to a club on the strip to meet with his dealer. I voiced my concerns about even trying the stuff after all of the articles I had read about people getting addicted the first time they tried it and all of the deaths that have been linked to it in the media. I also wasn't interested in using needles to get high, since I hated getting shots even when I was forced to, which was how I had managed to avoid them for so long. Just the thought reminded me of back in high school when I got into trouble and my dad grabbed my arms to check for tracks which I found both amusing and insulting at the same time. But this was 1998, and Dewayne had a way of talking me into at least trying different things before knocking them. In my own way, I trusted him with my life. He was the voice of knowledge and experience and I had become quite the guinea pig over the last four years so why shouldn't I see what all the fuss was about? Not only was I borderline suicidal anyways but if my father knew I was doing this, he would be so ashamed of me. At least this time I gave him a good reason.

When we entered the club, there was a local Marilyn Manson-like band playing on the ground level that sounded pretty good even if the crowd wasn't getting into it. We then climbed the stairs to the second level which had a bar and several booths. It was lit by lanterns and candles and was so dark that you couldn't see the person sitting across from you. Dewayne asked me if I was willing to pitch in some money to get some cocaine too, so he could mix up a lethal concoction to give us the ultimate "speedball" experience when we got back to my place. I knew that this combination was deadly but I found it intriguing in my own twisted way. Some people climb Everest to get their adrenalin rush from heights but I use illegal narcotics to get mine so I handed him what I had to spare. Eventually, a guy joined us in the booth and sat beside Dewayne to make the exchange. A few minutes later, we were back on the road and headed to my place with enough drugs in my car to not only be put in prison, but be put *under* the prison. I was ready to get this party started.

I hated heroin from the first time it hit my vein. It just didn't agree with me at all. It was not the right high, even mixed with cocaine, which made me one of the lucky ones. We did this lethal combination for a couple of weeks until we went too far. One night, while we were in the midst of an epic "speedball", I received a call from Justice. She had just got back in town after a photo shoot in the Caribbean and she sounded like she was already fucked up on something herself. She insisted that she was coming over to my place to party and although I didn't want her to see me like this, I reluctantly agreed, just to get her off the roads. At least, I could look after her and put her up for the night until she came down off whatever she was on. I had no intentions of letting her touch the heroin under any circumstances and since we only had two syringes, she probably wouldn't even bother to ask anyways.

When she got there, she was in rare form. She said that she had taken an ecstasy pill earlier and was rolling pretty hard. She started being a bit flirty with Dewayne and started giving *him* a lap dance like she had Daisy some months before. I felt like it was so disrespectful that she would do something like that not only in front of me but *in my own fucking house!* I didn't say anything this time and when she noticed that it didn't visibly bother me, she stopped on her own. I distracted her by saying that with her red hair and curves, she was a spitting image of the life-size, realistic looking poster of Mary Jane Watson, from the Spiderman comics, that was on my dining room wall. She posed in the same manner as Mary Jane in front of the poster and the resemblance was uncanny. We even took a photo of her but I think Dewayne stole it because I only saw it once.

Then Dewayne and I needed another fix so we headed for the kitchen, hoping Justice would stay seated and not come in there to see what we were doing. As soon as Dewayne was shooting it into my vein, she entered the room and saw us. "What are you guys doing?" she asked. "Heroin and cocaine, sweetheart... but don't get any ideas because we only have two needles and you don't want to share one right?" I asked, thinking that was going to be the end of that conversation. "I wanna try!" she said to my horror. "What? Are you out of your mind?" I asked before Dewayne interrupted and said "You know that we can sterilize one of our needles and it would be like a brand new one." There was no point in trying to talk her out of it then. I asked Dewayne to use mine since I was recently tested and knew that I was clean but for some kinky or sadistic reason, he used his, which pissed me off considering that I didn't know where *he* had been. Justice watched the whole preparation process and appeared to be getting nervous. I was hoping that she was having second thoughts but unfortunately she wasn't and there wasn't a damn thing I could do about it.

    Not long after Dewayne injected her, she literally collapsed on the couch. She had passed out due to the excess and I couldn't wake her up, so I carried her down the hall and placed her on my bed in the back so she could sleep it off. She looked so beautiful lying there and the room instantly smelled like her perfume. I could easily just forget that the whole Jonah thing ever happened just by staring at her. I wanted to lie down beside her and hold her but I knew that if she was sober, she wouldn't have wanted that, so I closed the door and continued partying for the rest of the night. I would check in every hour to see if she was awake or needed anything but she was out until morning. I told Dewayne that we should be ashamed of ourselves for what we have done and if he wants to do heroin again, count me out. That was indeed the last time that we did *that* drug together.

    Although I was off of the heroin, I had gotten used to the sting of the needle and the high that cocaine gave me when it went straight into my vein. It was quicker and didn't have those "side effects" that came with shoving it up my nose. I had never prepared my own needle or stuck myself before but I had watched Dewayne do it many times so I thought that I knew enough about it to try it on my own...big mistake. One night while I was at home alone, I gave it a go and nearly killed myself. I had put too much coke in the syringe and when I injected it, it hit me so hard that within seconds I was suffering from chest pains. I was sweating profusely and my heart was beating so fast that it felt like it was just going to explode. I just knew that I was going to go into cardiac arrest. I had obviously overdosed and all I could think of was the legacy that I had left behind once they finally found my body. Luckily, by the grace of God, I survived to tell the story and will probably never know how close I was to death.

3

I always said that if my habit got so bad that I found myself in either a "crack house" or the projects trying to score some dope, it was time to stop. Then it happened for the first time when Dewayne told me about a place that we could go to get high that wouldn't cost very much since we were both already broke. He didn't go into much detail, just said that they were good "friends" of his and that it would be ok. He had never steered me wrong before so I had no reason not to trust him. I drove him out to a part of town that I had never been to before to this guy's house, and we knocked on his door. An old black man answered the door, greeted Dewayne, and let us in.

Once we got inside, there were people everywhere. We saw Dewayne's former backup DJ, that we were still trying to replace, sitting there at one of the tables. He left soon after he saw us, but was quickly replaced by someone else as people were coming and going nonstop. I was starting to figure out where we actually were and instead of being freaked out about it, I chose to just be myself and enjoy the endless supply of crack. The owner of the house was the guy who came to the door. His name was "Max" and he turned out to be a pleasant, friendly man who just happens to be a drug dealer. I liked him and his middle aged, white girlfriend named "Shelly" who kept providing me with one pipe after another without asking for money. I always tried to make the best out of any situation and this was no exception.

As we partied deeper into the morning, Shelly started talking about how she wanted to just pack up a few things and move to Chicago and never look back. We could tell that she was dead serious about it and high enough to carry it out without a second thought. Then all of a sudden, Max decided that he was going too and he couldn't think of a better time to leave than the present. So they grabbed a few things and away they went, leaving Dewayne and me to an empty house. We were stunned by this series of events and decided to leave as well. As we were walking to my truck, I noticed three police cars parked across the road, pointing directly at us. They must have been watching the place all morning, possibly searching and arresting people as they were leaving. My first thought was wondering if they got Max and Shelly in cuffs somewhere. If that was the case, we were probably next.

When we pulled out onto the road, one of the cruisers started tailing us. I knew it was going to be only a matter of time before we got pulled over. About a mile down the road, he turned on his lights and siren. Dewayne suggested that we should pull over but I wasn't about to do that. I just drove casually down the road like I didn't see him for several minutes. I knew that although we didn't have any drugs on us, all he would have to do was look at our dilated pupils and we were going to jail, so I wasn't stopping. Then a miracle occurred: he just turned off his lights, took the next exit ramp, and just like that, he was gone. I pulled over to the side of the road to collect myself, baffled about how I had escaped incarceration once again. I thought Dewayne was going to hug me, and I wouldn't have blamed him if he had.

    I was so shaken that I couldn't get any sleep before work that afternoon so I was a nervous wreck at the club. When Dewayne saw the condition I was in, he came down from the booth and handed me a pill. "Take this. It will relax you" he said. I didn't even think to ask him what it was and to be honest, I didn't care. I just took it, no questions asked. I started feeling better while I was sitting in my chair but as soon as I stood up and tried to walk, my legs were like rubber. Needless to say, there were some assholes acting up and I had to figure out how to get to their table without falling on my face, so I just kept grabbing anything I could along the way to hold myself up. The customers looked puzzled, even somewhat sympathetic, as I approached them with such great difficulty. They must have felt pity for me because they were on their best behaviour after that. Gene had seen the whole thing and just sat at the bar shaking his head. Eventually it wore off and I was back to normal but it was rough there for a couple of hours. I still don't know what I took but I certainly don't recommend it.

4

After countless applicants and several failed experiments, we found our backup DJ: a big black man that looked like he just stepped off a football field who I called "The Captain." A lot of the girls knew him already from that nameless club across town where he used to work. Gene originally brought him in as a bartender, but he wouldn't stay there for very long after filling in as the DJ one fateful night. He was a natural who fired up the crowd like no other and we all took notice. He and I became friends straight away and partied together quite frequently. He not only made the girls feel safer when he was around, but he also made me feel safer as well, because he *always* had our backs.

    He would join us at Dewayne's house every so often to do some coke. On one occasion, he brought one of the girls from the club along with him. Her name was "Sky" and she, much like the Captain and I, enjoyed smoking it more than doing it any other way, so we were hitting the pipe in the living room. Sky would even "shotgun" her second hand smoke with us, which usually ended up with whichever one of us that was receiving it, getting a kiss as well after she exhaled. Meanwhile, in one of the other rooms, Dewayne was shooting himself up with his dope while Daisy and the other girls were snorting their powder upstairs. I was jumping from room to room, taking it in all three ways without anyone really noticing. It wasn't until I did too much and got too high that everyone caught on to what I was doing and started freaking out. Once again, I had done enough cocaine in one night to kill a horse and survived. My legend was starting to grow.

    The Captain was the one who introduced me to a bar called "Micheal's" in west Knoxville. From the first time we went out there after hours and ran into Justice, to the day they closed their doors for good, that was my hangout. From a distance, you would think that it would be a place that someone like me wouldn't be caught dead in. It had a strict dress code, with expensive spirits and even more expensive food. The waitresses looked more attractive than many of our girls and only socialized with the older, wealthier customers. You had to earn your spot there, otherwise you were practically invisible.

It had pool tables, dartboards, poker machines, even a dance floor. There also were TVs everywhere, airing every major sporting event going on at the time. I would usually find The Captain sitting at one of the pokies, with his glass of wild turkey on the rocks, having the time of his life. There was always cocaine in the building too if you knew where to look. Whether it was one of the dealers who practically lived there or one of the staff members who pushed their powder for extra cash, we always found them. To me, it was the closest thing to heaven on earth that I had ever seen. I have so many great memories of that place and spent a lot of time there over the years. The staff, regulars, and even the owner became like family to me.

When we weren't at Micheal's, The Captain always knew where the party was, and they weren't the same type of "parties" that Dewayne and I used to go to either. One night in particular, he took me to this mansion on the outskirts of the city. When we arrived, we had to walk through a basement full of college kids having a "keg" party. We saw Jessie and her best friend, and fellow dancer "Simone" there, but The Captain didn't come to drink beer so we climbed the stairs leading into the house. Once inside, the living quarters were filled with older folks sipping their wine and telling stories. The owners of the house were among them and excused themselves as soon as they saw The Captain standing there. They came up to him and greeted him, then pulled him over to a quiet corner so they could talk in private. A few minutes later, he came and got me. As we passed through the remaining rooms, we saw rooms filled with people either smoking weed while watching movies, or rooms filled with people tripping their asses off to psychedelic music and staring at nothing. We climbed yet another set of stairs to the top level that had been declared off limits to everyone else. There the owners of the house brought out their personal stash of cocaine, and we spent the rest of the night up there getting high away from the chaos around us. It was an epic night, to say the least…

5

This was around the time that Adam decided that he would try his hand at doing some dealing himself. He was already a part of a large steroid ring coming out of Mexico but he felt like he was ready to go into the big leagues with a much more profitable drug. He then took one of his shady doctor friends with him to New York to purchase his supply of cocaine at a cheaper price. He came back with not only the coke but a shitload of heroin as well. He asked me if I was interested in pushing some of the powder for him but I declined on the grounds that I would probably end up doing it all myself and owing him a huge debt. "Users don't make good dealers" I said. He understood but wanted me to sleep on it first before not considering it. One code that I had always lived by was avoiding owing drug dealers money. Everything else could wait till they were paid in full. The bank or any other bill collectors don't usually show up at your doorstep with firearms and that made them less of a priority in my eyes.

Adam did, however, recruit one of his best friends to help him out since I wasn't interested. His name was "Toby" and he shared the same look as Adam: bald head, bad attitude, and bulging biceps. His arms were bigger than my legs and that's not an exaggeration. Let's put it this way: if you saw those two guys walking toward you in a dark alley, you would go in the other direction… no matter how badass you thought you were. Toby was one of those guys that Gene offered a job to at the club and Gene wasn't exactly known for offering jobs to anyone who had a penis but even *he* was overwhelmed by the sheer size of this kid. I think that Adam made a wise choice by picking Toby to be one of his "runners". Who the fuck would try to doublecross this monster with the word "fear" tattooed on his lower lip? No one, that's who…

    The plan was simple. Adam was going to divide his portion of the coke up into so called "fat" $20 bags, and sell them to the girls inside the club. It was a total rip-off, as there was only enough powder in those things to make you want more. Girls who didn't want to spend much money but wanted a buzz throughout the night, like Sky for example, was paying several times more for their dope than if they just bought a large quantity outright. It worked like a charm. Toby, on the other hand, was hitting the college circuit and even the hoods. Adam had to be making some serious money, but when you mysteriously start increasing your income dramatically with nothing to show for it on the books, you draw the attention of the people that you don't want watching you, just biding their time just waiting for the right moment to strike. Within just a couple of weeks, Adam had increased his income tenfold and even had a new girlfriend but his carelessness with his activities was about to cost him everything. If he was going down, he was going to take me with him…

6

Adam wasn't the only person expanding their business. Gene had decided to open a second club and send Tommy and Adam over there to get it up and running. Adam wasn't happy about it because that would mean that he would no longer be working with his new girlfriend. The first location he chose was in the historic Old City portion of Knoxville right next to one of the most popular nightclubs in the area. Since that club always featured up and coming rock and metal bands several nights a week and served alcohol, we were literally asking for trouble. If that wasn't enough, where the building sat, drew a lot of bad press from the locals and caught the eye of any politician or law enforcement agency looking to make a name for themselves, so it was doomed from the start. I was forced to help with the move and when I arrived at the club, there was a tour bus parking next door. I asked one of their staff members who was on that bus and they told me that it was a band called "Cold" and that they kicked ass. I was carrying chairs into our building while they were bringing their equipment and instruments into the other. As we passed each other, I stopped and had a chat with them but didn't bother asking for autographs. It would be a couple of years down the track before I really gave them a listen and realized that I fucked up. Within the first week, the police raided our club twice. The first time, the only shut it down for the night but when they came back later in the week, they shut it down permanently. However, Gene did have a plan B in case this happened.

He had his sights set on a club on the other side of town called "the PPK" that was owned and ran by a crackhead. It had a really bad reputation and was on life support but Gene saw potential in the place so he closed our club early one night and had the entire bar staff and a couple of the girls go check it out. We intimidated the hell out of everyone in the building that night, which was a great strategy to get the papers signed. We left the proud new renters of the building, which was to be christened "The Last Chance 2000" when it reopened after we did some renovations. Once again, Gene was going to let Tommy run the place and have Adam as his doorman. The place was known to draw a rough crowd so it certainly wasn't going to be easy to get it cleaned up. In the weeks to come, Adam would persuade me to sell cocaine in the main club while he sold in the new club, doubling his profits and helping to support my rock star sized habit. I was about to become the most popular guy in the club for all the wrong reasons when all I wanted was to be invisible.

-DJN

CHAPTER IX-*"MELANCHOLIA"*

1998-1999

    Adam was the true Dr Frankenstein when it came to drugs and needles. If you compared him to Dewayne, it would be like comparing a tattoo artist to a scratcher. He was knowledgeable due to his years of steroid use. He had read many books about the effects of drugs on the human body and ordered syringes by the case on a weekly basis. Getting high with him was like a lesson in chemistry, as I learned many things from being his lab monkey. I permitted him to take me places that I had never been and knew that he could always get me back home.

    Doing cocaine with Adam was a three stage process. He would inject Nubane, which is a strong painkiller, into my arm to relax my muscles before we ever got out the coke. This was a drug that many bodybuilders, like Adam and Toby, used after a workout to heal and recover. Several minutes later came the cocaine and more syringes. We only powdered our noses while he prepared our needles for the next shot. While we were high, I usually picked out which CDs that we listened to, while he whined about his new girlfriend. He was in a bad predicament that I was so recently familiar with: his girlfriend had another man back in Georgia that she was also in a relationship with. Sometimes he was optimistic about it, thinking that she would eventually leave the other guy, and other times he was clinically depressed... even carving her name into his furniture with a knife. I never knew what kind of mood he was going to be in when I got there. Once I even walked in and found him passed out in a chair with the needle still sticking out of his arm. I often wondered if I was going to find him dead one day but luckily that never happened.

Then there was level 3...when we wanted to come down and go to sleep. He would put Valium into much larger needles and inject us both with them separately. Within only a few minutes, we were out like a light and would wake up a few hours later totally refreshed with no lingering effects. He was a genius when it came to taking drugs and made the whole routine run smooth as silk. We always repeated this same cycle, never straying far from the path. It was only when we experimented with other narcotics that things really got hairy.

Our first trial and error was when he wanted me to try something called "k4 dilaudid." As he was putting it into my vein, he warned me that I needed to sit down because it was going to knock me on my ass in about ten seconds. I didn't believe him and started walking around as he counted down. As soon as he got to one, it hit me like a motherfucker. Sweat started pouring from my forehead as I literally felt like my body was going to burst into flames. I started freaking out and stuck my head in the air conditioning vent on his kitchen floor. He was now worried that I might be dying and came to my aid. I had never felt this way before with any drug that I have taken, and that made both of us panic. I snapped out of it a few minutes later and vowed to never do that shit again. Adam, who was quite pale from watching my episode, agreed and apologized.

When Christmas rolled around that year, he brought out the leftover heroin from New York. I could have cared less if I ever saw that stuff again, but he insisted that I do some with him. He had already impressed me with his skill of using needles for everything else, so I decided to give it one more chance. We ended up doing so much heroin that we passed out on Christmas Eve and woke up two days *after* Christmas! Once I realized what day it was, I started thinking about my parents who were probably worried sick after I missed Christmas dinner and wasn't answering my phone. But I had a bigger problem: I had to be at work in less than an hour and I was too out of it to even open my eyes fully, much less drive to or function at the club. I didn't know what the hell I was going to do.

Then I blacked out again and was awakened this time by two imposing silhouettes standing over me, discussing how to get me fully awake and moving about. It was Adam and Toby, and they knew what I needed to get on my feet. Toby poured out a line of cocaine that was nearly as long as the coffee table that it was sitting on and handed me a straw. I snorted the entire line in one attempt, and like Popeye, after eating his spinach, got an unbelievable boost of energy and sprung up to my feet. "I need a shower" was the first words out of my mouth. I jumped in the shower and was on the road in record time, getting there just as the doors were opening. I called my parents soon after and make up some elaborate lie to cover my ass. I would never touch heroin again and avoided anyone who was associated with it from that moment on.

2

Back at Dewayne's place, our circle was expanding. A couple of the girls from the club, "Sugar" and "Blaze," had joined us every now and then. I had a brief history with Sugar when I was still a customer. She was married to one of the most promising up and coming boxers in the area until he got on drugs and his career went down the drain. She didn't bother to tell me this until I took her home one night and was introduced to him. I avoided her after that. Adam had told me when I first started at the club that these two ladies went down on him together in the parking lot one night for his "tip". Dewayne had even told me his own story about how he and his former backup DJ had an orgy with them one night at his house while they were all high. The stage was set for something interesting to develop for me but before that moment could happen, I told them both to not get any ideas because when I got high, sex took a backseat. Cocaine was my mistress then. That look of disappointment on their faces were priceless but I wasn't being cruel, I was just being honest.

Dewayne also was known to date girls who had a direct link to me. When I first met him, he was dating the girl who kept me from going to Florida: Blair. By the time we started running around together, they had broken up so I never saw her. But now he had gone from the frying pan into the fire when he started dating Dakota, the girl who left me stranded on the other side of town to go home with her husband. She had just returned to the club and was pretty much picking up where she left off. Dewayne was constantly complaining that her husband was randomly showing up at his house and trying to pick a fight with him. She even left with him afterwards most of the time. I couldn't help but wear a cheeky smile after hearing that someone else was going through practically the same shit that I did.

One of the funniest, yet disturbing, incidents took place around this timeframe. We were having our usual party at Dewayne's house when The Captain showed up with this nasty looking skank that he had picked up somewhere along the way. She was falling all over the place, and immediately stripped down to reveal a perfect pair of breasts. For some reason, she seemed to take a particular liking to me. I snuck off to the kitchen to do a few bumps and she followed me, naked as a jaybird. She pinned me against the counter trying to kiss me but I wasn't letting her get anywhere near me. She then grabbed my crotch, dropped down to her knees, and started unzipping my pants. For a split second, I considered letting her blow me before I looked down and saw something swinging between her legs. It was a fucking penis! Apparently, she/he had it tucked or something and when she/he got aroused, it broke free. I came running out of the kitchen with that thing in close pursuit. As soon as Dewayne saw her/him, he wanted it out. Adam was ready to kill it before The Captain said he would take care of it himself, since he brought it in the first place. He left with that thing and returned a few minutes later without it. He was obviously embarrassed by the whole thing but handled it with a sense of humour. He later confessed to me that "it gave him the best blowjob that he ever had on the way over" and that he had "left it on the side of the road to find its own way back after we kicked it out." We could all finally share a good laugh about it after all was said and done.

3

There was a new girl at the club named "Star" that started coming over to Dewayne's house to party with us. She was a beautiful, yet quite skinny, blonde gothic chick who always wore black and had something about her that made me want her badly. Her first night there, I made a pass at her and got nowhere so I never tried again. In time, we became close friends which led to me meeting her live in boyfriend "Martin." He was the typical wannabe musician, whose stripper girlfriend would drop him off at band practice on her way to work. He had no car or license and wasn't interested in having a real job, and shockingly, Star seemed ok with that. Although I didn't approve of his lifestyle, he hit it off with me immediately, which led to me apologizing for coming on to his woman the first time I partied with her. He seemed very nonchalant about the whole thing, almost as if it didn't bother him at all. I was both relieved and a bit confused but that was just how he was.

However, one thing that he did have was a great singing voice, which gave me what I thought at the time was a great idea: I offered him the lead vocalist role in a band that I was putting together called "Melancholia" and he gladly accepted it. I had made it clear that I wrote all the lyrics and the rest of the band collaborated on the music...no exceptions. Once he read my lyrics, I received the same reaction that I had gotten used to over the past few months: they were good but way out there as a result of me writing them all while I was high. He compared them to something that the band "Tool" would write which was the closest thing to a compliment that he gave me. He was concerned with whether people would "get" them or not, which could become a problem, so he insisted that I explain to him what each individual song was about so he would have a better understanding of the message I was trying to convey through him. Then he asked if he could alter a line here or there which was forbidden, as far as I was concerned. This led to weeks of lengthy discussions and loud disagreements over the product which kept us from moving forward with the project. Some of this material is strategically placed within this book and dated within the timeframe of the late 90's when it was written.

With me being a drug dealer, I was starting to feel as if they were more interested in doing my dope than thinking about the future. They would come by my house several times a week out of the blue, since they "just happened to be in the neighbourhood and thought they would drop in to see how I was doing" which made no sense since they lived almost an hour away. I think we would have a chat for around 10 minutes or so before they would ask me for a bump, then we would spend the entire night getting high instead of doing anything constructive. They were becoming more of a nuisance than an asset and Melancholia was still sitting in limbo. That's when I met up with that record producer in west Knoxville that suggested that I should drop Martin and be the face of the band myself. If I didn't hate the sound of my own voice so much, I would have considered it and possibly taken lessons to learn how to sing but instead I chose to stay on course with my original plan of just being the bass player. Things may not be progressing very fast, but I wasn't too concerned. I had all the time in the world after all...

4

I may have gained a couple of new friends but I was about to part ways with another. Dewayne had just got caught by his hippie roommate with cocaine and although he shared some with him and thought he wasn't going to rat, he told the other members of their "community" anyway and they wanted him out. All those months of partying right under their noses without them finding out was now a thing of the past. I always found it amusing that they were all about smoking weed and taking acid but they hated anyone who did cocaine. It just wasn't tolerated in this sanctuary and the penalty for breaking this rule was dismissal so Dewayne was now homeless. He stayed at my house briefly until he found another place and once he left, I started seeing less and less of him in the weeks to come until it got to where I only saw him at work. But even that was about to change.

After working too many days in succession without a day off, Gene asked Dewayne to fill in for me on one of my shifts so I could finally spend a nice relaxing evening at home. His position that night was to keep an eye on the VIP room and collect money from the girls as they came out. At some point during the night, he decided to steal a portion of Gene's dance money. He thought if he could share some of this money with the girls, they would keep their mouths shut. The problem was that Gene had his spies and Dewayne made the mistake of trusting one of them and they betrayed him costing him his job. When I heard the news the following day, I was very upset that he would do something so stupid but I knew that somewhere down the road, I would probably see him again. Dewayne's position as the primary DJ would be quickly filled by The Captain and would bring about the hiring of "Lars", who came from the West Club, to be his backup.

5

The day had finally come. It was the grand opening for our sister club "Last Chance 2000" which meant that a lot of changes were about to take place. Tommy was promoted to general manager over both clubs but was going to spend most of his time at the new club where he was a partial owner. This meant that the manager position at the main club was vacant but Gene already had someone in mind to take over: the returning Bear. Adam was also going to the new club, leaving me as the lone bouncer for a short time until Gene hired more staff.

Walking into the new club was like stepping out of a time machine into the year 1994 again. The bartender there was the old one from Bambi's, the waitress was a former dancer from the South Club called "Phoenix" and even half of the current roster that went on stage every night consisted of girls who had either left our club willingly, or was fired by Gene personally over the years. The rest of the staff came from the former "PPK", which included the manager, DJ, and the other half of the performers.

Some people enjoyed working in that place but others thought it was purgatory. The crowds were smaller and rougher, which meant that whether you were a dancer or any other staff member, you were going to make less money for sure. Gene would send disobedient employees there as punishment instead of firing them and losing their services altogether, which I always thought was a clever move indeed. It kept most of his staff in line and even got him laid on many occasions in an effort to possibly change his mind about sending them across town once they got on his bad side. Either way, you were fucked...whether it was Gene in the main club or the always horny Tommy on the other end, who many girls felt "obligated" to spread their legs for in his office to keep their jobs. Looking back on it, it wasn't a pleasant work environment at all. You had two men who knew that sexual harassment wasn't frowned upon, and was nearly impossible to prove in a courtroom while working in this profession, and they used it to their advantage for fucking *years*. The irony is that most of these ladies, to this very day, think that I am a bigger piece of shit than either of them which I find astounding.

6

Adam was now selling dope at the new club while yours truly was pushing it at the main one. I was doing over half of my profit myself and selling the rest at ridiculous prices to cover my ass...and the girls were reluctantly paying whatever I asked. I even picked up a protégé along the way who owned his own carpet cleaning business and looked up to me like I was a god. His name was "Oliver" and he followed me around like a little brother. When I told him that I did cocaine on a regular basis, he had to try it, so I sold him about $20 worth of coke for $70 because he didn't know any better. He had never taken drugs before but by the end of the week, he was buying cocaine nightly from me and getting ripped off royally in the process. I didn't care whether he was doing it all or flushing it down the toilet, as long as he continued to pay me triple what it was worth.

    That was when I met the first angel of my "Holy Trinity." Her name was "Lena" and although she had been working for us for nearly a month, this was the first time I had ever laid eyes on her. I had heard Adam ranting and raving about how beautiful she was for a couple of weeks, but after seeing her in person, he could have been accused of just being modest. She had a lot of Native American features, like her long, dark hair with matching skin and her big sexy brown eyes. She was, without question, the most beautiful woman I had ever seen walk through that door and take the stage. She walked straight up to me very cautiously, hesitated for a moment like she was having second thoughts, then finally turned and faced me. I could tell that she had been crying about something before she approached me but I wasn't about to get involved in whatever it was. I had no idea what she wanted because we had never spoke before. She cut right to the chase. "Some of the girls in the back told me that you were the guy to see. Do you have anything? I'm going through a tough time right now and I need something to help me get through the night." I wanted to hook her up but the only thing I had left was my personal stash and she wasn't getting that. "I'm sorry sweetie, but I'm drained" I said. She was visibly upset and obviously disappointed, nearly starting to weep again. She turned and walked away, only speaking to me once or twice when she had to in the next couple of weeks but never about dope strangely enough. If only I knew at the time that this special young lady was going to still be haunting me in my dreams even in this day and age.

7

Whether it was my late night shenanagans or some other unknown reason, the Hell's Angel that lived behind me decided to move and was quickly replaced by a young married couple. They reminded me of my marriage to Angie in almost every way. I could hear them bickering and arguing both day and night until the wife left him and ran off with the husband's best friend. I took the kid under my wing and he started looking up to me as well since I was always giving him advice on how to cope with a bad marriage since I had already been there and done that myself. I was starting to build a group of followers, or even disciples, if you will, and it made me feel like a natural leader for once.

For months, I had wanted to get a cat but never got around to it. When the kid's wife walked on him, she left her two female cats "Smokey" and "Bandit" behind. He often complained that they reminded him of his wife, and that he was thinking about getting rid of them, so I offered to take them off his hands. He eventually agreed and I took them both to my trailer. One of them kept getting out and running away, while the other seemed quite content with her new home. I renamed her "Gabrielle" and when the young couple reconciled and wanted their cat back, there was no way I was letting her go.

A few weeks later, a stray female kitten wandered up on my parents' doorstep and was trying to get into their house. My mother got attached to her straightaway, started feeding her, and named her "Brandy." The first time I saw her, I wanted her. I thought that she would be a great companion for Gabrielle so I pleaded with my mother to give her to me. At first, she didn't want to until I reminded her of all the cats we had lost to the road over the years and she wisely changed her mind. Now I had two cats that became my "children" and were great company on those lonely nights when I didn't want to leave the house.

They were useless when a big white field rat ran down the hall one night and rested on a pillow I had sitting on the floor. They just sat on the couch, too terrified to even move until it went back down the hall. I grabbed a baseball bat and chased the fucking thing but lost it somewhere in the bathroom. I just didn't understand how a rat, the size of one of the cats, managed to give me the slip. I also wondered how the damn thing even got in the house in the first place. However it got in must have been the same way it escaped and that worried me. Luckily, neither I, nor those cowardly cats, ever saw the bloody thing again.

8

Back at work, I had received word that Justice had resurfaced and was now working at the new club with certain "enhancements" to her body. Oliver and I met up there one night to see her and it turned into a total disaster. I brought in a bottle of Everclear and shared it with Oliver which was a terrible mistake. We had a great time throughout the night and Justice topped it off when she asked me to follow her back to her new place after she got off work. When I went to get into my truck, Oliver was sitting behind the wheel, daring me to move him. I asked him nicely the first time to get out but he ignored me. I then looked over at Justice who was just patiently waiting there oblivious to what was about to happen. I *told* him the second time to get his fat ass out of my seat but he still didn't listen. Now I was furious and just reacted. I yanked the door open, grabbed him around his neck, and slammed him headfirst into the pavement which not only opened a huge gash on his head but made blood start flowing from his mouth as well. I just kept bouncing his head off the ground as I began choking the life out of him. Blood was everywhere and he was nearly unconscious before the bouncers got there to pull me off of him. Tommy and Adam came out after they heard all the commotion and started yelling at me for beating my so called "friend" within an inch of his life. It wasn't until then that I realized what I had done and saw how badly he was hurt. When I turned back to look at Justice this time, she was petrified and getting into her car. She left me standing there in a trail of dust...obviously disgusted by my actions on this night.

    Seeing that I just had a change of plans, Tommy's friend "Punky" asked me for a lift home. As we were loading up into my truck, Punky asked what I was going to do about Oliver, who was still lying in a pool of his own blood. At first, I was going to just leave him there but Punky talked me into taking him home since he was both drunk and seriously injured and obviously in no condition to drive. He was in and out of consciousness and bleeding all over my seat the entire way back to his place. When we got there, the porch light came on and a woman, who I will assume was his wife, met him half way down the sidewalk. She started bashing him over his already injured head with a broomstick as we were driving away. I never heard nor seen him again after that night, but I wasn't really expecting to either.

    Needless to say, Justice didn't speak to me for a couple of weeks after what she saw that night. But when she started hanging around with Star, that all changed due to the fact that I was Star's dealer. From what I had heard, Star had already spent the night with Justice a couple of times and I knew what that probably meant due to her track record. When they both started coming over to my place to get high, things always got a bit interesting to say the least. Once they even recorded a sexy message on my answering machine for anyone who couldn't reach me. It used to drive my mother crazy every time she heard their voices on that recording but I personally loved it. As quickly as she appeared, Justice vanished once more but when she came back the next time, she might have unknowingly saved my life and for that she will always have a place in my heart...   **-DJN**

CHAPTER X - "PIN CUSHION"

1999

In my drawn out adolescence, many nights my hands shook and my legs quivered, as I awaited the pain only she could deliver. Revenge is still sought and she's ready to settle the score. To her, this world is spoiled, and rotten to the core.
(She picked us off one at a time... "An eye for an eye leaves the whole world blind.")

On bare feet over the hot coals, she begins to dance, to the beats of the pounding drums. Separating body from soul, she falls into a trance, before the loa comes...

She made a wax figure of me, burning it until it melts, like a baptism by incantation. Now I am just a toy in her hand, with every action felt, a puppet to her strings...now I'm just her pin cushion.

She wants me to walk the plank, wants my head on a platter, because she holds me responsible. Now I'm tortured by the faint sounds of shovelled earth, after witnessing my own funeral.

She gave me an ointment, but I don't know its composition. I'm starting to yield under its influence, like a lake of truth, in a pint of poison. There was no potion to revive me, and I heard the doctor pronounce me dead. Yet somehow I am aware of my weeping daughter beside my deathbed.

She buried me alive in a shallow grave, with her little dolls and shrunken heads. I'm becoming her slave... I'm becoming one of the undead. I'm stigmatic, carve a cross into my footsteps or shoot my picture with an arrow. I'm catatonic, without character or will, just awaiting the death blow.

She hears the pounding drums, as the ritual is nearly complete. She is possessed by their rhythm, cringing with every beat.

Consecrated in the fumes of Saturn, she sticks the pins in me. Pricking them into my member, she gets water, before placing my hands where my legs should be. Sweet as honey, but bitter as bile, champagne in four corners of the square... She pours salt on the pigeon's heart, and fills its nest with my hair. (The plate needs the spoon and the spoon needs the plate)

I'm just the mannequin in her window, she's not able to part with yet, so blindingly pristine...I'm just the mannequin in her window, and she's my ventriloquist, when I'm nothing more than prosthetics and cosmetics, groomed with feminine hygiene. I'm made of clay, stuffed on her mantle, knowing that someday, I will be sacrificed to her idol...

-Denny Noland "Draven" From my song "Pin Cushion"

Written in 1998-1999   Copyright 2015

After that massive purge between the two clubs, there were a few new faces and the return of some old ones that rounded out that void in my club. We had gained Punky as a bartender, and "Suzanne" as our new waitress. I had been a fan of Suzanne since I met her years ago as a customer and was delighted to be working with her at last. I had a serious crush on her back then but because she was not only married, but married to a guy I had developed a friendship with over the years, I considered her off limits. However, that didn't stop her husband from playfully insinuating that I would do his wife if I ever got the opportunity, which I could never honestly deny even though I did try.

We also added a new bouncer named "Jackson" since Adam was no longer with us. He was actually bigger than I was as well, which prompted Bear to come up to both of us and say, "I wish I had a camera...just look at us. This is what bouncers are supposed to look like. We can handle anything they throw at us." Bear, although a professional kickboxer and wrestler, seemed to be a little scared when there was a confrontation, which didn't make any sense to me whatsoever. Several times when someone said that they were coming back later to kick his ass after work hours, he would ask me to stay back. I don't know if he was afraid of what they could do to him or vice versa but I was always there just in case...yet nothing ever happened.

A few weeks later, Jackson would bring in his best friend "Homer" into the fold as a bouncer as well. Homer was a great bouncer but was always chasing tail even when he had a girlfriend which put his job in jeopardy. He was also way too aggressive toward the girls, which made them uncomfortable, and that just created a whole new problem. One night, I took him out to Micheal's with me and we ran into one of our new girls "Odyssey." He asked her if she would like to dance and they hit the dance floor as I watched from afar. He just kept trying to grope her the entire time against her wishes and before I could step in and intervene, she was already out the door. I was so pissed off at his actions that I took him back to his car and called it a night.

2
Later that week, Harley brought in one of her friends from Florida who had just got into town. Her

name was "Tristan" and I was very attracted to her so I asked Harley to "put in a good word for me" and ask her if she would be interested in going out with me the following night so I could "show her around town." Tristan had literally just stepped off the plane and already had me asking her out so I was expecting to be turned down…but I wasn't.

    I picked her up at the club early in the evening the next day but didn't know where we were going from there. I hadn't been on an actual date in so long that I had no idea what the hell I was doing. I ended up getting a bottle and taking her to a graveyard on Tellico Lake. It was there that I found out that she was under 21 so she wasn't legally supposed to be drinking. She insisted on it anyway and surprised me with her tolerance level. She had put down as much as I had but was still sober while I was buzzing my ass off. We talked for over an hour about her past including her dancing days in Florida and her experience of going through Hurricane Andrew. She was as fascinating as she was beautiful.

    When we got ready to leave, we realized that we had a slight problem: my truck was stuck in the mud. Realizing that if we didn't get out of there, I was probably going to jail for any number of reasons, I just kept spinning my wheels until we finally broke free. With my heart racing and nerves shattered, we went back to my place. Since she had an interest in UFOs, I put on a documentary and poured her another drink. After it was finished, it was getting late so we headed back to the club. When we pulled up, it dawned on me that I had never even tried to kiss her the entire night so before we got out, I was going to try my luck. I leaned in to kiss her and she planted an amazing, passionate kiss with a lot of tongue on me. This had obviously been building up for hours and she was determined to make it count. I even said to her, "Wow! I should have tried this much sooner." And she replied "Yes, you should have."

We then entered the club and basically went in two opposite directions. She was frustrated with my lack of aggression and I was feeling so embarrassed for showing her how boring my life actually was, that I had already decided to not ask for a second date. We did, however, go to the Waffle House with Adam and a few of the girls after all the clubs had closed, and the night started getting progressively worse if you could imagine that.

We had just arrived and ordered our food, when a couple of drunks sitting at the table across from us started saying vulgar, inappropriate things to the girl sitting beside me. She responded by flashing her tits at them which made the whole situation go from bad to worse. Things quietened down for a brief moment when our food came out, but before I could take my first bite, one of the drunks stood up and staggered over to our table to have a few words with the girls. Adam, who was sitting a few booths down, jumped to their defence and shoved the guy. Before we knew it, the cops were busting through the door and controlling the situation. They grabbed me first, and escorted me out of the restaurant since I was sitting closest to the door even though I hadn't done anything wrong, and the others quickly followed. We were told to never come back or we would be arrested. Still starving, we ended up down at the IHOP in Maryville later on and managed to actually have a meal without incident. Although, Tristan and I worked together for quite a while and became great friends in time, dating each other again was out of the question after all of this.

I did, however, find myself involved with Dakota once again, even after all the shit she put both Dewayne and myself through over the years. It started with a kiss here and there then evolved to full make out sessions in the parking lot. I ended up taking her home one night and she showed her appreciation by performing oral on me the whole way there. Once we reached her place, she asked me to come in and things escalated until we were nearly having sex before she stopped me once more. I suspected that her husband was also there, watching the whole thing from behind a curtain somewhere so I just left. This would be the final scene of this tragic play.

3

Now we come to one of the most controversial and memorable nights in my already intriguing sex life thus far. Bear had invited me to go out on the town with him and his lovely wife. I drove up to his house in Wears Valley that afternoon and we smoked some weed, then had a great workout in the full gym that he had in his basement, before hitting the road. At nightfall, we started out at the Last Chance where we had a few drinks and tipped the girls. Before we moved on to our next destination, we decided to buy a tabletop dance from the hottest girl there, which we all agreed was Lena. She performed like a champion and succeeded in arousing all of us in the process. It was setting the tone for a more elaborate plan that I never saw coming.

Then we went to Micheal's, which was more to my benefit than theirs, even though I thought Bear might hit the dance floor considering that when I was talking about becoming a male stripper, he was more than happy to show me a few moves of his own. I got some dope while I was there but kept it hidden from them just in case they weren't cool with it. I could tell that they weren't comfortable amongst the younger crowd so we wouldn't stick around for very long. As we headed down Kingston Pike, we came up to a sex shop called "The West Knox News" that caught their eye. They just had to stop and have a look. They ended up grabbing every "swingers" brochure they could find. By this time, Bear was fucking wasted and wanted to take the party back to his place so he relinquished his keys to the wife and we headed back out of town.

When we got back to Wears Valley, Bear wanted to pass out so I helped him to bed. As I was leaving the room to give him and his wife some privacy, I overheard a brief conversation between them where she asked him a question about something and he replied, "Do whatever you want. I don't care." I thought nothing of it and decided to crash out on the couch near the fireplace. I was just about to fall asleep when I heard someone throwing wood on the fire and using the poker to get it going. I could barely see the outline of a woman wearing next to nothing squatting down in the floor. It was Bear's wife wearing only a pair of panties. She turned and jumped on top of me, kissing me passionately. The first thing that ran through my mind was if Bear saw what we were doing, even in his condition, he would probably fucking kill me but I was so into the moment that I didn't want to stop. I remember thinking how beautiful she was without her glasses and how incredible she looked for her age. Her fake breasts and trim stomach made her look like she could have been a supermodel in a previous life. Before I had a chance to put on a condom, I was already inside of her. Bear was indeed a lucky man...and on that night, so was I.

We had been going at it for over an hour when I heard the clicking of the door and the turning of the knob. Bear had come out of the bedroom to take a piss, and to get to the bathroom, he would have to walk past us. Ok, now he was going to kill me with my pants down...great. He looked over at us and watched for a minute, then continued on his way. His wife didn't react at all which made this whole situation become crystal clear. Now I was started to remember Bear and his wife taking girls into the office at work and locking the door. Once Bear had even bragged to me that he had an open marriage and he could have his fun as long as he allowed his wife to have hers. He had always reminded me that my day was coming but I thought he was just kidding. Now I knew that he was dead serious. When he came out of the bathroom, he took a second look and then went back to bed without saying a word.

She was determined to get me off... unaware that that was much easier said than done. We lost track of time and the sun was starting to come up. We could hear the kids stirring upstairs, getting ready for school. Bear came tearing out of his bedroom, "Will you guys just fucking stop? The kids are awake!" he shouted. "What if they came downstairs and saw this? How would *you* explain it to them?" Neither of us could really say anything in our defence, so we just quietly got dressed and joined Bear and the kids upstairs at the breakfast table. That had to be the most uncomfortable room I had ever been in. Bear and his wife were talking to the children like nothing ever happened but only said a couple of words to each other. *No one* was speaking to me at all. It was almost like I had overstayed my welcome, and needed to get the hell out of there and the sooner the better so I obliged.

When I got to work that evening, it was more of the same. I was still getting the silent treatment from Bear which made me think that maybe he did have a problem with me so I was constantly looking over my shoulder waiting for that punch to the face.

This went on for a couple of days before he walked up to me and asked, "So what did you think? I told you I was going to throw her on you one day." I didn't really know what he wanted to hear or what I was expected to say, so I decided to just be honest. "She was incredible. I think I learned a few things that night." He laughed and said, "You owe me." I turned and looked him straight in the eye. "Owe you for what?" I asked. "I didn't ask to be with your wife... she climbed on top of me! I do appreciate the whole experience but I never agreed to return the favour." I couldn't tell if he was just fucking with me or being serious, but he just gave me a cheeky grin and walked away and we never brought that subject up again.

4

Although I was starting to get a few notches under my belt, I still wasn't confident when it came to the ladies. To me, kissing was more intimate than the act of sex and I seemed to enjoy it more. One night, one of our new girls came into the club, with a guy I assumed was her boyfriend, to get some of her belongings out of the dressing room. When she walked up to the barred window, I leaned in to ask her what she was doing there on her night off and she planted a long French kiss on my lips just before walking through the door. This would happen many times over the years with random girls entering or exiting the building but what made this time unique was the fact that every guy in the club wanted her and she was untouchable. She had already shot down everyone who had made advances toward her and I was the one that got a kiss. It made the other guys take me serious for once.

Adam was so envious and jealous when he heard. He thought she was the sexiest girl on the roster outside of Lena and called me a "lucky bastard" for getting to "swap spit" with such a goddess. He said, "Dude, you may not see it, but many of the girls like you. You are fully capable of getting any girl you want out of that place. I've known it all along. Just remember, they're not all like Justice, so quit letting one bad experience ruin it for everyone else." I had never looked at it that way before, partly because everyone I was associated it were in it for themselves and cock-blocked me every chance they got. That speech was something that I needed to hear because I had become my own worst enemy the past few months and never saw the forest for the trees. There was a new king that was about to be crowned and his queen had already taken notice even if her closest allies didn't even know it at the time. In the next few weeks, I was going to transform from a mere mortal to a god in the eyes of many practically overnight but a catastrophe had to occur first... one that would change my whole perspective on everything.

5

It was mid-afternoon when I heard the news. I've always known that selling dope in the workplace carried a high degree of risk and eventually you will get caught...it was just a matter of time. Someone called to warn me before I headed into work that Adam had been fired for dealing at the 2000 club, but they weren't sure if the rat who told on him knew about me or not so prepare myself for the worst. I had no way of finding this information out until I walked through that door later in the evening and I was scared to death. I remember thinking that this must be what it feels like when a criminal is only seconds away from the verdict on whether he walks free or goes to prison. For some reason, I didn't want to call Adam to ask him the full story, or if I was about to share the same fate as he did. I would rather just face the music or the firing squad when the time came.

    I walked in that day without a trace of coke on me, just in case they wanted to search my things. I tried my best to act normal but the sight of Gene, James, Tommy, and Bear sitting at the end of the bar giving me "the thousand- yard stare" when I entered the building, intimidated the hell out of me. Whether my name was mentioned or not, they all knew that I was involved somehow and they were determined to interrogate me until they got a confession. I was certain that they had no proof, even if I did nearly get caught once by one of Gene's minions doing an exchange in the hall but she didn't see what was in my hand even if she had a pretty good idea. I knew that she was the likely candidate if accusations started to fly, and I was prepared to make her life a living hell if that was the case. I wasn't going to incriminate myself by admitting to anything even if they had seen me do it themselves and had the evidence on film or sitting on top of the bar. I stood firm and answered all their questions, denying any involvement with any of it. I had prevailed but was left with the warning that they would be keeping a closer eye on me in the future so I had better keep my nose clean or I would be the next one to go. I heeded that warning…

    It would be about a week before I saw Adam again. I went over to his place to let him know that although I would still buy shit from him and help cut and split the product, my days of selling were over. He didn't take the news well, especially after he had just split from the Georgia peach that was two timing him named "Angelina," and wasn't happy about the quality of his most recent shipment. He insisted that I sample it with him so I pulled up a chair and we did a few lines. I honestly didn't know what he was talking about. I mean it wasn't the best I ever had, but to me, it was no different from anything else that we had been selling over the last few months. However, I couldn't convince him of that. The more he did, the madder he got, until he was in a fit of rage ready to go out to west Knoxville and kick someone's ass. Luckily, one of our new part time bouncers named "BJ" came over to visit. BJ was an impressionable 18 year old kid who didn't do drugs but was willing to participate in whatever it took to be part of the team. He was like a combination of Adam and me, thrown into a blender. He had piercings like me with a shaved head and big stature like Adam. His brother "Doyle" also got involved with us and probably *still* tells the story about the time he called me up to replenish his supply and I was in the middle of having sex. I made all the arrangements over the phone while still rooting whichever girl it was without losing focus on either task. From that moment on, he called me one of the coolest guys he's ever met. I knew that people like Doyle wouldn't admire me near as much and others like Star and Martin wasn't going to be coming around near as often once I got out of dealing but I was over it. I was ready to pass the torch to someone else. My decision was final.

    Adam, however, wasn't willing to let me ride off into the sunset so easily. Once he reached his breaking point, he had the tenacity to ask me to ride with him downtown to either intimidate or "rough up" the guy who supposably fucked him over but I refused. "Man, I'm out…that means everything" I said. Before he could respond, BJ stepped up and volunteered to go instead, leaving me to hold the fort until they got back. Everything worked out without anyone getting hurt and I was finally set free…just in the nick of time too.

I would only see Adam a handful of times after that. I heard that he got a job as a driver at a local vitamin depot and I even saw him once on the road in his truck but I wanted to sever those ties. It was one of the smartest moves I ever made. Only a few weeks later, the guy who rode up to New York with him got busted and started naming other people to reduce his sentence. Adam was arrested soon after, and started giving out even more names... making himself a marked man. Once he got out on bail, one of his steroid partners nearly beat him to death as soon as he found him. He was dead to everyone in that town as far as the underworld was concerned. He lost every friend that he ever had and would never be able to regain their trust. He had gone from being somebody to becoming nothing more than a ghost in the span of only a couple of weeks.

It was a scary time to say the least. There was a narcotics officer who had started camping out across the street from my house. Now I was not only being watched at work, but at home as well. It wouldn't be long until he started pulling me over every time I left the house, especially when I drove the Thunderbird, and demanding to search my vehicle. He never found anything since I was now only transporting my own stash late at night. However, I did get pulled over one evening by a different cop on my way home from the club. I had just taken a large bump of coke and still had the baggie sitting open on my console when I saw the flashing lights. I didn't have time to hide it before they were close enough to see what I was doing so I just left it there and tried to keep cool. I just casually pulled off the road onto someone's driveway and patiently waited until the beautiful young female cop walked up to my window. She shined her flashlight on my face and politely asked for my license and registration. In the meantime, two other cruisers also pulled up but they didn't approach my car...they just open their doors, squatted down behind them, and held me at gunpoint. Seeing this, I asked the lady why were they pointing guns at me if this was just a routine traffic stop and she replied "When I ran your plates, it came up that this is a stolen vehicle." The first thing that I could think to say to that was "Honestly, if I wanted to steal a car, I wouldn't steal a piece of shit like this." She busted out laughing, which relaxed me enough to playfully flirt with her. This tactic usually doesn't bring success for most people, but on this particular occasion it worked like a charm as she was eating it up, nearly blushing. This distraction allowed me to hide a gram of cocaine in plain sight and keep her from noticing that I was actually quite drunk at the time as well. After everything checked out and I was free to go, I couldn't believe that I had done it again. As I watched them all pull out, I looked in the mirror at my face and was horrified by what I saw. On the right side of my face, there was a trail of cocaine that ran from my nostril down to my chin. It was there the entire time. Since she only shined her torch on my left side and I never turned my head, she never saw the right side of my face. I wiped my face clean and sobered up pretty quick before heading back towards home.

    Not even a week later, I had another encounter with that same asshole who had been stalking me for nearly a month. He was sitting in the parking lot across the road facing my house, just waiting for me to leave to go somewhere. When I pulled out onto the highway to go to the gym, he started tailing me as he always did, but I wasn't in the fucking mood on that day to put up with his bullshit. I tried to just casually hide among the traffic but he nearly caused a couple of accidents to stay behind me. He literally followed me all the way into town, which was a distance of several miles, before pulling me over once again. That just fuelled my anger even more. I pulled into the parking lot of an old, abandoned building and watched in my rear view mirror as he stepped out of his car, adjusted his pants, and came strutting up toward my car. I just fucking lost it. I jumped out of my car and got into his face before he even got half way up to my vehicle. "What is your fucking problem?" I asked. He was speechless. "You know, you have searched my car several times and you have never found anything. I'll let you search it one more time but if you don't find anything again, and I can tell you right now that you won't, I'm going to file harassment charges against you." Once I said that, the cockiness and arrogance disappeared, and he became very apologetic all of a sudden. "Look, that won't be necessary. I was just told that you were moving narcotics from Knoxville into Blount County on a daily basis but maybe my information was wrong. I won't bother you again" and he kept his word.

Over a period of time, I had made friends with a state trooper who used to come into the club. I never learned his real name but he had an Opie Taylor look about him so I secretly called him "Mayberry." One night when I was working the door, I sneaked outside and went to my car between customers to chop up a few lines for a quick fix. I had a look around before I got out the mirror and the coast seemed to be clear. I cut out three lines in my seat and folded up a dollar bill to snort them with. I did them all at once without incident but when I laid my head back and did a massive inhale, I saw two figures approaching from the side of the building. I knew that only cops parked back there to keep their cruisers out of sight from customers so I was probably fucked. As the two figures got closer, I saw the trademark trooper hats which verified my fears. They had seen what I was doing so there was no point in stopping then. I heard one of them ask the other "Shouldn't we go over there and check him out?" Then I heard a familiar voice reply "No, he's cool. It's all good." It was Mayberry and he saved my ass from going to jail once again. Between this incident and all the others over the past month, I was starting to consider getting clean before my luck ran out.

Been in the darkest hole, within its grim confines, been the blackest soul, in the jaws of a lion…been on the highest mountains, been where eagles dare, been on every island on the oceans, been to the dragon's lair…

When it was lightning, I've jumped into the shower. I've cut the red wire without shutting off the power. I've been on top of a skyscraper during an earthquake, smoked a cigarette in bed before I was fully awake.

When there was a tornado, I've taken cover in a trailer park. I've used the Lord's name in vain under a steeple. I've watched scary movies in the dark, and gave speeches in front of thousands of people.

I've always lived life in the fast lane, like a biker on his Harley, with no speed limits or stop signs, then wrapped my car around a pole or tree, before I crossed the finish line. "The dead have highways, they have cities too. When the saints come marching in, let them walk a mile in my shoes.

Finally it draws to its apparent conclusion, which has taken a lifetime to decipher. After making the proper calculations, we have found a common denominator. I'm sending this message to the next generation: "You may feel closer to God, feel like His chosen one, but remember, we've all driven endless miles with the devil riding shotgun."

Like taking precedence over all claims of men and religion, "faith without works is dead." Like a whirlwind of human philosophy, and perverted revelations, and "hitting the proverbial nail on the head."

I've always gotten pleasure from doing what was wrong…always on the outside looking in, never finding where I belong. I'm never really satisfied…always thinking that the grass must be greener on the other side. I'm sure that once I've died, my wings will surely be denied. I've went the distance many years ago. If you want to stroll down memory lane, I'm going to pass. This is my motto: "If you ain't the lead dog, your head is in someone's ass."

One day while my extremities were impaired, the cops pulled me over and arrested me. After years of meddling in my affairs, I was put on trial for crimes against humanity. They sealed my connections and made racial slurs, putting the weight of the city on my shoulders. And her I am, here I stand, giving all you pigs the finger. I know no colour or creed, and its time I raised my flag. I don't discriminate, I hate everyone equally, let them all die for the colour of my rag.

When you really need them, you can never find a cop. They are either cornholing some drunk or raiding the nearest donut shop. Are they going to reprimand when I try to speak my peace or will you read in the paper about a defenceless man getting taken down by the local police? I ask of you only one thing: look at all the evidence, before you reach a verdict, cause I don't want any misconceptions. Believe in the innocence of your client, even if you know you are being blinded by deception. Just throw the book at me, put an

endangered species on death row. Send me to the chamber, so I can meet my maker, it's how I deserve to go…
 -Denny Noland "Draven" From my song "Silent Testimony"
 Written in 1998-1999
Copyright 2015

6

Just when I thought that my life was getting back to normal, I started having problems with my kidneys again. One night at the club, I started getting severe pain in my lower back and felt like my bladder was going to explode. When I went to take a piss, all that came out was a stream of blood. Knowing what I know now, it was probably kidney stones but whatever it was, it frightened me enough to consider getting off the dope. Between that and my recent run-ins with law enforcement made it a much easier decision to make. I couldn't stop thinking about all those nights that I used to sit at my kitchen table with enough cocaine to probably get me put away for the remaining years of my life, and the cops outside watching every move I made, just waiting for either a warrant or permission to kick down my door. It could have happened at any given moment. I was *that* close…and it made want to rethink my life and possibly go straight for a change.

I think Bear knew what was going on but chose to help me instead of lecturing me. He gave me some Goldenseal and told me that it would flush out any toxins that are in my body within a couple of days. Just as he had said, I was feeling like a new man by the end of the week and I used this to my advantage by getting off the cocaine. This was the first time that I was thinking clearly without drugs in my system in several years. I hit the gym even harder than I was before, using my newfound sobriety as motivation. It was a fresh start and being clean gave me a new lease on life.

With drugs out of the picture, sex became my new obsession. Up till now, I thought I had been very selective about who I slept with and was confident that I knew what the exact number of women that I have bedded was. Then I realized that I had forgotten a few one night stands along the way. On more than one occasion, I would run into a girl either at a club or somewhere else around town that I didn't recognize who would approach me and usually say something like "I have seen you since that night we slept together. How have you been? Why didn't you ever call?" Most of the time, I would pretend that I remembered just to keep from hurting their feelings, but other times when I was seriously having doubts, I would ask them a series of questions that would prove that they didn't have me confused with somebody else. They always passed the test with flying colours. They would give me directions to my house, describe how it was decorated, and even tell me intimate details about my body that only someone who had seen me naked would know. I had obviously been a much busier boy that I had originally thought. What I couldn't understand was how I had completely forgotten so many significant events in my life and even to this day, I still have amnesia and can't remember any of them. Drugs and alcohol had obviously not only taken a toll on me physically, but mentally as well.

Then on one fateful night, when a new girl named "Diamond", ran the gauntlet with almost all the male staff including me, it flushed out a girl who I would have never suspected would have the hots for me. Since all the ladies hated Diamond so much that they would hold her down and burn her with cigarettes, the fact that I would root her made this unacceptable, even unbearable, for this girl to comprehend. After I slept with her and returned to my desk, I saw Lena walking with purpose in my direction. What would come out of her mouth was something that I wasn't expecting, even in my wildest dreams. "You know, I can't have sex with you now that you've been with *her*." I was speechless and must have had a stunned look on my face because after Lena saw my reaction, she gave me a cheeky grin. All I could say was "But…" She interrupted, "Its ok, I've went through a few stages in my life when I've been a bit of a slut myself. I will forgive you…this time!" The stage was set. It was 1999 and we were quickly approaching the new millennium, and I was about to face "the storm of the century."

-DJN

CHAPTER XI - "STORMCHILD PART II"

1999

Not since I was a teenager, have I liked a girl this much. The problem was that everyone knew that she was in a long term relationship with her live in boyfriend and that they shared a house with her young daughter from a previous marriage. Even if she decided that she wanted to be with me, things were going to get complicated. It wasn't going to be easy for the little girl to adapt to a new guy in her mother's life and the different surroundings that came along with it. Then there was the fact I didn't really like kids and my history of being in relationships with single mothers have all ended badly. I took all these things into consideration at first, and didn't fall under her spell right away, but there is only so much that a man can take when such a beautiful woman was pouring it on like she was.

Her constant flirting made her irresistible and I couldn't help but retaliate. After just a few days, she had broken me down and I couldn't stop thinking about her. One night, while she was sitting at the bar talking to one of her regular customers, I just couldn't take it anymore. When I went up to the bar to get a refill, she started her usual flirting so I leaned in for a kiss, to see if she would allow it or not, and she surprised me by not only letting me kiss her, but doing so in front of her customer and everyone else who just happened to be in the club that night. We were pretty much in the middle of the room so anyone looking in our general direction would have seen us. The kiss itself was incredible and left me wanting more. I apologized afterwards because I knew that it was inappropriate, but she stopped me in my tracks. "There's nothing to be sorry about. We have amazing chemistry. If I didn't want it, it wouldn't have happened. *I* don't regret it, do *you?*" I told her that I didn't and she replied, "There's more where that came from. I've got a feeling that we're going to have a lot of fun together this summer." Then she got up and went to the dressing room. I sat there for a minute, thinking about that delicious kiss that I could still taste on my lips, then threw my clipboard down on the bar and followed her to the back. I walked straight into the dressing room, which I had hoped was empty, but was actually filled with a majority of the other dancers putting on their makeup or costumes and saw Lena standing in front of the mirror in the back corner where she always got ready. I walked straight through the crowd and right up to her. She turned around with a seductive look in her eyes and a sexy smirk on her face. I grabbed her, pinned her against the wall, and gave her a proper kiss with lots of tongue. It was so passionate that we forgot where we actually were for a couple of minutes until we turned around and there was probably twenty girls staring back at us. Star was one of them and she was smiling from ear to ear. "You two are so fucking hot…"she said before exiting onto the main floor. However, the rest of the room was in total silence… they were either both happy and excited about what they had just witnessed or was in total shock. Most of them had either met Lena's boyfriend at some point, or knew him quite well. The funny part was that there were quite a few of them who couldn't stand him and thought he was a total asshole. They were the ones who were overjoyed by what they just saw. Maybe Lena was finally going to listen and get rid of this jerk who took her for granted. It was on…and someone was inevitable going to get hurt when it was over. I was just praying that it wasn't going to be me.

At closing time, I walked all the girls out while Lena waited in her car so we could talk and make out some more to end the night on a positive note. When everyone else had cleared out, we sat in her car making out passionately until she stopped and reached into her purse for something. She pulled out a little baggie of cocaine and asked me if I wanted a bump. In her defence, she didn't know that I was trying to break the habit. It would have been extremely difficult to refuse in any situation but at that particular place and time, it was fucking impossible. She poured a sizable bump on her fingernail and I snorted it, kissing my few weeks of sobriety goodbye.

We would then talk for nearly an hour about what had just developed between us and the trials that lie ahead. Obviously, we couldn't be seen together outside of work and I wasn't allowed to call her at certain hours. She also had to be home within a particular timeframe so her boyfriend didn't get suspicious. She did, however, claim me as her own and asked me to not see other people, which I felt wasn't really fair considering *her* situation. I also wasn't supposed to say anything about us in front of select people so our affair wouldn't get back to her partner. I knew that I shouldn't be doing this but she was already holding my leash and had me whipped before we ever even had sex. Before we parted ways, she gave me what was left of her cocaine, as she would every night before heading home. She only partied at the club and led an entirely different personal life and I respected the hell out of her for that. Her willpower to just stop on a whim was off the charts and I could only wish that I was capable of doing the same but I knew better. Of course, I would be at the club on my nights off to not only see her, but to bring her cocaine and a bottle of Sutter Home wine as well. This would put her in the mood to fool around once she got off work. I was her obedient pet, and would have done *anything* to make her happy.

2

The club was going through another metamorphosis yet again. Bear was leaving once more and Punky was declared the new manager. We would also bring in a couple of people that ironically knew Lena quite well. One was her best friend from her old club, "Sika", and a bartender named "Jayden" who not only used to date Sika, but had been one of Lena's regular customers and closest friends for years. Both would provide me with useful information about Lena's past and give me an idea of what I was in store for in the future and the forecast wasn't good. Although, they loved her to death, they warned me that when she's finished with someone, they are never the same again. Our backup DJ, Lars, echoed that statement when he told me about one of her exes, who he watched go from a notorious womanizer, to getting hurt so badly by Lena that he couldn't even be in the same room as her without breaking down into tears. "This thing you're doing, being the other man, is playing with fire and you're definitely going to get burned." he warned. I don't know why I even bothered to ask them anything because I wasn't listening to a word they said unless it was something that I wanted to hear.

I would spend a lot of time getting to know Sika, thinking that maybe she could help me with my quest for Lena's heart. We would do coke together and talk about strategy over breakfast. When we worked together, especially on nights when Lena wasn't there, I would go up and tip her and she would always do the same routine. She would walk up to me and lick her lips while opening her robe. She would proceed to kneel down and kiss me square on the lips right in front of everyone. I was always worried that her actions would get back to Lena and create problems so I broke down and told her about them myself. She seemed to find it more funny than upsetting, which was a relief. Sika would also take me over to her and Lena's personal drug dealer's house to get some dope on several occasions but I would always have to wait in the car since he didn't know me. Sometimes it really bothered me that I couldn't reveal myself to her *whole* world, instead of just bits and pieces of it.

    One night while Tristan was teasing me about Lena, and I was feeling like I was on cloud nine, I got word that Lena's boyfriend was picking her up after work since her car was in the shop. I had never seen this kid face to face before and Lena wanted to keep it that way. At the end of the night, he was late of course and Lena was getting frustrated. She had tried to call several times and he wasn't answering so she was stranded. I offered to take her home as a last resort and she was just about ready to get into my truck, when he came tearing down the parking lot. As soon as he pulled up, Lena yanked the door open and threw her bag inside. She got in before I had a chance to see what he looked like but I heard him ask her who the "big goon" was that was glaring at him when he arrived. That was all I heard but that was enough. I wanted to punch him right then and there. When I asked her about it the next day, she defended him by saying that if she had been in his shoes, she would have probably said the same thing. That didn't help his case at all. He disrespected me in my house, now it was my turn to retaliate.

The next day, Jayden and I drove out to the cigar shop that Lena's boyfriend worked at to size this guy up. We walked in and pretended to be looking at different cigars but the kid recognized us and watched us like a hawk. If looks could kill, we would have died right then and there. I must say that I wasn't impressed by him at all. He looked just like any other punk that I brutalize on a nightly basis. I was contemplating on whether to say something to him or not but Jayden, who had a background in law enforcement, advised me to just walk away. I had already sent my message loud and clear. Now he knew that I obviously had a problem with him and I knew where he worked…he just didn't know *why* I had a problem with him. When I got to work that night, Lena confronted me and asked me if I had gone into the cigar shop earlier in the day. I told her the truth. "I was looking to buy a cigar." I joked. She wasn't buying that. "Why would you go in there while he was working? What were you hoping to accomplish?" Before I could answer she interrupted, "I think he knows. Someone must have told him something. He's been asking me a lot of questions about you ever since he saw you at the club that night. And then you do *this*? What the hell were you thinking? Do you even consider the repercussions before you act? Do you want to see me and my little girl thrown out on the streets? Don't ever do something like that again or we're over!" Lesson learned.

She didn't speak to me for most of the night and that drove me crazy. When it got to the end of the night, I wasn't going to let her leave without giving me a goodbye kiss and I was determined to give her one that would rock her world. As she passed through the lobby to get to her car, I grabbed her and pinned her against the wall and gave her one of the most passionate kisses she has probably ever had in her life. The rest of the staff and ladies had all went past before our lips and tongues finally detached. I wanted to take her right then and there and she was more than willing to give it to me. The only reason why we hadn't made love yet was because we had nowhere to do it. I wanted it to be special. She deserved better than the backseat of a car or a seedy motel. I couldn't take her back to my place because it was too far away and we couldn't go to her place for obvious reasons so we were going to have to settle for the next best thing: the club itself. Hell, I felt comfortable enough to have sex with other girls there so why not Lena? I asked Tommy, who just happened to be training Punky that night, if I could have the security code to the alarm system and the keys to lock up. Much to my surprise, he agreed without a second thought. I think he didn't want to be the one who kept us from being together. It's been a long time coming...no pun intended.

Once Tommy and Punky left the building, we were all alone. There was a couch just inside the security door and Lena pulled me down on it as she kissed me. We got undressed while we made out but I pulled back so I could go down on her. She tasted as good as I thought she would, if not better. After only a few minutes, she pushed my head away and told me that she wanted me inside of her. I pulled out a condom, even though I didn't want to, and put it on before I entered her. I knew she wouldn't touch *me* without protection because I had "been around." She had said that on several occasions. Once I penetrated her, she moaned like it was the end of the world which made it sound rehearsed. She was also whispering stuff in my ear like "You feel so good" and "I've wanted you for so long" which was turning me on more than I can even put into words. This was, without a doubt, the first time I had ever made love to a woman. There was a difference between this experience and all the others. We went at it for quite a while and would have kept going had Lena not looked down at her watch. It was getting late and she had to get home, putting an end to a night that neither of us will ever forget.

The next day, when I arrived at the club, I was still smiling...until I saw James. "So, you had a little fun last night I hear." I nodded my head. "Where did you put your used condom when you finished?" I looked at him puzzled, wondering where he was going with this. "I'll answer that for you. You put it on top of a table that was sitting beside the couch you obviously used last night. I guess you didn't notice that I had just painted the damn thing yesterday and left it to dry overnight. I came in today and had to pry the fucking rubber off of it which ruined the paint job. Look, I like to play around a little too but clean up after yourself next time and watch where you put things." I apologized and told him that I would more careful next time. This day wasn't starting as well as I had hoped.

On the flip side, Lena was following me around like a lovesick puppy all night. Every time I turned around, she was there in her cute little schoolgirl outfit, with a cigarette in one hand and an alcoholic beverage in the other with a big grin on her face. I loved it but Gene had also noticed that we were providing a distraction for each other and wasn't happy about it at all. I didn't want her to stop chasing me but I knew that Gene would separate us if it became a problem and neither of us wanted that to happen. Unfortunately, she ignored my warnings and kept doing it anyway, putting me in harm's way. Gene would always get rid of a bartender or a bouncer before he would ever consider losing one of his girls. Lena made him money...I costed him money. Who do you think the sacrificial lamb was going to be? The Last Chance 2000 had already started calling my name. It was only a matter of time...

3

Now that we had been intimate, Lena trusted me enough to introduce me to her drug dealers. Their names were "Nathan" and "Connor" and I had seen them in a club numerous times but thought they were just a couple of Lena's regular customers. I liked them both and would usually talk about professional wrestling with them for hours. I think that they knew that there was something going on between Lena and me but I'm not sure if they knew the extent of it. Lena would go over to Nathan's house a couple of times a week to buy her coke and I would sometimes go over there to party but we were never there at the same time to avoid exposure. It was tearing me apart inside that there were so many rules and restrictions between us but I just learned to live with it. I would often confide in both Nathan and Connor about Lena, partially to find out what they knew about her relationship... whether she was actually happy with her boyfriend or was she considering a split without directly telling them why I wanted to know. I had befriended everyone that I knew she was close to, hoping that it would pay off somewhere down the road. Sometimes I felt like it might be working, and other times I didn't but I was willing to do *anything* to show her how much I cared for her.

I almost felt sorry for my own friends who had to listen to me talk about Lena for hours on end... especially Star and Martin. They had heard her name brought up so many times that they were getting sick of it. Martin was always very encouraging and supportive but Star, on the other hand, was never convinced that I ever had a fighting chance. It was almost like she knew something that I didn't. I thought some of that might be due to the fact that she had unresolved issues with me that had been building up inside of her for the past few months and she had started resenting me a little since then. It started after a night of partying at Adam's house only weeks before he got busted. She had just dropped me off somewhere and to show her my appreciation, I told her that I loved her and gave her a tender kiss on the lips. I didn't mean anything by it other than a friendly gesture, but it seemed to have been much more than that to her. When I saw her that night at work, she pulled me to the side and said "I've been thinking a lot about that kiss…" and that was all she got out before I cut her off and walked away. I didn't like where this was all going and left her standing there before she had a chance to finish her sentence. I was hoping that this was where all of the negativity was coming from but I've been wrong before. I just prayed that this wasn't one of those instances.

    When doubts started getting to me, Lena would do something to make me start second guessing myself. One example of this was when Tommy had a skeleton crew one busy Saturday night and Gene sent me over to help him out. As soon as Lena heard the news, she was devastated. "I don't want you to go!" she screamed. "There's going to be a lot of girls that are going to be hitting on you and you might give in to temptation. You are mine…remember that." After hearing those insecurities, I knew that she must have some feelings for me, whether she wanted to admit it or not, otherwise she wouldn't care. Right before I left, she made one last plea for me not to cheat on her, but that wouldn't be enough to stop me. The way I saw it, she was cheating on me every fucking time she went home to *him* and it was time for me to dish out some payback.

    I had only been there for a few minutes before I had already talked one of the girls into providing me with alcohol. Within an hour or so, I was very intoxicated and flirting with the beautiful young waitress on duty that night. No one said a damn word to me about anything because they knew better. I was in the right state of mind to just leave if someone pissed me off and everyone was fully aware of that. By the end of the night, I had my tongue down the waitress's throat in the parking lot but had no intentions of sleeping with her even if I was technically single and had every right to do so. As I was leaving, she asked me if she was ever going to see me again and I replied, "Probably not." Since we closed earlier than the main club, I drove across town to catch Lena before she headed home. She was surprised and ecstatic to see me walk through that door. She ran straight up to me to give me a hug and a kiss, not caring who saw us. Then she said "Tell me you didn't touch another girl while you over there tonight." And I replied "Of course not, baby. I am *yours* right?" She smiled and gave me another kiss. "Will you take me somewhere so we can talk in private after we close?" she asked. "*Anything* for you sweetie…" I replied. "Two can play this game." I thought to myself.

    At last call, she grabbed my hand and took me to the VIP room to give me a dance that I'm pretty sure was illegal. It was so sexual that if a cop saw it, the club would have been shut down. When the song ended, she sat back on my lap and whispered in my ear "That dance turned me on so much that I'm actually wet." I told her that I didn't believe her, so she reached between her legs and wiped some of it on her finger, then rubbed it across my lips. "Now do you believe me?" she asked, just before getting up and heading to the back to get changed. I didn't know what we were going to do now that her shift was over but I was definitely looking forward to it.

With nowhere to go, we ended up in the parking lot of the supermarket just down the road from the club. We made out and talked for about an hour about our future. We covered everything from how much we liked each other to where she and her daughter were going to go once she broke up with her boyfriend. This was the first time that she had actually admitted to me that she was seriously considering leaving him. I was so close to having Lena as my girl that I could taste it and that alone made me happier than I had been in a very long time, maybe ever. We were also both incredibly aroused but couldn't really do anything about it. She did start rubbing between my legs, which led to her unzipping my pants like she was about to perform oral sex on me but I stopped her in her tracks. I felt like it was both demeaning and disrespectful to allow her to go down on me in her car whether she wanted to or not. "Not here." I said. "There will be plenty of time for that later." We shared one last kiss before she took me back to my truck.

The following week, while we were fooling around at Lena's car in an otherwise empty parking lot, a group of guys pulled in very slowly and made a circle around us. "We're closed!" I yelled out. Lena was sitting on the hood of her car with her arms and legs wrapped around me literally shaking. As they got near one of the guys looked at Lena and said, "You sure have a pretty girlfriend." I replied "I know, now get the fuck out of here and leave us alone!" I was so angry that I wasn't the least bit concerned about what they might do. I was willing to take them all on to protect my girl, and they were going to have to kill me to get to her. I knew that although I probably couldn't win, I was going to at the very least, take a couple of them down with me. They must have known that because they weren't interested in taking me on. They just told us to have a nice night and left. Lena looked up at me with those big brown eyes and said, "I feel so safe when I'm with you." I just smiled at her and said, "If you were *really* my girl, you could feel that way all the time." She just rolled her eyes and said, "I know that. Just be patient with me and it may happen someday…very soon." I know that I would often go a little overboard protecting her, especially when I would thrash some poor guy for touching her, often times without a warning, but that was just how it was and she accepted that.

    Sometimes she would come up to me and say something like "Do you see those two old guys sitting over there? Can you believe that they offered to pay me $1000 to come up to their room at the Hilton after work for a private party…" that really got to me. I knew that they were more interested in trying to have sex with her than watching her dance and I was already starting to understand why so many of the girls actually *hated* men and became lesbians. Hell, if I was one of them, I would probably be gay too. We would see men behaving at their very worst every night of the week and that gave all of us a bad name. I always tried to say that I was different, but everyone knew better. Gene always told me that he would rather just come out and ask a girl how much it would cost him to have sex with her, than waste time spending even more money buying her roses and taking her out to dinner. "You get her out of your system and you move on to the next one. Let her husband or boyfriend spend the holidays with her, while you do whatever you want." I knew that he was right and that's how I should have looked at Lena but it was easier said than done.

4

We were now in the middle of summer and Gene decided to bring back a couple of familiar faces to draw larger crowds once more. Raquel Darringer was the first and this time she brought her boyfriend with her as well. He was a cool guy and quite a character to say the least. Everything ran like clockwork all week until her final show that Saturday night. Two rednecks, who I called "Dumb and Dumber" decided to make their appearance and in typical fashion got too drunk and got thrown out for grabbing Raquel while she was on stage. Once we got outside with them, they started talking shit like they always did but before we could re-enter the building, Raquel's boyfriend had already joined us holding the baseball bat that we kept at the door in his hands. He stood behind us running his mouth as well, while swinging that bat around like he was Babe Ruth. We made him go back inside because he was making everything worse and we didn't want him getting hurt if things started getting out of hand. Once we got him out of the mix, it started cooling off, allowing all of us to finally come back inside and watch the security camera to see if they were going to leave...no such luck. They walked back up to the front door with their *own* baseball bat and started hitting the door with it. That only lasted for a couple of minutes before they got in their car and left. Luckily, no one came through that door while they were out there, or they could have been seriously hurt. I used to say that they were like herpes, they might lie dormant for a while but they always came back. We all knew that we hadn't seen the last of them.

A couple of weeks later, Mallesia Renee was back with us. Before she had even been picked up at the airport, Gene told me that I was solely responsible for looking after her the entire week. That meant that once she arrived at the club, I was to stay by her side anywhere she went except for the bathroom. We would be working *very* closely together which wouldn't go over well with Lena. I think that was probably Gene's intentions by putting us together. He usually didn't care who I was involved with as long as it didn't affect my job and it wasn't on display for customers to see. Lena had already broken the first rule and she was well on her way to breaking the second one.

The proverbial final nail in the coffin was going to happen later that week. Although we were definitely attracted to each other, Mallesia and I had remained professional the entire time and not acted on it. During one of her final performances, while I was standing behind her on the stage to make sure that the gathering crowd didn't touch her, she leaned back to ask me if I wanted to do a live sex act on stage. I told her that I didn't think Gene would like that very much and she replied, "We could make *a lot* of money." I was shocked that she would suggest such a thing when there were so many people that were within hearing distance, and to be honest, I still don't know what a live sex act even implies. Unfortunately, both Lena and Sika were among the crowd that heard the whole conversation. They just happened to be standing near the stage to tip her as it happened. Their smiles turned to rage and as soon as Mallesia exited the stage, they were waiting for her. I just stood there and watched as two gorgeous women had a heated discussion about me and my biggest concern was the Gene was also watching it all go down. Had a punch been thrown, I wouldn't have to worry about being sent to Clinton Highway, I would be going home. When I saw Mallesia in the dressing room afterwards, I asked her what Lena said to her and she replied, "She told me that you were her man and was off limits. She warned be that I had better keep my hands off you." Then I asked her what she said and she replied "I told her that I was sorry...I didn't know. Then I told her that she was one lucky girl and that she had great taste in men." I thought to myself "I wonder if she saw Lena's real boyfriend if she would still feel the same way?" but I wasn't about to go there. When I walked back out on the main floor, I got a hero's welcome. Guys were doing the "we're not worthy" bow and patting me on the back while saying things like "You da man!" Everyone had figured out what happened and for one night at least, I felt like a celebrity.

    Mallesia and I were on our best behaviour for the rest of the week and on her last night with us she told me that she couldn't do this anymore. She was sick of being on the road and wanted to do something else with her life. Over the past week, we had gotten to know each other quite well and developed a friendship, so I wished her luck with her future endeavours, and told her that it had been a pleasure to work with her over the last few days. I also gave her a hug and said "If I don't ever see you again, please take care of yourself" then gave her a quick kiss on the lips. She replied "Wow! I wasn't expecting that! Thanks for the kiss." Then just before she got into the waiting car and sped away, she said one more thing "Please be good to Lena. She's such a beautiful girl and you guys are great together." I gave her my word that I would and a man is only as good as his word...

<u>5</u>

Since I was known by pretty much everyone at both clubs, I was invited to a party thrown by a gothic chick from the Last Chance 2000 named "Cynthia." A group of us which included Tommy, Punky, and me met at the main club to catch a buzz beforehand. This terrified the bouncers on duty because they knew that we were uncontrollable. To make matters worse, Tommy and I were both hammered and looking for a fight. However, we did manage to keep our cool until it was time to go. As I got about half way through the door to leave, Tommy, who was coming out behind me, kicked it as hard as he could. The door struck me in the head and snapped my neck back. At the time I seemed ok and had a good laugh about it as we smoked a couple of joints on the way to the party. By the time we arrived, all was forgotten.

The party was going well until we heard Cynthia's son screaming out from the den. He was in there playing video games when a shit faced Punky wandered in wanting to play too. The kid started freaking out when Punky had been sitting there for several minutes thinking that he was playing...without a controller in his hands! Tommy and I dragged Punky through the house and dropped him in the front yard. We jokingly told him that if he fell asleep, we were going to do him in the ass. He must have thought we were serious, because as I was leaving, I saw Punky propped up against a tree in the dog's pen passed out but still on his feet. People were laughing hysterically and taking pictures of the poor bastard.

When I got back to the club, instead of going inside, I got in my truck and drove down to Micheal's to get some dope first. When I returned, I was high as a kite and acting like a madman. I demanded that Lars play a song for me and when I finally heard it, I starting swinging from the lattice fence that went around the DJ booth. What no one bothered to tell me was that I had cocaine residue in my moustache and goatee for everyone to see. I wouldn't hear about it until weeks later. It was a wild night for sure and one that none of us was going to forget anytime soon.

    The next morning I woke up with a pounding headache and dizziness. I originally thought it might be a hangover but as the day went on, instead of feeling better my symptoms kept getting progressively worse. They continued for a couple of days before I began to panic. I started thinking the worst. Did I have a brain tumour? Was I about to have a stroke or an aneurysm? I couldn't go to work because I couldn't stand up much less drive so I went to the hospital to find out what was wrong with me. After a series of X-rays and scans on my head, they found nothing of any concern. It was a mystery. As I sat at home, thinking that I was going to die, only two people other than my parents bothered to call to see how I was doing: Tommy and Lena. None of my other so called friends seemed concerned at all.

    Somewhere along the way, someone suggested that I see a chiropractor. I was hesitant at first because I had been told over the years that they were in the same category as witch doctors in the eyes of many in the medical profession. I had suffered so much that I was willing to try anything at this point so I made an appointment. As soon as I went in and told them about my ailment, they sent me in for an X-ray to look at my neck instead of my head and found the problem right away. My neck was severely out of line due to an intense trauma or impact and it was affecting me my body to such a degree that I couldn't function. I immediately knew what caused this affliction: Tommy kicking the door that night. I was so fucked up at the time that I didn't realize I was hurt so I never made the connection. They managed to pop my neck back into place and there was instant relief but the bad news was that I would need additional therapy to strengthen my neck and it wasn't going to be cheap. I never made those sessions because I couldn't afford them, and every now and then, I have a relapse that can last up to several weeks before it clears up on its own.

6

Once I was back at work, I was getting into trouble again. First there was the night that Punky got drunk and told me to do some wrestling chops on him. I really laid them in there but wasn't doing them correctly and ended up severely bruising his chest. I don't know why he did it, but Punky showed the bruises to Gene, and I was accused of bullying my boss. Then I foolishly asked one of the girls to pour some straight Crown Royal in my cup while I was working the floor and standing on the stage. She just kept refilling it every time I asked and I eventually got plastered. Later on, while Lena was doing her set, one of the guys tried to touch her causing me to spring into action. Unfortunately my momentum in doing so caused me to lose my balance and fall. Luckily, there were some young lads who had pushed their table against the side of the stage. They caught me in mid- air and placed me back on my feet before I hit the ground. From a distance, it probably looked like I was crowd surfing at a rock concert but my clumsiness could have got me fired or seriously injured.

But it wasn't just my relationship with Gene that was about to take a fatal hit: Lena was ready to make a critical decision about our possible future together as well. It might have started out like any other night but by the end of it, I would know the truth about where I stood with her. Did she really legitimately like me or was she just using me all along like everyone said? I was about to get all the answers I had been seeking. On that special night, an up and coming band called "Dial 7" came into the club and we bonded almost immediately. They ended up inviting BJ and me out to their RV for drinks and autographs after closing. Once we got out there, they encouraged me to keep chasing my dreams of being a rock star and gave me some valuable advice on how to get my foot in the door of the music industry. I was so wrapped up in this conversation that I completely lost track of time and didn't realize that Lena was still outside waiting for me.

When I opened the door to the RV, I saw her standing there with hellfire and brimstone in her eyes. "You need to decide whether you would rather hang out with *them* or have sex with *me!*" she screamed. I apologized and embraced her to calm her down. We got into my truck and drove to a seedy motel just down the road from the club to get a room. Once inside, we stripped down and crawled into bed. Lena was on her knees just staring down at me while I was lying on my back. I couldn't tell if she was really focused on me or her thoughts were elsewhere but at that moment she looked so beautiful that words can't even begin to describe her. I rose up and began kissing her passionately as our naked bodies became so entwined that we were as one. I then spun her around and got on top of her. I entered her and was thrusting her so hard that my sweat was literally pouring into her mouth. I leaned in closer, causing my long, wet hair to drape over both of us which made it difficult for her to breathe so I had to back off again. As I gazed into those beautiful brown eyes, I felt that the time was right to tell her how I felt about her. "What is more intimate than pouring your heart out to a girl while you are inside of her?" I thought to myself. So the words just came out, "I think that I'm falling in love with you." After saying that, I could tell by the expression on Lena's face that I had fucked up. We had told each other that we loved each other many times before but never in *this* way. She not only didn't respond the way I wanted her to do, but she said nothing at all. I would compare how I was feeling to someone hearing from the doctor for the first time that they had inoperable cancer. A part of me had truly died in that very moment and the scar would remain for the rest of my life. I went limp soon after and slipped out of her. The moment was gone and I was no longer in the mood, so I quickly got dressed and cut out a couple of lines of cocaine on the bedside table for us before I took her back to her car. There was a painful silence on the way to the club and for the first time I couldn't wait for her to get out of my sight. I wanted her to just leave and never come back.

Unfortunately, I would have to see her the next day at work. I still had hope that we might have a future together, despite what happened the night before, because she didn't verbally tell me that it was over. I would find that getting to the bottom of this was going to be impossible on this night, because she was so drunk that she could barely walk. When I tried to touch her, she resisted and laughed it off. Even her friends, who used to be on my side, was coming up to me and asking me to leave her alone and respect the fact that she had a boyfriend. Everyone was turning on me literally overnight, and all of a sudden, I had become the bad guy in this whole scenario. Lena left without even giving me a kiss for the first time in months which told me all I needed to know.

I would get officially dumped the following day on the grounds that she had started feeling guilty about cheating on her boyfriend and wanted to start over to give their relationship another chance. After ripping my heart out and stomping it with her heel, she promised that "If anything happens or it just doesn't work out, I would be the first to know." I guess she felt that at this point, a few more lies and broken promises weren't going to hurt anything.

It was love at first sight, but her heart belonged to another. Said, "It wouldn't feel right, cause I was like her brother." But then it happened one night, and we became lovers.
First it was a one time thing, no rings, no strings…Then a harmless fling, that meant nothing. She wanted all the perks of hooking up with me, minus the responsibility. We never was, and we never will be…
She used to come out and play, until the sun went away. Wish I could cut off my ears, so I couldn't hear, pluck out my eyes, so I wouldn't cry.
In the heat of passion, I told her, "It's not just an infatuation, I'm falling in love with you." I could tell by her reaction, she was the last person I should have said that to. We were never meant to be together, and I think we both knew.
She said, "I can't do this anymore…I have to go…I should be with him. This has to end, but can we still be friends? But if anything happens, I promise you will be the first to know." I haven't heard from her since, hadn't seen her in god knows when.
Like a moth to the flame, I held a candle for the one who never came. I have the burns to remind me, to put her behind me. Now I'm just a fool, left

standing in the rain. You can't tame what's meant to be wild, teaching me was when she smiled...
-Denny Noland "Draven" From my song "Storm Child"
Written on August 14, 2006   Copyright 2007   -DJN

CHAPTER XII- "THE STAR CHAMBER"

1999

Gene had decided to throw out some of the old couches that had been sitting around in the club for a while, and the one that Lena and I had sex on for the first time was among them. I decided to take it home as a keepsake so I fumigated it and left it in my yard for a couple of days to air it out. The club had been infested with cockroaches for as long as I could remember and I certainly didn't want the bastards in my house. Unfortunately, I missed an egg somewhere because within a week, I had a new pest living in my house and I just couldn't get rid of them. It was funny how the cockroaches were seldom seen during business hours at the club, but as soon as the music shut off at the end of the night and the lights came on, they were fucking everywhere. The vibrations may have kept them at bay for a majority of the time, but they were always around, just waiting for the opportunity to scatter in search of food. Now my house had become their new home and they took it over in no time. I was starting to wonder what was going to happen next.

Between my new uninvited guests and all the shit that went down earlier in the week, I didn't even want to be in my own house. It was just too quiet, and silence made me start thinking about everything, so I turned to Lars for help. On an unusually slow Sunday night, the girls got bored and began practicing their routines on the pole while there were no customers around. When Sika went up on the stage, Lars joined her and it turned into a full blown make out session. Lars and I had already made plans to party after work at his house but now there was someone else thrown into the mix. When we got back to his place, Sika and Lars did a few lines and headed to the bedroom to have sex, leaving me alone in the living room with no one to talk to. I did a couple of lines myself, before turning on the TV to drown out Sika's moaning in the background. The movie "Urban Legend" was on but my mind was somewhere else. I wished that Lena was here with me. It would have been perfect… but obviously that could never be. After Lars and Sika had worn each other out, we all partied together until the sun came up. I felt like this was a wasted trip so I planned to try it again later in the week.

When the time finally came, it was just the two of us. We partied hard that night…even going through all the various stashes that he had hidden throughout the house over the years. I had managed to avoid bringing up Lena's name the entire night but that was about to change. When Lars brought a couple of hits of acid out of his fridge to keep the party going, it would change my mood entirely. All I said was that I thought I still had a chance with Lena, and that prompted Lars to say something that I had heard one too many times before. He said, "It's never going to happen, man. You need to move on and put her behind you. Don't hate her, all she did was spread her legs for you. You should be grateful instead of bitter towards her." I went ballistic. I pushed him out to his balcony and threatened to throw him off the motherfucker for saying such a thing. He stood his ground, not backing down at all. In a moment of clarity, I realized that he was just being honest with me, even if it was a bit blunt, and that made me come to grips with reality. I wanted to cry but kept it all inside until I got home and then took it out on my furniture.

Tristan was another friend who stood by my side during this difficult period in my life. When I took her and her roommate "Witt" out to breakfast one night after work, I started feeling very sick. I was so strung out from doing too much cocaine that I was having trouble breathing. Not only were they concerned about how ill I was, but I was also driving, which meant that I literally had their lives in my hands. Tristan looked at me and said, "When I first met you and we went out that night, you were larger than life and full of confidence. Over the past few months, I've watched drugs slowly make it all disappear. Now when I look into those eyes, I don't see that fire burning in them anymore. Sometimes they are so far away, it's almost like I'm looking straight through you. There is such blankness in them that I feel like you are just not here anymore. You know that I care for you and I worry about you a lot. I pray that you get clean before it's too late. I miss the *real* you." She always knew what to say. I often wondered if I had made a terrible mistake by letting her slip away after just one date. There was a definite connection between us that night and I could tell by how she kissed me afterwards that she was into me but I dropped the ball. Although we had remained close friends throughout, it was too late to for it to be anything more at this point. She was already caught up in a love triangle of her own and well on her way to preferring girls over guys anyway. She would start dating a girl named "Nadia" a few months later and be sent to the Last Chance 2000 as punishment for breaking one of Gene's rules. However, she would get the last laugh. Instead of going to the other club, she and Witt packed their things and went back to Florida. I never saw either of them again.

"He is critically ill," said one of the nurses, "better call in the family." For months, I've had angina pectoris, from the hardening of my arteries. I'm a fallen hero, in my death throes, put me out of my misery. Don't want to depend on life support, I wish they would pull the plug on me.

When it was time to serve my country, when the battle lines were clearly drawn, I had to deport. When it went beyond the call of duty, I became their pawn, when it was my last resort. If given the opportunity, I would have been gone, even if it was a crime to abort. It didn't matter if we all died, as long as it was with honour, cause we were disposable. By the time we found out our government lied, they were placing dog tags in her mouths instead of giving us medals.

I was no Spiderman and you were no Mary Jane. I was no Superman and you were no Lois Lane. Someone must be the prey, for there to be a predator, and I'm that weapon of mass destruction, the spear of the warrior, shooting your white flags to ribbons.

From crossing the tracks, before a speeding train, to running into burning buildings and jumping out of airplanes, to being electrocuted by a hair dryer while I soaked, to performing the heimleck manuever on someone as they choked, I've already had All Timers and suffered a stroke, eaten down to the bone by cancer, from second hand smoke. This is how I get rewarded from doing all those things I did. From the cradle to the hearse, "the rumours of my death have been greatly exaggerated."

Now my muscles start twitching, followed by convulsions, code 99. A simple faint, a missed heartbeat, then flatline…as the defibrillation paddles slam me with two hundred joules, they know my life is nearly over. The doctor said, "There's not much I can do. Death can only be postponed, but never conquered." Two metal discs on my chest and wired to a machine, the quoting of the scripture and John 3:16.

"Be still, and the dead will overshadow thee..." I take a minute to beg for forgiveness for all of my sins... then prepare to board the ferry, to cross the river Styx straight into Hades, with a handful of coins. In the distance, I see familiar faces of long deceased relatives waiting for me to enter the light, as I leave this cruel world forever tonight.

Blood comes from my lips and bowels, now I'm nothing more than food for maggots, and fertilizer for flowers. Place quarters in my eyes, and pull the sheet over my face, tag my toe, and close the drawer.

If you didn't have time for me while I was alive, don't bother attending my funeral. I'm sure it won't bother you much that you missed it. I don't care if there's anyone left to carry my casket to its burial, just throw me in a ditch somewhere and pretend I never existed.

-Denny Noland "Draven" From my song "Fallen Hero"

Written in 1998-1999   Copyright 2015

When I needed to just get away, I started hanging out at Micheal's more frequently. I started dating one of the waitresses for a minute but lost interest within a week or two and just let us drift apart without having to say anything. The Captain did, however, introduce me to a new source to get my powder from: a former dancer from yesteryear and her husband. They were always at the bar sitting on the pokies with a plentiful supply of cocaine on hand. I started buying from them and developed a close friendship with both to the extent that they invited The Captain and me over to their apartment one night to do some free blow. I didn't know that the one bartender who I didn't get along with at Micheal's was going to be there as well until we walked in and saw him. As we all got high, I started talking about how I was sick and tired of Mexicans coming across our borders and getting great jobs and benefits yet can't speak a word of English while there were so many qualified Americans who are still unemployed. This subject triggered the bartender to jump into the conversation by making a lot of racial slurs that took it far beyond where I was planning to take it. To keep the peace, I was agreeing with everything he said. What I didn't know, but would find out later, was that *he* was Mexican, even though he didn't look like one or have an accent, and was only saying all that shit to make fun of me. Apparently, he was also making faces and obscene gestures at me every time my back was turned so everyone in the room could see them except for me. I was so pissed off that no one let me in on this until he had already gone home for the night and I couldn't do anything about it. I did, however, understand why they didn't but that was beside the point. Although, I remained friends with them for a long time after this incident, I never went back to their apartment again.

    The next time I saw The Captain at the bar, he had Diamond with him. I hadn't seen her since she quit the club. The doorman at Micheal's just happened to be a close friend of ours and took an interest in Diamond as soon as he saw her. He invited the three of us over to his place after his shift ended to do some coke. I wasn't feeling well so as soon as we got there, I crashed on his couch while they partied. One thing led to another and our host started going down on Diamond. The Captain would eventually join in, making it a threesome, but I had no interest in participating myself. I had already been with her before so I was determined to sit this one out... but Diamond had other plans. I had been watching but was starting to nod off when I felt someone's hands rubbing between my legs. Before I even realized what was going on, Diamond had my pants down and was giving me head. I wasn't about to stop her at that point. Meanwhile, The Captain got behind her and started putting a condom on. Her ass was straight up in the air so he started throwing it to her while she blew me. After a few minutes, The Captain pulled out and screamed "The damn condom just broke!" and everything stopped. Our host, who had been watching from his recliner, said, "You guys are welcomed to stay as long as you like but I have to drive to Atlanta this morning." He then walked over and kissed Diamond on her hand and said "And you sexy girl, taste better than any woman I've ever been with. Thanks for coming, tonight." We followed him out and went our separate ways.

2

I had recently bought a synthesizer to help with the whole writing process. As soon as Martin saw it, he asked if he could borrow it so he could get his voice in key. I agreed to lend it to him without a second thought. Hell, it was a step in the right direction to get the ball rolling. Only a couple of days later, Star quit working at the club. I wasn't too concerned as first, because strippers were known to come and go on a regular basis. It wasn't until one of her friends told me that they had left town that I realized that I had been duped once again. The worst part of it was that no one knew where they had moved to so any chance of getting my synthesizer back went right out the window.

My luck wasn't any better when I went out to that nameless strip club near the interstate to see some fresh meat. I had no problems getting in and probably sat there for ten minutes or so when a familiar face walked by and spotted me. "Well, hello there stranger" she said. As soon as I heard that voice, I knew for certain that it was indeed who I thought it was. It was Natasha…looking as beautiful as ever. I hadn't seen her in years so this was a rare treat. "My sister told me that you have been working for Gene for quite a while. How do you like it?" she asked. "To be honest, working there has not only changed me, but how I feel about the business as well. It has ruined it for me. Now I see how pathetic I must have appeared back in the day" I replied. She laughed and we continued chatting for a few minutes before she asked me if I would like a dance "for old time's sake." There was no way I was going to refuse…hell, I never could. "Well it's settled then. We'll do the next song" she said. I could hardly wait…

Not long after the song started, I caught some suspicious activity out of the corner of my eye that indicated to me that this dance was probably going to be cut short. A guy, who I assumed was the manager, pointed me out to the bouncers and within seconds, I was surrounded by not only the bouncers but the security guard that was stationed outside as well. "We know who you are" one of them said "and we know why you are here." I had no idea what they were accusing me so I simply asked. They responded with "You are not stealing any more of our girls. You need to leave now." They were stern but smart enough not to touch me. Maybe they did know who I was after all. Natasha was probably as angry as I was about the whole thing and asked if she could at least finish her dance first but they weren't having it. "But he didn't do anything" she pleaded but to no avail. She looked at me as I was being escorted to the door and yelled out "I'm sorry Denny... that I work for a bunch of assholes!" I responded back with "Yeah, me too. It looks like I will have to take a raincheck on that dance sweetie." She nodded and looked down disappointingly to the ground. I left and headed to the Last Chance... where I was always welcome.

    When I got back to the mother ship, Tommy was standing outside talking to one of the new girls who obviously had the night off. I stopped to have a chat with them and somehow the conversation went from being casual to Tommy daring the girl to give him a blowjob right then and there on the stairs just outside the front door during business hours. She said "Ok, whip it out" and he did, so she dropped to her knees and started giving him head while he was leaning against the handrail at the entrance. It was still daylight outside and I was just watching the cars passing by, thinking that at any moment, someone was going to either pull in or come out of the club and they were going to not only get caught, but be in a world of trouble to boot. I wasn't going to play a part in any of this until she started rubbing my crotch with her hand while she was waxing him. I then pulled my penis out and just before she was about to move over to do me, Tommy whispered in my ear "When she looked up at me a minute ago and smiled, I noticed that her fucking gums were bleeding. Pull your pants back up man!" He didn't have to tell me twice. I immediately went inside to wash my hands and Tommy came in not long after with a bottle of whiskey. He pulled his penis out and emptied the entire bottle on it. When I asked him what they hell he was doing, he replied "Sterilizing and disinfecting." Just another day at the office...you might say.

Strangely enough, I started going through a stretch where female customers were starting to notice me. Up to that point, the only attention I received from them involved a lot of swearing, due to those poor ladies watching me kick their partner's ass right in front of them. This was a nice change of pace. The first one was a Hooters girl from West Knoxville who used to gather up a large group of her fellow staff members to come out to our club after they closed up for the night. She was so beautiful and very forward about her attraction to me. She would tease me through the window before coming in, then run around and hug me when she came through the door. She would always ask me what she needs to do for me to throw her out and make me promise to be as physical as possible while doing so. Her male friends used to warn me that I was in trouble because she wasn't going to stop until she got what she wanted. I would usually walk them out and she would jump into my arms so I could carry her to their vehicle. Every time she was about to drive away, she would beg me to come down to Hooters sometime and she would provide me with free food and alcohol but I foolishly never went. I think that deep down, I felt like she was too good for me, especially with my lifestyle being what it was. I liked her too much to put her through all of that.

Then there was another attractive girl who came in with her boss one night and started asking Harley about me. She wrote her number down on a dollar bill and got Harley to hand it to me. When I asked Harley about the girl, she replied "Well, she's beautiful and got a lot of money. What else do you need to know?" then walked away. Apparently, that wasn't enough to get my interest because I never bothered to call her.

But one customer boldly went where none of the others were willing to go. Her name was "Tiffany" and she actually came in with a guy as well but they got into an argument in the lobby and he left her there. We had a strict rule that we enforced about women coming into the club without a male escort, so I was torn about what I was going to do with her. I chose to break the rules and let her in anyway so she wasn't lingering around outside by herself in the dark. She took a seat right in front of my desk and kept coming up to me throughout the night telling me how sexy I was. Each time she approached me, she turned it up a notch. First, she acted like she was going to whisper in my ear then stuck her tongue in it instead. The next time she licked all up my neck until she got to my mouth and then French kissed me. Finally, she just blatantly asked me if there was somewhere we could go to have sex. There were many people that saw what was going on and reacted accordingly. Tommy came over and tried his magic on her but got shot down in flames. He was followed by a couple of our girls who came up to ask me if I knew her or not since they had seen us making out several times. I would always say "Never seen her in my life. But I might be getting pretty close to her later tonight."

 I tried to persuade her to stick around until after closing so I could take her back to my place but I could tell that she was getting bored and anxious. I had no other choice but to call her a cab to take her back to the hotel so she could meet up with me later. When the cab arrived, I paid the driver with my own money and even threw in a little extra so we could have one last kiss before we parted ways. While we were kissing passionately for several minutes, Tiffany held my ass and began to cry. When I asked her what was wrong, she replied "I want you so bad. Are you *sure* that there is nowhere in this building where we could have some privacy?" I assured her that there wasn't before we exchanged phone numbers so I could call her when my shift was over. I watched her leave before I went back inside. Once I returned to my desk, James came walking over and said, "That girl really liked you a lot didn't she?" I replied back with "Yeah, too bad I couldn't hook up with her while she was still here." James looked at me with a puzzled look on his face. "You know, you could have taken her back to Bambi's. I have the keys and would have gladly watched the door for you." I had completely forgotten about the new bar that Gene had opened in the back of our building for customers to purchase their beer without having to get behind the wheel to do so. It had taken the club's original name and was only open on the weekends, and I'll give you one guess who was the bartender. I couldn't fucking believe it. It would have been perfect but it was too late now. Tiffany was gone. I rang her as soon as I finished up and she was already half way to Gatlinburg, where she supposably owned her own business. I pleaded with her to turn around but it wasn't happening. She thanked me for everything and invited me to come up to her place sometime so we could finish what we started but I never bothered to call her again either. Another one bites the dust...

3

While Lena was involved with me, I told her once that I didn't understand why she chose me out of all of the guys that liked her and she said "I think you are quite a catch. There's just something about you that makes me weak in the knees." Unfortunately, all of these isolated incidents that I just wrote about occurred when she wasn't around. I can only speculate about how she might have reacted if she had been there to witness them. However, when she was in my presence, she was still my dream. She would do little things to fuck with me because she knew I wasn't over her. One example of this was the night Tommy's manager from the Last Chance 2000, "One Time", (I will explain how he earned the nickname later on) came over to party with us. He, like pretty much everyone in the club circuit, had heard about Lena and myself and wanted to play a joke on me. I was just sitting at the end of the bar minding my own business when I smelled Lena's perfume. I knew her scent so well that I identified her towel once just by sniffing it. I knew that she was close, possibly even sneaking up behind me. Before I could turn around and look, she was sticking her tongue in my ear and sucking on my right earlobe. Then I felt the same sensations on my left side, and when I turned in that direction, I saw that it was the other resident goddess, Nadia, that was licking and sucking on that side at the same time. Most normal men would have probably prematurely ejaculated had they been in my shoes at that moment and I must say that even I was having a hard time dealing with it myself. This went on for a few minutes and about the time I was I got really worked up, they stopped and walked away. It was vicious and cruel and I was ready to punch One Time in the nose when it was over, which made him laugh even harder.

    Now I felt like I had to do something drastic in order to make a statement. I vowed to come in on my next night off and sleep with whichever girl who just happened to be on stage when I walked through the door. It turned out to be a new girl who had just started that night named "Trixie", that I had never seen before, who became my next victim. I walked up to the stage to tip her and when she knelt down to spread her garter, I said "You are coming home with me tonight." She replied "Ok" without a moment of hesitation and I had sex with her later that night.

    Since I was still out of my head and on the rebound, what was meant to be only a one night stand turned into a month long affair. To say that this was one of the strangest periods in my life would be an understatement. Trixie's adoptive mother was also a stripper and worked with us at the club. She would give me massages on a nightly basis right in front of Trixie and she didn't seem to mind at all. Trixie would also tell her mother everything, no matter how personal it was. One night, while Trixie and I were shagging in my bed, we jarred a ten pound weight that I used to hold down the door on my CD player off and it not only smacked her in the back of the head, but bounced off and hit me square in the mouth. The next day Trixie's mother informed me that she knew how her daughter got that huge lump on her head. If that didn't make me uncomfortable enough, Trixie would sometimes bring her infant child with her when she came over. Now I had a child's car seat in my truck when we went somewhere and that didn't feel right either. Combine all of this with Lena and my colleagues accusing me of lowering my standards and settling on the first girl who came along, I knew what I needed to do: devise a plan to break it off with her but make it appear that she is breaking it off with *me*. It would take a few days for the stars to align but eventually it did happen and I was ready. Homer came up to my desk one night and told me that Trixie was dancing a little too close to a customer in the VIP room. I didn't believe him nor did I really care either way but this was the perfect opportunity to start up a fight with her that could put an end to this once and for all. I tore into her as soon as she got near me, and after a few minutes of bickering, she said those magic words that were music to my ears: "If you think I would do something like that, then maybe we should stop seeing each other." I responded back with "Well, if that's what you want, then that's how it's going to be. As far as I'm concerned, we are over!" As soon as she was out of my sight, I couldn't hold back a smile. Mission accomplished…

4

It was nearing the end of summer, and there was an outbreak of celebrity sightings in our club. First there were three members of the metal band "Pantera" (minus lead singer Phil) who came in and the girls absolutely loved them. Although, they didn't really spend any money or buy any dances, it was how they treated the girls with respect that won them over. Everyone was thrilled to be in the presence of such greatness. I wish I could say the same about a certain baseball player who played for the Colorado Rockies that showed up in a limo with his entourage. I saw them carrying several cases of beer into the lobby after the 1am curfew. I tried to explain in the nicest way possible that although we would be more than happy to let them in, we couldn't allow the alcohol through the door because it would be against the law. When the ball player heard this, he worked his way through his people to my window. He then said that one line that celebrities try to use to get special favours that I hate with a passion: "Do you know who I am?" Every time I heard that phrase, it reminded me of a story my uncle told me years ago about an incident that occurred at Disneyland, where he was head of security, involving himself and Madonna. She had said exactly the same thing and my uncle told her, "I don't give a damn about who you are. I was told specific instructions to not let *anyone* have a free pass today. You are going to have to pay like everyone else... otherwise you are not coming in." I couldn't remember if he said she paid or not, but that part of the story was irrelevant. Despite my efforts, the ball player chose to have a shouting match with me instead of accepting our rules and regulations and he never made it inside that night. He must have called me every name in the book on his way out and even gave me the finger before he went out the door. But me being who I am got the last word in: "You know what? I'm an Atlanta Braves fan. The Colorado Rockies suck!" which wasn't exactly a lie at the time, then flipped him a bird of my own. Looking back, I still can't believe how unprofessional this guy acted that night, and I never thought much of him since.

One of the girls used to hook up with a former WWE superstar from the Attitude Era when he would come to town. He would drop into the club to see her and wait for her shift to finish. We never had any problems with him once he understood why we were taking his beer away at 1 am. Her association with him paid off big time when Monday Night Raw came to Knoxville and she got a gig as one of The Godfather's "hoes" on national TV. She was ecstatic about not only the experience itself but being able to meet all the boys in the back.

Then there were the UT football players. When I first started working at the club, there were a couple of players, one was black and the other was white, that used to come in every week. From my understanding, they both eventually went on the NFL to become offensive and defensive linemen for their respective teams. They always made me feel more comfortable when they were around because they stood beside me on more than one occasion when my fellow bouncers didn't. One example was just after the Florida Gators came to town and beat us yet again to knock us out of contention for the national championship. Let me say that Saturdays at the club during football season, mainly when the Vols were playing at home, was always a nightmare. We would start out slow but as soon as the game let out, we were stampeded by a mob of visiting fans that were either talking shit about beating us or pissed off because their team lost. Mix that with our own intoxicated fans and you had a volcano that was on the verge of erupting at any moment. On the night in question, we had a rowdy bunch of Florida fans that came in acting like they owned the place. I could sense that something bad was about to happen when one of the loudest, most obnoxious of the group headed into the VIP room with one of our sleaziest girls. It only took a matter of seconds before that jerk grabbed her on the ass. When I stepped in to warn him, instead of thanking me for doing my job, the bitch told me that she had told the guy that he could touch her if he wanted. I told her that it wasn't her choice to make and then told the bloke to keep his hands to himself. As soon as I turned to leave the room, I glanced back and saw his hands on her ass again. I stopped the dance and escorted the gentleman out which caught the attention of all of his buddies. They all came to back him up which meant that I was cornered and hopelessly outnumbered. Those two football players saw all of the commotion and came over to help me out. The guy who purchased the dance didn't like the fact that a black guy had got involved so he screamed "Don't touch me you nigger!" Now I had to step in and separate them before it became a scene out of "Road House." Luckily, no punches were thrown so we didn't make the 11:00 news.

Sometimes a large group of the players would come in after a game and that required a chaperone to keep them out of trouble. He would always come up to me and say something like "If any of the boys get out of line, let me know and I will deal with it. We don't want any bad publicity that might tarnish the team's image in the newspapers." Gene would usually help them along by telling the bartender or waitress to give them free mixers or buckets of ice when they were already fired up and then turn around and say, "Well, I'll see you guys tomorrow. I'm going home." leaving us to deal with them. Most of the time, they behaved like perfect gentlemen, but one night the chaperone was concerned about a player who tagged along that normally didn't. He said that he never worried about the ones who let out their emotions… it was the quiet ones that you have to watch. "Everyone on the team is afraid of this guy" he said. "He always stays calm no matter what. We think that if he ever gets really mad, he's going to do a lot of damage to someone."

As luck would have it, he was talking about the guy who had been eyeballing me since they came in. He eventually approached me and explained why he had been staring at me and his reason wasn't what I was expecting. He actually wanted a VIP dance from Dana but was too shy to ask her so that's where I came in. When I first told Dana about him, she wasn't interested… claiming the she didn't dance for black people. That was unusual considering how many of our girls "went black and never came back." I asked if she could make an exception this time and I promised her that I would be watching very closely to make sure that he didn't do anything inappropriate. She wasn't happy about it but she agreed to do it anyway just to shut me up. I might have been many things but racist wasn't one of them. Just the idea of hating someone because of the colour of their skin was and still is the most ridiculous excuse ever. I used to have girls that I liked at the club tell me "If you were black, I would definitely have sex with you" over the years and I still despise them to this day. To make a long story short, not only was the dance clean and without incident but even Dana admitted that it wasn't as bad as she thought it was going to be. The young man actually came out and shook my hand afterwards… thanking me for talking Dana into it when he could sense that she would have rather been somewhere else. Not everything I did was thoughtless and negative but that's all people seem to remember about me

    I'm going to California, headed to the big city. I'm over being average… I'm ready to be somebody. I want to decide how I am marketed, going to call all of the shots, so I won't become another frustrated starlet, like you hear on the jukebox.
    Going to be on that stage every night, ready to rock… want to write my story, about a hitchhiker on his way to glory, be every daughter's fantasy, while I make her parents sick. From the day I was discovered, to my writer's block, now that's what I call music.
    Not just another singer in the studio, who can't clear his throat…not another soprano, who can't hit the high notes, just give me a guitar, and I'll be a rock n roll star…From starting in a garage, to going on tour, from having a huge entourage, to doing yet another encore, I'm going to make millions, turn these gold teeth platinum.
    Take me to the Star Chamber, so I can make a demo, cut a record, become the next one hit

wonder. From rags to riches, and back to skid row, the curtains have been closed on this show.

They say I was an infiltrator, that nothing I've done is original, say I'm a perpetrator, nothing is legit, it's all counterfeit... not capable of producing a single. You make think I'm so fucking cool but I'm actually playing you for a fool.

I'm going to make a video, so controversial that it can't be aired on MTV, only HBO. Once you buy the CD or DVD, you won't fast forward...only rewind and play. Then watch the director's cut, and believe me, it'll make hard-core porn look like classical ballet.

Then I'm going to have my own reality show, one hour to corrupt the minors, construct new sex offenders, with no commercials. Allow me to step out of the tube, before you change that channel. Before this series can be renewed, it's going to be cancelled.

Cherish these moments when I'm still on top, it's not the fall that hurts so much, it's the sudden stop. One day I will become irrelevant, and my ratings and record sells will drop. I will try to hold on to these memories as long as I can, because that's all I've got.   -Denny Noland "Draven"
From my song "The Star Chamber"
Written in 2001-2002
Copyright 2015

5

Although, I had kept my emotions in check, for the most part, since the breakup with Lena, there is only so much I could take considering she was still in the picture. I had played around with a few girls since she dumped me, but every night when I closed my eyes, all I thought about was her. No one could fill that void... only provide a temporary distraction.

I paced around that club constantly like a wild animal hoping that someone would provide me with an outlet. One night a group of Asians came in and did just that. After one warning that I'm not sure they understood, I grabbed one of them and picked him up out of his chair. This caused it to topple over with the legs still sticking straight up in the air. Seeing this, I slammed the poor bastard down on it, notching one of the legs straight up his ass. He just froze for a minute in obvious pain as a sudden hush fell across the crowd. When he looked up at me, I could see fear in his eyes and that gave me great pleasure. I could tell that he was extremely embarrassed about what just happened so I taunted him by doing my best "Karate Kid" impression of "the Crane" to show him that it wasn't an accident and to entertain the crowd, which had now gone from total silence to deafening laughter. He eventually limped out the door to never return.

I humiliated two other customers later in the week when they got into a scuffle with each other at their table. I saw which one started it so I ran over and picked him up off of the ground in a chokehold. I tossed him through the air and he sailed over a table, hitting the floor with a resounding thud. I climbed on top of him and said, "If you want to fight someone, motherfucker, fight me! Hell, I will fight both of you at the same time in the parking lot right now if you want." Unfortunately, they both declined. When I came back inside after walking them out, the Captain played Tom Petty's "Learning to Fly" over the system and dedicated it to me. I had become careless and reckless, spiralling out of control. I was attacking people first, and asking questions later. Gene held out as long as he could but his patience had worn thin. I needed to go...and no better time than the present.

On the following weekend, I was on floor duty and standing at my usual spot at the back of the stage. I noticed that Gene and James were sitting at a table near the stage instead of at the bar where they would normally sit so I knew that something was going down. It was one of the few nights that I wasn't high or drunk so I was very focused and alert. It would pay huge dividends when a customer sneaked a camera in, which was against club policy, and attempted to take a picture of one of the girls on stage. When he jumped up on his chair to snap a photo, I sprang into action. I literally leaped from the stage to this guy's table which coincidentally was beside where Gene and James were. I grabbed his camera and smashed it in one motion before he even had a chance to press the button. I could tell that Gene and James were impressed by what they saw. Gene even gave me a little smirk and a nod of approval but it was already too late. Gene had not only made his decision to send me to the Last Chance 2000 , but also informed me that I was banned from the main club until further notice due to my addictions to drugs and alcohol. I had made my own bed and now I was going to have to sleep in it. I had no one to blame but myself.
-DJN

CHAPTER XIII- "THE EX-FILES"

1999

    I wasn't the only one who was getting punished for their sins. Punky had got demoted for drinking on the clock as well which left Homer as the best candidate for the manager position. This really stepped on my toes since I had been there much longer than he had, but there wasn't anything I could really do about but sit back and watch everything unfold. I suspected from the beginning that he had a hand in me getting banned since he saw me as his biggest competition with the ladies. He also seemed to be afraid of me since he watched me use a fully charged Taser on my penis and balls on three separate occasions in the same night while I was drunk to show everyone that I was a bad motherfucker. He also found me to be dangerous when I would wander in wasted on my nights off and wouldn't listen to reason. I believe that I told him and Jackson to "fuck off" more than once and he hadn't forgotten that.
    This was kind of sad since I considered them both to be my friends. When I got into a fight with a customer one night and the guy tried desperately to hold on to the counter so I couldn't toss him out, I saw Homer racing across the room to lend me a hand. He actually pried the guy loose so I could do my thing. I slammed the customer's head unintentionally into the weakest part of the wall in the lobby instead of the bricks, which knocked a hole in it, and got me a scolding from Gene. He threatened to make me pay for the repairs if it ever happened again. We also had fun isolating troublemakers in the bathroom and intimidating the hell out of them in the process. A few times it did

blow up in our faces when their friends caught on to what we were doing and would join in the fray leaving us outgunned and outnumbered, with no choice but to retreat. That was then. Now I wasn't allowed in the club that I played a significant role in cleaning up, which was being policed by people who I had trained. I had been forced out of my own kingdom by the peasants, but I knew that everything would work itself out in the end and I would be back to take my throne. I just had to give them enough rope and they would hang themselves. They always do...

In a nutshell, the Last Chance 2000 was a circus, but a more laid back environment to work in. Gene only came in once a week leaving Tommy to run the show however he saw fit, which basically meant that the place was nothing more than a glorified orgy. Since we were never really that busy, we had to find more creative ways to pass time. This alone created some interesting entertainment to say the least. Some nights, a new girl would rehearse then disappear into Tommy's office where he was napping and wake him up with a striptease and a blowjob. Other nights, a girl would be criticizing another girl about spreading for Tommy, after everywhere that he has been, saying "I would never have sex with him. He's probably got something" then the next time you saw her, usually on videotape, she was bent over something with Tommy standing behind her with his trademark hat on, doing you know what. Sometimes, one of her friends was included in the meat triangle as well as a bonus.

But without a shadow of a doubt, the strangest thing that I ever witnessed back then was the night that I walked into the office to get some paper and saw Punky and the girl who gave me my inaugural first blowjob at the mother ship, when I had just started working there, fooling around. She was on her knees with her back turned to me as I entered the room, going down on Punky while Tommy was just standing there watching. As soon as she stood up and bent over to get more leverage, I could see a light bulb appear over Tommy's head. He grabbed a beer bottle off the shelf and took the lid off of it. He began slowly inserting the drinking end into her vagina, causing beer to trickle down her leg, and she barely flinched. I had seen enough, but it was such a small room that I was actually trapped in the corner and couldn't get out so I was forced to watch. He then looked at me and said, "Watch this." He flipped the bottle around to the holding end and started easing it into her privates. It actually went in without much of a problem which amazed both of us. All she did when it entered her was let out a pleasurable moan. I know it sounds farfetched but it actually happened. I wouldn't have believed it myself had I not seen it with my own eyes. As he pulled the bottle out, I could tell that he was getting aroused so when he leaned over to get a condom out of his desk, I made a run for it. I don't know what happened after that and I didn't want to know either.

(Warning: explicit content) I know Victoria's secret, and I'm not keeping it. She's been faking orgasms, cause she never has them. She would rather masterbate, than fornicate...consummate...the hell with the boys, all she needs is her toys, on her waterbed, or with a detachable showerhead, why would she need me, when she can do it manually.

She wanted to vomit, when giving fellatio, wanted to spit, but always swallowed. Always in the missionary position, and that routine was getting boring. He got a nut, in about two minutes, yet she wasn't finished, and before he could get the job done, he was already snoring... (Back to the spin cycle on her washing machine)

She reaches into her panties, and touches my lips with her wetness. When she craves that release, it's time to thaw the ice princess. Now she's a nympho, tossing her dildo, holding onto the headboard, with her head in the pillow. She's going to be too sore to walk tomorrow.

I'm frantic, tantric...counting sheep cause I can't sleep. Every night I hear her libido, and I always come to her window.

When I'm hungry, will she be my sex on a plate, ready to be ate? We'll make the earth move, or at least a mountain. When I'm thirsty, will she let me dehydrate, or drink from her jade fountain?

I hear her moan, as I enter her erogenous zone, playing with her nipples, as she fondles my family jewels. She got off every time she got on, not just singles but multiples. There's nowhere to hide, her g-spot will be found. She slides her panties to one side, showing me how she touches herself, when I'm not around.

I'll be her gynaecologist, and I'm playing doctor, after she gets her Brazilian bikini wax. She's an exhibitionist, who wants me to watch her, as she's about to climax.

-Denny Noland "Draven" From my song "Pillow Talk"

Written on September 25, 2006   Copyright 2007

It was Jackson's birthday... so Homer wanted to get him laid. None of the girls at the main club were interested, no matter how much money he threw at them, so he had to resort to calling Tommy and asking if there was a whore available that might be game to come over and make some extra cash. He would find one but he had already planned to hook up with one of his old flames and couldn't take her over there. His only option was to ask Gene if my ban could be lifted for one night so I could take her instead, and he got the green light. I was looking forward to seeing the boys again because I had a few choice words to say to a couple of them but I decided that this wasn't the time or place to do so.

I could feel a little friction and animosity in the air as soon as we got there, but everyone pretended like they were glad to see me. I took a seat at the bar next to the Captain, One Time, and BJ while Jackson and Homer ironed out all the details, exchanged money, and made all the necessary arrangements with their whore. Jackson ended up taking her to one of the couches in the VIP room, while Homer watched like a proud papa through the beads. He wisely threw a towel over the security camera and they went at it until Jackson fired his money shot on her tits. Several minutes later, BJ went in there and started sucking on her puppies, unaware of what was all over them. We were all either gagging or laughing, causing him to turn around and ask us what was so damn funny. I asked him if her breasts tasted a little salty and he replied "A little. Why?" I replied, "How does Jackson taste anyway?" He knew what I meant straight away and nearly spewed. He ran out of there, so embarrassed that he went home soon after.

Now we were all sitting on separate couches in the VIP room as she was giving us our own personal lap dances. When she got around to Jackson, Tommy came out of nowhere with his pants already down to his knees. He had let himself in while we were all preoccupied, obviously feeling unfulfilled after spending the last couple of hours banging his old girlfriend. He was having trouble getting an erection by jacking off, so he shoved his unwashed penis into the whore's mouth while she was still straddling Jackson. The scary part was that she either didn't taste the other girl on him or she just didn't mind because she started going down on him like a champion. She would go on to blow and shag every guy in the building that night for a certain price, except for me. She was a beautiful girl and all but I wasn't paying *anyone* to have sex with me, much less being the caboose on that train. I was just enjoying my buzz and minding my own business when she came up to me and grabbed my hand. She led me back into the now empty VIP room and said "I saved the best for last." I let her know right off the bat that she wasn't getting any money out of me. She replied, "This one is on the house. I actually want *this*."

She unzipped my pants and started giving me head for several minutes until I got hard. Then she tried to put it in before I had a chance to grab a condom, but that wasn't happening. "Denny, please don't wear one of those. I'm rubbed so raw down there already, I don't think I can take it" she said. I replied "If you want me, this is how it has to be. I've watched you have sex with five different guys tonight and two of them didn't use protection. I'm not taking any chances. As a matter of fact, I might wear two." She eventually saw it my way and we ended up going at it for quite a while. I kept seeing the guys peeping through the curtain at us but that was the least of my worries. I noticed when we were getting dressed afterwards that the towel had fallen off of the camera during our session so it was all, or at least parts of it, videotaped. I wasn't happy about participating in another sex tape, especially without my knowledge or consent. I knew that Gene would be overjoyed when he went back to watch the cameras the next day and saw the footage and he was. He held this over my head for years, using it to blackmail me into doing things that I didn't want to do. The night didn't get any better for the whore either. She told me that when they dropped her off at her house the next morning, her boyfriend was still up and horny so she had to have sex with him too before she had a chance to recuperate or take a shower. For a moment, I felt for the guy but the feeling went away…

2

It was a night that I will never forget. I had been teasing Odyssey off and on for weeks but I had no idea that it had made her look at me differently. When I went up to the booth to talk to the DJ, "Lynn", she was in there picking out her music. I don't remember what I did to her, but she said, "Denny, if you don't stop, I'm going to kiss you. I swear!" So, I did it again to see if she meant what she said and she did indeed keep her word. I was in a good mood for the rest of the night and I was certain that nothing was going to change that. Then the clock struck 1:00 a.m. If you hadn't been paying attention, this meant that it was time to take away all the alcohol. There was a biker and a redneck sitting together near the stage who hadn't been much of a problem throughout the night but they weren't going to give up their beer willingly, leaving me no other choice but to start removing it myself. The biker didn't take that too well. When I say that this guy was a biker, I mean that if you looked up the term "biker" in the dictionary, this guy's picture would be there. He was an older gentleman that was covered in tattoos and sporting a long, grey beard. He probably weighed in at around 300 pounds…give or take a few. Let's put it this way: he looked like someone you wouldn't want to scrap with if you could avoid it. Unfortunately, I was going to have to. When I attempted to take their ice bucket, the big guy rose up out of his chair, grabbed me by the still injured neck, and shoved me into a section of empty tables. I might have been intimidated by this guy's brute strength had he not put his hands on my neck but he went there. I got up and dusted myself off, then proceeded to go into a full sprint and spear this dude so hard that he not only went through a table, but took out Tommy as well, who was coming up from behind to restrain him. He was clearly out of it, and unable to defend himself, as soon as his head hit the ground but I still placed him in a chokehold in an effort to show this guy that he fucked up. The redneck was pleading with me to let him go since he was turning blue and although he was trying to submit, no words were coming out. His face had also become a crimson mask and the blood was covering my hands before I realized that I was killing him. I finally snapped out of it before I took his life. When he finally made it back up to his feet, he had no idea where he was or what happened, until the redneck pointed me out as the one who kicked his ass. I stood there with fists clenched just in case he wanted to start round 2 but all he wanted to do was apologize, get his shit and leave.

    I was still quite shaken, at just the thought of reinjuring my neck, so I went into the office to collect myself. A few minutes later, Odyssey came in and pretended like she was looking for something but I knew what she really came in for. I held her in my arms and planted a long, passionate kiss on her lips. Afterwards, I asked her what the real reason was for her coming in there and she told me the truth. "I wasn't sure how I felt about that first kiss so I had to have a proper one to know for sure" she said. "Well, what did you think?" I asked. She replied, "I liked it very much. I'm sure I will be thinking about it all night." She wasn't the only one.

Odyssey could have easily been my girlfriend had she ever considered it. We would flirt and make out every day in front of everyone, including customers, but she had no interest in either dating or sleeping with me. She was one of several over the years who fit into that unpleasant category. Sometimes, she would even go out to breakfast with me after work, but we were never alone. We were always in a small group. One night, Tommy was with us and she dared me to order and eat a steak that was so rare that it was practically still kicking. Since I had been drinking, I actually won the bet and kept it down. She was kissing me throughout the meal and when we walked her to her car, she made out with me like we were a lovesick couple. Tommy even asked if we were actually dating and I said "Maybe" while Odyssey replied with conviction that "we most definitely were not." We would play this game for years. Even when she fell pregnant and the guy left her, I stood by her side and wanted to be with her but she still wasn't interested. We never became a couple but she would be the more than willing to let me know when someone I was dating was cheating on me. She always told me that she was "too much of a handful" for me to deal with but I begged to differ. To this day, I just don't get it, but maybe I wasn't meant to…

In the following weeks, I would get into several more significant fights. The first would be with an older gentleman who said, "Why don't you get a real job?" when I told him to stop doing something. After I tossed him, he got into my face and let me know that he was a carpenter and I was beneath him. I reacted by shoving him as hard as I could over the flowerbeds, making him trip and fall between two parked cars. Had he landed a foot or two in either direction, he could have hit his head on a bumper and would have been paralysed or worse but I never considered that. Once he realized how close he came to being seriously injured, he shut his mouth quickly and got off the premises.

Only a few days after that, a man came in and was showing Odyssey some pictures that he had stored on his camera that he had taken at a bikini contest somewhere in Florida. He insisted that she show them to me as well even though I wasn't really interested. After she ran them all past me, she handed the camera back to him and went back to the dressing room. He pulled it back out and started examining it a few minutes later, then approached my desk. "I think that you have broken my camera. Do you know how much I paid for this thing?" I was petrified…even if I did know that there was nothing wrong with it while we had it. If he pressed the issue, it was my word against his and "the customer is always right" even in this business. I worried about it all night until I noticed something that he was doing that made me a little suspicious. He was going out to his car every few minutes and wiping his nose every time that he came back in. Being a drug addict myself, I had a pretty good idea what was going on. I just had to time this just right and problem solved. I watched him go out once more, waited a few minutes to give him time to prepare his next bump, and then walked up to his window to catch him red handed. He had several lines of crystal meth on his mirror when I shined the torch on him. Now *he* was scared to death and I was holding all the cards. I made him roll his window down and I told him that if he didn't get off our property immediately, I was going to call the cops. I even bluffed him by saying that I already wrote down his licence plate number. All of a sudden, his stupid camera was the least of his concerns and Odyssey and I were home free. He left immediately and I never heard from him again.

I had been in this business for a couple of years before someone actually threatened me with a weapon. The first time it happened was when a hood rat pulled out a switchblade in an effort to scare me. I can't say that I was shocked that some gutless coward would eventually stoop that low, but I was surprised that I had made it this long. When you threaten to cut someone who is a troubled, depressed drug addict who was already border-line suicidal with a broken heart, it is actually doing them a favour. At least, I would have died a hero and that's what people would remember me for. I just told the guy that if he intended to use that thing, he had better make sure that he killed me and not just wound me otherwise I was going to kill his entire family, ending his bloodline. He wisely put the blade back into his pocket and got into his car.

It wouldn't be long until someone else would take it a step further, and point a gun at me. Once again, I felt more insulted than afraid, inspiring me to approach the guy, practically begging him to pull the trigger. I even grabbed the gun and placed the barrel against my chest so he wouldn't miss but this seemed to turn the tables and freak *him* out, causing him to run away with his tail between his legs. No one inside the building knew that all of this was going on, because I had a tendency to go outside for some fresh air quite often. I wanted to die so I put myself in situations that would get the job done if the right person was on the other end. Unfortunately, no one had the balls to follow through with it, so I continued on in a world that I never belonged in.

The term "the bigger they come, the harder they fall" was indeed true, as I had proven time and time again, so it was the little guys who concerned me the most. They could take anything that you could dish out and just keep coming. One of these pint-sized hellions crossed my path one night and gave me the fight of my life. He touched a girl on stage after I had already warned him causing me to switch into attack mode. I went to grab him but he held on to the rail that surrounded the stage. He was so greasy and sweaty that my own momentum caused me to just slide off of him and send me flying across the room. I'm sure that from a distance, it looked like he just swatted me away like a fucking fly. Embarrassed and humiliated, I dug my fingers into his ribs, which made him let go immediately, and body slammed him on the concrete floor. I got on top of him, and began swinging away at his head while screaming "Who do you think you are? Do you know who you are fucking with? I'm not in the mood for this… you piece of shit!" I kept throwing punches until I saw blood coming from his mouth and one of his eyes nearly swollen shut. I walked him outside, thinking that it was over, when he decided to take a cheap shot at me. I grabbed him in a headlock, and hit him several more times in the jaw while his blood started staining my white t-shirt. He said that he would leave if I would release him, so I did and went back inside. Just as I was about to take a seat, he came through the door and sat back down at his table. Punky walked up to him this time and asked him to leave. I went out the second time with Punky but I let my guard down, allowing the customer to pop me in the eye and knock one of my contact lenses out. Now he was being beaten down by two of us instead of just one and he had finally had enough. I was so winded and exhausted afterwards, that I nearly collapsed when I got back in the building. I was then approached by a couple of the girls, who normally didn't acknowledge me at all, and asked if I would like to go into the office with them because watching me fight turned them on. I politely declined their offers because I was much too worked up already to appreciate their advances. All I wanted to do was catch my breath.

Later that night, Tommy sent me over to the main club to drop something off to Gene. I had just walked in the door when I saw Lena racing across the room to embrace me. "I heard that you got into a fight. Are you ok?" Before I could say anything, she saw the blood on my shirt. "Oh my God, you are bleeding!" she screamed. "Don't worry. It's not *my* blood" I replied as I held her tightly in my arms. For a brief moment at least, all was great in my world. This almost felt like a fairy tale, just the way I pictured it. Then she got called up to the stage and that ruined the moment. She turned as she was walking away and said "I've missed you." Too bad, she meant that as a friend and not a lover. As I was leaving, I saw a new girl named "Mercedes" doing a tabletop dance for a group of Mexicans. They were trying to stick a dollar bill up her twat and she was doing her best to fend for herself. I looked back at the bouncers and none of them were paying attention so I took matters into my own hands. I snatched the main culprit up in a full nelson and began dragging him toward the front door. Finally, one of the bouncers noticed all of the commotion and gave me a hand. We literally lifted this dude off the ground and carried him out the door then dropped him on his ass. To this day, Mercedes still talks about that incident when my name is mentioned. I had made it painfully obvious that night to everyone that Gene can hire as many blokes to replace me that he wants but none of them can fill my shoes whether he would admit it or not.

But even I wasn't prepared for what happened next. It was a typical night at the Last Chance 2000 until a group of five guys came into the building together. One of them was much larger than the rest of them and seemed to be the leader. He kept scanning the room, sizing up all of the bouncers, and plotting something. The first time that I had words with him was in the bathroom and I could tell that he wasn't taking me seriously. When he joined the others at their table, Tommy was already there, with cigar in mouth, handing out free admission passes to the entire group as a way of keeping the peace. I knew that it was a lost cause but he was the boss. I had only looked away for a second when I heard Phoenix scream and point in their general direction. I turned around and saw Tommy grab the leader by the throat and start pushing him toward the door. Lynn was next to the scene and I wasn't far behind. We got him out finally and his posse followed, not getting involved. There was the usual trash talking and threats but we went back inside hoping that they would just leave…but they didn't. When we had a look on the security camera, the leader had pulled a baseball bat out of his car and was smashing my windshield, then walked over to Tommy's car and smashed his. He then jumped into their car and they peeled out of the parking lot with gravel flying, which was hitting everyone else's cars, causing significant damage to one poor customer's new paint job on his corvette. We thought it was over but they returned a few minutes later to either cause more damage or to have another look at what they had already done. Tommy grabbed his pistol out of the office and ran to the backdoor. He fired a shot at their gas tank as they passed by then went back inside to call the cops. The group got arrested in the parking lot at the Wal-Mart just down the street where they were obviously planning their next move. To this day, I don't know what the leader said or did to get thrown out but I knew it was coming from the moment they walked in the door. However, the biggest mystery was how did that asshole know which cars belonged to us in a packed, dimly lit parking lot. They weren't there when we got to work that night and we had never seen them before, so there was no logical explanation, unless it was an inside job and that was highly doubtful. Tommy and I met up with the customer at the police station and we all pressed charges against the leader of the group, who we would find out had just got out on bail for a number of other crimes that he had committed somewhere else. Tommy and I just wanted him to pay for our windshields to be replaced but it would be a while before we could get a court date. More on that later...

3

Going to the Last Chance 2000 opened a lot of new doors for me when it came to one of my original boyhood dreams of becoming a professional wrestler. When a former WWE/ECW superstar came out to the club one night, we bonded right away. I was having trouble out of a couple of bodybuilders who were showing off in front of their girlfriends, and the wrestler told me that he was going to take care of it. "Watch and learn" he said. He proceeded to grab a chair and pull it up between one of the musclebound freaks and his girlfriend. He only had to sit there for a few minutes before the entire group got up and left. He rose up out of his chair, turned and smiled at me. He said, "Typical young punks who have done a cycle of steroids and think that they are something special...I used to fuck guys like that in prison." Considering that he was almost seven feet tall and tipping the scales at over 300 pounds, not to mention that his stints in the big house were well documented, he was probably telling the truth.

Now in his eyes, I owed him one, and what he wanted in return was for me to find him some cocaine. Although Jonah was in the building, I had no intentions of getting this monster high so I lied and told him that the club was dry. I knew that if something went haywire, he would be virtually impossible to control so I wasn't taking that risk. Jonah, on the other hand, introduced himself and took him outside to give him a fix. All was going great, until Jonah ran out and the monster wanted more. As I had predicted, he got hostile and agitated and everyone was in grave danger if I didn't think of something pretty quick. Jonah had already run to the hills at the first sign of trouble, leaving me to deal with this beast alone. Luckily, our new friendship played an important role in talking him down and getting him to leave before he snapped and hurt someone.

We had a bouncer named "Junior" at the club who, like Tommy, was a local wrestling star. He had trained under the tutelage of WWE Hall of Famer "Mr. Fuji" at his wrestling school in Knoxville. Fuji's own son even worked at the club from time to time, so wrestling was all around me. I talked Junior into bringing in Mr. Fuji so I could meet the man who managed everyone from the "Magnificent" Muraco and the "Powers of Pain" to "Demolition" and "Yokozuna". I was truly honoured to shake the man's hand and listen to his stories. He offered to take me on a student but I couldn't really afford it so I declined.

We also had "Who's Your Daddy" Terry Landell and "Nature Boy" Buddy Landell, who were both close personal friends of Tommy, in the club quite frequently. Tommy was actually working for Terry at his small regional promotion when they booked a venue. He usually worked "squash" matches against young upstarts who had no idea how to carry a match. He would often tell me about his days in the old NWA, like how "the Great Muta" was so smooth in the ring that although his moves looked devastating, when he actually hit you, you didn't feel a thing, to "Dan Spivey" beating the crap out of him on national TV. He also told me about a local televised match between himself and "Kevin Sullivan" that was so brutal that it almost wasn't shown on the air due to its graphic nature. All of this played a part in my decision to break into the business. With Tommy volunteering to train me in the old Smokey Mountain wrestling ring that sat in the centre of Terry Landell's wrestling school, how could I say no?

    When WCW brought Monday Nitro back once more to Knoxville, Terry asked Tommy and me, if we would like to attend the show with him. There was no way we were going to let this opportunity pass us by. We met up at the school and while we were waiting for Terry to get ready, I spotted his heavyweight championship belt resting on his mantle. I asked if I could have my picture taken holding the belt in my arms and he obliged. I still have that picture in storage back home. We arrived at the arena early, so we walked around the stands so Tommy and Terry could get some attention from the local fans. Terry, somehow, managed to get us backstage and past security. I asked one of the guards if my hero, Kevin Nash, was around and he told me that we literally had just missed him. We walked down the hall toward the dressing room and passed "Daffney" between a pair of security guards. She gave me kind of a friendly, yet flirty smile when she saw me which made me blush a little. We saw

"Ric Flair" sitting at a table talking to a couple of beauties. Terry stopped and said, "There's the man himself. Watch this." He approached the "Nature Boy" and placed a free admission pass on the table before him and said, "Come out to our club after the show." Flair barely reacted and said nothing at all. He looked down at the card but never made eye contact with any of us, even though we were only a couple of feet away from him, then continued to talk to the ladies. Needless to say, he never showed up. We were just outside the dressing room at this point, as "Konnan" and "Rey Mysterio" was stretching, getting ready for their match. The show was just about to start now, so we went and took our seats so we could watch the show. It was cool to listen to two guys, who were also in the business, sit and analyse every match frame by frame.

It was around this time that two significant events occurred at exactly the same time. Sara had returned from her hiatus and wanted to pick up where she left off with me. We shared a brief kiss in the DJ booth first, then a passionate kiss in the dressing room later. After that second kiss, Sara said "You've changed." She was right. When she last saw me, I was an innocent and naïve kid...now I was a drug infested, battle scarred pessimist that didn't give a damn about anyone but himself. For some unknown reason, she was attracted to what I had become and quickly claimed me as her own, without asking me how I felt about it first. This really pissed me off and was going to create a problem. I wasn't really interested in her anymore, but I felt like she owed me something, so I decided to play along for a little while before I showed her what this "new" me was capable of.

The second event was that I started my training for professional wrestling. Tommy even brought in local legend "Rick Connors" to advise and observe to see if I had the makings of a star. Although I had been a fan of wrestling since 1984, and used to mimic everything I saw on TV, once I stepped into the squared circle for real, I realized immediately that I had no fucking idea what the hell I was doing. I had heard former football players who crossed over to sports entertainment say on numerous occasions that training for professional wrestling was much harder than football ever was, and as a guy who had done both myself, I can vouch for that. It was brutal and required a lot of stamina and endurance to be successful, and unfortunately, I had neither. I was not only a smoker and a drug addict, but I had just completed a two week trial of steroid pills that didn't agree with me and I was still suffering from severe headaches long after I stopped. I did do cardio at the gym, but it was a lost cause once you factor in all of these elements. Tommy always stressed the importance of stamina in this business through stories about being in the ring with guys who had million dollar bodies but once that had to pick up the pace and get moving, they couldn't handle it and were throwing up under the ring during the match. I thought I was in decent shape until I stepped through those ropes for the first time. I wasn't near as prepared as I thought I was.

Being a slow learner, I had trouble with the move sets and sequences. I tried to make up for this by showing Tommy and Rick how tough I was by bouncing back up to my feet as quickly as possible which caused me to get a lecture about not "selling" the moves. Just before we were about to call it a day, we practiced getting thrown from the ring and onto the arena floor. On one of my attempts of going the middle ropes, somehow I got spun the wrong way and my eye caught the top rope giving me a painful burn. My contact had fallen out of that eye and it was beginning to swell but I was determined to keep going. Rick, who was standing outside the ring, noticed that I was having trouble seeing what Tommy was about to do and was favouring my eye. He made Tommy stop before I hurt myself and ended the session before inviting us out to dinner. About halfway through our meal, the pain was starting to really set in. By the time we finished eating, I was so sore that I could barely move at all. It was like every bone and muscle in my body was hurting at the same time. I had never felt so beaten up in my entire life as was starting to wonder if all this was going to be worth the trouble.

When we got back to the club, Sara came running up to me to give me a hug and a kiss. I tried to stop her before she got to me but I wasn't quick enough. I nearly shat myself when she embraced me due to the intense pain so she took it upon herself, since she was supposably "my girl", to take me to the back and rub oil on my body to give me a decent massage. As soon as Tommy saw what she was doing, he wanted a massage too… but not from her. "Brother, why don't we ride out to Oak Ridge and I'll pay for you to get a *real* massage?" he asked. At this point, I was down for anything or so I thought.

He ended up taking me to an "Asian Spa" and although I had heard rumours about what goes on in these types of places, I didn't really believe it. We walked in and Tommy paid the girl at the desk an undisclosed amount of money before we parted ways with our respective ladies. My girl took me to a table that was sitting in the centre of a large shower room. As she unravelled the hose, she asked me to take off all of my clothes and lie face down on the table. She lathered up everything from my heels to the crack of my ass with soap then rinsed it off with warm water. Now it was time to flip me over and clean the other side. She thoroughly scrubbed and rinsed every inch of me, including my privates, then handed me a robe and told me to follow her. We entered what looked like, and could only be called, a bedroom. Once again, she asked me to lie on my stomach with my head in the pillow. She straddled me and began rubbing everything… starting at my neck and working her way down to my toes. Then she asked me to turn over and repeated the process, this time starting at the top and working her way down until she reached my crotch. She paused there and looked at me. "What do you want me to do about that?" she asked as she pointed at my penis. I was confused. "What do you mean?" I asked. "We have reached that point where you need to let me know how far you want me to go" she said as she showed me the price list. She was a gorgeous woman and I wanted her badly but I wasn't willing to give her my hard earned money, especially when I could get laid for free at the club if I wanted to. Then I had a thought: "Maybe Tommy will pay for it…" I persuaded her to interrupt Tommy and ask him for more money even though I actually had enough cash in my wallet to get the full VIP treatment but I wasn't about to tell her that. She came back a couple of minutes later and told me that he only had enough money left for a hand-job after he paid for the *two* girls that were in his room… doubling his pleasure. At first, I was pissed off but a hand-job was better than nothing, especially when all I actually came in for was a massage. She took her top off and put on some gloves before lubricating me up. She got me off fairly quickly then pleaded with me to throw in more money so she could have sex with me. She even offered me a discount but I just couldn't do it.

When I walked back up to the counter, Tommy was standing there with a big grin on his face. My girl came out shortly after and literally begged me to come back and see her again. She looked at Tommy and said, "He has very nice penis." Tommy wanted to know more. "Do you mean quality or quantity?" he asked fishing for an insult. "Both" she said to his surprise. As we went out the door, Tommy said, "I think she wanted you bad." I replied, "Yeah, an Asian girl thinking that I have an incredible penis…why don't I feel as flattered as I should be?" We both shared a laugh as we headed back to the club.

Although Buddy Landell was very encouraging and supportive about my wrestling training, even promising to teach me how to do his old finisher "the corkscrew elbow", Terry and Tommy was losing patience fast. Terry already had an idea for my gimmick: changing my name to "Denny Nash" and have me play the character of being a "relative" of "Big Sexy." I wasn't sold on the concept unless it meant that I was going to win matches…which it obviously didn't. That was why I was on the receiving end of so many beatings. You have to be "over" with the fans before you can deliver them. Because I got such a late start, I wanted to skip all the bullshit and jump right into the main event but that wasn't going to happen. I was already starting to lose interest.

It didn't help when Terry was only criticizing me, and when fellow wrestlers like Junior was asking Tommy how I was coming along, and he would tell them that I was having trouble even learning how to apply a simple arm-bar. The only feedback I ever got was negative and it was killing my determination. I was on the verge of giving up when fate made the decision for me. While taking a body-slam from Tommy, I landed on the ball of my foot and nearly crushed it. I couldn't walk for several weeks… much less wrestle. I had to go to work wearing only one shoe until it healed, which rendered me useless and ineffective at the club. That's when my training stopped and my potential wrestling career was all but over.

But that wasn't the only thing that was coming to an end. Sara was really starting to annoy me and it was time for her to go. I haven't felt anything for her in years and nothing she could do was going to change that. The last straw was when I volunteered to take something over to the main club after hours just to avoid spending time with her. As I was getting ready to leave there, I heard the front door swing open and heard Jessie say "I brought your girlfriend over so you can take her home tonight." I just couldn't get away from her, no matter how hard I tried. We ended up doing coke together for the first time that night in my truck but I wasn't about to take her anywhere I was planning to be, so I dropped her off at a friend's house instead. She kissed me on the lips and wrote down her number before she crawled out of my truck. I waited until I got out of sight then tossed her number out the window, even though I promised that I would call her later. She never came back to work and I never saw her again.

Remember that girl who was missing her front teeth that I almost hooked up with back when I was still just a customer? She's back…and this time she was working at the Last Chance 2000. She still had a thing for me but she knew that I wasn't going to touch her willingly, so she asked me how much it would cost for me to sleep with her. I told her $300 because I knew that she didn't have the money and there was no way that she could draw that amount in one night. What I didn't anticipate, however, was someone loaning her the money as a practical joke. Phoenix did just that. When the girl handed me the money, I actually considered following through with my end of the bargain, using the thought of how much cocaine I could purchase with it as inspiration and motivation. It was the combination of Phoenix telling me after she tipped her on stage that the girl's vagina looked like it had been hit by a chainsaw, and the changing of the rules and stipulations by the girl herself that changed my mind. Now she was insisting that I had to also go down on her, and pretend like I was enjoying it while doing so, that was just too much. Although I was flattered that she wanted me enough to pay for it, which no one had ever done before, it still wasn't enough to seal the deal. I did, however, see Jonah sticking his tongue down her throat later on that night so maybe she did get lucky after all.

4

Another night I will not soon forget was the time that One Time threw a party at his house. He lived in one of the roughest neighbourhoods in the city and just the thought of us getting together in this location was absurd. There were two different groups of personalities that made the party branch off into separate circles. In his living room was where all the pot smokers gathered and in the kitchen was where all of us coke heads and speed freaks found ourselves. The party was really happening until there was a knock at the door after everyone was accounted for. I looked in the direction of the front door and all I could see was a massive cloud of smoke. I remember saying to the others in the kitchen that I hoped that the cops weren't outside cause they would have a field day with all of us considering how many illegal narcotics were floating around the house. When One Time answered the door, it was confirmed that our biggest fear had come true...it *was* the cops! Jonah, Homer, and I decided to start hiding our cocaine in everything from cereal boxes to loaves of bread…basically anywhere that was out of the open. We were all scared to death and praying that this was just a nightmare that we could wake up from, but unfortunately it wasn't. I was just about to make a run for the backdoor, which would have been a mistake of biblical proportions, when I heard the cops leaving. What had actually happened was that someone had parked their car in one of the neighbours' yards, and they wanted it moved at once, so they decided to let the police handle it instead of causing a scene themselves. Luckily, they weren't interested in busting us, only making the neighbours happy, so they turned a blind eye toward what they saw and smelled. Needless to say, most of the stoners left soon afterwards but we partied on…once we found all the dope that we had hidden that is.

It was the next morning and two eight-balls later, when we ran out of cocaine. Jonah, who had supplied us throughout the night, wasn't interested in getting more. However, Homer and I wanted to keep going… unlike the lightweights. He told me that he knew a place just down the road where we could definitely get some, even at that hour, so we grabbed a bottle of whiskey and got into his car. Unfamiliar with the area, I had no idea what I was in store for. We literally drove over a bridge and we were somewhere I had been before but swore I would never go again: the projects. We pulled up to a traffic light where there were several black kids standing in the median and Homer rolled his window down. "Have you got any powder?" he asked. One of the boys nodded his head and walked up to the car. "We want $100 worth" he continued. I couldn't believe that we were buying cocaine at 10:00 in the morning in the middle of a busy intersection in front of everyone. This just didn't seem right in more ways than one. The boy handed Homer a baggie, but before money was exchanged, he realized that we had been duped and pulled the note back before the boy could grab it. "I said powder, not rock!" he screamed. Just as we were about to drive off, the boy punched Homer right in the eye and made one last attempt to snatch the money out of his hand. Everything was going so fast that my mind was having trouble catching up, but we weren't out of the woods yet.

I had noticed that there had been a car tailing us ever since we left that traffic light and that worried me. I asked Homer to pull over so we could see what this man's problem was. He walked up to our car and flashed a pistol that was hidden under his jacket. "I saw what you did to those kids. They work for me you know and you try to rip them off?" he said. "*We* ripped *them* off you say? Look at what they handed us. Fucking candle wax!" Homer screamed. The man examined the contents in the bag and apologized for those kids' actions before letting us go. That morning was getting crazier and crazier but it wasn't over yet.

Homer then tried a different strategy. We went up and down the road slowly, seeking out black teenage boys who might be able to help us. I must confess that I felt like a sexual predator stalking his next victim. The first boy we came up to got scared and ran away, as expected, but the second one was just what we were looking for. We caught him as he left a convenience store and asked him if he knew where we could get a gram of cocaine. He said that his cousin was a dealer and he would hook us up if we took him to his house. However, he did warn us that his cousin hated white people or "crackers" and if he saw one of us in his house, he would probably put a bullet between our eyes so we would have to be very careful. We both agreed that it was worth the risk so the boy got in the backseat. As Homer was reversing out, he slammed into a fence that separated the market from the police station. There were two cops who were walking toward their cruisers at the time and witnessed the accident. They raced to get into their cars but we were too far away for them to catch us so we left them in a cloud of dust. The boy started screaming at Homer, calling him a moron among other things, and telling him that he was starting to have second thoughts, until I calmed the situation down. Once we reached the cousin's house, the boy told us that only one of us could go in. I volunteered to enter, telling Homer to stay in the car and keep it running just in case something went wrong. The boy and I went inside and I handed him the money before he ventured upstairs where his cousin was. I waited quietly at the bottom of the staircase with a million things going through my mind. What if I get killed here? They would never find my body. Hell, no one even knows where to look. What if things go haywire and Homer leaves me here? I was sure putting a lot of trust in someone who had already stabbed me in the back once already. A few minutes later, the boy returned and we made the exchange. I was out of there without even testing or sampling it, but luckily, it was the real thing this time around. Back at One Time's house, a majority of the crowd had either left already or were passed out on the floor, so Homer and I returned to the kitchen and restarted the party. We ran out again in the afternoon but continued drinking until I looked down at my watch and realized that I had to be at work in an hour. I was fucking wasted... but there was no way I could call in sick since Tommy knew where I was last night. I ended up working all night in this condition, and managed somehow, even if I couldn't remember a thing about it afterwards.

Later in the week, Punky and I rode out to Micheal's with One Time to have a few drinks. Once inside, we bumped into the whore that I took over to Jackson's birthday orgy and the boys managed to talk her into leaving with us instead of the guy she came in with. Since we all couldn't fit in the front of the truck, I had to ride in the back with her. Just like before, she drove me crazy because she would never stop talking, so it gave me an idea. I unzipped my pants and suggested that she should give me a blowjob. She didn't hesitate to go down on me again, even going down the street where everyone could see. I'm sure that everyone who was sitting beside us at a traffic light was getting quite a show. Every now and then, I saw Punky watching through the window but I didn't really care. I noticed that One Time was trying to drive around until I finished but with my stamina, he would probably run out of gas first, so I made her stop and I pulled my pants back up. One Time took her to the club, which was closed for some reason that night, so he and Punky could have a little fun. I really wasn't interested so I went home to get high.

There were always ladies who would come into the clubs to sell roses to either customers, or in my case, employees who was willing to buy one for their favourite girl. I had used roses on several occasions when I really liked a girl or was trying to pour it on to get into someone's pants. The rose lady at the main club was a sweetheart, who used to tease me because she knew what I was up to, but the one who came in the 2000 club fell hook, line, and sinker into my trap. I used to buy *her* roses because I could tell that she had a crush on me. One night I talked her into sticking around for the rest of the night. She had a few drinks and started feeling a little tipsy and by the end of the night, we were in her car making out hot and heavy. I almost had her naked before she got paranoid and went home. We didn't speak much of it afterwards and remained friends like nothing ever happened.

5

There was yet another change in management between the two clubs. Homer had got caught with his pants down by Gene and was being sent over to purgatory. One Time was chosen to take his place since I was still banned and only allowed in the main club when I was there "on business" usually after closing. About a week after he got there, he came out to see me to deliver a message from Lena. Her birthday was coming up soon and she was having a party at Micheal's to celebrate it. "She told me to tell you that she already knows that you are not working that night and it would mean a lot to her if you attended. Then she said that you had better show up or else. She misses you and she wants to see you" he said. Was this the moment that I had been waiting for such a long time? Come hell or high water, I was going to that party. Although, I had played around quite a bit since our split, I would erase everything to be with her. I had decided to try one last time to make this happen…it was time to sink or swim.

The night of the party, I had a stomach bug and had been either in bed or in the bathroom literally the entire day but I was going to drag myself to Micheal's if it fucking killed me. When I got there, just getting a moment to talk to Lena in private was practically impossible. Hell, I couldn't even sit close to her. I got some coke from one of my sources that worked there and started getting high as I always did, and spent almost the whole night in the bathroom either doing a line, throwing up or sitting on the toilet. When the party started breaking up and Lena was about to leave, I finally got a chance to spend some time with her. We sat out in the parking lot in her car and did a few lines together. She asked me where I had been all night and I told her that I wasn't feeling well. She thanked me for coming with a kiss on the cheek. I used this act of kindness and compassion to tell her once more how I still felt about her. So much had changed between us since she dumped me and I truly felt like an outsider looking in at something I could never have again. Gone were the days when I could say something sexy to her and she would have a quick comeback like "You know we could take that out in trade" or "Do you want to shag now or shag later?" Even when I kissed her on the lips a couple of times in the car that night, I felt like it was forced and unwanted. I still told her that "If anything happens..." Before I had a chance to finish this familiar phrase, she finished it for me. "Oh, you will definitely be the first to know" she said as I held her face in my hands. I kissed her one last time before getting out of her car. That would be the last time our lips would ever meet or we would ever discuss a possible future together. Too bad, the last thing she said to me with any emotion or feeling was not only a broken promise, but a fucking lie.

Over the past few years, I had looked after people when they were going through some bad times in their lives. When Tommy fell in love with a girl and couldn't have her and used alcohol to help him cope, I was there to talk him through it. Even when Bear came into the club drunk as a skunk one night with a buddy just before he quit, Tommy and I let him vent without judgement and made sure that he didn't hurt himself or someone else. But I had no one who cared enough to just give a few minutes of their precious time to listen and help me come up with answers. It has always been that way. That's why I have grown to despise families that are very close and people who have friends that are reliable. I have never had that. I've had to deal with everything in my own self destructive way. It's all I know.

    I am going to take a minute to talk about my views on homosexuality, and you will understand why a bit later. I am not going to exploit or condemn anyone's sexual preference because it is not my place to judge, however I do want people to know where I stand on this sensitive topic. When I was a teenager, I used to get so aroused by watching two beautiful women kiss each other. It was so taboo back then, but after spending several years at the club, seeing it happen as often as it was, my opinion was beginning to change. Night after night, I saw the same damn thing: a so-called "lesbian" would get drunk, forget she was gay, and end up making out with, or attempting to seduce, either myself or one of the other guys who worked there. Considering that they had partners who tried their best to look and dress like men, I questioned their true sexuality. I never understood why certain homosexuals chose this route. Wouldn't a gay man want the most masculine man they could find if that was what they were truly attracted to and not be interested in the feminine ones who showed the same characteristics as the opposite sex? Some lesbians were guilty as well. I would see a beautiful woman who was capable of getting any man or woman they wanted but would settle for a butch with either a mullet or a shaved head that always wore flannel clothes? Were they really into women or was this a trust issue that developed after years of bad experiences? Maybe they required a certain "sensitivity" that they weren't getting from men that only another woman could provide. I just wish that someone could explain this to me so I can have a better understanding, that's all.

Then there were the other ones…the ones who are, for the most part, "straight" but chose to always play around with their own gender when they are intoxicated. We had plenty of this type at the club as well. They often used this as a tool to draw attention to themselves, but a majority of the time, it worked against them when they tried it on me. However, one night at the 2000 club, even my defences were broken down. Nadia and Lena were both sent over to us for the night because we had a shortage of dancers. When I saw Lena in that building, I was overwhelmed. This was going to be the first time that we had worked together in a while and I just had a feeling that it was going to be a night to remember. I couldn't have been more right. For some reason, Nadia and Lena both got wasted and were playing around with each other throughout the night. As it got later, Nadia's boyfriend came in and got involved as well. I knew that he was trying to take advantage of the situation, perhaps get Lena to go home with them for a possible threesome. He would go up to tip Lena and she would rub her body against him like a bitch in heat. She was playing along, as I had seen her do in the past, but teasing and giving false hope was what she did best. I knew that better than anyone. The poor bastard wasn't going to have a three way on that night for sure. Back in the dressing room, as the girls were getting ready to leave, Nadia made one last attempt to get Lena to come home with her but got rejected again. To be truthful, I had known Nadia for a while and she loved being with other beautiful women and wasn't used to be turned down by *either* sex. This was actually the first time I had ever seen anyone resist her, no matter how hard they tried. As Lena was grabbing her bags to leave, Nadia said, "Well if I can't be with you, can I at least have a kiss then?" I immediately turned around to see what Lena was going to do. She put her bags back down and they locked lips and tongues for one of the most passionate and longest kisses I had ever seen two women engaged in that wasn't on film. Even the other girls stopped what they were doing and watched. One even pulled up a chair and said to me, "That is so fucking hot." I don't think I even took a breath until they finished. I had an instant erection that kept coming back every time I thought about it for years afterwards. I wasn't really jealous, which was unusual, but maybe that was because I did have both their tongues on me at the same time before and felt like I was actually a part of this. I was just going to leave it at that but then Lena had to go and tarnish it for me. She looked at me with one of her cheeky grins and said, "Did you like that? Well, tomorrow night Nadia and I will be working together again at the other club. We are going to be doing more of that but this time you won't be able to watch." I didn't know what to say to that. Lena knew that comment got to me and enjoyed every minute of it. She was even laughing about it as I walked her to her car. I don't know why she enjoyed fucking with me so much, especially when it was uncalled for. If she didn't want to be with me, why even bother? Just leave me alone and let me heal…

When I've got a boner and need a shrink, I never heard my dick was like a bull's. She said I was a goner on the brink, a mechanic with a very small tool. She made a sandwich, and put me in the middle. Who's the butch and who's the bitch, when I'm playing second fiddle, to peanut butter and her cocker spaniel?

But I'm very good with my hand, it never tells me no...thinking about being stranded on a deserted island, with Alyssa Milano.

Through these eyes, it was a bad idea, like feeding pigeons, but it may be a blessing in disguise...the tossing of the salad, the icing on the cake, yet the conclusion is uncertain. Will we conceive a world, will we duplicate? Will the eggs hatch, will the water break?

She had me by the short hairs, I didn't wear protection, never thought about infections, she sat on Santa's lap, but her present wasn't wrapped, the penetration caused premature ejaculation, and the next morning I was scared, when that cunt said, "if I get pregnant, I'll throw myself down those stairs."

Sip pennyroyal tea, and list my deficiencies, pick the scab until it festers...cut the scar that shames me of nudity... (I guess size does matter) You can lead a horse to water, but you can't make it drink. I fell more limp than ever, when I dipped my pen in company ink.

As she thinks of another metaphor for the word slut, and starts pointing her finger, I'm on the killing floor, spilling my own guts, and what should be kept behind closed doors, ends up on Springer.

From the coronal ridge to the London Bridge, sixty nines and Sutter Home wine, dirty Sanchez, golden showers...one day it will be time to repay. Tight lipped, but sink ships later, when I finally have my say.

Would rather cut off my genitals, than see another nun be defiled...would rather be rendered barren, than give an inch when she wants a mile.
-Denny Noland "Draven" From my song "Through These Eyes"
 Written on December 3, 2006
Copyright 2007

6

When I was down and out, and didn't think I could go on, my phone rang. The person on the other end was the only human being on this planet that could lift my broken body back up off the ground. It was Justice. She had just returned from Atlanta, where she had a life changing experience that opened her eyes on a number of things she had done in the past. For some reason, she thought of me and how she never really gave me a chance. She was ready to fix that. She told me that she wanted to date me for real this time and see what develops. Although I wasn't interested when Sara tried the exact same thing, Justice was different. Obviously, I didn't feel as strongly about her as I once did, but I still had enough feelings for her to give it a shot. "Maybe she *was* the one that I was supposed to be with all along…" I thought to myself.

We went out on dinner dates like before and we even spent an entire day at the old "Ogle's Water Park" in Pigeon Forge. However, it was what we were doing at night that would become our downfall. We were partying constantly…whether it was cocaine or some over the counter, new age recreational drug that she introduced me to. In other words, we were constantly high and that wasn't good. It created an unstable atmosphere where anything could, and often did, happen. For example: one night she brought her boa constrictor out and placed it on her bed while she listened to music and sorted her wardrobe. I don't know whether it was the vibrations from the speakers or something about me that it didn't like, but the snake had become stressed, and was aggressive toward Justice when she tried to pick it up. She was freaking out because it had never done that before and asked me to help her catch it. We threw a blanket over it to keep from getting bitten and eventually got it back in its cage. It was just surreal being in this environment, because it was so unpredictable. I don't think I was ever really comfortable being there.

We did, however, finally have sex. It only happened once, and I can't remember who or what initiated it, so the details are sketchy to say the least. I can only recall how she felt when I entered her and what she said to me afterwards. She told me that she thought that my condom had come off during intercourse but I assured her that it hadn't. We then took a hot shower together to wash the scent off before going to sleep. I didn't know how much being intimate with her had helped me get over Lena until after we were already over. To this day, Justice has no idea how significant the night actually was to me...until now of course.

We only dated for a brief period of time before everything fell apart. If you blinked, you might have even missed it. Sometimes I wonder if my heart was even in it at the time. I could have been unknowingly sabotaging the relationship all along and just didn't care. But strangely enough, it wasn't me that ended the whole affair...it was Justice, and I never even saw it coming. We had been partying all night as we always did, and we ran out of coke at around 9:00 in the morning. We might have had a minor disagreement or something beforehand, but as I was ready to wind down and sleep it off, Justice started having a fit. She was screaming and crying hysterically before she called her mother and told her everything. She confessed to having a drug problem and even suggested that she might need to go to rehab. I was just lost. I couldn't believe how quickly she went from being "normal" to whatever the hell you call this. It was like someone just flipped a switch. As soon as she hung up the phone, she told me to get out of her house. Let's just put it this way: I wasn't in any condition to drive yet and I wasn't too keen on putting my life at risk if I didn't have to, so I asked her if I could at least sober up first. She refused…even appearing insulted that I would ask such a thing, so I left and miraculously made it home in one piece. Needless to say, I wasn't interested in her anymore and it was over as far as I was concerned.

(UPDATE: A few years later, while I was on my honeymoon with my second wife in Gatlinburg, I saw Justice, but I don't think that she saw me. I wouldn't have wanted it any other way. I would also hear her voice on the radio several times over the years, but even that didn't make me want to talk to her. However, that all changed when I joined Facebook in 2010. I found her and sent her a friend request which she accepted. We messaged each other back and forth several times until I told her that she was still just as beautiful as I remembered her and she didn't respond. I think that she might have assumed that I was coming on to her but I was only trying to throw her a compliment…nothing more. We had very little interaction until she read that I was writing this book. She has been very supportive and encouraging about the project, even flattered that she was going to be a part of it. I will eternally be grateful to her for helping me through one of the most painful and difficult times of my life even though she was actually unaware that she was doing so.)

Was a romantic epiphany, I couldn't take my eyes off of her, from across a crowded room. Maybe, we'll never have that luxury, maybe, the riches this world has to offer, will never do. Always

seeking someone unattainable, need to stick to my own kind, never felt so invisible, is this world that dark, or am I just that blind?

I'll be the jerk, that causes all the fireworks, too bad she don't believe in fairy tales…instead we'll repeat the pattern: "I'll be at home getting hammered, while she's out getting nailed."

I'm so hated, and she's so jaded, we both need an attitude adjustment. We need to believe it, to receive it, or we'll never have anything permanent.

I know what she's thinking about, "Have I been working out?" when I look like shit, I loved the way she touched me, oh, how well she knew my body, we ate from the same fork, and broke the habit, by throwing away all the spoons. Every time I come back from war, she's there to lick my wounds.

So many roads, so many detours, and she's running on empty. As she takes a long drive up the coast, I'm pacing the floor, cause she left so abruptly. Hit the brakes in the snow… tell me there's a light, at the end of the tunnel. See the approaching tornado… tell me it's going to be alright, in the walls of the funnel.

No more stress or PMS, no more pick-up lines, like "What's my sign?" let's paint the town red, she needs this, like another hole in her head, tastes me on her lips, smells me on her skin, carpe diem…then at midnight, I'll turn back into a pumpkin.

Don't want to depend on anyone, just her lithium. Now she's gothic, wearing black lipstick, with a pale complexion. (Let me hold your hair while you throw up) "Come to bed," said the spider. "I hate to sleep alone." Caught in her web, she's like cancer, eating me down to the bone.
 -Denny Noland "Draven" From my song "Love Song"

Written on January 14, 2007   Copyright 2007

7

There were a lot of girls making big bucks in Knoxville back in those days, and word was spreading fast. In the past, we had picked up Nadia, her sister "Carla," and Adam's ex Angelina, from the south and now we were being invaded by a wave of dancers from Johnson City in the north. The first four that appeared were two quite attractive ladies, a nasty skank who hated me from the start that would later call me "a wannabe anything" and a girl who was so thin that Gene nicknamed her "Skinny Minnie." He used to say that "if she stood behind the pole, she would have to stick her tongue out so you could see her." Homer and I took the two pretty ones in the VIP room so we could check them out. One of them was a gothic chick with multi-coloured hair and huge store bought tits named "Chardonnay" and the other was a more down to earth, natural looking blonde named "April." I managed to get a kiss from April during the dance but that was as far as we went. Chardonnay, on the other hand, went much further. She took me out for a meal after work and the understanding was that we were going back to her motel room to have sex after that. I was a perfect gentleman to her in the restaurant, even opening doors, pulling out her chair and taking her coat. I thought that was what she wanted but she didn't like it at all. It actually made her change her mind about everything because I was "too nice of a guy to be taken advantage of." We still made out in her car until sunrise then parted ways. I would find out the next day that she was actually married and was planning to either place an audio recorder, or just call her husband beforehand and leave the phone under the bed while we were having sex, so he could listen. Apparently, he got off on his wife being with another man, especially a total stranger. Honestly, it wouldn't have made any difference to me as long as I was getting laid. I had been in a similar situation before, but don't tell her that, because she already had me figured out. I don't want to hurt my rep... right?

In time, Chardonnay would see how I really was and reconsider but on the night in question, I had other offers...two in fact. One was a beautiful but noticeably overweight girl from my hometown named "Alicia" who wanted me and a new girl from Johnson City named "Samantha" who sounded like Fran Drescher in "The Nanny" when she talked. All three of these ladies called dibs on me that night but wasn't willing to share so I had a choice to make. Alicia was a bit too plump for my taste, and I was still angry at Chardonnay for what she did to me last time, so Samantha was looking like the front runner. One Time was in the club that night and had already taken a liking to her until he walked back to the dressing room and saw us kissing and he knew that crushed his chances. I nearly blew it when I thought Sam wasn't looking, and I shared a kiss with Alicia only for her to turn around at the last second and catch us in the act. I managed to charm my way out of it by playing the victim so we were back on. The beautiful part about this particular club was that most of the girls didn't like each other so they rarely talked. I would take advantage of this countless times over the years.

Our little rendezvous at the motel went beautifully until there was a knock at the door the next morning. Samantha jumped up out of the bed and screamed, "Oh my God, Dad is here! I forgot that he was coming by this morning!" I tried to calm her down by telling her that he doesn't have a key. "He *does* have a key, that's the problem. I told him to come on in if I didn't answer the door" she replied. She had barely finished the sentence before he was standing inside the room, staring at us on the bed. I was only in my underwear and Samantha had on a see through gown. The look the bearded redneck wearing camos gave me was indescribable... but he never said anything to me about violating his daughter. I intended on this being just a one night stand, but there was just something about this girl...

However, that didn't stop me from having sex with Alicia at my house the next day. Since she only lived a couple of miles away, she just showed up at my doorstep unannounced for one reason and one reason only. We started kissing on my deck then I led her to my bedroom. I went down on her first before I took her top off. I must admit that she had made an art out of wearing skimpy clothes that covered up her love handles. At work, she never exposed her belly and now I knew why. As she was giving me oral, I only looked at her face, which was quite beautiful compared to her body. I reached out to my bedside table for a condom and she stopped me in my tracks. "No protection needed baby" she said. "I've had my tubes tied." I had just had unprotected sex with a different girl less than 24 hours ago, and now I was feeling like a venereal disease waiting to happen, yet I went through with it anyway. She mounted me while I was lying on my back and everything was going great until I reached up to squeeze her sides to help me to penetrate her deeper and got two handfuls of flab. I lost my erection immediately... and despite her best efforts, it wasn't coming back. She left the house disappointed and would drag my name through the mud at work to anyone who would listen, but miraculously Samantha wasn't one of those people. The way I saw it, she was a nuisance that was lucky to get what she got from me. She also drove me crazy constantly talking about having sex with the guy from my school who left the scar on my chin when I played football, like I cared. Although she always ran me down to the girls in the back, she still kept trying to have sex with me again to no avail. I often wondered why these girls who always did, and probably still do, criticise me every time my name is brought up, would still drop their panties in a heartbeat if I asked them to. If I was so terrible, why even go there again? Go figure…

I still didn't let the criticism get to me. My arrogance was shown only a few days later, when I saw Homer going down on a girl in the VIP room. I could tell that she wasn't getting into it, so I offered my services to her. She sat back down on the couch and spread her legs and I got her off soon after. She said, "You really know what you are doing, don't you?" I came back with the clever response "I was taught everything I know by a lesbian." She would repay that debt one night when I had been drinking heavily and feeling down. Tommy, being the friend he was, asked her if she would like to go into the office and "cheer me up." She didn't think twice. She came in and we fooled around for an hour at least before she had to go back up on stage.

8

We are going to change gears for a minute. There were a lot of myths, legends, and ghost stories that surrounded both clubs. The main club was actually sitting near, if not on, part of an old cemetery. I know that for a fact because I've explored the woods behind the building and saw the graves for myself. There were even a few old caskets sitting on top of the ground that had obviously been washed out over the years and were dated back to the 1800's. Although I had never experienced anything inside the building, Gene apparently had. He told me about the time that they were getting the place fumigated and something happened that he couldn't explain. He and the manager at the time had covered all the tables with sheets and placed the chairs up on the bar before locking the club up for the night. When they came back the next morning to air out the building, all the sheets were pulled off the tables and lying on the floor and that wasn't even the creepiest part. The chairs that were sitting up on the bar were now neatly placed around their respective tables! From that moment on, the manager was scared to be in the building by himself. He always heard strange noises and saw shadows and was convinced that the place was haunted.

However, the 2000 club was rumoured to have a much darker history. I was told by a number of people that back before it became a strip club, it was a house of ill repute. The legend says that the upstairs attic was the scene of a grisly murder. An escaped convict had sex with one of the prostitutes up there and when it came time to pay, an argument ensued. The man apparently pulled out a knife and stabbed her repeatedly until she was no longer breathing. I never bothered to verify this story, and still don't know whether it was fact or fiction, but I will tell you what I legitimately experienced in that building. One night, a few of us stayed back after closing to have a few drinks when we heard a pop like someone just turned on the sound system in the DJ booth. Then we heard a number of mysterious voices that seemed to be coming across the microphone ever so faintly. We all looked at each other like we had just seen a ghost. I thought that someone must have snuck into the booth when we weren't looking to play a prank on us, so I tiptoed to the entrance to trap them inside since there was no escape. There was only one way in and one way out, so it would be practically impossible to make a run for it without someone seeing you. To my surprise, no one was in there and the sound system was all lit up like Christmas. I turned off all of the power and told everyone that the booth was empty. That was when Phoenix told us about seeing an old man in ragged clothes standing at the bar earlier in the night. She asked him what he wanted and he said that he needed to use the phone. She turned her back for only a few seconds to grab the phone for the old man and when she turned back around, he had simply vanished. She thought it was odd because she didn't see this guy come in and no one saw him leave. I was sitting at the door all night and didn't remember seeing anyone who fit that description enter the building either. Needless to say, everyone was a little spooked then and wanted to go home immediately. A few nights later, all of the bouncers, including myself, were determined to prove that we weren't afraid by staying back one more time with all the lights turned off and just listen. I think that there were about five off us in there that night... all grown men who wouldn't back down from anyone, and we didn't even last five minutes, before the lights were turned back on. That place had a way of sending chills down your spine, especially at the witching hour.

9

One thing I thought for certain that I would never see was Dewayne working in one of Gene's clubs again but he resurfaced once more at the Last

Chance 2000. Things were different this time around between us, as I pretty much gave him the cold shoulder in an attempt to steer clear of him. The only notable event was the night that one of the girls had just given me a blowjob only minutes before she was seen making out with Dewayne up in the booth. The girl's name was "Toni" and she was a real trooper…a valuable asset to have around a bunch of horny guys. We all benefited from having this lovely lady working for us at one time or another, but Dewayne obviously wasn't aware of that. After having a good laugh watching what he was doing, I had to ask him "Well, how did I taste?" He knew exactly what I meant and nearly spewed. After that, he had second thoughts before attempting to shag every girl who would give him the time of day.

The funny part was that I was supposably in a relationship with Samantha during all of this. I was fooling around with other girls practically right in front of her without her noticing. One of those girls was Toni, which was ironic considering that when Samantha's brother came in for a visit, she actually set them up together to get him laid. Toni wasn't shy about just coming up to me and asking if she could give me head. Of course, I wasn't going to turn her down. She went down on me several times in the office while Samantha was just outside the door. I did this because I never fully trusted her for some reason. I just knew that she was going to be unfaithful to me at some point, if she hadn't already, so I justified my actions by cheating on her every opportunity I could. This would lessen the blow when I found out about her infidelity.

One of those times that Toni waxed me in the office, I asked her to go make out with Tommy afterwards, like she had previously done with Dewayne. I thought that it would be hilarious to play a prank on him but it didn't quite work out the way I planned it. When she walked up to him and leaned in for a kiss, *he* grabbed *her* and planted a big French kiss on *her*, and he knew for certain where that mouth had just been. That took the fun right out of it. Even when I tried to humiliate him verbally, he said "Well, I figured that she had either swallowed or at least gargled afterwards. If not, you tasted alright." There was no way to embarrass or shame Tommy…he would just turn the tables on you and make you feel like the fool instead.

Speaking of making a fool out of myself, I was about to take that to a whole new level. One night, while Samantha was going down on me back at my place, her tongue ring went into the hole of my penis by mistake. I let out a scream that probably woke up the neighbours but we kept on going despite my agonizing pain. We were so wasted that we passed out on the couch and didn't think anything else about it. Samantha left early the next morning while I slept in. When I got up later on to take a piss, it felt like someone was holding a lighter beneath my penis. In a panic, I rang Lars to ask him what he thought was going on since I had no recollection about what happened the night before. He said, "You don't have anything to worry about unless it burns when you pee." I was now very concerned. "It's almost like I'm pissing fire" I replied. "That's not good man" Lars said. "You probably have some blockage up in there. You need to go to the doctor immediately. They will probably have to stick something up the end of your penis to clear it out. It's going to hurt like hell but you will feel much better afterwards." I just knew that Samantha had given me something and I was determined to make that bitch pay for whatever medical procedures I needed.

I got to work early that day and waited in the parking lot for Samantha to show up. When she arrived, I walked straight up to her car before she had a chance to even open the door. "I want you to know that you have passed on something to me last night. I expect you to fix this." I was shocked that she thought the whole thing was funny. "You don't remember what happened last night do you? You don't have anything unless you picked it up somewhere else because I've been tested for everything and I'm clean. I can, however, explain why you have that burning sensation." She then refreshed my memory about the freak accident the night before. I felt like the village idiot but was relieved to finally know the truth. I was as good as new a couple of days later.

Samantha had also begun to get quite jealous when other girls started giving me attention. Case in point, the night Simone came over to work with us. She greeted me with a hug and a kiss, since she hadn't seen me in ages, and Samantha didn't take it too well. She followed Simone to the dressing room to stake her claim but it didn't exactly work out the way she wanted. Simone immediately came up to me and asked if Samantha was my girlfriend and I replied "Sort of...why?" even though I was pretty sure I already knew the answer to that question. "Well, that little bitch confronted me in the back and threatened to kick my ass if I put my hands on you again." I had to ask her what she said in response to that and she replied, "I told her that if I wanted you, I would have you. I also warned her that if she got into my face again, I was going to prove it to her." I can't imagine why I felt insulted by what she said, even if it was 100% accurate.

It was hilarious to listen to Samantha tell everyone how bad she was, and how much she loved to fight, especially when you saw how tiny and petite she was. However, there were two girls that worked in the club back then that was taller than most men. Their names were "Shannon" and "Destiny" and wouldn't you know that I had brief connection to both? I used to make out with Shannon occasionally but she never seemed to enjoy it. She wouldn't ever turn away but she would bitch and moan about it afterwards which was intriguing considering that I saw her trying to have sex with an old man and a midget on separate occasions. Maybe I was too natural and normal for her...who knows? The only time she seemed somewhat interested was the night I saw her at Micheal's with a group of older men and she was quite drunk. I always felt like that was only the alcohol talking though. Destiny, however, was an enigma. I had heard rumours that she liked me a lot but she rarely talked to anyone, especially me. When she was publicly linked to someone, it was usually another girl. It wasn't until she saw me kissing one of the flavours of the week and took offense to it that she actually muttered a few words of anger and frustration in my direction. Although she was gorgeous, she wasn't really my type, if I had one, and nothing ever developed.

    Then there was the lovely "Amanda". She was a girl who was always there to tell me when my relationships were falling apart that my significant other "didn't realize how lucky she was" to have me. Sometimes she would take it even further by saying something like "I wish that I was the one that got your attention instead of her. I would actually appreciate it." There were several girls who threw little daggers at me like this over the years, but they all missed their mark just the same. On a number of occasions, I saw this girl at an after- hours nightclub called "The Boiler Room" doing a little ritual that turned everyone's heads in the room, male and female alike. She would grab a chair and sit down, then put another coat of lip gloss on and place her hands behind her back like she was handcuffed and wait. Eventually, one of the other strippers would straddle her and they would lock lips for several minutes, usually to a rousing ovation. I started teasing her one day after watching one of these shows the night before. She was so drunk at the Boiler Room that night that she couldn't even remember who she kissed the next day. She even asked me if we kissed or not. When I told her that we didn't, she replied "Too bad…we will have to change that." We didn't wait until we got to the Boiler Room to have that kiss, it happened in her car at the end of the night. There were a couple of other times here and there that we played around a bit, but we never went "all the way" even if we both wanted to.

10

It was around this time that the Insane Clown Posse came into the club, without their makeup on of course. They were sitting only a few feet in front of me the entire time and I had no idea until one of the girls told me. They seemed pretty cool to me, despite random girls coming up to me throughout the night telling me that they were being assholes.

We were also frequently visited by a man who claimed to be Metallica's road manager. I didn't believe him because in this business men would say anything if they thought it would get them a piece of ass. It wasn't until I went back and watched an old Metallica documentary and saw the man being interviewed on film that I realized that he was indeed who he said he was. One of his crew members even drove one of Jason Newsted's cars to the club one night to show it to me. They were all great guys and were never any trouble at all. I used to wonder why there were so many people who were associated with Metallica in town when they weren't on the road. It all made sense when I read that the band's "official" fan club was based in Knoxville.

11

While Samantha was away for a while to visit her family, I got briefly involved with yet another girl at the club. Her name was "Rachel" and she had just ended a long relationship with a former acquaintance of mine. She came up to me one night at the club to let me know that she was officially single and asked me if I would like a private dance in the VIP room. To be perfectly honest, she had never been on my radar until that very moment. She took my hand and led me to the first couch we came to on the next song. Once I got seated, she took her panties off and shoved them into my mouth. Her tongue quickly followed and I realized right away that this wasn't going to be just any ordinary dance. When she stood up on the couch and placed her vagina close to my mouth, it was on. I went down on her until the music stopped. There was another girl with a customer in there with us, who watched the whole thing while doing her own performance, that was smiling at me every time I came up for air. She had our backs though...cleverly shielding her client from seeing what we were doing.

Later that same week, not only did I have Rachel at my house, but her two besties "Keisha" and "Lindsey" were also in attendance. As soon as I got out the blow, Lindsey hit the door. Although she didn't want to party, Keisha was more than happy to stay until we ran through my entire stash. We ended up loading into my truck and driving to

Micheal's to get more a couple of hours later. When we got back to my house, Keisha asked if she could use my phone. As she picked up the receiver, two cockroaches came darting across the counter to my embarrassment. She let out a scream that would curl your hair and left soon afterwards, leaving Rachel and me alone. I was so ashamed of my living conditions, especially considering that I had offered to let Rachel crash at my place until she found an apartment, that I was no longer in the mood to do what we came there to do. To her credit, Rachel stretched out on my couch and waited patiently for me to make my move for hours before she asked me to drop her off at Keisha's on my way to work. That just goes to show once again that although I got a lot of ass back in those days, I *could* have got a lot more if I wanted to.

Now Samantha was back in town...which meant that I was going to pull off the heist of the year if I could keep her from finding out about Rachel, especially with them both working in the same building. One night, when I walked into the dressing room, I saw Tommy going down on Keisha. As I turned to leave the room, Keisha said "I want Denny to eat me now." I declined until both her and Tommy called me out by saying I was chicken. I told Keisha to meet me in the office so we weren't out in the open. Hell, both Samantha *and* Rachel were both in the building somewhere and I wasn't interested in getting caught. Not today.

Once we were both in that infamous office, we started kissing as I pulled down her panties. I placed her in Tommy's chair with her legs spread and I dropped to my knees. I tore into her with a passion but I was about to experience something that I had never experienced before: dissatisfaction. She wasn't enjoying it at all. This was a real shock to my system, because I had never heard any complaints about my oral skills...even from girls who had grown to hate my guts! I took great pride in my work and believed that I could pleasure *any* woman with my tongue until I did her. As I went to change my approach and try a different strategy, I heard the doorknob turn and the key being inserted. It was One Time...who had come out to get plastered on his night off from the main club. "I just came in to get my hat" he said. "How did you get the fucking keys?" I asked. "Phoenix gave them to me" he replied. That was enough for Keisha...she was already standing up and getting dressed. I kissed her one last time before we went out separately to avoid suspicion.

When I exited the office, Samantha saw me and motioned for me to come over to the other side of the bar where she was sitting. I wasn't sure what to expect. "Did she know what I had been doing?" I thought to myself. When I took a seat beside her, she gave me a deep, passionate kiss and told me she loved me. I was so paranoid that she could taste Keisha on my lips or smell her on my breath, but apparently she couldn't, which was a miracle if I had ever witnessed one. She would have killed both of us if she knew where my mouth had just been...especially since she didn't like Keisha at all.

Just when I thought I had cheated certain death, the unexpected happened. For some reason, Keisha had started feeling guilty about what she had done and confessed everything to Rachel. Now, all of a sudden, they were both in tears and hugging while I had become the sorriest excuse for a human being that ever walked this planet. This had all escalated to quite a dilemma and was going to get far worse if Samantha figures out who they are talking about. Fortunately, she remained oblivious to the whole thing, mostly due to her excessive drinking. As far as she knew, I was still the perfect would be boyfriend and I was determined to keep it that way.

Samantha's brother "Timmy" decided to come down to Knoxville for a fresh start resulting in the two of them moving in with our bartender, who had daughters either the same age or older than Samantha. I always knew that he had a thing for her, but never considered him to be a legitimate threat, yet something about this whole scenario just didn't feel right to me…so I did something about it. I drove out to his house and invited both Samantha and Timmy to move in with me instead. They jumped at the offer, so I threw all their shit into my truck and took them to their new home.

Timmy would find a job soon after, working for one of Samantha's regular customers who just happened to own his own tree trimming company. Even with his extra income, I never asked him to pay rent or chip in on groceries. I was just happy to have someone looking after the house overnight while Samantha and I were working. I basically treated him as if he was family, and in time, I would live to regret it.

Not long after she unpacked all of her things, Samantha gave me a sincere, yet unexpected, warning. She told me that when she was a little girl, she had a bad experience with the Ouija board. Apparently, something attached itself to her and never left. It continues to follow her wherever she goes. Although it was no secret that I was fascinated with the paranormal, I thought nothing about what she told me. Especially after she also told me that she had been diagnosed with ovarian cancer some years before but was too scared to go through with the treatment. I think you will see how that might have overshadowed the so called "ghost." I actually forgot all about it until a couple of weeks later.

It all started with minor things like the cats reacting to something that I couldn't see or objects being moved from where I left them and it only seemed to happen when I was in the house alone. I blamed it all on either coincidence or an overactive imagination. Then the footsteps started. I was in the shower one night when I heard them for the first time. They were so clear and distinct that I would have bet my life that either Samantha or Timmy had come home and were walking down the hall to the bathroom and stopped just outside the door. The only problem was that no one was there and there were no evidence that anyone had been there either. If that wasn't creepy enough, I heard those same footsteps another night while I was lying in bed with the lights off. Once again, the sounds started at the other end of the hall and kept getting louder the closer they got until they reached the door… then silence. I summoned up enough courage to open the door and have a look but came up empty handed yet again. I was so freaked out that I never slept in that bedroom again.

One night, while Timmy and I were both home and Samantha was away, I was about to bring up the topic to see if I was indeed going crazy or not when Timmy brought it up instead. I was so relieved to hear that he was witnessing the same paranormal activity as I was. It would go on until Samantha and I split about a year later and all of her belongings were out of my house. I would find out down the road that the guy who not only bought my house, but also pretty much lived in a shed in my front yard at the time when all of this shit was happening, had an experience of his own. He said that he woke up one night and couldn't move. When he opened his eyes, he saw what could only be described as a "shadow person" holding him down. This was coming from one of the most honest, god fearing men I've ever known. Since this occurred around the same timeframe that I was hearing footsteps in my house and only a few feet away from where I was, was this "shadow person" the same entity that walked my hall and terrorized me as well? You be the judge...

12

Now it was time to meet her parents. First, we headed up to Kentucky where her father lived. I was concerned about how he was going to be towards me, especially after seeing me in bed with the daughter the last time we were in the same room. But before I could be too worried about that, I had to brave the elements in order to get there. As we crossed Jellico Mountain late that night, we hit heavy snow, which caused slick and treacherous road conditions, not to mention low visibility. I just took my time and got us there safely. The scenery up there was absolutely stunning, especially with snow on the ground. It actually could have been on a postcard...it was that beautiful. Although I wasn't looking forward to that road trip at first, I was now starting to enjoy it.

When we got up to the cabin, Samantha's dad was pretty cool. We sat and watched movies with him and discussed the fast approaching Y2K dilemma and how we were preparing for it. He was what they now call a "doomsday prepper." He lived out in the middle of nowhere with a pet raccoon and an endless supply of eggs, courtesy of about ten ostriches that he kept in his barn. He took me out there to see them and I foolishly entered the barn like he had a litter of kittens instead of a flock of large birds that were capable of ripping me apart with their claws. The ostriches were all sitting in a circle and what did I do? I walked into the middle without a concern in the world. One by one, they all gradually stood up. I asked Samantha's dad what was going on and all he said was "Start backing up slowly. No sudden movements." I followed his advice and got out of the barn before he slammed the door shut. "What happened?" I asked. He replied "They felt threatened by you. Had I left you in there, they would have probably killed you and I couldn't have done anything about it." We both agreed to go back inside, where it was safe, to thaw out. The sleeping arrangements were that Samantha and I could sleep in a sleeping bag on the floor in the living room which basically meant that we were having sex that night…and we did. But this time, at least, we were dressed and packing when he entered the room the next morning. We said our farewells and left around midday but our journey home didn't go as well as either of us would have liked. Samantha's car broke down on the interstate near a hotel that looked like something out of Stephen King's "The Shining." We would get a room there for the night but wouldn't stay for very long because my dad, upon receiving word about our car trouble, picked us up in his van and took us the rest of the way home. Samantha's family would have her car towed and repaired in the following days.

    Then it was time to meet Samantha's mother and three children. We would travel to Bristol, Virginia this time and once again it was snowing. I didn't have any problems until I saw the driveway. It was a long and winding gravel road to the top of what Samantha would call "Turkey Holler." Her mother lived in a house up there and I had no other choice but to at least attempt to get the car up the snowy path. I just floored it and never touched the brakes even if I felt it sliding and made it up on the first try. I was so proud of myself.

I liked her family very much, even if they were a bit on the redneck side. Her stepdad took us for a drive in the snow that scared me half to death. We went to a bridge just down the road and he would purposely slide all over the icy road just for fun. I was in the backseat nearly having a heart attack but didn't say a word. He got us back safely and we had a wonderful dinner before turning in for the night. I would receive a message from back home telling me that Gene wanted to move me back to the main club. He even sweetened the deal by letting Samantha come with me. We were on the road to Knoxville the next morning and I was back "home" the following night. This was going to be interesting…

When I walked back through the doors again, everything was different. Not only was this the first time that I had an "official" girlfriend on the premises, but you could almost smell the fear that the media had installed into everyone over the Y2K bug. We were literally counting down the days until doomsday, and business was already suffering because people weren't willing to spend money on recreational things until this threat came to pass. This allowed me to have a few extra days off around Christmas and Samantha wanted to utilise them by heading back to Virginia to see her kids one last time. I was all for it until I saw that they were predicting heavy snow again but that wasn't going to stop Samantha. She was going to go without me, if need be, and there was no way I was going to let her do that, so I started packing up a few things.

We had barely reached the outskirts of Maryville when I felt the transmission slipping every now and then. I asked Samantha how long it has been doing that and she replied "For quite a while. It's nothing to worry about." I wasn't so sure. We actually made it all the way to Virginia, and were on the road leading up to her mother's house before the transmission went completely out. We rang her mother and the family came down to get us. Not wanting to leave the car on the road and unable to get a tow, someone came up with the idea of using the 4x4 to push Samantha's car the rest of the way. Her little brother got the spare tire out of her car, sat down on the hood of the 4x4, and held the tire between the two bumpers the whole time so they didn't touch. It was dangerous but effective...as it actually worked.

When we finally got up to the house, we were packed in there like sardines. There were 11 of us total and half were already sick. This time when we crashed on the living room floor, there were other people in the room. One of Samantha's kids was sleeping on the loveseat, while her lesbian sister and her partner were sharing the couch. We still managed to find a way to have sex without waking anyone except the lesbian partner, who continued to watch while pretending to be asleep. The next morning we woke up to several more inches of fresh snow, which meant that we were going to be stranded there for a couple of days until some of it melted. Samantha's family would take us back to Maryville when we could finally get out, but we had to leave her car behind. This meant that she was now completely dependent on me to take her everywhere.

When Christmas rolled around, we spend it with my parents. Samantha and I decided to do some blow before we went, which was a bad idea. I was too stoned to sit still, so we got a football out of the car and started throwing it around in near freezing temperatures to try to come down. It didn't work. When it was time to eat dinner, the drugs had also killed my appetite so I barely touched my food... which was a first. I was so high that we ended up leaving early so I could do more dope. All that cooking that my mother did was basically for nothing and the gifts were unappreciated.

    Those last few days of the year went so fast and before we knew it, it was New Year's Eve. I had to work, as usual, but Samantha and Timmy had the night off, so they came out to the club to ring in the New Year with me. They took a seat at the table nearest to my post and started drinking. Not long after, a customer decided to join them at their table and kept putting his hand on Samantha's knee. Part of me was fuming, but when I saw that Samantha didn't seem to mind, I became angrier at *her* than him and let it slide. Then the door swung open and there she was…Lena had arrived, wearing party attire and yellow tinted sunglasses. I could tell that she was already in rare form so I had to say something. "Damn girl! You started the party early didn't you?" I asked. She replied, "Yeah, I'm tripping my ass off. I took a hit of acid earlier." That just showed how fearless and unaffected she was about the potential "end of the world as we know it" scenario. I gained even more respect for her at that moment. No wonder I fell in love with her. The rest of the night was a light party atmosphere with a touch of doom and gloom. I could see the expressions and moods change in the final minutes and seconds of 1999, even if they tried hard to cover it up. There was so much concern and uncertainty about what was going to happen when the clock struck midnight. Then I had a pleasant thought: if this was indeed the end, at least Lena was with me. That was kind of sad considering that my so called "girlfriend" was also there but in reality, I would drop her in a second if Lena changed her mind. They both knew that whether they wanted to admit it or not. Then I heard the music stop and the Captain begin his countdown through

the speakers. "Let's get this over with..." I thought to myself. I took a deep breath and waited in anticipation as he called out five, four, three, two, one...
-DJN

CHAPTER XIV - "SEEMS WE WERE DREAMING..."

2000

Trade the cross for a swastika, our holy temples now for the wicked... words not in our vocabulary, now spoken after years of great efforts and difficulties, from five tongues not naked.

Somewhere the meaning gets lost, in the framework of each religion. Who needs to hear another sermon? Ten different assholes, ten different opinions...can I get an amen?

They take up their collection, and sing another hymn, with their red wine and communion wafers. They are there to worship the church, not the redeemer. Let's spread His gospel, and bow to our new Messiah, let us bask in His light, while He allows volcanoes to spew their lava and seas to swell to mountainous heights.

There's a lack of honest, god fearing citizens, who cares if there is a tomorrow. You can't extend your hand to those who suffer, when everything is sorrow. Is this world ever going to end?

Year 2000, third anti-Christ, third world party, a world of new laws and customs...Y2K, stock market crash, from an artificial conspiracy, called the bug of the millennium.

Push of the button, storms of bombs and rockets...World War III. The moon eclipses the sun, storms of meteors and comets...paradise found finally...

I seek divine intervention, but I'm yet to see a miracle. I seek many answers, but knowledge is impossible. Modern science can't confirm, with any conviction or authority, than the earth could successfully evolve, by their big bang theory.

> Tomorrow's headline: "Uncovered by time, dust, and cinders, the faults lay bare, ruled by forces we can't control. When the earth tremors, no one will be spared, already the death knell tolls…" If I was God, you would all die…
> -Denny Noland "Draven" From my song "Paradise Found"
> Written in 1999
> Copyright 2015

Nothing happened. As I saw everyone kissing each other and heard the horns blowing, I couldn't help but think about how nice it would have been to have kissed Lena at that very moment. But, in reality, I had to reluctantly kiss Samantha instead. I would have been content to not have to kiss anyone at all. I loved Samantha in my own way, but like so many before her, I wasn't *in love* with her. Although Justice had pulled me out of my depression, I was still in love with Lena at the end of the day. I just learned how to live in denial and accept things for what they were. I had tried everything, but there was nothing I could do to make Lena care for me again…if she ever did.

Nathan and Connor were also in the club that night. Nathan, now in a festive mood, invited not only Lena, but Samantha and I over to his house to party once we closed. He left around 1:00 am and Lena managed to leave early as well. I finished out the night thinking about how I couldn't wait to see Lena outside of work to see what happens. By the time that Samantha and I arrived over an hour later, Lena had already left. I was so disappointed…even if I did understand how awkward it would have been to be partying with not only me and my girlfriend, but my girlfriend's brother as well. After buying a significant amount of blow, I was told that that I was welcomed to use Nathan's hot tub. "You can have sex in it if you want" he said. "But promise me one thing beforehand though...don't ejaculate in there." Little did he know that I hadn't gotten off during sex in years, and I wasn't about to do so tonight either. I had been my own birth control for so long, that I didn't know any different anymore.

Samantha and I stripped down naked and got into the hot tub. We had a couple of beers and a few lines cut out just outside the tub so we could refuel without feeling the cold winter chill. Samantha wasted no time as she pushed me against the side and began kissing me. She then performed an impressive feat that I wasn't expecting: she went under and started giving me oral. Just being able to do that in normal water was difficult enough, but this was *hot* water. Although she only lasted a few minutes, it got me hard as a rock. She mounted me and we went at it for only a couple of minutes before I got too overheated and we had to stop. My blood runs hot by nature so I just can't withstand activity in extreme heat for very long without feeling ill and nearly passing out. We got out shortly after and joined the others inside. I remember thinking that maybe it was a good thing that Lena wasn't there when we arrived. I don't know how she might have reacted after seeing this.

2

Against my wishes, Samantha decided to get a matching tattoo. She wanted to get my "vampire girl" tattooed on her shoulder. Throughout history, when someone either got a matching tattoo or someone's name put on their skin, it was a curse... but she insisted on it anyway. It reminded me of when I got my last two tattoos on my arm, a wolf and a bloody sword that said "no fear", back when I was courting Lena. She, in her own smartass and sarcastic way, told me that "another tattoo is just what I needed." I replied, "It's my body and if I want to make it a living piece of art, that's my choice." She dropped the subject immediately...and now I was doing the same.

I took Samantha to the same place where I got all of my work done and for doing that, she was rewarded with a discount. The artist did alter the colours a bit, but the picture itself was exactly the same. I wasn't sure how I felt about this. In a way, I was flattered, especially when the only time that a girl did something similar to this was when I dated a certain psycho bitch many years ago. While we were talking on the phone, she let me know that she was carving my name into her leg with razor blades. I think we broke up only days later but she has the wear that scar for the rest of her life. Now Samantha would be in the same boat. No matter where she is or who she is with, she's going to think of me every time she looks in the mirror. I wouldn't wish that on anyone...

3

With the Captain being held in such high regard by Gene, he was able to bring in some of his friends to fill in some of the gaps. This added a little colour to our staff, which suited me fine. First, there was a black man named "Andre" who would serve as a replacement to Lars, who was being sent to the Last Chance 2000. The Captain also got another black man named "Tyrone" a job at the other club as a bouncer. Tyrone looked and even sounded so much like Dewayne "the Rock" Johnson that it was uncanny. He was just a little darker... otherwise he could have been his twin.

I had just worked with Andre a couple of times before one of the strangest incidents in club history took place. A large group of both whites and blacks came in together and started disrespecting the girls. While one of the black guys was tipping, he started rubbing the dollar bill across the girl's ass that was on stage. She had been sitting with this group all night and was known to favour black men over her own race. I stepped up beside him and warned him to stop before returning to my seat. The next time the girl went back on stage, he did it again and I approached him once more. All of a sudden, another black man in the group started yelling at me from his table. He was calling me a racist and asked me why I only scold the black men that do something wrong and ignore the white men who were doing the same thing. I honestly had no idea what the hell he was talking about or how to handle this situation.

I just stood there screaming and pointing but didn't go towards him. I could hear other customers, mostly white, that wasn't affiliated with the group, calling me a racist as well. Even the girl who I was trying to protect turned on me. I felt like I was in the Twilight Zone and it was me against the world. I knew that if I put my hands on him, someone was probably going to get hurt so I kept my distance. Before it all got real ugly, Andre came out of the booth and pushed the culprit out the emergency exit. The rest of the group followed, which cleared out that side of the room. The girl who was at the centre of all of this was also forced outside in her dancing attire and was never seen again. I thought I was prepared for anything until this happened. Andre, on his way back to the DJ booth, turned to me and said, "Why did you just stand there? Were you afraid or something?" I thought that I did the right thing but I ended up looking like a coward.

Andre and I would become close friends later on though. I used to see him at Micheal's every so often, usually when I couldn't find any blow. He would always be standing there with a smile on his face, looking as if he wanted to tell me something. One day at the club, he finally spat it out. "You know that I'm a coke dealer right? I used to see you at the bar looking for coke when no one had any and I just wanted to tell you that I had it all day long. Just don't expect me to bring it into the workplace. We'll have to make other arrangements." He would become my primary dealer for a little while and I would become one of his biggest pains in the ass.

Things weren't much better at home either. Timmy was homesick and wanted to go back to Virginia... so we took him. A few days later, I wanted to listen to a particular CD and I couldn't find it. I did notice, however, that several other discs were missing from their cases. Someone had stolen them and I knew right away who it was. I told Samantha that the next time I saw Timmy I was going to kick his ass. To my surprise, Samantha didn't say a word. She didn't confirm or deny whether he was capable of stealing from someone who had put a roof over his head and food on his plate for the last few weeks. Her silence told me everything that I needed to know.

Samantha was also turning into quite a slut. I would get her off every day before she went to work, usually by going down on her, but it wasn't enough. She was starting to like girls more than me and was notorious for going after every girl in the building that I was with before her. When Rachel came to the main club, Samantha went after her. They got drunk one night and things happened in the dressing room. Samantha came up to me, kissed my lips, and asked me who she tasted like. Then it was Rachel's turn to bust my balls. She told me what they did and was having a good laugh about it, until I reminded her that when she was with Samantha, she's actually with me as well. She snapped back with "Honestly, that never crosses my mind when I'm with her. I'm just focused on *her*." When Rachel failed to get inside my head, Samantha knew who would really get to me so she set her sights on Lena. Fortunately, it didn't work. Lena had better taste than to let someone of Samantha's calibre lay a finger on her...much less *in* her. I was relieved because that one would have stung.

Samantha would also mess around with Mercedes and her best friend "Wendy." If only she knew how much this act was going to come back and haunt her down the road. All of this fucking around was taking its toll on me. I was more annoyed and irritated about it than I was jealous or hurt. I watched Samantha shoot down girls who came on to her at parties for her own bizarre reasons, but she was a totally different person at the club. She had become nothing more than a drunken slut and I wasn't down with that anymore. I had reached a breaking point and had to do something drastic to make it all stop.

I finally did one weekend to everyone's surprise. As I scanned across the room during roll call, I saw five girls who I had been with, each with their own personal reasons for hating my guts. As they passed by my desk to go to the dressing room, they would either give me a look like they wanted me to drop dead or said something insulting to me. There was only one thing that could make all this tension go away: just leave. I did just that. I walked over to One Time and told him that I was quitting. I walked out and felt instant relief as soon as I went out that door. When I got home, I took off my shoes and enjoyed the peace and quiet like "normal" people did. It was nice… even if it did feel alien to me.

I did, however, have to return to the club to pick up Samantha. While I was waiting outside, Lena came out and had a few choice words for me. She wanted to know why I walked out and what I was going to do for money now that I was no longer working the clubs. I told her that I didn't know yet but I have had "real" jobs in the past so I wasn't too worried about it. She just looked at me with an unconvincing grin and walked away. Samantha, who was unaware that I had quit until I was already gone, was supportive but was concerned about the possibility of being the breadwinner, and have to pay the bills by herself until I found something else. She wouldn't have to stress over it for long.

Although she had lost her license, she got a new car so she could sneak around and continue to drive. One day, while we were driving into town, Samantha got caught speeding by a K-9 cop who was coming in from the opposite direction. We had a little time before he could turn around and pursue us, so I told Samantha to park off the road so we could switch drivers. By the time he caught up to us and pulled us over, I was behind the wheel…but he knew that Samantha was driving before and that pissed him off. Now he was suspicious that we must have been hiding something, so he made me stand against his cruiser away from Samantha's car, and made her stand beside it. The fucking dog was barking right in my face through the glass and I was starting to get angry. Thinking that there were no drugs inside of her car, I told the cop that he could "search the fucking thing if he wanted."

As he tore the car apart, all I could think about was all those times that my car used to get searched and there was no way that I was going to let history repeat itself. What was annoying me the most was watching Samantha kiss his ass and crack jokes nervously, while I was sizzling in the sun... next to an animal that would love to tear me apart if given the opportunity. The cop didn't find anything, which led to me verbally abusing him while Samantha begged me to shut my mouth. She still got a ticket for driving without a license and I got nothing even though I could have been thrown in jail for my behaviour. As we drove away, Samantha pulled out a bag of weed that she had hid up in a hole underneath the seat that she had "forgotten" to tell me about. I couldn't believe that the cop was so close to it but never found it and that he chose not to use the dog, who would have found it immediately. All I could think about was how close I came to get arrested over drugs that I didn't know was in the car. Samantha's lying and deceit was almost never-ending and I was getting so sick of it.

As bad as that was, that was nothing compared to when Samantha's mother and stepdad brought the kids down so we could take them to Pigeon Forge and Gatlinburg for the day. Samantha and I had already been bickering all afternoon, so when we were on our way back, she insisted that one of the kids should ride with us to calm the situation down. As we were coming down Kingston Pike to get gas and to drop me off at my truck, we started fighting again. Samantha snaps and punches me right in the mouth, while I'm driving in rush hour traffic with her kid in the backseat. I wanted to hit the bitch back but I couldn't do it...especially in front of her daughter who was already freaking out. Every time I tried to speak, she would hit me again. This happened three times before we got to the gas station. When I got to the pump, I got out and walked the rest of the way to my truck. Before I got across the street, I heard her stepdad, who was behind us on the road with her mother and other two kids, ask Samantha why she was hitting me. They saw the entire thing through the rear window...which meant that the other kids were watching too. I couldn't believe that she could be so stupid and irresponsible. She would apologize later but "I'm sorry" just doesn't make everything alright after something like this.

Karma would bite her on the ass and she would find her way back to the Last Chance 2000 due to her actions. Not wanting to deal with a "real" job again, I swallowed my pride and asked Gene if I could have my old job back. He would send me back to the 2000 club with Samantha for one last tour. I would, however, get called to fill in at the mother ship when needed...which wasn't often. Samantha's jealousy and insecurities would lead to us breaking up and her moving out of my house not long after our return. I will never forget hearing Limp Bizkit's "Re-Arranged" playing in the club when I dumped her. Every time she tried to say something, I would just sing along with the song to drown her out. Homer, who was the DJ that night, assisted me by harmonizing over the microphone.
It was classic.

4

I made two new friends at the 2000 club. Both were fellow bouncers just breaking into the business. "Duane" was a big guy who, other than his shaved head, was often asked if he was my brother because we had similar facial features. "Mac", however, couldn't have been more different from me if he wanted to. He was a handsome, clean cut kid, fresh out of the Marines. There was a certain innocence to him that was just asking to be corrupted...and I was, unfortunately, the man to do it. I set up his first piece of ass out of the club and took him under my wing somewhat. He had also never tried cocaine until I cut him out a line. He was an impressionable young man with a bright future ahead of him and was smart enough to do drugs in moderation, unlike myself, so he knew when to stop and be responsible. I told him the night after I got him laid that he "had the potential to get any girl from either club that he wanted, including the ones that was out of my reach." Needless to say, he didn't let me down... nor did he need any more help from me in doing so.

Lynn had invited the three of us out to a driving range that he owned on the outskirts of town. We stopped and picked up a case of beer on the way and finally arrived about midday. We were the only ones there that day, so Lynn rolled up a "fatty" and asked us if we wanted to get stoned. We refused his kind offer, but we did start drinking and by the time we actually picked up a club, we were practically drunk. It had to be comical watching us either send the ball in the wrong direction or, in my case, miss the ball completely and break the club on the ground... which I did twice. Lynn never complained... no matter how rowdy we got or how much damage we did. He knew that none of us knew what the hell we were doing. As an ex baseball player, I tried to swing the golf club like I used to swing a baseball bat, and anyone who has ever played golf before knows how well that works. Sometimes the ball never lifted off the ground...it would just roll a few feet in front of me, no matter how hard I hit it. At least, Duane and Mac weren't doing much better.

If all of that wasn't humiliating enough, Lynn's young son came out and showed us how it was done. In frustration, Mac was determined to not be outdone. He put the ball on the tee and swung as hard as he could. Not only did he miss the ball but the club went flying out of his hands. Lynn had a dog chained up to a tree that had been barking all day until Mac's club landed in that tree above its doghouse. Avoiding all of the leaves and branches raining down on it, the dog went into its house and never came back out. It didn't bark again either for the rest of the day.

The party didn't stop there. We went down to Micheal's once we got back to Knoxville to continue drinking and shoot some pool. Mac and I got some cocaine to take the edge off, but Duane wouldn't touch the stuff and we respected that, so we never teased him or tried to push it on him. Mac and I weren't shy about doing our blow in the open but when Duane was around, we always went to the bathroom. Anyone who has done coke before knows that often times, it has a way of "cleaning out your system" if you know what I mean. Mac and I would get into separate stalls, side by side, and do the "number two" while doing bumps. I was never comfortable enough around *anyone* to relieve myself while they were in the same room until I met Mac. I don't really know why he was different but he was. Anyways, we all had a great time that day and night and I couldn't wait to do it all over again but it never happened.

5

With me "back on the market" again, I started making up for lost time by playing the field at not just one club, but both clubs simultaneously. It started with a girl named "Bev" who I had known since I was a customer. I kissed her one night and she enjoyed it so much that she considered it to be the best kiss she ever had. After hearing several girls say those very same words to me, I was starting to believe my own hype. I would see Bev and Blaze down at Micheal's one night with a drug dealer who was filling them with drugs and using them for his own private entertainment and amusement. As soon as Bev passed me in the lobby, she begged me to kiss her again. With Blaze standing beside her, I got an idea. While I was kissing Bev, I started touching Blaze. She took the hint and joined in to create my first "three way" kiss. It lasted for several minutes and was seen by the entire crowd... including the staff. I was so turned on but chose to walk away instead of offering to take the girls home with me to spare them from another night of humiliation.

    One night while I was working at the 2000 club, Bev came in with some black girl that I didn't know. She saw me outside and wanted to make out behind the building. I kissed her yet again which led to her going and telling Phoenix about how great of kisser I was, and that she wanted to have sex with me when I got off of work. Unfortunately, Toni also came out for a visit and was interested as well so I had to pick between the two. Since I knew that we were going out to Toni's place if I chose her, and I had no idea where Bev was going to take me, it was a no-brainer: I was going with Toni. When I saw Bev distracted, I asked Tommy if I could leave early. Since it was a slow night, he had no problem with it so Toni and I slipped out the backdoor.

    When we got out to her place, I started second guessing myself. Although her apartment was clean, the building itself was a dump. Her mother was sitting there on the sofa holding a newborn baby that belonged to Toni that I didn't even know about. After her mother left, Toni told me that she had been married and divorced since she last saw me. She also said that she hadn't had sex with anyone since the split, and although she had went down on me several times in the past, she always wondered what it would be like to be with me. That's why she came out to the club that night: to seduce me. I was flattered...I hadn't been used for sex in a long time.

What she didn't know was that there was a chink in the armour that I had been battling all week: jock itch. Any guy who has ever had it knows that it itches like hell, and makes your balls smell even more disgusting than usual, especially once they start sweating. I had already decided that I was wearing a condom and I wasn't letting her face or nose get anywhere near my crotch. After some hard kissing, I pulled out my condom, but before I could put it on, she told me that she was allergic so I couldn't wear one. I thought about stopping right then and there, but she started kissing me again and I knew that if I told her about my ailment now, she was going to be pissed. So we kept going.

I had never been anyone's first but she was the closest thing to it. I couldn't believe how tight she was, especially after just having a baby only a few months before. I literally pushed and pushed until I was exhausted just trying to get it in. I finally got inside after several minutes and we went at it until I slipped out and almost broke my penis. I asked her how it was even possible to be that "closed off" and she just laughed and said, "I guess you are just too big." Now I was laughing too. "I've never been told that before and probably never will again. Thank you for the kind words even if it was total bullshit" I said. I went home afterwards and never heard from the girl again.

I received a phone call from Tommy the following week. He was in a bind and needed someone to help him around the house, so I went over there to lend a hand. When I got there, he had one of the girls who I have had issues with in the past sitting in his living room. She needed someone to drive her around town to run some errands. I got drafted for the job since Tommy couldn't be bothered doing it. The whole time she was in the car, she kept talking about how she had found religion and changed her ways. She was now basking in God's light and got high from loving Jesus instead of from taking drugs. That lasted until we reached west Knoxville and she got to a pay phone. I overheard her talking to her dealer about how she had come into some money and she needed a fix. Apparently, Tommy, whose heart was sometimes bigger than his brain, fell for her newfound faith and helped her out by lending her an undisclosed sum of money. We had just got back to Tommy's place when I was asked to leave so they could have some privacy. I was told later that they had sex the entire afternoon until Tommy had to go open the club. Tommy was left with a smile on his face and an empty wallet... I was left scratching my head.

    I was then asked to work at the main club for a few days. Now that Trixie wasn't working there anymore, her stepmother, who was always a bit flirty towards me, turned up the juice a little. While I was watching the VIP room, she walked out to pay me after finishing up her dance. I stuck out my pierced tongue at her and she licked it. This led to her asking if I would like a VIP dance for myself. Aroused and curious, I got One Time to fill in for one song so this could take place. When we got in there, she started licking from my neck down to my navel. She then dropped down to her knees and gave me head through my pants. Most of the girls did this because it was the closest thing to an actual blowjob that they could legally do. It always left the customers wanting more. I'm not sure if it crossed the line or not but Gene often overlooked it because it made heaps of money. I enjoyed the hell out of it, even if I had been with her adopted daughter many times before and the only thing that was separating her lips from my penis was my underwear and pants. I would kiss this woman several times later on but never with tongue. We never slept together...even if I would have if I had the chance.

About a month before all of this, a new girl named "Christine" started at the club. Her boyfriend at the time used to brag to us about how many attractive girls she could bring home for them to play with. I had no reason to doubt this after I had seen her tear into Amanda at the Boiler Room and even saw her at another club with one of our other new faces: a young girl named "Velvet." This was all long after the boyfriend had vanished. I was one of the few guys who got to make out with her. It happened in her car one night while we were both drunk. Lars and I also ran into her once at Micheal's and she was surrounded by a group of hopeful or hopeless, depending on your point of view, guys. When the lights came on as they were closing down, she started singing Madonna's "Like A Prayer." It was such a beautiful rendition that everyone in the room turned to see where this angelic voice was coming from. She now had everyone's attention, including Lars, who had taken a seat beside her. Long story short, Lars struck out...and had to go home for a cold shower. This was the first time that I saw this self-proclaimed "stud" get rejected but it certainly wasn't the last.

With Homer getting fired yet again for not being able to keep his penis in his pants, Lars was now working exclusively at the Last Chance 2000. In a shocking twist, he actually got into a relationship with one of the girls who also worked with us. They were notorious for getting various girls high and talking them into having threesomes. One night, I somehow got caught in their web and ended up at one of their victim's houses to observe how all of this hoopla worked. Their usual strategy of seducing the girl with drugs wasn't going to be an option this time because this particular girl didn't drink or get high. I watched Lars, who was beyond messed up, make a complete ass out of himself. The potential victim had spread out a blanket on the floor so she could sit and watch a movie. The girlfriend sat beside me on the couch that was on the other side of the room, to watch everything unfold. Lars kept trying to get under the blanket with her but she kept pushing him away, much to his surprise. I could respect his persistence but if he went too far, I was prepared to end this party in a heartbeat. I looked over at his girlfriend, whose expression was either one of disappointment, or disdain, it was hard to tell, and busted out laughing. This ritual was so pathetic that I couldn't help myself. Nothing happened that night… except for my stomach hurting from all of the laughter. I lost a lot of respect for Lars and his girlfriend after that.

    It shouldn't have been a surprise when Lars's girlfriend came out to the club one night and asked me if I would have sex with her behind his back…but it was. Apparently, Lars was going to be away for the night, meaning that the house was going to be empty, so there was no way that we could have been caught. I declined the offer but she wasn't about to take no as an answer. She kept asking over and over but I wasn't going to be talked into it. Despite the fact that I was no stranger to cheating, even at this age, I *never* did so if it involved hurting someone that I considered to be a friend. Unfortunately, when the tables were turned and the roles were reversed, Lars didn't feel the same way. I would find this out from a reliable source down the road.

Another time, I went out the mother ship and met two beautiful young ladies who were a little overly affectionate towards me. One was a blonde and the other was a brunette who called herself "Felony." Tommy, who had turned up to have a few drinks with Gene earlier in the night, told me about Gene and him tag teaming on the blonde for money before I arrived. That really wasn't much of a deterrent since I was drawn to Felony, who to my understanding wasn't involved. I thought I had it in the bag until a group of young guys came in and offered the girls a large sum of money to do a "private party" for them. Since it was their first day on the job, they were allowed to leave whenever they wanted. This killed any chance of competing with those guys over Felony's company. As they were leaving, Felony stuck her tongue down my throat one last time. For some reason, the blonde joined in for yet another three way kiss. All I could think about was where her lips probably were earlier in the night and how I prayed that she brushed her teeth or at least gargled sometime in between. Felony liked the kiss so much that she was having second thoughts about doing the party...she wanted to be with me instead. The blonde literally grabbed her arm and dragged her away, leaving me standing there at the entrance. I would find out the next day that not only did they not get paid, but Felony was sexually assaulted by one of those young guys. Neither the guys nor the ladies ever returned. Only days later, it happened a second time with a different pair of ladies. This time the blonde liked me and was talked into doing a private party after their auditions. I don't know what their story was and how it went that night because they never came back either.

Out of the archives of the strange but true, I have yet another story to tell. There was this girl at the

2000 club that I was working on that invited me into the VIP room. We started making out which led to me sticking my finger inside of her. I immediately pulled it back out when I felt a second hole. It turns out that her ex-husband had shot her in the vagina with his pistol during a drunken rage a few years back. I immediately lost interest and wanted nothing more to do with her despite her efforts. Phoenix appropriately nicknamed her "Shot Pussy." Is it me or does that sound like it should be a character on "The Sopranos?"

6

The following weekend, I was working the door at the main club when the road manager and crew of "The Red Hot Chili Peppers" came up to my window. I swear he looked like someone who would have been at the casting call for the movie "Rock Star." He was quite a character, almost animated. He took to me instantly, telling me about Anthony and Flea's recent sobriety, which was ironic considering that I was high during our conversation. "Anthony is doing quite well" he said. "Flea, on the other hand, is a different story altogether. He's literally bouncing off the walls and pacing the floor wanting to get high. That's why they stayed at the hotel...to stay out of trouble and away from temptation." I totally understood and respected that, even if I was disappointed that I didn't get to meet them in person.

A few hours and several drinks later, the whole conversation changed. Now he was coming up to me and asking me if I knew where he could get some blow. He said "If you can find three eight balls of cocaine and bring them to the back gate of the arena tomorrow night before the show, you write your own ticket my friend. Anything you want. You can have an all access pass to go anywhere and see anyone you want." Although I was against the concept of getting drugs for a band that was trying their best to overcome their addictions, I still called everyone I knew but all my dealers were dry. I had to tell the guy that I failed. He thanked me for trying and told me to still come to the back gate the following night and he would take care of me anyway. After they left, Lena came up and asked if I got an invitation. Like it was written in the stars, we were the only two people who got them. We made plans to meet at the arena at a particular time to avoid confusion. Were we coming together again? Could this change everything? Not exactly.

I had already made other plans. Now that Wendy had broken up with her boyfriend "Slim", she was now free to see anyone she wanted, so she picked me. I had already promised to go over to her apartment on the night of the show to have sex. Unlike others who had come and gone from my life, I kept my promises, so I chose to go that route and have been kicking myself ever since. Our brief little affair didn't last very long at all, maybe a week or so, with the highlight being a day long sex-fest that ended with her having a seizure and having to go to the hospital. This also pushed her back into Slim's arms and made me a not so distant memory. I only wish that I would have been content and left things where they were but life had other plans for the two of us.

However, in that short period of time, one of the new girls "Sapphire" thought we looked so great together that she asked if she could go to a hotel with us on her dollar. We both declined. We had grabbed a lot of people's attention literally overnight which got people talking. Now that we were split, hanging out at the Boiler Room after work became especially painful for Wendy, considering that I was used to seeing her with Slim and now she was watching go on with my life right in front of her. One night I even heard her crying to our mutual friend and co-worker "Mitzi" about how she couldn't handle seeing me with other women. Mitzi told her not to worry about it because it wasn't worth it. I took that personally and confronted her in an empty dressing room the following night. She defended herself by grabbing my face and planting one of the deepest French kisses on me that I ever had. She ended the kiss by licking my lips and grabbing my penis. When she looked into my eyes afterwards, she had to laugh a little. It was amazing how fast I forgot what I was even mad about. It wasn't every day that a so called "lesbian" put something on me like that. To make a long story short: she was forgiven without even really apologizing.

    Then I heard the news that Lena had finally ended her relationship with that loser. Of course, everyone knew about it long before I did and that pissed me off royally. I made the mistake of taking Mac out to the main club with me one night and as soon as Lena saw him, I knew I was fucked. I had never had gone into any detail about my feelings for her to him, if I even mentioned her name at all. I had two ways I could play this. Either I could make a fool of myself and look even more pathetic than I already have over the past year, and probably get rejected again, or I give him my blessing and let the chips fall where they may. I chose the latter since I felt like I had already been humiliated enough. He thanked me by putting his hands all over her and rubbing her crotch right in front of me, while she moaned and panted like she was about to have an orgasm right there on the spot. I knew that she was an expert of "over-selling" but this was ridiculous. As much as it hurt at first to see all of this, I think that in the grand scheme of things, I needed it badly. When you add that to the terrible things that Mac told me she was doing for money that caused them to stop seeing each other only a few short weeks later, I was glad that she had chosen him over me. I never looked at her the same again. Although, she may have looked and smelled like the girl I used to love, it was like she was just an imposter wearing her skin. I would call her a cheap imitation even. The Lena I knew and loved was truly dead and all that was left was this shell of what used to be. Finally I was over her once and for all.

At this time, the drug "ecstasy" was everywhere. I think that you could safely say that it was the new craze. We were rolling at work every night then taking the party to the Boiler Room after that. There were so many crazy events that occurred when everyone was taking that shit. One example was the night that I rode out to the Boiler Room with a couple of the girls. So horny that they couldn't wait till we got to the Old City, they started making out going down the road while one of them was driving. I was in the passenger seat watching their truck nearly go off the road and into oncoming traffic several times before I asked them to stop. I had girls come out of the VIP Room at our club so aroused after doing a dance that they were actually wet, then put their fingers in their moist vaginas and rub their wetness off on my lips as a tease. I even caused two lesbians to nearly break up because one of them sat on my lap and start making out with me while the other was getting drinks. You never knew what was going to happen.

At the Boiler Room, and most of the other clubs across Knoxville for that matter, we always got treated like royalty. We often got free or discounted drinks, could always jump to the front of the line and walk in without waiting, paying an entrance fee or being searched and when a fight broke out between one of us and another customer, the bouncers would always toss the other guy and never say a word to us, even if we started it. Hell, most of us even had sex in a dark corner or in a bathroom stall without repercussions. It was awesome. We always tried to look after any of their people too when they came out to our club to return the favour. Law enforcement, however, was hit or miss. We had some of them in our pockets but others weren't exactly friends. When a state trooper came in one night that I hadn't seen before and looked over at me sitting outside the VIP room, he knew I was wasted. I was so fucked up in fact that I couldn't look anyone in the eye. He noticed that and stared a hole through me but couldn't do anything about it but make me uncomfortable. He had no business being there so he couldn't arrest anyone. As he was leaving, I gave him a cheeky smile and a wave. If looks could kill, the one he gave me would have stopped my heart for sure.

There was a girl named "Chloe" who liked me and wanted to ride out to the Boiler Room with me. The first night I took her, we shared a pleasant kiss the next morning when I dropped her off back at her car. The following night, things got a bit complicated. When we walked into the Boiler Room, I saw someone that I never thought I was see again: Adam. He basically looked the same in the face, yet was much smaller in physical appearance. I thought to myself, "That's what jail can do to you... you sorry bastard!" He yelled out my name over the loud music and started approaching me. He extended his hand to shake but I was hesitant to take it after what he had done to me. "What the hell are you doing here?" I asked. "I'm here with my girlfriend" he replied. Before I had a chance to ask him who his girlfriend was, Carla darted across the dance floor and leaped into my arms. She then proceeded to wrap her legs around me and start kissing me passionately. All I could think about was how Adam was reacting to this and whether I was going to have to duck a punch in a minute or two. When our lips parted, Carla whispered in my ear "I've liked you for a very long time, Denny." By the way she kissed me I had no reason to doubt that. When I looked over at Adam, he wasn't angry...he was actually smiling. Then Carla's sister, Nadia, walked up and started making out with Adam. I was confused and wondered what the hell was going on. After he finished kissing Nadia, he turned to me and said, "I must say that it's great being with Carla. I can have her sister too if I want. She doesn't care." This was just too much...especially after I had watched him attempt suicide twice over Carla's best friend Angelina and now he's dating *Carla*. Talk about keeping your friends close and your enemies closer.

Trying my luck at Nadia, I kissed her a couple of times but she had her eyes on a cute little blonde that she met that night. As we approached the sunrise, Adam invited Chloe and me to follow him and his entourage back to Carla's place. I reluctantly agreed for the free drugs if nothing else. It turned out that she lived in an apartment complex in Maryville, just behind the flea market that I used to visit every weekend as a kid to search for comic books. So there we were: five of us rolling our asses off in the living room. While my back was turned, I felt a sting in my shoulder. Adam had stuck a needle in it without asking, which infuriated me. "Don't worry...you'll like it" he said. After a few minutes of cursing, I asked him what he had put into my body and what was it going to do to me. He told me that it was called "Special K" and that I was going to go through several stages of being high and will probably hallucinate. Now I was very angry because I fucking hated hallucinogens! I always liked being in complete control and now I was out of my element. This was going to be a very interesting night to say the least.

    It wasn't long before Adam and Carla retired to the bedroom, but not before Adam injected Chloe with the drug as well. Now we were sitting on the couch, extremely messed up, watching Nadia and her female companion make out on the other couch right across from us. Eventually, Nadia dropped down to the floor between the other girl's legs and it was on. A few minutes later, they were gone as well, leaving Chloe and I alone in the room. Carla had a pet boa in a cage near where we were sitting and that inspired Chloe to reach in and pick it up. She started rubbing the snake across my face and arms, which was both weird and erotic at the same time. She then put the snake back in its cage and took a seat beside me on the couch that Nadia and the blonde were sitting on earlier. We started kissing and touching each other and before we knew it, we had taken all our clothes off. She asked me if I had a condom and I told her that I didn't. She looked at me with obvious disappointment. "I'm sorry. I didn't think that I was going to be having sex tonight" I replied. She straddled me anyway and we went at it until I was getting winded and wanted to stop. Chloe got down on all fours on the floor in doggie-style position and said, "Let's do it this way now." I had nothing left and I told her as much, so we got into the shower to wash off instead. I can't remember anything that happened in there or what happened afterwards. We could have gone at it again in the shower for all I know. Everything was a complete blur once the warm water hit our sweaty bodies.

7

The following night, Chloe and I went back to the Boiler Room again. We saw Adam and his entourage once more, but this time I ran into Samantha at the bar. When Carla saw her, she kissed her on the lips then kissed me straight after, which seemed to catch Samantha off guard. I must admit that Samantha was looking very sexy and I reacted accordingly by sitting her up on the bar and tearing into her right in front of everyone. Of course, the bouncers did nothing but stand there and watch. Occasionally, a patron would pass by and pat me on the back or cheer me on, but that was about it. I decided at that moment that Samantha was taking Chloe's spot later on. I didn't even know where Chloe was half the time and when I finally located her, I told her that she needed to find her own way home. It was a cold and heartless thing to do but that was who I was back then. When we got ready to leave, Samantha loaded up into my truck and we followed Adam's van out of the city. Samantha voiced her concerns about what was going to happen when we got to Carla's apartment. She didn't want to be with anyone but me despite Carla's advancements. I was ok with that and gave her my word that she was there for me and no one else.

We would never make it there. When we got to the turnoff, Samantha and I watched Adam drive right into a parked car. It happened so fast that we had no idea what happened. All I could do was drive past the accident and turn around because I was sitting in the middle of the road. There were already people, who had been setting up their booths at the flea market, on the scene who witnessed the whole thing. They were actually running toward Adam's van just after the moment of impact. As I headed back down the hill towards Adam's car, I saw the girls walking towards me. Nadia had broken her glasses, but was still wearing them, as tears rolled down her cheeks. Carla was carrying Adam's pouch which was full of ecstasy pills and other narcotics. "What the fuck happened?" I asked. Carla, who was still quite shaken up herself, told me that Adam had fallen asleep or passed out behind the wheel. "But he was driving normal until he crashed. How could he drift off that quickly?" I asked. She just shrugged her shoulders and began to cry as well. "I don't know" she said. "He just handed me the pouch and told us to flee the scene as soon as possible." I told them all to get in the back of my truck and I would take them the rest of the way to the apartment before the cops got there. They were all intoxicated and carrying enough narcotics to put Adam and themselves away for a very long time. I got them all home safely before going back to check on Adam. When I got back to the crash site, the cops were already there and had him in cuffs. I made the decision to just keep driving, since there was nothing I could really do, and stopping would have incriminated Samantha and me. We talked about whether we had done the right thing all the way back to my place. Despite the backstabbing in the past, I still felt bad for him…even if he did deserve everything he got.

8

Samantha and I were back together. This time around though, we didn't live together. When she was in town, we stayed in a private suite at my favourite hotel in West Knoxville. It had a swimming pool and hot tubs just outside our door. We would take a bottle and some cocaine out there late at night when no one was around and have a great time. We even had sex out there a few times. The location was convenient because I had talked to my friend Don at the West Club and got Samantha a job there and even one of my dealers, Andre, was just a hop, skip, and a jump away. If we wanted to go out, Micheal's was just down the road as well. It was kind of like our "city home" and we spent a great deal of time there.

The important part was that if we started fighting, I could just leave and go home. I never had that option before. It came in handy many times because we were still like cats and dogs. I was actually prepared to break up with her until she told me that she was taking me, her mom and stepfather, and the kids to Myrtle Beach, South Carolina… all expenses paid. I hadn't been there since I went there with my brothers nearly a decade before. That ended with a catastrophe and this had the potential to be its own entity with the same result. My goal going in was to enjoy myself and try my best to tolerate Samantha and the children until we got home then drop her like a bad habit. It wasn't going to be easy, but I had faith that I could pull it off.

In the meantime, I decided to dye all of my hair black including my goatee and beard. When I walked into the club that night, no one even recognized me. The only person who seemed to like it was Cynthia. She said that it "brought out the colour in my eyes", but unfortunately, no one else agreed. Samantha said that she could fix it and I made the mistake of letting her try. I ended up looking like a fucking clown or a bag of skittles by the time she finished. Before I could even get it repaired by a professional, I had to go to work. I wore a rag over my head to hide my rainbow coloured hair and was terrified that I was going to get into a fight and it was going to come off… but thank God it didn't! The next day, I got it all stripped and I was back to my original blond after about three hours of sitting, several clumps of hair forever lost, and around $200 out of Samantha's purse.

    Once we arrived in Myrtle Beach about a week later, it was more of the same. I will admit though that going to the beach with the kids during the day was quite pleasant. We would build sand castles, and just float around on air mattresses in the ocean while basking in the sun. But at nightfall, everything changed. Since we were all sharing a single room, with only a curtain like they have at the hospital that wrapped around our section to separate us from everyone else, there was absolutely no privacy. Living in such close quarters for a couple of weeks put everyone on edge, especially Samantha and me. We couldn't even go shopping, or go anywhere for that matter, without having an argument. We usually walked back to the room separately. I was always walking ahead while Samantha dragged behind with a look on her face like she was the "Ronda Rousey" of her generation. But I still tried to make the most of it anyway, knowing what I was going to do to her once we got back to Tennessee was going to make it all worthwhile.

    Our last night in South Carolina, I wanted to do something special for Samantha to show my appreciation and gratitude for letting me take this final vacation with her, so I took her out to dinner at the restaurant on the pier. As the sun was setting, we were served our appetizers, which included shark meat among other things, while we sat over the ocean waiting for our table to open. Once inside, I told Samantha to order anything off the menu that she wanted. It was the least I could do considering that she had paid for the entire trip thus far. We ended up having a delicious meal and drinks which tallied up to over $200. Afterwards we took a long romantic walk down the beach, hand in hand, and even attempted to have sex, but were rudely interrupted by the police. When we got back to the room, we were relieved to find that it was empty. We made love for the final time that night while everyone was away.

The next day we were back in the car and back at each other's throats again. I was literally counting the miles until we got home. When we finally arrived in Virginia, I got into my truck and drove back to Knoxville. I felt like the weight of the world had been lifted off my shoulders. Despite all services rendered, I had no remorse or regret. In the coming days, I ignored all of Samantha's phone calls until they eventually stopped. I was finally enjoying life again. I had hoped that she got the message without me having to actually come out and say it, but it turned out that she had been thrown into jail again and couldn't reach me for a few days. When she got back to Knoxville, I officially ended our relationship. She reacted by threatening to drive her car through my house and telling any girl who she thought might be interested in me that I had a small penis. I wasn't bothered though. I just wished that some of these broads could come up with some new material because this routine was getting stale. Honestly, I don't think any of them were capable.

9

One person who was immune to Samantha's poison was Wendy. She had never completely got over me. We started talking again and she told me that if I was willing to put everything I had into a relationship, she would kick Slim to the curb immediately. Just like I could tell any woman that I love them while I was inside of them, whether it was true or not, I could do the same with any woman who let it be known that they had feelings for me. I could tell them *anything* that they wanted to hear and look sincere while doing so. People who know me will tell you that I am one of the most honest people that they know, but I could be a great liar when I wanted to. Long story short, what I said to Wendy made it happen and we were dating for real this time.

At this point and time, I was working exclusively at the Last Chance 2000, and only made an appearance at the mother ship on the night that Wendy and I got the ball rolling again. Working at separate clubs made life much easier. Since Wendy lived in a low income apartment complex off Merchant's Road, which was just down the road from where I was working, it became quite handy. It gave me options. Instead of driving all the way back to Maryville, I would crash at her place. Eventually, I was practically living there. It was the kind of place that was misleading. It looked like a nice place to live, but the tenants were at times dodgy and shady. You were always hearing about robberies, drugs, and domestic violence cases. When a car door slammed in the parking lot after dark or you heard voices outside, it was a good idea to go check it out. It didn't help that the actual "projects" were just on the other side of the fence. It is safe to say that there was never a dull moment.

Although Wendy and I didn't fight very often, we still had our share of problems. Her son wasn't exactly bonding with me at home and Samantha had also returned to my club to torment me. Every time Wendy came into the building, something would happen. Usually, Samantha would run up to her and try to kiss her on the mouth to remind me that she had actually been with her first. Wendy would wisely always turn away to avoid any misconceptions, but that didn't stop Samantha from trying. One night, one of Wendy's closest friends "Chanel" grabbed Wendy as soon as she entered the building and took her to the infamous VIP room so she could go down on her while I watched. I wasn't exactly impressed. As a matter of fact, I told Chanel that "Anything you can do, I can do better." She wasn't amused and never did it again.

Every weekend, we would go to the Boiler Room together. I would take a couple of ecstasy pills to enhance sex later while Wendy would take half of one and spend the entire night with her head buried in my lap, afraid to open her eyes. Needless to say, we could never roll together and have any kind of intercourse. Even when Mac started dating Chanel, and we would take Viagra or liquid acid together, Mac would get naked under the blanket with Chanel and they would start going at it, while I was deprived and frustrated, because Wendy wasn't in the mood. It just wasn't fair.

10

I considered Mac to be one of my closest friends at this time. He would come by the house and take cocaine with me all night, then hit the bottle in the morning before we went to the gym in the afternoon. Since I didn't have air conditioning, sometimes it was so hot in the house that we were literally in our underwear pouring buckets of sweat but he never complained... not once. One day, we decided to go to the local steakhouse to grab a bite to eat after working out. We both ordered expensive steaks and hit the hot bar while we waited. About an hour later, they brought out a slab of fat, with a hint of actual meat in the middle, and placed it before me. I was furious and demanded a refund after I saw the one they brought out to Mac.

It wasn't helping that Mac was saying stuff like "Man, this is the best steak I ever had" and "Don't you wish your steak looked like this?" The waitress didn't see anything wrong with my steak, and wasn't cooperating, so I took matters into my own hands. I took my plate and filled it with every vegetable I could find and dumped it all over our booth. I repeated that several times until the table, seat, and windows were completely trashed. All the while, Mac was enjoying his steak and laughing at my behaviour. I left without paying for my food and never ate there again.

I had also became quite close with Andre and spent a lot of time at his house buying drugs, hanging out, and playing Playstation. Most of the time, I was the only white boy in his crib but there always seemed to be a number of white girls stopping by. Andre would often say, "I wish you would just come over to see me as a friend instead of your dealer sometime. I want you to get off that shit but I know that if I don't sell it to you, you will just find it somewhere else. That's why I keep doing it." He was right of course. Eventually, he did cut me off even though I didn't owe him anything so I went elsewhere.

One night he invited me out to the Boiler Room with him and his crew. There was a gas station on the outskirts of the Old City that most people were scared to pull into... especially at night. It was the type of place where you pumped gas with one eye on the nozzle and the other looking over your shoulder. It was also a good idea to roll up your windows and lock your doors when you went inside to pay as well. However, when I pulled up with Andre and his crew, with "Dr. Dre" blaring over his sound system, everyone else were locking their doors and staring at us. Although I was the only white guy in the car, I never felt safer in my life. It was incredible.

Then there was "Jake." Here was a good looking kid who obviously had a lot of money and was apparently hung like a horse as well. The first time that we met, it wasn't exactly pleasant. We got into a heated exchange over him not following the ever-changing dress code. I would hear some of the girls talking about meeting up with him after they got off work. I would also find out later that another one of Wendy's closest friends was actually his "baby's mama." Wendy had known this guy for years through her and told me that he suggested that she should have sex with him on numerous occasions because "she might like it" but Wendy refused for obvious reasons. However, Jake was plowing through the rosters at both clubs like a champion and eventually worked his way around to Lena. I was actually present when her number came up while she was at the Boiler Room. I saw them dancing and leaving together later on. I was told by mutual friends that had either been in his house or at a party while he was rooting a girl that heard sounds coming from the room that was similar to what they say used to come out of Stu Hart's dungeon.

He started bringing another young man with him who I called "Cajun" because of his thick Louisiana sounding accent. One night Cajun hooked up with one of our girls and she literally couldn't walk the next day. Cajun, like Jake, always had my back when shit went down and no one else was around. Although we weren't the closest of friends, we all had a healthy respect for one another. Jake would even find cocaine for me when I couldn't find it anywhere else. He always told his dealers to "take care of me because I was his boy" and they always did. Andre and I even dropped off a "package" or two at his house when he was throwing a party there. Usually, I knew a majority of the people there, but like a vampire, I never entered without an invitation. Besides, I always seemed to have better things to do elsewhere...if you know what I mean.

11

Several weeks later, Tommy came up to me at the door and told me that Gene was coming in specifically to talk to me about something important but didn't elaborate on the reason why. I naturally expected the worst and was already planning things for the future. When Gene arrived, he asked me to get into his car so we could take a little drive. We had just got out on the highway, when Gene cut to the chase. "How would you like to be the manager of the main club?" he asked. "I would be honoured sir." I replied. "I will be honest with you Denny" Gene said. "You would have been in that position long ago if you weren't on drugs. But by the same token, you have paid your dues as far as I'm concerned." My mind was now racing with a number of questions. "Who do I answer to?" I asked. "You will only answer to me" Gene replied. "You will have the power to change anything you want. The bar staff...the dancers...you are in complete control." I couldn't believe how far I had come. I had gone from a lowly customer, to assistant manager at the Last Chance 2000, to *the* manager at the Last Chance. I had used a fully charged taser on my balls not once, not twice, but three times to prove how tough or crazy I was. I've been overpowered and had my clothes ripped off by the girls out on the main floor, just because they were bored. I've even taken the stage twice myself, once at each club, to entertain the girls on a painfully slow night for extra money. I've even worked all night tearing out old carpet and helped Gene move into his new house for next to nothing. I had earned this spot. It was time for me to take my rightful place at his side. It's been a long time coming…

We arrived at our destination: my new kingdom. The reason I was given this opportunity was because One Time fucked up. He was screwing around with a couple of the girls and they were receiving special treatment while he was treating the others like shit. The roster had been so depleted that they barely had enough girls left to make a schedule. I made it a top priority to get those girls back and make that club thrive again. It all sounded great and looked good on paper, but the girls had heard all of this before. Many of them probably thought they would be asked to blow me now that I was in charge to leave early or get a night off and that would be the only difference. They didn't know what I had in store for them. I was about to prove all my critics wrong.

When Gene dropped me back off at the Last Chance 2000, I pulled both Duane and Mac to the side. Duane and I weren't as close as Mac and I was but we had definitely become friends. Although we rarely saw each other outside of work, we always threw a football around before work and had many good conversations along the way. The most important quality that he had was that I trusted him and I didn't trust anyone. I tried my best to persuade him to go work for me at the other club but he was happy where he was. The extra money didn't matter to him. He was content and there was nothing I could do to change his mind. Mac also refused because he was thinking of getting out of the business altogether. The concept of working a full time schedule didn't appeal to him whatsoever.

It was looking like I was going to have to build my crew from the ground up.

There was only one bouncer already there that impressed me enough to keep him employed: a young black man named "Tyrell." That meant that my first days on the job were going to be spend doing interviews. The first guy I saw was a guy who I had just thrown out of the Last Chance 2000 on my final night there. He was intoxicated and looking for a fight that night, so I thought he would be a welcomed addition if he just showed that much fire and emotion on the other side. Unfortunately he didn't, and was fired a couple of days later when he was too afraid to confront anyone sober. Next I gave one of the Captain's friends a shot, and had to fire him on his first night because he got caught tipping the girls in the back with Gene's own money. This wasn't starting well to say the least.

I ended up hiring my ecstasy dealer, unaware or uncaring that he was dating one of our top girls which could present a problem. I had also brought Andre back so I had a cocaine dealer on hand as well...even if he *never* brought drugs into the club itself. I was pretty well set until my ecstasy dealer started having jealous outbursts concerning his girlfriend. He was often overheard accusing her of "cheating" or "enjoying a dance a little too much" which led to a soap opera every night in the parking lot after hours. One night, my tolerance level just wasn't there so I grabbed the guy and slammed him against the wall in front of his girl. "Look you idiot, you are dating one of the classiest and most decent girls on the roster. I have worked with her for years, and she is not a slut. You should consider yourself lucky that she even gave you the time of day" I screamed. He turned to her and apologized immediately. Now I had gone from breaking up an argument to watching them kiss all over the premises in front of everyone. A couple of days later, it started up again and I had to let him go too but I had gained a new fan in the process. His now ex-girlfriend was telling everyone that I was her "brother" which was basically her way of reminding me that even if I wanted her for myself, I had no chance. I actually grew tired of hearing it, especially when *my* girlfriend Wendy was always in the building somewhere listening to all of this.

After all of these failures, I settled on a white guy who turned out to be a "Judas" in the long run and a friend of Andre's named "Murphy." Judas was from Chicago and had a tendency to get under my skin. There was something about him that I didn't like from the start. I always felt like he was up to something and wanted to take my spot. When he found out that I partied, he went home to Chicago one weekend and brought me back an 8-ball of so called "better quality product than what these rednecks and hillbillies have." He then sat back and laughed as I sampled it, like we were smoking a joint instead of doing lines. Little did I know that he had already started whispering in Gene's ear, and was setting me up from the beginning...

Murphy, on the other hand, was the total opposite. He wasn't a big guy by any means, but wasn't afraid of anything or anyone. He wanted to work seven days a week if he could and fully had my trust. After I hired him, Gene wanted to talk to me in private. "The customers have been complaining that there are too many black people working here" he said. "They are saying that they are trying to take over and that makes them uncomfortable." I couldn't believe what I was hearing. "Well, that's very unfortunate" I replied. "To be truthful, every white man that I've hired has proven to be untrustworthy. At least these guys are reliable, dependable, and don't have hidden agendas." Gene just looked at me as if he knew *who* I was talking about specifically. "I'm not firing anyone that has done nothing wrong, just because of the colour of their skin. If that's what you are suggesting, you can fucking forget it." I turned and walked away.

Judas wasn't the only person who was working behind the scenes to have me ousted from power. Dana, who had been vocal numerous times about how much she didn't like black people, was still Gene's eyes and ears when he wasn't there. When Tyrell and Judas got into a heated argument, that turned physical when Tyrell swung a bar stool, I told them both that if they wanted to fight someone, step outside with me and I would be more than happy to kick both their asses. Both of them quickly cooled down, apologized to each other, and shook hands. Although I handled the situation without anyone getting fired, Dana felt like Gene needed to know about it anyway, so she told him as soon as he walked through the door. Gene was ready to fire Tyrell on the spot but I wouldn't allow it.

They were also both instrumental in letting Gene know what they thought I was doing in the office when I kept the doors locked. I was indeed chopping lines nightly on Gene's desk, rolling on ecstasy while I did the paperwork and counted the money on the weekends, and even had sex with Wendy on the couch just before she went on stage a time or two. She literally had me running down her leg while customers were unknowingly trying to get as close to her vagina as possible. How they knew what was literally going on behind closed doors is anyone's guess. I just denied everything and continued doing what I was accused of…claiming my innocence even when the evidence actually fell out of my nose and onto the bar right in front of Gene more than once.

12

Now let's talk about what I brought to the party...the good things I did for this business. The first order of business was to rid the club of all the hoes that One Time was involved with, so I could replenish the roster with more deserving ladies, and keep him out at the same time. I remember him coming over to my club once and having a look around. When he didn't see any of his minions, he left and stayed across town because none of the other girls would touch him. It only took me about a week to get all the cancers out of the building, but it was obviously going to take much longer to replace them.

Gene ran an ad in the paper but I wasn't impressed with the girls who were answering it. Most of them didn't make the cut when I was there because my philosophy was "if I wouldn't pay to see her, why would I expect someone else to?" So Gene and James did all their damage on my nights off. I would come in the next day and there would be a girl on stage that had no business being there, who was obviously hired by two old men that had too much to drink the night before. I would usually send them to Tommy, because he always needed girls too, and wasn't near as picky as I was. He, and the girl, would usually thank me for it...except for one night in particular. James and Gene had hired an obese girl, who hid her physique well under her loose fitting clothes, while they were drunk. She didn't get to audition that night, so she was going to take the stage for the first time in front of me the following night. I, like most of the crowd, was horrified by what I saw. I walked up to Gene and James and screamed, "What the fuck is this? Is this your idea of a joke? Are we trying to get customers in and trying to scare them away? I'm doing *all* the hiring from now on. This is pathetic!" Shockingly,

Gene agreed. He found the girl just as repulsive as I did once he was sober and saw what she looked like naked. She had to go…immediately if not sooner.

I called Tommy and told him that she was on her way but didn't warn him about what she looked like ahead of time. She had probably been gone for about an hour when Tommy rang me back. "What the hell is that about?" he screamed. "Did you even see what she looked like underneath before you hired her?" I chuckled then replied "I didn't hire her. Our fearless leader did." There was a short moment of silence before Tommy spoke again. "Well…don't send me anymore girls who look like that ok? I still don't know what I can do with her" then hung up the phone. I could just then picture the look of Tommy's face as he watched her strip, and it cracked me up.

However, sometimes the joke was on me. I hired a cute little Asian girl once who kept getting into trouble so I sent her across town as well. She tried every way in the world to have sex with me to keep her job but I just couldn't do it. Unlike all the other managers before me, I separated business from pleasure. Besides, with Wendy working for me under the same roof, my chances of getting caught increased tenfold. I had to do what I had to do. I was told later that the first words that came out of her mouth when she saw Tommy was "It looks like you are going to be eating Chinese tonight." I won't elaborate any further.

Another new girl, named "Mena," who became one of Lena's closest friends later on, asked me "if there was anything she could do to change my mind" when I told her that her boyfriend wasn't allowed in the club because it was against policy. I don't know *exactly* what she meant for sure, but that was what she said. I had just hired her and she had been working for me only a few days before she tried to sneak him in and got caught. Once again, I didn't take advantage of a beautiful lady when I could have… and probably wanted to.

Every now and then, Gene would take me over to Tommy's club to have a look at their talent. As soon as I walked through that door, I was swarmed by a number of the ladies. They would often want a hug or a soft kiss on the lips, and sometimes they would just come out and ask if I would like to go out on a date sometime. I knew why I was getting all of this attention, and so did Gene, who was usually sitting at one of the tables laughing his ass off. It was because I held their financial future literally in the palm of my hand. They knew that I was their way back to the main club, so they kissed my ass every time I came there. The irony was that they were now working with One Time again…the same bastard who sent them there to begin with. Don't get me wrong, not *every* girl wanted greener pastures. Some were content working for Tommy, and that was understandable. He was a great boss and although he did run a tight ship, it was loose compared to Gene. That reason alone was enough for a few girls to stay put. However, I did bring back a handful of girls that I had worked with in the past, who had been unfairly dismissed. I told each of them that "it was time to go home… so pack your things." It felt good to put a smile on a few faces that had given up hope.

Back at the main club, Gene and I were butting heads on a number of things. When I found one of our best girls "Kellie" crying in the back uncontrollably, I asked her what was wrong. She told me that her mother had died and Gene wouldn't let her have a few days off to mourn because she was scheduled to be at work. I was not only sympathetic, but was also ashamed that someone that I considered to be a father figure or mentor could do such a thing. I told her to take off as many days as she needed. "But what about Gene?" she asked. "I can't afford to lose my job." I put my hand on her shoulder and said "Let me deal with Gene. You have enough to deal with already." She hugged me as she wiped her eyes. "Thank you so much" she said. "I will see you when you get back ok?" I replied. "Absolutely…you can count on it" she said as she was changing her clothes.

When Gene came in later that night and asked where Kellie was, I let him have it. "How could you treat one of our best girls that way?" I asked. "She is reliable, she's never late, and she makes the club and *you* a lot of money. These are the girls you should be looking after. Wasn't it *you* who told me that the girls are what kept us in business all these years, because no one is going to pay to see us?" He nodded his head. "I told her to take off as much time as needed by the way. Don't worry about the schedule, I'll sort that out. If you have a problem with it, don't take it out on her…I'm the one who gave her permission so I'm the one held responsible" I screamed. He didn't say another word about it…and Kellie never forgot either. She would pay me back in a big way a couple of years later.

However, there was one lady who never took me seriously as a manager and had no respect for my authority whatsoever: Lena. She often tried to throw her weight around even though my girlfriend at the time, Wendy, didn't. This led to a few verbal altercations in the back about me. From my understanding, Lena asked Wendy how she could be with a guy who couldn't keep it up and Wendy's only defence was "Well, at least he's great at oral. Didn't he ever go down on you?" Lena nodded her head no…which was obviously a lie. I only heard Wendy's side of the story, so I questioned Lena and she admitted everything. Somehow, word of this got back to Gene and he started plotting to separate Lena and I once again. Had I still been just a bouncer, I would have found myself back on Clinton Highway, but with me being the manager, that tipped the scales in my favour this time.

We were having an issue with certain girls being late to the stage and delaying the show on a nightly basis, and Gene wanted to put a stop to it. He told me to fine the girls $50 *every time* they weren't ready when their names were called. This kept most of the girls in line… but not Lena. She didn't like anyone telling her what to do, so she ignored the warnings. She wasn't laughing when Gene ordered me to collect the money from her after just one violation. Of course, she thought that I was just enforcing the rule to get back at her, so she took it personally and began to hate me. On my next night off, Gene fired her for his own personal reasons, but told her that I had asked him to do it because of our history so he wouldn't have to look like the bad guy. I knew nothing about it until I got to work the next day. Often times, this procedure was just part of the job. It just came with the territory, so to speak, but this was a little different from all of those times Gene would want a girl gone and pay me extra to get her out of the building without him having to interact with her. This was Lena…and now she has every reason in the world to believe that I was behind this travesty. I had a motive, and Gene used that to his advantage and made me his scapegoat. I almost threw up in my mouth. I had no way to make this right.

13

Although my bar staff and DJ's were up to par, my bouncers were letting me down. It was just stupid things that they were doing without thinking that was getting on my nerves. One example was when a group of guys came in and spotted a small snake hanging down from one of the lights. The bouncers were scared of snakes, so one of the customers caught it and got bitten accidently. All we heard all night was that dude talking about how trained he was in the martial arts and how I could throw a hundred punches at his sensei and never make contact. The longer the night went, the more obnoxious he became, and the bouncers just took it with a grain of salt.

    Something similar happened when two older gentlemen came in and stayed until closing. They wanted to sit in the parking lot after hours and watch the girls come out. I told the bouncers that I wanted them gone but ended up having to go out there myself to see why they were still there. As I was approaching, I heard one of them asking one of my guys if he knew who the other customer was. Apparently he was a legend in his own mind. As I drew near, the self-proclaimed celebrity slammed his hand into the windshield of his buddy's car in an effort to crack it. I guess that was supposed to either frighten or impress us but it did neither. Eventually, after several minutes of negotiations, they left on their own accord, but now my guys were contemplating attacking them until I told them to go back inside. I felt like a disappointed father.

    Also on that same weekend, I watched a group of kickboxers come in and my guys didn't hesitate to toss one of them which could have been a critical error in judgement had they put up a fight. At the end of the night, as a disgruntled customer was leaving, one of my guys kicked his car as he passed us which led to an unnecessary fight. I was starting to realize why Gene never wanted to fire me. A good bouncer was hard to come by and almost impossible to replace. Hell, I singlehandedly ran Dumb and Dumber off after they made the mistake of crossing me on Clinton Highway, when I had already warned them that I wasn't in the mood, after months of terrorizing the staff at the mother ship. I guess dragging one through gravel on their back got the message across. No one had seen hide nor hair of them since.

It was no different when the celebrities came in. One night, when David Keith and his entourage walked through that door, his bodyguard took a seat up at the stage where he wasn't allowed to sit. I told Tyrell that he needed to say something to him and although he didn't want to, he took off his tie and confronted him. They left shortly after without much problem but I could tell that Tyrell resented being sent up there. He complained to me throughout the remainder of the night like I threw him to the lions. "I would never ask you to do something that I haven't done a hundred times myself." I said to him. I knew right then and there that he wasn't going to make it. He got me back later on when I threw a Mexican out the door and slammed him on the concrete with his beer in his arms. The beer started spewing everywhere like someone was popping champagne bottles when the clock struck midnight on New Year's Eve. I started feeling bad for the guy and helped him to his feet. As soon as he stabilized himself, he took a cheap shot at me. Tyrell opened the door, saw that we were going at it, and instead of helping me, went back inside and sat down. I ended up knocking the Mexican unconscious and left him for dead before I had a little chat with Tyrell. "Listen, you motherfucker! Up until this regime, the managers only had to point a finger and we went to work. They were the absolute last resort… the last line of defence. Now I find myself out there rolling around in a puddle of beer while you are sitting here on your ass. You ever do that again and it will be the last time. You feel me?" He nodded in agreement as I stepped out for some fresh air.

The first thing I saw when I opened the door was a police car sitting at the bottom of the steps. The little Mexican had not only awakened, but had walked to the gas station down the road, used the payphone and rang the police. The cop got out and asked the Mexican what was going on and he told him that he had purchased a VIP dance and the girl refused to have sex with him after he paid her. The cop's expression was one of disbelief. "You do realize that prostitution is illegal don't you? What did you expect her to say?" he asked as the Mexican continued to plead his case. The cop had heard enough. He handcuffed the little guy and read him his rights. I didn't even get the opportunity to tell my side of the story...it was irrelevant. In the following day's newspaper, under the column for dumbest criminals, was a summary of what happened on that night. Hopefully, when he sobered up, he realized that he wasn't in Tijuana anymore.

Things quietened down for a few weeks after that, and the club finally ran like a well- oiled machine, until the band "Papa Roach" came to town and was standing in the lobby. I saw them on the security camera discussing something with Tyrell through the window then he motioned for me to come over there. "The band Papa Roach is out there and they want free admission because of who they are." I was so sick and tired of wealthy people wanting handouts when everyone else had paid to enter. "Tell them that we would be grateful to have them in our establishment...as long as they paid the cover" I said. I stood out of sight and listened as Tyrell repeated what I said word for word. I could tell by his expression that it wasn't working. "They want to hear that from you personally" he said. Now I was annoyed. I walked out there and told them what they Tyrell had already told them several times before. We got into a short, heated argument and they ended up not even coming in...because they thought they were above having to pay to enter our fine club. I wasn't much of a fan before that and I definitely wasn't about to be one now.

Now it was time to be tested once again. The night was winding down and there were only a couple of customers lingering around that wasn't spending money, so the girls asked me of there was any chance we could close early. I could really see no reason why we couldn't, so I walked up to the DJ booth and told the Captain to play two more songs and pull the plug. When I went to the back to check on a couple of things, I heard the song finish and the Captain say, "I have just be told that we are going to keep this party going a while longer." Before I could react, someone was already knocking on my door. When it swung open, there was a lynch mob of angry girls waiting to rip me a new one because I promised them we were closing. I had to get to the bottom of this...

When I got to the end of the hall, I saw Tommy come walking down from the DJ booth. I darted past him and headed toward the Captain. "Didn't I tell you two more songs before?" I asked. "Yeah, but Tommy told me it was too early to close. There are still people in here" he replied. "Who is the manager of this club?" I asked. "You are..." he replied. "I say that *this* is the final song" I stated firmly. "Not a problem" he replied. We ended up closing and Tommy didn't say a word to me. The Captain, however, did. "Damn, I respect you" he said. "That took balls to do what you did." The next day I explained to Gene what happened and his response was "You did the right thing, Denny. Tommy can't overrule you in this club...only I can. The next time he disrespects you, you got my permission to ask or even tell him to leave." That was all I needed to know.

    I was finally getting the respect and credibility that I had been seeking for the past few months but it was too late. I was already burned out from having to live that damn club every day of my life. When repairs needed to be made, I would not only have to come in and unlock the doors for the tradies, but I couldn't leave them alone in the building without supervision so it wasted my entire day. All the hiring and firing, and trying to keep nearly forty women happy and productive, just wasn't for me. At the end of the day I was still a drug addict, whose dream would be to isolate myself from the rest of the world and stay high every waking hour without interruptions. I couldn't be any further from living that dream if I tried. Something had to be done...

    On one of my heavy partying nights, I ran out a little later than usual and needed sleep urgently. I only had about four hours to go before I had to open the club, and I knew that I was going to have problems dozing off, so Wendy offered me a handful of Xanax pills to help me sleep. Unable to tell how many was too many, I might have come close to an overdose, because I slipped into such a deep sleep that I slept through multiple alarms clocks that we had set and ended up waking up about two hours *after* I was supposed to be there. Still groggy and in a daze, I called James and told him that I had overslept and asked him if he would go to the club and let everyone in. It was so late that the entire staff and dancers would have been there by then...some had probably been waiting outside for a couple of hours. As I drove across town, a

million things ran through my mind, including turning in my keys with my resignation. I wasn't sure what I was going to do until I got there. As I drew closer, the answer became as clear as the nose on my face. This was the end... let's get this over with so I can go back to bed.
-DJN

CHAPTER XV - "TIL DEATH DO US PART PART II"

2001

Now I was home and unemployed again... fresh off of losing my grandmother on my father's side to a stress related illness only weeks before. I always thought that she would outlive my grandfather, who suffered from both diabetes and high blood pressure, when she was thin and petite with as far as we knew...a clean bill of health. But she did worry a lot about her own mortality. If her clothes rubbed against a mole and it changed colour, she was at her doctor the next morning. She was obviously afraid of dying and eventually *that* killed her. When she fell ill, it came out of nowhere. The team of doctors couldn't identify the problem...all they knew was that her organs were shutting down, one after another, until she was gone. Of course, I was too strung out to attend the funeral which hurt my dad's feelings, but at the time, it didn't seem to matter much to me at all. It's amazing how drugs can numb you to everything in the outside world.

After months of watching me do unlimited amounts of cocaine right in front of her, Wendy decided to start getting high with me. She was already popping pills daily and smoking weed but she avoided the powder...that was my baby. Unlike every other woman in my life, who did at least take responsibility for their own actions, Wendy will probably *still* tell you that she was the victim here, as ridiculous as that sounds. Forget the fact that an older black gentleman used to stop by the apartment randomly, and asked for Wendy, who just happened to sell crack. Also don't take into consideration that I was a selfish and greedy prick when it came to my blow and try to imagine someone being foolish enough to make accusations that I *forced* drugs on them...that was my Wendy. She even had the audacity to try to sell that story to my parents down the road, but like anyone else, they knew it was bullshit. I thought that it was time to get away from this scene and I knew just the place.

    For some reason, Wendy was forced to downsize her apartment so I talked her into moving into my trailer in Maryville to escape the madness. If it didn't work, we still had a new, smaller apartment to move into in the same complex. In the meantime, we could use it as storage for all of her belongings that wouldn't fit into my place. Wendy wasn't thrilled about it at first, but was willing to give it a shot. That was all I asked for.

    It would be an understatement to say that she didn't like living out in the country, especially when she decided to start working in Johnson City instead of Knoxville. Being out there meant that she had just added an addition hour to an already lengthy commute four nights a week. I never understood why she chose to work up there, considering that there were so many girls that were coming to Knoxville because there was no money to be made in that area at the time. But at least she was working...that's more than I could say. On her nights off she was so exhausted, but I insisted that Mercedes come and stay with us to give her someone to talk to. Tension was starting to build between us and space was a needed remedy.

    That was when she started planting stupid ideas in my head about a number of ways I could really "stick it to the man" which would benefit me in the short term but affect decisions that I still make even to this day. Selling my trailer and moving back to the city was the first topic brought up. Since I was never there anyway, it made perfect sense to take the money and run. I would sell it quickly for the same amount that I gave for it to "Rico"...the same guy who had experienced paranormal activity in that shed while Samantha was still around. I obviously didn't consider where I was going to live if Wendy and I ever split. Thinking ahead wasn't part of my repertoire back in those days.

The next thing she went after was my perfect credit rating. She told me about how one of her friends maxed out all of her credit cards, filed bankruptcy, and not only didn't have to pay the money back, but also got to keep the stuff. It sounded like free money as I was naïve about the lasting effect it would have on my life. So we got a credit card everywhere that would grant me one. Wendy was buying jewelry and clothes at such a rapid pace that I was constantly getting harassed by the creditors. We were living it up and weren't even dipping into our own money. We then rented a moving truck and were back in Knoxville later that week. It seemed only logical to take the next step.

That was when marriage was discussed. I must admit that I never considered it, and didn't really want to do it again, until Wendy mentioned it. In my defence, at least we had lived together for a while, unlike Angie and me, who never "drove the car before we bought it." I thought that was going to make all the difference in the world, but what did I know? Obviously, not a damn thing...

The unstable relationship between Wendy's son and me had reached the boiling point. I panicked when Wendy, who was prone to seizures, felt one coming on while making dinner. I might have raised my voice, not out of anger, but concern and her son overheard from his bedroom. He thought we were fighting and despite Wendy's best efforts of trying to explain the situation to him, he was already talking about wanting to go live with his father. Once again, I had come between a mother and her child leading to a change of custody. Now it was just Wendy and me and my two cats. Although it was unintentional, I was kind of glad that he was gone. The house was so much more quiet and peaceful without him being there.

It was also no secret that Wendy wasn't too fond of the cats. Because of that very reason, I had let Gabrielle out while Wendy and I were still living at the old apartment. She was used to being outdoors and always found a way to get out every chance she could, so I thought I was doing her a favour. Just before I sold the trailer, I stopped by after being away for a month to get some clothes. As I was leaving, she appeared out of nowhere and ran into the house. Out of fear, she ran behind the oven and wouldn't come out. I had a hard time just getting to her and nearly electrocuted her in the process but I managed to grab her. I took it as an omen that maybe I should keep her after all.

We already had two cats when we moved into the new apartment, which was plenty in my book, but Wendy wanted a third cat: a kitten she named "Panthor," obviously inspired from one of the characters in the "Masters of the Universe" toy line that covered the wall in her son's old room. We were supposably allowed to have two cats, but three was a violation of our lease which created a number of problems during inspections, but if the landlord only knew what else was going on under that roof, we would have been gone long ago anyway. We would have also been told to vacate the premises if it was discovered that Wendy's son no longer lived with us, so we kept his room looking as if he was still there. I made it clear to him that he wasn't allowed to touch those toys on his wall and he never did. I also told him that if he wanted a certain toy, I would buy him his own, but under no circumstances, was he allowed to open any of those figures. They were actually worth a small fortune and I wanted to keep them that way. Leaving them on that wall gave the room a child's touch which helped to deceive the landlord.

2

When the big day came around this time, it was a little different. We didn't have a wedding...we just showed up at the courthouse with Mercedes and her friend, who served as our witnesses. I wanted to just wear jeans and a t-shirt, but Wendy insisted that we should at least dress up for the occasion since there was going to be plenty of photo opportunities, so we did. The actual ceremony was short and sweet, and before we knew it, we were back at Mercedes's house getting high. However, before we were on our way to our honeymoon, Mercedes and her friend covered my truck with shaving cream. Luckily, it started raining soon after, which washed away all the remnants before we got on the road.

We were only a block or two away from Mercedes's house when I came up to what I thought was a four way stop on the road. I saw a police car coming from my left and assumed that he had to stop but unfortunately he didn't. As I went to cross, he had to swerve to keep from hitting me. I was in deep shit. Not only was I high, but I had over three grams of cocaine on me. The cop motioned for me to pull into the church parking lot across the road. He was furious and a little shaken as he walked up to my vehicle. "What in the hell do you think you are doing? You could have killed us both!" he screamed. I tried my best to talk my way out of a ticket but he felt like he had to do something, so he wrote me a ticket for $20 for not wearing my seat belt without searching my car. This was obviously before the law had passed otherwise the outcome would have been much worse. What a way to kick off my second honeymoon...even if I was lucky to avoid hurting someone or going to jail.

    We did, however, end up going back to Pigeon Forge and Gatlinburg, just as Angie and I had done nearly a decade before. I paid for everything from our marriage license, to our drugs and accommodations, with my credit card so we treated ourselves to any and everything we wanted. Unlike with Angie, we consummated our marriage then partied together instead of arguing over petty things. It was a pleasant change from the mistakes of the past.

    The following day, as we were walking around Gatlinburg, we ducked into one of the places where you get your picture taken dressed in Old West attire. There was a young couple posing for the camera while the parents looked on. The girl looked so familiar that I got goosebumps like I had just seen a ghost. She was a spitting image of Justice and could have even been her for all I knew. If it wasn't, she had an identical twin and I just found her. Either way, I got the hell out of there just in case, before the girl saw me, to Wendy's confusion. Other than that awkward situation, we had a great time and were eager to get home and begin our new lives together.

3

    About a week later, we walked into the Last Chance 2000 to see if Wendy could get a job there since Gene wouldn't allow her to work at the mother ship due to my actions. Tommy not only gave her a job, but offered me a role in his excavating company during the day. We both accepted. Now with our combined incomes, it took all the pressure off of Wendy, who had now gone from working out of town to just five minutes away. I had a number of issues adjusting to getting up early in the morning, because I had been a night owl most of my working life. I was still waiting up for Wendy to get home every night so I could stand on the balcony and watch her come up the sidewalk to make sure you got into the house safely. Then we would usually start partying and sometimes that lasted until it was time for me to start getting ready for work. I tried coffee to keep myself awake, but would usually drink until I was sick to my stomach and jittery, yet I was still fatigued. Those memories are why I still don't drink coffee to this day. It just made a bad situation worse, since I had no clue what I was doing half the time, and was generally a nervous wreck anyways. I don't know how useful I was to that business or what I brought to the table, but Tommy kept me around for some reason.

 Because I was now in some serious debt, I had neglected quite a few of my bills in the process. I was fairly certain that I no longer had insurance on my truck, which made every commute a treacherous one, especially driving across town from our place to Tommy's farm in Seymour during rush hour every morning. I knew that one day an error in judgement either on my part or someone else's was going to cost me dearly, and eventually it did. I had just crossed the Henley Street Bridge one morning and was running a bit late. The light had just turned green and there was a line of cars in the left lane while the right lane was completely empty. As I went to overtake everyone, I just had a feeling that someone was going to cut in front of me… underestimating the speed that I was going. As I approached a van filled with elderly people, I saw the wheels slowly creeping over into my lane so I increased my speed to try to close the gap and avoid it. I wasn't fast enough and the van clipped my bumper. As luck would have it, there was a cop sitting at one of the lights who saw the whole thing happen. We all pulled to the side of the road and everyone got out of their vehicles to survey the damage. Before I reached the rear of my truck, the cop said, "If I hadn't seen it with my own eyes, it would still be easy to figure out who was at fault here" as he pointed down at my bumper. The van's bumper had come off during the impact and was lodged behind mine. Other than that, there wasn't a scratch on my truck even though the van was pretty smashed up. The cop asked if I wanted to press charges after getting the details of the other driver but never asked me for anything because I was the one who got hit. I was so relieved and felt like doing the right thing so I let the other driver walk instead of being an asshole. I only asked the cop if he would assist me in prying the van's bumper from mine so I could continue on my merry way. Needless to say, I called the insurance company after that to make sure that I was still covered and I actually was the entire time.

4

On one of my many trips to Maryville, I ran into Kaine which was always a pleasant surprise. It was great to have a real buddy to confide in, which was something that I hadn't had in a long time. He started coming by the house, which he called the "Ewok Village" due to all the walkways leading into the various apartments, every now and then. He also renewed my interest in collecting toys and comic books, which gave me a hobby and something to think about besides just getting high.

If only I knew how much I was going to need him in my life in the weeks ahead.

Wendy was also having friends over constantly, so my life of isolation and privacy went up in smoke. Suzanne came over once to party with us, which was a complete shock to me, because I didn't even know she got high in all the years I've known her. One of the other girls from the club came over to do Wendy's hair once and made the comment when I left the room that she had never noticed how hot I actually was until she saw me in shorts and a tank-top with my hair down that day. This was coming from a woman who was sarcastic and annoying in my eyes even after saying that.

Things got a bit more interesting when certain other people came over. When one of her old friends from Chattanooga visited us, she brought some crystal meth for me to sample, as well as her kids and some local guy who she used to know who was obviously still in love with her. Our house was filled with screaming children, and people that I didn't know too well, which made me paranoid and very uncomfortable in my own home. I didn't say anything because she had bribed me with free drugs ahead of time but I made it clear that this wasn't happening ever again.

You never knew what was going to happen when we started buying cocaine from one of the girls at the club either. On one occasion, in particular, I was sitting in the living room getting high while watching TV, and the girls were lying on the bed, talking, with the door open. I could tell that they were plotting something, because they were whispering and looking out at me every few seconds. All of a sudden they yelled out to me, "Hey Denny, why don't you come in here and lie down between us." I had a pretty good idea of what their intentions were and I didn't want any part of it. For all I knew it could be a trap, a setup, to see if I would bite or maybe not, but I politely declined and avoided the bedroom at all costs until she left.

But the biggest potential disaster was after Mac started dating Mercedes and we all took ecstasy together, except Wendy of course, while we were at the Boiler Room one night. When they followed us home afterwards was when it all got out of control. Mercedes was so messed up and aroused that she asked Wendy to lie down with her on the couch. As Wendy was cuddling her, Mercedes started kissing her and trying to talk her into taking it further. Mac and I were enjoying the show, watching in anticipation to see what Wendy was going to do, but she stopped it from progressing any further because she thought it would piss me off. Honestly, I didn't care what happened that night...as long as I got to play too. I knew that if I wasn't there, Wendy would give in so I was very disappointment with her fake loyalty and morals.

When she couldn't seduce Wendy, she moved on to me by asking if I would go into the bedroom with her so that we could have a talk in private. I knew that this was a bad idea, but I played stupid so I could see how this was going to play out. I was always attracted to Mercedes so this was an opportunity I wasn't about to let slip. We both got on the bed and she started telling me about how much Wendy loved me and how happy she was that we were married. Then she began to complain about how hot it was in that room and asked me to blow on her neck to cool her off. I did so from a safe distance at first until she demanded that I kept moving closer until my lips were literally touching her skin. It was only natural that I started kissing her. She started breathing heavy and panting, even squirming as I made my way around her neck until I got to her mouth. Then I planted a soft kiss on her lips as she arched her back and extended the kiss much longer than I was expecting. She had also wrapped her legs around me as she started kissing me deeper and I was now completely lost in the moment. About that time, I heard Mac and Wendy's voices on the other side of the door, followed by a heavy handed knock. I pulled away from Mercedes because I knew that I hadn't locked the door. Mercedes didn't care. She grabbed my head and pulled me back down on top of her and started kissing me again as I heard the door click and squeak as it swung open. When I looked up, I saw Wendy and Mac standing there with their arms crossed and tombstones in their eyes. I had managed to end the kiss before they caught us but Mercedes had not removed her legs from around my body. Busted!

After getting yelled out and told to return to the living room, Mercedes asked if I would carry her in my arms because she was too messed up to walk. No sooner than I had picked her up, she kissed me one last time as Wendy turned her back to lead the way. When we got out there, no one really said anything but you could just feel the tension in the air. A couple of hours later, everyone went to their rooms and turned in for the night but the games weren't over yet.

When Wendy and I got to the bedroom, we had great sex courtesy of Mercedes getting me aroused well ahead of time. In the kid's old room, Mac was working on Mercedes while Wendy, in typical fashion, thought of something she needed out of that room so she could have a peek. She was notorious for doing that whether ever she meant to or not. When she returned to bed, it was my turn. I kept making up excuses to leave the room, hoping that I would run into Mercedes out there somewhere but apparently, Mac was keeping her quite preoccupied.

The next morning, there was still an uneasy silence in the room, except for the smacking of Mac and Mercedes's lips as they made out every few minutes in front of Wendy and myself, who was sitting on the couch facing them. I started feeling bad about my actions the night before after seeing how much Mac really liked Mercedes. I broke my own rule of not fucking around with a buddy's girl and I did so in front of my own wife for god's sake. I knew that this was never going to be forgotten, no matter how hard I tried to sweep it under the rug. I was going to get mine in the end.

<u>5</u>

A few weeks later, while I am sitting at home by myself after a hard day's work, watching "Haunted History" on the History Channel and getting high, I received a disturbing phone call from Wendy with a cryptic message. Apparently, there was a whole chapter of bikers creating chaos inside the club. They were touching the girls and harassing and intimidating the other customers while the bouncers did nothing. "What about Tommy?" I asked. "Oh, he's sitting at the bar getting drunk with their president, ignoring everything that is going on" she replied. "Start getting dressed, I will be right there" I told her as I grabbed my keys. "Tell Tommy you are going home." I arrived there a few minutes later and entered the building, going through anyone who stood between me and that dressing room. Wendy and Mercedes were both back there having a discussion when Tommy and the president wandered in. I watched as the president yelled at Mercedes, calling her every name in the book. I was waiting for Tommy to step up and do something but he never moved or said anything so I knew I was on my own. Mercedes drew back to slap the president in the face but was intercepted by Wendy. Meanwhile, the president made a move toward the girls so I grabbed him and forced him out the door. I then took Wendy by the hand and guided her out of the building safely. It went down without a hitch but left a lasting impression with the president who I would see again one day.

    I might have been the hero that night, but our marriage was on the rocks. Within days, Wendy was either leaving quite frequently or not coming home at all. When she would call me, she was always with Slim, and claiming that she was sleeping on the couch, not in his bed. I knew better. One day, she just walked in and told me to get out of her house. I pleaded with her to give it another try, but she didn't have one in her. For a short time, I gained a little respect for her. I had treated women like whores in the past, tossing them aside like yesterday's garbage, and now someone was doing the same to me. The future might look bleak now… but I will be ok. I always find a way.   **–DJN**

CHAPTER XVI - *"TIN MAN"*

2001-2002

They say, "Never judge a book by its cover," and I think it's noble to be honest. I have many layers...one day I'm her knight in shining armour, when she's the damsel in distress, then I make a 180 turn, show my true colours, and don't care who gets hurt in the process.

Cut me off at second base, no one remembers who came in second place. Don't hate the player, hate the game. I've already erased her number, and forgotten her name. Like a quarterback, heading for the sidelines, trying to get out of bounds. Like a catcher, flashing signs, to the pitcher on the mound. Three strikes and you're out...

They all became a part of me, and then gone without a trace, but no one can take their place. Where my heart was, is now just an empty space. When push came to shove, I showed them what I was made of, been collecting dust, and I'm starting to rust, and I'm left wondering what the hell happened, why everyone I've ever loved, goes away in the end.

Was a gigolo, with reasonable rates, banging everything in sight, and turning lesbians straight. I've hauled all their cargo, all their freight, if I was Superman, they were my Kryptonite.

Through my path to mediocrity, to my trail of casualties, this is for those lost along the way, who fell like dominoes. You won't hear any apologies, "you can't rape the willing," they say, "it takes two to tango." Let's make one thing crystal clear, there were no victims...only volunteers.

Many are called, but few are chosen, just a small fish in this huge ocean. When you get your fins, have to dive right in, sink or swim. It's a smorgasbord, and I can't come ashore.

Let's wipe the slate clean, I feel like the guest who wouldn't leave, already worn out my welcome. Been concerned about my legacy, how everyone will remember me, just grieve and move on, I no longer pass for a gentleman.

I don't think we are in Kansas anymore, click your heels three times, and say, "There's no place like home…" -Denny Noland "Draven" From my song "Tin Man"
Written on October 2, 2006   Copyright 2015

Although I swore I would never do it again, I called up Kaine and told him the situation, hoping that he would offer me a place to stay. Ironically, he lived behind the flea market in the same complex where Carla and Adam used to live. Luckily, he welcomed me with open arms and I repaid him by getting wasted every night. One night I was so out of it after a trip to the South Club that I woke up in the middle of the night needing to take a piss. Instead of going to the bathroom like normal people do, I walked past the bathroom and out the front door, stood at the edge of the stairway and let it fly. It was strange because I remember doing it but was powerless to stop it. It wasn't until after Kaine, who was awakened by the sound of the door opening, had already started yelling at me that I snapped out of it. "What the hell are you doing out there?" he screamed. "You are going to get us kicked out of here!" I felt like a damn fool…especially the next morning when there was still a trail of urine going from the top of the stairs to a little puddle down at the bottom which was literally right outside another tenant's door. Miraculously, no one reported the incident.

Later on that week, when Kaine had a comic book convention to go to in Durham, North Carolina, he insisted that I go with him to get out of the house. I think he did that for a number of reasons. First and foremost, he probably didn't want to go alone and he sure as hell didn't trust me to look after his apartment in my present condition either. It was an unpleasant trip for me because I was out of drugs and going through withdrawals. Although I loved going to those things under normal circumstances, I did want to be there this time... not in the state I was in. All I could think about was getting home so I could get high. It just seemed like a wasted trip to me.

The following week, Kaine wanted to take a couple of boys from work out to the Last Chance 2000. I decided to go as well, even though I knew Wendy was going to be there... bad idea. It was all good until I got drunk and started pouring my heart out to Wendy, only to be rejected. Out of anger, I walked into the office and got Tommy's loaded shotgun. I sat down in his chair, placed it into my mouth, and was about to take the safety off and pull the trigger, when Wendy walked in to check on me. She let out a piercing scream and ran back out the door to grab Tommy, who was only a few feet away. He managed to yank the gun out of my hand without it firing and said, "If you are going to blow your head off, do it somewhere else. I just had these walls painted and I don't want to have to clean up the mess." Even in my fragile state, I saw the humour in that and had a quiet chuckle. Within minutes, word of this got back to Kaine and the boys who had already decided to get me the hell out of there. The next few days, Kaine spent a lot of time by my side, being uncharacteristically nice, until I realized that killing myself wasn't worth it. There was no way I was letting her off that easy.

2

Kaine's lease was up for renewal when Tommy made me an interesting offer. He was purchasing a duplex from Gene and offered it to Kaine and me. This opened up a number of options. We could either live together and share the entire house or live separately on different floors for a combined $650 a month. We jumped at it foolishly, without looking at it first. There were a number of problems that we weren't told about before we started moving in. There was actually a hornet's nest *inside* the house, above the staircase leading to the second level. There was a shower downstairs that leaked behind the tiles so we couldn't use it and only a bathtub on the second floor which we had to share. There was a full kitchen on both levels, but other than the fridge upstairs, the rest of the appliances were defective...meaning that if you wanted to eat upstairs, you had to go downstairs to cook it, then walk outside and up the stairs to get back to where you were. There was a strip heater in some of the rooms that put out very little heat due to the house not being properly insulated. As far as air conditioning went, we were shit out of luck...often relying on fans to circulate the dry air inside. It was definitely not worth the price we were paying with all those issues, but it was better than living in my car and trust me, I would know.

It took several trips to get all of my stuff out of Wendy's apartment, and each time she saw me, her feelings started changing more and more. As soon as Kaine and I got the duplex, it was like I woke up one morning and I didn't want Wendy anymore. That was just the way I healed...all at once. I had a well- documented history of doing just that, which was unfortunate for Wendy, who was heading in the other direction. Eventually, she would call to ask me if I wanted to come over for a booty call, since we were still technically married. I took her up on her offer…under one condition. "It's just sex and nothing more" I explained. "When it's over, I am going home, no questions asked. Don't take it as the first step toward us getting back together." I thought she understood but apparently she didn't.

As soon as we did the deed and I got up to get dressed, she asked me where I was going. "Home" I said. "But you are home" Wendy replied. "I thought this meant---". I cut her off right there. "I already explained this once before" I said. "Don't you love me anymore?" she interrupted. "It's over. It's actually been over for quite a while. It just took some time to get that through my head, but I've got it now" I replied. "Don't you have a heart? You are a tin man! That's what you are! Heartless…" she sobbed as she slapped me as hard as she could right across the face. We lived together for several months and were married for about three, and things never got physical until that moment. I just walked away before things escalated, with a new nickname that I planned to have tattooed on my arm someday.

Wendy started dating a new guy for a little while so the calls stopped temporarily. I was told by one of the girls that he was a nasty bastard with greasy hair and dirt under his fingernails. I couldn't say that I was really surprised at all, nor was I surprised that as soon as they broke up, she was calling again. I went over for what would become my last booty call that night. When I got there, she was asleep in the bed so I got undressed and crawled into bed beside her. She didn't wake up but did throw her leg over me to let me know that she knew I was there.

All I could do was lie there and stare up at the ceiling, wondering why the fuck I even bothered coming around. Then I thought about the fact that she had that nasty bastard inside of her and I nearly lost my lunch. I slowly removed Wendy's leg and lightly rose from the bed. I went into the other room and got dressed because I knew that my clumsiness would probably wake her. I grabbed a few of my belongings and left as quietly as possible. I was probably half way home, when she called me to ask me why I left. It was simple. I just found her repulsive now and I needed to go on with my life. Of course, I didn't tell her that. Maybe I had a heart after all.

    I felt like it was probably a good idea to get all of my remaining belongings out of Wendy's apartment, so I took Kaine with me when I knew Wendy wasn't going to be there. We loaded up both of our trucks to the sounds of little Panthor crying from the bathroom. Wendy had obviously locked him in there because she hadn't had the patience to train him how to use the litter box properly. I was tempted to take him with me, so he could be reunited with Brandy and Gabrielle, but at the end of the day, he was still Wendy's cat so I had to leave him behind. When we were having one last look around the house, I said to Kaine, "Too bad I can't stop her from watching the cable TV that's still in my name." I saw Kaine's eyes light up. "But you can…let me handle this" he replied, as he pulled all of the wires out of the wall and disconnected everything so it was rendered virtually useless. "She won't be watching anything now, my friend" he said. Then we had a good laugh before we left. I almost felt remorse about what he had done…almost.

3

After all of this, I started doing healthier recreational things like attending a local wrestling event with Kaine in honour of "Freebird" Terry Gordy, who had just recently passed away. I saw Buddy Landell there, and we hugged it out like long lost brothers. When the other wrestlers saw that Buddy knew me, they all joined in on our conversation. It was very cool. Tommy was in the main event against an up and coming kid that obviously hadn't learned the ropes yet, and out of frustration, ended up squashing him. I felt sorry for that young man after Tommy pinned him. I asked Tommy why he was so hard on the lad and he said that it was because he didn't know how to make a proper comeback, and that pissed him off, so he stretched him. That could have easily been me if I hadn't got injured.

I also attended a football game at my old school. There were a lot of familiar faces but I didn't talk to anyone except for the new head coach, who was one of my old teammates. He spotted me as the team was about to come back out on the field after halftime, and asked me how I had been. It was just funny how I stood there surrounded by the players and was still bigger than most, even with their pads and helmets on. I must admit that it felt great to be home again, even if most of the people in this sleepy little town wouldn't piss on me if I was on fire.

For some reason, the school was open so I walked through its hallowed halls. This was only the second time I had been in the building since graduation ten years ago. My mom was working for the school as a cleaning lady, so I stopped in to say hello a few years back while she was cleaning my old kinder-garden classroom. It was amazing how it still looked exactly how I remembered it. However, this time I had access to a majority of the building which was normally off limits. There were ghosts everywhere. The last time I roamed these halls, I was innocent. Despite my reputation, I had only been high twice and that was what defined me in the eyes of many. Some of the more popular jocks dabbled into drugs more than I did but never got caught… which was the only difference. I was also a virgin throughout school because girls looked at me like I was a leper, due to my family's name and my misunderstood after school activities… which were more than a little exaggerated. I needed this to heal and put it all to rest. I was feeling so nostalgic and euphoric. It was like I had stepped back in time and I didn't want to go back. Unfortunately, one of my former teachers saw me and told me that they were getting ready to lock the building up so I needed to get out immediately. I had just walked back outside when I got a phone call…one that I wished I hadn't answered. It snapped me back to reality.

    It was Wendy…and as usual, a friendly discussion turned into a heated argument. I don't even remember what it was about but somehow, her new old boyfriend Slim got involved because he "didn't appreciate how I was talking to his girlfriend." I never had a problem with Slim. He always respected our relationship and stayed out of the picture until now. Hell, we even hung out at the Boiler Room one night, against Wendy's wishes, and nearly started a riot after I told him that I bet we could whip everyone's asses that were in the building that night. He agreed and grabbed an empty bottle to use as a weapon before Wendy intervened. She loved to stir the pot and create unnecessary drama, especially by calling me while her partner at the time was listening in. She not only did that with Slim, but also Homer later on when she was sleeping with him. She would even put her "friend" Jackson on the phone with me which gave it away. I knew that wherever Jackson was, Homer wasn't too far away so it blew her cover. All I told Slim on the phone that night was "She may be your girlfriend, but she was still my *wife* so stay out of it." He didn't listen and kept running his mouth so I hung up on him. I knew that Wendy was enjoying this too much so I let it go. Of course, this put a damper on the entire evening, so when I got back to Knoxville, I used it as an excuse to get high…like I needed one.

4

I will never forget where I was on September 11, 2001. I was at home suffering with an infection in both eyes. I had been battling this affliction for over a week. It had gotten so severe that I was literally sitting in the dark because even dim light was too much for my eyes to handle. I couldn't walk outside or go to work because it was just too irritating and painful. I had just made an appearance at the club days prior with Tommy and had to wear sunglasses to get around inside the building at night. That was how bad it was. The new DJ, who called himself "Marky Mark", immediately thought I was a joke because he thought I was just wearing them in an attempt to look cool. Later, one of the girls explained it to him and then he understood. I had tried wearing a patch over the original eye that showed signs of infection while at work, in an attempt to keep myself from either rubbing it or getting more debris in it, but it managed to spread into the other one anyway within a couple of days. It was completely disrupting my life so I forced to stay home until I got better.

That morning started like any other. Kaine came downstairs before heading off to work, Brandy jumped down out of the window onto my face and farted, and I went into the kitchen for a beverage and a snack. It wasn't until I flipped on the TV after Kaine left that made it different. I could barely see the image of a building burning but couldn't read the headlines. I turned up the volume and got within a foot or two of the screen to try to see what the hell was going on. About that time, I saw a plane flying toward a second building and my heart just sunk as I watched it crash into it and burst into flames. Oh my God! What is happening? Once I realized that this horrific act was being carried out on American soil, I just sat there in silence. I could feel a tear running down my cheek. These were my people and they are dying right before my eyes on national TV. I was devastated and wanted to enlist to kill whoever was responsible for committing this heinous and cowardly act. I died a little more as I watched both buildings come tumbling down.

    I made it back to work a couple of days later and it was like I was on a different planet. I could just feel the love of a nation united for the first time that I could remember. Everyone treated each other like they were family. It didn't matter if you were straight or gay, black or white, Republican or Democrat, you were an American and that was the only thing that mattered. We were one and we could overcome anything. I loved the world that I saw then, but I knew that it wouldn't last and it didn't…too much greed and corruption around for that to happen. I even said those very words to someone on that day when I overheard them talking about it. Sad but true. Then we heard a rendition of Live's "Overcome" on the "Mancow Muller" radio show which had footage of not only one of George W. Bush's inspirational post 9/11 speeches but the original news broadcasts audio mixed into the song, and we were nearly brought to tears again. No one said a word...

5

I had some great times working for Tommy over the years and even more funny stories to tell. Once we were both working in Bristol, Tennessee near the racetrack clearing out some land that they wanted to convert into a park. Since I couldn't operate the machinery, I was almost insignificant. Tommy was paying me though, so he thought of something I could do: drive the dump truck around on the premises. I couldn't drive stick, so Tommy showed me in a couple of minutes all that he felt I needed to know. He showed me where reverse and first gear was and how to raise and lower the bed. They were loading my truck with tons of rock and dirt and I was driving up to the top of the hill and dumping it. Since I was only driving in first gear, I was going so slow that they were hauling small loads themselves while they were waiting for me to bring the truck back. One thing that Tommy had forgotten to show me was the angle that the truck should be sitting before I unloaded it to keep it from tipping over. The thought of weight distribution never crossed my mind. I had already made several trips and dumped before one of the boys stopped me and told me that if I continued doing it the way I was, I was going to end up toppling down the hill and killing myself. I took his advice before tempting fate again... then gave Tommy an earful afterwards.

Since we were so far from home, we had to get rooms at the local hotel for a few days. I shared a room with Tommy which was interesting to say the least. We all headed out to a fancy restaurant that first night to have dinner. I had the husband and wife maintenance duo of "Blackie" and "Linda" sitting across from me. Someone made the mistake of cracking a joke while I had a mouthful of mashed potatoes and I blew them all over Blackie. They were in his beard, his hair and eyes, even his food. He reminded me of Mr. Edwards on Little House on the Prairie when he came bursting through the door after he walked through that blizzard to give Laura and Mary their cups and shiny new pennies. I thought he was going to kill me. He wasn't a big guy by any means but he was a biker and Linda could probably kick a few men's asses herself. Luckily for me, they thought it was hilarious and the table just erupted with laughter. Whew!

Then there was the time that Tommy and I was digging a septic tank and I made the mistake of leaning up against a tree covered with poison oak. It started as only a single spot, but by the next morning it had spread to several more areas because apparently I had been scratching in my sleep. Within a week, I had it everywhere except for my face and crotch. I had literally wrapped myself like a mummy so the blisters wouldn't leak but it wasn't helping. The itching was fucking unbearable, no matter how much medication I used. I eventually went to the clinic and got a shot in my ass to clear it all up. When the doctor first saw my skin, he said "In all of my years practicing, I have never seen a case of poison oak this severe. You must have gone through hell." I just smiled and said, "You have no idea doc." It turned out that almost every tree there had poison oak on them, as we would later discover. But, I must say the whole experience made me learn how to identify it, and steer clear of it in the future.

My favourite by far was when Tommy bought a houseboat and a speedboat from Gene. We went to get the houseboat first off the lake and we had just started moving it when it started taking on water.

Tommy decided to patch the hole and leave it until the next day, so now we were taking the speedboat instead. Tommy then suggested that we should take it for a spin before loading it onto the trailer. There were four of us on that boat and all could swim, except me, even if I was an accomplished dog-paddler. We got out to the middle of the lake when it started taking on water too. One of the guys said, as he was using a bucket to dip some of the water out, "I guess we are going to have to swim back to the shore." Fear overcame me as I pleaded with them to turn the boat around and head towards the dock. By the grace of God, we made it back to dry land without the boat sinking and I didn't embarrassed myself or drown. I wasn't exactly afraid of the water but I wasn't confident in my swimming either. One of the guys figured that out and started teasing me about it but I played it off in a way that made him stop pretty quickly, before the others realized that he was on to something.

We were supposed to pick up the houseboat the following morning but Mother Nature had other ideas. It wasn't just raining… it was pissing rain for three days straight. By the time we got to the boat, only the top of it was still above the water. Tommy went and bought some cheap scuba gear so he and one of the guys could dive down to the bottom and hook chains underneath the boat so we could hoist it back to the surface. It took all day, nearly a dozen men, and most of Tommy's heavy equipment, but we got it out of the water in one piece.

Getting it back to Tommy's house wasn't going to be easy either. Between the one lane roads and how much the boat was hanging over on both sides of the trailer presented a number of potential disasters but we managed. Of course, we were in the lead truck waving the flags to let everyone know that a wide load was coming and to get the fuck out of the way until we got to the highway. What people couldn't see was that Tommy and his driver were both naked because they wanted to get out of their wet clothes and let the warm air dry them off. They kept making comments back and forth about each other's penises and I was thankful to be in the backseat fully clothed. I was just waiting for Tommy to reach into the glove box and pull out a tape measure but fortunately the thought never crossed his mind or he probably would have. That damn boat was still sitting there in the same spot beside Tommy's house some years later, full of dead fish and stagnant water. Somewhere I could hear Gene laughing...

6

Now I was starting to miss the club, but wasn't sure if I had even a snowball's chance of ever working there again. I had already burned Gene not once, but twice, and the last time was a doozy. I also didn't know how certain girls were going to react if I returned, especially since I had liberated them from One Time then abandoned them to fall under his regime again. I just wasn't much of an asset to Tommy's business and if I wasn't a friend, he would have fired me long ago. I swallowed my pride and had a meeting with Gene one last time. He reluctantly agreed to hire me back as a bouncer under one condition: if I ever felt burned out, just let him know so he could arrange some time off...don't just walk out on him again without letting him know how unhappy I was. Times like these, and when Wendy and I wanted to have a child together but she had her tubes tied, and Gene offered to pay to for the surgery to reverse it, showed me how much I meant to him. I was determined to not disappoint him this time around. He didn't like many people but he took me under his wing for some reason. I owed him my loyalty at least. The next time I left this business, it was going to be for good. I swore to myself that under no circumstances was I ever coming back.

My original plan was to do double duty like Tommy. I was going to work full time for him during the day and work overnight for Gene. This would give me a steady income, since there was always an uncertainty of when I was actually getting paid working for Tommy. I got paid when he got paid, and often times, customers weren't in any hurry to let go of their hard earned money, or just couldn't afford to pay for our services in one lump sum. Things had gotten so tough at times that Tommy was either counting out his loose change or digging deep into his freezer to find us something we might be able to eat for lunch the following day. Then out of the blue, we would get paid for several jobs all at once and our pockets were filled. Tommy always paid me everything he owed me but I hated the inconsistency. The club was about to remedy that.

On the day of my big return, I worked a gruelling shift for Tommy until it was time for me to report to the club. The guys kept saying their goodbyes because they were confident that I wasn't going to be able to handle doing both, despite what I was telling them. Unfortunately, I didn't have time to take a shower in between so I walked in with my work clothes on and Gene was not impressed. "I want you to make a decision right now" he said. "Either you are working for me or you are working for Tommy. You can't do both. This is just unacceptable." Needless to say, I didn't make it to work the following morning. Tommy understood and didn't really seem surprised. The only way he was able to juggle both jobs was because he was the boss at both. He would roll into the club sometimes whenever he felt like it and generally slept in the office during working hours to catch up on his rest. I didn't have that option. I had to be awake and alert at all times. That was my job.

I was amazed at how different the club looked that first day. The Captain was no longer at the helm of the DJ booth... that was Marky Mark's baby now. There were also new bouncers and bar staff and a few new girls who already seemed to know me somehow. Lena wasn't working there still, yet was making appearances at special events, like contests for example, on the weekends from time to time. Jessie and her future husband weren't tending the back bar anymore either, which was disheartening and very unfortunate, since I had never told her how I really felt about her. It was like this every time I came back and I always felt guilty about leaving once I saw that certain people wasn't just simply waiting for me and had moved on with their lives without me. I had fucked up...yet again. I guess I was very good at something after all.

7

As unlikely and unusual as it seemed, after such a rough start, I became instant friends with Marky Mark. We couldn't have been more different. I was a drug addict living in a shithole not caring what anyone thought, while he focused on making money and living the good life. He was against drugs and often encouraged me to get myself clean and get my shit together before it was too late. He was also very picky with the calibre of women that he associated with. He was actually dating a feature dancer at the time that spent a lot of time on the road, travelling around the country selling merchandise and signing autographs. When I told him that I grew up madly in love with Alyssa Milano, he informed me that his girlfriend actually did a private one on one dance for her while in LA touring the club circuit. I wasn't sure if he was telling me the truth or not until his girlfriend verified the story later on. Marky Mark had a tendency to brag a lot so I never knew when he might be stretching the truth a little. Overall, I saw him as a positive influence on my life that was much needed at the time.

We even discussed possibly resurrecting Melancholia with him as my new lead singer. I thought that he was probably going to be my best chance of getting this project off the ground, but it never made it beyond the early development stages due to my drug problems and later on, my deteriorating health. Since his girlfriend was usually out of town, I would often stay overnight at his home in Kingsport. I would occasionally bring cocaine with me to take the edge off, unbeknownst to him, and sneak off to the bathroom to do a bump whenever I could get away. I would feel terrible afterwards about disrespecting him in his own house, but I felt like I couldn't live without it. Hell, I kind of needed it to stay awake since he never slept. We would either be watching movies or playing video games until about two hours before we needed to get up. Then we would take a short two hour nap and hit the showers before loading into his car for a long two hour drive to work that he did daily. I honestly didn't know how he could bring so much energy and enthusiasm to the microphone every night without any rest, or without any help, but he did. That was just how he was. It was almost like he was high on life.

Speaking of getting high, I also made friends with a trio of drug dealers led by a guy named "Reese." They became an easier source for not only ecstasy and cocaine, but also crystal meth, which had become increasingly hard to find. One of the guys "Kris" lived just down the road from me, and usually had a constant supply of all three that he was pushing, so I saw him more than the other two. The only uncomfortable thing about that was how his girlfriend looked at me when he wasn't paying attention. I would find out that she was totally into me when she started working at the club but I wasn't going there. The third guy was named "Darryl" and he was more of a follower than anything else. I had known him since I used to be associated with Jake. He used to idolize him before he met Reese. He would sometimes do a drop out to my place when Reese or Kris had other shit going on. At this point, they were very valuable because Andre was just starting to have thoughts about possibly cutting me off because he could see that I was lost. Reese didn't care about all that sentimental shit, business was business. I was making him very wealthy.

    Reese was a cowboy, careless to the point that he thought he was untouchable. He was far too accepting of people and trusting of them and anyone could see that it was eventually going to be his downfall. He had literally only just met me when he invited me over to his house. I was sitting on his couch in the living room when he told me that he needed to take a shit. The bathroom was straight down the hall from where I was. He went in there, dropped his pants, and continued the conversation with the door opened. I had never talked to anyone while they were on the toilet, especially someone I just met, but Reese had no shame. That was just how he was…he just didn't care.

    He had also tried to get me involved in his affairs by talking me into going somewhere with him for different reasons, but these trips always ended with a drug deal. I remember being lured into meeting some girls once in a restaurant parking lot. I didn't really know that anything was going on until a police car passed by and Reese said, "If that pig pulls in here, you better be ready to roll. I've got thirteen ecstasy pills and we are eating every one of these motherfuckers or we're going to jail." A couple of incidents like this, and I wasn't going anywhere with him anymore. I had just narrowly escaped a prison record several times in the past. Once I got pulled over when I was well and truly beyond the legal limit by Blount County's finest. I passed all the sobriety tests but wasn't asked to take a Breathalyzer test even though the cop smelled alcohol on me. Instead, he asked me if I knew someone close by that could look after me until I sobered up, which was unheard of. I told him that my uncle was head of security at the Wal-Mart just down the street and he could take care of me, so the cop drove me down there, leaving my car on the side of the road. My uncle took me to his apartment, which sat above an Asian spa, and let me sleep it off. I tried to convince him that I was sober and pleaded with him to take me back to my car until he said, "You don't get it do you? You caught a break tonight. I guarantee you that he will be keeping an eye on that car and if he catches you anywhere near it, you won't be so lucky next time." Point well taken...

    Then there was the time that I passed out momentarily while driving home one night on ecstasy and crashed into the side of a bridge. My front tire on the driver's side literally exploded on impact. Because I was so high, I thought that it was hilarious. There were two cop cars sitting on the other side of the road that had to have heard the collision, yet never came to investigate. Tommy ended up coming to the rescue and changing my tire because I couldn't even stand up. He even followed me home to make sure I arrived safely.

There was also the night that I was driving home and the alternator started going out on my car. I literally drove across Knoxville with headlights that were dimmer than two flashlights and getting weaker by the moment. I knew that once I turned off the ignition I was fucked, so I was determined to drive it as far as possible before stopping. Of course, I was intoxicated that night too. I made it to the exact same bridge that I had the accident on, and the car just died. I got out to inspect it and noticed that it was actually on fire underneath due to an oil leak as well. There I was…dousing the fire with jugs of water that I had stored in my trunk for the radiator until I got it put out. I called dad and he came out to help. No sooner than when he got out of his car, we heard a crack of thunder and saw a flash of lightning. Dad was worried because we were sitting over the river, which increased our chances of getting struck significantly. He put the hot battery out of his car into mine, and placed my battery into his, so he could charge it while my alternator was pulling his down. This was so we could inch our way closer to the house. We must have stopped several times and switched batteries before we got home. My dad could be brilliant at times and this was one of them.

It wasn't even the fact that we were making deals in public places that bothered me either. Andre would never come over to my house, unless it was when I was living with Wendy, and that was only because he had a thing for her. She could talk him into anything. He was basically doing it for *her* not *me*. So a majority of the time, I either had to go to his place or we would meet somewhere in the middle, usually at the IHOP on Kingston Pike. He would usually ask me to park in the front, preferably near the ever present police cruisers. I used to think that he was out of his mind until he explained the method to his madness. "Who in their right mind would ever suspect that someone would be stupid enough to be dealing right out in the open in plain view of the cops? They would probably go somewhere hidden like perhaps the back of the building. Well, that's where the cops look too because it appears suspicious." He was telling me this as we looked in on two police officers through the window having a meal, who just happened to be paying us no attention whatsoever. "Sometimes you got to think outside the box" he added. "Like reverse psychology I suppose?" I asked. He nodded. I had never thought about it that way before, but it did make sense. The difference was that I had agreed to be involved then. I don't like it when people deceive me. It can wreck a friendship or a partnership in this case.

8

Then there were the women in my life at this time. I had been nicknamed "0069" from Marky Mark due to my James Bond persona and way with women. I had tried a couple of more times to enter that nameless club on the other side of town, but was asked to leave both times. I took Mac down there once when I wasn't even working at the club at the time and neither of us made it out of the lobby. The old lady at the desk saw me, then looked at Mac, then reached under the counter for something. She finally stepped away for a minute to talk to someone in the back before taking our money. When she returned, she demanded that both of us must leave at once, no questions asked. I don't know if they had pictures to identify us or some disgruntled former employee of ours who pointed us out to them, but they always knew who we were…especially me for some fucking reason.

The interesting part of all of this was when I went once with Tommy and we both got in. I don't know if they were afraid of what Tommy and me were capable of once we had already had a number of drinks beforehand or what, but they opened their doors to us. Homer was working as the bouncer there that night and was scared to death that we were going to get out of hand and cause trouble. He kept kissing our asses, especially Tommy, because he knew that Tommy never liked him. We pretty much broke every rule in the book that night and had nothing said to us. This would be the last time I ever tried to enter that shithole.

When looking abroad wasn't working, I searched within once more with little or no success. The first girl was named "Melanie" and she grabbed my attention in the same manner that Justice had done so years earlier. When she put on a particular two-piece red leather outfit and hair extensions, I became putty in her hands. I started buying her roses and sweeping her off her feet until One Time got involved. He had told her that I had been bragging about what I was planning to do to her once I got into her pants, which was a boldface lie by the way, and she bought it without even asking me first. I don't know why he did this unless it was because he wanted her for himself. I was upset at first, until I realized that he might have been doing me a huge favour.

It just so happened that we had a club meeting later that week. Before it got started, Gene pulled me off to the side and said, "I don't know why you are chasing Melanie, she only likes girls. Of course, if you throw enough money at her, she will consider it. I've had her. If you don't believe me, just ask her." Obviously, I had to ask her the first opportunity I got, and she didn't deny it. I couldn't believe that she would do such a thing. He was old enough to be her grandfather for god's sake. When I turned to look back at One Time, he was laughing his ass off. I couldn't believe that someone who claimed I was his friend was behind all of this. This bastard owed me everything. The only reason he was in the position he was in, was because I gave it up. He wasn't even Gene's first choice as my successor. Judas got his shot first and failed miserably, leaving Gene with no other choice. And this was how he showed his gratitude? He could go fuck himself as far as I was concerned.

When a girl named "Celeste" started working for us, I had no idea that she liked me until she stood on her tiptoes and kissed me on the lips out of nowhere one night in front of everyone. Since I had been drinking heavily all night, I wasn't going to let it stop there. As she was getting ready to drive past, I motioned for her to stop. When she did, I poked my head through her window and we engaged in one of the longest, wettest, sloppiest kisses I have ever had. Her tongue was so long that she was nearly choking me. If only I would have stayed on my best behaviour that night, it could have led to something but it's me we are talking about. I would later make out with another girl outside of her car. Kissing this girl was different. It was slower, softer, and more sensual instead of sexual. She hated the fact that she had to leave me standing there afterwards. Both of these girls were in serious relationships but I didn't give a fuck. I wanted some lip service so I made it happen.

I was running a little late for work the following night, so when I got there, both girls was waiting at the door for me. Neither of them knew who the other was waiting for until Celeste opened her mouth. "Denny and I played around a little last

night" she told the other girl. The look on the other girl's face was pretty self- explanatory.
"Hmmm...well that's interesting. Denny and me played around a little last night too" she said. I had no idea that both girls would were affected by the events of the previous night or I would have been more careful. They obviously took it more seriously than I did, and the only way I knew to react to it was to keep walking and try to avoid them the rest of the night. Strangely enough, neither of them seemed too bothered after all, and was willing to "share" me to my delight. But it was about to become even more complicated.

Once again, a third girl would join the fray when she made the mistake of letting me know that she had a sexual dream about me. She was very young and naïve so it was fun to fuck with her head. She would eventually start kissing me on the lips every time I tipped her, especially on my nights off when I was getting drunk. Some nights I would rotate back and forth with the three girls, telling them everything that they wanted to hear. However, the joke was on me. Celeste and the young girl had become close friends, and although I never slept with either of them, the young girl's boyfriend was rooting them both. It was just one more step toward me writing off women altogether, even if I had brought this all on myself.

I just kept putting myself into these situations, and paid for it accordingly. I made out with a girl everyone knew was a lesbian at the 2000 club one night a year prior then shared another moment with her around this time. She told me that I was a sexy motherfucker and that she was going to "screw my brains out" one day. I knew it was never going to happen and it didn't. This was a common theme back then. There was one girl named "Sabine" who liked me and kept flipping back and forth on whether she was single or not. One night we would be kissing at her car and planning our next move, and a week later, she was back with her boyfriend and everything was cancelled. There was another named "Rochelle" who approached me one night and asked if I we could just have sex without any strings attached. I was ok with that but it never happened either, despite the same question being asked on several other occasions as well. Then there was Adam's ex Angelina who got friendly with me one night before she left town. She French kissed me very passionately in an empty dressing room until she realized that the security camera was recording everything. She pulled away quickly and didn't say another word until we stepped outside. She then informed me, as so many others have before and even after her, that she had wanted me for a long time. She even told me that she should have started having sex with me back in the day instead of Adam…especially after everything turned out. I ended up teasing her all night about the kiss, saying things like "It wasn't so bad was it?" and she was playing along throughout, without dropping even the slightest hint that we were probably never going to see each other again. My anger just kept building up, but they just kept pouring it on, one after another.

    Finally, it happened. I saw a girl at the deli down the road that appeared to have the qualities and attributes that interested me…and she wasn't even a stripper! I know that every guy has been in this situation before. There's an attractive girl and a cute, yet severely overweight, friend that liked you first, which makes the one you do like a little hesitant about dating you. Of course, I wasn't aware of this until I asked her out and to make things worse, they not only worked together but shared an apartment too. When the girl agreed to go out with me, the fat friend got jealous and stopped speaking to her which created quite a rift between the two. Now we were limited to when we could spend any time together. Kaine and I had an agreement that no girls were allowed in our house overnight, so we could only have privacy at her apartment while her roommate was at work. We might have gone on a handful of dates before we were ready to "get down to business." I had met her little girl and spent the entire day at the park with her before we dropped the kid off at her grandmother's house. I then stopped by Andre's to get some cocaine and although she didn't say anything verbally, I knew that this wasn't going to end well. I did a few bumps going down the highway that probably terrified her, but that was just what I did. If she didn't like it, that's too bad.

    This girl acted different when I kissed her than most did. You would think that I was her fantasy or something, by how she reacted when my lips met hers. I even pointed it out by saying "You act like my kisses burn or something." She just smiled and closed her eyes as she puckered up again. Magnify that tenfold when I went down on her. She acted like she had never had an orgasm before. It was going as planned until she took her shirt off. She was pale as a vampire and had really badly done tattoos in the wrong places that I found repulsive. I was even having trouble staying hard while she was giving me oral. I was tempted to ask her to put her shirt back on but I didn't want to hurt her feelings. I thought that once I was inside her, there would be no problems but I was wrong. I might have gotten in a handful of thrusts in before I went soft and was down for the count. She insisted on more foreplay, but I wanted to sleep on it and try again tomorrow. We then stopped by the house briefly so I could do more coke and Kaine was there. He had admired the girl from a distance himself and didn't seem surprised at all that I had already bedded her. Since we weren't staying, he wasn't upset. However, I just had a feeling that she wasn't going to be in my life for very long anyway. I had been through this before… except this particular girl drank bourbon and smoked marijuana, but didn't want to be around cocaine because it was bad. We just kind of ended it without saying anything. I didn't have room in my life for a fucking hypocrite anyway.

9

I wasn't buying my dope from Andre much anymore since Reese had come into the picture. I was, however, still hanging out with him occasionally, and that led to me finally meeting the "big dogs" who supplied him. This was the first time I had ever met someone that high on the totem pole. This pair of "brothers" weren't just petty drug dealers…they only dealt with large quantities and was responsible for bringing up most of the cocaine into this area from Florida. It was no surprise that I recognized both of them from the club. They weren't exactly thrilled to see me sitting on Andre's couch as they began carrying in their bags and suitcases but Andre somehow convinced them that I could be trusted. Of course, Andre was in one of those moods and wouldn't sell me anything so I made a phone call.

I found myself at Kris's house about a half hour later. I don't remember where my head was that day but I decided to buy three grams of crystal meth instead of cocaine. Anyone who knows anything about meth will tell you that you should never do it in the same manner that you do cocaine. It is not necessary. I actually used to call it "the poor man's cocaine" because you could get as high off a small amount of meth as you could an unhealthy dose of cocaine. It was also more dangerous to large quantities of meth due to the fact that it was made from household chemicals found under your sink. I was fully aware of all of this, yet did the entire three grams overnight into the next morning, without stopping, until it was all gone. I must say that I never felt better in my life. I felt young, like I had been born again, and that was without any food or sleep. I never wanted to come down from this high. I felt no pain or fatigue for the first time since I was a child. I went to work that night feeling like a new man… so alert and full of energy. This was too good to be true. Something was definitely wrong…

    About half-way through my shift, I felt like I needed to piss so I headed off to the bathroom. I was hit suddenly with severe pain in my lower back and collapsed to the floor. I was in the fetal position for a few minutes, until the pain eased up enough for me to get back to my feet. I tried to piss but all that would come out was blood again. It felt like kidney-stones but I wasn't sure so I went to the emergency room. A couple of hours later, I had an X-ray done, and the doctor found a huge stone lodged between my kidneys that was going to require surgery to have it removed. I couldn't help but wonder if this "stone" was comprised of calcium like the ones before, or was this the result of my body not being able to break down such a large amount of crystal meth? The doctor even asked me if I had been taking any kind of drugs that night and I told him the truth, even explaining to him what crystal meth was made of, since he had never heard of it. He told me that it was impossible to tell what this stone was caused by until it was removed and examined. He then asked if I had medical insurance and I told him that I didn't. "I have to send you home then, son" he said. "We're not legally obligated to treat you, unless you are literally on your deathbed, if you don't have an insurance card." I couldn't fucking believe that patients were being turned away under any circumstances. It just seemed so un-American to me. This was supposed to be the greatest country in the world. I suppose it still was, unless you got sick. So I went home to suffer.

Within days, I was burning up with fever and my skin was literally turning green from infection. I was in constant pain and just wanted to die. I was missing a lot of work because I was too sick to even function. This went on for nearly two months until my parents found a way to get the procedure done. My mother had found an insurance company that I could pay a fee and get a card immediately... but that was just to get my foot in the door. They told me up front that they weren't covering the costs of anything other than that. I was already in serious debt after the whole Wendy debacle, so I was hesitant to add endless hospital bills into the equation as well, but I had no other choice. I had been suffering for way too long. I needed to do something before it killed me, so I gave in and booked my appointment.

In the meantime, I started talking to a girl named "Victoria" at the club. As I was sitting on the step at the bar one night, she walked up to me and shoved my head into her crotch. I looked up at her and said in my own arrogant and cocky way "You could possibly be my next girl." She just laughed and walked away. You see, Victoria wasn't really interested in my kind at all. She wasn't into dating drug addicts, she went after the *dealers.* She had her eyes on Reese after I got him a job at the club because she knew that he had drugs and money. But when it came to being narcissistic, she had met her match. Although he did have her over at his house once, he wasn't into her at all so he ditched her. That was probably the only time that has happened to her in her entire life.

The earliest signs of things to come started with Victoria. I was starting to distance myself from women and devote myself exclusively to cocaine. Sex just wasn't important anymore. In fact, women were more of a nuisance than an asset at times. If I had one in my life, that meant that I had to share my drugs and I was no longer willing to support anyone else's habit anymore...only my own. I would keep pursuing Victoria aggressively until we would set a date, then it was the same result: I would do some coke, get really high, and decide to stay home instead of showing up. The first couple of times, I cleverly covered my ass with lame excuses. The best one was on Halloween night, when I convinced her that I was actually at a costume party when I really wasn't. I had been known to dress up as "the Crow" in the past, and I was almost certain that others at the party would be thinking the same, so I lied and told her that I was there as Eric Draven and even waved to her a couple of times but she never acknowledged me. She responded with "I think I did see you there. I'm sorry that I didn't recognize you. I feel terrible. I'll have to make it up to you." My plan worked to perfection. She fell for it. Then I would repeat the process over and over again until she just gave up. I didn't need her in my life anyway.

On the night of my first surgery, I was so drunk that I actually passed out before they even put me under. I don't know how they didn't notice. Had something went wrong, they would have been in some serious legal trouble and deservingly so. When I came to after the procedure, I was pissing on not only myself but the poor nurse who was looking after me. My kidneys were in a constant spasm so I couldn't control them. My parents were just outside the room and entered when they heard my voice. "How are you feeling?" dad asked. "I feel worse than before the surgery" I said as I looked over at the attractive nurse whose scrubs were now stained with my blood. "A lot of that is probably due to the fact that you have a stent shoved up your penis" the nurse said. I had no idea what the hell a stent was, or how much discomfort it was going to cause me over the next few days, but by the time it was over, I would be able to write a paper on it.

After my parents dropped me off at my house, I did something that was borderline insane. I called Andre and arranged to meet him at West Town Mall to get some dope. When he saw me, he was horrified. I had blood stains on my clothing from my little accident at the hospital and was still way too impaired to be behind the wheel. I was unaware that everyone was staring at me because I looked like I had just stepped out of a slasher film. "Where did that blood come from?" Andre asked. "I just got out of surgery about an hour ago" I replied. "Are you out of your fucking mind? This is it! Don't bother calling me again. If you are trying to kill yourself, you're not doing it on my watch" he said as he handed me the blow. "The only reason I'm letting you have this is because I took the risk of getting it to you. Man, you need help. If you want to continue with this habit, you better find someone else because I'm done." He was true to his word. This would be our last transaction as we parted ways forever.

I wasn't able to go to work very often but when I did show up, there was never a dull moment. The girls actually pitched in and gave me several hundred dollars to help me pay my bills which meant a lot to me. When I asked one of the girls why they did this, she said "You are our Denny and we love you. We know that you are running out of money and we felt like it was the least that we could do." Sometimes these girls were the only thing keeping me going. I remember a couple of years before when I was working on my birthday, and they managed to sneak a cake in without me noticing. The Captain actually announced it over the microphone and stopped the show so the girls could bring out my cake and sing "Happy Birthday" to me. I got a hug and a kiss from every girl that was working that night. It was indeed a special memory just like this one. Of course, I spent all of the money that they gave on blow but it was the thought that counts.

One Time had also been busy while I'd been away. He has started sleeping with a cute young girl named "Misty" who supposably had an abusive boyfriend. One of the nights I was at work, the young couple got into an argument at the end of the parking lot after hours. One Time, Marky Mark, yours truly, and two other bouncers went up there to break it up. Seeing that he was clearly outnumbered and being circled by an angry mob of guys itching to tear him apart, he apologized to Misty and was backing up slowly to leave, keeping an eye on Mark and me. About that time, One Time popped him right in the mouth while he wasn't looking, breaking his jaw instantly. We were all furious at him for taking a cheap shot, especially when he gave himself the nickname "One Time" once we were back safely inside the building, because it only took one punch to break the unsuspecting kid's jaw. I remember telling him that "Karma was going to get him back for gloating over this cowardly act that he should be ashamed of...not proud of." He just laughed it off.

Now it was time to go back to the hospital to see if the surgery took care of the stone or not. When I got the results, I was not happy. Apparently, the incompetent doctor missed the stone entirely so I had to go back for a second surgery. I had a lengthy conversation with this clown about how much all of this was going to cost. He said, "Well, I don't charge you anything for my services, but every time I turn this machine on, it costs $5000." Then he gave me a sarcastic laugh. "But you botched the first surgery. Why do I still have to pay?" I asked. "That's not how the health system works, son. I guess I will see you in a couple of days" he said as he left the room. I was ready to go postal but somehow managed to keep my cool.

Instead of being drunk, I was high on cocaine when I arrived at the hospital this time around. So high, in fact, that I didn't go under like I was supposed to. I was awake but couldn't move or talk. I watched as several beautiful young nurses prepped me. I even saw the doctor putting on his gloves and what the machine looked like before the picture faded out. I woke up hoping that this time would do it, but the x-ray was inconclusive, so I had to have another one in a week or so to be sure.

The next couple of weeks would be nothing less than a fucking nightmare. When I arrived home from the hospital, I found out that Kaine had his girlfriend over for the entire night since I wasn't there. I wasn't exactly in the mood to say anything so I let it go. He would also inform me days later that he was moving out to be with her, which left me without anyone to talk to. He did pay up all the utility bills and transfer them all into my name before he left which was greatly appreciated. Now I was alone again and not well. The timing couldn't have been worse.

I now had to go back to work against doctor's orders. Gene knew that I was limited to just watching over the VIP room and he was ok with that. I couldn't risk getting punched between the legs or in the gut, especially with a stent that was still in me that should have been removed weeks before. It was literally tearing up my insides, leaving me in constant excruciating pain. I was praying that the night would go smoothly, but when a bachelor party came through that door, I was starting to have my doubts. They were already drunk and rowdy before they got there, so placing them in this environment was not going to be good. I was known to watch the monitor while I was on the door, and had prevented a lot of trouble from ever getting inside without anyone knowing, because I ran them off beforehand. But on this particular night, I wasn't on the door. Instead we had a so called "black belt" pretty boy who was more concerned with the size of his penis and how he looked than the safety of the girls. He had let them all inside without a second thought, and within five minutes, they were already starting trouble. The main culprit had unbuttoned his shirt and was touching the girl on stage while no one was paying attention. I looked around to see if anyone was going to do anything and no one moved, so I rose up out of the chair and limped up to him. I made him put his shirt back on and told him the rules before taking my seat again. It was quiet for maybe twenty minutes before he did something else and got tossed out along with the rest of the group.

    It could have ended right there, and would have, had One Time not came out from the back and got involved when it wasn't necessary. He took it upon himself to grab the main culprit around the waist from behind and attempt to throw him down on the concrete. Unfortunately, it's always slippery out there and I can tell you that from experience. When he went to toss him, he lost his footing and the culprit went one way while One Time went another. Now it was a race to see who could get to their feet first and gain the upper hand. One Time lost...and was hit with a full on body punch to the mouth... shattering his jaw. Although, he got a few hits in after the fact, the damage was already done. What went around came back around. One Time got a broken jaw from just one punch... just as I predicted weeks earlier. Don't fuck with karma, you always lose.

In the meantime, I watched all of this unfold right before my eyes on the security camera...unable to do anything about it. One of the girls, who saw what happened, urged me to go help but I was in no condition to even defend myself. She made me feel like I was letting everyone down, but I had been through so much over the past few months that I wasn't about to put myself at risk of yet another setback. Gene himself had even advised me not to get involved because he needed me back at a hundred percent as soon as possible. Although I was eager to be on the front lines, like I always had been any other time, I had to sit this one out.

Although our bouncers had done their jobs and got everyone out of the building, the war had only just begun. It was so chaotic outside that customers were afraid to leave. One of them even called the cops, which could have been the scarlet letter had one of Gene's buddies not answered the call. The main culprit even tried to pick a fight with the fucking cop! Like going through a hurricane, we had literally reached only the eye of the storm. It was quiet and peaceful for a short while before several fights broke out in the parking lot among the members of the bachelor party. They were beating each other senseless in the courtyard and even in the limo as we all watched on in disbelief. In all of my years, I had never seen anything like this. I felt like we lost the battle and I never even fired a shot.

After the dust had settled and we had closed up for the night, Tommy and I made a trip to the local hospital to visit One Time. I had spent so much time at that place over the last few weeks that I already knew my way around. I apologized for not throwing myself into the lions' den but One Time understood why I didn't and didn't hold it against me. This was the first step to building a great friendship between us. I made the decision that night to not report back to work until all of my health issues had been resolved and the whole ordeal was over. If I couldn't pull my own weight, I was giving everyone a false sense of security and I couldn't live with that. Someone else could get hurt as well and next time it could be one of the girls. I wouldn't be able to just put that in a box and bury the motherfucker like I did this…

A few days later, I went in and got a second X-ray which delivered even more bad news: they hit the stone but only split it in half. It was still too big to pass which meant that I was going to need yet another surgery. However, there was some good news as well. The doctor told me that they were going to remove the stent while I was under so I wouldn't be going through the usual painful procedure of having done while I was awake. In a weird coincidence, Gene, One Time, and I were all in the same hospital at the same time but on different floors. I didn't care though. I was just happy to finally be on the road to recovery.

I was rarely seen in the club for the next few weeks, but when I did make an appearance, a lot of people noticed Victoria and I having conversations in private. It misled everyone into believing that something romantic was going on between us finally, but in reality, she was only being a friend concerned about my health. After that third and final surgery, I was close to returning full time to work. I avoided the club completely until New Year's Eve. I wasn't about to miss that party. I didn't stay for very long, but I did pose for a few pictures with Victoria and have a nice chat with Mark and his girlfriend before I left. Within a week or two, I was finally whole again and it felt so good.

While I was on the mend, I had received news that Gene had lost his lease on the Last Chance 2000. It was sold to a veterinarian who I only knew as "the Doc" and was renamed, with my old friend Lynn as the new manager. Reese wanted to go check it out and I was game to see something new, so we went out there one weekend. I had just walked through the door when I saw Slim sitting at one of the tables, which meant that Wendy must be in the building somewhere. Lynn noticed me straight away from across the room and approached me with his hand extended. I only got to talk to him for a few seconds before Wendy noticed me and make a beeline in my direction. She whispered something in Lynn's ear before she grabbed my hand and let me into the office. "Oh my god, I heard about all of your health problems. Are you ok?" she asked. Before I could even answer her question, she grabbed my face and started kissing me deeply. "I love you...and I want you right now!" she screamed as she led me up into the so called "haunted" attic that was now decked out like a private little hideaway for staff members to go when they were about to do something that they didn't want on film. I stopped her before she got my pants unzipped. "I don't feel like doing this" I said. "To be honest, I don't know if I can even physically do this right now if I wanted to." She nodded her head with a look of disappointment. "But I will go down on you though." She didn't hesitate to pull her panties off and let me service her, even though her boyfriend was literally only a few feet away and floor beneath us. We cleaned ourselves up and joined the others on the main floor afterwards. Lynn was grinning from ear to ear, because he always wanted Wendy and me to work things out someday and get back together. To him, lending the office and attic to us was really no big deal. We were still legally married at the end of the day. As soon as Lynn got called away, Reese joined me and asked if Wendy was my wife and let me know that he thought that she was very attractive. She did look great that night I must admit, but I kept my distance from her anyway, as I spent the rest of the evening listening to Lynn tell me about how he and the Doc were cleaning the place up and how much more pleasant the working environment was compared to when Gene had it. Before I left, he told me that if I ever needed a job, I could always come and work for him. I thanked him and told him that I would keep that in mind.

    A couple of days before I was cleared by the doctor, I walked into the Last Chance and just sat at the bar minding my own business when a beautiful young lady took a seat near me. She must have just started working there while I was in the hospital because she had no idea who I was. I just threw a compliment her way by telling her that she was very attractive and she responded with the classic "Well, you aren't too bad yourself." That was the green light to ask her out and she accepted, asking me to take her to a wet t-shirt contest that she was competing in the following night at one of the new clubs in the city. I was pretty pumped about it until the next day after an all- night cocaine binge. I still kept my word and picked her up, along with one of our mutual friends from the club that got thrown into the mix as a safety precaution I suppose. It was an unpleasant and quiet trip to the bar, for me at least, as I just didn't think we were meshing well at all. When we got to the bar, I wished her luck and couldn't wait to be away from her. When I went to get a drink, I saw that one of my friends was tending bar so he was giving me free shots of bourbon...one after another until I was quite drunk. By the time the contest started, I could barely stand up. I ran into a few other friends outside on the balcony afterwards and joined them in a feeble effort to avoid my date. She managed to find me eventually but I was such an asshole to her that she got the message pretty quickly and found her own way home. At the time, I had two separate cell phones and one of the guys asked me why. I told him that one of them was strictly for my drug dealers and the other was for everyone else. He just laughed because he thought I was joking but I was being serious. Later on, I used the "special phone" to ring up one of my boys at Micheal's to let them know that I was on my way. One of my buddies said, "You were serious about the phone weren't you? That's fucking awesome!" I just smiled and left the party to go to another one, leaving the two girls behind. It was awkward when we worked together after that and although she didn't deal with it too well, it was nothing new to me.

10

There was one drug floating around that I hadn't done. They call it PCP, or "angel dust," and I was about to be introduced to it by one of my friends. They called him "the Milkman" because he didn't give out his real name to many people. It was a Sunday night and I wasn't working, but was in the club out of boredom when he came in. He told me that he had some PCP in his van if I wanted to try some, so we stepped out for a moment and took a little walk. He pulled out a small bottle of something and dipped our cigarettes in it then we went inside.

There was an off duty cop friend sitting beside us at the bar as we smoked our "cigarettes." The scent that the smoke produced was very unusual but not identifiable to an untrained nose like marijuana. He was literally a couple of feet away from two guys smoking PCP yet he never suspected a thing. The Milkman got up to tip one of the girls and left his cigarette burning in the ashtray. Jayden was bartending that night and accidently dumped Milkman's cigarette in the garbage can. When Milkman came back, he noticed that his cigarette was gone. He panicked and started digging through the rubbish trying to find it to no avail. I was pissing myself laughing. I actually felt normal until I tried to stand up and I nearly collapsed. The floor felt like it had turned from stone to a mattress. Every step presented a new challenge as I probably reminded the cop of watching a newborn calf walk for the first time. He just thought that I had too much to drink. I could see why people liked this stuff. I may not be able to walk but my body was so relaxed, which was much needed, after what I had recently gone through.

    Now it was time to test a few friendships. When I got word that Mac had gotten really drunk and started mouthing off about how Wendy and Slim made a better couple than Wendy and I did and it was good thing that our marriage was over because I "treated Wendy like shit anyway," I was just biding my time to have my say. Eventually, he called me up to party and was bringing the favours for once, so I seized the moment to kill two birds with one stone. I got high with Mac then brought the subject up. He owned up to it and apologized then we put it behind us.

    Then at Clinton Highway, while jonesing for cocaine, I went to Sapphire and flirted hard to get some from her, not knowing that she had been sleeping with Duane in recent weeks. She had some really bad quality "club dope" that had been stepped on more times than a spider under a girl's shoe, but it was better than nothing. She told me that she was going to do a bump in the bathroom and then I could have the rest, so I took a seat next to Duane and waited. She came out a few minutes later and walked up to me. "I'm sorry, but there wasn't as much in that baggie as I thought, so I can't give you anything. You can, however, lick the remnants off my tongue if you like. It will give you a decent buzz" she said. I grabbed her and we French-kissed for a couple of minutes, literally right in front of Duane, but his expression never changed, so I thought nothing of it. A few minutes later, we were making out at the bar passionately, which led to me bending her backwards over the counter, while pulling her hair and nibbling on her neck, which was turning her on big time. She never asked me to stop...only that I didn't leave any marks. She had made it clear several times in the past that she wanted to shag me and that had never been more evident than at this moment. She asked me to go home with her one last time but I turned her down flat again. Someone told me later that the initial kiss was only to make Duane jealous but then it escalated to something more right before his eyes. I had betrayed a true friend and wasn't even aware that I was doing so because he was being so passive about the whole thing. I felt terrible but I was too much of an asshole to even apologize to him after I found out the truth. I just left to avoid the situation, like I was known to do.

    If I hadn't done enough damage already, I ran into Misty one night at Micheal's. It started off innocently enough but would evolve into something more. She was there with her sister, who had already noticed me and liked what she saw. The feeling was mutual but Misty wanted to step outside and try to sell her sister to me anyway. That was a not a good idea. After a long conversation about life, and very little of it concerning her sister, Misty and I realized that we had a connection too. We made out and smoked cigarettes for nearly an hour, before she had to go home to her boyfriend and baby. Here I was, with a beautiful *single* girl inside dying to get to know me better, and I end up spending the evening with her *married* sister who had already brought enough trouble and guilt into my life over the past couple of months. I never went back inside because I didn't want to face her, especially if she had seen or heard about what Misty and I were doing in the parking lot. I never told One Time about that night, but if I could remember correctly, I owed him one anyway.

    Unfortunately, I had to watch Reese follow in Adam's footsteps. As I had mentioned before, he was far too trusting in strangers and that would lead to his incarceration. The seeds were planted one night while we were at Micheal's with a couple of lovelies. One was Reese's on again off again girlfriend, and the other was either her sister or a friend of hers. The friend saw a guy that she was attracted to and asked him to join us. He obliged and hit it off with not only her but Reese as well. I can honestly say that there was something about him that just wasn't right from the outset to me but I just couldn't put my finger on it. Before I could warn Reese of this gut feeling I had, he had already told him that he was a drug dealer and had invited him back to his girlfriend's place to party with us.

    When we got to Reese's girlfriend's house, the stranger went to the guest room with his girl, and Reese took his girlfriend to her bedroom for privacy, while Darryl and I continued the party together in the living room. We didn't see anyone else until we

were getting ready to leave the next morning. For some reason, I felt the need to put some distance between the boys and myself for a little while after that night. I would hear some disturbing news several weeks later. That guy that I was suspicious of *was* an undercover cop. He had gained enough trust in Reese in the weeks that followed their initial meeting to buy large quantities of everything from ecstasy to meth until he had enough to charge Reese with a felony. When Reese went down, so did Kris and Darryl, but they only got a slap on the wrist in comparison. When they took Reese down, they busted him with pills, cocaine, meth and a number of other drugs that he kept in his house. Let's just put it this way: I don't think he will be getting out anytime soon. Such a fucking waste...
-DJN

CHAPTER XVII-"777"

2002

    We are warriors, going through the landscape of Las Vegas, jump on the bandwagon, the Mercedes, and watch us go opposite ways on the same rail. I have a scholarship, but I'm bagging groceries, graduated from the school of hard knocks, and saved by the bell.

    If only I could have bigger paychecks and a pension, for once the creditor, and not the debtor, giving no refunds. If only I could form a union, so I don't have to see them outside, like the homeless, holding up their signs. When their checks bounce, I see them outside, in protest, walking the picket line.

    To you, money was never an object, got plenty of it buried in mason jars. Yet you have all the food stamps and welfare, heading to Wal-Mart to fill your shopping cart.

    The loosest slots, the biggest jackpots, know when to hold, and when to fold, need a royal flush, never settle for a straight...Spin the reels, spin the wheels, like high stakes poker, hold the trump, but end up as the joker, it's like a game of chess, and every move is a stalemate.

    I'm your love handles, caused by your gluttony. I'm your wrinkles, after your plastic surgery. I'm the bottom dollar, I'm your money woes. I'm the running meter on every ho. One eyed Jacks, and aces, thinking I have it made. Like Russian roulette, when the devil's hand is rolling sixes, it's all given back in spades.

    I'm the cutthroat pragmatist, when inflation hits double digits this fiscal year. I've sold out to the almighty dollar, the buck stops here. I've been all over the world, and this is what I've seen: I found where God is in America and it's the colour green.

Like having the revenue, to buy and sell stocks each day on Wall Street…Like having a new pair of shoes, when everything is rocks and stumbling blocks, and all you need is something concrete. Like filing for custody, and getting a restraining order… like filing for bankruptcy, after being the bread winner… Pay the premium, pay the alimony, based on my income, garnish my wages until I'm making below minimum.

I'm ready for the fight, if given the opportunity. Let me become the merchant with the golden scales that fixes our economy. It could be like a demolition derby, and when it hits too close to home, some will call it quits. Even if my engine blows, and my car is towed, at least I made it out of the pits…

-Denny Noland "Draven" From my song "777"
Written in 2002   Copyright 2015

I desperately needed to get away again. I had heard Gene talk about a place called Tunica, Mississippi where he and James had spent at least one weekend a month at since I've known them. Tunica was like a poor man's Las Vegas, made up of casinos without all the extra hoopla. What was most appealing to me was that as long as you were gambling, all of your food and alcohol was provided free of charge. If you impressed them enough, you would be offered a free room or suite the next time you came out there. So when One Time asked me if I would like to give it a try, I simply said, "You're the manager…make it happen!"

We left right after work one night. We had been sneaking around drinking all night and I had already bought about three grams of blow to take with me.

It is debatable whether we should have been on the road in the first place in our present condition, but off we went anyway. We had literally reached the outskirts of Nashville and I had already gone through half of my stash, so I backed off a bit and eventually passed out between Nashville and Memphis and didn't wake up until we reached Tunica.

We stayed at the Horseshoe and I must say that I was impressed. Everything that you could possibly need was under one roof. The hotel was on the upper floors with sauna, steam room, gym and swimming pool. The casino was on the ground level with several restaurants that served everything from southern cooking to seafood to pizza. There was even a grocery store in the building and a large venue that featured nightly concerts and comedy acts from the past. If I remember correctly, the 80's band "Journey" was there the night before we arrived and comedian/actor Don Knotts was paired up with someone else to do stand up on the first night. There were also lesser known bands and comedians who played or performed all night on the various smaller stages scattered throughout the casino. There was literally so much to do that you couldn't get bored, and I was having a blast I must say.

It was easy to get wasted in this environment and at times, not even realize it. There was fresh oxygen being pumped into the building at all times, which kept you from feeling how drunk you actually were until you got into the elevator and then it hit you like a ton of bricks. The waitresses looked like models and rivalled the beauty of our top girls. They came around every five minutes to top up your drinks and were very hard to say no to. Before you knew it, you would have a pyramid of shot glasses up to your waist but still felt sober as a bell. It was a clever strategy to keep everyone gambling and making stupid decisions. The higher you were, the higher the bets and the larger the risks. Add that to the fact that I was sneaking off to the bathroom and doing bumps every few minutes, and you pretty much had a general idea of how I was starting to lose my ass. However, I was smart enough to avoid the tables and stick to the slots or it could have been much worse.

One Time and I rarely saw each other through the whole trip. I kind of went and done my own thing while he barely even moved from the slots for anything. He didn't sleep or eat at all, only getting up to get another drink or use the bathroom. My internal clock was all messed up due to the fact that there were no windows in the casino, and that I had no reason to go outside to notice whether it was day or night. I went to bed whenever I felt exhausted and pretty much had the room all to myself anyway. I remember waking up once thinking that it was probably mid-afternoon so I went down to get a pizza. When I got down there, all I saw was breakfast food everywhere. It was actually three in the morning instead of three in the afternoon, making me realize pretty quickly that I really needed to buy a watch.

However, we did come together on the last night. He had broken even while I had gone through all the cash that I had brought with me. Instead of just sitting and watching him play, I asked if I could borrow $20 off of him but he made me a counter-offer. "I've got probably a little more than that left on this machine if you want to play the credits off. I want to try the one beside it anyway." I sat down and rolled the wheels a couple of times before I noticed that the button had stopped working. I was so drunk that I didn't notice that the machine had landed on 7-7-7. I thought I had broken the damn thing. Then came the delayed sounds of ringing bells and sirens and people staring. I looked over at One Time and asked him what the hell was going on. He laughed and said, "You hit the jackpot! You've just won $2500!" I still thought he was kidding until security surrounded me and strangers started patting me on the shoulder while congratulating me. I had gone from loser to big winner in the matter of seconds and I was hooked. I paid One Time his twenty dollars with interest and I was already planning to come back to Tunica the first chance I got. This had turned into quite a profitable trip after all.

We wouldn't be waiting long for our next trip out there, except this time Mark was coming with us. We would get drunk on the way, leading to a heated argument between Mark and myself over a new girl named "Lexus." You see, over the last few weeks between these road trips, I was hearing my name still getting dragged through the mud by my old friend Lena. Although I was under the impression that we had patched things up the night she came into the club with a "client" and I explained to her that I had nothing to do with her getting fired, and we hugged it out in front of a room full of approving smiling faces, she just couldn't leave it well enough alone. When we saw each other at East Town Mall later on and she had a guy with her, we were on seemingly good terms. Although I was trying to avoid a conversation at first, Lena and I talked for several minutes and it was actually refreshing. Now I was hearing from this new girl, Lexus, who had hanging out with both Mena and Lena in recent days, that Lena had told her, and a number of other "newbies," all about our little fling a couple of years ago. At this point, I hadn't even mentioned Lena's name to anyone in a long time... and I never brought her up before then to people who wasn't there and didn't already know about us in the first place. Other than Lexus asking for my side of the story like an ambitious young reporter after the big scoop, the thing that annoyed me the most was Lena's answer when Lexus asked her how we got together. She had nothing except "Everyone makes mistakes." I don't know why I was even surprised.

However, the big surprise came when Mena had a temporary falling out with Lena and started showing up at these contests by herself. If anyone had heard every single detail about Lena and me, it would be her…Lena's best friend. She couldn't wait to fill me in on what she knew. One of the most intriguing things that Lena told her was that I had written a song about her. Mena even knew that the title was "Storm Child," which, to my knowledge, was only mentioned once while Lena and I were intimate, so the fact that she could remember that at all was remarkable. I wasn't sure about Mena's intentions after telling me this. Was she fishing or trying to bait me into saying something to go back and tell Lena? Who the fuck knows? Even when she looked me straight in the eyes and said, "I don't know why you would bother writing a song about her…she doesn't deserve it." I was baffled. I didn't know whether she saw that I wasn't as bad as Lena made me out to be or was she just saying all of this because she was angry with her at the time. I suppose I will never know the truth.

So when Mark started talking about how innocent young Lexus was and I disagreed, we were ready to pull over and start throwing punches. Cooler heads prevailed before we got to Tunica, but just like last time, everyone went their separate ways once we got to the Horseshoe. I had been sent a brochure for my own free room about two weeks prior in the mail, but One Time had a suite that was big enough for the three of us. I didn't see a reason to stay in a separate room on a different floor by myself so I went down to the front desk and turned in my keys so someone else could have my room. Although I thought I was doing a good thing, the receptionist didn't see it that way. She took my keys but seemed offended about the whole thing. Needless to say, they never offered me another free room after that...ever.

No one saw each other that first night. The next morning we surveyed the damage and it wasn't good...especially for Mark, who had lost $1500 of his girlfriend's money at the tables. He made a rookie mistake of not only hitting the tables, but drinking heavily while doing so. He started off winning, but got selfish and began to raise his bets before his luck took a turn for the worst, causing him to lose a shitload of money. He was pretty much finished in less than twenty four hours, and I wasn't far behind him. With us both discouraged and frustrated, we started taking in the sights. We visited the neighbouring casinos and tried our luck there to no avail. At one point, an old lady kept waiting for Mark to finish up on a slot machine then she would throw a dollar in and hit it on the very next spin. At first, he was pissed but eventually even he had to break down and laugh about how unlucky he was. We still had fun without spending very much money.

The next day we went to the gym, and tried out the sauna and steam room before heading down to the pool. The water in that pool was fucking freezing cold but Mark was determined to take a swim. He looked at me and said, "You know what they say in the military don't you? Sometimes you just have to suck it up!" He then jumped in the water before trying to convince me to join him. Not to be outdone, I jumped in as well and I thought my heart was going to stop beating. We had only just begun to adjust to the temperature when Mark said, "Watch this." He flipped over underwater and began walking on his hands toward me. What he didn't realize was that when he did that, his bathing suit fell down to his knees so what I saw was a penis and a pair of legs coming straight at me. I tried to get as far away as possible but got pinned in the corner. I could literally hear the "Jaws" theme playing in my head. Then I heard the latch on the gate click. A middle aged woman was bringing her two little boys to the pool. She looked up and saw what was going on in the pool, shielded her children's eyes, turned around and exited the pool area immediately. About that time Mark surfaced, unaware that he had not only flashed me but a stranger as well. He was embarrassed and we had a great laugh about it. I was just grateful that he came up for air when he did, otherwise his penis would have been right on top of me because I literally had nowhere to go.

 On our final night, I pulled my last $20 bill out of my wallet and put it into a machine. I was down to my final spin when I hit the jackpot again. This time it was for $1500. I was ecstatic and offered to loan some of it to Mark but he wouldn't accept it. I may have played off about $200 of it out of boredom, but I sat on the rest. I went home ahead of the game like before, and hadn't been inside of a casino since.

 On the journey back home, we were discussing the ladies that have come and gone over the years and Chloe came to mind. I always felt bad about how I dumped her at the Boiler Room that night so I made it a top priority to call her when I got back into town. When I rang her, some guy answered the phone. As much as she used to like me, I thought that there would still be enough remnants of those feelings still lingering around to be able to sweet talk my way back into her arms. The guy put her on the line and I could tell from her yawning and that scratchy voice that I had woke her up. I tried everything but I could not sway her to give me another chance. She was already in a happy relationship and wasn't really interested in me anymore. You never know until you try and I left her alone after that.

    I would stay at Mark's for a couple of days before returning to work. His girlfriend's cat had left little presents all around the litter box while he had been away, instead of in the bloody thing, so I began to worry about the damage that my two cats might have left for me to clean up when I got home. And they didn't disappoint either. Brandy, in fact, had crawled into my clothes basket full of clean clothes and pissed all over everything. I just lost it. I tossed her into the pet carrier and drove her down to the nearby factory to turn her loose. She was crying so hysterically that I almost had a change of heart until she bit and clawed the hell out of my hand when I reached in to grab her. My flesh looked like I had been wrestling with a barbed wire fence and lost. I was hoping that *someone* would see her and take her home with them the next morning and was relieved to find out that they did. Now there was only me and Gabrielle.

2

On one of my last visits to the infamous Boiler Room, I had Jayden as my designated driver. He was one of those guys who dreamed of being a police officer but didn't quite make the cut, so he befriended and idolized any cop that would give him the time of day. This was common knowledge to everyone who knew him. Although, I took drugs in front of him several times, he never lectured me or got me into any kind of trouble so I trusted him enough to be my chauffeur. On the night in question, I was on ecstasy and seriously messed up. I had run into Lena, Sabine, and two other girls from the club that I had played around with in the past who was also taking ecstasy, and making plans to get their freak on at a friend's house after the lights came on. I had been coming on to Sabine all night, but for some reason, she didn't seem to be very receptive which was unusual for her, but after an invite from one of the girls to join them later on, I was sure my luck would going to change.

There we were…standing outside as the sun was coming up with four lovelies all dressed in black, and looking sexy, discussing how we were going to follow them back to the friend's place, when one of the girls suggested that maybe they should call the friend and let them know that we were coming along too. I knew the friend very well and suspected that he was a possible drug dealer but wasn't sure until the girl hung up the phone. She said "Denny, you can go but Jayden can't come. He doesn't trust him. Sorry…but it's *his* house so he makes the rules. There's nothing I can do." Now I was in a dilemma. I had no car and the girls didn't have room for me in their car so I had run out of options. I was going to have to sit this one out and go home to an empty house instead of possibly scoring with one or more of these beautiful ladies. If you have ever been on ecstasy around someone who wasn't on it or been alone while the high was peaking, you can only imagine what I was going through. What a terrible morning it was indeed.

I also had two brief affairs with married women around this time. The first was with Phoenix, who had come over to work with us after Gene lost the 2000 club. While we were both drunk one night, we started flirting and ended up making out at the bar.

Nothing happened between us that night, but I was delighted to find out the following day that she did end up in a threesome with Tommy and Gene after I got her worked up and left. We would find ourselves in the days that followed, groping each other's bodies, with our tongues down each other's throats, both on the main floor in front of the fellow staff, and in the back in private, with the culmination being an encounter in the ladies' restroom when she pulled her panties down and bent over the sink, begging me to put it in. I didn't exactly carry condoms in my wallet because I rarely used them, so when she warned me about how fertile she had was, I had second thoughts and nothing happened then either. Eventually, the whole fling just faded away and I moved on to the next one.

Next up was a girl named "Jennifer." We had a great working relationship for months but things got confusing during one of her drinking binges. I was up at the DJ booth talking to Mark when she staggered in to pick out her music. She noticed that I was staring at her and thinking naughty things so she called me out on it. "You look at me like you want to kiss me" she slurred. "Not going to happen." Although her observation was accurate, I played it off like she had it all wrong anyway. Later on, while I was watching the VIP room, she came over to continue the conversation. "I know you want me. I can see it in your eyes. But you can't have me." After a few wisecracks back and forth, we shared a passionate kiss right outside the VIP room. She wasn't the only one who could read people's eyes.

As the night progressed, her mood changed as she began to sober up. She was having problems with her marriage and was thinking about leaving her husband if she only had somewhere for her and her little girl to stay. That was where I came in. I had an entire floor that was fully furnished and empty so I offered it to her. She thanked me but declined my offer. This was one of those times that Gene wanted all the guys to wear shirts and ties to perhaps bring in a different crowd even though business suffered, because our bread and butter was rednecks in blue jeans and t-shirts. At the end of the night when I walked Jennifer to her car, I made the offer again, letting her know that it didn't mean that we were in a relationship if she took me up on it. She would still have her independence. She took her seat behind the wheel, reached up, grabbed me by the tie, and asked for one more kiss. She then pulled me down to her waiting mouth and we shared yet another passionate kiss. I told her goodbye and reminded her that if she changed her mind, my offer still stands. I watched as she drove away and wouldn't see or hear from her in years.

    I think that the walls outside of the VIP room, probably has as many stories to tell about me as any other part inside or outside of the building. One night, I saw one of the girls dancing for a handsome gentleman and getting a little too close. When the song finished, she started making out with him in front of other customers. I had done similar things in the past but that was me. I gave the girl a lecture when she came out and she responded by sticking her tongue down my throat, which left me breathless and wondering what the hell I was mad about in the first place. Even Dana, who I didn't like, came in as a customer one night wearing black leather pants. You all know what leather does to me and so did she. She started dancing between my legs and grinding her ass on my crotch right in front of her husband. She then turned around and started licking my nose, which was coated with cocaine residue. Being so against drugs, she surprisingly didn't say anything. I'm sure her tongue was numb for a few minutes after our little private show.

That very same night, I was still feeling a bit playful after work so I attempted to make out with Harley like I had many times in the past. What I didn't know was that she was in the middle of a crisis and needed to go. She didn't really have time for any of this kind of crap, so when I got a little carried away, she pushed me away and drove off. I had come to the realization that something was changing inside of me and it had started after I got sick. All those months of enjoying my seclusion and isolation had worn off. I was starting to get a bit lonely and was craving female companionship again. I didn't care about the just getting laid part anymore... I needed someone to be there when I needed them the most. The problem was that there weren't many girls in the workplace, at that point, that I didn't have some form of history with, and if I didn't, there was probably a good reason for that. I wasn't about to look elsewhere because every time I did that, my lifestyle and profession became too much for them to handle causing a rift and eventually a split. However, there was someone who I had sensed a connection with over the years that might fit the bill, but even I couldn't have imagined how complicated the whole picture was about to become.

The girl used the stage name "Britney." She was a tall girl with a lovely face, store bought breasts, and long flowing hair down to her ass. I had noticed many times over the years that when we were slow at work and she was on stage, she would *always* turn in my direction, spread her legs, and look at me with those dreamy bedroom eyes. Sometimes she would just walk up to me after she had just arrived to work and give me a little kiss on the lips randomly. I thought nothing of it really. Even when she would party with me and let me lick the cocaine off her fingertips, then she place her finger in her mouth, it didn't register. Hell, I would often catch her staring at me while she was sitting with one of her regulars and every time I did, she would give me the same seductive smile but I still didn't get the hint.

Of course, it wouldn't be that simple. There would be a second girl named "Torrie," added into the mix, who literally started liking me overnight and she just happened to be Britney's best friend at the time. She was a beautiful girl who I was very attracted to, but there was one problem though: she not only had a boyfriend who I considered a friend, but they had children together as well. To make it even harder, the boyfriend would arrive early to pick Torrie up and wait in the car with the kids until she got off of work. When she would come out, often times they would stand outside and kiss for several minutes like a couple truly in love. That was why I couldn't understand how or why she started wanting me.

I just couldn't do it...but damn, I wanted to. She made it very difficult to resist her when she was doing things like pulling up my shirt and licking my nipples, and turning her head when I would go to kiss her on the cheek, using the old Blair move so my lips would touch hers. She even borrowed a car a couple of times so she could come alone and give us some privacy after work, but I still wouldn't let it happen. I think that made her want me more... as it would. Of course, everyone at the club knew that she wanted me, including Britney, who backed off to keep from ruffling her feathers. Lexus, the resident Oprah, filled me in daily about what she was saying in the back and it sounded like she had it bad. I finally had to have a long talk with her about the situation, and thought everything was sorted until one fateful night.

    I was sitting at the door when One Time and Britney came up to the desk. "Would you like for me to watch the door for you while you take Britney somewhere private?" One Time asked to my confusion. I looked over at Britney and she gave me that cheeky smile and a little nod. "Sure" I said as I led her to the only place that was available at the time, which was the kitchen. I closed the door and flipped on the lights. The place was a fucking mess, and the make matters worse, the door wouldn't lock. I was so high that I wasn't exactly comfortable with this situation, but the opportunity presented itself, and I knew that I would regret it later if I didn't seize it. We kissed briefly before I went for it. I pulled down her panties and shoved my tongue as deep inside of her as it would go. I was very shaky and I could tell that she was worried about someone walking in on us, so I would only go down on her for a few minutes before she nervously pulled away. "What's wrong?" I asked. "I can't do this here. I am afraid that the door is going to swing open any second and we are going to get into trouble." This was very likely considering that the dressing room was just outside the door. We could see people coming and going the entire time through the cracks. I replied, "Fine, but promise me that you will let me finish this one day." She smiled as she nodded in agreement, and we made a run for it when the coast was clear.

    Within an hour or so, everyone knew about our little rendezvous. I don't know how but they did. Torrie was not happy about the whole thing and felt betrayed. I don't know what was said behind the scenes but whatever it was, it kept me from Britney. She barely spoke to me after that and ended up dating other fellow employees as I faded into the background. Although, I saw Britney as a potential girlfriend, I didn't exactly try to finish what we started either. The whole thing fizzled out as quickly as it started and it would be years before we would talk about it again. It turns out that she didn't take me seriously because of my track record. It didn't help that I never told her how I felt until it was too late. Life had passed us by but we are still close friends to this day thanks to social media.

3

Thanks to Mark's recommendation, we hired another guy from the Tri-Cities area named "AJ" to fill in for Mark on his days off. He had long, flowing blond hair like I did and was known to be quite the stoner. The first night he came in, he was getting picked on by some customers while he was bringing in his gear. I defended him and probably kept him from taking a beating. You would think that he would probably do everything in his power to befriend me, but he actually did just the opposite. I don't know why he had beef with me, whether it was professional jealousy or something else of that nature, but for some reason he hated my guts from the start. He would be nice to my face but talk shit behind my back. I despise people like that and he was no different. Little did I know at the time that he would be someone I would have to rely on in the future to resolve a very personal matter.

As we continued to bring in fresh faces, I seemed to make more enemies. My drug problem had escalated to the point that I had become lazy and uncaring, and it was being noticed by everyone. I was now the smallest bouncer we had and was content with just "mailing my performance in" so to speak, allowing everyone else to do all the work. I basically felt like I had paid my fucking dues in this business and it was time for me to relax and let someone else earn their stripes for a while. This was an unpopular decision, understandably so, but that was just how it was going to be. Don't get me wrong, I never backed away from a fight or left anyone alone in the trenches but I was sick and tired of being on the front line all the time. No one respected my decision or supported it, but I didn't really give a damn.

One typical Sunday night, while I was on the door, James and Simone came up to my desk. I was told to let a couple of black dudes in that Simone knew that was supposably of age but didn't have their ID's with them. I wasn't in the best of moods already. I had run out of blow and was crashing hard, so I let James know how I felt about it. "Why do I even bother to check anyone's ID's when they come up to the window anyway? I should just ask one of the fucking girls if they look old enough or not!" I screamed. Simone looked shocked and puzzled. She just quietly walked away and went to the back. She returned a few minutes later and said, "Hold out your hand." She handed me her personal stash and said, "I think you need this worse than I do." She figured out what was wrong and what I needed to snap out of it. I will never forget what she did. It was one of the most thoughtful and unselfish acts I had ever witnessed in this business. I felt like such an asshole.

4

It was a time of brawls and potentially hazardous scenarios. An example of this was the night that a group of five guys came into the club looking for trouble. The two younger guys were massive and confident that we didn't have the manpower to remove them if they got out of line. They were already giving me an attitude over prices, resulting in the one of the big guys just grabbing his beer and entering without paying. I was about to tackle this guy when one of his mates apologized for his actions and offered to pay. I knew that there was going to be trouble but I felt like these arrogant punks needed to be taught a lesson and knocked down a peg or two. I thought I saw one of the giants grabbing Celeste only minutes after entering, but I wasn't sure so I didn't want to make a scene. I knew that they weren't going to be a problem long. One of our guys will catch them eventually and it was going to be on.

    Within the hour, my prediction had come true. Our floor guy took down one of the giants but paid the price by having his tie used as a weapon against him nearly causing a serious injury. It took all the bouncers, Jayden, who was bartending that night, a regular customer, and two visiting bikers to get this big bastard out. Luckily the rest of his crew left without putting up a fight or we would have been in trouble. I remember Jayden standing on the other side of my barred window throwing punches at the giant as we passed by. I can't remember who it was, but one of the guys had grabbed our police strength pepper spray on the way out. This giant had been humiliated and was determined to force his way back in until someone dropped him to his knees with some mace in his eyes. He was done for after that, literally crying like a baby on the ground. We were criticized heavily by the two bikers for using pepper spray, prompting One Time to ask them to leave as well. Now it was a circus outside. On one side, you had the big guy lying on the ground screaming while Tommy attempted to flush his eyes, while on the other, two bikers were threatening to have their boys, a gang that none of us had ever heard of, come back and "level the place." Not in the mood to hear threats, I told them that if they returned, I would be waiting on the roof with Tommy's shotgun, picking them off one by one as they came down the hill. Thankfully, they never returned.

Speaking of bikers, remember that chapter that terrorized the 2000 club a while back that I had to rescue Wendy from? Well, they came back. The president was the first one through the door. I recognized him straight away and was hoping that he had forgotten about me. As soon as I spoke and he looked at my face, he knew exactly who I was. "Hey, I remember you! That night on Clinton Highway...we had a little misunderstanding" he said with a smile on his face. The longer he stood there, the friendlier he became, and that was what worried me the most. He came in and immediately shook my hand, which was in this business, a red flag. He took his boys to the back bar and out of my sight to my relief and I became hopeful that maybe, just maybe, I might make it through the night in one piece.

As the night progressed, I realized that I hadn't seen them in a while and had assumed that they had left. I stepped outside for a smoke and a bump and was on my way back inside when I heard, "Hey! Come here!" I turned and saw the president and four of his minions standing there staring at me. They hadn't gone anywhere. They had just been in Bambi's having drinks all this time. I had two choices here. I could turn tail and run and look like a coward, or I could stand my ground and take whatever they dished out on me like a man. I was already thinking strategy of who I was going to take out to decrease the numbers. I knew I couldn't take them all and no one was coming out to help me, but I was planning to at least take a couple of them down with me regardless.

I walked toward them and got face to face with the president. I could see the other guys surrounding me like a pack of wolves ready to strike at a moment's notice, if necessary, in the corner of my eye. For some reason, I was concerned but not really afraid. I had lost the will to live long ago, and if this was the way I was destined to go, so be it. I took a deep breath and prepared for the worst. The president looked me in the eyes and cracked a smile, then extended his hand once again. I took his hand and held it tightly as he spoke. "Look, I'm sorry about disrespecting your wife that night. I was out of line. If you ever need anything, and I mean *anything,* you let me know ok? Tommy knows where to find me. You are a stand- up guy and I respect that." I was touched. "Thank you...and the same goes to you" I replied as I released his hand. I went back inside feeling good about myself and never had an issue with these guys again.

Much to my dismay, Samantha popped back up again and this time she brought her new boyfriend with her. He immediately knew who I was and started kissing my ass, even asking me to respect that she was *his* girl now. I could barely keep a straight face when I said "You got nothing to worry about I assure you." Samantha would go through phases at times, when she would want to make out "for old time's sake" but neither of us was willing to take it further than that. I must admit that a part of me will always despise her and got a lot of pleasure out of watching her get her ass kicked by the girlfriend of one of the bouncers one night in the office. The sad part was that she expected me to jump in and help her and I didn't. Why should I? I was too busy laughing anyway.

Later in the week, I had to do my laundry so I began my normal weekly routine of driving down to the laundromat at the end of the street. I never knew what to expect or who I might see there so it was always an adventure. On this particular occasion, the girl who I briefly dated from the deli a few months back was there with some guy. If she recognized me, she didn't acknowledge it, but of course, it's hard to notice anyone when your mouths are constantly stuck together like Siamese twins. Strangely enough, the fact that she was there displaying so much PDA didn't bother me but this guy who kept staring at me like he wanted to root me, did. I swear he looked like someone who would be sitting outside of a school trying to trick some kid into getting into his car. His behaviour and mannerisms weren't much better. He was just plain creepy!

    I put my clothes in the dryer and went home to do a few lines as I always did. When I returned, the creepy bastard was still there. When I walked in, I saw something disturbing. He had not only taken my clothes out of the dryer and folded them, but I caught him sniffing my underwear! I grabbed my basket and said a few choice words to him before leaving. When I got back to the duplex, I parked around back where I always did and went inside. I kept hearing a car go up the road slowly, turn around, and come back down the other side. When I looked out the window, he was passing the house again, staring up the driveway obviously looking for my truck. I had forgotten all about letting it slip that I just lived up the road earlier in the day. I came tearing out of the house with a pen and a piece of paper in my hand. As he made another pass, I wrote down the number on his plates. When he saw me, he stopped and I let him know that if I saw his car again, I was turning him in to the cops if he was lucky. If not, his family may never see him again. He nodded his head and drove away without saying a word.

I had a few other scares in the weeks to come. While I was upstairs getting high one afternoon, I heard a knocking on the door. I looked out the window and saw an unmarked police car. As I threw on some clothes, the knocking got more intense until it sounded like he was trying to beat the door off of its hinges. When I answered the door, the cop looked confused. He asked me if I knew someone that used to live at my address, and I had seen the name on some mail that I had received in the past, but I had never met the guy. Whoever he was, he had the police looking for him. Had they known how many drugs I had in the house at the time, they would have forgotten all about that guy.

I was also showing my vulnerability by showing up at Tommy's house in the middle of the night in terrible shape. He didn't know how to help me except to invite me to move in with him. He would try to get me up the next morning to go to work with him but I couldn't move. He would always end up leaving me there to come to my senses. I would go home that afternoon and repeat the whole process all over again. I was slowly and willingly losing my mind and killing myself in the process. There was nothing anyone could do to help me.

Then something happened that made me reconsider my chosen profession. I stepped out for some fresh air one night at the club and a white pickup truck pulled into the parking lot. It had tinted windows so I couldn't see what the driver looked like. He was just sitting there, revving up his engine, with his lights on me. All of sudden, he just headed straight for me and I had to jump out of the way. He then tore down the driveway and back onto the highway, leaving me lying on the ground. I had so many enemies that it was impossible to even name a suspect. It could have been a disgruntled customer, one of the girls' husbands, a drug dealer,

anyone…I just knew that if I didn't get out of the business soon, I was going to end up in a body bag either from drugs or someone was going to kill me.
-DJN

CHAPTER XVIII- "LETTERS NEVER SENT"

2002-2004

She was toxic, in her French maid outfit...her negligee, her lingerie...She said "Do a line off my chest, off my breast, and let's fuck like rabbits, to these delights of the flesh."

She said, "I love it when you put on the blindfold, so I cannot see, then tie me to the bedpost, take control, have your way with me. Bite my nose, pull my hair, suck my toes, smack my ass bare...But there's nothing I like better, nothing gets me wetter, than when you take off your belt, and leave those pretty welts."

Menage a trois...two may be company, but three is a party, there's always room for one more. As she prepared for rear entry, she said, "Please bone me, in my exit only" as she feels the beads, being pulled from her backdoor.

She shot me with her poison dart, and we popped another pill, forgot about her bills then she ripped out my still beating heart, and stomped it with her heel. Together we had such chemistry, but when I reached out to her, she wouldn't lift a finger to help me.

To all those chemicals, we became co-dependent. Now I'm going postal, wishing these words had never seen print, wishing that letter had never been sent.

Wanted to read her favourite Cosmo issue, apply the Revlon, take her farther away than Calgon. But when she was full of it, full of shit, I was the tissue she wiped her ass on.

Like a stern mother, to the bastard who disobeyed, she said "You are going to learn, to stop being so stubborn, it's my way or the fucking highway."

I would rather die on my feet, than live on my knees…I would rather be back on the streets, than stay at home with my disease…

Can't believe what I've done, what I've become, she will never be forgiven. When I was at rock bottom, she always got her kicks in. Then one day, my bags were packed, and I never came back. When I stopped returning calls, she remembered something she used to say, "Sometimes life throws you a curveball."

 -Denny Noland "Draven" From my song "Letters Never Sent" Written on September 4, 2006 Copyright 2007

During my seemingly never-ending quest to find my next girl, Mark had someone in mind. Her name was "DeLynn" and she was a feature dancer who had done a few photo shoots and interviews in some lesser known, sleazy pornographic magazines. Just reading her comments in the articles made me cringe at times, but her looks overruled, so I was willing to give her a chance. Mark and his girlfriend arranged for her to compete in one of our weekly contests so I was going to inevitably meet her whether I wanted to or not.

When I met her, she was just as I had anticipated. She wasn't near as glamourous as she looked in the magazines, and her attitude reminded me of my sister and why I didn't like her either. She was so whiny and unpleasant that I just wanted to avoid her. Although she might have been a huge letdown, she brought someone with her that was everything she wasn't… her cousin "Vanessa." There hadn't been anyone in years that I was this interested in. She was so beautiful with those qualities that I couldn't resist: fake breasts that were almost too big for her frame and long flowing brown hair down to her ass. I raced up to Mark's girlfriend and began asking questions about Vanessa. Apparently, Vanessa had already spoken to her about me because in the matter of minutes she came over to me and initiated a conversation. We had an instant connection that impacted many people in the room.

DeLynn, for one, was furious and jealous which was understandable, but there was someone else who had taken notice as well. Lena just happened to be in the building that night for the contest and she knew exactly what was going on. She took it upon herself to make her presence felt for some unknown reason. As she passed to pick out her music, she looked over at Vanessa and said, "You better be careful with that guy. He's trouble." Vanessa just looked at me suspiciously and must have seen the terror on my face. "Who was she and why would she say such a thing?" she asked. I was trying to think of something fast but my mind was blank from the panic. Then I saw Lena approaching and I could sense the impending doom... but she surprised me by saying "I was just kidding. He's really a great guy." She then gave me that trademark smirk that said a thousand words. It was like her way of letting me know that she approved this time. She had made it known several times in the past that I deserved better than what I settled for, but this girl was different. She was worthy...a suitable replacement. At the time, I didn't even think about the significance of that moment in time, or I would have appreciated it more...cherished it even. It would be the only time that Vanessa, Lena, and me would knowingly be in the same building at the same time and actually interact. As a matter of fact, it would be the only time that *any* combination of my "Holy Trinity" would share of moment together in my entire life. Those were also the last words Lena ever said to me. I found her on Facebook in 2010, and tried several times to reconnect, but she wouldn't accept my requests. I sent her various messages, and even an apology, and although she does read them and leaves that window open, she has never responded with a single word. It is what it is I suppose.

At the end of the night, Vanessa invited me back to their hotel room for a drink. DeLynn wasn't about to allow that to happen, so she made up several excuses to keep us apart. Since DeLynn was driving, Vanessa couldn't do a damn thing about it so our night ended early. I was hoping that I would see her again the following night but DeLynn had taken Vanessa back to Johnson City unexpectedly against her wishes. I was devastated…fearing that I would never see the girl of my dreams again.

The following week, DeLynn came back, but this time she was alone. She immediately went to work on me by telling me shit like "I could have sex with you all night and not even talk to you tomorrow" and even attempted to grab me by the tie and force me to kiss her, but I managed to turn my head in the nick of time despite her death grip. She was all about control, but I just wasn't into all that S&M crap, or her in general to be honest. When she eventually got the message, she backed off and found a submissive girl to torment instead. The more I got to know her, the more I disliked her. I just wanted her to go away and leave me alone.

Not knowing where to turn, Mark offered to help. He told me that he would talk to Vanessa the first chance he got since they both lived in the same area 100 miles from Knoxville. He stressed to me to clean my act up in the meantime, because Vanessa didn't do drugs, and liked well- groomed men. I followed his advice concerning my appearance, but wasn't willing to stop getting high for anyone. I waited and waited for Mark to help me out, but nothing was happening, so I started exploring other options. A girl like Vanessa didn't stay single for long, so I needed to find a way to reach her somehow before someone else did.

It took a couple of weeks before I found the solution. During that time, my personality changed significantly. I became more arrogant and focused, ignoring the girls in the process. Now it became a competition to see who could seduce me first, but no one even came close. I knew who I wanted and no one else could fill that void. When one of my closest female friends in the business asked me what was going on with me, I told her that I was waiting for Vanessa. She thought it was ridiculous. "Do you not realize how unlikely it would be that you guys will ever be together? You are living in a fantasy world. Shit like that only happens in the movies…not in real life! I wish you the best of luck but it's only a dream." Those words didn't discourage me, they motivated me. Now I was determined to find her and tell her how I felt. Then I stumbled across some information that changed everything, but I was going to have to rely on someone who hated me already to put my plan in motion.

It just so happened, that AJ lived in the same apartment complex that she did. Just asking him to talk to her for me wasn't going to work since he specialized in talking shit about me behind my back. I needed to try a different tactic. It came to me when I heard one of the girls dancing to the metal group "Flaw" and the song just happened to be called "My Letter." I hadn't written a love letter to a girl in a decade but maybe I still had it. I knew how powerful and magical they could be to certain girls who appreciated them, and maybe Vanessa was one of them. I was about to find out. I literally spilled my heart out to her in that letter, and ended it with my phone number. If only I could get AJ to give it to her...

I ended up paying him an undisclosed sum of money to see to it that she got it. He laughed about the whole thing and even tried to humiliate me by saying things like "How do you know that she will even bother to read the letter?" but it didn't deter me in the slightest. Somehow I knew in my heart that she would. "Just make sure she gets it, ok? The rest will work itself out, trust me" I said with great confidence. "Well, it's your money" AJ replied. "You have my word." I had really put my neck on the line this time. If it didn't work, I was going to be the laughingstock of the entire club, but I was willing to take that risk to win her heart.

All I could do now was pace the floor like a worried father waiting up for his daughter to get home from her first date. I actually had an ace up my sleeve but wasn't aware of it at the time. AJ's girlfriend and Vanessa's best friend was one and the same, and just happened to be the one person on the planet that had absolutely nothing bad to say about me. She was Kellie...the girl who I ended up overruling Gene and giving time off to mourn her late mother when I was still manager. I hadn't seen her in years but she never forgot what I did for her, and she felt like this was as good of a time as any to return the favour. When she was asked to deliver that letter to Vanessa, she was honoured. I got that phone call that I was praying for later that day.

I was worried that she may not remember me but that wasn't the case. Her response was "Are you kidding? After I read that letter and saw that it was from you, it actually made my day. Then after I heard about what you did for Kellie after her mother died, there was no chance that I was going to let you slip away." We would then talk for hours, just getting to know each other, which led to an invitation to her apartment the following weekend. The topic of drugs was never brought up as I had no intentions of letting my addictions scare yet another girl away.

I was very familiar with the roads between Knoxville and the Tri-Cities. I had been up and down them so many times with Samantha and Mark that I had lost count. However, I had no idea where anything actually was, so finding the suburb where Vanessa lived was going to be difficult. I managed to find the club where she worked and told her to meet me there. Ironically, this was the same club where Wendy also worked when we were married, so the two girls obviously had worked together before and probably knew each other quite well. This was going to be a bump in the road, considering that in the eyes of the law, we were technically *still* married. I was hoping that Vanessa wouldn't piece it all together.

When we got back to her place, we had a few drinks and started to get to know each other better. I learned that she had just recently divorced an older man, who didn't work, but did everything around the house for her so she wouldn't have to lift a finger. She told me about dating a member of the rock band "Slaughter" before that. He apparently cheated on her while he was on the road so she dumped him. Imagine that...a rock star screwing other women while touring. What a shocker! She then pulled out a photo album with pictures of them together to back up her story. She would also go on to introduce me to her cocker spaniel, and let it be known that the dog meant more to her than anything, and it trumped *any* man that would enter her life. When I mentioned that I felt the same about my cat Gabrielle, her expression changed. "If we get serious and we start living together, Gabrielle will have to go. I'm...uh...allergic to cats." It just sounded like she was lying by the tone of her voice but I will never know.

I think that it was the way she presented herself that concerned me the most. She was oozing with self- confidence, carrying herself with so much elegance and arrogance that it literally overshadowed every other quality that she had. I was beginning to think that I was in over my head until she asked that million dollar question that my relationships have either built upon or torn down by literally overnight, "Do you party at all?" I had decided to just tell the truth and watch it all crumble but she surprised me. Instead of telling me to leave and showing me the door, she said "Good! I was thinking about calling my dealer and getting a little coke. Are you comfortable with that?" This changed everything. Obviously, my buddy Mark didn't know her as well as he thought.

I don't know whether it was the lack of sleep, or my anxiety about having our first date, but for some reason, the coke had not agreed with me. I was so nervous and jittery that several hours had passed, and I had yet to even try to kiss Vanessa. She eventually just got tired of waiting and asked for one. I gave her a quick, pathetic dry kiss that didn't satisfy her at all. "Um...that's good and all but I wanted a real kiss." I giggled and planted a second one with tongue that was weak and unenthusiastic as well, but she seemed to like it anyway. As the night progressed and I began to sober up, I became more affectionate. We were literally making out every few minutes, and the sessions were growing more intense as we went along. When we retired to bed, we continued to make out for hours but *didn't* have sex the entire weekend. The timing just wasn't right yet.

For the next few days, we only talked on the phone until I went up to Kingsport to see Mark. I was intending on avoiding Vanessa until the following weekend, but as soon as she found out that I was back in town, she kept pleading with me to come and spend the night with her. Mark and I went out to dinner at Damon's in Kingsport and later went to see Star Wars Episode 2-"Attack of the Clones" at the Imax Theatre in Abingdon, Virginia. I remember pulling into town and hearing a rumble as loud as thunder while we were sitting at a red light a few blocks away from the theatre. I asked Mark what that sound was and he replied with a smile, "That's the movie, man." I hadn't seen or heard anything like it. By the time the movie finished, I had so many messages and missed calls that I finally gave in and called Vanessa. She asked if Mark could drop me off at the club so she could drive me back to her place for the night. He reluctantly agreed. I knew at that moment that not only was I falling for her, but she was falling for me as well.

We got high together that night... and made love over and over again. We were so into each other that we never made it into the bed... we did it several times at the foot of the bed! We had such a natural chemistry and compatibility that it made it almost seem like we were meant to be together. I was truly in love for the first time in a very long time. I might have just been "dating" Vanessa when Mark dropped me off, but when he picked me back up the next day, Vanessa was my girl. I went back to Knoxville in a long distance relationship, and that simply wasn't going to work. Something drastic needed to be done and fast.

I received some good news later that week. Vanessa was coming down to Knoxville to attend an Eagles concert with some friends on the weekend, and had already arranged to be dropped off at the club after the show, so she could ride back up to Johnson City with me when I got off work. Now everyone could see that we were a genuine couple. No one had actually seen us in the same room since the night we met, so this was going to be a treat for everyone. No one, including myself, would have ever guessed that this was going to be one of the final times I would ever be seen in that building again.

Vanessa arrived at the club around midnight, and took a seat next to me at the door. Over the final couple of hours, many of the girls greeted her and Mark even played the Flaw song and dedicated it to us. We were the centre of attention that night, but for us it seemed like it would never end. We hit the road around the witching hour and arrived in Johnson City just before sunrise. We spent the rest of the weekend together and I was supposed to be back in Knoxville for work on Monday afternoon. I didn't make it. I became one of those guests that never left. I wanted to put everything I had into making this relationship work and I couldn't do that by living a hundred miles away...not to mention I couldn't exactly afford it either. I did, however, return to Knoxville a few days later to officially hand over Gabrielle to the neighbour who had been looking after her in my absence, and to slowly start moving my belongings to the Tri-Cities. In the weeks to come, the duplex was nothing more than a two story personal storage building. Life was grand for a little while...until Vanessa taught me the art of "freebasing" cocaine and revealed her true self. Sometimes when you jump into a serious relationship without taking the time to get to know the other person first, it comes back to bite you. This was about to be one of those times.

She had a number of quirks and fetishes that seriously got on my nerves. I managed to either just accept them and move on, or work around them if I had to. Before she could even get out of the bed in the morning, two things had to happen. First, I had to go downstairs to walk *her* dog and clean up any "accidents" that might have happened overnight, because she just couldn't stomach it first thing in the morning. Then I would have to get her a diet coke and a number of pills from the kitchen before she could face the day. When she was finally up and moving, I would usually have to drive down to Burger King to get her a burger and fries with no salt. If even one drop of salt was on anything, it fucked up her entire day and mine too. I just had to tolerate it because I wasn't working and she was…even if it was only whenever she felt like going.

She missed her calling. She should have gone to college and majored in chemistry because she was brilliant at not only cooking up the perfect rocks of cocaine, but even repairing other people's mistakes. Freebasing brought out the best and worst in me. Unlike the effects cocaine had on me in any of its other forms, freebasing gave me an instant erection that could knock a hole in the wall, leading to some of the most incredible sex that I had ever had. Add that to Vanessa's natural and unnatural beauty, and I was whipped…and she knew that. On the flip side, it made me incredibly paranoid. I must have worn out the blinds, peeping out every time I heard the slightest noise. It had gotten so bad that I was literally hiding in the closet at times because I thought that we were being watched. Combine that with her dog barking every time she heard a car or voice outside, and I almost had my reservations to the local nuthouse.

    Vanessa and I had such a volatile relationship, that I could never guess what was going to happen next… case in point: the first time she broke up with me. It was just one of those days when she was bitching about the fact that I didn't have a job and backed me into a corner. I said something along the lines of "You call dancing a job? Where do strippers go when they are not working? They usually dress up in a revealing outfit and go dancing at a club, that's where. Since they do drugs and drink on the job, what's the fucking difference?" Well, she didn't like my answer and made it public by telling some of the other girls at the club what I said. Of course, they got defensive and took her side, as they would, and invited her to go shopping with them the following day. While Vanessa was getting ready, she gave me a list of things to do around the house while she was gone. I knew that the other girls had got to her and she was intending on kicking me out regardless, but I completed all the chores anyway. All I could think about was how she must have been talking about me the entire time, and those girls were probably advising her to get rid of me. When she got home, she checked everything thoroughly and found one spot I missed underneath the toilet seat. "This is unacceptable!" she screamed. "You have just proved how worthless you are. You can't do anything right. I want you to pack your shit and get out of my house…today!" I couldn't really do or say anything, because it was legally *her* place, so I did what she asked. I remember driving down the road feeling free and in good spirits at first, but started missing her soon after. She felt the same way, and called me when I nearly halfway home, asking me to turn around and come back. *This* particular time, I did, against my better judgement.

We would break up several more times in the coming months over the most ridiculous shit. Once we split because I dropped Vanessa's pill bottle in the sink and some of them either got wet, or went down the drain. Knowing that I was going to be yelled at, I wasn't planning to tell her, hoping that she wouldn't notice. Unfortunately, she went downstairs and caught me red-handed, then hit the ceiling. I felt so terrible that I got into my truck and drove back to Knoxville without saying a word. I ignored her phone calls during the trip and didn't see her again until she cooled off. There were so many of these scenarios that the neighbours must have got out the popcorn several times and just sat back and enjoyed the show. Sometimes we would get into a fight and Vanessa would kick me out, then as I was leaving, change her mind and either climb on top of my truck and try to pry the door open, or jump in front of it to keep me from leaving. Jerry Springer would have proud... for we could have been the best "reality" show on TV.

2

We did have some good times among the madness though. You know what they say about makeup sex... we definitely proved that it wasn't a myth. We had sex in the private pool, scaring the hell out of some kids who were thinking about having a swim until they saw us. We went over to her mother's house and had complaints filed against us by a neighbour for lewd behaviour on a lawn chair, so we took it further and had sex in that pool as well. We were like two starving animals when it came to sex and cocaine, even if we had nothing in common anywhere else.

I introduced her to the "Star Wars" universe by taking her to see "Attack of the Clones," which only seemed logical since Mark saw us as a real life "Padme" and "Anakin," and we watched all the other films together as well. She liked to make out during movies, but I wouldn't allow it during Star Wars films. I would always say something like "You are missing an important part" or "You know I'm going to quiz you later to see if you were paying attention" to disrupt any intentions she might have had.

She, in turn, introduced me to Frank Sinatra songs and mobster movies, as well as guilty pleasures that I still love today, like the Reese Witherspoon film "Sweet Home Alabama." We would also watch hour after hour of the TV shows "Friends" and "the Sopranos" until I literally had most of the dialog memorized. We rarely went anywhere or did anything... other than sit at home, get stoned and have sex while one of these shows or discs were playing in the background. It wasn't a glamourous life by any means, but we enjoyed ourselves and that was all the mattered.

At times, I was starting to feel as if the foundation of our relationship was built around using one another. We did have amazing sex and had a great time partying with each other, which was all I needed to stay interested, but on the flip side, I had become her servant and slave. Even when I would head down to Knoxville for a few days and come back, before I could sit down and relax, I would have to do a few things around the house first. Walking the dog was always the first job and then she would usually say something like "Do you mind taking out the trash? I've put it in the downstairs bathroom." I would open the door expecting a couple of bags, and instead it was usually stacked halfway to the ceiling from all the parties she had while I was out of town. I couldn't believe that she was too lazy to walk across the parking lot to the bin. She would rather wait until I came up, and stink up the house in the meantime, than dispose of it. She could be so annoying and predictable at times, but I was whipped so I put up with it.

3

I had already begun to sell off my toys and comic book collections to support our habit, which was something that I had sworn to myself that I would never do. Tommy had also noticed that something was going on, and being already resentful towards me for not paying the rent since Kaine left several months ago, began showing the house without letting me know. One day while I was in town, I stopped by the duplex to grab a few things. When I pulled in the driveway, I noticed a moving truck parked in my back yard. As soon as they saw me, two girls got out of the truck and approached me. I recognized them from the club and I wasn't too fond of either one. When I asked them what they were doing on my property, they replied "Tommy promised us the bottom apartment but we didn't feel like it was right to move in without checking with you first." They also informed me that Tommy had even had sex with one of them in Kaine's old bed about a week earlier and was snooping through my things afterwards. He apparently wasn't happy with all of the empty baggies lying around in the open, so he had a field day looking through the rest of my stuff. He had found my voice recorder and listened to what was on the tape, which was an outline of the songs I had written, and what each one of them meant in the event of my death. It changed his perspective of me somewhat. Now he had confirmation that I was seriously fucked up in the head and he wanted to get me the hell out of there.

As the night progressed, and we started drinking, we no longer talked about the house. Instead the girls were coming on to me. I knew that the older of the two had liked me for a long time, and the other wasn't shy about sharing, so this was starting to get interesting. Had I not been in a relationship with someone that I actually loved, knowing me as well as I do, there would have been only one possible outcome, but something just didn't feel right. All we had done was watch "Jay and Silent Bob Strikes Back" and cozied up together over a few drinks but I felt like I was cheating already, so when we ran out of beer and I went to get more, I called Vanessa and told her everything. Luckily, when I got back to the house, the two girls were cuddled up in my bed asleep. I watched them for hours…then asked them to leave and never come back once they awakened. They were so disappointed and angry that they never bothered me again.

4

This lone incident seemed to bring us closer together for the most part. I would meet her entire immediate family and I felt like it was finally time for her to meet mine. I planned out the entire day. We would go eat dinner at the same restaurant that I had taken every girl I had ever cared about in Lenoir City before stopping by the park to feed the ducks. Then we would head over to my parents' house to relax before getting some blow and having drinks at Micheal's. The first part went without a hitch until Vanessa met my mother. Mom saw right through her from the start, but when Vanessa told her about making me cover my tattoos and take out my earrings before meeting her dad and grandmother... that was the last straw. The way mother saw it, and rightfully so, if I could proudly express myself to my own family and every other girl's family that I ever dated, why did I have to pretend to be someone else around hers. What made her so damn special? She made a valid point as far as I was concerned, but love makes you do stupid things and make ridiculous compromises sometimes. From that moment on, mother dubbed her "Little Miss Beautiful" and she didn't exactly mean it to be as complimentary as it sounded.

The night didn't get any better when we got to Micheal's. Vanessa didn't like the quality of the cocaine that I bought, and to make matters worse, was being stalked by a black guy from the moment we arrived. I was used to guys staring at her everywhere we went and usually just laughed it off, but this guy took it to a whole new level. He saw us come in together and even asked me directly if she was my girl, but just wouldn't stop following her around. When she went to get us drinks, he came up behind her and grabbed her ass as I watched helplessly from the other side of the bar. Before I could get to the guy, one of the bouncers who knew me stopped me and said, "Let us handle this." They tossed the guy out on his face without me even having to touch him. That could have been a bad thing, because no matter what Vanessa did to lighten the mood failed miserably. I would remain in a bad mood for the rest of the night until we got back home.

About a week later, Vanessa suggested that I should apply for a job as a bouncer at one of the local bars. Honestly, I wasn't keen on the job because I wanted to do something else with my life, but to make her happy I agreed to look into it. When we walked in, I immediately didn't like the place. There was just a bad vibe in the air that didn't agree with me at all. It was the type of establishment that I despised and avoided over the years. There were country music blaring, pool tables and a hostile crowd of drunken rednecks looking for a fight. I just couldn't see myself happy in a shithole like that.

We had only went a few feet into the building when we saw one of Vanessa's friends: a girl named "Nikki" who had heard so much about and been lusting over in photos for several months. She looked as beautiful in person as she did in Vanessa's albums and seemed like a really sweet girl. After a brief introduction and conversation, we parted ways and got down to business. We met with the manager, who pretty much hired me on the spot, then headed to the bar to get a drink. There were two girls giving me the eye while we were waiting on our shots. In an effort to get my attention, since nothing else was working, they started making out. Vanessa busted out laughing because she knew how that did nothing for me at all anymore. I just rolled my eyes and turned my back to them. What I saw when I looked the other way, was a sight indeed. It was DeLynn with an entire entourage of people with her. My night was about to go from bad to worse.

It started off as a game. Vanessa would kiss me to make DeLynn jealous then DeLynn would make out with one of the random guys in her flock to retaliate. I was not in favour of throwing salt in the wound but Vanessa kept pouring it on ruthlessly. Eventually DeLynn came up to Vanessa and called a fake truce with her but called me every name in the book. I was baffled at why this girl hated me so much. I never did anything to her personally to give her a reason to dislike me but she was badly scorned. She was out for blood on this night...*my* blood.

She and her posse continued to circle us like sharks in the water everywhere we went. The only time Vanessa was out of my sight was when she had to go to the bathroom. That was when DeLynn and one of her redneck girlfriends came up to me and told me that Vanessa wasn't coming out looking the same as she went in. I went and got one of the female bouncers to go in and check on Vanessa after that threat. She came out and told me that the girls were just "talking" and I had nothing to worry about. A few minutes later, the girls emerged laughing and hugging it out like they were the best of friends again. That was when Vanessa told me that DeLynn had accused me of not only sleeping with her but giving her a venereal disease in the process. That was supposably why she had such a problem seeing Vanessa and I together. That would be understandable if there was any truth to it but it was all lies. The sad part was that I had already told Vanessa exactly what happened when DeLynn came back to Knoxville without her, yet she was now buying her bullshit and starting to doubt me. I had to point out the obvious to her to make her believe me again. "We have been having unprotected sex for months" I said. "Wouldn't you have it or at least noticed something by now if I actually had something?" She had nothing to say to that because apologizing wasn't in her vocabulary.

    I could sense that the atmosphere was getting tenser by the minute, and that I was going to get jumped at some point by someone...I just didn't know who. It was inevitable. So I informed the bouncers, my future co-workers, of the situation and asked them to please watch my back. They gave me their word. It was probably fifteen minutes later when it all went down. DeLynn came up to us with all of her minions backing her and started arguing with Vanessa. I stood close to make sure that it didn't get physical. Out of nowhere, a punch comes from over DeLynn's shoulder, while I wasn't looking, and catches me in the corner of the eye. I turned to see where Vanessa was, and she was already sprinting across the floor to get help. In the meantime, this coward is throwing punch after punch and landing them on my face. He managed to rip the buttons off the new shirt that I was wearing that Vanessa had only bought me days before. With Vanessa safely out of the picture, I block his next punch and overpower him. I put him in a headlock and start pounding him with uppercuts. He was helpless. I could have done anything to him that I wanted to.

    Then the unthinkable happened. I could feel multiple fists hitting me on the back of the head. I just kept my head down and kept punching the coward until I could feel the swelling start then I released him. I was shocked to see that I wasn't being attacked by any of DeLynn's bystanders… it was the fucking bouncers who was supposed to be helping me! This led to a number of altercations between us and them where we had went from enemies to being on the same side. We both left the building as the police were arriving and ironically were parked beside each other in the parking lot. There weren't any words exchanged toward each other, only to the so called security. Obviously, this changed how I felt about the job and I ended up not reporting to my first shift. I would only see this guy once at a gas station later on, but there wasn't any actions taken on either side. I would only run into DeLynn once in the months to come, and that would be while I was in the local Wal-Mart with Mark. She was still very upset and distracted by me but nothing happened. Mark insisted that we fuck with her and her boyfriend by following them to the parking lot, but I had seen and heard enough from her already, so I chose to let her leave without incident.

After the bouncing job didn't appeal to me anymore, I took whatever I could get. The first couple of jobs were at gas stations but neither worked out due to a number of reasons too numerous to list. Then I tried my hand at hospitality. I got hired at a sports bar as a cook even though I had absolutely no experience whatsoever. The manager told me that there was a decent learning curve so I would be properly trained before I would ever be in the kitchen alone. That was a bald-faced lie. I would find myself alone only days later, not knowing how to prepare anything except for French fries and chicken strips... even then I almost gave a poor waitress food poisoning from undercooked poultry. I was about to walk out, when the lady who hired me came in and took over the grill until help arrived. A hippie that everyone called "Soup" was supposed to show me the basics, but got so frustrated with me that he requested that I be sent home. He claimed that I was worthless and only in his way. I wasn't *that* easy to get rid of. I stuck around just to piss him off.

All along there had been a number of guys who Vanessa made top priority over me. A couple of them were "sugar daddies" who she could depend on anytime she needed money, whether she was actually in a bind or just didn't want to go to work for a few days. She was notorious for being unreliable at the club, but had enough seniority to get away with it. She called it "job sabotage" and could care less whether they fired her or not, as long as she had these guys to fall back on. The man who she held closest to her heart was an older gentleman named "Herb" who lived in Charlotte, NC with his wife and children. All she had to do was make up some lame tragic story to pull at his heartstrings and he would wire her several hundred dollars without hesitation. Unbeknownst to his sick wife, Vanessa had literally drained his savings and retirement to almost nothing over the years. She bragged about it like she was proud of her actions, and seemingly had no remorse. When she called him wanting money, she wasn't about to take "no" for an answer, so he always found a way to come through and send her whatever she asked for.

Every so often, when they hadn't seen each other in a while and Herb wasn't able to get away for a few days, Vanessa would make the trip to Charlotte. He would usually put her up in a hotel and buy all of her meals or anything else that she required, making it a pretty profitable trip overall. Vanessa was afraid to drive on the interstate, so she usually took DeLynn with her to do all the driving, but now, after their falling out, I had assumed that responsibility. The problem was that I had to work that night, and wasn't going to get any sleep, but that didn't matter to the princess. What Vanessa wants…Vanessa gets. This was going to be no exception.

We left early the next morning. Between my natural ability to find my way without a map and Vanessa's foggy drug infested memory to guide us, we had no problems getting to Charlotte. There was, however, a minor incident at a dodgy gas station along the way. When we pulled up to the pump, we saw two shady guys sitting on the sidewalk in front of the store with their mangy dog. I just had a feeling that they were going to walk up to the car for some reason, so I told Vanessa to stay seated. Sure enough, they approached the car as I was filling up and instinct took over. "That sure is a pretty dog you have there, lady" one said to Vanessa as they peered into the window at her cocker spaniel. I immediately walked up and got between the two guys and Vanessa. "You have a pretty dog too" I replied as I began plotting which one I was going to attack first if they made the wrong move. The conversation lasted about five minutes, and I never took an eye off of them for a second. Eventually they left without anything significant happening and our journey continued.

I checked Vanessa into the hotel then had to get back on the road immediately. I literally had time to get back home, take a shower and change my clothes before I had to go to work. If I got lost along the way somewhere, I was fucked because I had very little time to spare. All that was going through my mind was how nice the bed was going to feel after work and how much I was going to enjoy not having Vanessa or her dog around the house for a couple of days. I ended up making it to work on time and looked forward to a nice, quiet evening in an otherwise empty house afterwards. It didn't exactly work out the way I planned. As soon as I walked into the house that night, the phone was ringing. It was Vanessa and she wanted to come home. Not tomorrow, mind you, but right then and there. She was turning on the waterworks until I agreed to get back into the car. I was so tired that I could barely hold my eyes open. I had a hell of a time getting across the mountains outside of Asheville in heavy fog on only a two lane road. I was sure that I was going to get into an accident...either by falling asleep at the wheel or driving off the mountain, but fortunately, I made it. I impressed myself by driving directly there without missing an exit or getting turned around, even though I had only driven up there once before. She was ready when I arrived, so we were immediately inside the car again driving back to Tennessee. In less than 24 hours, I had worked an eight hour shift and driven back and forth to Charlotte twice without any sleep.

When I finally did crash, I think I was out as soon as my head hit the pillow.

5

Ever since the day I moved up to Johnson City, we used Vanessa's drug dealer "Preacher" when we wanted to get high...which was pretty much every day. He was an older fellow, who was so careful and paranoid about meeting new people that I had to leave every time he came over. Many nights were spent roaming around the shops for several hours, waiting for that call so I could come home. It was a hard pill to swallow at times, but the end result of having Vanessa all to myself with vast quantities of free blow made it worth it to me. Preacher was a lonely and unattractive man who was obviously in love with someone he couldn't have: my Vanessa. If she let him hang out at her house and let him watch a few "private" dances while he got high, he would pay her with a mountain of dope, otherwise she had to pay for it with cash in hand. We couldn't afford to support our habits, so sacrifices had to be made. This went on for a while until she found another source.

There were two brothers who lived on their parents' farm on the outskirts of town who came into Vanessa's club quite frequently. Very few of the girls knew that they were drug dealers, but Vanessa was one of the first to figure it out. They would bring the shit right to our doorstep anytime we called them and I didn't have to ever leave the house either. It was great...except that we had to pay for it. One of the brothers worked as a supervisor at a telemarketing firm that specialized in selling time shares. He helped me get a job there and after two weeks of paid training, watching the professionals make their commission with relative ease, I quickly realized that I couldn't sell rain to a bloody desert. All I did accomplish was break up a few marriages by exposing infidelity through hotel records that was at our disposal to provide us with names and personal details of potential clients. I was told to be put on certain customers' no-call list and was even given advice on what other fields of work I should consider looking into. Meanwhile, I listened as the girl beside me sold package after package, bringing home nearly a grand a week. I eventually gave up and quit the job because I wasn't making any money. The whole time I was there, I only made one sell and I had to work my ass off to keep from losing that one. About a month after I stopped working there, Vanessa and I saw on the news that the brothers had sold to an undercover cop and had not only fucked their lives up, but the rest of the family as well. They were on the verge of losing the farm last I heard before the media tossed their story aside.

This was around the time that Vanessa suggested, out of the blue, that I should look into being a truck driver. Such a thing would have been unheard of when things were going great, but at this point and time, things had gone sour again. This would be a perfect scenario for her. I would be on the road all the time and the only time I would see her, I would have a pocketful of money. I actually met with the recruiter, and attended a local class, but my real training was going to be in Arkansas. With no running vehicle of my own and unable to use Vanessa's car for the trip, I gave up on a trucking career before it got started. Vanessa had seen enough…one more time.

It wasn't even a week later when Vanessa threw me out again. However, this time was slightly different: my truck wasn't running so I couldn't go anywhere. She called her mother to ask if her boyfriend could come over and have a look under the hood. I would find out later that he had another reason for being there: to make sure that I left peacefully. He worked tirelessly for a couple of hours and even had a couple of other mechanics have a look as well, but no one could pinpoint what the problem actually was, so I had no other choice but to call my dad. He had been on the road all day, driving around North Carolina while taking in the sights and was already exhausted. The last thing that he wanted to do was to go anywhere else, especially to work on someone's car, but he did. He drove straight up to Johnson City and got it started but even he didn't know what the issue was. He suspected that someone must have poured sugar into my gas tank or something. I immediately thought of DeLynn. She knew where Vanessa lived. She knew what I drove. She had a problem with me that had escalated to violence only weeks before…you do the math. I made it home several hours later and my house looked like a tornado had hit it. There was shit everywhere and Tommy was doing some landscaping in the yard. I hadn't been gone that long but times were definitely changing.

6

I now found myself living at Tommy's place with a revolving door of other tenants… one of them being a midget wrestler who wrestled under the name "Butch Cassidy" in the WWE and around the world. Butch and I became fast friends and would often get drunk and play NCAA football on the old Playstation 2 while Tommy was at work. It kept us out of trouble for the most part. I would also start working at an Italian restaurant as a dishwasher and was so great at my job that I would sometimes work Sunday mornings by myself…which usually required two or more people to get the job done on a normal basis. I was the model employee until Vanessa and I were on speaking terms again. Then I started calling in sick pretty frequently and my stock went down practically overnight.

One person who stood by me through it all was one of the waitresses, a beautiful blonde named "Kate." She would see me struggling at times and would encourage others to lend me a hand when I needed it. Because she was such a popular and respected woman, when she talked, everyone listened. However, I had no idea that she liked me until Valentine's Day rolled around. There was a guy that I worked with in the kitchen that everyone called "Crazy Cooter" that was trying to talk Kate into giving him a little kiss in the true holiday spirit. She refused but said "Dennis, on the other hand, can have a kiss if he wants." I thought about it for a few seconds then followed her to an otherwise empty breakroom and we shared a tender kiss. From that moment on, she was always in the back of my mind every time Vanessa and I would have a fight.

Kate watched my relationship with great interest. She pleaded with me several times to leave Vanessa because she felt that Vanessa was taking me for granted. She would say things like "If you were with me, you wouldn't even have to work. I would keep you up. Remember, I own my own business... I would be so good to you." I never doubted her sincerity for a second. I knew that she was a great person...one capable of getting me off drugs, and putting my life on the right track, but I wasn't ready for that. I still wanted to get high, so I kept pushing her away.

My life was playing out like a broken record. Vanessa and I would break up, then Kate would ask me out for some drinks, and I would accept, but by the end of the night, Vanessa would call and reconcile and we would get back together...leaving Kate out in the cold. This repeated over and over and over until Kate got sick of it. Add that to what she was telling Cooter on a daily basis about how I was "missing out" on something, whether she was referring to sex or her companionship, I never bothered to ask, and my ignoring it, the fire slowly fizzled out. By the time I came around, she was quitting her job at the restaurant. We shared one last kiss on her final night there, and as she wiped the lipstick off my lips, she asked me to come with her but I couldn't. Foolishly, I let her leave without trying to stop her. This wasn't over by a long shot.

7

The winter of 2002-2003 was a weird one indeed. When a huge snowstorm came in only an hour before I had to drive down to Knoxville, I wasn't concerned. Normally, the heavier snow hits the northern half of the state while the southern half either gets light snow, flurries, or nothing at all. This time, however, was quite the opposite. I had only gone a few miles south, when I noticed that the lines on the road were already covered. The snow appeared to be growing more intense the further I went. I literally had to drive in the freshly made tracks that were quickly filling in, hoping that the person in front of me had some idea where the road was because I sure as hell didn't. I had to get gas so I slowly eased down the exit ramp around Jonesborough. I had just started coming down the hill when I lost control of the truck and slid sideways. All I could see ahead of me was a semi sitting at the stop sign at the bottom of the hill and I was heading straight for it without brakes. I knew I was a goner and just braced for the impact. At the last minute, I regained control of my car and was able to correct myself before I faced certain death. I managed to get to the gas station with no problems after that but I wasn't out of the woods yet. I was only about half way home and the weather was getting worse by the second.

    I managed to get all the way to Knoxville and was literally a mile away from Tommy's house when the unthinkable happened. While sitting still at a red light, my truck began to slide forward towards the car in front of me. Apparently, I was sitting on an icy patch on the road that was somewhat sloped and my tires just didn't have enough tread left on them to keep me stable. All I could do was turn the wheel and go into the ditch while the people in front of me sat there and watched. It was quite embarrassing but I wasn't the only one that it happened to. As a matter of fact, I barely got stopped before I hit one of the stationary cars already resting in the ditch. I immediately called Tommy but he wasn't available because he was already assisting others on the other side of town. I then called Butch and he couldn't help me because he was already drunk. I had no other choice but to call Tommy again. He came up with an alternate plan. He was able to reach the former Hell's Angel who had done most of my tattoos and got him to pull my truck out. He lived nearby and was literally there in five minutes or less to assist me. He tied a chain from his 4x4 to my truck and yanked me out so fast that I nearly didn't turn the wheel fast enough to miss the car parked in front of me. He towed me to the fire station just down the road from the site then gave me a lift to Tommy's. I couldn't believe that I had driven over 100 miles with all those twists and turns and made it this close to home and *then* go off the road when I wasn't moving. It would be a day or two before the snow melted enough to get my truck home.

Then there was my 30th birthday on February 7th 2003. I had just worked my shift at the restaurant, and driven up to Johnson City to celebrate it with Vanessa, when the phone rang. It was my mother, who I was expecting to hear from to wish me a Happy Birthday. Unfortunately, that wasn't why she called. My dad had suffered a heart attack and was in stable condition at the hospital after being revived by paramedics in the living room at my parents' house. Mom wanted me to get back into the car and drive back to Knoxville, but I was already intoxicated from cocaine and alcohol. I tried to explain to her on the phone that I was in no condition to drive, and that I would be there first thing in the morning, but she kept insisting that I come to the hospital immediately. This led to a huge argument that resulted in me going on a binge that would keep me from returning the next day. By the time I made it down a few days later, dad was back at home and recovering. To this day, he remembers my birthday because of the heart attack, when they had forgotten it a couple of times in the past.

A few days later, another strange event took place: Vanessa sprung a leak in one of her breast implants. She needed to go to the doctor immediately but wasn't about to go to just any doctor, she wanted to see the artist that did her surgery originally at his office in Nashville. There was a rainstorm of biblical proportions going on outside for the past couple of days that was causing flash flooding and heavy fog, so travelling for any reason wasn't recommended or advised by the National Weather Service. I thought we were going to wait out the storm, as we had agreed upon, but after freebasing cocaine all night, Vanessa changed her mind. She pitched one of her tantrums until she got her way, as always, despite my attempts of talking her out of it. This was going to be a trip for the ages...

Vanessa cooked up some rocks for us to smoke on the way just to keep me awake. We thought we were running late, so I wasn't exactly following speed limits. A couple of times I glanced down at the speedometer and we were doing over 100mph. With the road conditions being what they were, had I lost control of the car at any point, they would be peeling our remains off the road a quarter of a mile away or further. Several times I actually felt the car lift up off the road from the rising water beneath but not enough to cause an accident. We were cruising at breakneck speeds until I saw flashing lights behind us in the rear-view mirror. I had literally just got my first speeding ticket in my life only days before but if the cop just saw me hitting that pipe, and found how much cocaine and paraphernalia we had sitting on the console, we were fucked. So I decided to pretend not to see him like I did years before leaving that crack-house in Knoxville, and believe it or not, it worked a second time! This one was more bittersweet because I avoided getting arrested by a state trooper instead of the measly local police. I slowed down a little after the near miss... but continued to drive at deadly speeds for these extreme conditions.

We ended up getting to Nashville an hour early...not because of my reckless driving, but because in my drug infested haze, I had forgotten all about entering a different time zone on the other side of the plateau. This basically meant that I put our lives at risk for nothing. Overall, the appointment went well, but going back to Johnson City was going to be much more difficult journey since we ran out of dope on the way to Nashville. I didn't drink coffee, and Vanessa fell asleep before we left the city limits, so I pretty much had to fend for myself. I smoked countless cigarettes and rolled the window down all the way to stimulate my brain so I didn't pass out. I had been awake for a day and a half at this point so to say my eyes were a bit heavy would be an understatement. I was driving about an hour before I realized that I had seriously fucked up. My fatigue had caused me to take the wrong exit a long way back and head into the wrong direction. I needed to turn around immediately and go back into Nashville... all the while hoping that Vanessa didn't find out. This would prove difficult because it was now rush hour. I might have miraculously survived this trip so far, against unbelievable odds, but Vanessa was going to be the death of me.

    I had literally just entered Nashville when I nodded off for a split second. When I opened my eyes, I saw that traffic had come to a standstill just ahead of me and I was approaching it at about 80mph. I took evasive action and slammed on the breaks, literally skidding into the other lane which luckily was empty at that particular moment. This woke a frightened Vanessa up from her deep slumber as she held on for dear life. We managed to get stopped only mere inches from the car ahead of us. Vanessa immediately asked what happened and when I told her, she scolded me harshly for not pulling off the road and taking a nap before I got that fatigued. Then she asked where we were, and when I told her that we were still in Nashville because I had taken a wrong turn somewhere, she went through every emotion imaginable. First she started screaming at me then broke down into tears because she missed her dog. Although she kept insisting that I pull over and sleep for a few minutes, she would turn around and reprimand me immediately after for not being closer to home by now. I just kept driving and fighting sleep until we got back to Johnson City.

8

Our house over the next few weeks was being invaded by a number of bisexual sluts from Vanessa's workplace. They would come over and get high, then make a pass at Vanessa or me at some point, and get booted out. One girl was so obsessed with Vanessa, that she stole some of her clothes and other personal belongings as a memento or a souvenir before she went out the door. This increased traffic through our home wasn't helping with my ever growing paranoia. All those years, even when I knew the DEA was watching me, I wasn't really paranoid. It wasn't until I started freebasing that everything changed. I only trusted one of Vanessa's friends and that was Kellie. Everyone else just didn't seem trustworthy. Take for example, her male friend "Liam." He welcomed me into his house with open arms when Vanessa and I were having problems, yet when things were good and Vanessa, who was all about "public displays of affection," would sit between my legs and be all over me in front of him, would call her ex-husband and tell him all about it as soon as we parted ways. To make matters worse, Vanessa would sometimes be a little too affectionate towards him to make me jealous. I really couldn't handle being around all these clowns anymore. If this relationship was ever going to really amount to anything, we needed new friends and a change of scenery.

My first attempt was in Knoxville. I quit working at the restaurant and got a job pressure washing semis with Cooter during the day. A week later, I got a job working at the same grocery store that didn't hire me when I applied there a couple of years earlier while I was still with Wendy. Although I had bought some stuff to "clean out my system" or at least cover up the narcotics in my bloodstream, I still failed the drug test. Since I was taking everything from cocaine to ecstasy in those days, a representative from the store didn't call to tell me the results…a doctor did. He told me that he had found nine different drugs in my urine and that I not only didn't get the job, but I needed professional help. He gave me the phone numbers and addresses of several people and rehab clinics around town that could assist me with my addictions…and I told *him* to go fuck himself. I was hoping that enough time had passed that I had fallen off of their radar and thankfully it had. I now had two full time jobs and would be making plenty of money with little time to spend it. Vanessa wouldn't have to lift a finger anymore if she didn't want to.

    There were only two problems that I faced to make all of this happen. One was the lack of sleep, and the other was that I would be spending most of my time in Knoxville…away from Vanessa. There was a new resident at Tommy's house: a wannabe cowboy named "Aiden." He didn't work but had a number of stories about things he had done in the past. Apparently, he was in Somalia when the Black Hawk helicopter went down…which would have been remarkable since he would have been a kid at the time. When we watched the movie "Road House" together, he told me about working at a club out west that was so bad that it made the "Double Duece" look like "Cheers." Yeah…he was one of *those* guys… always sitting in front of the TV, making the stories he watched his own. He would, however, become my backup alarm clock if there was ever a possibility of me oversleeping, which came in handy on a number of occasions.

Most days I averaged about four hours of sleep, but sometimes Tommy would ask me to help his dad in the hay fields and I would get even less. I literally had to do coke every day to get through my shifts and even then I nearly fell asleep at the wheel several times on the way to work. My days off weren't much better because instead of resting, I would drive up to Johnson City to spend time with Vanessa. We would party the entire time and go to bed a couple of hours before I had to drive back, then Vanessa would want to have sex so I was lucky to get an hour. My body just couldn't take it anymore after three months. They sprung a surprise drug test on me at the car wash one rainy day that detected traces of cocaine in my urine, which came as no surprise considering that I was smoking it that morning in the parking lot as I waited for the doors to open just to stay awake. I was told to go home until the results came back from the lab and I wisely never answered their calls or showed my face there again so they couldn't fire me. I didn't need that on my record.

At the store, I refused to suck up to the grocery manager who had hired someone else to compete against me for the role. All I would hear every night was how much everyone respected him and it drove me crazy. I was also being pressured by both sides relentlessly to join the union and that annoyed the hell out of me too. I eventually just had enough and walked away... leaving me unemployed once again. In three months, I had gone from making more money than I could spend to having no income at all. Drugs had once again played an important part in fucking up my life but I hadn't seen anything yet.

Our next move would leave both of us scratching our heads later on. We accepted Herb's invitation to *move* to Charlotte for a week or so to determine whether we wanted to reside there permanently in the future. This was all a ploy to get Vanessa under his nose and under his watchful eyes. He already had our apartment picked out and paid for, and even had Vanessa a job at the nearest strip club. He had all the bases covered. It was an offer that would have been foolish to refuse considering how messed up our lives were at the time, so we packed a few things and away we went.

Our apartment wasn't quite what we expected. Unlike the hotel that we usually stayed at, which had a swimming pool that we would often times have sex in… much to the delight of the Mexicans who worked at the restaurant next door, this place was a dump. It was dirty and we literally had to close the blinds straight away because dodgy people were walking by and pressing their hands up to the glass to look at not only us, but all of our personal belongings as well. I felt so insecure that when I was unpacking the car, I would close the trunk and lock the doors every time I walked inside. This was not a great neighbourhood at all… but we owed it to Herb to at least give it a shot.

I took Vanessa to work that night and when I returned to the apartment, there were a group of people standing out in the parking lot, staring at our front door like they were plotting something. I fearlessly walked past them and went inside. For the next few hours, I just sat on the bed watching TV and staring at my watch. I kept hearing voices and strange noises coming from outside my window and that was enough to make an important decision. There was absolutely no way I was staying in this place another day. I left early to pick up Vanessa, meaning that I was either going to be waiting in the car or inside the club and I chose the latter. Vanessa saw me sitting at the bar so she took a seat beside me. "Is everything ok?" she asked. "I don't like it here" I replied. "Me neither" she said to my delight. "Don't get me wrong, this club is ok. I've made a lot of money here tonight but that apartment..." I stopped her there. "Do you want to go back home tomorrow?" I asked. She nodded her head in agreement. "But Herb is going to be devastated" she replied. I just looked at her and said "He'll get over it, sweetie. We'll leave first thing in the morning." And that was exactly what we did.

When we got home, we found out that Vanessa's mother was going out of town for a day or two and she wanted us to look after her house. Vanessa used this as a forum for Preacher and me to finally meet each other. We didn't exactly get along from the start as I had hoped. He was obviously jealous of me because he wanted Vanessa for himself, and he came across as an arrogant asshole to me to boot. This wasn't good considering that I had animosity towards him already for constantly getting booted out of my own house every time he wanted to party. We did put aside our differences until I made the mistake of saying "Maybe we shouldn't smoke out here on the porch since the neighbours can practically look out the window and see what we are doing." This either made him extremely paranoid or pissed him off because he left in great haste and went back to not wanting me around again when he was. I decided right then and there that this clown needed to go and the only way to do this was to move somewhere and not tell him where we had gone. So that was exactly what we did...

9

With our lease running out, we made the move to the little country town where Vanessa grew up. It was called Elizabethton, TN and it was only a few minutes away from Johnson City. The idea of this particular spot came from Vanessa's dad and stepmother, whose best friend owned a trailer park and was willingly to give us a reasonable monthly price to relocate there. I had only met this fellow once and that was at a Christmas party held inside the barn that sat near our trailer. I really had no opinion of him, or his son, who would be looking after us a majority of the time. Vanessa, however, had known both of them most of her life and that was what sold the idea to me.

    Within a couple of weeks, I got a decent paying job working at a junkyard. I made enough money that Vanessa didn't have to strip anymore and could basically sit at home and do nothing without having to worry about anything. I had made quite an impression at the workplace by coming down with the flu just after I got hired and still coming to work every day without calling in sick at all. Since I worked outside, I wasn't spreading many germs so at least I wasn't exposing others to my illness. I was constantly running a fever and that was what kept me warm as I stood there with snow flurries falling around me when I should have been in bed. With Christmas approaching, I knew that if I could suck it up for a few days, I would have a long weekend to recuperate. I kept pushing myself until I finished the week and then I slept for nearly three days… meaning that I completely missed out on Christmas. It was worth it. I felt like a new man on Monday morning and it was time to shine.

    There was one thing that didn't seem right though. After the holidays were over, I noticed that there was something wrong with my pay: I was making more money than I anticipated. A part of me just wanted to keep my mouth shut but I was afraid that someone was going to find out and make me repay all that extra money, which I no longer had, so I went and told the manager. He yanked my payslip out of my hand and looked at it, then tore it to pieces and cut me another check. There was no "thank you" or nothing…it was almost like I had scammed them out of money intentionally. When I told a couple of the guys about the incident, they told me that I should have never let them know that I was making as much money as the truck drivers. "We never get a raise here… yet your workload constantly increases" they said. "When it's all said and done, you will regret it." I already regretted it…

10

On the flip side, at least for a while, we lived a clean normal life like everyone else. We went and got groceries on the same day every week, went out to dinner every Friday, and even visited the family every other week. There was only one problem though: Vanessa was bored. Since I had lost the keys to the ignition of my truck, she was often stranded without a car. This could have helped to extend our sobriety but I will never know. All it took was her mentioning getting some dope "occasionally" to make us both fall off the wagon again. We were doing so good too… even making plans for the future like marriage and kids. Three months was as long as we could stay on the right path before things went back to the way they were. We just didn't have the willpower to fight our addictions any longer.

We were also finding out pretty quick why you don't rent from family friends. Although they would do small repairs around the house, when a big problem like a hot water leak in the wall of the shower came up, their solution was to let it go until we received an enormous water bill, then just go outside and cut the water off at the source. They even put a lock on it so I couldn't turn it back on.

That meant that we had to go over to Vanessa's mother's house to even take a shower. I believe that it was their way of getting us to leave, without actually coming out and saying it, but we had nowhere else to go so we just dealt with it the best we could.

With all the anger and frustrations building up, it wouldn't be long until I quit my job at the junkyard. Over a short period of time, my crew had diminished, leaving me to rely on the welders to help out when needed. That became the deciding factor the day a bus pulled in, filled from top to bottom with scrap metal that could only realistically be unloaded by hand. The welders refused to help because it was going to be a lot of hard work, leaving me and the customer to finish the job alone. It literally took us the entire day…meaning that I never got lunch. I knew right then and there that once I punched that time clock, it was going to be the last time and it was…

Now we were both at home and using again…which meant that Preacher was back too and forcing me out of my own house once more. However, this time around, I had no car so I couldn't leave. Instead, I either stayed in my own car for hours on end, only wandering outside when I needed to use the bathroom, or I walked around in the nearby woods until I got bored. After Preacher would get a good buzz and Vanessa had a chance to cook up enough rocks to sneak them out to me, she would execute a brilliant plan. She would take the dog out for a walk near my truck and give me a signal somehow to let me know when she was ready for me to roll down the window. She would then drop a container full of rocks and a couple of pipes into my seat before returning inside. It worked like a charm for the most part, except for the fact that I nearly froze to death several times waiting for her in sub-freezing temperatures.

Outside was where the real paranoia took a hold of me. The first drag would sharpen my senses so much that I could hear everything from branches and leaves falling from trees a great distance away, to small animals lightly scurrying across the ground. I also spent a great deal of time staring back at the road, thinking about how there was only one way in and one way out. If the cops ever came up to the trailer, we were trapped without any means of escape. I was usually a nervous wreck until I saw the sun coming up and heard Preacher's car leaving the next morning. I would then go inside and not question what went on overnight. We would always party until the sun was going back down again… then repeat the whole process again.

Thanks to a spying neighbour, the landlord and Vanessa's stepmother found out that Preacher was back in Vanessa's life again and tried to intervene. The wicked stepmother even came by the house once while Preacher was there. I just happened to be taking a piss behind the house when I saw her car coming up the hill towards the house. I managed to crawl under the deck just in the nick of time to avoid being seen, and watched in horror as she stomped right above my head and began pounding on the door, yelling out many threats and obscenities. Of course, no one answered the door and she ended up leaving in a fit of rage. At least her appearance cut the party short and kept Preacher away from the house for a few days.

She would return a few days later with the landlord, when I was home alone, and managed to talk her way into the house. They sat me down and tried to convince me that Vanessa was corrupting and manipulating me, and that I would be better off without her in my life. They also claimed that

Vanessa was sleeping with Preacher, as well as some of her "regular" customers, right under my nose but I was too blind to see it. It was just odd how they saw me as the victim, and Vanessa as the root of all evil, but I have to admit that some of the things that they told me was starting to make a lot of sense whether I wanted to admit it or not. A couple of hours later, Vanessa turned up unaware that right behind her was her stepmother *and* her father. They tore into her verbally as I stood there like a scarecrow, not knowing what to say. Vanessa's dad offered to help me any way he could to get home if that was what I wanted to do while Vanessa was pleading with me to get into her car. Part of me wanted to take him up on his offer, but I chose to leave with Vanessa and spend the night at a hotel downtown, having sex and getting stoned.

When we felt like things had cooled off enough to go back to the trailer, we returned. A couple of hours later, my mother rings me up and invites me to a family reunion the following day. I tried to get out of it by claiming that I didn't have enough money to get back to Maryville but my parents were willing to drive up to Johnson City to give me enough money to fund my trip both ways. I agreed to meet them in the parking lot of a local grocery store, instead of the trailer, since Vanessa was cooking up a large amount of dope in the kitchen and the house was fucking wrecked.

They were both shocked and perhaps even horrified by my appearance that day. I had lost nearly 80lbs since they last saw me. I stunk from the toxins coming out in my sweat and my hair was short for the first time in nearly two decades because Vanessa wanted it that way. I was so high that I couldn't really make eye contact and tried to get it all over and done with as quickly as possible so I could get another fix. I was so sick and frail that

I could no longer hide it so I didn't even try anymore. I was a true junkie in every sense of the word now, and was beyond help. I was ready to die because this world had made me nothing more than a worthless piece of shit. I wouldn't attend that reunion the following day. I was too busy getting stoned with the money that my parents brought to me.

11

Over the next couple of months, we learned a lot about each other sexually. Although we always had a healthy sexual relationship, if nothing else, we really hadn't opened up about our fantasies and preferences. Vanessa had always teased me by calling me a "man-whore" but when we sat down one night and listed all of our sexual partners, her list was three times as long as mine. There were both men and women on there and it even included relatives of our shady landlord which disgusted me. But that was only the beginning…

She also introduced me to a different, kinkier side of her personality. She loved to be spanked and I'm not talking about love taps either. She wanted me to hit her ass until it turned beet red and had welts rising on her skin. I was never comfortable with doing this because it seemed almost abusive but she insisted and at times even begged for it. Add that to pulling her hair and calling her a "dirty slut" and we had a party. She did, however, take me to levels of sensitivity and ecstasy that can never be matched by anyone without certain substances being included. She would put on some porn to get me in the right frame of mind as she made the rocks and then let me take the first hit while she went down on me. I've never felt anything like the pleasure and sensations that she gave me. It was almost like she knew my body better than I did. She ruined it for everyone else who came after her by setting the bar so high. I was never the same again...

Despite how great we were in bed, we knew that our relationship was built on sex and co-dependency, and that we were only still together out of habit, so we agreed to call it quits. She had been bitter and resentful toward me ever since I accidently dented her car by reversing into a pole at her mother's house. She never really got over that and threw it in my face almost daily. Our living conditions had also become so poor that we were practically homeless, often having to stay in hotels just to feel clean. Over time, I had left some pretty disgusting things buried in the yard and even hung bags of my own excrement in the trees to make a statement for them turning off our water. The day eventually came when we just couldn't live like that any longer. Overall, I considered the whole relationship an epic fail and a complete waste of time that probably took several years off my life.

Vanessa's immediate plan was to move in with her mother, which basically meant that we could no longer live under the same roof even if we wanted to. I was broke and didn't even have the money to call a locksmith to make me a key, so I was stuck with nowhere to go. Vanessa ended up loaning me the money for the key and all I could do was pray that the battery had enough charge left to at least start the engine. I got lucky and it turned over right away. I then packed up all my things and hit the road before the sky opened up and dumped heavy rains on the valley. I took one last look in the mirror at what I was leaving behind and all I saw were those bags of feces swaying in the wind. I had a brief chuckle.

-DJN

CHAPTER XIX - "CHANT OF THE WANDERER"

2004

When I touched down in Knoxville, the first thing I did was give Kate a call. Instead of a simple yes or no answer about providing me a place to stay and finally trying to have a relationship, she gave me a heartfelt, somewhat inspirational speech that lasted nearly 30 minutes, about what she had been doing with her life and her plans for the future. What I gathered from it all, was that she didn't want me in it anymore. That ship had sailed and I missed it. Since I was only a couple of minutes from Tommy's house, I thought I would try to go back there. Unfortunately, no one was home so instead of waiting around, I went on to my next stop: the Last Chance.

When I got to the club, I saw Mark and a couple of the girls getting out of their cars. Mark had to do a double take to recognize me and then one of the girls started to piece it all together. "Denny?" she asked. "What happened to you? Your hair is gone and you've lost so much weight." I foolishly played along, pretending that I still had my confidence. "Well, is it an improvement?" I asked, although I already knew the answer. I don't actually recall what the girl said but it didn't exactly boost my ego from what I remembered. I did, however, appreciate her honesty. Mark turned to me and asked what happened with Vanessa, and did I need anything, so I swallowed my pride and said, "If you can spare a little cash, it would help a lot." He handed me a $100 bill, which I would spend on dope later that night.

I went inside and took a seat at the bar directly in front of the stage. Girl after girl went on stage, looked right at me and didn't acknowledge me at all. I didn't understand why I was getting the cold shoulder until Blaze was up and stopped in the middle of her routine to say "Oh my God! That's Denny!" I then heard a couple of the other girls, who were sitting with customers, yell back "No it's not! That guy does resemble him somewhat but that can't be him." It wasn't until I nodded my head and flashed that trademark smile that they believed her. I was, at this time, so sick that even girls who had been intimate with me before didn't even know who I was. I could have stood in a police line-up and they would swear that I was an imposter and not the real thing. I had become nothing more than a Big Lots version of my old self. I left both embarrassed and ashamed of myself, and wouldn't return for several years.

    Something wicked this way comes… taunt me with visions, haunt me with apparitions, as I collect keepsakes from my loved ones. I'm coming home, if I can remember the way. Life has dealt me some bad hands, but I have one more card to play.
    Back from my hiatus, I have flown the coop and been thrown for a loop, once a virtual unknown and now I'm the shit. From the outhouse to the penthouse, now I shake hands with the crowd, even kiss the babies… I guess you can say I've mellowed a bit.
    The clock seems to tick faster, and every year gets shorter. Mother, don't you recognize your own handiwork? Father thinks that I am a waste of sperm, building from the ground up a life on my own terms. Mirror Mirror…My reflection has never looked clearer…who is the man I see looking back at me? It seems like only yesterday they were rocking my cradle and changing my diapers. Oh,

how I've grown to hate those same people, no longer helping the weak and feeble. Mirror Mirror on the wall, I've seen and done it all… just finish my life and watch me fall.

Every dog has his day, every son of a bitch…

Forget my past, erase those memories, can you please make them fade away? Forget my past, erase what used to be, can you ease the burden I carry every day? "Never expect a handout, just look for a start, and don't wait too long to say what's in your heart."

Tonight a boy becomes a man…

Almost as if rehearsed, and only for me, the same sad scene replays, "Live for the moment, and make each one count," she used to say, "For the future is filled with uncertainties." "Someday, when your skin is like parchment, and your hair is thin and grey, you will wish you had stopped and noticed the scenery."

My life has been a disaster of biblical proportions, bet it makes you wish you had an abortion, and for that you have incurred my wrath. Forced onto me your religion, when only my journey was written, not the destination… I've embraced many sins, learned to sail in all winds, yet you still try to stand in my path.

I am a product of sex, drugs, and violence…sad but true. God will judge me one day, but not you. So what if I chose not to live the way I was raised? It's too late now to kneel beside you and pray… I've been down for years, holding my ticket to nowhere, still haunted by your ghost, the spectre of failure and despair. My American Dream has turned into a grisly nightmare…

Tossed aside like a sack of unwanted kittens, I'm so tired of being of being a talk show punchline or tabloid staple. Now that I've fallen off the planet, like a wretched tree that beared such ugly fruit, I'm

holding you all accountable...
-Denny Noland "Draven" From my song "The Homecoming"
Written in 2000
Copyright 2016

    I arrived at my parents' house early the next morning. My mother insisted that I take a shower immediately because I wore a foul stench that smelled like a combination of toxins and dog that I had grown used to and never really noticed. She even rewashed all of my "clean" clothes and disinfected them before she put them away. It was obvious that she was trying to get rid of any remnants of Vanessa and everything that came along with her. She then went into the kitchen and made me the first hot meal I've had in months. Although my stomach couldn't handle it, it reminded me to appreciate the little things in life that most take for granted. It changed my outlook on life from then on.
    With the weekend just around the corner, my parents were in a dilemma. They had grown accustomed to going camping and were obviously concerned about leaving me at the house alone...especially my dad. He didn't trust me at all. I was insulted when he told me that he thought I was capable of stealing some of their personal belongings in exchange for money or dope. I had never taken anything from either of them without asking in my entire life. Eventually, I talked them into going and gave them my word that the house was going to look exactly the same when they returned, but I can assure all of you that it was probably one of the least relaxing trips they had ever taken.

2

Although our relationship was supposably over, I was still receiving calls from Vanessa at home... almost on a daily basis. She had a plan for us to be together and it involved her moving to Knoxville and working at the West Club. I really just wanted her to go away but every time I heard her voice, all those feelings came back. She was staying at a hotel in the city and that was where I would start freebasing again. What made it unbearable was that wherever Vanessa was, Preacher wasn't too far behind. Now I was back in that same situation a third time, only now it was on my own turf, which made it even worse. Needless to say, she never made it to work and although we were being intimate again and claiming each other as our own, something had changed between us. Affection wasn't given as freely as it once was. It was more forced and often felt unwanted or even burdensome. Sometimes I wondered why we were even trying.

On the day that we were supposed to move all of her stuff, a few things happened that could only be called "divine intervention." An argument ensued where she told me that the dog meant more to her than I did, and she reminded me of how she had to get her brothers to do repairs and services because I didn't know how to do anything. I was so angry that I wanted to leave both her and her dog standing on the side of the road. But I wouldn't have to. As we were pulling into a restaurant to have a feed, the gas petal on my truck malfunctioned leaving us stranded around Jonesborough. I had to get a tow to the closest Ford dealership which just happened to be the next exit down the highway. I got grossly overcharged for my trouble after being told that the driver was quite reasonable with his prices. I had no choice but to pay the guy what he wanted. I was then told some other terrible news: they didn't have the part they needed to repair my truck, so they would have to order it. This would take a couple of days, meaning that Vanessa and I were going to have to get a hotel room. The expenses kept piling up as did the tension between us. By the time my truck was roadworthy again, we weren't even speaking to each other anymore. I took Vanessa back to Johnson City and that was that. It was over...for the last time, as far as I was concerned anyway.

Now I was searching for a job again. Even if I wasn't focused on doing so, my parents were constantly reminding me. I got hired at a franchised grocery store to work as a cashier in the fuel center and only lasted a couple of days before I quit out of boredom. The only perks of the job was the cute girls from Maryville College that came in from time to time. Once or twice, a girl would lock eyes with me, then blush and giggle, which created an uncomfortable situation for me. I knew that I was going to be teased once the parking lot was empty and I was. If working in a shoebox is your thing, then this job is for you. I'm too claustrophobic for that shit myself.

Then I tried to get my job back at the restaurant, and although they considered me to be an incredible worker, my reliability costed me the job. They did, however, have an opening in the kitchen at one of their new locations in West Knoxville, so I took the job. I think I made it through one shift before I left due to a lack of communication. Most of the employees there were Mexican, and couldn't speak a word of English. I just couldn't see myself playing Pictionary every night just to get my point across.

The following day, I turned in applications all over Maryville. When I went into a store I affectionately called "the FC," they were interested right away, due to the fact that I had worked for one of their competitors, not once but twice. They asked me a series of questions before letting me go and told me that they would be in touch. I literally had just walked into my parents' house, when the phone rang. It was the store manager asking if I would like to start that night. I ate some dinner and went straight to bed because it was going to be a long day indeed.

When I met my team later that night, I saw a familiar face. It was Rico, the guy who bought my trailer. He was a legend in that place, breaking records on speed and efficiency. He was so well known and respected that other stores knew about him. He was simply the best...hands down. The rest of my team was nothing more than a circus act. We had one guy who was obsessed with fat women and the pet aisle. We caught him eating dog food one night and he resigned soon after. We had another scrawny dude who asked me one night if I had my tickets yet. I just looked at him, completely puzzled, and asked "Tickets to what?" He rolled up his sleeves and flexed his miniature biceps. "To the gun show baby!" he screamed. I was almost rolling on the floor, especially since he was being serious. Gun Show was his new name after that, as I started giving all the losers nicknames, mostly because I couldn't remember their real ones.

Gun Show was quite eccentric to say the least. He was dating a much older woman and claimed to be in the Navy. He said to me one day "You can ask me anything except for how many people I've killed...I don't want to talk about it." This guy had supposably seen so much combat and wasn't even old enough to buy alcohol. He was always so sincere about everything, which made it sound believable, no matter how farfetched what he was telling me actually was. I can remember the night his girlfriend left him for another man, who she had been cheating on him with from the beginning. He was so devastated that he was crying out on the sales floor and playing Breaking Benjamin's "So Cold" over and over until I went from liking the song to almost hating it. With him claiming to be either a national hero or a national treasure, she must the dumbest woman alive to dump such a celebrity. I should have been honoured to be working beside him every night.

    Our manager "Chandler" and his assistant "Charles" rounded out our team. Chandler was probably the one I had the most in common with. We were both long haired hoodlums, who liked metal music and horror films, and had a fascination with the paranormal. He also had a thing for overweight chicks, but he preferred his pale as a dead whore, and into the occult. His wife was a prime example of this. She claimed to be a Pagan with magical powers, who was also borderline manic depressive. Many times I would go over to Chandler's house to play video games after work and I rarely saw her. She was always locked in her room. When she would come out, she barely said anything to anyone, including Chandler. She was a special girl indeed…

    Charles, on the other hand, couldn't have been more different if he tried. He was a 30+ year old divorcee living at home with his mother and stepfather. He was just an average guy scorned by a failed marriage and forking out a large chunk of his pay every week for child support. He was a great guy but was the one you had to keep an eye on. If you got on his bad side, he would use his seniority and influence to get rid of you. Other than that, I had nothing but great things to say about him.

There were, however, more familiar faces around the store. My estranged sister was working in the bakery with one of my least favourite cousins. We were on opposite schedules so we seldom crossed paths, but when we did, I made sure that our conversations were brief. The FC had strict rules about family working together so I wanted to keep it all quiet, but unfortunately, my sister doesn't know how to keep her mouth closed. She never did. Within a couple of weeks, everyone except for the store manager knew that we were all related, despite the fact that we all had separate surnames. I really liked my job, and the people I worked with, but was constantly living in fear of the wrong people finding out, and it costing me my job.

One night, the refrigeration went down, so Chandler and one of the female office managers had to pull out all of the stock out before it went off. Although the girl appeared to be much younger than me, there was just something about her that caught my attention. As soon as I could get Chandler alone, I began asking him a lot of questions about her. I found out that her name was "Courtney" and she was only 20 years old, which meant that there was a 12 year age difference between us. I was also told some other disheartening news: she not only had a boyfriend, but he worked at the store as well. That was enough to make me start second guessing myself, at least for a little while that is. Besides, no matter how far I had come to piece my life back together, I was still a drug addict at the end of the day. I didn't want to drag anyone in that mess...

When I would bump into my sister on those rare occasions, she would tell me about a different girl who was interested in me. Her name was "Rebecca" and she worked in the seafood department. It was weird, because when I would talk to her, she was always trying to fix me up with an older woman in her department that was apparently quite wealthy, and was only working there to "meet interesting people." After careful consideration, I rejected the cougar's offer and decided to cast my line back out there to see who bites.

    As part of the healing process, I was back in the gym within a week with my new training partner and spotter Rico. I called it "building the perfect beast" as I worked harder than I ever had to get back in shape. I was literally growing stronger at a much more rapid pace than any other time in my life. My maximum bench press was increasing at least 10lbs per week, and I was already seeing positive results on my body. It was also nice to stay at my old trailer every now and then, which had been renovated somewhat over the past couple of years by Rico, instead of going to my parents' house. Sometimes I even slept in my old bedroom. It was almost as if I had a second chance to redeem myself by going back in time. The good that this all did for me cannot even be put into words...

<u>3</u>

    Just when everything started heading in the right direction, Vanessa would surface again. She was calling me at all hours of the day, just like before, except now it was both at home and at work, practically begging me to come up to Johnson City to spend the night with her. She used every weapon in her arsenal to lure me back in, including reminding me of all the great sex we used to have, and how her award winning dope, which she had a seemingly endless supply of, used to make me feel. The only excuse I could think of for turning her down was that I didn't have enough money to make the trip. She would counter by offering to give me some money if I would just show up. It took everything I had to maintain the willpower to resist her charms. She knew me like no other but obviously not well enough.

The last two phone calls I ever received from Vanessa sent chills down my spine. I had been avoiding her by having either Rico or Rebecca answer the phone and tell her that either I wasn't there or just wasn't unavailable, but she tricked them once by telling them that it was an emergency. My hands were literally shaking because I suspected that she could be pregnant. It was a false alarm as she just used that because she knew that I would pick up the phone if I thought something was wrong. Nothing she could really do would surprise me…or so I thought.

For some reason, I took her call that night. The first thing out of her mouth was "I think I might have got raped last night." Her voice had very little concern in it, unlike what you would expect to hear from someone who had just been sexually assaulted. "And I think the guy stole my car" she added. I was overwhelmed and confused due to her passive delivery. "The guy was a friend of my ex-husband. He had been coming on to me all night, sometimes forcefully. I woke up this morning lying naked on the bed and my car was gone. I don't remember anything else. Maybe he slipped something in my drink." My first reaction was anger, then profound sadness, as she changed the subject by telling me how she thought the FBI was watching her at all times. She even thought that they were outside her door listening in on our current conversation. She told me that she still loved me and blamed herself for our failed relationship, then proceeded to ask me for money since I put a dent in her car a few months back. I didn't have to, but I immediately wired her the money to avoid a lengthy argument. I knew what she really wanted the money for because I had heard the same guilt trip used on Herb, and other clients in the past, when she was desperate to buy more dope. It was my way of having closure and moving on with my life. She called me about an hour later and verified that she had received the cash. The last thing she said to me was "Oh my God! They are trying to get in!" then she was gone. I didn't know what was going on and I didn't want to know either. I was just happy to be free again.

4

(UPDATE: After years of speculating about whether Vanessa was either dead or in prison, I would get my answer in 2015. I found her brother on Facebook and sent him a friend request. He accepted and told me that Vanessa only got worse after we broke up, and had even served a little time. She was, in fact, in jail when we had that conversation but was getting out in a couple of weeks. I asked if he would put me in touch with her as soon as she was released. He must have kept his word because she turned up on Facebook when she got out and sent me a friend request a few days later. We didn't exactly have what you would call a long, elaborate conversation, but I did let her know that I tried my best to make it work between us and she responded back that she was fully aware of that and it was all her fault. She has since found God and a new man in her life and is still, as of this writing, beating her addictions. I told her about my sobriety and made her promise that before she gives in to her cravings, to please talk to me first. So far, I haven't heard from her. I hope she knows how proud of her I am...)

-DJN

CHAPTER XX - *"A PRAYER FOR THE DYING"*

2004-2005

Shortly after I started at the store, Chandler was demoted and replaced by an older gentleman named "Henry," who was on the verge of retirement and could smoke weed with the best of them. I could always smell it on his clothes and see it in his eyes every night when he came in, which made me feel sick. I had developed allergic reactions to marijuana while I was with Vanessa, nearly landing myself in the hospital on more than one occasion. At best, it caused severe vomiting, even worse than a case of food poisoning. For that reason alone, I tried to keep my distance to avoid any exposure.

Henry and I didn't get along at first...and we butted heads for the next couple of years about almost everything, but overall, he was a great manager. I didn't see it until he was gone and my regime started. He always kept the store managers off our backs, and had enough pull to tell *them* how it was going to be instead of the other way around. We only faced his wrath yet were oblivious to everyone else's. Since he was handpicked by our main manager, he got his way a majority of the time just out of pride alone.

Strangely enough, I actually enjoyed working at the FC, and dreaded my days off. Living under my parents' roof and following their rules when I was over 30 years old, having already been through two failed marriages, was no fun at all. I was bored to tears with the environment and getting very little sleep working the graveyard shift due to Mom's daily cleaning routine. I started spending my nights off at Micheal's, so I could get high and have a few drinks while trying to maintain some kind of social life. One night I ran into Jake and his entourage and he bought me a drink as we discussed how many strippers we had slept with over the years. The difference was that his numbers were still rising while I fell out of the game. Sex, to me at least, had become an unnecessary evil. Cocaine, on the other hand, was something I felt like I couldn't live without. I didn't usually leave Micheal's until the doors closed and then I would find myself in some alley somewhere, finishing off my nightly stash. I would usually head home the next morning, after dad had left for work, and try to sleep it off while my mind was replaying something or someone from my so called "glory days" that now seemed to be a lifetime ago. I hated my life and prayed for answers for what I should be doing next to get my independence back. Despite how bad things were with Vanessa, I was happier with her than where my life was going without her.

2

I had become a passionate Boston Red Sox fan after watching them fall to the New York Yankees in the 2003 ALCS. Now they were in the playoffs again and facing the rival Yankees. I literally watched every Red Sox game at Micheal's while under the influence of cocaine and alcohol. I was ecstatic when they made their historic comeback in that series against the Yankees and won their first championship in over eight decades. With baseball season over, I had nothing to distract me from my growing depression. I started getting lonely again but had no idea how to talk to a "normal" woman anymore because I had spent the last decade dating only strippers. I wasted many hours in the garage, just listening to music and reliving the past, afraid that I would never adapt to life outside the club.

Meanwhile, at the store, we lost Gun Show to a broken heart and the other guy went to another store, leaving two openings. Rebecca ended up transferring from the seafood department to our crew, much to both Rico and Charles's delight, and they brought back some idiot who claimed to be "Twisted steel and sex appeal" that had been on workers comp for the past year due to a back injury. Twisted Steel, as he would be known, was put on light duty at first to see his limitations before adding him back to the team. He had his nose so far up Charles's ass that he could have told you what he had for lunch in an effort to replace me and take my spot. It would only take me a couple of weeks to do something that pissed Charles off enough to endorse him.

It was common knowledge that Charles and Rebecca had been out on date months prior, and it wasn't exactly a pleasant experience for either, so as far as I was concerned, she was readily available. I jokingly asked her one night if she wanted to go up on the roof and make out and she responded back with "OK" so while we were in the back alone together, I puckered up and leaned in for either a kiss or a slap. She met me half way and we shared a great kiss, followed soon after by another. That was all there was until I made the mistake of calling her a couple of weeks later, while I was staying at a seedy hotel with a serious boner, after coming down off drugs and alcohol. No matter how hard I tried to get her up to my room that night, she wasn't budging. What I didn't know was that she had put our entire conversation on speakerphone because she had developed a mutual crush on Rico and didn't want him thinking that we had something going on. By the time I came back to work the following day, I was nothing more than a joke...with a target on my back. Charles tried to rally the troops to turn against me and vote me off the island so Twisted Steel could step right in, but no one would join his cause. All he got was a warning from upper management to let it go or else, because I wasn't going anywhere. About a week later, we were on a skeleton crew so Henry asked Twisted Steel to help us out. About an hour into it, he grabbed his back and went back on worker's comp again...just as he wanted. This just made Charles look like the fool instead of me. Within a couple of months, Henry got Rico a better job and he left. He married Rebecca soon after and they had a child together. They are still happily married to this day.

Now we had two spots to fill again. They hired a tall slender guy from Boston who was covered in tattoos and looked like the love child of AC/DC's Brian Johnson and Marilyn Manson. His name was "Pauly" and he was a self-professed conman and thief who claimed to have links to the Mafia. He was a good worker when he wanted to be or when it was convenient to do so, but often times he was a little on the lazy side. He made it clear that he wanted to be the boss from the moment he walked through the door, and thought he could talk his way to the top. There was only one thing standing in his way: me.

The second spot was filled by a young kid named "Rhett," who liked to race go-karts and believed that someone from Nascar was going to watch him compete one day and sign him a contract. He was a hard worker...when he bothered to show up that is. He was as reliable as I used to be at the restaurant and that wasn't good. He, like Twisted Steel before him, followed Charles around like a lost puppy. He was constantly trying to impress him, almost as if he actually looked up at Charles like a big brother. I would have my problems with both of the new guys in the year to come.

3

Despite all the obstacles that stood in the way, I finally asked Chandler to talk to Courtney for me. To my surprise, he informed me that she was interested in me too and wanted to get to know me better, so a few nights later, we went on a little drive. She took me down Highway 129 toward Chilhowee Lake where I used to take Salena many years ago. We held hands the entire way until we reached a deli/motorcycle repair shop that I've passed so many times in the past. Ironically, her aunt and uncle owned the joint and she worked there on the weekends for extra money… meaning that she was not only a student, but she worked two jobs as well. I didn't know how she even had time to have a relationship, to be honest, but that wasn't going to stop me.

We must have talked for the better part of an hour. As always, I was completely honest with her about everything. I told her about my addictions, my once promiscuous lifestyle, even how I felt about marriage and kids. She told me about how she wasn't happy in her relationship anymore but didn't know how to break it off. I told her that I didn't like sneaking around behind his back, so when she figured it all out, let me know. Until then, I didn't want to see her again. I've been down that road too many times in the past and I wasn't about to do it again. We shared a brief but tender kiss before she dropped me back off at the store.

It took about a week or two, but she did eventually dump her boyfriend of four years for me. I had to hear their arguments over the phone, but chose to stay out of it. He did confront me one night, not to fight mind you, but to verify that Courtney and I were, in fact, seeing each other. He asked me to be good to her, which was quite ironic considering that she told me that he had sexually assaulted her before. It was awkward for a few weeks there since we all worked together, especially when he started bringing his new girlfriend in to fuck with Courtney's head. He did eventually leave the store and all was well.

    Now we were attached at the hip and finally a genuine couple. We had only been together a couple of days when she called from some bar, drunk off her ass, wanting me to take her home. I was asleep at the time and had to be at work in a couple of hours, so I was already thinking that I had made a terrible mistake. I had to get Rico to drive me to the bar so I could drive her car back which was embarrassing enough, but her behaviour once we got back to his place was the icing on the cake. She was stumbling and falling all over his furniture… while finding the whole experience hilarious. I was already furious for a number of reasons. When I got to the bar, the skank that she was with tried to convince me that she was ok to drive when she couldn't even walk. Besides that, the bartender was serving Courtney alcohol, fulling aware that she was underage. I told her on the way to her parents' place that if she ever pulled a stunt like that again, we were over.

    To make matters worse, when I got her home, she kept trying to get me to come inside so she could seduce me. Her parents were home and I had yet to meet them, not to mention I wanted her to remember our first time together, so I took a raincheck. I wouldn't have to wait long though. That weekend, while my parents were gone camping, I broke a promise to my parents by making love to

Courtney on *their* bed. She would also lie to *her* parents a couple of days later, when she told them that she was staying at a friend's house, when we were actually in Pigeon Forge having sex in a four star hotel.

All of this deceit had helped Courtney decide that it was probably time to meet the parents. I met her father at a gas station one day while we were filling up the truck and he shook my hand while looking at me like he wanted to tear me apart. He reminded me of "Dale" from "King of the Hill." He always had the trademark cap on his head and a cigarette sticking out of his mouth. He was a retired military sergeant who was also an alcoholic. He didn't trust the government. He watched CNN religiously and had a vast collection of guns for when "the shit hit the fan." Most people were scared of him because of his mood swings and unpredictability when he had been drinking, but I always felt comfortable around him.

Her mother was also military yet more down to earth. She had a very sarcastic and pessimistic personality, much like Courtney, as the acorn didn't fall far from the tree… in this case anyway. Courtney's brother was one of the brightest kids I've ever seen for his age. He was absolutely brilliant, except for when it came to drugs and women. They were his weakness and downfall. Overall, I liked her family very much. They were good people, despite their flaws. I would spend a great deal of time with each of them in the future.

When it came to visiting the family, time wasn't exactly divided equally. When we were visiting her family, it was always an all-day affair. I would often have to take a nap in Courtney's room, and even when I woke up several hours later, she *still* wouldn't be ready to leave yet. For instance, we attended a party there one night before I needed to go to work. We arrived early, so I crashed in Courtney's bed until I was awakened by the sounds of gunshots and fireworks. I exited the bedroom into a house filled with total strangers, except for Courtney's drunken dad, who had a young black kid pinned down in a chair in front of a large group of frightened spectators, telling him how it didn't matter what colour he was, he would always be considered family. I walked outside and couldn't find Courtney anywhere in the darkness. About an hour later, she finally turned up, but only momentarily, before she vanished again. I ended up leaving without saying goodbye because I didn't have time to look for her. That was not how I wanted to end the night.

 It was just the opposite when we went to see my folks. Courtney was content for about fifteen minutes before she started throwing little hints through body language that she was bored and wanted to leave. This would usually result in an argument right in front of my parents that carried over to the drive home. She wasn't too keen on talking otherwise, which annoyed the hell out of me. I would eventually just give up and start going over there alone so I didn't feel rushed. Unfortunately, I still had to go over with her once a week to see her family regardless.

4

 It was getting close to Christmas when my dad gave me an ultimatum. He said, "I think that it's time for you to leave. We have given you plenty of time to save up enough money to find your own place so you need to start looking." The following day, I did just that…and I found a place. It was in the same trailer park where my old trailer still sat occupied by Rico and Rebecca. Although I never liked trailers, especially in high winds, due to their tendency to shake and even shift, this one was an upgrade. It had two bathrooms and a huge washroom, unlike my old trailer, and had obviously been very well kept by the previous tenants. Had it not been all that it was, I probably would have still taken it just to get away from my parents.

    We never discussed it or anything but Courtney gradually moved in with me over time. Our place was decorated just the way I wanted. There were Halloween decorations everywhere and the entire trailer was illuminated by flashing rope lights much like the club. I can't say whether that was done intentionally or was just a coincidence because my brain was all over the place at the time. I also uncharacteristically kept the place virtually spotless, even though all of our furniture was second hand. As a housewarming gift, my landlord gave me my old coffee table back from the original trailer. He had found it sitting at the bin after Rico moved in and decided to keep it for some reason. It's no surprise how quickly you learn to appreciate the little things more, when everything you had left would fit into a couple of garbage bags not so long ago.

    After the move was complete, we were invited by a couple of friends to Dollywood to see the Christmas lights. Foolishly, I didn't check the weather forecast, nor did I take into consideration the significant contrast in temperature between where we were and the higher elevations... especially after the sun went down. Of course, I was severely underdressed, despite warnings from Courtney and her friends to put on extra layers. I knew I was in trouble when we got there and the clerks were advising me to buy clothes instead of souvenirs. We all nearly froze to death that night as the temperature reached below freezing. The lights were indeed beautiful but not worth fighting the elements to see them. The worst part was that, as usual, I had to go to work afterwards. I couldn't stop shivering the entire night…even in the warmth of the store! I had just recently gotten over the flu, which I had willingly exposed myself to by insisting that Courtney make out with me while she was sick and obviously running a fever. I didn't want to go through all of that again, especially this soon, but luckily I thawed out the next day with no lingering effects.

5

Due to Courtney and me loving animals as much as we did, I decided to get another cat. I picked a black cat from the local pet shop and named him "Azreal." From day one, that darn cat had a bad attitude. He hated everyone, including me, the hand that fed him. At least he hated me less than everyone else it would seem. A couple of weeks later, I was awakened by loud purring and little paws crawling up my chest toward my face. Courtney had brought home a second kitten that I would name "Gabriel." He had a completely different personality than Azreal, and would become my pride and joy, my little shadow, for years to come.

However, this was also a time of great tragedy, as I would lose both my last living grandmother and my uncle Jay within days of each other. My grandmother was expected, because she had been bedridden for months and had stopped eating, but Jay, on the other hand, no one saw coming. From what I've been told, he woke up that day feeling great…so great in fact that he worked all day in his garage as he normally would. Things took a darker turn when he came in for supper, and was complaining about pain in his chest. He told my aunt that he thought he had pulled a muscle or something, and that he was going to take a shower to see if that helped, while she was putting the finishing touches on supper. My aunt heard the water turn on...followed by a loud thud. When she went to check on him, she found him lying on the bathroom floor. He took one final breath... then he was gone. The doctors told her later on that Jay's heart literally "exploded." Even if it had happened at the hospital, there would have been nothing that they could have done. I took both deaths pretty hard, but Courtney never left my side. She was there for me every step of the way.

6

Although Courtney knew that I was an addict, she never saw me high. I did everything behind her back to keep her in the dark and she never asked...probably because she didn't want to know whether I was still using or not. It took only one slip up to change all of that. I voluntarily took her to work one night, in *her* truck, and was supposed to pick her back up eight hours later. I took a right out of the parking lot, instead of a left, and found myself at Micheal's about an hour later. I bought two grams of cocaine and went back home. I got really messed up, really fast, and started writing terrible songs as I watched the clock closely. Before I knew it, my time was nearly up and I still had cocaine left. I used the severe thunderstorm that had blown in as an excuse to delay picking her up and buy me some time to finish it off. I did about a half of a gram of cocaine in the next ten minutes or so, then headed out on the slippery roads, thinking that I was going to be a master of disguise and keep her from finding out.

It didn't quite work out the way I planned. I was so jacked up that my hands were trembling, my voice was shaky, and my eyes look like an owl's. She knew something was up as soon as she got into the truck. I had never lied to her and I wasn't about to start now. I admitted to what she already knew and prepared for the worst. She surprised me though. There was no yelling or lecturing... only a look of disappointment and obvious concern about whether she should put her life into my hands in my current condition. No one had ever taken this approach with me before, so I didn't really know how to react to it. I was used to anger and criticism, and usually responded by doing even more drugs out of spite. But something strange and different was happening on this night: I was actually feeling bad about what I did! It had been such a long time since remorse was even a word in my vocabulary.

When we got home, Courtney said to me, "If you have any more of that stuff, we'll do it together and be rid of it." I told her that there was nothing left but I was craving more. She pulled out a deck of cards and poured me a cold drink in an effort to distract me from thinking about it. Then I started crashing hard...feeling sick and irritated. She did everything in her power to keep me as calm and comfortable as possible until I eventually passed out cold. I woke the next morning feeling like an asshole for hurting her with my actions the night before. I felt like it was finally time to kick this addiction right in the balls before it killed me or someone I loved. It just wasn't fun anymore...

A wise man once said that you only have so many drinks in your life and when they are used up, the party's over. In my opinion, this applied to drugs as well. I hadn't been clean and sober in well over a decade and where has it gotten me? I've lost friends, lovers, houses, cars, and enough money to fund an early retirement. I was miserable...even if I had tricked myself into thinking that I was happy. Then there was this thing they call sleep. I hadn't slept longer than four hours at any time in fucking years. I was sick and tired of feeling sick and tired. I wanted to live for once before I died.

   I was craving cocaine more with every passing day, especially on my days off, when I had nothing to keep me preoccupied. I had no real hobbies anymore to distract me from thinking about doing what I had been doing in my spare time for such a long time. I felt like a werewolf who needed to be shackled and chained on the night of the full moon to keep from hurting someone. It was very touch and go for several weeks, as I fought to stay sober and resist temptation with everything I had. It was, arguably, the toughest battle I've ever fault. I was so very close on multiple occasions to cave in but by the grace of God, I didn't. Otherwise, I probably wouldn't be here today to tell the tale.

I'm the last of a dying breed, but I carry on a legacy...passed down to me...so ignore all the things you read, because I'm about to rewrite history.

   When the moon is full, I'm matted with blood, and bristling with dark fur. It's not really anything supernatural, merely the workings of nature.

   My nose to the wind and my ears folded back, I already feel the pressure. Into the grassy open pampas, I lift my hind leg...marking with a stream from my bladder.

   We are the aspects of many themes, with this ecological plight. We are the snarling dogs of God...we are the children of the night...
When you hear the howl, the pack is on the prowl...

We are the lunar deities that no one can exorcise. Last night, the moon dripped blood and the hills had eyes…

I'm the last of a dying species, I am lycan…lupine…it's in my bloodline, it runs in the family…I'm a scavenger of urine and feces, never knowing the precious vestige of humanity.

Always been an enigma, shrouded in mystery, with such stealth it becomes a cloak of invisibility, my curse eradicated, my face contorted, my belly lifted…my rib cage contracted, my throat constricted, my shape shifted…

Little Red Riding Hood, come sit in Granny's rocking chair. Oh, the sweetness of human meat, the menstrual blood, the soft of skin, the gloss of hair. They will discover her motionless form disembowelled in an alley, her body still warm… her blood still runny…

Restrain me with a spiked collar, and chain me to the wall…better heed my warning. Load your gun with silver bullets before the moon falls or you won't make it until morning. I don't feel alive until it gets dark, then wake up naked the next day on a bench in the park.

We appear normal in the day, but it's just a disguise…last night, the moon dripped blood and the hills had eyes…

 -Denny Noland "Draven" From my song "The Hills Have Eyes"
 Written in 1998-1999
Copyright 2016

Sleeping made everything even harder, as I was tormented by dreams, much like the one in the opening of this book. Sometimes, they were about my old girlfriends, often replaying a familiar scene with a number of different outcomes that were

usually much worse than what actually happened. Other times I dreamt of getting high, even waking myself up on several occasions, in total darkness, reaching for an invisible crack pipe. I felt everything as if it was real. I quickly realized that I needed a new hobby to take my mind off what I was going through, so I went back to something that interested me since I was a kid: the paranormal.
–DJN

CHAPTER XXI- *"SOMETIMES THEY COME BACK"*

2006-2007

With drugs finally out of my system, I focused on my new passion. It started out with just the three of us: myself, Chandler, and a mutual friend named "Ryan," who was game for pretty much anything. We would use everything from the internet to local urban legends to find supposably "haunted" locations to investigate every Sunday morning after work. One thing that we realized pretty quickly was that once you took out all of the listings that were either private property that was guarded by the police, which made them off limits, or buildings that have already been torn down, there weren't many places to visit anymore. What was supposed to last all summer was all but over only a few weeks in. We did, however, share a few bizarre and unexplainable experiences over such a short span.

We went to investigate an old abandoned church one day that had a history of satanic cult activity. There were stories on the internet of animal sacrifice and even a demonic presence that was supposably still lurking on the premises. When we got there, the only remnants that it ever existed was a pile of ash and rubble. We were still determined to get something out of the trip, so we got out our cameras and took photos of the ruins. Chandler and I had no problems at all, but Ryan, who had his dad's expensive camera, which looked like something you would see a Japanese tourist with, had a number of issues. He couldn't get it to focus at first and when he finally did and took a photo, the background had turned crimson red. When he got home and tried to upload it onto his computer, it crashed and he lost everything. Was there something in that picture that didn't want to be seen or was it just a simple camera malfunction? Who knows? In case you were wondering, nothing strange turned up in any of the photos that Chandler and I took unfortunately.

One of the strangest things that had ever happened to us during our investigations was when Chandler told us about a secluded graveyard that he had found in the middle of nowhere near Tellico Lake. He generated a lot of interest with the place when he claimed that there was a headstone of a young boy, who had only recently passed, that mysteriously drained his batteries every time he pointed a camera at it. I had heard of this occurring sometimes when a spirit is trying to manifest itself from watching shows like "Ghost Hunters" on TV but I still wasn't sold on it yet. Besides, Chandler had a tendency to "stretch the truth" from time to time. Ryan and I were intrigued enough though to ride out there with him with a pack of brand new batteries just in case.

The hike there was through a lot of heavy brush along a dirt trail until we reached a clearing where the graveyard was. The young boy's freshly dug grave sat right in the middle under a large oak tree. The first thing that caught my eye was the creepy photo of the boy on the headstone. It seemed to not only go out of focus the closer you would get to it through a camera lens, but it appeared to do the same with the naked eye. I watched with anticipation as Chandler tried to take a picture and couldn't. I then pointed my camera right at the headstone and the same thing happened. When I turned the camera on, I had a fully charged battery but as soon as I turned towards the boy's grave, the meter began flashing red and then shut off. I proceeded to reach into my pocket and pull out more batteries that had only been bought that morning, and they also went flat as soon as I tried to focus on the headstone. It took an entire pack of batteries just to get a couple of good shots! When we got back to the car, out of curiosity, I tested all the batteries and they not only worked, but they were still fully charged as they should have been. I didn't even know how to explain away what I had just seen.

It wasn't always so serious… there were other occasions where it was just downright comical. When we went to the "Bleeding Mausoleum" in Cleveland, Tennessee, we made the mistake of not being satisfied with just getting shots of the mausoleum, we wanted to get pictures of the church that it was connected to as well. None of us took into consideration that it was a Sunday morning and people were starting to pour in for the morning services around the time we got down there. Here we were…wearing heavy metal t-shirts and jeans, strolling around the yard taking photos like the paparazzi, and making as much noise as possible, whether intentional or not. We were getting a lot of stares and fingers being pointed at us but no one bothered to ask us to leave. This inspired Chandler to actually walk in to touch the signature book at the front door in an attempt to prove his manhood. We stood back and had a laugh until the preacher caught him in the act and we thought we were all in trouble. He simply asked us politely what we were doing there and I thought out some elaborate lie about how we were admirers and students of architecture and really appreciated the craftsmanship of old churches especially. He bought my story and spent about 20 minutes telling us about all the renovations that they've made to restore the building to its former glory. We were allowed to take as many pictures as we wanted while he sipped his coffee and waited for his congregation to arrive. I would abuse this privilege by spotting a very attractive young lady standing near the altar and focusing my attention on taking pictures of her instead of the church itself. Little did I know that the preacher was looking over my shoulder... fully aware of what I was doing. He never said anything but I did suggest that maybe we should leave before I got struck by lightning or something. The gang agreed.

With Ryan drifting out of the picture, Chandler and I started bringing our ladies along with us. The irony of that was that they didn't really like each other very much. Conversations in the car were usually only between Chandler and myself as if the girls weren't even there. Then there were those staring contests in the mirror between the girls that nearly caused a number of accidents. Eventually we just decided to leave them at home, and not long after that, we just stopped doing investigations together at all, but still remained friends.

As the summer heated up, ghost hunting took a backseat to just going to local tourist attractions with Courtney. We went everywhere from the Lost Sea to Dollywood to Ripley's Aquarium of the Smokies to Splash Country to Cades Cove. However, when September and October rolled around, I was back investigating the paranormal again. Courtney and I would stay at various "haunted" hotels overnight with the hope that we might share an experience together but nothing ever happened. That was until I got a room in the heart of Gatlinburg where someone had been murdered in many years ago.

When I asked the lady at the desk about the place actually being haunted, she reacted harshly. She got very defensive and told me to not "believe everything that I read on the internet." The way Courtney looked at me made me even angrier. In her eyes, I was out of line and shouldn't have asked such a ridiculous question. It was not a good way to start our night together and it got even worse when a group of rednecks checked into the room beside us. They were making so much noise that if something did happen in our room, we would have never heard it. It was a very frustrating night and I was starting to feel like it was a total waste of time.

    I woke up the next morning feeling cheated and very disappointed. Courtney quietly helped me pack the suitcases before loading the car. I told Courtney that I was going to do my usual walkabout around the room to make sure that we didn't leave anything behind. While I was in the bathroom, I heard a click and the static sound of the TV turning on, followed by the audio of whatever show was airing at the time. I thought nothing of it, just assuming that Courtney must have got tired of waiting and decided to watch TV. When I entered the room only a few seconds later, Courtney was nowhere to be seen. I looked out the window and saw her sitting patiently in the truck with the engine running downstairs. There was absolutely no way that she would have had time to have played a prank. Stranger still, the remote had been moved from where I had left it and was facing the opposite direction than the TV. There was no way to rationalize what I had just witnessed. I just had the experience that I was longing for, and it happened at the very last minute for only me to see.

2

    I wanted to go somewhere really cool for Halloween, so I booked a room for three days in Adams, Tennessee, so Courtney and I could investigate the infamous "Bell Witch" legend. For those of you who have never heard of her, there were a number of books written and films made about the story, most notable and recent was the film "An American Haunting" released back in 2005. When I heard that the land used to be ancient Indian burial ground, and the spirit of the Bell Witch was supposably living in a cave on the property, I couldn't wait to get there and start my investigation. Add the fact that the present owners had also restored the old cabin to look exactly as it did back in 1817-1821, even using some of the old wood from the original cabin, and I was like a child on Christmas morning. This was going to be the best way to celebrate the spirit of Halloween that I could afford on such short notice.

 We left Knoxville the day before Halloween, and reached Nashville a few hours later. Of course, we touched down at rush hour so traffic was a mess. I had to rely on Courtney to read the map and navigate which was always an adventure. When we reached a split in the road and I needed to know which way to go immediately, or we were going to be lost in the heart of Music City for what could be hours, she was uncertain and confused. She was saying that I should turn left but my gut was telling me to turn right, so at the last second, I swerved between two semis in a foolish and extremely dangerous move to follow my instincts. It may have turned out to be the right move but it led to a serious argument between Courtney and me. It was just another example of why we couldn't travel together.

 A couple of days before we started our vacation, a hard sneeze while I was lying down on the couch had my heart feeling out of rhythm. I even had numbness in my hands. I could have had a mild heart attack for all I knew and this constant bickering and arguing was causing me to have chest pains again. By the time we reached Adams, I wasn't feeling well at all. I never told Courtney about any of it, because I knew that with her being a nursing student, she would have probably cancelled the trip and had me admitted into the hospital instead. There was no way I was going to let that happen so I kept it all to myself.

Once we got settled into our room, we drove out to the location. There were people everywhere, preparing to take the cave tour. Everyone was excited but calm except for one lady who claimed to be a "sensitive." She was freaking out to everyone else's amusement, except for the children who were being frightened by this woman's antics. I found her to be more annoying and unnecessary than anything else. For all I know, she could have been planted there to put the crowd on edge before they entered the cave. If that was indeed the case, she did a horrible job. If anything, she made everyone take the tour less seriously by hurting its credibility with her ridiculous performance.

The tour itself was disappointing…with the exception of seeing the open grave of a Native American child sitting in one of the rooms within the cave. Obviously, not only was the ground above the cave ancient burial ground but *inside* the cave was as well. I also got a cool picture of a red lizard that was lurking inside with us but as far as seeing or feeling anything supernatural in nature, I had nothing. Courtney, however, was overcome with a feeling that we shouldn't be there, but after shelling out that much money and getting nothing in return, I was starting to feel the same way.

It was even more discouraging when we took the cabin tour. Although you were allowed to take pictures on the outside of the cabin, cameras weren't allowed inside because "flashes would damage the interior over time." Instead, we were forced to sit quietly and listen to a tape of the Bell

Witch story like a bunch of kids in a classroom. I would also go on to waste a large sum of money on t-shirts, books, and even a DVD with some of the cheapest sets and worst acting I had ever seen. I left with a bad taste in my mouth and felt like I had been ripped off overall.

Halloween was a whole different ballgame entirely. Courtney and I drove out to a corn maze in the evening and it was like a scene out of a horror movie. Here we were...walking around an abandoned farmhouse surrounded by a massive cornfield. We could not find anyone on the premises to take our money so we left before the knife wielding maniac saw us. By now, it was dusk, so we headed back out to the Bell Witch cave and cabin. This time around, there were only the owners and a lone female teenage tour guide there, as everyone was still waiting for sunlight to completely disappear before coming out. I wasn't interested in buying souvenirs or sitting in that cabin again, so I simply asked the tour guide if I could take a private tour into the cave. She was hesitant at first, but eventually agreed when I told her that she didn't have to do or say anything... only accompany Courtney and me so we could get in. She reluctantly let me to go much deeper into the cave than the tour would ever allow anyone to go, so I got some amazing shots that no one else had, while the girls shared a pleasant conversation. By the time we exited, a crowd was gathering, so Courtney and I were out of there. I was finally satisfied with what we had accomplished, so we grabbed some dinner, and went back to the hotel to relax.

Feeling like we had pretty much done everything we could do in this little town, we decided to come home that night instead of waiting around until checkout time the next day. By doing this, we made incredible time and missed out on all of the traffic.

As we entered Oak Ridge a few hours later, I saw a building that brought back a few memories. It was the Asian spa that Tommy took me to several years before when I was training for wrestling. It was now closed down and in ruins. I couldn't help but giggle quietly to myself so Courtney wouldn't hear me. The last thing I needed was for *that* to be brought up in a conversation.

    You think of a twitching nose Samantha, with a flying broom and a pointed hat, a Prue, Piper, or Phoebe…or a teenage Sabrina, with a magic wand, and a black cat, but her coven, not exactly the charmed ones, with the power of three (blessed be)
    After three degrees of initiation, was a graduation, to become a true magician, not just another dabbler in the occult. After chanting in ancient syllables, cursing often in riddles, now she gets the desired results.
    She could prepare a herb potion, to heal any affliction or cool any fever. From the womb to the tomb…love is thy poison…she beckons, with one crooked fever, preventing procreation, by depriving man of his virile member.
    During the Inquisition, in Salem, September 1692, there were persecutions, when the gods of the Old Religion, became the devils of the new…
    After the bang of the gavel, and she's been sent to the gallows…there will be cakes and ale, for death is a time of celebration. From the long drop, to the sudden stop, there will be no Book of Shadows, no casting of spells, only her belief in reincarnation.
    In the season of Samhain, there is an ancient fertility rite. It can only be Beltane, when in the

darkness, the goddess, is impregnated with the seed of light.

She can control the weather, change water into wine. She can foresee the future, with the cards she divines.

Want someone killed? Like the Fates, she is the spinner of the threads. Or made fairly ill? Perhaps when we ate, at last night's dinner, there was fungus on the bread.

After the testimonies, of the men of low repute, using the water of antiquity, thumbscrews, strappado, or the boot…In the town square, seated in a heated iron chair, revealing what man may never know, and women must never tell, then roll her down the hill in a barrel, the sides and ends, stuck full of sharp, pointed nails.

Accused of worshipping Diana, and the brightest star in the sky… Accused of having the evil eye, and practicing the craft of the wise…Guilty of bestiality, and the kiss of infamy, guilty of heresy…pile up the rocks, till she can't take the weight, but instead of the pine box, burn her at the stake.

-Denny Noland "Draven" From my song "Fire Song"
 Written on June 26, 2008   Copyright 2016

3

2006 would be the year that I would lose my last living grandparent: Pa Noland. Everyone knew that it was only going to be a matter of time as he dealt with both diabetes and All Timer's Disease. At his funeral, I ran into Mac, who I hadn't seen in years. It turned out that his grandmother had been looking after my grandfather when dad wasn't, so he knew him quite well. She was now willed most of his belongings while the property and estate went to the kids to be sold with the profits split. I wouldn't receive anything, which had been a common theme over the years. The only thing that I had to remember anyone by was a music box that I got when Nanny died that didn't work...except when it decided to start playing music on its own at significant dates, like the anniversary of Nanny's death. Instead of being creepy, it was actually quite comforting, like it was her way that she let me know that she was still looking after me.

To just get away and clear my head, Courtney invited me to attend a week long family reunion in Wears Valley. Her mother had gotten together with other relatives who had also pitched in to rent two luxurious and secluded cabins in the mountains. I didn't really want to go at first, but I knew how much it meant to Courtney, so I took one for the team. I was pleasantly surprised when I saw the cabins. They were nothing like what I had pictured in my head. They had two levels with scattered dens, bedrooms, and bathrooms. They even had pool tables and hot tubs! Staying there was more like staying at some kind of resort than in a cabin, so I was glad that I changed my mind. I even got along with her family very well which was the icing on the cake. However, it was awkward sharing a bed with Courtney around almost her entire immediate family...especially while we were being intimate, but I tried not to think about that very much.

Our nights may have been filled with passion, but our days were spent at various locations around Pigeon Forge and Gatlinburg. Restaurants, amusement parks, and even nightly local ghost tours were often on the itinerary as we made that week as unforgettable as possible. I must admit that the week couldn't have been more perfect and it literally flew by. Before I knew it, people had started leaving and returning to their everyday lives and I was back at work, hoping that we could do it all again one day.

Back at work, a new guy had joined our team. His name was "Lucas" and he had somehow convinced our store manager to hire him after he had just walked out in the middle of his shift at another of our stores. He had a hearing problem and a smartass mouth with a poor work ethic. Needless to say, I didn't like this guy very much at all. Within days, we nearly got in a fight after he accused me of stealing his knife when he had simply just misplaced it. There was no hope of us ever going to afternoon tea together after that. I had somehow thought that guys would just naturally respect me due to my background of street fighting and bouncing, but no one seemed to care. I had been disrespected by a number of the fly by night stockers that had come and gone over the years. Most notably, Rhett, who had the audacity to challenge me to a meeting in the parking lot after work over a small disagreement. I knew that he had no chance and that he would more than likely get seriously hurt if we got into a fight...not to mention, we would probably both lose our jobs in the process. There was no way that I was going to come out of this without looking like a bully due to the size difference and would probably have assault charges brought up against me to boot. I had all but talked myself out of beating this kid's ass by the time we finished our shift. Hell, I wasn't even mad anymore. I just wanted to go home.

    When we met up outside, I explained to him that I didn't really want to fight, but if he was still eager to put on the gloves, I would drive him over to a nearby parking lot off the premises so we could settle this. I was hoping that it didn't come to that because I knew me. Once I got in that state of mind, only one of us was coming back and I would have bet the farm that it was going to be me. Luckily, he didn't want to go either, as we had a long conversation about why we were really angry and how to fix it without blood being spilled. We never had a problem with each other again. Later on, I was thanked by both Courtney and Charles for not making that kid famous, but I often wondered if he took my compassion as a sign of weakness.

4

2006-2007 were great years all around from an entertainment and recreational perspective at least. All of my sports teams won major championships: the Red Sox won the World Series again, the Texas Longhorns won the National Championship in college football and the Steelers won the Super Bowl. This would also be the year of my greatest Halloween tour and investigation ever… as Courtney and I booked our tickets to Gettysburg, Pennsylvania! This destination is every ghost hunter's dream and was prepared for and planned out very carefully over the past year. We rented a car so we wouldn't have to use one of our own and booked a room at the Holiday Inn that sat on the outskirts of the battlefield months in advance. This wasn't Adams, Tennessee…this was a place that had endless things to do and places to see, whether you were into the historical side of things as Courtney was, or the paranormal like myself. We had saved up enough money to do whatever we wanted in the time we were granted, so I was going to try to squeeze in as much as possible.

We had a plan to leave around 2 am in the morning after Courtney did her final shift and I was supposed to nap during the day so I could watch game 4 of the World Series that night and at least be rested enough to make the trip. It didn't happen. Courtney's dad came over to the trailer in the evening to drop something off and ended up staying for a couple of hours. He was insisting that I should drive on up to Washington, DC and check out the nation's capital before heading back but that wasn't in the cards. After he left, it was time for the game to start. If I had any plans to sleep after the game, they went out the window when the Red Sox won the World Series for the second time in four years that night. It would be late before the adrenalin wore off and just as I was nodding off, Courtney walked through the door. The car was packed and for once, she was actually ready to go. The problem was that I was too fatigued to drive so I asked to take at least a short nap. Courtney would cuddle up beside me and we both slept for probably an hour or two before we found ourselves in the car heading north. I was just praying that I didn't get us both killed.

 I was struggling big time until we reached Virginia. The sun was just starting to come up so we grabbed some breakfast to a beautiful mountain setting. My goal was to get a shot glass from every state that we passed through to add to my collection. This wasn't a problem in Virginia and West Virginia, but Maryland proved to be more difficult due to the fact that we weren't in the state for very long. I pulled into a seedy gas station off the exit ramp that just happened to be in one of the worst parts of town. I was impressed that even they had shot glasses! We both had a laugh and soon after crossed the line into Pennsylvania.

 Out on a lonely stretch of road, heading into Gettysburg, was a strip club. I just thought that was the strangest place to have one considering that Amish country was only a few miles further down the road. I was fascinated with the Amish, and their ability to not adapt to modern society. It was just so cool to see people still living simple, traditional lives. In some ways, I envied them. There were horses and buggies everywhere and several shops where you could buy arts and crafts but unfortunately, I was too exhausted to actually stop. We did, however, see a vineyard and winery outside of town that grabbed our attention. It was definitely going to be blessed with our presence at some point during this trip.

    Once in the city limits, I saw an unfamiliar sight: a roundabout. Not knowing exactly where that our hotel was, I got in the outer lane…which happened to be a turning lane that went straight to the Holiday Inn. A deep sigh of relief later…and we were there. Although I was so tired that I felt like I was going to collapse after carrying in the luggage and settling in, I went out on foot to purchase tickets to keep us busy for the next few days. Once I got back to the room, I took a nap because we had a long night ahead of us.

    On the first night, we investigated the Jennie Wade house, which just happened to be literally across the road from our hotel. Jennie Wade was the only civilian casualty during the Civil War and was actually killed by accident as a stray bullet killed her in her own home. The bullet hole is still in the door to this day, and of course, I had to stick my finger in it and take pictures of it. The only experience we had, was seeing the chains that kept the crowds back, start swaying back and forth when no one was around. We would soon discover that many of the floorboards were loose and when people would be walking across certain areas, it would create a slight "see-saw" effect that was just enough to give the illusion of possible paranormal activity. Although nothing really significant happened, I thought that it was still an awesome tour and a great way to start out the week.

    I had only been there for a day yet I had already fallen in love with Gettysburg. I could feel certain energy as soon as we got there, like the place had its own aura. Chandler had told me about how he felt like there were invisible eyes watching him everywhere he went when he had gone there the year before, but it wasn't exactly what I was feeling. I loved the people, history, climate and atmosphere, pretty much everything…so much in fact that I extended our stay for a few days until I absolutely had to go back to work. I even recall telling Courtney that I wanted to live there one day. Only time will tell.

Our second night was spent at the Farnsworth House on Baltimore Street. The building was filled with over a hundred bullet holes that had been there since the Civil War. We spent a great deal of time in the attic where sharpshooters used to sit patiently awaiting their next victim over a century ago. We also got to hear EVPs that had been recorded there ever since. I also spent a lot of money in this building because it was the official headquarters of the "Ghosts of Gettysburg" tours and famous resident Mark Nesbitt. I didn't know until we took the tour that you can actually stay in the house if you book it well in advance as it is also doubles as a bed and breakfast. Some of the people that were staying there just happened to be on the tour with us and was frightened to hear about how haunted the place actually was. I almost offered to swap rooms with them but I don't think Courtney would have appreciated that very much.

The following day, we took a bus ride around the battlefield to learn where everything was, then got into our rental car and explored the sights on our own afterwards. I took pictures at every significant location including "the Devil's Den", "Culp's Hill", "Triangular Field", and "the Round Tops" as well as from any watchtower that overlooked the battlefield. We spent the entire day out there and saw nothing ghostly in nature, but the vibe some of these places had was nothing short of overwhelming. I believed in my heart that if there were really ghosts, this was where you would find them. Just because we didn't experience anything while we were there didn't mean a damn thing. I've never felt closer to seeing a spirit and finding the Holy Grail in my whole life. There was something there…I just can't say for sure what it was.

That night, we took a tour around Gettysburg College, which had been used as a field hospital during the war. We saw the window where the "blue boy" had been seen and the area where battlefield doctors used to throw body parts after amputations. We didn't find any evidence but a stroll around campus was still quite amusing regardless. A few of the gorgeous female students came up to us and praised the local tours while telling us their own personal ghost stories and experiences. Just when I thought that nothing that happened would really surprise me, a group of young men came tearing out of a nearby bar wearing nothing but their underwear and ran down the street. When the guide asked me how I was enjoying my Gettysburg experience, I told her that I hadn't seen or heard anything ghostly yet which was a little disappointing. She said, "You know that this entire town is sitting on part of the battlefield… right?" I nodded. "There have been paranormal activity and apparitions seen or heard in every business, whether it was the restaurant or hotel down the street or where we are currently standing. Ghosts are everywhere in this town. Just pay more attention and I promise you will have your own experience before you leave" she continued. She wasn't lying…

That was one of the many things I loved about Gettysburg: they embraced their haunted history, instead of sweeping it under a rug like other towns and cities often did. However, the following day was spent chasing different kinds of spirits as Courtney and I drove out to the vineyard. I must have sampled ten different types of wine while we were there. I was so intoxicated afterwards that Courtney had to drive us back to the hotel. I remember lying on the bed watching Two and a Half Men for the very first time while waiting for both my buzz and the sun to go down. We had places to go and people to see...

After we had been all over Gettysburg throughout the week and didn't really have an experience, it would be on our final night that I would get some hard evidence. That night was so intense that it made Courtney a believer when she took such pride in being a skeptic. We returned to the Farnsworth House again on a different tour and ended up in the basement. It was filled with toys left by tourists for the spirit of a young boy named "Jeremy" who had been trampled to death outside the Farnsworth by a buggy in the 1800's. Our guide was using dowsing rods to supposably communicate with his ghost, which made Courtney and I both unimpressed and sceptical. About midway through his demonstration, everyone in the room, including the guide himself, smelled the aroma of both food and cigar smoke. He reminded us that the kitchen above us closed several hours ago and there were no restaurants nearby, and even if they were, we were underground. We shouldn't be able to smell anything from the streets above. He then continued to talk to Jeremy, while everyone began to look around at each other.

At the end of his presentation, I walked up to him and asked if I could try my luck at "talking" to Jeremy. To my surprise, he was more than happy to hand over the rods. I held them straight out as tight and still as possible. As soon as I asked if Jeremy was there, the rods crossed despite my best efforts of resistance. "What does this mean?" I asked. "Jeremy is standing right in front of you" the guide replied. I looked over at Courtney and her eyes were as big as saucers. I would ask a series of questions to Jeremy and he would reply by crossing the rods for yes and spreading them apart for no. I couldn't believe what was happening, nor could anyone else who witnessed it. I could have stood there for hours... but it was time to go to the next guide for the second part of the tour. Things were about to get even more interesting...

The second part of the tour began on the outskirts of the battlefield, since it was illegal to be on the actual battlefield at night due mostly to reports of vandalism. We stood under a tree that was so old that it had been dated to have been there during the Civil War. Our guide was telling us stories about full body apparitions that had been seen around this area over the years, when the familiar scent of gunpowder filled the air around us. There was no logical explanation for smelling the past but even the tour guide acknowledged it and stated the obvious. I had my back to the forest but Courtney was facing them. I noticed that she kept staring out into the woods with a frightened look on her face. I kept turning around to see what she was looking at, but I couldn't see a damn thing. After the tour guide finished her speech, she took us down to the very edge of the battlefield itself so we could take a few pictures. Courtney wasn't having any of it... as she wanted to go back to the room, by herself if she had to. This was a girl who was afraid to walk to the mailbox by herself at dusk, and now she was willing to walk several blocks down the street on her own in a strange town. Something was going on... but there was absolutely no way I was leaving without getting a few shots of the battlefield after dark. This was our last night, and I may never get this opportunity again, so I had an idea that would kill two birds with one stone. I saw a woman standing under a street light a short distance away, that was waiting for someone also, so I took Courtney there so I would know exactly where she was at all times. Of course, as luck would have it, the woman left Courtney alone only a few minutes later, so my plan backfired somewhat, but I did take my pictures and managed to get Courtney out of there before she completely lost it.

It was a quiet walk back to the hotel and an even quieter stay overnight. Courtney just didn't want to talk about what she saw, so I didn't press, because I knew that she would tell me when the time was right. The next morning was stormy and dark and would have been a perfect day to have been on the battlefield but I had extended this vacation as far as I could. Hell, I had to literally be back at work in a few hours so we *had* to leave right then. We got to about Maryland before she finally told me what had been bothering her. During the final tour, she had seen shadow people in the forest, moving about and peering at us from behind trees while everyone else was distracted by the scent of gunpowder. Since she didn't believe in ghosts, she didn't know how to handle what she had just seen. I could tell that she wasn't just fucking around... she was being sincere. Needless to say, it changed her opinion completely about the paranormal.

We got home late in the evening and I needed to hit the bed, so Courtney and her mother dropped off the rental car without me. I don't know how I made it through the night but I did. Other than a few local investigations with Ryan, primarily in Gatlinburg, my hobby of ghost hunting was all but over. Sometime around 2009, Ryan and I did go do an investigation in Jonesborough, Tennessee, with a douche bag guide, who rudely ask me to be quiet during his tour and rolled his eyes every time I asked him a fucking question. I had planned to take a large group of people with me to Waverly Hills Sanatorium in Louisville, Kentucky for an overnight investigation and even offered to drive everyone up there, but as Halloween night approached, everyone backed out and the trip got cancelled. As of this writing, I hadn't been on an investigation in over 6 years…but that could be subject to change very soon.

    We did do the cabin thing again in 2007, but it wouldn't go as smoothly as it did the year before. Apparently, there was a falling out over money and who was supposed to be chipping in to help pay for these extravagant getaways. There was tension in the air this time around which resulted in some people leaving early and others to isolate themselves from everyone else. The yearly tradition was pretty much broken before it ever got started. Courtney and I had a great time and that was all that really mattered…to me at least.
-DJN

CHAPTER XXII- *"ME, YOU, AND THEM"*

2008-2009

Although we had our ups and downs over the years and overcame it all, Courtney and I were quickly approaching the end. It was just a depressing time for everyone. Chandler and his wife's marriage had also ended when he came home early one night from work and caught her in bed with another man. Without their combined income, he could no longer afford the mortgage, so he went into survival mode and started stealing what he needed from the store to save money. He was obviously inspired by my method of getting beer past the cops when I was underage and working at that store with my aunt. He would fill a shopping cart to the brim with empty boxes, pretending to be moving house, and have the one at the very bottom filled with a number of essential and nonessential items that he didn't pay for. To make matters worse, he always carried a backpack which he also stuffed with everything that he could as well. He had gotten away with it for so long that he became overconfident and sloppy.

His biggest mistake was leaving those carts unattended in the breakroom every morning, while everyone else was just arriving and we were finishing up. Someone eventually became suspicious, after a month had passed and he was still supposably moving, and informed management. They searched not only the trolley, but his backpack as well without him knowing then notified the police. Had Chandler left early like he normally did, he wouldn't have been caught, but for some reason, he decided to stay back and keep me company that day. We had just gone on break when I stepped outside to have a quick cigarette. When I returned, Chandler was gone without a trace, but both the contents from his backpack and trolley were spread out across the table. There was everything from food to hairspray to wrestling magazines in his bags but no receipts for any of it. In the few minutes that I had been away, the cops had taken him out in handcuffs and he had already confessed to stealing thousands of dollars of merchandise over the past few months. I had missed the entire thing!

Although we all suspected that he was stealing, we never *saw* him take anything. He was our friend so we never searched his bags...probably because if he was doing it, we didn't really want to know. I did, however, tell him the night before he got busted what everyone's suspicions were and asked him to stop if they were true. He just laughed and pleaded his innocence. I let it go after that. A few hours later, he had not only lost his job and went to jail, but now he had a criminal record. I wasn't happy about losing another friend because they were hard to come by, but I tried to talk some sense into him beforehand. He just didn't heed my warning. Now someone else was taken from me prematurely and I would never see him again. I would talk briefly to him on MySpace in 2010 before I came to Australia but that was the extent of it.

2

Courtney would make a foolish decision to alter her appearance somewhat by cutting off all of her beautiful long hair... using the excuse that her teacher in nursing school was constantly complaining about it. I wasn't buying it... especially when most of her classmates had long hair too and apparently that was ok. I let Courtney have it until she softened the blow by telling me that she was donating it to "Locks of Love" so they could make wigs for cancer patients, and promising to grow it back. All I needed at the time was something else to decrease my sex drive. Our sex life was now limited only to Wednesday nights and I was sleeping on the couch every other night of the week. We were now more like roommates than lovers… but at least we were financially secure and that made me comfortable.

However, my eyes were starting to wander a bit. There were a couple of women who were married but let me know that they were willing to have an affair if I was interested. One worked during the day on the stock team, and blatantly asked me if I would ever "date a married woman." My response was "Probably not. I don't like constantly looking over my shoulder wondering if I'm going to get shot." She appreciated and respected my answer. We did continue to flirt after that but nothing serious. The other, however, was a little more outspoken and persistent. She used to stare at my crotch when I was talking to her at times, and would often invite me to a hotel after work. Sometimes she would ask me if I have ever had sex in a pool, or something of that nature, that she must have thought was kinky or taboo, that I had done countless times in the past. She told me once that she was interested because of my "reformed bad boy image" and that Courtney didn't deserve me.

Nothing ever happened while we were both at the FC, but after she got fired and became employed at the local Wal-Mart, which just happened to be one of my regular stops, we did make out a few times right on the sales floor. All of this time, I thought she said she was married to a truck driver, when in fact she was married to a cop. That killed any interest that I might have had as I started avoiding her like the plague. There was also another older married woman at Wal-Mart, who I had known for years through my uncle, that I started talking to that went nowhere as well. I didn't know what I wanted anymore.

 Then one day while I was leaving the store, an attractive woman from the bakery approached me and asked, "You don't remember me do you?" Honestly, I had no idea who she was. I couldn't even guess. "I'm Jennifer. We worked together at the club years ago" she said. It took me a minute to figure out that she was the same Jennifer who considered my offer to move in with me to get away from her husband, then vanished without even saying goodbye or a simple "fuck you." Once I pieced it all together, I didn't exactly go out of my way to socialize. Up to this point, I had successfully avoided everyone from my past but now someone was right on my doorstep and I wasn't thrilled about it either. She would go on to tell me that she had heard that both Gene and James had only recently passed away, which caused me to feel guilty about not stopping in to see them again while they were still alive. Just Jennifer's appearance, or anyone else from that era to be honest, was probably the worst thing that could have happened to me. It made me nostalgic again. I realized right then and there that one day, somewhere down the road, I had to go back to that place for some closure.

3

 I would soon receive a double dose of what I thought was good fortune that would turn out to be more of the same bullshit. First and foremost, I was offered a house from Courtney's father that was near the city and much closer to work. I jumped at the opportunity to become a homeowner, especially since it was never going to happen under any other circumstances with my credit rating being what it was. Oh, how I was looking forward to living in a building that was stable enough to not sway every time the wind blew. The only thing that I didn't like about the situation was how our agreement was nothing more than a handshake, because he was hesitant about drawing up a written contract. He would always stall or delay the paperwork, so nothing was actually ever signed, leaving me no legal "leg to stand on" if he wanted me out for any reason. I now felt pressured to stay with Courtney out of fear. If we did ever break up, blood was thicker than water so I would probably be back out on the streets again. Despite the risk, I took the house and a week off from work to move all of our belongings and start settling in.

I also got promoted to manager after Henry retired. Charles wasn't interested in stepping up so it came down to Pauly and me and I was chosen for the job. This would only make Pauly resentful and bitter, even though I got him a title, security code, and a raise as my third in charge. It still wasn't enough to satisfy him. My weekend crew was a joke anyway…made up with impressionable, and often incompetent, outcasts from every walk of life with everything from drug problems to mental disorders. One kid used to even talk to, and even yell at, cans before he placed them on the shelf. One Friday night, he just decided not to show up for work. When the assistant manager rang him to ask him why he wasn't coming in, he just simply replied, "What's it to you? It's really none of your fucking business!" Obviously he was fired immediately…then replaced by someone worse.

What really pissed me off about it all was when Charles was around, everyone at least made an effort, but when I was in charge, no one gave a damn about schedules or repercussions. To make matters worse, I was constantly getting phone calls about refrigeration issues that kept me from doing my job. This meant that Pauly was often watching over the crew in my absence. Without me, they goofed off and took constant breaks that got us further behind. We were always running late and even though no one said anything at first, it was drawing the wrong type of attention. Eventually I had not only the big boss, but also his teenage assistants criticizing me on a daily basis. Hell, they even came to work with us for a week at a time and even held meetings to threaten everyone's jobs but nothing fixed the problem, because at the end of the day, everyone knew that I was just a figurehead. They weren't actually going to let me get rid of anyone...otherwise I would have fired everyone but Charles and started over. I was running out of excuses and had grown tired of having to explain to someone every morning why we couldn't get the job done.

    I tried everything from losing my temper to asking nicely but no one ever listened. I even ordered less stock but all that did was make everyone work slower and cause the boss to complain about the shelves being empty. In reality, the shelves weren't empty...low maybe, but not empty. No one ever walked into that store and didn't get everything that they came in for, unlike every other fucking store that I've ever shopped at. Yet, I was the sorriest excuse for a manager ever. I could only take so much criticism before I snapped and asked to be demoted back to just a filler after only a few months. Predictably enough, the boss was praising Charles before the stock was even on the shelves when he ordered his first truck after I stepped down. All of a sudden, the store was miraculously "full" and "looked great" practically overnight. I never forgot that and held a grudge until the day I left.

The new manager that replaced me wasn't Pauly. After all of the problems that he caused me by constantly whispering in everyone's ears, he didn't want the job after all. Instead, it went to an outsider, who was instantly treated with respect by both management and my crew. To throw more salt into my wounds, they finally repaired all of the refrigeration issues before he got there so he didn't have to deal with that either. This was all a slap in my face in almost every way imaginable.

4

Although I may have been out of the corporate inner circle, Courtney wasn't. She would invite me to attend a Knoxville Smokies game with her using the company reserved press box behind home plate. The team was being managed by Hall of Famer Ryne Sandberg at the time and all food and alcohol was free. That was all I needed to know. I would eat just before first pitch, then grab a case of beer and take my seat so I could watch the game. Courtney, on the other hand, never left the press box. She chose to socialize with everyone instead of spending time with me. The only time she even looked toward the field was when a foul ball nearly took out one of our associates while he was coming down the stairs with his beer. I ended up getting pretty drunk and spent most of the evening alone.

It would more of the same when we went to a hockey game later that year…except turn it up to ten. I only went because of all the times that Courtney had tried to spend time with me and I couldn't be bothered. She also bribed me with a bottle of Crown Royal, which was just asking for this night to get out of hand. There were four of us going...two guys and two girls. The plan was to have dinner before going to the arena, but I had already started chugging straight bourbon from the bottle before we even left the FC parking lot. I was pretty wasted by the time we reached the restaurant and wasn't interested in eating at all, so I spent the majority of my time standing outside near the car, smoking one cigarette after another. I could tell that Courtney was already upset with me so it came as no surprise that she never came out to check on me herself...she would send her girlfriend instead. That was a terrible mistake, because it would cause the two party animals of the group to focus more on each other than the other two for the rest of the night. When we got to the game, we fed off of each other. She would flash her tits at the crowd then I would flash mine. We bought each other drinks and never offered to buy them for our partners. The drunker we got, the more obnoxious we became, not thinking about the fact that we were representing the store. Hell, we even sat together and made Courtney and the other person sit behind us. Although she didn't act like it was bothering her, Courtney was very upset and let me know all about it on the way home. I never got invited to any other company related events after that night.

    As much as I enjoyed going to concerts, I hated going with Courtney. We went to a "Nine Inch Nails" concert once and I was so exhausted and bored during the opening act that I actually fell asleep...proving once and for all that I could literally fall asleep anywhere doing anything. We're talking about the same guy who passed out before during sex for goodness sake. This annoyed Courtney because she had purchased the tickets. I did wake up when NIN came onstage, but the crowd was really irritating me. I had two obese lesbians sitting in front of me and one of them kept using my knee to pull her fat ass out of her chair every few minutes. On the other side of Courtney were a couple and their teenage son. When the band played "Closer," the wife jumped up out of her chair in her cheap hooker outfit and grabbed the pole in front of her. She pretended to be a stripper as she bumped and grinded on her husband's crotch right in front of their kid. I was disgusted by both her behaviour and pathetic rendition of an exotic dancer, as it was distracting me from watching the show. To make matters worse, Courtney wanted to leave before the encore to beat traffic because she had to get up early the next morning, so we missed part of the show. I wasn't a happy camper at all.

She pulled a similar stunt when "Staind" came to town. She wanted to leave even earlier because the band "wasn't enthusiastic enough" and acted as though "they didn't want to be there" because they weren't jumping around on stage during their set. I guess she had never seen a concert where the musicians just stood there and played their instruments. This fight on the way home was the final straw. We would never go to another concert together again.

As her final act of desperation, Courtney gave her best shot at rekindling our romance by renting a smaller cabin for just the two of us. We had a full week to let things work itself out. The cabin was two stories, and had everything we needed with even a few extra accommodations upon request to suit me. We had a PlayStation 2, DVD players in every room, and cable TV. We even had a small study, with a bookcase stocked full of books for various interests. It was perfect for what it was. Hell, Courtney's mother even came up one day and was impressed. I couldn't have planned this trip any better myself.

Then things started taking a turn for the worst. We had an infestation of bees in the cabin. They were practically everywhere and we just couldn't get rid of them. Then a bear or raccoon climbed up onto the balcony and got into our trash, leaving one hell of a mess for me to clean up the next morning. Even after all of this bad luck, I still didn't lose my temper until Courtney wanted to have sex. I foolishly attempted to jump into bed with her... but hit my head hard on the low ceiling upstairs in the process. I was seeing stars and nearly gave myself a concussion, but Courtney kept coming on to me. I was certainly not in the mood anymore. All of her concern and humour quickly turned into anger as she voiced her frustration. After this unnecessary argument, I didn't care if we had sex at all the entire week and we wouldn't.

Just when I thought that nothing else could possibly go wrong, I started getting extremely thirsty at night, and was urinating like a horse every couple of hours. Courtney, who was a nursing student, knew the signs and suspected that I might be diabetic. It wasn't a far stretch since both of my parents suffered from this condition. I still didn't want to believe it though, and wasn't fully convinced until blood tests and urine samples confirmed it once we got back to Maryville. The doctors said that I could have had this condition for a very long time, but it never surfaced because of the combination of speed and other drugs in my system and my intense workouts may have been covering it up over the years. Now that I was clean and taking a break from the gym, it finally reared its ugly head. My first concern was how I was going to afford the extra expenses of the medications for the rest of my life when I was barely getting by as it was. As soon as word spread into the FC, instead of people taking it seriously, they made it out to be a joke. Just the way they asked me about my diabetes on a daily basis made a mockery of the whole thing because it sounded more sarcastic than serious. I wanted to tell everyone to get fucked, but didn't really feel like drawing any extra attention, so I tried to not bring it up again.

Then the worst possible thing that could have happened…happened. While trying to push a large pallet of groceries up the ramp, I lost my footing and hit the concrete with a thud. Since I had someone on the other side of the pallet pushing and not being able to see why the pallet stopped moving suddenly, he rolled it up on my foot by accident. Now I was stuck…with several hundred pounds of weight directly sitting on my foot and couldn't free myself. The guys quickly rushed to my aid and got me loose but the damage was done. I couldn't stand up and could literally see the bones through my bruising skin. To make matters worse, it all happened in front of the assistant manager, so I had to go to the hospital immediately or she was held responsible. I limped to my truck and drove myself to the house so Courtney could take me to the emergency room. When I got there, she seemed to be more bothered by the fact that I was interrupting her activities than my foot being injured. She reluctantly drove me to the hospital and I waited for over eight hours to be treated. My foot was ok…no fractures or bones broken, but so severely bruised and swollen that I couldn't support my own weight. By the time I dropped the results off at the F.C., my crew had already finished the truck, and were on their way home. It was so pathetic how I left while we were pulling out the stock and had spent the entire night in that damned waiting room, yet I was still out and about while they were at home resting. I couldn't fucking believe it.

5

When Christmas rolled around again, instead of going over to our parents' houses like we always did, I invited everyone over to our place for Christmas dinner. Before sending out invitations, I talked it over with Courtney because she was doing all the cooking and she thought it was a great idea. It was a big deal to me because my parents *never* came for a visit and if this didn't go well, they probably won't do it again. Courtney's mother and brother got there early and helped out in the kitchen while I nervously waited for my parents to arrive.

As expected, they showed up late but just in time to exchange gifts before dinner. They never really went out of their way to find gifts once the kids were grown, but it was the thought that counted as far as I was concerned. Whatever they got Courtney didn't impress her much, as she briefly thanked them before turning her back and continuing the private conversation she was having with her mother, who she had been talking to for a couple of hours already. She completely disrespected not only me, but my family as well, as she virtually ignored them the entire evening. My dad, who rarely showed emotion, pretended to watch a movie while my mother went into the kitchen to do the dishes. I was so angry and embarrassed that I wanted to toss not only Courtney, but her entire family out of the house but I didn't want any drama on Christmas day. My parents didn't stay very long because they could sense that Courtney didn't want them there. That would be the first and only time that Christmas dinner was ever held anywhere other than their place. I was so pissed that I spent a couple of hours out in the cold before coming back inside because I could have ended the relationship right then and there...and probably should have.

If our household wasn't already unstable enough, Courtney brought a stray dog into the house that her dad found named "Molly." The poor dog had obviously been abused at some point because she hated every man than she saw...including me. She obviously wasn't too fond of cats either which was a bigger problem. Courtney had immediately put the dog higher on the food chain and started resenting and neglecting the cats, which turned them completely against her. Courtney and I bought a fence to go around the house a couple of days later, so Molly could stretch her legs without us standing over her all the time and we started putting it up immediately. I only got the posts in the ground before we got into a fight and I went back in the house. She called her brother and they finished the job while I slept it off. This animal was only going to create a larger rift between Courtney and me over time as I grew to despise the fucking thing.

6

Courtney's graduation from nursing school was upon us, and traditionally, her family rented a cabin for everyone out of town where the ceremony was to be held. Although, most of the family didn't attend, there were still quite a few that did. Her grandparents and her favourite aunt and uncle made the trip, and even her father and brother were coming, even though they avoided all of the other reunions in the past. Courtney, her mother, and yours truly went up early to get checked in and get everything ready. Of course, we couldn't get the key until a couple of hours after we arrived, which put everyone in a bad mood. Courtney was already distracted and different...not because she was nervous or excited, but because all of her nursing friends was coming up in a couple of days and renting their own cabin in the area. That was all she really talked about as her family seemed far less important all of sudden.

When she was still in regular college, Courtney was the girl that everyone knew and loved, but as soon as she got into nursing school, she changed dramatically. Her behaviour at Christmas the previous year was a prime example. It was almost like she thought she was better than everyone else, especially me and my family. I don't know if her fellow students were influencing her somewhat, or she just started trying to change her image on her own but I didn't like it at all. The sweet girl that I met several years before had now become an arrogant bitch.

Once the family got there, Courtney seemed unappreciative and uninterested. She appeared to be almost resentful because I think that deep down she wanted to stay with her friends instead of her loved ones. When she received that phone call… the one that she had been waiting for, to let her know that her friends had arrived, she immediately came out of her depression. After the girls unpacked, they came by our cabin to say hello and to give us directions to where they were staying. From that moment on, Courtney kept trying to persuade me to go pay them a visit…no matter what our plans were at the time. I couldn't restrain her for very long but I tried my best.

The first night after her friends arrived, Courtney's father and I were sitting out on the balcony, having countless beers and cigarettes after a wonderful dinner, and bonding like Courtney had wanted us to do for the past few years. We must have drank two cases of beer before it got too dark to even see each other's faces and we had to go in.

During that time, we discussed how difficult both Courtney and her mother could be at times. We even had a laugh when we asked our partners to bring us more beer and they both said exactly the same thing, "Your legs aren't broke...go get it yourself!" It was getting late when we finally came in and all we wanted to do was crash. However, Courtney had other ideas...for me at least. She wanted to have sex and then meet up with her friends around midnight. This obviously wasn't going to end well... especially with me being as drunk as I was. While we were having sex, I could tell that she was getting anxious and her mind obviously wasn't on what she was doing. After we finished, she begged me to jump into the car and head up the mountain. I kept trying to convince her of how dangerous it was to go on such narrow roads, that you have never ventured down before, in the middle of the night. "We'll go first thing tomorrow, ok? That way, we can at least see where we're going" I said. "They assured me already that we won't have any problems getting up there" she argued. "Sorry babe, but I'm not putting our lives at risk because people that I don't really know gave me the green light." She wasn't happy at all and even threatened to go alone but it didn't work because I knew that she was afraid to. Eventually she settled down and fell asleep.

    I kept my word. We drove up there the next day and I was pleasantly surprised to see that there were guy nurses there as well. Everyone was pretty cool...except for all the girls constantly gushing over the recently released "Twilight" film and its star "Rob Pattinson." They were playing a song that he was doing the vocals on and claiming "to be wet already" just by hearing his voice. After a few beers, this gave me all the material I needed to make fun of them. I provided the entertainment for the evening once I got drunk. I had everyone laughing... even at themselves. We left late in the evening and wouldn't see them again until they were wearing caps and gowns.

It was Courtney's big day...and I couldn't be prouder. Despite our ups and downs, she worked her ass off to get here. This was her moment and I was just glad to be a part of it. That was until she gave her private acceptance speech and forgot to thank one particular person: me. I had just sit through an inspiring story about a skydiver thanking the one who "packed his parachute" and I thought that I was the one who packed hers. Every time she thought about dropping out of school, I was there to keep her on course. When she had to attend symphonies and other events for a credit, I went with her, even when I had better things to do. Hell, even when she had to practice using a needle and no one else would be her pin cushion, I let her stick them in me. I went to work with bruises on my arm on multiple occasions looking like a heroin addict. But in her eyes, I did nothing and deserved no recognition or credit. It hurt my feelings a little, I must admit, and that's not easy to do as heartless as I've been known to be.

Courtney was about to write a new chapter in her life...turn over a new leaf if you will. She even volunteered to drive home that day, which was a rare sight indeed, to prove that she was gaining confidence and ready to have her independence. I think that those new friends had already got to her and convinced her to drop her much older boyfriend. I honestly wasn't concerned with it because I didn't think that she had it in her, so I was shocked when she attempted to break up with me a few weeks later...on the grounds that I wasn't giving her enough attention. I managed to persuade her to give me another chance... for no real reason other than that I needed her to maintain a certain lifestyle. She was finally working in the medical field, even if it was at the same looney bin that her father was also working at as a security guard, and making some serious money I might add, as she waited patiently for something better to came along. I felt like I deserved this and sacrifices had to be made, so I gave it everything I had, whether my heart was really in it or not. After about a week, Courtney asked for some space, because I was now "too clingy" and it was smothering her. That's when I sat her down and asked her what she really wanted from me. She had no idea...

We were now coming up on Fourth of July weekend. Courtney and her fellow nurses decided to go back to the cabin that they had during graduation. She had carefully thought it through to where there was absolutely no chance of me being able to get off work to go. She smoothed it over by lying to me about how this particular trip was "for the nurses only... so spouses and boyfriends were not allowed." Then she forgot her own lie and let it slip that not only were a couple of husbands going, but they were also bringing some of their single male friends along as well. I suspected the worse and tried to talk Courtney into reconsidering but that wasn't happening. I was now watching my long-time girlfriend head off to a sausage fest, while I was left to not only work, but to look after a fucking dog that already hated my guts. I had already been in this situation before and we all know how that ended.

It was Independence Day, and I was awakened early by the usual sound of fireworks. I tried to take Molly out before I left for work because I wasn't going to be home for at least 8 hours. The problem was that she was spooked from all the noise and refused to go into the yard. I called Courtney for some advice, since it was *her* dog, and she went off on me in front of an audience. "Why are you interrupting my party with this? You are just wasting my time!" she yelled. "I just didn't want to come home in the morning to a mess. Sorry to bother you..." I replied. "Can't you just leave me alone?" she snapped back. I then threw the fucking phone against the wall and broke it. The next morning, I was cleaning up multiple piles of dog shit throughout the house...just as I predicted. By the time Courtney got home, I was furious and ready to kill that mutt. I warned her that she better never leave me alone to take care of that dog again or she would regret it.

When things finally settled down a few days later, I was looking at the pictures on *my* digital camera and saw several photos of Courtney with some random guy at that cabin. They were both in their bathing suits hugging and cuddling like young lovers. That didn't go over too well. Of course, Courtney defended herself by accusing me of invading her privacy, and claiming her innocence. Maybe nothing did happen... but that was irrelevant now. Within days, Courtney and I had split up for good. Unlike the first time, I didn't put up much of a fight. I wanted her gone and the sooner, the better. She moved back in with her parents, and I kept the house. That probably had more to do with Courtney's father being a man of his word than Courtney actually doing the right thing. I never had a problem with her family, my issues stemmed from *her* and her alone. I still maintained a great relationship with her father, even after the way things ended. At least she had those dodgy friends to fall back on, I had no one. It was time to try again and chalk it up as yet another learning experience.
-DJN

CHAPTER XXIII- "THE EXES AND THE WHY"

2009-2010

As in the novel, "Bram Stoker's Dracula," used to have a castle in Transylvania. There's no Buffy, or Van Helsing, in New Orleans, where I live in the trunk of a tree, underneath the autumn leaves.

I'm a creature of the night, never seen in broad daylight. Like Vlad, or Lestat, with a tuxedo and a cape, can appear as a bat, or any colour or shape.

Gave up humanity, for immortality...in the mirror, cast no reflection, cannot enter, without an invitation...

Oh, Mother Lilith, oh, Father Caine, my castle lies in ruins, my armies all slain. I am Abel, from the mating of gods and mortals, in the land of Nod. Refuse my tender shoots, my brightest fruits, for thy brother's sweetest animal.

Four centuries, I've been in limbo, after becoming one of them, (the forsaken) seems like an eternity I've been in the shadows, awaiting my next victim. I am but a virus, in the world I now tread. When I'm contagious, oh, how the infection spreads.

Hypnotized by my stare, paralyzed by my glare, sucking your veins, with my fangs...When you bleed, I feed, untying every knot, counting every seed. So hang up your garlic and a branch of wild rose. Grab your crucifix and put nets in your windows.

Oh, Brother Seth, Oh, Dreaded Uriel, bleeding for me in a bowl, is a dove and a beautiful dancer. Punished with ceaseless hunger, I am ever in her thrall, of mixed berries and delicious elixir.

> **When in the coffin, my hair and nails still grow. I'm like a soul, without repose...strong as twenty men, I never age or decompose.**
>
> **Find my tomb, have it exhumed, in hallowed ground, buried face down. Before I reanimate...better decapitate, or have water that's been blessed, or be ready to drive a wooden stake through my chest.**
>
> -Denny Noland "Draven" From my song "Blood Song"
>
> Written on May 9, 2007   Copyright 2016

Apparently, I still had a lot to learn too. After months of spending my spare time playing video games and watching endless movies and paranormal shows on the Travel Channel, I was desperate for a woman. Somehow, Jennifer's name was brought up from a mutual friend during a conversation, and it got me to thinking. Maybe her turning up in my life after such a long hiatus was destiny...fate perhaps. Either way, it wasn't much of a gamble to at least try, so I sent her my phone number through the friend.

Jennifer would call me later that evening and we would talk for hours about the club, the store, Courtney, and a number of other topics. She was one of the first people to actually ask me why I chose Courtney, because she wasn't really my type. Jennifer had seen me surrounded by beauties almost the whole time she's known me and Courtney just didn't fit the bill. I told her that I was trying to be less superficial in my old age and we both had a laugh.

The conversation eventually got more serious, as we started discussing how we now had a second chance at a potential relationship. Her situation was a bit awkward, as her supposably now ex-husband was still living under the same roof but working out of town a lot. She assured me that the marriage was indeed over and that they were no longer intimate. He was apparently only there for their young daughter. I bought into the whole story and changed the subject back to us again. She appeared to be very interested in dating me, even discussing what it would be like to kiss my lips again. She invited me to her house later that week. I was eager to see what might happen and what might develop.

    I never knew that she lived close to where my old trailer was. I had literally driven by her house a thousand times over the years and had no idea. When she answered the door, I leaned in for a kiss on the lips, and she turned her head slightly, so I got the side of her lips and a portion of her cheek. That caught me off guard, especially after our phone conversation, but I didn't say anything. It was obvious to me that she only invited me over to chew gum, smoke cigarettes, and talk. And that was exactly what we did. I thought that it might have been because her daughter was there, so I completely understood. Over the next few hours, we talked about many things, but with her being a published author herself and me thinking about writing a book, that became our main topic. She advised me on how to go about outlining my stories and warned me to change everyone's names. We never left the kitchen table until it got late and I had to go to work. As I was leaving, I slipped her some tongue outside and she moaned with pleasure, until it dawned on her what was happening and she pulled away. "We have to stop" she said. "I don't want my daughter to see us and get confused." Now I was wondering if she was actually single or not... and if she was, were we going to have to sneak around the entire time. I left more confused than I was before I got there, especially when she asked me not to tell *anyone* that we were dating.

The longer we saw each other, the weirder it got. She would ask me questions about my skill level and whether I would be willing to give up my house if things got serious between us, then be cold and distant, like she was when I left Thanksgiving dinner with my family early to see her like we had planned for weeks, yet she called and cancelled while I was on my way, because she suddenly "wasn't feeling well." In so many ways, she was brutally honest with me. She told me what she wanted and expected from me if we ever became a couple. I was going to earn all the money and she wasn't going to work. Then I would do everything around the house so she didn't have to lift a finger if she didn't want to. Her drive and ambition was lacking to an unbearable degree, but I liked her a lot and made excuses for her... even in my own head. There were so many reasons to walk away but I just couldn't. She had me by the short and curlies, and never even slept with me yet.

I tried to make up for my shortcomings by doing everything that I could to always be there when she needed me. She called me once because she was cleaning house and had a truck load of trash that needed to be hauled away, so I got into my truck and disposed of it for her. I met her mother that morning and she thought that I was a "very good looking guy" and started asking Jennifer questions. I have no idea what Jennifer told her and didn't want to know either. All I did know was that Jennifer agreed that I did look damn good that day, because she told me as much, and that was good enough for me. Then there was the time that her daughter wanted a puppy, but for one reason or another, Jennifer didn't qualify to get the one that her daughter picked out so I had to be the hero again. I drove up to the shelter and adopted the puppy for her, then gave it to her daughter. I immediately won her daughter over by my actions but Jennifer still was hesitant. I honestly didn't know what else to do. I had tried everything at this point and still nothing.

 Then there was the day that she invited me over while her daughter was in school. We sat at our usual spots at the table with another couple, talking about everything from sex to the store. When the guests left, Jennifer pulled out a bottle of wine…then another…then another. We drank three bottles in total, and were very tipsy, when she started asking me about the women that have come and gone from my life. Lena's name was brought up, because Jennifer knew her personally, and was around during our fling. She started analysing the rise and fall of that near relationship and it was getting really annoying and upsetting. She noticed that I was getting angry so she sat down on my lap and held me. She was wearing a pair of shorts and a t-shirt that made her boobs really stand out as they pressed against my face. Out of nowhere, she grabbed my face hard and stuck her tongue down my throat. It was so passionate that I was literally gasping for air. I pulled away once to catch my breath yet she kept pouring it on. Five minutes later, it was like it never happened. We made out briefly in the living room afterwards, but with very little passion, before she looked up and noticed the time. Her daughter was going to be home in a few minutes and she didn't want her to see either of us drunk… especially me, since she was really starting to like me. I was asked to leave, even though I was pretty wasted. Jennifer walked me to my truck and we started kissing again, forgetting all about her daughter until the bus came into sight. I tore out of the driveway before it got to the house and drove home. A couple of hours later, Jennifer called me and told me that her daughter was very upset with her, and if that wasn't bad enough, Jennifer herself was claiming that she couldn't remember what happened between us earlier. I gave her the rundown and she said that we couldn't let that ever happen again. I couldn't believe what I was hearing. I finally got somewhere with Jennifer and she was now ashamed of it, even though she initiated the whole thing. I thought that it was time to put some distance between us and Jennifer agreed.

    We made it through Christmas with very little contact and it was now New Year's Eve. I had no plans except for getting a bottle of Crown Royal and chilling out at home. I had just started getting drunk when the phone rang. It was Jennifer, and to this day, I still don't know why she originally called, but once she realized how fucked up I was, her plans for the night changed. Since her ex-husband was watching the kid, she kind of invited herself over to my place. We both hit the bottle hard, especially me, as I was already wasted at this point since I got a head start. All I remember was Jennifer leaning in for a kiss once and me kissing her... then everything gets blurry. I vaguely recall starting to feel sick, and Jennifer going into the kitchen to cook something to sober me up. I passed out at some point and when I woke up, Jennifer was nowhere to be found so I went to bed.

    Around 6:00 a.m. on New Year's Day, 2010, I was awakened by the phone ringing. One again, it was Jennifer, but this time she was calling from jail. She had gotten into an accident after she left my house the night before and couldn't remember even driving home, much less what happened along the way. I couldn't comprehend what she was telling me because she appeared to be quite sober the last time I saw her. She was being charged with DUI but wasn't calling me for bail money…she was calling to dump me over the phone. Since her ex-husband came and bailed her out, she decided to give the relationship another chance. "He didn't have to do that" she said. "He must still love me." Still technically drunk and half asleep, I thought I must have been having a nightmare until I heard the ex-husband's voice in the background. I had become familiar with it over time, because around the holidays, he was often in the room when she would call me. She talked to me as if I was only a friend in front of him but apparently he knew that we could potentially be more than that. The fact that she insisted on ditching me over the phone, where he could hear her, pretty much verified that. I was so upset that I couldn't face anyone at work for a couple of days…especially with them being as supportive of us getting together as they were. I felt like an idiot for letting her do this to me, not once, but twice in my lifetime. It could have been much worse though. I would have done anything for her, but she didn't "milk me for all I was worth" like she could have or some other women might have. That's why I don't hate her today. She could have taken everything from me and then broke it off but she didn't. I am eternally grateful for that at least.

2

Without Courtney's extra income to help me out financially, I chose to take a different route than my old friend Chandler. I got an interview with a local factory to try to better myself. What I didn't know, was that they were having it in a classroom with another twenty or more candidates. We were told that we were going to be taking a two part test. The first part was a math test and the second part was a "character" or "personality" test that no one could supposably fail because there were no right or wrong answers. We were given a certain time limit to complete each part and was assured that we wouldn't be penalized by how many questions we answered...just how many we answered correctly. It was all bullshit.

The math test consisted of everything that I haven't used since I was in school, so I couldn't remember how to solve most of the problems. Then there was the personality test, where they asked stupid questions like, for example, "If you found a dollar lying on the ground outside in the parking lot, would you just stick it in your pocket or would you go inside and ask everyone in the building if it belonged to them?" We all know what most people would do in that situation, and I answered all of the questions as honestly as I could, thinking that was what they wanted. I finished both tests feeling confident that I had passed with flying colours and was going to get hired.

Then they called out my name to tell me the results. I could tell that the lady who graded the test was either disgusted by my appearance or annoyed that someone like me was wasting her time. She tore into me like I was a piece of shit. "You should go get your GED, before trying to get a job here!" she screamed, not knowing that I actually did graduate high school. I noticed that she was looking at me up and down like I was trash while she was talking. Then she picked up my personality test, looked me in the eyes and said, "And this...No! I'm not even going to bother going over this with you. Please leave! You application was unsuccessful..." I didn't mind that I didn't get the job but I was furious about how I was treated by that old bitch. She disrespected me on every level and I didn't say a word. The worst part was that I went to this interview before my shift at the FC, so I was pissed off the entire night and I took it out on everyone who didn't deserve it.

    I applied at a gas station across the street from the FC a few days later...primarily because I was very attracted to the manager. This job obviously wasn't going to pay the bills, so I wanted to use it for extra money on my days off from the FC. The manager didn't have an opening but she was interested enough to create a position for me to give me work. She was a real sweetheart, as beautiful on the inside as she was on the outside, and I never saw a ring on her finger. However, the place was extremely busy, and the customers were mostly men for a good reason. Between her and her head cashier, there was enough eye candy to bring in business. It wasn't until our janitor informed me that she was actually married, but didn't wear a ring at work, that I stopped pursuing the role and her.

    Although I wasn't actually asking anyone out, I felt like I was getting rejected anyway. Every woman that I was interested in was already taken and I was running out of options fast. On a nightly basis, people from that factory that I applied at came into the FC to get groceries after their shifts. There was this beautiful young lady who appeared to be around my age that asked me where something was one night. She reminded me of someone that I had a crush on back in high school, and that led to a brief and pleasant conversation. She started coming into the store more frequently after that, and always found me to say hello. I thought she was just being nice but my co-workers didn't agree. They all believed that she liked me and tried to encourage me to ask her out on a date. I wanted to but I never did… and eventually she stopped coming into the store. Sometimes I was my own worst enemy when it came to these types of things.

For some reason, I felt like going to the club...not to find a woman or to get my old job back, but to have some closure and put some demons to rest. When I arrived, I noticed that the place not only looked different but the name had changed once again. Yet when I stepped out of my truck, ghosts were everywhere I looked. I could look over to the left and see the spot where Justice and I made out in my truck many years ago, look to the right and see where Lena used to sit on the hood of her car and wrap her legs around me while we shared our forbidden kisses. Look near the centre and see where I had made out with Celeste and Tristan during our short flings. Everything was swirling around like leaves in the brisk autumn wind. It had been a long time since I had been on this sacred ground. Way too long...in fact.

I was pleasantly surprised when I recognized the doorman. He was one of the many guys who I had a hand in training over the years. He pretty much filled me in on what I had missed out on in my absence. There were very few fights in the club anymore and with Gene's passing, and the place going to his long-time girlfriend, the whole building had a much more relaxed atmosphere overall. I also recognized the DJ's voice. It was AJ, and he still didn't like me enough to acknowledge me, which was ok with me. All of the girls, on the other hand, were new except for two...who were practically babies in this business when I left years ago. They both came up to me to say hello and give me a hug. They hadn't forgotten who I was either. I was then introduced to the next generation of bouncers, who had obviously heard stories about me and seemed excited to finally meet me. I felt like I had regained a part of me that had been dormant for ages, and it felt awesome. The prodigal son had finally returned home.

I decided to take a seat at the bar and just couldn't help but look across to where Gene used to sit so he could watch the whole room. It wasn't the same without him being there. Between that and the fact that the old stage was gone and replaced by a new one, I started to get a little sad. Then I was pulled out of the moment by the young female bartender asking if I wanted something to drink. I wasn't going to drink alcohol for a number of reasons...one being that I knew what it would lead to, especially in this environment. I asked her about Gene and James, and although Gene was gone before she started working there, she did know James, and we shared a couple of stories before I was interrupted by a beautiful blonde coming my way.

The girl immediately stood between my legs and threw her arms around me. Then she whispered into my ear "You're cute. Do you want to go to the VIP room with me so I can ride on your hard long cock?" I busted out laughing. I couldn't help myself. "What are you laughing about?" she asked looking insulted. "You are an incredibly beautiful girl" I replied. "You don't have to say shit like that to get a dance. You are trying way too hard princess. That kind of approach might work on some guys but being classy works on all of them." She apologized and then asked politely. I still turned her down because I wasn't there to spend money. I told her who I was and she claimed that she had heard of me also. She didn't ask for a dance again. She did, however, tell all of the other girls who I was and before I knew it, I had the entire roster sitting around me except for the two girls who used to work with me. They sat together from a safe distance, and just watched and listened as I gave the girls advice and tips and told funny stories from the past. By the time I was ready to leave, I had spent less than ten bucks and felt like I had just exorcised a few demons. Then it dawned on me that on this particular night, I was sober in that building for the first time. I felt like I had really accomplished something and was glad that I went there that night...even if it would be the last time I ever walked through those doors.

3

When I ran out of options on potential job opportunities, I decided to take on a roommate. I didn't have any friends who I trusted enough to share my house with, and there was only one member of my family that qualified: my niece "Tegan." She was still young and hadn't yet been corrupted or heavily influenced by my sister. She grew up next door to my parents and they thought very highly of her, especially my dad. When I first mentioned that I was thinking of moving her into the house, my dad reminded me that she was my niece and that touching her inappropriately was not only wrong but a sin. This was just how my dad was. He didn't trust me with anything or anyone, even though I never gave him a reason not to. I was both offended and insulted by his remark, but sadly not really surprised, considering how low he thought of me.

Just like her mother and cousin before her, Tegan also worked at the FC. I saw her one morning as I was leaving, and made her an offer. She didn't say yes straight away but was intrigued by the idea of having her independence. She said she would think about it and get back to me in a couple of days. Just like my dad, the other members of my family were against it as well, thinking that I might be a negative influence on her, thanks to my "checkered past." Being a rebellious teenager, I think that was what made her decision for her. She was sick and tired of everyone telling her what to do with her life. She called me and told me the good news within a couple of days as promised.

The arrangement was simple. Tegan splits the house payment and buys her own food, while I pay the other half and all of the other bills. This was so she would have some spending money and I could save some cash for a rainy day. It worked out pretty well since she was home at night while I was home during the day. She had her own bedroom and access to thousands of movies if she got bored. She also brought a computer so I paid for the internet services. Then I got into something that would change my life forever: social media.

For years I despised Myspace and Facebook. I used to make fun of Courtney because she was always posting pictures and status updates. I just thought that the idea of being in contact with people that were no longer in your life was futile. But now I was longing for something but I wasn't sure what exactly. When I found out that Tegan was on Facebook, I persuaded her to open me an account and teach me how to use it. Within days, I had a thousand friends and didn't know but a small portion of them. I made friends with everyone who would accept my requests, including people from school that I liked and didn't like, both of my ex-wives, family members, and fellow employees from the present and the past. I was just asking for trouble and I found it almost immediately.

I realized that some people just never grow up no matter how much time has passed. There were still people from school who rejected my friend requests because I had tattoos and long hair in my profile picture. They thought I was a junkie when I actually wasn't, and obviously because of my appearance, I must still be. Then there were those who unfriended me soon after because I didn't praise Jesus on my posts or quote scripture. I foolishly thought that people who actually knew me would want to hear from me, but very few actually gave a damn. The more interactive that I became, the more I got deleted. Even when I didn't post anything for a few days, I still got cut for not being online enough. I hated the fact that I ever opened a fucking account. It was doing more harm than good.

But then I got to thinking. I had written a long bio on my information page about all of the stuff I had been through in life, and hinted about possibly writing a book someday, which was all well received from a number of people. I had also rewritten a majority of my songs back in 2006-2007. I took all of the emotion out of them, from when I originally wrote them both high and love sick. Although they had only grabbed the attention of shitty record companies that were trying to screw me out of money, they were good enough to grab *someone's* attention. Maybe I could even find the right musicians to reform Melancholia through social media since my range had gone from local to infinity. I had the best intentions to make the most of it all, but my own stupidity always got in the way. Still does in fact...

Honestly, I should have been more selective of who I allowed to be in my business. I added everyone from Courtney to my estranged sister, who I have never been able to get along with, and every slut and psycho in between. One "girl" messaged me and told me that she not only wanted to kill me but she would bathe in my blood afterwards. Another teenage girl uploaded my profile picture and placed it within one of her own personal photo albums claiming me as her boyfriend. She would threaten to just show up at my doorstep one day so we could be together, but I got rid of her before that could ever happen. Courtney was watching my wall closely, always poking fun at me for my self-induced drama. But what was annoying me the most was the people that I saw every day in real life, whether it was at work or just hanging out, that couldn't distinguish between reality and Facebook. They would sit back and read my statuses but never comment, then ask me a million questions when I saw them in person about what each status meant, like they were encrypted or something. I put a stop to this pretty quickly by telling them not to be concerned with anything that they read. If there was something that they should be concerned with, I would let them know face to face, not over social media. I still feel the same today.

    Some days I just felt like turning off that damn computer and doing something productive and recreational. I would either go hiking with my uncle or ride around my parents' property on a four wheeler. Sometimes I would even return to my favourite spot on the lake and just sit for hours gazing at the water or the sky, just thinking about things. It was like I subconsciously knew that my life was going in a different direction soon. Therefore, my time was short so I had better cherish every moment like it was my last. I was probably closer to my family during this time than I had been in years.

4

    When I got home one day, I had a message waiting for me from a total stranger through Facebook. She was a beautiful 21 year old girl named "Emma" and she was from my hometown. I had never talked to this girl before and, more than likely, probably never would have either. I was weary about reading her message… especially after all of the heat I had received over the past few weeks. However, I was pleasantly surprised by what she had to say. She said that she found me very attractive and we had just too many things in common, like for instance, our taste in music and movies, to not go out on a date if I was, in fact, single. She also mentioned how inspiring my bio was to her, as she had been through much of the same. I didn't believe that for a second, not at her age, but I humoured her anyway.

If she wasn't so cute, I would have turned her down flat, especially with the age difference being even greater than Courtney and I. She was practically the same age as my niece. They even went to school together and knew each other quite well. Hell, in this day and age, I was almost old enough to be her father! But being as superficial as I was, I accepted her invitation for drinks at Cancun's the following night.

As luck would have it, when I showed up that night, she wasn't there. Thinking that I had been stood up, I raced back home very angry and upset. When I got into the house, I noticed that the answering machine was flashing as I had a missed call. It was Emma, telling me that she was running late and begging me not to leave. I got back into the truck and drove back up there but this time *she* had to wait for *me*. She had apparently arrived just after I had left. This was already not off to a good start at all.

When I got back to Cancun's, Emma was standing outside and she was looking simply ravishing dressed in black. I instantly forgot why I was even mad at her. We went in and had a few drinks before stepping out for a cigarette in the crisp March air. We had an interesting conversation along the way before heading back to my house to watch a movie. Probably ten minutes into the movie, I asked for a kiss. She replied, "I thought you would never ask. I've wanted to kiss you since we were at Cancun's." Seconds later, we were making out hard. Emma was, without a doubt, the best kisser I had ever had the pleasure to lock lips with...and that's saying a lot. After the movie, I took her back to Foothills Mall where her car was, and we shared one final passionate kiss before parting ways. This date may have taken a while to get started but it was well worth the wait.

    The next day I did the dumbest thing possible: I posted something about it on Facebook. I meant it as a compliment to Emma and it was well received by all of my friends. The problem was that everyone liked it except for the one person who mattered...Emma. She saw it as me trying to be a "Facebook celebrity" and she didn't appreciate it. Here was a girl who had a Myspace account and two Facebook accounts yet she had a problem with everything I did on social media. It would become an ongoing issue between us in the days to come. It was, in fact, the only issue that we ever had.

    After everything settled down, Emma rang me and asked if she could come over and bring pizza. Of course, I wasn't going to say no, even though Tegan was home as well. I met Emma at the gas station down the road because she wasn't sure how to get to my house. We kissed passionately through the window for a few minutes before she followed me to my house. I found it comical that she brought a small pizza over for three people to share. That balanced out to practically one piece per person. Tegan hugged Emma when she walked in and they talked for several minutes while I decided which movie to watch. I heard Tegan say that Emma was very popular in school and Emma replied "That doesn't mean anything at all. It doesn't take much to become popular in that school." I thought to myself "If that was indeed the case, what in the hell happened to me then?" When I joined the conversation, Emma brought up the name of a friend of hers who knew everything about everyone who ever went to that school, past or present, and she was going to ask her about me the next time they talked. I knew that if she did her research, she wasn't going to like what she found.

I ended up putting "Zombieland" in the DVD player, but Tegan just couldn't take a hint to leave us alone and give us a little privacy. She sat on the sectional behind us, feeding her face and belching loudly like she always did. To keep from being embarrassed, I would kiss Emma and let our lips smacking together drown out my obnoxious niece's rudeness. Once I even got on my knees and just looked Emma in the eyes. She grabbed my face and said "Come here" just before she began to kiss me deeply again. When the movie ended, Emma said that she had to get going because she had to be up early the next morning. I talked her into going into my bedroom first. Once we got back there and the door was locked, I picked her up and placed her gently on my bed. I crawled on top of her and we started kissing again as I felt her legs wrap around my body. I nibbled on her ear and whispered softly "I can't wait to really taste you." She grinned and said "Me either." I knew that if she was human, she had to be dripping wet. I had her...if she didn't have to leave. When she left that room, her hair and clothes were seriously messed up and she could barely walk. As soon as Tegan noticed, her face turned beet red and she gave me a cheeky smile. I thought to myself "One more night and she's mine."

That was when things got bizarre. Emma called me the next day, late in the evening after I had already gone to bed, and asked if she could come over when she got off of work. Although I had to work that night, and was already exhausted and desperately needed sleep, as long as she either called beforehand or knocked very loudly, I would still let her in. She seemed ok with that. But something happened somewhere between when she left her job and came over to the house that not only changed her mind about spending time with me that night…but any other time as well. Maybe she talked to her friend about me. Maybe she didn't like the fact that I put my responsibilities before her. Maybe she did come by and I didn't answer the door. Maybe it was because I waited until the next day to call her back. Who knows? But for whatever reason, the alarm was what woke me up that night. When I finally did reach her, she wanted some space because she felt like we were moving too quickly. If that was the truth, then why did she call in the first place… then suddenly change her mind?

Over the next few days, we had minimal contact. Only cryptic messages about me trying to be someone I'm not on Facebook from her end and apologies from mine. I wanted her so bad that I humiliated myself in front of 3000 "friends" for her amusement. All I could do then was bury my head in the sand and wait for a response. I would get that on St. Patrick's Day. Kaine, who I had reconnected with over Facebook, and I went to an Irish pub to hear some music and drink some green beer. I went to take my mind off Emma but spent most of the evening talking about her and dissecting the entire brief relationship. Kaine had been following, like everyone else, all of the drama that unfolded between Emma and me. He asked me what the problem was and I told him that she was accusing me of pretending to be more popular than I actually was on social media. His immediate response was "Does she not actually know you? You kind of are." He then told me that it was out of character for me to let a girl that I barely knew get to me the way that she had and advised me to let her go because she obviously wasn't worth the trouble. I totally agreed. We went on to have a great time and I didn't mention Emma's name again.

That was until I got home and saw that I had a message from her on the computer. I was so drunk that I couldn't read the screen, so I had to get Tegan to read it to me. It simply stated that she was very impressed by the lengths I would go to secure her, and that she accepted my apology, therefore she wanted to see me again. I invited her on a day trip to Ripley's Aquarium of the Smokies and Dollywood the following day. We were only going as "friends" and just take it from there to see what happens. Everything was grand...for a few hours that is.

The next morning I decided to delete my Facebook account and create a fresh one to eliminate all the riff raff. I thought that was what Emma wanted but all she saw was that, for a brief moment, I had two accounts. She sent me an angry message about how I haven't learned a damn thing and cancelled our plans for later in the day. I had seen enough at this point, and completely lost my temper. I called her a few select names and she told me to "enjoy my popularity on Facebook because that was the only place I would ever have it." How ironic that she came to me through social media and I lost her because of it. Facebook giveth...then it taketh away. Over the next few months, I would see Emma a couple of times, but never said a word to her. I did, however, send her an apology through her Myspace, since she had blocked me through Facebook, before I left the States. She did read it but never gave me the time of day. Looking back, she didn't even deserve that, but I felt like it was the right thing to do at the time. I've changed a lot since then. The funny part was that I was unknowingly still friends with her mother long after our fling. Emma could have been following me through her mother's account after she blocked me, and I would have never known. As soon as I figured it out, I deleted and blocked her mother and the chain was broken forever... as far as I know that is.

5

Ever since I've been on social media, there have been a number of girls from different countries that was interested in me, while girls in America stopped noticing me at all. I was pretty popular in Europe especially. There was one girl from Germany who wanted me so much that she used to talk dirty to me every morning and even called me a couple of times long distance. She had even planned a trip to America in the summer just to spend a week with me. But before that could ever happen, fate would have someone else in mind.

Back when I was still talking to Jennifer, she read my tarot cards. They said that I was going to meet someone very special in March or April that was going to change my life forever. I didn't believe in fortune telling, but I did think that this was perhaps her way of letting me know when we could take our "relationship" to the next level. That obviously wasn't the case. I think that we could safely agree that Emma did fit the description either. But there were two girls that came into my life at that time that did. I met them both through Facebook also.

One was a single mother from Baltimore named "Christie." We started talking after one of her relationships fell apart and she was down on herself. All I did was provide an outlet and an ear to listen and then tell her that everything was going to be ok. There could have been a little flirting going on as well. The attraction between us grew out of

that. As the days passed, her biggest concern was how we were going to actually date, living in different states and all, and then what we do if things got serious. I assured her that if something like that did develop, I wouldn't hesitate to relocate to Baltimore. That was when she informed me that she would be driving down to Florida in a month or so. We agreed that would be the perfect opportunity for us to finally spend some quality time together. Everything seemed to be falling into place one would think. Then the unthinkable happened: she simply vanished for a while. Without that constant communication, what we did have was started to fade. In the meantime, I was exploring other options and so was she. What I had been looking for my entire life was right under my nose… but it wasn't going to be easy to obtain it. I couldn't have imagined in my wildest dreams a more difficult challenge that what lied ahead.   -
DJN

CHAPTER XXIV - *"THE PERFECT COMES"*

2010

    From the day she was born, she knew she was my destiny. She was a petal that wasn't torn, a celestial body, made just for me. We were so compatible, without scorn, without thorns, and when I held her in my arms, spread her legs, she fit me so perfectly.

    Come with me, on my final journey, I am the wind, and you are the feather. I have such sights to show you. Think deeply, be with me… let's soar higher than birds, through showers of light and waves of dew.

    Take my hand… let's sail off into the late evening dusk, to the spot where we first met, building castles in the sand, with the aroma of floral nectars and sheer musk, under a light red sunset.

    I've sown my wild oats, now I'm humble. Thank God it's over, all in the past. I've made pebbles float, made mountains crumble, I've found my four leaf clover… I've saved the best for last.

    Come with me, on my final journey, I am the wind and you are the feather. I'll take you places you never knew you wanted to go. Think deeply, be with me… as I find the treasure at the end of the rainbow.

    Take my hand…let's sail off into the early morning mist, to the hill overlooking the ocean, where we first kissed, under the dark blue heavens.

    From out of my imagination, the perfect comes…

 -Denny Noland "Draven" From my song "The Perfect Comes"

Written on August 24, 2006
Copyright 2007

    Now let's talk about the other. She was a stunning goddess from Australia named "Sepi." Although we had a very strong connection, she was the dark horse in the race for a number of reasons. First and foremost, was where she was lived…I may have had a chance back in school to come to Australia as an exchange student but the idea of living there one day permanently never appealed to me. Besides, as far as Sepi was concerned, she was already taken. She had been talking to a single father from Texas for a very long time and had already made plans to come to America to be with him. So I guess you can say that neither of us was each other's first picks. The problem that she ran into was her health issues and the "red tape" that I would get to know too well later on. She was a type 1 diabetic and was having procedure after procedure to keep from going blind due to an abundance of faulty vessels behind her eyes that wasn't detected until they were out of control. So without proper health care in the States, and already suffering from a pre-existing condition, coming to America was starting to look like a bad idea.
    Around the time that Christie was avoiding me, Sepi's partner pulled the same stunt, leading us toward each other. Sepi was about to go back to the eye clinic to get more lasering done, while I was starting to piss blood again. I had hoped and prayed that I wouldn't have to go through all of that shit again, but apparently, my prayers fell on deaf ears. At least I had insurance this time, but it would become a fucking nightmare anyway. The doctors that they sent me to tried to tell me that I had a

simple kidney infection and refused an X-ray. I knew that I had a stone because I knew all too well what they felt like. Hell, I could pretty much tell them exactly where it was. But they just gave me some good drugs and sent me home multiple times without bothering to give me an X-ray. Eventually, I got my dad to take me to the hospital where my plan paid 90% on the bill. We wasted an entire day there only to be told that it was only infection and to "stay the course" and everything would be alright. Although I demanded an X-ray, once again I was told that there was no need. Inevitably, I ended up at the original clinic again, and by that time, I was so sick that they immediately referred me to a specialist. The specialist didn't waste any time. He took me in for an X-ray straight away and told me what I knew all along: that I had a stone that was going to require surgery. This was after several visits that didn't accomplish anything but drain my bank account. This had dragged out for so long that I had run out of sick days, so now I wasn't getting paid either. I was in dire straits.

Through all of this, Sepi was there for me. She didn't have to be but she chose to. I wasn't the easiest person to get along with at this time, especially when I was heavily medicated. Tegan was giving me a few dollars here and there to help out, but when the house payment was due, she didn't feel like she should have to contribute because she chose to do that. This would lead to our first argument. I had also said a few derogatory remarks on Facebook, while I was medicated, that led to me losing a lot of my friends, and the few who did decide to stick around, was put through a roller coaster of emotions, depending on how I was feeling at the time. The only person that could cheer me up was Sepi and now she was the only one who mattered.

The night before my surgery, I received a phone call from a number that I didn't recognize. I thought that it might be someone wishing me luck, but it wasn't. It was the company who owns the machine that they use to do the procedure. Someone had noticed that the last time I owed the hospital a large sum of money, the bills went to a collection agency. They threatened to cancel my surgery if I didn't send a $100 deposit within the next hour. I got them their money but it reminded me of how crooked the medical field could be at times. No patient should ever be turned away whether they can afford the treatment or not the way I see it, but that's not the way it works. That fucking phone call just made me resent them even more.

When I went in for surgery the next day, they took me straight in as dad waited patiently in the waiting room. They put me on a slow drip at first since there were several people in front of me. Now I was both relaxed and drowsy, and in true diabetic fashion, desperately needing to piss. This was a problem obviously, as one of the beautiful young nurses had to walk me to the bathroom and wait outside holding my drip. Unfortunately for her, she couldn't close the door properly so before I finished adjusting my gown, I had already given her and everyone other nurse and patient in the room an eyeful of both my penis and ass. I was too out of it to either care or be embarrassed about it though. "I'm sure this happens all the time" I thought to myself.

Finally, it was my turn...so they started putting me under as the wheeled me in for my operation. Counting backwards from ten, I made it to about seven before everything went black. I woke up in recovery with that familiar pain of not only the procedure itself but of having a stent inside of my penis again. I was starving on the way home so I talked dad into stopping at Burger King, despite the fact that the anesthesia always made me sick to my stomach. I nearly hurled with every bite but I forced it down anyway. I may have been very sick but I had promised Sepi that I would let her know as soon as I got home and I kept that promise.

Having missed so much work already and bills piling up, I tried to go back to work early, only to be sent home because I didn't have the proper medical clearance. Later that same week, Tegan took me to get the stent taken out. I had no idea what I was in store for, considering that I was lucky enough to be under the last time I had one removed after the multiple surgeries. I had heard horror stories over the years, but I always prided myself for having a high tolerance for pain so I wasn't worried. Then the nurse grabbed my penis with her gloved hands, and the doctor attached the machine to the tip of it. It was bad enough that I had to see all of this but there was nothing they could give me to numb the pain either. "There is a local that I can give you" the doctor said. "But my patients have always told me that it makes no difference. They still felt *everything*." Therefore, I decided to just take it like a man.

The doctor tried to distract me from what was about to happen by talking about sports. I just looked at him and said, "Doc, I don't think that there's a damn thing that you could do or say that's going to take my mind off of this. Just do it!" I gripped the side of the table and squeezed tightly as I prepared for the worst. Then I took a deep breath and closed my eyes as I waited for that crucial moment. It was over in seconds...but can I say that in all of my life, never have I felt such excruciating pain. The machine literally yanks the damn thing out while it flushes water into your bladder to keep blood from going everywhere. This immediately gives you the sensation that you need to piss even if there is nothing in there to come out. Needless to say that the journey across town to get my scripts made the pain ten times worse, but at least having a near death experience, courtesy of Tegan's driving, took my mind off of it briefly. When I got home, once again, Sepi was waiting to hear from me. Things were starting to change between us and we both noticed it. We were falling in love…

Although most people were starting to figure out what was going on, others just didn't care. One former wrestling valet, who wasn't near as famous as she thought she was, kept trying to get me to go out with her. She kept inviting me to just hang out with her and her girls all the way up to the week before I was leaving for Australia. She appeared to be cool and sweet so I did consider it briefly until Sepi asked, "If the shoe was on the other foot, and I was coming to America to be with you and some guy wanted to "meet" me before I left, how would you feel?" Point well taken…I never met her and she ended up deleting me after I left the country. Then there was another local girl who offered to come to my house and "see if everything was still working right" after my surgery. I turned down her advances several times and then deleted her. Sepi and I may not have been technically in a relationship yet, I still felt a sense of loyalty to her anyway. I didn't totally like where this was heading, but I couldn't stop it.

Now I was back at work and although my kidneys were back to normal, I started suffering from a severe toothache. I tried every over the counter remedy on the market and nothing was working, so I eventually had to go to the dentist. It turned out that not only had a section of one of my back teeth rotted and fallen off, leaving the nerve exposed, but a wisdom tooth was coming in right behind it and needed to be surgically removed. I had literally just returned to work so the boss wasn't too happy to hear that I needed more time off. I didn't like it too much myself. I had been an ironman the first four years I worked there, never taking even one sick day, yet now I was the most unreliable person on the crew. The boss told me that he was giving me an entire week off to heal because "no one he has ever known had been able to return to work earlier than that." I told him that I would be back in three days at the most. He just laughed and said, "OK then, I'll see you in a week." To his amazement and disbelief, I was back in three days as promised. Within weeks, all the doctor bills started coming in, eleven in total, and I was up shit creek financially again after I had worked my ass off to get back on my feet.

2

The animosity between Tegan and I only increased in the weeks to come. It started when her mother, my sister, asked if she could come over and use the computer to "look for a job." I was strongly against it but Tegan promised to keep her under control and out of my hair. From the second my sister sat down in that chair and logged into the internet, she started bitching and whining. Instead of admitting that she didn't know what the hell she was doing and asking for help, she claimed that the computer wasn't working right. Then she said that the internet was too slow, even though I had the fastest speed available in that particular area. She might have even slammed her fist down on the keyboard a time or two out of anger and frustration. Eventually my niece took over and showed her what she was doing wrong, and then several hours pass and she didn't want to leave. I needed to get to bed, and I didn't want my sister wandering around the house unsupervised, so I pulled Tegan to the side and told her to get rid of her or I would. About an hour later, my sister finally left and I was telling Tegan that she wasn't coming back…ever. She didn't like it but it was my house and my rules and what I say goes, whether she agreed or not. It was not a democracy. She should have read the fine print before signing.

Then there was the night that she called me at work and told me that the cops had just left the house. When she got home from work, she forgot to turn the alarm system off. A few seconds later, the alarm went off followed by the phone ringing. In a panic, she forgot what the password was so the local police paid her a visit. After several minutes of scolding, they warned Tegan that if there was another "false alarm" I would be receiving a bill for their troubles on top of everything else. I lost my temper when I heard this, and let Tegan have it. I didn't know how anyone could be so stupid. Did she not notice the constant beeping that always reminds you to punch the code in when you enter the front door? How about the fact that I even had the password wrote down for her in case this ever happened and she completely forgot that too? I was starting to think that I was wrong about her. Perhaps she had too much of her mother in her for me to tolerate. I was ready to send her and her shit back to my aunt the first chance I had.

This was around the time that I asked Sepi to be my girl, as ludicrous as that sounds with us being on opposite sides of the planet. Her answer made me the happiest guy in the world. We would begin talking on the phone first but it got too damn expensive quick so she suggested Skype. I went out the next day and bought the best web cam I could afford and a couple of speakers. She then told me how to install the program and taught me how to use it. Now we were talking for hours on end every single day until we fell asleep. I will never forget how funny it was when the picture would freeze mid-sentence and how sad I got every time we would hang up for the day. It always felt like it was the last time I would ever get to see her and talk to her. Eventually, I just dragged the couch near the computer so I could watch her sleep and vice versa. I loved her deeply and I knew that one day all of this just wasn't going to be enough. That was when the notion of moving to Australia first entered my mind.

While Tegan was living it up... throwing all night slumber parties with as many as five of the young ladies from the store in the house at a time, I was plotting my next move. I'm sure it probably looked bad to Sepi on web cam when girl after girl would come out of my bedroom in the morning in their pajamas, but thank God she trusted me. I had already called the Australian embassy in the States and got false information about being able to legally work once I got to Oz. However, one particular woman did advise me to avoid extending my visa to six months otherwise I would have to come back to America once it expires no matter what happens. "I probably shouldn't be telling you this but go over on a three month visa and if you decide to get married before your time is up, there is a procedure to stay in the country. But you have to do it exactly the way I tell you ok?" She would go on and tell me how to beat the system, even if it meant that it could be a very long time before I could walk on American soil again. At least I would be with Sepi until she got sick of me.

In order for me to be with Sepi, I had to go to her. There was absolutely no way I was letting her come to me even though she wanted to. She was in the middle of receiving treatments for her eyes and we could never afford any of them without Medicare. Unlike in America, as long as I didn't have

AIDS, Hepatitis, or anything else contagious, my health wasn't going to be an issue in Australia. I was going to be picked up by Medicare instead of being treated like a fucking leper. There was only one answer: I absolutely had to move to Australia or end my relationship with the only woman who really got me. I've always said that if I found "the one" I would do *anything* to be with her. I wasn't just whistling Dixie, I meant every word. I just wished that I didn't have to give up *everything*, but it was what it was.

After applying for and being granted my visa and passport, it was time to set a date: August 20, 2010. This would give me a couple of months to sort out a few loose ends. I broke the news to everyone within the next few days. My parents accused me of just doing it to hurt them. My friends thought I had lost my damn mind and the boss reacted by saying "Why do you have to go to Australia to be with someone? Can't you find a girl here?" I even had a few people who I hadn't seen in years stop by the store to see me one last time. Then there were those who were sent to test me, like Jennifer, who called me up and wanted to "date for real" this time since her reconciliation with her husband didn't work out. At least this time around, I rejected her and that felt pretty good.

My original plan was to go over to Australia for a few months while Tegan remained in my house. I was going to send money to her each month to help her with bills until I got back. When I first mentioned it she was on board, but as time passed and tension increased between us, she changed her mind. She wanted to go back to my aunt where she had no responsibilities. I totally understood but I had a favour to ask: I needed a computer to stay in touch with Sepi until I got over there. Tegan agreed to let me keep it until a day or two before I left and then she wanted it back. I hated that everything went sour toward the end between us, but she still did come through for me when I needed her the most. I would have very little contact with her in the weeks to come. She lost her job at the FC and I would only see her once before I left and that was when she came by to pick up her computer. I did, however, interact with her briefly online when a man was killed in my aunt's front yard when he crashed his ATV into her well house. He was obviously going too fast around the curve and lost control. I was told that it was a horrific scene. He wasn't wearing a helmet so his head was mangled. Tegan and my aunt were still finding his teeth in the yard months later. Around 2011, Tegan deleted me from her Facebook friend list because she hadn't heard from me in a long time. She kept Sepi, however, even though they never interacted at all. Yeah…I don't get it either but that's Tegan logic for you.

    There would be even more backlash from Courtney, who had kept an eye on this developing story. Instead of criticising me for eventually walking away from everything, she was furious because I hadn't mentioned it to her father yet. He had to find out just like everyone else did through Facebook. As time passed, I began to realize that the only reason that she cared was because she wanted the house. I made a deal with her that benefitted both of us. I would let her keep all of the electronics, and even the bed, if she just paid her dad a little money to reduce my last house payment somewhat. That way, I could save some money to take to Australia and not have to find somewhere to store them. Although she agreed to all of this, she didn't tell her dad. When he came over with Courtney's brother to collect the final house payment, it was all news to him, but he reluctantly accepted anyway because of how close we had become. I had earned his trust...even enough for him to let me know that he thought that the idea of moving overseas for any woman is ridiculous. "Now if you told me that you were going over there for any other reason, I would understand but when you tell me what you've just told me, it sounds crazy" he said with sincerity. All I could say was "Trust me I know what I am doing." He knew that was total bullshit but he chose to keep his mouth shut and spend the rest of the evening saying goodbye and wishing me luck. I was definitely going to miss *him* at least.

There were two other problems though. I was still under contract for the alarm system that we had installed in the house and breaking the contract wasn't going to be easy. I was delighted when Courtney said that she wanted to keep it on, but getting the name changed on the account was like pulling teeth...even if she had to co-sign for me to get it in the first place due to my less than stellar credit rating. She supposably paid a decent amount of money to switch it over, but failed to change the banking details, so I was still getting billed for it through direct debit even after I left the States. Since she had immediately deleted me on Facebook as soon as my feet left the ground, and she had what she wanted, I had no means to contact her anymore. I had no other choice but to close my account in America, ending any chance of paying off my debts from afar.

Then there was the issue of what to do with the cats. When Courtney broke up with her next boyfriend, she talked to me in length about what went wrong in our relationship and spoke of how much she missed the boys. Although she didn't come out and say it, it felt like she might have wanted to get back together. Then she started dating a fellow nurse from the nuthouse, where she worked with her dad, and she changed. A couple of weeks before I was scheduled to leave the country, she brought this guy over to check out the house, even though we had agreed that she would come alone. Maybe I might of read the guy wrong, but I felt like he was disrespecting me in my own house, and that is never a good idea. Anger was racing through my veins as this uninvited guest pranced around the grounds like he already owned them. Courtney was trying her best to distract me by being very polite but it wasn't working. Then I thought of Sepi… and how an assault charge at this stage could prevent me from going to her, so I let it ride. When I mentioned the cats this time around, Courtney didn't want them anymore. I begged and pleaded with her to no avail. Now I had no idea what to do with them as time was running out quickly. Taking them to a shelter wasn't an option…they deserved better than that. I had 4000 friends on Facebook at the time, and several hundred of them lived in the area, yet not a damn one of them would adopt the cats either. My heart would break every time I looked at them. They had no idea what was going on. If only I could have afforded to take them with me I would have. The thought of leaving them behind in the house so Courtney would have to take care of them did cross my mind briefly, but I was afraid that she may not be moving in for several weeks and they would run out of food and water before then. I had to find another way. I needed a miracle…

3

At the FC, I had agreed to work up until the day of my flight. There were so many memories and so many people there that I will never forget. From the guy that we called "the Worm," who was always late and had an amazing excuse each and every time. Once he told us that there was an accident on the road and he pulled both the driver and the passenger out of the flames. Strange how a heroic act like that never made the news or the papers. The last time we saw him, he was confronted by two drug dealers outside the store one morning. They had literally been waiting in the parking lot all night to collect some money that he owed them. They didn't touch him on the premises but no one knows what happened later that day. We never had a chance to ask him. If we had, I'm sure it would have sounded like a movie script.

Then there was the guy we called "Ed" because when they hired him, we were given a speech from the boss about how we probably wouldn't like him or get along with him because he was an "educated man." No one really knew what that was supposed to mean. Was the boss calling us a bunch of dumbasses? Ed was kind of an asshole but I got along with him and understood his dry sense of humour. We also had an assistant manager who was one of the nicest guys while he was still in training, but after he got his own store and then got demoted for having an affair with one of the married staff members, came back with a vengeance. He now talked to everyone like they were trash and never smiled. When he first heard that they might need to replace me because I was moving to Australia, he thought it was all a myth. He never believed it until I turned in my notice.

There was even a casualty along the way. A kid that had only been working with us for a few weeks came in seriously fucked up on something one night. He could barely walk and was pouring sweat so we had to send him home. He died from heart failure after an overdose an hour or two later. I even nearly got killed one night on my way to work when some pale girl wearing black was walking on the side of the road. By the time I saw her, it was almost too late. I had to swerve into the other lane to miss her and then get back over before I hit a truck head on. I didn't get over fast enough so our mirrors smashed into each other. I was scared to death even though it could have been much worse. The guy that I clipped never saw the girl at all and unfortunately she had disappeared into one of the houses after the accident instead of sticking around. If she had been off the road, this would have never happened, but hopefully she learned her lesson.

    Honestly, I don't know what my crew thought of me. The only times I was really likeable was when I was sick and heavily medicated. One example of this was when I got a prescription for liquid hydrocodone. Since I refused to call in sick no matter what, I took a big dose of that delicious stuff and had everyone laughing all night and don't even remember what I did. However, what I do remember was the following day when I got paid. I only lived about five minutes from my bank and needed to cash my check. It usually took twenty or so minutes to really kick in so I took a dose and got behind the wheel, thinking that by the time I got back home it would hit. For some reason, it hit me much quicker this time and as luck would have it, it was as I was approaching the drive thru window. The beams on both sides of the lane seemed to be closing in so I could possibly hold the record for the slowest speed ever up to that window. I couldn't even look that woman in the eye as she gave me my money because I felt so fucked up and probably looked the part too. Thank God I made it home safely. Needless to say, I never did that again. I hope that it's the comical stuff like this that people remember when they think of me.

We were now in the final days and I was selling off everything that didn't have sentimental value. I was selling my toys and comic books to one guy in the video department, while another guy in produce was buying the bulk of my DVDs. I still had two cars to get rid of so I sold one to our floor guy "Harry." Harry was a great guy who I liked a lot. He may have been a little burned out but aren't we all? Everyone tried to give him a hard time but he always took up for himself, even if a strong gust of wind could potentially blow him away. He was much better than the old bastard that he replaced, who always talked about Gene like they were the best of friends. Apparently, he did some plumbing for him back in the early nineties and they have been mates ever since. I always thought it was funny that I had worked for Gene off and on for a decade and never heard this guy's name mentioned once. I must have heard the same damn story a hundred times about how Gene let him snort cocaine off a stripper's ass once. I always wanted to say to him, "To you, that might have been a special night that you are proud of and will never forget, but to me, that was only Friday" but I never got the chance because he always either interrupted me by talking over me or just ignored me completely. Hell, if I had a dollar for every stripper's ass that I've snorted cocaine off of, I could pay his wages for a week!

All of this time, I was still spending all of my spare time talking to Sepi on Skype. I knew in my heart that she was the one… the final girl in the Trinity… so I proposed to her even though we had never felt each other's skin or even been in the same room. She accepted. Now I not only had to buy her an engagement ring, but the biggest rock I could afford. I went to my jeweller in Foothills Mall in Maryville, where I had bought all of my previous rings, and picked one out. I was ashamed of how small of a rock all of the money that I had saved up could buy, so I kept upgrading every time I sold off more of my belongings. I was finally satisfied a couple of days before I had to leave. I knew that whether she would ever admit it or not, once I announced our engagement over social media, a part of Courtney probably died. For nearly five years, she waited for me to propose to *her* and it never happened. I always used the excuse that I was never getting married again, and at the time I meant that, but now I was getting married to someone I have physically never met. No wonder she hated my guts.

4

The last week flew by and now we had reached my final night in the United States. I had been gradually having everything disconnected until the only thing that was still on was the electricity. Tegan had taken her computer so I had only my cell phone to keep in touch with Sepi. I had planned to spend as much time with my family and friends as possible but it didn't exactly work out that way. Instead, I became a hermit and barely left the house. It was my way of letting things go…letting the world I've known my entire life just fade away without thinking about it too much. A part of me was a little hurt that no one had really made any kind of effort to stop me or talk me out of leaving. I wouldn't have listened… but it would have still been nice to have known that someone actually cared…but they didn't. Life was already going on as if I had already left. They had replaced me with not one, but two guys at the FC. I even had the opportunity to play a huge part in their training over the past few weeks. There was a brutal tug of war going on inside of my head. One side wanted to stay and the other couldn't wait to be with the love of his life.

I don't know why I did it, but I worked my shift at the store instead of spending my last hours with family and friends. One of the girls from the front asked to be taken off the register so she could help me split the truck. She was always very shy and didn't really say goodbye with words but with actions. I had a number of other people come up to me during my shift with well wishes and farewells, but the only part that really bothered me, and made me emotional, was saying goodbye to my crew the next morning, knowing that I would never see them again. Each one of them shook my hand and wished me luck. It was hard to hold back tears. I had worked with some of them for several years and never dreamed this day would actually come. Before I could walk out the door, I was told by one of the managers that the boss was on the phone and wanted to talk to me. I didn't believe her at first and laughed it off until I heard the voice on the other end of the line. It was indeed him...thanking me for all of my years of service and wishing me luck. His last words were "If something happens or things don't work out for one reason or another and you have to come back, you will always have a job here." That nearly did it. It was all I could do to keep from turning on the wetworks but I held them back until I got to the van then I let it all out. It would be a few minutes before they stopped but I felt better afterwards. I had so much to do before I caught that plane so I didn't have time to get too caught up in the moment.

I tried to get a couple of hours of sleep before packing my suitcases, but I was dealing with too many emotions for my brain to rest, so I went ahead and filled the van up with all of my belongings and drove to my parents' house. As I walked across the yard, I took one final look around at my childhood home. I took notice of everything from the clean country air to the beautiful hillsides and mountains surrounding me. I wanted to remember everything exactly as it was, in all of its glory, because there were no guarantees that I would ever see it again. I tried to do the same with the house, but my mother was pissed off that I hadn't changed my mind about leaving. We got into a shouting match that dad had to break up and I ended up leaving without even saying goodbye. It was not what I was expecting or wanting to happen but I had no control over how my mother was going to react.

Dad wasn't very supportive of me either, but he did handle it like an adult at least. He didn't agree with my decision but he did respect it and admired me for having the balls to follow through with it. In the weeks leading up to this big day, he had given me some great advice about airports and how to handle flying for the first time. He would also help me on this day by driving me around to run a few last minute errands since I no longer had a car. He took me to the bank so I could activate the international use of my debit card and then to the FC so I could fill all of my scripts in the pharmacy. However, he was quick to voice his opinion when some of my former fellow employees told me that I was making a mistake. He also warned me that if I went to Australia and fell on my ass, don't call him to bail me out. He even refused to drive me to the airport, leaving me with no other option but to call a cab.

When he dropped me back off at my nearly empty house, he hugged me and told me to please look after myself. My last words to him were that I could be very resilient when I needed to be and that everything was going to be fine. Then I went into the house and faced the cats. They could sense that something was wrong and change was coming. Most of their old hiding places were gone and the TV that I always left on for noise hadn't been turned on in days. There was just an eerie silence that filled the room now. The saddest part was that I still didn't know what the hell I was going to do with them, yet my cab was going to be there to pick *me* up in a couple of hours. My thoughts were elsewhere and everywhere... as my life literally passed before my eyes and I didn't like what I was seeing. All of the drug use and near death experiences, combined with the childhood ridicule and a lifetime of damaging relationships had scarred me beyond repair. I needed to move on and start over and this was my big opportunity. There was no one who could come into my life that could possibly be the perfect fit that Sepi was. I knew once and for all that I was doing the right thing but it still didn't really make it any easier to walk away. I had run my course...worn out my welcome in this fucking town and I desperately needed something to put that sparkle back in my eye and bounce in my step. If I needed to travel to the other side of the world to obtain it, so be it.

    Then a miracle happened to set in all in motion. Kaine called me and not only volunteered to drive me to the airport personally, but also offered to take the cats off my hands and find them a good home. Lord knows we have had our differences in the past but he came through at the last minute and fixed everything singlehandedly. I could never possibly thank him enough for what he did. If it hadn't been for his perfect timing, I would have been in quite a dilemma once my cab arrived. I can't even begin to imagine how that could have potentially played out.

    Kaine was running a little late, mostly because he had never been to my house before. I couldn't really assist him in any way except verbally over the phone. When he finally pulled down on my street, I could have hugged his neck. We chatted for a bit, then rounded up the cats and loaded my luggage into his truck. I took one final look around the house before locking it up and hiding the key under the mat. I really loved the place, and if I only had a contract saying that I was actually buying it, it might have affected my decision to leave. Kaine and I said our goodbyes on the way to the airport. He knew exactly where to drop me off, which was very handy and time saving. I shook his hand and thanked him again before I cuddled the cats one last time. They were terrified and had been crying since we left the house. I felt like I had lost another piece of myself as I watched Kaine drive away. This was definitely the most difficult thing I had ever done in my life.

My itinerary read that I was supposed to fly from Knoxville to Dallas, then from Dallas to Los Angeles, and finally from Los Angeles to Sydney. Once I got to Sydney, I had a two hour bus ride to Canberra. It was a very tight schedule with a few minutes to spare here and there but I was fucked right out of the gate. The flight out of Knoxville was delayed for more than an hour, so it was going to take a miracle for me to be at the station in time to catch that bus. I called my mother to pass time as she had finally calmed down enough to talk. Finally a plane did show up, but before I could board it, I was told that it was headed to Chicago instead of Dallas so I would have to wait longer. By the time my plane did arrive, I was a nervous wreck. If having everything searched through customs didn't do me in, running this late did the job. I really wished that *someone* would have at least come to the airport and surprised me but I ended up leaving both hurt and disappointed.

Despite all of the warnings from both my Kaine and my father about how scary taking off and landing could be for a virgin flyer, I was too bitter to be afraid even though the first plane was quite small. I had booked window seats the whole way except for the long flight from Los Angeles to Sydney, which didn't really matter since it was overnight anyways. I spent my time admiring the view from high above and staring at the wing that was literally just outside my window. It seemed like we reached Dallas in no time at all. I was intrigued by my view of that massive city from the clear blue sky. When my feet touched the ground, all I wanted was to take a piss and grab something to eat in that order before heading out to LA.

Once we landed, the first thing I found was the bathroom. While I was zipping up my pants, I heard an announcement over the loudspeaker that my flight to LA was departing in ten minutes. Now I had to race through that huge airport trying to find my gate. Anyone who has ever been there can tell you that it is no easy task. I asked one of the employees if I was close and she told me that I couldn't be much further away. I needed to catch the tram to get to the other side of the airport and fast. Of course, she couldn't tell me where the tram was so I wasn't much better off. Five minutes had passed when I glanced over instinctively and saw a young couple sitting on what looked like a tram. They just happened to be going to the gate beside the one I needed to get to. I took a seat beside them and got to my plane just in the nick of time. I was the last person to board that plane. They were literally closing the door when I walked up. Of course, this meant that my carry- on bag, which had Sepi's engagement ring in it among other things, couldn't be placed anywhere near me. My eyes never strayed far from that area until I memorized the exact spot. Then I relaxed a little...

Now I was on a larger plane... and from the moment we left the runway, my ears started aching. At times, it was all I could do to keep from screaming out in pain. However, I was blessed to be seated next to an elderly couple who were coming home from visiting relatives in Chicago. They were lovely people, saying all the right things to keep me going forward without second guessing myself. They also became my tour guide as they pointed out all of the sights as we flew over Los Angeles at sunset. I saw the crowded LA freeway, and even the Hollywood sign. As a matter of fact, that sign would be the last thing that I could remember seeing on American soil. Then there was the descent at LAX airport, that made my ears feel as if they were going to explode. The whole experience felt surreal, as I kept pinching myself to make sure that I wasn't dreaming.

I instantly fell in love with Los Angeles. Just walking on the grounds that so many legendary performers have walked on at some point in their lives was magical. You could almost feel it in the air if you've never been there before. I spent around three hours wandering around LAX. When I went to the gate that was on my itinerary, I noticed an abundance of Chinese people there. It turns out that my itinerary was wrong, unless I wanted to go to China. Now I had to continue searching for the area I was supposed to be in. Once I found it, I ordered some food to stop my stomach from growling and took a seat. I had been running on pure adrenalin but it was starting to run out.

Although my Qantas international flight to Sydney was also running late, we were promised that we would touch down in Australia right on time due to the jet stream and otherwise perfect flying weather. I had my doubts but there was nothing I could really do about it. One way or another, this was going to be a very long flight, and the plus side was that my seat was at the very back of this massive plane near the bathroom. I was sitting beside a gorgeous young English girl who kept falling asleep on my shoulder. Then someone sitting in front of us started either freaking out or getting sick and ended up getting moved towards the front of the plane. When they moved, the entire family moved as well leaving several empty seats. One of the stewardesses asked if I wanted to sit in that area where I would have room to really stretch out. I peeled the girl off of my shoulder and moved to that row.

Now I had three TV monitors instead of one. I put one on music videos, one on the GPS so I knew exactly where we were at all times, and the other one on movies. I watched "Hot Tub Time Machine" and "Chloe" hoping that I would eventually fall asleep like everyone else but I was wide awake. I watched as we flew over Hawaii and endless miles of ocean. I even watched the sun come up the next morning. Although I didn't get any sleep, I did freshen up a bit as it would be my last opportunity to do so before I saw Sepi. About mid-morning, we were served breakfast and was told that we would be in Sydney in a couple of hours. That meant that the pilot obviously knew what the hell he was talking about. We were actually ahead of schedule! Before we were allowed to land and get off the plane, everyone had to fill out some information card to turn into customs. By the time we arrived at Sydney airport, I was ready to kiss the ground. I had finally arrived... **-DJN**

CHAPTER XXV - "PARADISE FOUND?"

2010-2011

Now I was standing in the centre of Sydney airport and couldn't find my luggage. I was so fucking angry that I was swearing out loud where everyone could hear me. Eventually a middle aged bloke came up to me and said, "G'day matey! Can I help you?" I just looked at him in disgust like any arrogant yank would, not even really meaning to. It turned out that I had been searching in the wrong place but I wasn't about to apologize for my mistake…or my language for that matter. I'm sure that everyone had heard worse. I only got more irritated when I got to customs and saw the long line of people in front of me… mostly from third world countries and being searched thoroughly. Fortunately, I was only in line for a couple of minutes before one of the officers pulled me over to the side. She let the dog smell my bags and then allowed me to exit out onto the street. I was a little confused but wasn't about to say anything. When what I thought was going to take forever, and I get waved through with very little fuss in the matter of five minutes, who am I to complain?

My body went into shock once the winter air hit me. It doesn't get terribly cold in Sydney but when you go from 99 degrees in the shade in the heart of summer to the middle of winter in just under 24 hours, it's hard to adjust to. I was also confused about what day it was because technically I lost a day once I crossed the ocean. Then I learned a quick lesson about expenses when I went to buy a pack of cigarettes. They were nearly 4 times as expensive as they were back in the States. When you leave

America and enter a new country, you realize how good you actually had it pretty quick.

All I could do was sit out on the sidewalk and wait for the bus. I avoided cobwebs like the plague because I had watched way too many documentaries about all of the insects and animals that could potentially kill you here. Then I started to worry about Sepi. What if she had second thoughts and wasn't there to pick me up after I came all this way? I couldn't already hear my father saying, "I told you so." I really tried not to think about the possibility but people-watching was starting to bore me. In three hours, I would finally know whether she meant every word she said or I was the dumbest piece of shit on the planet.

When my bus finally arrived, I was seated next to an elderly woman who could barely speak a word of English. She kept leaning on me, even falling asleep a couple of times as I held her up. Since I was sitting on the outside, every time she needed something out of her bag, I had to get it for her. That got annoying pretty quick. However, when she wasn't bothering me, I was enjoying the beautiful scenery which was often interrupted by the driver having to slam on his brakes nearly sending me flying. I couldn't believe how people drove in this country. I've always said that they are either some of the best drivers I've ever seen or the worst, depending on your point of view. They give new meaning to the term "defensive driving" as I would need a calculator to add up how many near misses we had on that highway. Obviously, some of these morons had seen too many action movie car chases and couldn't distinguish between fiction and reality. To this day, I still dread getting into the car when I used to find it relaxing overseas.

Three hours later, we arrived at the bus station in Canberra. I looked out the window and saw Sepi sitting in her car looking down at her phone. I don't even know how to put into words how relieved I was to see her there. She got out of the car and stood outside the bus waiting for me to come down the stairs. When she saw me, she ran up to me and we shared a long embrace before getting into her car. Once inside, we kissed for several minutes before leaving the premises. Our first stop was at a gourmet pizza joint to pick up some dinner, then she took me to my temporary new home. I could see why she loved the place. It was a beautiful two story townhouse with multiple bedrooms and a huge master bedroom all upstairs. We also had three bathrooms...two upstairs and one downstairs. The unit was so big that she took on a roommate, who had his own living quarters with the exception being the kitchen. It was a damn shame that the new owners and the real estate agent lied to her about it remaining just an investment property. The new owners decided they wanted to move in out of the blue and gave Sepi only three weeks to get out. I could see that it was still very upsetting to Sepi that we had to move literally a week after I got there but there wasn't really anything we could do about it. She had cried her eyes out over the webcam when she broke the news to me. She thought that she had let me down and I would likely change my mind about coming after she told me. I explained to her, the best way that I knew how, that I wanted to be with *her* and I didn't care if we had to live in the car. Hell, I've been there and done that a couple of times already in my lifetime. She had nothing to be ashamed of. She found a much smaller one story townhouse in the same complex so we did have somewhere to go.

    My days were spent being locked up in Sepi's room, often playing around on the computer until she got home from work. I would sometimes cross paths with the roommate when I got hungry and went downstairs, but I tried to keep my distance. I usually just logged into Facebook and smoked cigarettes for hours on end. I didn't really miss home very much in those days because I felt like I was on vacation instead of accepting the fact that I had actually moved away. I didn't venture outside very much either, and when I did decide to take a stroll to the mailbox one day, I got lost and almost went into the wrong house because they all looked so similar. My nights were spent packing things once again which I wasn't exactly thrilled about. Even worse was that the roommate informed us that he was coming along too which was both a blessing from a financial standpoint, and a curse because we were going to have less room. It was such a difficult time for all of us and it was beginning to show.

    When moving day was upon us, the new owners, who weren't supposed to be there until the afternoon to give us time to vacate the premises, showed up a few hours early. Now we had two different removalist companies in each other's way. Our roommate, who was supposed to arrange his own moving, decided that he was going to use our truck as well at the last minute. His mother and stepfather made an appearance too...not to help in any way, but to take him out to dinner while all of this was going on. Meanwhile, the new owners were inspecting the house to try to get some money out of us. They were the typical overpaid, arrogant public service couple. He was short and fat and wasn't attractive at all, with a trophy wife that looked half his age. Now there was bickering back and forth between us and them while the movers were passing each other in the courtyard. It was an awful mess and there were already tension between Sepi and myself ever since I volunteered to take her showerhead off the night before and broke the damn thing. This would become an ongoing tradition around the Noland household in the years to come.

The week had started off so well and now it was so hectic and stressful. Since I had only proposed to Sepi over a webcam, I dropped down to one knee and did it properly our first night together. She was now wearing that ring that I had brought all the way from Maryville, Tennessee. However, over the last couple of days, there had been trouble in paradise. It had gotten so bad that I had even told her that if she thought that this relationship and soon to be marriage wasn't going to work, I would leave now before we said our vows and tied the knot. Thank God she still believed in us and decided to keep me around. We both knew that we weren't the problem, everyone else was. Once this move was over, maybe we could enjoy each other's company for a while.

Our part of the move went well... except for the fact that we got charged $600 to have our stuff moved across the complex without even getting on the main road, and we were late getting our keys to the new place. I even impressed the movers so much by helping out that they offered me a job! I politely declined but took their card anyway just in case. Of course, since the roommate's shit was also thrown on the truck, we got some of our money back which stopped some of the bleeding as well. We did stick around long enough to hear the new owners argue with their removalists about how to get their furniture to the second floor. It could only be described as "trying to put 20 pounds of shit in a 10 pound bag." As big as our old place was, it wasn't big enough for all of their junk. They ended up having to take the fence down and bedroom door off to get their shit up to the balcony and make it fit.

Our new place might have everything sitting just inside the front door but at least it was *inside*. That was more than those other ass clowns could say. Karma can be a real bitch sometimes. My heart was bleeding...not!

2

We definitely had some interesting neighbours at the new place. On one side we had an insane elderly couple who looked like Santa and Mrs Claus... but far more annoying. The old man was retired, and was usually left home alone during the day, so he was obviously bored and lonely. He would either invite himself over or wait outside for me to walk through the gate and grab my attention then. He was usually either wearing food or coffee in his thick grey beard that he must have been saving for later. He had a garage full of wine that he sipped on all day...which might explain why he wasn't shy about saying whatever he was thinking, whether it was appropriate or not. I would find out down the road that he wasn't right in the head after having brain surgery years ago... which explains a lot. The wife was less annoying but I rarely saw her, which might be the reason why. It got to the point to where I had to do a recon mission before I even went to the mailbox to avoid being seen. I kept spacing out when I interacted with him until we didn't talk at all.

On the other side of the wall was a young military couple with a toddler. He was usually overseas, leaving *her* alone as well. For extra money, she started babysitting other people's children too. Since the walls were so thin, all I heard throughout the day was either babies crying or nursery rhymes. What made matters worse was when the husband came home and they would have sex. We could hear everything from their creaking bed to her loud moaning and pillow talk but thankfully it would only last for a minute or two. She would play an important role with my visa issues by being a character witness on my behalf. I liked them a lot but when they decided to move, they didn't even let us know. I had to hear about it from the old bastard next door.

3

I think that one of the main reasons that women keep men around, other than fixing things around the house and opening jars, is to kill spiders... and boy, do they have a lot of creepy crawlies in Australia. One day, when Sepi yelled out to me in horror to come into the kitchen quickly to kill one, I was expecting the typical small common house variety that I used to find in the States. What I saw was what is called a "Huntsman." It had a leg-span as wide as my hand, and I have very large hands. I had brought a simple flyswatter and dropped it onto the floor. I looked over at Sepi and said, "What the hell is this place? Jurassic Park? I've never seen a spider so big in my fucking life!" I had a grab a shoe to squash the damn thing! But even the Aussie version of a "common" house spider is a little different than what I was used to. It is quite large, black in colour, and poisonous to some people. Our house was already being infested by them. When I saw one on the ceiling over the bed one day, I got under it and was prepared to swing the flyswatter when it detached... and landed right on my face! My reflexes shook it off before it had a chance to bite me. The problem was that it landed on the bed... which just happened to have black sheets on it as well. I knew that if I didn't find it, Sepi would not sleep that night, so I hunted for it until I located it and eliminated it then I brought the carcass back to show Sepi so she could rest easy.

I was literally killing one of these pests at least once a day, so we notified our real estate agent and requested an exterminator to spray the house. Our agent was a bitter and strict old lady on the verge of retirement. She took her job way too seriously and was impossible to please. She treated us as if we were common criminals. The house was never clean enough to suit her, no matter how hard we scrubbed. And the courtyard...well, if she saw a single weed that I missed, she would make a note of it on her report. Although we never actually failed a house inspection, but she always found something to bitch about. On the flip side, heaven forbid you needed something repaired because it took an act of Congress to get her to take action. She would always say, "Oh, you can probably live without that" and not bother to notify the owners. I don't know how but Sepi managed to persuade her to order an exterminator. Of course, it would be the cheapest one that she could find but at least it was *something*.

A couple of days later, the exterminator stopped by. He was a young guy from Amsterdam and he liked me right away. We compared stories about our wild pasts over a few bottles of Jack Daniels and Coke after he finished. He, just like the removalists, offered me a job working for him. I wasn't quite ready to join the workforce yet but I thanked him and accepted his card in case I changed my mind. He also invited me to go with him to a club or pub sometime in the future but I never called him. Sepi was impressed at how people were naturally drawn to me. I just smiled and said that it was "my curse." Of course, the strong southern accent wasn't helping either. Too bad, I hated people...especially when they weren't *my* people.

4

    This was around the time that the first flaws in the Australian immigration process were exposed. I had tried to do everything right but every time my case got passed along to another person, I would receive a letter in the mail telling me that some of my paperwork had been lost and that I needed to provide it once again. This was getting quite expensive and frustrating, especially when everything had to be signed by a notary. With no car, I had to rely on Sepi to take me everywhere without missing much work. Just when I thought that the process couldn't get any worse, I found out that even after we got married, I couldn't legally work in the country of Australia for up to a year until I went on another visa. I was also warned that if I got caught working for cash in hand, I would not only get deported, but be banned from entering the country for several years. Up to this point, everyone had been lying to me and it didn't matter to them whether we could keep a roof over our head and food on the table or not. I was starting to think that I could have come over as a refugee on a boat illegally, and been better off.

    Here I was...offered two jobs and pretty much already hired at a local grocery store down the street, basically doing what I was doing back home, yet can't provide legal documentation needed to actually go to work. We were now in a very bad place. I had to close my bank account overseas to keep from paying for a service that I no longer had, I couldn't pay my doctor bills without that account, and all the money that I had saved and brought over from the U.S. had vanished due to the extremely high cost of living here. My diabetes medication, that I had once stockpiled, was now running low as well, so I was skipping pills to make them last as long as possible. The sad reality was that our idiot of roommate, that I couldn't wait to get rid of, was now a necessary evil and he fucking knew it too. He never got in any hurry to pay his half of the bills and had already started questioning why he was paying half when there were three of us living in our townhouse. Sepi had to constantly remind me to keep my lips sealed to keep from scaring him away, so I pretended to be his friend to get money out of him instead of beating the shit out of him like he deserved.

    I did have one option that I didn't give much consideration: going back to the U.S. until the red tape was cleared up. Sepi and I had set a date for October 31 to get married and I wasn't about to leave my new bride for even a day...much less a year or longer. If we had to eat Ramen noodles and spaghetti seven days a week and not go anywhere or do anything for the first year, that was what we were going to do. It seemed like there was almost no hope. The price of my visa was going to end up costing twice as much as we were originally told, as it genuinely felt like those wankers were making up the rules and prices as they went along. I had several Facebook "friends" back home who offered to take up donations and even sell some of their personal art to help us out, but we never saw a dollar from any of it. I felt like a loser...like I was no different from Sepi's ex-boyfriend, who spent all of his money on weed instead of contributing on bills, food, and all of those other necessities of life. She was basically supporting me like she did him. The only difference was that I came from the other side of the world to live off of her, and it was tearing me apart inside. I even said to Sepi multiple times that if I had known that we were going to suffer like this our first year together, I would have never bought that ticket. I would have been doing her a favour...

Well, we couldn't get married on Halloween as we originally planned because of the day of the week that it fell on, so we had to settle on October 29th instead. Although Sepi, much like yours truly, didn't have the best of relationships with her family, her mother did, in fact, attend to be one of our two witnesses. Her brother, on the other hand, did not attend because he had "better things to do." Now we needed a second witness and the only other person we could think of that we could rely on was Sepi's GP. The problem was that he was at work on the other side of town and his shift didn't finish until only a few minutes before our ceremony was supposed to start. Although the ceremony itself wasn't stressing me, certain things that were out of my control was, therefore I was a wreck.

We arrived at the courthouse in Queanbeyan, New South Wales, with Sepi's mother about an hour early. That certainly didn't help matters any considering that we had to delay the ceremony for a while anyways as we waited for the doc to show up. I was pacing like a caged animal, constantly looking down at my watch. If something happened and he couldn't make it, we were fucked. My visa was set to expire within two weeks so if we didn't get this done today, there may not be another opening before time ran out. My future was literally in his hands for a brief moment.

When he finally walked through that door, I took back all of the things that I had been thinking. The ceremony was very straight forward and simple and took only a few minutes. The doctor didn't stick around for very long afterwards, but Sepi's mother invited us over for a feast that she had been preparing since the night before. It was a pleasant change from our usual pasta and we ate so much that we were in no condition to consummate our marriage. That could wait until tomorrow. We immediately hit the bed when we got home so we could go to sleep and try to digest our meal overnight. We had the weekend to relax before we had to make an appearance at the immigration department on Monday morning.

5

Instead of going on a honeymoon like normal newlyweds do, we spent the next few weeks in the eye clinic at the local hospital. The specialist had given the back of her eyes so much laser that they had ran out of room so they had to try something else. There was still a lot of swelling that had to go down and the only procedure left was an injection. Yes, that's right...a needle right into her eyeball! If just the thought of that makes you cringe, it gets worse. Every time that she had it done, the open wound got infected, leading to constant itching and discharge. Within a few hours, her eyes would get so blood red that she looked like something out of a horror movie. My heart went out to her as I watched her suffer continuously for nearly a week each time. This went on for several months until she got the faulty vessels somewhat under control.

When our first Christmas together rolled around, I was reminded of why I despised roommates. Ours decided to invite his brother and father up from Melbourne without asking. Now we had two total strangers walking around the house that we had never met before over the holidays. We were pissed but couldn't really say anything once they were already here. Christmas already felt strange, especially with it now being in the middle of summer. I was used to wood fires and snow flurries, not sweating profusely by the swimming pool. I've been here nearly six years as of this writing and I still haven't got used to the seasons being so out of whack from what I had known for 37 years. Hell, my birthday is on February 7th and it used to snow on that day every year. Now there is no chance of that happening on this continent.

On New Year's Day 2011, Sepi and I decided to go to the National Zoo and Aquarium. It was a stinking hot day so I wore a tank-top and shorts. As we were walking along the trail to see the tigers, I felt something either sting or bite me on the leg. I swatted the culprit away before I could identify what it was. I went about my day like nothing happened, focusing more on my blistering skin than anything else. Over the next few days, that place on my leg went through a series of changes. It turned black and scabbed over, then itched and burned like hell. I was starting to develop kidney pain like I had another stone but I didn't make the connection. I just assumed that it was an unrelated event. To treat the wound of my leg, I soaked it in bleach because bleach kills almost anything. Whether it was actually helping or not was debatable, but it did cause all the dead skin to peel off, exposing two puncture marks underneath. When I visited my doctor about a month later for another ailment, I showed him the spot on my leg which had now left a small scar. He informed me that I had been bitten by the notorious "white tail spider." The reactions that most people have after being bitten is similar to the infamous "brown recluse spider" back in the States. The venom can, if you are allergic, rot the flesh from the inside… and more often than not, it takes amputation of that particular limb to save one's life. There had even been reports of the bite returning to the very same spot every year to torment the poor victim. Thank God that I wasn't allergic is all I can really say…

I have always been somewhat immune to bee stings and spider bites over the years. I got bitten on the same leg by a black widow while cleaning out my old clubhouse when I was young. I had numbness in my leg for a couple of weeks but never got sick or needed to go get treated. There have also been many occasions where I have looked under certain objects that I had picked up without gloves multiple times that had not one but several nasties nesting underneath. I don't press my luck anymore as I have grown a bit wiser with age.

6

Our first few road trips together were always to Sydney, and usually to concerts. Sepi would always book our no lower than 4 star hotel weeks in advance and it was usually within walking distance of the arena. That just made life easier... as we didn't have to get into the car until we were ready to go home. I was usually stressed out until we checked in, mostly due to the heavy traffic and the tedious streets whose lanes often ended without notice that you had to deal with in order to get there. Sydney was also the only city that I had ever been to that charges you money before you could either enter or leave. There are actually several toll booths on the outskirts of the city that you have to go through before you could do either, unless you wanted to drive well out of the way to avoid them. To us, it just wasn't worth it, because that was going to cost you about as much.

The first show that we went to was to see the rock band "Disturbed." We made the mistake of purchasing general admission tickets on the floor which had its own pros and cons. The good part was that by the time the band took the stage, we were literally only a few feet away from them. The bad part was that we were packed in there like sardines. I hated the stench of body odour and sweaty bodies brushing up against me. The Australian fans were much rowdier than American fans, mostly due to the fact that bands rarely come out here so when they do, people get a little over excited. I bonded with a group of "good old blokes" that were in front of us with their ladies who was just wanting to watch the show and wasn't interested in all of the hoopla that surrounded us. There was some young head-banger behind us that kept jumping over my shoulder and landing on my new friends. We teamed up to teach this scrawny bastard a lesson before he got his ass kicked. About midway through the band's set, a mosh pit appeared. Everyone was slamming into each other like a demolition derby, and all I cared about was protecting Sepi, who had only recently had her eyes done. I wrapped her petite and fragile body in my arms like a blanket and became her human shield as I got hit from all sides. Eventually, I got fed up and shoved a majority of the crowd into the fucking wall. I did this several times, just waiting for someone to take it personally, but unfortunately no one did. By the time the show finished, I was exhausted from fighting the crowd all night and couldn't wait to go back to the room. Once we got there, I sat out on the balcony with a beer and a cigarette and watched the sea of heads go back and forth on the streets below from several stories up. I felt like someone had beaten me with a baseball bat and probably looked that way too. Sepi, on the other hand, didn't have a scratch on her… so I did my job.

The next concert was meant to be "Avenged Sevenfold/Sevendust" but we found out once we got to Sydney that Sevendust had cancelled. Sepi was furious because it was like the third time that she had bought tickets to see that band and they never bothered to show up. Instead, we ended up with a local band that sounded very good and Avenged Sevenfold playing a longer set to try to give the fans their money's worth. Of course, Sevendust fans were still upset but appreciated the effort. The third and final show that we went to was "Motley Crue/Bret Micheals," which I was stoked about since I had missed both acts back in their heyday for one reason or another. As with Avenged Sevenfold, we bought seats instead of open admission on the floor so we could watch the chaos instead of being part of it. We laughed as fights broke out and people were being escorted to the exit before the curtains even opened. This sort of thing was probably happening at Disturbed but we were completely unaware of it. I was getting too old for this shit. I would rather just sit back and observe than actively participate nowadays.

7

I had been in Australia for just over a year and still wasn't homesick yet. It saddened me that I was so bitter and resentful toward the people in my previous life that I could so willingly detach from who I was and just become someone else with relative ease. It did, however, come with a price. Since I hadn't driven a car in such a long time, I had lost my confidence. I felt like my reflexes weren't sharp enough anymore to be behind the wheel. I had also lost most of my muscular physique and replaced it with cellulite. My hair was falling out faster than it could grow. I felt so unattractive that I was starting to lose my sex drive completely because I hated to see myself naked. I had never looked this bad in my life. I felt like Sepi didn't sign on for this and deserved better. If I couldn't stand to look at myself, imagine how Sepi feels. All of this insecurity caused my old neck injury to return as well. Each and every day, I found it difficult to move my neck without excruciating pain. I also went through stages where I felt like I couldn't breathe...like my windpipe was being closed off by some unseen object. All I did everyday was play "Star Wars-The Force Unleashed" to keep my mind distracted from this mystery condition. It took almost two full months to completely recover.

Now Christmas was upon us again and we would receive some shocking news: the roommate was moving out. We were barely keeping our heads above water as it was and now we had lost part of our income. Sepi was panicking but I kept my hopes up that somehow this was going to work out for the best. We had been backed into the corner several times over the past year and we always came out swinging. We had overcome every obstacle that had been put before us and this would be no different. I sent a letter to the Department of Immigration that explained our financial situation and why I needed to start working immediately. Within a couple of weeks, they responded by lifting my work restrictions. It was the best Christmas present ever. I thought that all of our problems were solved. If I had known had difficult the road ahead was going to be, I wouldn't have been near as excited, but we agreed to not think about it until after the holidays. We just cherished the moment before we faced the world with clenched fists once again...

-DJN

ACKNOWLEDGMENTS

FIRST AND FOREMOST- God, Mom and Dad, Sepi Noland, Darth Paws "Paws" Darth Whiskers "Whisky"

THE EXTENDED FAMILY

Stacy Mealer, Jonathan McCall, Tory Perdue, Jason Rollins, Bryan Tipton, Bill Morton, Richard Challender, Cody Tucker, Robert Tree Corder, Tommy Pitner, Jane Burch Barber, Greg Barber, Christine Guinn, Michelle Cornett Alexander, Marsha Lainey King, Rebecca Sykes, Melissa McCarter, Heather Bright Thompson, Salena Burkett Garza, Angela Pritchett Mullins, Amy Wright, Denise Martinez, Annette Thwaits Tomko, Natashia Gilbert Goins, Christie Gerber, Wendy Hurst Barbieri, Gary Garner, Terry Martin, Lisa Mullins, Bianca Catherine Knight, Morgan Ramsey Lovejoy, Andrea Wilde, John Pedigo, Scott Duncan, Ashley Makusevich, Coreen Matthews, Dianne Blair, Shannon Herron, Tara Lynn Bell, Rebecca Barnette Rowland, Stephanie Yester, Lisa Coffey Stewart, Don Rowe, Misty Hawkins, Jennifer Alexander, David Russell, Sinthia Domina, Nicci Hodge, Leslie Elmore, Hunter Farley Seymour, Mitzi Isbill Branch, Jennifer Justus Thompson, Audra Angelle, Wendy Navarre, Nikki Phillips Gibson, Heather Watters, Lesley Burnett, Jason Parrot, Randall Paige, Roger Russell, Shannon Branson Boyd, Shiloah Wyatt, Rachel Lianne Ford, Contonia Lee Jung, Jill Regenia Hamilton, Kelly Clark, Kris Todd, Denise Lyall, Katey Goforth, Michelle Hulsey, Dwayne Singletary, Mark Powers, Stephen Jeter, Mark Hutson, Iain Sibthorpe, Cheri Jones, Ryan Melton, Joyce Johnson, Joseph Gardner, Dawn Holloway, Richard Wilson, Mark Cartright

TEACHERS

Ann Dunn Tallent, Renda Poe Crowe

IN MEMORY OF
Arthur Moses, Carrie Moses, James Noland, Louise Noland, J.E. Bradburn, Brian Williams, Brian Bowling, Ed Ramsey, Gene Lovelace, James Irwin, Jenna Alexander, Rachelle Marlow, Jackie Rucker, Angela Centers, Kandi Gerber-Wetzel, Ted Sanders, Robin LaDon, Dennis Barnette, Travis McCammon, Shawn Knox, Bob Shaffer, Judy Mealer, Peggy Tipton, Kasee Cope, Tonya Baker, Gene & Betty Moses, Angela Gates

www.ingramcontent.com/pod-product-compliance
Lightning Source LLC
Chambersburg PA
CBHW071357230426
43669CB00010B/1377